lonely planet

CRUISE PORTS
MEDITERRANEAN
EUROPE

A GUIDE TO PERFECT DAYS ON SHORE

D1338351

Virginia Maxwell, Kate Armstrong, Brett Atkinson,
Alexis Averbuck, James Bainbridge, Cristian Bonetto,
Gregor Clark, Duncan Garwood, Paula Hardy, Anna Kamin_
Catherine Le Nevez, Hugh McNaughtan, Kate Morgan,
Kevin Raub, Simon Richmond, Brendan Sainsbury,
Regis St Louis, Greg Ward and Nicola Willi_

Contents

POLAND

UKRAINE

AGUE ✪
CZECH
REPUBLIC

SLOVAKIA

VIENNA ✪ ✪ BRATISLAVA

✪ BUDAPEST

Odesa ◉

HUNGARY

MOLDOVA

ROMANIA

BLJANA ✪
OVENIA

✪ ZAGREB
CROATIA

STRIA

BUCHAREST ✪

BELGRADE ✪

Black
Sea

BOSNIA &
HERZEGOVINA

SERBIA

SARAJEVO ✪

PLIT p329 ◉

MONTENEGRO

BULGARIA

DUBROVNIK p347 ◉

KOTOR p367

SOFIA ✪

Adriatic
Sea

İSTANBUL p475

SKOPJE ✪

NORTH
MACEDONIA

Sea of
Marmara

TIRANA ✪

Bari ◉

Naples ○
○ Pompeii

ALBANIA

Thessaloniki ◉

Thasos

Gökçeada

Limnos

TURKEY

GREECE

Lesvos

İzmir ◉

CORFU p383 ◉

Lefkada

Evia

Aegean Sea

Chios

Andros

Samos

ATHENS p437 ✪

Catania ○

Kefallonia

ly

Ionian
Sea

Zakynthos

MYKONOS p463

Naxos

Kos

RHODES p423

Santorini
(Thira)

Kythira

Karpathos

Sea of Crete

VALLETTA p287 ✪

TA

HANIA p395

Crete ◉

IRAKLIO p407

MEDITERRANEAN
SEA

OLI

EGYPT

Welcome to Mediterranean Europe

Part history tour, part beach vacation, part culinary odyssey, this region offers a veritable feast for every traveller, whether in world-class cities or zipping around tiny islands.

Sailing the Mediterranean for trade and conquest was a rite of passage for every civilisation that rose to prominence in the Mediterranean Basin, from ancient Persians and Minoans to the Greeks and Phoenicians. As you tour Malta's 5000-year-old Tarxien Temples, climb up to Athens' 2500-year-old Acropolis or pretend to be a gladiator at Rome's relatively young 2050-year-old Colosseum, you can't help but feel part of that antiquity.

For many holidaymakers the Mediterranean's main appeal is the promise of summer sun and long, lazy days on the beach. While not all visitors head straight for the coast, many do – and with good reason. The Mediterranean's beaches are superb, ranging from idyllic Sardinian hideaways to rocky platforms on Croatia's craggy Dalmatian coast.

Eating well is one of the great pleasures of everyday life on the Med, and it doesn't have to cost a bomb. Picnicking on a loaf of freshly baked bread with cheese and olives and a bottle of wine bought from the local market could well turn out to be a holiday highlight. For dedicated foodies, France and Italy are the obvious destinations, but each country has its own culinary specialities – think tapas in Spain, kebaps in Turkey, souvlaki in Greece. And for wine buffs, the Mediterranean cellar is really quite something, with everything from world-famous vintages to thousands of cheerful local labels.

Ancient ruins, legendary cities and sun-kissed beaches – Mediterranean Europe is a visual and sensual feast. Visit once and you'll be hooked for life.

A veritable feast for travellers, whether in world-class cities or zipping around tiny islands.

Kotor (p366), Montenegro
S-F/SHUTTERSTOCK ©

Contents

Left: Pizza margherita, Naples;
Top right: The Golden Gate (p333)and the Statue of Grgur Ninski
(p340), Split
Bottom right: Windmills (p470), Mykonos

TICHR/SHUTTERSTOCK ©

ELLA HANOCHI/SHUTTERSTOCK ©

Plan Your Trip
Mediterranean Europe's Top 25

PECOLD/SHUTTERSTOCK ©

Barcelona, Spain

The genius of a visionary architect

Barcelona is famous for its Modernista architecture, much of which was designed by Antoni Gaudí. His masterwork is the mighty La Sagrada Família cathedral, which remains a work in progress close to a century after its creator's death. It's a bizarre combination of crazy and classic: Gothic touches intersect with eccentric experiments and improbable angles. Even half complete, it's a modern-day wonder.

From left: La Sagrada Família facade (p52); La Sagrada Família exterior (p52)

NARVIKK/GETTY IMAGES ©

Florence, Italy

Exquisite streets packed with art

Home to Brunelleschi's Duomo and Masaccio's Cappella Brancacci frescoes, Florence contains one of the greatest concentrations of renowned artworks in the world. It's where the Renaissance kicked off and artists such as Michelangelo and Botticelli rewrote the rules of creative expression. The result is a city packed with artistic treasures, blockbuster museums, elegant churches and flawless Renaissance streetscapes. Top: Duomo (p178); Bottom: Frescoes of Brancacci Chapel

AMIRRAIZAT7/SHUTTERSTOCK ©

Dubrovnik, Croatia

A spectacular walled city

Dubrovnik's main claim to fame is its historic ramparts, considered among the finest in the world, which surround luminous marble streets and finely ornamented buildings. Built between the 13th and 16th centuries, the walls are remarkably intact and the vistas over terracotta rooftops and the Adriatic Sea are sublime, especially at dusk, when the fading light creates dramatic hues and unforgettable panoramas. Pile Gate (p358)

3

İstanbul, Turkey

East meets West

İstanbul is bursting with a millennia of history. The megacity formerly known as Constantinople and Byzantium was the capital of a series of empires. The fact that the city straddles two continents wasn't its only drawcard – it was also the final stage on the legendary Silk Road linking Asia with Europe. Top sights include Aya Sofya, Topkapı Palace and the Blue Mosque, but there's a sultan's treasury of other sights and activities. Blue Mosque (p490)

Valletta, Malta

A city of knights and fortresses

Malta's capital is a remarkable place. Only 1km by 600m, with every street leading to the sea, the walled fortress city contains a harmonious ensemble of 16th- and 17th-century townhouses fronted by traditional Maltese balconies. The last few years have seen Valletta bloom with exciting restaurants, renovated buildings and an emerging nightlife scene. New galleries, museums and art spaces have boosted Valletta's cultural credibility, and you'll sense the excitement immediately. Valletta street leading to the Grand Harbour

Venice, Italy

A magical city seemingly floating on water

A sunny winter's day, with far fewer tourists around, is the perfect time to lap up Venice's unique and magical atmosphere. Ditch your map and wander the shadowy back lanes of the city while imagining secret assignations and whispered conspiracies at every turn. Then visit one of Venice's top galleries, the Galleria dell'Accademia, with its catalogue of Venetian art from the 14th to 18th centuries.

6

MATTEO COLOMBO/GETTY IMAGES ©

Rome, Italy

Classical ruins mixed with contemporary style

From the crumbling Colosseum to the ancient Forum, few sights are more evocative than the ruins of ancient Rome. Two thousand years ago this city was the centre of the greatest empire of the ancient world, where gladiators battled and emperors lived in unimaginable luxury. Nowadays it's a haunting spot: as you walk the cobbled paths, you can almost sense the ghosts in the air. Temple of Saturn in the Roman Forum (p208)

7

Nice, France

Riviera high life for savvy urbanites

There is no better city for soaking up the glitz, glamour and hedonistic lifestyle of the legendary French Riviera. Undisputed queen of this Mediterranean kingdom of shimmering seas, idyllic beaches and lush hills, Nice is one of France's smartest urban hang-outs. Its old town is gorgeous, its street markets buzz and it knows how to party.
Promenade des Anglais (p129)

VIACHESLAV LOPATIN/SHUTTERSTOCK ©

BELLENA/SHUTTERSTOCK ©

ALVARO GERMAN VILELA/
SHUTTERSTOCK ©

9

Pompeii, Italy

An ancient city destroyed by Vesuvius

Frozen in its death throes, the sprawling, time-warped ruins of Pompeii hurtle you 2000 years into the past. Wander through chariot-grooved Roman streets, lavishly frescoed villas and bathhouses, food stores and markets, theatres and even an ancient brothel. Then, in the eerie stillness, with your eye on ominous Mt Vesuvius, ponder the town's final hours, when the skies grew dark and heavy with volcanic ashes. From left: Ruins of Pompeii (p240) overlooked by Mt Vesuvius; Ruins of an ancient snack bar (p245)

BLUEJAYPHOTO/GETTY IMAGES ©

ANIBAL TREJO/SHUTTERSTOCK ©

OLGICA65/BUDGET TRAVEL ©

Cinque Terre, Italy

Five dramatically picturesque fishing villages

For the sinful inhabitants of the Cinque Terre's five sherbet-coloured villages, appeals for forgiveness involved a hike up the vertiginous cliff side to the sanctuary. Scale the same trails today through terraced vineyards and unfurling heavenly views, and it's hard to think of a more benign punishment. Those seeking less exertion can hop from one village to the next on the train. Clockwise from top: Vernazza harbour (p171); Monterosso beach (p171); Vernazza village (p171)

JAN ZABRODSKY/SHUTTERSTOCK ©

Sardinia, Italy

A wild island of peaks and beaches

Words fail to accurately describe the varied blue-green hues of the sea surrounding Sardinia. While models, ministers and perma-tanned celebrities wine, dine and sail along the glossy coast, much of Sardinia remains a wild, raw playground. Slather on that sunscreen and explore the island's rugged beauty, from the hilltop citadel in Cagliari to the intriguing archaeological ruins of Nora. Nora ruins (p278)

ENKI PHOTO/SHUTTERSTOCK ©

Sicily, Italy

An island of diverse flavours

Sour, spicy and sweet, Sicily's flavours reflect millennia of cross-cultural influences. No other regional Italian cuisine is quite as complex and intriguing. The Mercato di Ballarò in Palermo has stalls bursting with local delicacies: Bronte pistachios, olives, swordfish and nutty Canestrato cheese. And leave room for a *cannolo* (pastry shell with a sweet filling of ricotta) or a slice of *cassata* (a mix of sponge cake, cream, marzipan, chocolate and candied fruit). Cannoli and cassata

VESNA CELEBIC/LONELY PLANET ©

CGE2010/SHUTTERSTOCK ©

Split, Croatia

Balance between tradition and modernity

Experience life as it's been lived for thousands of years in Diocletian's Palace, one of the world's most imposing Roman remains. The maze-like streets of this buzzing quarter – the living heart and soul of Split – are full of bars, shops and restaurants. Getting lost in the labyrinth of narrow streets and courtyards is one of Croatia's most enchanting experiences – and it's small enough that you can easily find your way out again. Top: Zlatna Ribica; Bottom: Diocletian's Palace (p332)

13

MILAN GONDA/SHUTTERSTOCK ©

Iraklio, Greece

The epicentre of Crete

Crete's capital city is home to several of the island's top sights, many of which are wedged within its walled historic town: the Palace of Knossos and the superb Heraklion Archaeological Museum are standouts. In Iraklio it always seems to be six o'clock (official 'drinking' time in some countries); there's a lively cafe scene here, and a nearby wine region of repute. Exhibits at the Heraklion Archaeological Museum (p416)

14

15

Marseille, France
Two millennia of Mediterranean heritage

The Greeks loved it and so will you: hot, sultry Marseille grows on visitors with its unique history, fusion of cultures, souk-like markets, millennia-old port and hair-raising corniches (coastal roads). The icing on the cake: the striking Musée des Civilisations de l'Europe et de la Méditerranée (MuCEM), a state-of-the-art museum showcasing Mediterranean history and mind-blowing panoramas across one of the Med's most bewitching cities. Cathédrale de Marseille Notre Dame de la Major and Musée des Civilisations de l'Europe et de la Méditerranée (p104)

16

Kotor, Montenegro
Romance, ambience and living history

Time-travel back to a Europe of moated walled towns with shadowy lanes and stone churches on every square. It may not be as impressive as Dubrovnik's or as shiny as Budva's, but Kotor's Old Town feels much more lived-in and ever so dramatic. The way it seems to grow out of the sheer grey mountains surrounding it adds a thrill of foreboding to the experience – as if they could at any point choose to squeeze the little town in a rocky embrace. Kotor City Walls (p370) and moat

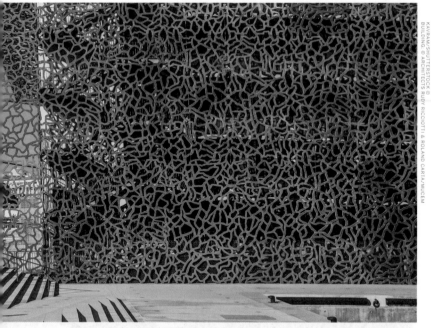

MARTIDIS IOANNIS/SHUTTERSTOCK ©

Athens, Greece

Mixing history and edginess

The cultural and social life of Athens plays out amid, around and in landmarks that are centuries – if not millennia – old. And although individuals endured difficult circumstances during (and after) the economic crisis that began in 2008, the city crackles with energy generated by art shows, political debates and even the walls of derelict buildings – Athens is one of Europe's most noted spots for street art. View of the Acropolis (p440) from Monastiraki Sq (p452)

17

Palma de Mallorca, Spain

Mallorca's capital and greatest asset

Visually magnificent, culturally spoiled, historically fascinating and geographically blessed, Palma should be better recognised as one of Europe's great destinations. Visitors enjoy its many wonders: crooked medieval streets lined with aristocratic mansions, galleries packed with the works of renowned artists, a broad bay bristling with the masts of maritime wealth, restaurants showcasing the great innovators of modern Spanish food, and endless acres of shopping.

19

Mykonos, Greece

A glamorous, fun-filled island

Mykonos is where the party is – a hedonistic paradise that, in high-season, draws celebrities (real and wannabes) and posturing fashionistas. Each major beach has at least one beach bar that gets going during the day. It also boasts a traditional whitewashed maze of a main town with a well-preserved and colourful harbour, and an active dining scene featuring top fusion restaurants alongside traditional tavernas. Mykonos bay (p466)

20

Rhodes, Greece

A window into times past

The footprints of everyone from Greeks and Romans to crusading medieval knights, Byzantine and Ottoman potentates to 20th-century Italian bureaucrats, are found here. Sealed like a medieval time capsule behind a double ring of high walls and a deep moat, the Old Town is a mind-boggling maze of cobbled streets and twisting alleyways, but never far away are sprawling beaches and wooded valleys. From left: Rhodes Old Town (p426); Palace of the Grand Master (p430)

DZIEWUL/SHUTTERSTOCK ©

DZIEWUL/SHUTTERSTOCK ©

Hania, Greece

Crete's most evocative city

You will be enthralled by Hania's old town. At its captivating Venetian harbour, historic townhouses rim the waterfront promenade, where tourists and locals stroll, gossip and people-watch as the sea swirls between a portside mosque, lighthouse and the imposing Firkas Fortress. In the winding old streets radiating out from the quay, you'll find minarets, boutique hotels and some of the island's best dining options. Top: Venetian Harbour (398); Bottom: Mosque of Kioutsouk Hasan (p399)

21

S-F/SHUTTERSTOCK ©

Monaco & Monte Carlo

Small size, big attitude

Monaco is the world's second-smallest country, so you can see all its major sights very easily. First is the old clifftop town of Le Rocher, where you'll find the prince's palace, the oceanographic museum and the cathedral. North across the port is Monaco's second centre of gravity, the Casino de Monte Carlo. In between lies the waterfront, a popular spot for sundrenched drinking and dining with views of the yachts and cruise ships. Casino de Monte Carlo (p138)

22

Corfu, Greece

Mythic history and majestic architecture

The name Corfu, meaning 'peaks', refers to its twin hills, each topped by a massive fortress built to withstand Ottoman sieges. Sitting between the two, the Old Town is a tightly packed warren of winding lanes, some bursting with fine restaurants, lively bars and intriguing shops, others timeless back alleys where washing lines stretch from balcony to balcony. It also displays some impressive architecture. Clockwise from top: Corfu town; lane in Corfu; local restaurant

23

JAVEN/SHUTTERSTOCK ©

Genoa, Italy
Ancient republic of living history

Known as La Superba (the Superb One) to biased locals, Genoa ruled over one of the finest maritime empires in medieval Europe. At its centre, medieval *caruggi* (alleyways) untangle outwards to the Porto Antico and teem with hawkers, merchants and office workers. Along Via Garibaldi and Via XXV Aprile is another Genoa, one of Unesco-sponsored palaces, smart shops and grand architectural gestures. Palazzo Reale (p158)

24

GIANCARLO LIGUORI/SHUTTERSTOCK ©

Cannes, France
Sun, sand and cinematic splendour

Set on the famous Côte d'Azur, Cannes is blessed with sandy beaches and beautiful weather, but its main claim to fame is as the home of the world's most famous film festival. It's a city of glamour year-round, with designer bars and couture shops, not to mention the palaces of La Croisette. Its best-known beach has had a major revamp, with 95,000 cubic metres of sand added to its shoreline. Beach and La Croisette (p114)

25

Plan Your Trip
Need to Know

When to Go

desert, dry climate
warm to hot summers, mild winters
warm to hot summers, cold winters
mild summers, cold winters
cold climate

Venice
GO Feb–Mar
& Sep–Nov

Nice
GO Apr–Jun
& Sep–Oct

İstanbul
GO Apr–May
& Sep

Kotor
GO May–Oct

Barcelona
GO Year round

Rome
GO Apr–May,
Jul & Nov–Dec

Athens
GO May–Sep

Valletta
GO Apr–Jun
& Sep–Oct

High Season (Jun–Aug)

o Hot, sunny days and packed beaches.

o Peak rates in coastal areas; inland cities may have discounts in August.

Shoulder (Apr–May & Sep–Oct)

o Sunny spring days in April and May; September is still hot enough for the beach.

o Crowds and high prices in many cities; more space and lower prices on the coast.

Low Season (Nov–Mar)

o The coldest and wettest time of the year.

o Prices are at their lowest.

o Many coastal resorts close for the winter.

Currencies

Most Mediterranean countries use the euro (€). Croatia uses the kuna (KN), Turkey the Turkish lira (₺).

Language

English is often spoken in ports and large cities. It's helpful to learn a few local phrases.

Visas

Citizens of Australia, New Zealand, Canada, the UK and the US do not need a visa to enter most countries in Mediterranean Europe for stays of up to 90 days, but need a visa to enter Turkey.

Money

ATMs are widely available and easy to use.

Mobile Phones

Most European mobile phones operate on the GSM 900/1800 system, compatible with Australian and New Zealand phones. Some American GSM 1900/900 phones do work in Europe, but incur high roaming charges.

Time

Most countries in Mediterranean Europe are on Central European Time (GMT/UTC plus one hour). Greece and Turkey are on Eastern European Time (GMT/UTC plus two hours).

Costs For a Day in Port

Budget: Less than €40

- Museum admission: free–€15

- Local bus/train tickets: €5–10

- Quick bite from a market or supermarket:

Midrange: €40–100

- Restaurant meal: from €15

- Short taxi trip: €10–20

- Guided tour: from €10–25 per person

Top End: Over €100

- Lunch at a fine-dining restaurant €40

- Cocktail: around €12

- Souvenirs €50 and up

Useful Websites

Lonely Planet (www.lonelyplanet.com) Destination info, hotel bookings, traveller forum.

Cruise Critic (www.cruisecritic.com) Trip reviews, prices, ship and port info.

Visit Europe (www.visiteurope.com) Practical advice and useful links.

Opening Hours

Although there are no hard-and-fast rules applicable to all countries, most Mediterranean nations share some habits. See Directory A–Z (p520) for more information.

Wi-Fi Access

- Wi-fi is often available in public parks, at cafes and restaurants, in railway stations and at airports.

- Internet cafes are no longer widespread, though they do still exist, but you may be able to log on (€1.50 to €5 per hour) in department stores, post offices, libraries, tourist offices, phone centres and universities.

- If using your own kit, you will need a power transformer if your computer isn't set up for dual voltage, and a plug adaptor.

Arriving in Mediterranean Europe

Athens The **X96 Piraeus–Athens Airport Express** costs 6 and runs from Eleftherios Venizelos International Airport every 20 to 40 minutes 24/7. It stops near the port in Piraeus; take the inside-port shuttle to your gate. Average journey time is around 1½ hours. In 2019 a new metro line is opening between the airport and the centre of Piraeus (one way €10). Taxis to the city centre (inner ring)take about 40 minutes and cost €35 (€50 between midnight and 5am).

Barcelona There is no direct bus or metro service between the airport and the pier, so you need to switch buses/trains in the city. Frequent *aerobúses* (airport shuttles) make the 35-minute run from El Prat Airport into town (€5.90) from 5.35am to 1am. Taxis from the airport cost around €25.

Rome There is no direct train line between Leonardo da Vinci (Fiumicino) Airport and the port in Civitavecchia, 65km to the north: head towards Rome and change at Trastevere. Total journey time is about two hours and costs €12.60. From Civitavecchia, an Argo bus to the port takes less than 10 minutes and costs €2. A private transfer from the airport to Civitavecchia starts at €22 per person.

Venice ACTV (p327) runs bus 5 between Marco Polo Airport and Piazzale Roma (€8, 30 minutes, four per hour). From Piazzale Roma, a frequent free shuttle bus to the cruise terminal runs every 15 to 20 minutes from Monday to Saturday during cruise season and whenever a big ship is in port. Land taxis from the airport cost around €30 to €40.

For more on **getting around**, see p527 ➡

Plan Your Trip
Hotspots for...

Food & Drink

There's no finer place to indulge your appetite than the Mediterranean. With so many local specialities and traditional tipples to try, you'll be in seventh heaven.

MICHAEL HEFFERNAN/LONELY PLANET ©

Naples (p232)
Naples is one of Italy's gastronomic darlings. The bayside setting makes for some seriously memorable meals.

Pizzeria Gino Sorbillo (p247)
The best pizza in town? The debate rages.

Barcelona (p50)
Barcelona's food scene is combination of world-class chefs, imaginative recipes and magnificent ingredients.

Tapas 24 (p76)
Known for its gourmet versions of old faves.

Athens (p438)
Athens' vibrant restaurant scene is marked by a delightful culture of casual, convivial alfresco dining.

Kalderimi (p459)
Taverna offering Greek food at its most authentic.

Architecture

Mediterranean Europe is a dream for architecture buffs. Ancient temples stand alongside hulking Gothic churches, majestic mosques, baroque piazzas and avant-garde museums.

VIACHESLAV LOPATIN/SHUTTERSTOCK ©

Rome (p424)
Rome's architectural legacy is unparalleled: ancient ruins, Renaissance basilicas, baroque churches and *palazzi*.

Pantheon (pictured; p218)
The high point of ancient Roman engineering.

İstanbul (p476)
Architects and urban designers wanting to study the world's best practice need go no further than İstanbul.

Blue Mosque (p490)
Islamic style finds perfect form.

Barcelona (p50)
Striking Gothic cathedrals, fantastical Modernista creations and avant-garde works from more recent days.

La Sagrada Família (p52)
Gaudí's work-in-progress modernist cathedral.

Medieval History

Against a backdrop of almost constant conflict, art and architecture flourished during the Middle Ages, giving rise to some wonderful towns and cities.

TABAK LEJLA/SHUTTERSTOCK ©

Dubrovnik (p348)
Dubrovnik's medieval walls date to its heyday as an independent republic and rival to the Venetians.

Lokrum (pictured; p361)
Home to a large medieval Benedictine monastery.

Rhodes (p198)
Rhodes' Unesco-protected Old Town is lined with impressive buildings and surrounded by huge, thick walls.

Knights' Quarter (p426)
Fortifications built by the Knights of St John.

Kotor (p368)
Walled Kotor is dramatically wedged between the sea and the steeply rising mountainside.

City Walls (p370)
The city's fortified walls offer a spectacular climb.

Coastal Beauty

With spectacular scenery and shimmering seascapes, few areas can rival the Mediterranean. Its coastline is a magical mix of silky beaches, dreamy coves and precipitous cliffs.

ELITRAVO/SHUTTERSTOCK ©

Cinque Terre (pictured; p164)
These five ingeniously constructed fishing villages are set amid dramatic coastal scenery.

Belvedere di Santa Maria (p171)
Enjoy dazzling 180-degree sea views.

Nice (p124)
The sea and the Mediterranean climate made Nice a tourist magnet as early as the 1700s.

Promenade des Anglais (p128)
Possibly France's most famous stretch of seafront.

Sardinia (p272)
A coastline indented with bays, honeycombed with grottoes and punctuated by granite rock formations.

Poetto Beach (p281)
One of the longest stretches of sand in Italy.

Plan Your Trip
Overtouristed Ports

Each year about 200 million visitors pour into the Mediterranean region, making it the world's top tourist destination. But the swamping of popular destinations by multitudes of tourists has a significant impact on these cities and the people who live there.

Issues

With just a little time to visit each city, visitors tend to head straight for the same major sights; the resulting congestion is unpleasant for both tourists and residents. Property prices in these areas skyrocket, and traditional businesses are forced out. Some centuries-old sights in major cities are under threat of degradation and the local economy may be left with little to show for it – cruise passengers, in particular, are often ashore for only a few hours and spend little to nothing as meals have already been paid for back on the boat.

Residents have increasingly rallied against the ever-increasing number of tourists in their home cities. Anti-tourist graffiti has proliferated throughout the region. In 2017, a tour bus in Barcelona was attacked by masked protesters. Venetians demonstrated against cruise ships visiting their "fragile" city, worried the ships are threatening the foundations of old buildings. As this book was going to print, a cruise ship crashed into a dock and a tourist river boat on one of Venice's busiest canals, resulting in four injuries. Dubrovnik now limits the number of visitors to 4000 per day and plans to decrease the number of cruise ships docking at the port.

How Can I Help?

o **Visit in the off-season.** Many of the Mediterranean's most beautiful sights can be enjoyed year round. In this part of the world, it can be warm and sunny well beyond the summer months; the off-season is quieter and often cheaper.

○ **Choose less popular or well-known places.** Many top destinations are unique and do merit visiting, but depending on what you're looking for, a less popular or well-known destination could prove even more memorable. Beaches of jaw-dropping beauty can be found the length and breadth of the Mediterranean, and the old quarters of many less-visited cities often deliver a more authentic experience.

○ **Check out less well-known sites in popular destinations.** All the top cities in the region have many more sights than you could ever see in a day, so why not choose some of the less obvious museums, galleries or markets? They are often still utterly spectacular, but cheaper and less crowded. And there's no better way to get to the heart of a city than to choose a quieter neighbourhood and go for a wander.

○ **Support traditional and local businesses.** Locally run shops and restaurants not only give you a more authentic local experience, supporting them will also help

★ Most Overtouristed Places

Barcelona Home to 1.6 million people, close to 32 million tourists visit each year. Of these, around half are day-trippers.

Dubrovnik Almost 800,000 people arrived here on cruise ships in 2016 and the majority stayed for about three hours.

Venice Increasing numbers of tourists have caused a precipitous drop in Venice's local population, resulting in the closure of local businesses and amenities.

the city maintain its unique identity. And you might avoid paying tourist prices, too.

○ **Be respectful.** Don't litter, and try to minimise waste by bringing your own water bottle or reusable bag. Adhere to local customs as much as possible. Learn a few words of the local language: you may find locals receive you more warmly as a result.

From left: Luža Sq, Dubrovnik (p357); Elia, Mykonos (p467)

Plan Your Trip
Month by Month

February

☙ Carnival

In the run-up to Lent, Carnival is celebrated with wild processions, costumed parties and much eating and drinking. Events are held all over, but festivities are particularly exuberant in Nice and Venice.

April

Weather-wise April is glorious – sunshine and pleasant temperatures – but it can be busy, depending on when Easter falls. If travelling over Easter, expect crowds, memorable celebrations and high-season prices.

☙ Easter

Across the region, Easter week is marked by parades, solemn processions and Passion plays. In Rome, the Pope leads a Good Friday procession around the Colosseum and, on Easter Sunday, he gives his traditional blessing in St Peter's Square.

☆ Maggio Musicale Fiorentino

The curtain goes up on Italy's oldest arts festival, a month-long spectacle of opera, theatre, classical music, jazz and dance held in Florence.

May

Beautiful sunny weather makes May a wonderful time to visit and the festival calendar moves into top gear.

☙ May Day

A public holiday across much of the region, May Day traditions differ from country to country: the French give each other *muguets* (lilies of the valley), the Greeks gather wild flowers, and the Italians descend on Rome for a vast open-air rock concert.

☆ Cannes Film Festival

Mid-month, the world's most influential and glamorous film festival rolls out the red carpet for the Hollywood A-list. Onlookers

Above: Easter Festival, Valletta (p288)

crowd la Croisette to catch a glimpse of their celluloid heroes and debate potential Palme d'Or winners.

June

Summer arrives and with it hot, sunny weather and a full festival schedule. This is a great time for sunning yourself on the beach before the hordes descend and prices skyrocket.

🏆 Palio delle Quattro Antiche Repubbliche Marinare

Historic rivalries are rekindled in the form of boat races between Italy's four ancient maritime republics: Pisa, Genoa, Amalfi and Venice. Before the races, representatives from each city don medieval garb and parade through the host city.

☆ İstanbul Music Festival

Catch a classical concert in a sultan's palace or a jazz jam in a 4th-century church during İstanbul's month-long music fest. See http://muzik.iksv.org/en.

★ Best Festivals & Events

Carnival February
Easter late March or April
Cannes Film Festival May
Athens & Epidaurus Festival June
Festes de la Mercè September

☆ Estate Romana

Between June and September, Rome's ruins, piazzas and parks stage events organised as part of this sweeping annual festival. The program is eclectic featuring everything from film screenings to children's concerts, book readings and theatrical performances.

☆ Athens & Epidaurus Festival

The ancient theatre at Epidaurus and the Odeon of Herodes Atticus are the headline venues of Athens' annual cultural shindig. The festival, which runs from mid-June to

Above: *Presepi* (nativity scene; p38), Naples

August, features music, dance, theatre and much more. See www.greekfestival.gr.

July

Temperatures start to peak as schools break up for the long summer vacation. The coastal resorts are pretty busy and there are any number of festivals to check out.

☆ Dubrovnik Summer Festival

Dubrovnik's beautiful streets set the scintillating stage for Croatia's biggest summer arts festival. Local and international musicians, actors and artists perform at venues across the city throughout July and August. Get details at www.dubrovnik-festival.hr.

✵ Festa del Redentore

On the third weekend in July, gondola regattas serve as the build-up to a spectacular fireworks display in Venice. The much beloved festival was inaugurated in the 16th century to give thanks for the end of a plague epidemic.

☆ Nice Jazz Festival

International jazz greats lead this week-long party on the French Riviera. Louis Armstrong, Dizzy Gillespie and BB King have all headlined here, and the festival is a key date on the European jazz calendar. See www.nicejazzfestival.fr.

☆ Split Summer Festival

Music, drama and dance enjoy top billing at Split's annual culture fest, held from mid-July to mid-August. Shows cover the full range from classical music concerts and opera to experimental theatre performances and puppet shows.

August

The height of summer. Much of the region is on holiday – most people in France and Italy take their annual vacation this month – making for packed resorts, quiet cities and traffic jams on coast-bound roads.

✵ Feast of the Assumption

Celebrated on 15 August, the Feast of the Assumption is the busiest holiday day of the year. Across the region, beaches are crammed, cities slow to a standstill, and everyone basks in the summer sun.

☆ Mostra del Cinema di Venezia

At the end of the month, movie big-shots alight at Venice for the world's oldest film festival. The focus of attention is the Palazzo del Cinema on the Lido, a small slither of an island in Venice's lagoon.

September

This is a lovely month to be on the Med: the August crowds are gone, but it's still hot enough for sunbathing and swimming.

✵ Festes de la Mercè

Barcelona's great annual bash is a bombastic affair, held over four days around 24 September. Highlights include eight-storey human towers and a procession of dragons which parades through the streets accompanied by deafening fireworks and bangers. See www.bcn.cat/merce.

October

As coastal resorts wind down for the season, the focus returns inland.

☆ Romaeuropa

Established international performers join emerging stars at Rome's autumn festival of theatre, opera and dance. Events, staged between late September and October, range from full-on raves and avant-garde dance performances to installations, multimedia shows, recitals and readings. Get details at http://romaeuropa.net.

December
✵ Christmas

Christmas is accompanied by gift-giving traditions and family get-togethers. A highlight is Naples' elaborate *presepi* (nativity scenes).

Plan Your Trip
Get Inspired

Read

Barcelona (Robert Hughes, 1992) Witty and passionate study of 2000 years of history.

SPQR: A History of Ancient Rome (Mary Beard; 2015) Cambridge classicist conjures a bestseller out of Rome's ancient history.

My Brilliant Friend (Elena Ferrante; 2012) The first of Ferrante's bestselling novels about two Neapolitan friends.

Sea and Sardinia (DH Lawrence; 1921) Evocative account of Lawrence's sojourn on the island.

The Great Siege: Malta 1565 (Ernle Bradford; 1961) Rip-roaring read about the epic battle between the Ottoman Turks and the Knights of Malta.

Watch

A Room with a View (1985) Exquisitely rendered screen version of EM Forster's 1908 novel set in Florence.

La grande bellezza (The Great Beauty; 2013) Paolo Sorrentino's Fellini-esque homage to Rome.

L'oro di Napoli (The Gold of Naples; 1954) An anthology of stories set in Naples and featuring Sophia Loren.

Zorba the Greek (1964) The quintessential Crete-filmed movie, based on the excellent novel of the same name.

Güneşe Yolculuk (Journey to the Sun; 1999) Tackles discrimination against Kurdish members of the İstanbul community.

Listen

Le Début de la Suite (Bénabar; 2018) Modern French chansons.

Napul'è (Pino Daniele; 1977) Daniele's tender ode to his hometown is Naples' unofficial anthem.

Folk Songs & Music from Malta (1964) Comprehensive compilation of Maltese musical traditions.

Cesarica (Oliver Dragojević; 1994) Big singalong ballad by Dalmatia's soft-rock superstar.

Rembetika: Songs of the Greek Underground 1925–1947 Many of the classic songs you're likely to hear played in bars.

Above: French singer Bénabar

Plan Your Trip
Choose Your Cruise

There are many different kinds of cruises – if one type of experience doesn't interest you, another surely will. Whether you're looking for a seasoned operator that will take care of everything for you, or a smaller, more niche adventure, your options abound. Here's an overview of the different types of cruising on offer in the Mediterranean.

Megaships

It's not so much about the destination as it is about the panoply of amenities on board. These aren't mere cruises – they're floating cities stocked with every entertainment under the sun. The competition in this category is fierce, as cruise lines crack a bottle of champagne over new and improved vessels at a rapid pace. Some megaship cruise lines that trawl the Mediterranean include, but are not limited to:

Carnival Cruise Line (www.carnival.com) One of the largest cruise lines in the world. The "fun" cruise line woos party animals of all ages, including families and singles.

Celebrity Cruises (www.celebritycruises.com) Has long been one of the most innovative lines. Attracts couples, families and groups who want style and comfort without luxury-line fares.

Disney Cruise Line (disneycruise.disney.go.com) Easily the most expensive of the family-friendly lines, but you get what you pay for. There is no better choice for those travelling with children.

Holland America Line (www.hollandamerica.com) These venerable ships deliver minimalism and competence.

Norwegian Cruise Line (www.ncl.com) Attracts mostly middle-aged and older couples, but you'll also find young families aboard.

Princess Cruises (www.princess.com) This mid-priced operator attracts families and couples on shorter trips; longer cruises draw an older crowd.

Royal Caribbean International (www.royalcaribbean.com) Has some of the biggest cruise ships in the world. A great choice for families looking for a cheaper alternative to Disney. It's also ideal for sporty travellers, offering adrenaline rush–driven activities on board.

Luxury Vessels

These luxury lines promise a palpable uptick in service across the board. From small 100-person ships with sails to large 1000-person cruisers that feel more like floating five-star hotels, opulence and exclusivity are the major draw. Expect sweet suites and perks on board. Some luxury lines include:

Azamara Club Cruises (www.azamaraclub cruises.com) Specialises in destination immersion – longer calls and more overnights allow passengers more time to soak up the local atmosphere and to experience the nightlife.

Crystal Cruises (www.crystalcruises.com) Offers excellent service without stuffiness or dated formality. Also promotes social responsibility, encouraging passengers to participate in volunteering excursions on some trips.

Cunard Line (www.cunard.com) Operating since the 19th century, the atmosphere on these ships is sophisticated. Attracts an older crowd.

Oceania Cruises (www.oceaniacruises.com) Sophisticated with a casually elegant atmosphere. Known for its culinary program and foodie shore excursions.

★ Best Online Resources

Cruise Critic (www.cruisecritic.com)
Cruise Line (www.cruiseline.com)
Cruise Reviews (www.cruisereviews.com)
Cruise Mates (www.cruisemates.com)

Ponant (www.ponant.com) This French operator runs intimate, upscale ships with a social atmosphere.

Regent Seven Seas Cruises (www.rssc.com) These are the most all-inclusive cruises at sea. They've put great effort into providing consistency across the fleet.

Seabourn Cruise Line (www.seabourn.com) Competing in the ultra-luxury market, ships can dock in smaller ports. But you'll remember the on-board experience as much as the destinations.

From left: Sunbathing on the deck of a Princess Cruises ship; Azamara Club Cruises ship

Silversea Cruises (www.silversea.com) Expect formal service – couples in their forties and older dress for dinner.

Viking Cruises (www.vikingcruises.com) A fairly new operator that is growing rapidly. Their cruises are designed for travellers with an interest in geography, culture and history.

Windstar Cruises (www.windstarcruises.com) You'll find families with older teens and couples – including honeymooners – aboard.

Expedition Cruises

Explore the Mediterranean on these multipurpose vessels that mix the excitement of discovery with active excursions and on-board lectures. Some expedition lines include:

Adventure Life Voyages (www.adventure-life.com) Off-the-beaten-track locations and more adventurous itineraries are the focus here.

AdventureSmith Explorations (www.adventuresmithexplorations) This company offsets its carbon emissions and focuses on learning and adventure cruises.

Lindblad Expeditions (www.expeditions.com) If you're looking to discover nature with a small group of like-minded people, this could be the operator for you. Has had an alliance with National Geographic since 2004.

Peregrine Adventures (www.peregrineadventures.com). Offers small-group cruises. Local tour guides seek to offer travellers a more unique experience. They also promote responsible travel and offset their carbon emissions.

Charter Cruises

If the thought of cruising with multitudes of other passengers doesn't appeal, consider chartering your own boat with or without a crew. Vessels are available for all wallet sizes and levels of experience, from river barges to cove-to-cove island hoppers. Self-charter cruise options include:

The Moorings (www.moorings.com)

Nicholson Yacht Charters (www.yachtvacations.com)

Sailo (www.sailo.com)

The Yacht Week (www.theyachtweek.com)

BENSON TRUONG/SHUTTERSTOCK ©

LGBT+ Cruises

LGBT+ events are common aboard major cruise liners. Some companies, such as Celebrity, Holland America, Royal Caribbean, Oceania and Azamara, host LGBT+ charter cruises. Also check out the following operators:

Atlantis (http://atlantisevents.com) Hosts Europe's largest gay cruise.

Olivia (www.olivia.com) Organises lesbian-only cruises.

When to Go

Many Mediterranean cruises run year-round or close to it. Spring and autumn beat the high summer season of July and August in terms of crowds and heat. Timing your cruise to coincide with festival dates can add an extra dimension to your trip.

How Long Do I Need?

One week will give you a good overview of the western Mediterranean region – hitting several of the most popular places, such as Rome, Florence, Cannes, Mallorca, Barcelona and Naples – or eastern Mediterranean ports like Venice, Dubrovnik, Kotor, Athens and the Greek Islands.

Cruises that approach or exceed the two-week mark can take you from one end of the Mediterranean to the other, covering many major ports along the way. Alternatively, smaller luxury or adventure ships often delve deep into one specific zone, whether it be the Greek Islands or the Dalmatian coast.

From left: Windstar Cruises ship; Pool on a Norwegian Cruise Line ship (p40)

Plan Your Trip
Sustainable Cruising

SOLARISYS/SHUTTERSTOCK ©

Travelling on cruise ships isn't without significant impacts – choose your cruise line carefully.

Environmental Issues

Although all travel comes with an environmental cost, by their very size, cruise ships have a disproportionate effect.

Air pollution According to UK-based Climate Care, a carbon-offsetting company, cruise ships emit more carbon per passenger than planes – nearly twice as much. German environmental group Nabu put the figure at around 150 tons of fuel a day, which releases as much particulate matter into the air as about 1 million cars. Most ships burn low-grade bunker fuel – even while in port, to power their generators – which contains more sulphur and particulates than higher-quality fuel. The US and Canada are phasing in new regulations that require ships to burn cleaner fuel when they are close to land; in Europe, a proposal to implement a low-emission zone for ships in the region is supported by France, Spain and Italy, although Greece and Malta remain opposed.

Water pollution Cruise ships generate enormous amounts of sewage, solid waste and grey water, which often just gets dumped directly (or with minimal treatment) into the sea. Some countries are beginning to introduce legislation to curb this behaviour – in 2016, Princess Cruises was fined US$40 million for illegally dumping oil-contaminated waste and covering it up – but unfortunately legislation is lacking when it comes to international waters. As this book was going to print, Carnival and its Princess line acknowledged violating the probation terms from their 2016 case and were ordered to pay an additional $20 million penalty.

What You Can Do

Email the cruise lines you're considering travelling with and ask them about their environmental policies: wastewater treatment, recycling initiatives and whether they use

ERIC FRANKS/ALAMY STOCK PHOTO ©

alternative energy sources. Knowing that customers care about these things has an impact.

As consumer pressure grows, more ships are being equipped with new waste-water treatment facilities, LED lighting and solar panels. In some ports around the world (but no major Mediterranean ports yet), 'cold-ironing' allows ships to plug into local power supplies and avoid leaving the engine running while in port. In Norway and China, electric ships are already in operation, cutting emissions by 95%; this example will need to be followed around the world if cruise ships are to curb their environmental impact effectively.

When choosing a cruise, you might consider a smaller operator, as their environmental impact will also be smaller. Some even offset their carbon emissions. See Choose Your Cruise (p40) for more information.

★ Most Sustainable

According to Friends of the Earth, the most sustainable large cruise-ship company is Disney, followed by Cunard, Holland America and Norwegian. But of course, large cruise liners cannot compete with smaller ships for environmental sustainability.

There are also organisations that rate and review companies and ships on their environmental records:

Friends of the Earth (www.foe.org/cruise reportcard) Letter grades given to cruise lines for environmental and human health impacts.

World Travel Awards (www worldtravelawards. com) Annual awards for the 'World's Leading Green Cruise Line'.

From left: Norwegian Cruise Lines ship *Norwegian Jade*; Cunard Line ship *Queen Victoria*

Plan Your Trip
Family Time Ashore

HALFPOINT/SHUTTERSTOCK ©

Despite a dearth of specifically child-friendly sights and activities, the Mediterranean is a great place to travel with children. Kids are welcome just about everywhere.

Practical Information

You should have no problems finding baby food, formula or disposable nappies.

○ Shop opening hours might differ from those at home, so if you run out of nappies on Saturday afternoon, you could be in for a messy weekend.

○ Most restaurants will have high chairs, but numbers will be limited.

○ Restaurants often have a children's menu.

○ Most European countries have a pretty relaxed attitude to breastfeeding in public.

○ In several Mediterranean countries, museum entry is discounted or free for children under 18.

○ Hit a festival: many European festivals have a strong family bias and have been entertaining children for centuries.

○ The Mediterranean sun is strong and sunburn is a risk, particularly in the first couple of days.

○ For more information, see Lonely Planet's *Travel with Children,* or check out TravelWithYourKids (www.travelwith yourkids.com) or Family Travel Network (www.familytravelnetwork.com).

In Each Country

Croatia Croatia's relaxed dining scene means that you can take children almost anywhere. Even the more upmarket restaurants will have a kid-friendly pasta, pizza or rice dish on the menu.

France Children's menus (fixed meals at a set price) are common, Don't be shy in asking for a half-portion of an adult main – restaurants generally oblige.

Greece Ingredients such as nuts and dairy find their way into lots of dishes, so if your children

TRAVNIKOVSTUDIO/SHUTTERSTOCK ©

suffer from allergies, write them clearly in plain Greek to show restaurant staff.

Italy In restaurants, aside from the *menù bambini* (children's menu), it's also acceptable to order a *mezzo piatto* (half-portion).

Malta Many of the smarter restaurants don't permit very young children, but most restaurants are very child-friendly.

Montenegro You'll need to keep a close eye on small children given the generally lower standard of safety regulations (missing railings, unfenced pools etc). You'll struggle to get strollers along the cobbled lanes and stairways – a baby carrier or sling makes exploring easier.

Spain Adapting to Spanish eating hours can be a challenge. When kids get hungry between meals, it's sometimes possible to zip into the nearest *tasca* (tapas bar) and get them a snack.

Turkey While free or discounted entry to sights is common, facilities are often lacking and safety consciousness rarely meets Western norms. Breastfeeding in public is uncommon; best to do so in a private or discreet place.

★ Best Cruise Lines for Families

Disney (p40)

Carnival (p40)

Celebrity (p40)

Royal Caribbean International (p40)

Princess (p40)

Best Ports for Kids

Athens, Greece Ruins to clamber over, plus museums and child-geared sights to explore.

Dubrovnik, Croatia Lots of beach action and unique experiences; let the little ones off the leash in the car-free old town.

Valletta, Malta Sun and sea, forts and castles: there's lots for kids to see and do.

Naples, Italy Subterranean ruins in Naples, gladiator battlefields in nearby Pompeii, plus volcanoes, thermal pools and coastal caves.

Palma de Mallorca, Spain With its beaches, parks, castles, water activities and plentiful cafes and ice-cream shops, Palma is wonderful for children.

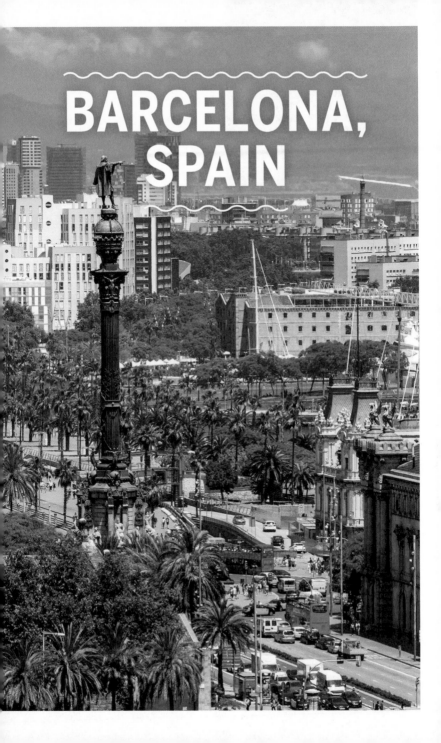

BARCELONA, SPAIN

Barcelona at a Glance...

Barcelona is a mix of sunny Mediterranean charm and European urban style. The city bursts with art and architecture, Catalan cooking is among the country's best, summer sunseekers fill the beaches in and beyond the city, and the bars and clubs heave year-round. Vestiges of Barcelona's days as a middle-ranking Roman town remain, and its old centre constitutes one of Europe's richest concentrations of Gothic architecture. Elsewhere are surreal spectacles capped by La Sagrada Família. Equally worth seeking out are the city's avant-garde chefs, who compete with old-time classics for the gourmet's attention.

With One Day in Port

● Start your day with La Rambla. Don't miss the human statues, the Miró mosaic, and key buildings including the 18th-century **Palau de la Virreina** (p67). Next is a stop at food market **Mercat de la Boqueria** (p67), one of the greatest sensory experiences in Europe.

● Head back down La Rambla and cross **Plaça Reial** (p57) before wandering the atmospheric lanes of the Barri Gòtic. Make your way to the magnificent **La Catedral** (p66).

● In the afternoon, head to **La Sagrada Família** (p52) and linger over the artistry of Spain's most visited sight.

Best Places For...

Tapas Tapas 24 (p76)

Churros Xurreria (p74)

Cava Can Paixano (p76)

Markets Mercat de la Boqueria (p67)

Plazas Plaça Reial (p57)

Previous page: Barcelona skyline from Montjuïc (p58)
MISTERVLAD/SHUTTERSTOCK ©

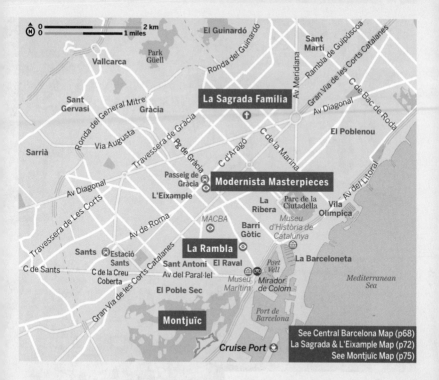

0 ─── 2 km
0 ─── 1 miles

El Guinardó

Sant Martí

Vallcarca Park Güell

Ronda del Guinardó

Av Meridiana

Rambla de Guipúscoa

Gran Via de les Corts Catalanes

C de Bac de Roda

Sant Gervasi

Ronda del General Mitre

Gràcia

Av Diagonal

La Sagrada Família

C d'Aragó

C de la Marina

El Poblenou

Via Augusta

Travessera de Gràcia

Pg de Gràcia

Sarrià

Passeig de Gràcia

Modernista Masterpieces

Av del Litoral

Av Diagonal

L'Eixample

La Ribera

Parc de la Ciutadella

Vila Olímpica

Travessera de Les Corts

Av de Roma

MACBA

Museu d'Història de Catalunya

Barri Gòtic

Sants

Estació Sants

Corts Catalanes

La Rambla

La Barceloneta

C de Sants

C de la Creu Coberta

Sant Antoni

El Raval

Av del Paral·lel

Port Vell

Mediterranean Sea

El Poble Sec

Museu Marítim

Mirador de Colom

Montjuïc

Port de Barcelona

Cruise Port

See Central Barcelona Map (p68)
La Sagrada & L'Eixample Map (p72)
See Montjuïc Map (p75)

Getting from the Port

One of the biggest in the world, Barcelona's cruise port has **nine terminals**. Located south of the city centre, the cruise port is just over 1.5km from the bottom of La Rambla. The north, south and east terminals are around 800m from this legendary avenue.

It's about a 25-minute walk to the heart of Ciutat Vella (Old City), and most sights worth visiting fan out from here. Barcelona is very walkable and distances are mostly short. The excellent metro can get you most places, with buses and trams filling in the gaps.

Fast Facts

Currency Euro (€)

Languages Spanish, Catalan

Money ATMs are in plentiful supply around Plaça de Catalunya, and along Via Laietana and La Rambla.

Tourist Information Oficina d'Informació de Turisme de Barcelona is located in Plaça Catalunya, about 2.5km from the cruise port.

Visas Generally not required for stays of up to 90 days; not required at all for members of EU or Schengen countries). Some nationalities need a Schengen visa.

Wi-fi The city has dozens of free public wi-fi hotspots. Look for the small blue signs with the blue 'W' symbol.

Passion Facade

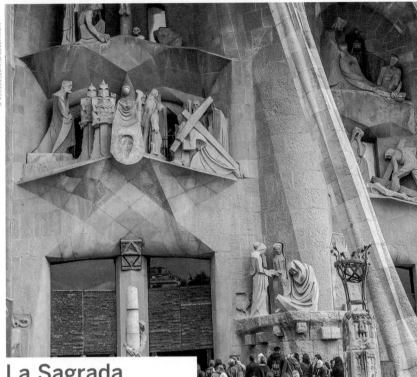

KIEV.VICTOR/SHUTTERSTOCK ©

La Sagrada Família

If you can only visit one place in Barcelona, this should be it. Still under construction, La Sagrada Família inspires awe by its sheer verticality in the manner of the medieval cathedrals.

Great For...

Don't Miss

The extraordinary pillars and stained glass, the Nativity Facade, the Passion Facade.

Gaudí's Vision

The Temple Expiatori de la Sagrada Família (Expiatory Temple of the Holy Family) was Antoni Gaudí's all-consuming obsession. Given the commission by a conservative society that wished to build a temple as atonement for the city's sins of modernity, Gaudí saw its completion as his holy mission.

Gaudí devised a cathedral 95m long and 60m wide, able to seat 13,000 people, with a central tower (representing Christ) 170m high above the transept and another 17 of 100m or more. The 12 along the three facades represent the Apostles, while the remaining five represent the Virgin Mary and the four evangelists. With his characteristic dislike for straight lines, Gaudí gave his towers swelling outlines inspired by the weird peaks of Montserrat.

Explore Ashore

Catching public transport from the cruise port involves changing transport types several times; the quickest and simplest way to get there is to catch a taxi (around €15). Allow a few hours to explore once you arrive.

❶ Need to Know

Map p72; ☎93 208 04 14; www.sagrada familia.org; Carrer de la Marina; adult/child €15/free; ⊗9am-8pm Apr-Sep, to 7pm Mar & Oct, to 6pm Nov-Feb; ⓂSagrada Família)

At Gaudí's death, only the crypt, the apse walls, one portal and one tower were finished.

The Nativity Facade

The Nativity Facade is the artistic pinnacle of the building, mostly created under Gaudí's personal supervision. You can reach high up inside some of the four towers through a combination of lifts and narrow spiral staircases. The towers are destined to hold tubular bells capable of playing complex music at great volume. Their upper parts are decorated with mosaics spelling out 'Sanctus, Sanctus, Sanctus, Hosanna in Excelsis, Amen, Alleluia'.

Passion Facade

The southwest Passion Facade, depicting Christ's last days and death, was built between 1954 and 1978 based on surviving drawings by Gaudí, with four towers and a large, sculpture-bedecked portal. The main series of sculptures, on three levels, are in an S-shaped sequence, starting with the Last Supper at the bottom left and ending with Christ's burial at the top right.

Glory Facade

The Glory Facade is under construction and will, like the others, be crowned by four towers. Gaudí wanted it to be the most magnificent facade of the church. Inside will be the narthex, a kind of foyer made up of 16 'lanterns', a series of hyperboloid forms topped by cones.

Museu Gaudí

The Museu Gaudí, below ground level, includes interesting material on Gaudí's life and other works, as well as models and photos of La Sagrada Família.

La Sagrada Família

A TIMELINE

1882 Construction begins on a neo-Gothic church designed by Francisco de Paula del Villar y Lozano.

1883 Antoni Gaudí takes over as chief architect and plans a far more ambitious church to hold 13,000 faithful.

1926 Gaudí dies; work continues under Domènec Sugrañes i Gras. Much of the **apse ❶** and **Nativity Facade ❷** is complete.

1930 Bell towers ❸ of the Nativity Facade completed.

1936 Construction interrupted by Spanish Civil War; anarchists destroy Gaudí's plans.

1939–40 Architect Francesc de Paula Quintana i Vidal restores the crypt and meticulously reassembles many of Gaudí's lost models, some of which can be seen in the **museum ❹**.

1976 Passion Facade ❺ completed.

1986–2006 Sculptor Josep Subirachs adds sculptural details to the Passion Facade including the panels telling the story of Christ's last days, amid much criticism for employing a style far removed from what was thought typical of Gaudí.

2000 Central nave vault ❻ completed.

2010 Church completely roofed over; Pope Benedict XVI consecrates the church; work begins on a high-speed rail tunnel that will pass beneath the church's **Glory Facade ❼**.

2026 Projected completion date.

TOP TIPS

➡ The best light through the stained-glass windows of the Passion Facade bursts into the heart of the church in the late afternoon.

➡ Visit at opening time on weekdays to avoid the worst of the crowds.

➡ Head up the Nativity Facade bell towers for the views, as long queues generally await at the Passion Facade towers.

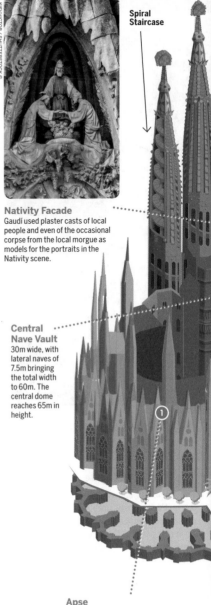

KIEVVICTOR / SHUTTERSTOCK ©

Spiral Staircase

Nativity Facade
Gaudí used plaster casts of local people and even of the occasional corpse from the local morgue as models for the portraits in the Nativity scene.

Central Nave Vault
30m wide, with lateral naves of 7.5m bringing the total width to 60m. The central dome reaches 65m in height.

Apse
Built just after the crypt in mostly neo-Gothic style, it is capped by pinnacles that show a hint of the genius that Gaudí would later deploy in the rest of the church.

Bell Towers
The towers of the three facades will represent the Twelve Apostles. Eight are completed. Lifts whisk visitors up one tower of the Nativity and Passion Facades (the latter gets longer queues) for fine views.

NIKADA / GETTY IMAGES ©

Completed Church
Along with the Glory Facade and its four towers, six other towers remain to be completed. They will represent the four evangelists, the Virgin Mary and, soaring above them all over the transept, a 170m colossus symbolising Christ.

Glory Facade
This will be the most fanciful facade of all, with a narthex boasting 16 hyperboloid lanterns topped by cones that will look something like an organ made of melting ice cream.

Museu Gaudí
Jammed with old photos, drawings and restored plaster models that bring Gaudí's ambitions to life, the museum also houses an extraordinarily complex plumb-line device he used to calculate his constructions.

Escoles de Gaudí

Crypt
The first completed part of the church, the crypt is in largely neo-Gothic style and lies under the transept. Gaudí's burial place here can be seen from the Museu Gaudí.

Passion Facade
See the story of Christ's last days from Last Supper to burial in an S-shaped sequence from bottom to top of the facade. Check out the cryptogram in which the numbers always add up to 33, Christ's age at his death.

YURY DMITRIENKO / SHUTTERSTOCK ©

MISTERVLAD/SHUTTERSTOCK ©

La Rambla

Barcelona's most famous street is both a tourist magnet and a window into Catalan culture, with cultural centres, theatres and architecturally intriguing buildings lining its sides.

Set between narrow traffic lanes and flanked by plane trees, the middle of La Rambla is a broad pedestrian boulevard, crowded every day until the wee hours. A stroll here is pure sensory overload, with souvenir hawkers, buskers, pavement artists, mimes and living statues all part of the ever-changing street scene.

What's in a Name?

La Rambla takes its name from a seasonal stream (*raml* in Arabic) that once ran here. From the early Middle Ages it was better known as the Cagalell (Stream of Shit) and lay outside the city walls until the 14th century. Monastic buildings were built and, subsequently, mansions of the well-to-do. Unofficially, La Rambla is divided into five sections, which explains why many know it as Las Ramblas.

Great For...

Don't Miss

The Mercat de la Boqueria, one of the world's most celebrated markets, on La Rambla's western side..

La Font de Canaletes

Explore Ashore

The nearest cruise terminal is about a 15-minute walk away. Or, catch the cruise shuttle to Mirador de Colom at bottom of La Rambla. A stroll down La Rambla is 1.5km.

❶ Need to Know

Ⓜ Catalunya (north), Ⓜ Liceu (middle) and Ⓜ Drassanes (south).

La Font de Canaletes

From Plaça de Catalunya, La Rambla unfurls down the hill to the southeast. Its first manifestation, La Rambla de Canaletes, is named after a pretty 19th-century wrought-iron fountain, La Font de Canaletes. Local legend says anyone who drinks from its waters will return to Barcelona. More prosaically, delirious football fans gather here to celebrate whenever FC Barcelona wins something.

Bird Market

In keeping with its numerous contradictory impulses, La Rambla changes personality as it gains momentum down the hill. Stalls crowd in from the side as the name changes to La Rambla dels Estudis (officially) or La Rambla dels Ocells ('birds', unofficially) in Barcelona's twittering bird market (under threat from ice-cream and pastry stands).

Plaça de la Boqueria

At around La Rambla's midpoint lies one of Europe's greatest markets, the Mercat de la Boqueria (p67), while almost opposite is your chance to walk on the colourful Mosaïc de Miró in the pavement (one tile is signed by the artist). Look also for the grandiose Gran Teatre del Liceu, then rest in the lovely **Plaça Reial** (Map p68; Ⓜ Liceu). The lamp posts by the central fountain are Antoni Gaudí's first known works in the city.

La Rambla de Santa Mònica

The final stretch of La Rambla, La Rambla de Santa Mònica, widens out to approach the Mirador de Colom overlooking Port Vell. Just off La Rambla's southwestern tip, don't miss the sublime Museu Marítim (p66).

CaixaForum, entrance designed by architect Arata Isozaki

NITOJ00/GETTY IMAGES © CAIXAFORUM ENTRANCE DESIGNED BY ARCHITECT ARATA ISOZAKI

Montjuïc

The Montjuïc hillside, crowned by a castle and gardens, overlooks the port and holds some of the city's finest art collections: the Museu Nacional d'Art de Catalunya, the Fundació Joan Miró and CaixaForum. Dominating the southeastern heights of Montjuïc, the forbidding castell enjoys commanding views over the Mediterranean.

Great For...

Don't Miss

The Romanesque frescoes in the Museu Nacional d'Art de Catalunya.

Museu Nacional d'Art de Catalunya

Built for the 1929 World Exhibition and restored in 2005, the **Museu Nacional d'Art de Catalunya** (MNAC; Map p75; ☎ 936 22 03 76; www.museunacional.cat; Mirador del Palau Nacional; adult/child €12/free, after 3pm Sat & 1st Sun of month free, rooftop viewpoint only €2; ☺10am-8pm Tue-Sat, to 3pm Sun May-Sep, to 6pm Tue-Sat, to 3pm Sun Oct-Apr; ☒55, Ⓜ Espanya) houses a vast collection of mostly Catalan art spanning the early Middle Ages to the early 20th century. The high point is the collection of extraordinary Romanesque frescoes. Rescued from neglected country churches across northern Catalonia in the early 20th century, the collection consists of 21 frescoes, woodcarvings and painted altar frontals.

Museu Nacional d'Art de Catalunya

⚓ Explore Ashore

The quickest way to get from the cruise port to Montjuïc is in a taxi (15 to 20 minutes, depending on traffic). Otherwise, the metro stops at the foot of Montjuïc; buses and funiculars go all the way.

★ Top Tip

Ride the Transbordador Aeri from Barceloneta for a bird's-eye approach to Montjuïc.

Fundació Joan Miró

Joan Miró, the city's best-known 20th-century artistic progeny, bequeathed the **Fundació Joan Miró** (Map p75; ☏93 443 94 70; www.fmirobcn.org; Parc de Montjuïc; adult/child €12/free; ⊙10am-8pm Tue, Wed, Fri & Sat, to 9pm Thu, to 3pm Sun Apr-Oct, 10am-6pm Tue, Wed & Fri, to 9pm Thu, to 8pm Sat, to 3pm Sun Nov-Mar; ☐55, 150, ☐Paral·lel) to his hometown in 1971. Its light-filled buildings, designed by close friend and architect Josep Lluís Sert, are crammed with seminal works, from Miró's earliest timid sketches to paintings from his last years. Highlights include Sala Joan Prats, with works spanning the early years until 1919; Sala Pilar Juncosa, which covers his surrealist years from 1932 to 1955; and Rooms 18 and 19 which contain masterworks of the years 1956 to 1983.

CaixaForum

The Caixa building society prides itself on its involvement in (and ownership of) art, in particular all that is contemporary. Its premier art expo space in Barcelona, **CaixaForum** (Map p75; ☏93 476 86 00; www.caixaforum.es; Avinguda de Francesc Ferrer i Guàrdia 6-8; adult/child €4/free, 1st Sun of month free; ⊙10am-8pm; ☒Espanya) hosts part of the bank's extensive collection from around the globe. The setting is a completely renovated former factory, the Fàbrica Casaramona, an outstanding Modernista brick structure designed by Josep Puig i Cadafalch. On occasion, portions of La Caixa's own collection of 800 works of modern and contemporary art go on display, but more often than not major international exhibitions are the key draw.

Casa Batlló

Modernista Masterpieces

The elegant, if traffic-filled, district of L'Eixample (pronounced 'lay-sham-pluh') is a showcase for Modernista architecture, including some of Gaudí's most treasured masterpieces.

Great For

Don't Miss

Casa Batllo is quite simply one of the weirdest and most wonderful buildings in Spain.

La Pedrera

This undulating beast is a Gaudí **masterpiece** (Casa Milà; Map p72; ☎ 93 214 25 76; www.lapedrera.com; Passeig de Gràcia 92; adult/child €25/14; ⏰ 9am-8.30pm & 9-11pm Mar-Oct, 9am-6.30pm & 7-9pm Nov-Feb; Ⓜ Diagonal), built from 1905 to 1910 as a combined apartment and office block. The top-floor apartment, attic and roof, together called the Espai Gaudí (Gaudí Space), are open to visitors. The roof is extraordinary, with its giant chimney pots looking like multicoloured medieval knights. Gaudí wanted to put a statue of the Virgin up here, but when the Milà family (who commissioned the building) said no, Gaudí resigned in disgust.

The next floor down is the elegantly furnished apartment (El Pis de la Pedrera), done up in the style of an early 20th-century well-to-do family. There are sensuous curves

Roof of La Pedrera

CATALUNYA LA PEDRERA FOUNDATION ©

Modernista
Masterpieces

Explore Ashore

Take the shuttle bus from the cruise port to Mirador de Colom. The closest metro station is Drassanes (L3), from where you can emerge onto to Passeig de Gràcia in L'Eixample.

❶ Need to Know

Four metro lines criss-cross L'Eixample, with Passeig de Gràcia and Diagonal the most useful.

window and skylights are dreamy waves of wood and coloured glass.

and unexpected touches in everything from light fittings to bedsteads, from door handles to balconies.

Casa Batlló

One of the strangest residential **buildings** (Map p72; ☎93 216 03 06; www.casabatllo.es; Passeig de Gràcia 43; adult/child €29/26; ⊗9am-9pm, last admission 8pm; ⓂPasseig de Gràcia) in Europe, this is Gaudí at his hallucinatory best. The facade, sprinkled with blue, mauve and green tiles and studded with wave-shaped window frames and balconies, rises to an uneven blue-tiled roof. The balconies look like the bony jaws of some strange beast and the roof represents Sant Jordi (St George) and the dragon. The internal light wells shimmer with tiles of deep sea blue. Everything swirls: the ceiling is twisted into a vortex around its sunlike lamp; the doors,

Beyond Gaudí

Casa Batlló is just one of the three houses on the block between Carrer del Consell de Cent and Carrer d'Aragó that gave it the playful name Manzana de la Discordia. The other houses are the Casa Amatller (p71), one of Puig i Cadafalch's most striking bits of Modernista fantasy, and the **Casa Lleó Morera** (Map p72; Passeig de Gràcia 35; ⓂPasseig de Gràcia), Lluís Domènech i Montaner's 1905 creation. Other Modernista icons to watch out for include Puig i Cadafalch's **Palau del Baró Quadras** (Map p72; ☎93 467 80 00; www. llull.cat; Avinguda Diagonal 373; tour adult/ child €10/free; ⊗11am-1pm Wed; ⓂDiagonal) and **Palau Montaner** (Map p72; ☎93 317 76 52; www.fundaciotapies.org; Carrer de Mallorca 278; adult/child €7/free; ⊗by reservation; ⓂPasseig de Gràcia).

Hidden Treasures in the Barri Gòtic

This scenic walk through the Barri Gòtic will take you back in time, from the early days of Roman-era Barcino through to the medieval era.

Start La Catedral
Distance 1.5km
Duration 1½ hours

Classic Photo La Catedral

1 Before entering the cathedral, have a look at **three Picasso friezes** on the building facing the square. After noting his signature style, wander through **La Catedral** (p66); don't miss the cloister with its flock of 13 geese.

2 Leaving the cathedral, enter the former gates of the ancient fortified city and turn right into **Plaça de Sant Felip Neri**. Note the shrapnel-scarred walls of the old church, damaged by pro-Francoist bombers in 1938. A plaque commemorates the victims (mostly children) of the bombing.

3 Head out of the square and turn right. In this narrow lane you'll spot a small **statue of Santa Eulàlia**, one of Barcelona's patron saints who suffered various tortures during her martyrdom. Make your way west to the looming 14th-century **Basilica de Santa Maria del Pi** (adult/concession/child under 7yr €4/3/free; ⏰10am-6pm), which is famed for its magnificent rose window.

4 Follow the curving road and zigzag down to **Plaça Reial** (p57), one of Barcelona's prettiest squares. Flanking the fountain are lamp posts designed by Antoni Gaudí.

C d'en Roca

C del Petritxol

Plaça del Pi

Plaça de Sant Josep Oriol

La Rambla de Sant Josep

3

La Rambla

C del Cardenal Casañas

C de la Boqueria

C d'en Quintana

Plaça de la Boqueria

Ⓜ Liceu

C de n'Arolès

La Rambla dels Caputxins

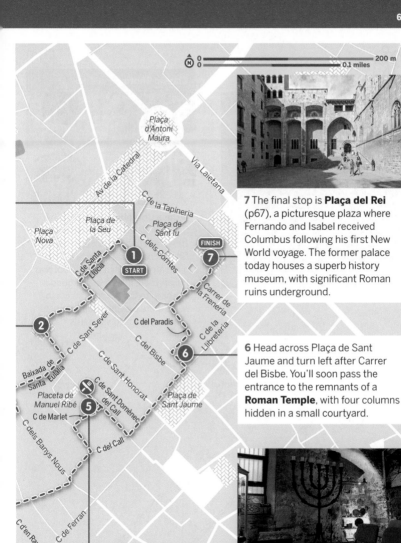

Plaça d'Antoni Maura

Av de la Catedral

Via Laietana

C de la Tapineria

Plaça de la Seu

Plaça de Sant Iu

Plaça Nova

C dels Comtes

START

FINISH

C de Santa Llúcia

Carrer de la Freneria

C de Sant Sever

C del Paradis

C de la Llibreteria

Baixada de Santa Eulàlia

C de Sant Honorat

C del Bisbe

C de Sant Domènec del Call

Placeta de Manuel Ribé

Plaça de Sant Jaume

C de Marlet

C dels Banys Nous

C del Call

C d'en Rauric

C de Ferran

C de les Heures

200 m
0.1 miles

7 The final stop is **Plaça del Rei** (p67), a picturesque plaza where Fernando and Isabel received Columbus following his first New World voyage. The former palace today houses a superb history museum, with significant Roman ruins underground.

6 Head across Plaça de Sant Jaume and turn left after Carrer del Bisbe. You'll soon pass the entrance to the remnants of a **Roman Temple**, with four columns hidden in a small courtyard.

Take a Break... In the heart of El Call, **Alcoba Azul** (Carrer de Salamó Ben Adret 14; ☎ 93 302 81 41; mains €6-10) is atmospheric.

5 Stroll up to Carrer de la Boqueria and turn left on Carrer de Sant Domènec del Call. This leads into the **El Call** district, the heart of the medieval Jewish quarter until the bloody pogrom of 1391. The **Sinagoga Major** (adult/child under 11yr €3.50/free), one of Europe's oldest, was discovered in 1996.

1 LORNET/SHUTTERSTOCK © 5 ESME FOX/LONELY PLANET © 7 MARK52/SHUTTERSTOCK ©

Modernisme in L'Eixample

Catalan modernism (Modernisme) abounds in Barcelona's L'Eixample district. This walk introduces you to the movement's main form of expression: architecture.

Start Casa Calvet
Distance 4km
Duration one hour

Classic Photo Casa Comalat

4 Casa Comalat, built in 1911 by Salvador Valeri i Pupurull (1873–1954), is similarly striking. Note Gaudí's obvious influence on the main facade, with its wavy roof and bulging balconies. Head around the back to Carrer de Còrsega to see a more playful facade, with its windows stacked like cards.

3 Puig i Cadafalch let his imagination loose on **Casa Serra** (1903–08), a neo-Gothic whimsy that is today home to government offices.

2 Casa Enric Batlló was completed in 1896 by Josep Vilaseca (1848–1910), part of the Comtes de Barcelona hotel. The brickwork facade is very graceful lit up at night.

0 — 400 m
0 — 0.2 miles

5 Completed in 1912, **Casa Thomas** was one of Domènech i Montaner's earlier efforts – the floral motifs and reptile figurines are trademarks and the massive ground-level wrought-iron decoration (and protection?) is magnificent. Wander inside to the Cubiña design store to admire his interior work, including the brick columns.

FINISH

Verdaguer

Plaça de Mossèn Jacint Verdaguer

Av Diagonal

C de València

C d'Aragó

SANT GERVASI

6

C de Girona

C de Bailén

Pg de Sant Joan

7 Puig i Cadafalch's **Palau Macaya**, 1901, has a wonderful courtyard and features the typical playful, pseudo-Gothic decoration that characterises many of the architect's projects. It belongs to La Caixa bank and is occasionally used for temporary exhibitions, when visitors are permitted to enter.

6 Casa Llopis i Bofill is an interesting block of flats designed by Antoni Gallissà (1861–1903) in 1902. The graffiti-covered facade is particularly striking to the visitor's eye. The use of elaborate parabolic arches on the ground floor is a clear Modernista touch, as are the wrought-iron balconies.

Take a Break... Check out **Casa Amalia** (✆93 458 94 58; www.casamaliabcn.com; Passatge del Mercat 4-6 mains €9-20; Ⓜ Girona) for hearty Catalan cooking.

1 Casa Calvet Gaudí's most conventional contribution to L'Eixample was built in 1900. Inspired by baroque, the noble ashlar facade is broken up by protruding wrought-iron balconies.

Gran Via de les Corts Catalanes

C de Casp

START

Via Laietana

Ronda de Sant Pere

Plaça de Joan Carles I

Urquinaona Ⓜ Plaça d'Urquinaona

⊙ SIGHTS

⊚ Barceloneta, the Waterfront & El Poblenou

Museu Marítim   Museum

(☎93 342 99 20; www.mmb.cat; Avinguda de les Drassanes; adult/child €10/5, free from 3pm Sun; ☉10am-8pm; ⓜDrassanes) The city's maritime museum occupies Gothic shipyards – a remarkable relic from Barcelona's days as the seat of a seafaring empire. Highlights include a full-scale 1970s replica of Don Juan of Austria's 16th-century flagship, fishing vessels, antique navigation charts and dioramas of the Barcelona waterfront.

Museu d'Història de Catalunya   Museum

(Museum of the History of Catalonia; ☎93 225 47 00; www.mhcat.cat; Plaça de Pau Vila 3; adult/child €4.50/3.50, last Tue of the month Oct-Jun free; ☉10am-7pm Tue & Thu-Sat, to 8pm Wed, to 2.30pm Sun; ⓜBarceloneta) Inside the **Palau de Mar**, this worthwhile museum takes you from the Stone Age through to the early 1980s. It's a busy hotchpotch of dioramas, artefacts, videos, models, documents and interactive bits: all up, an entertaining exploration of 2000 years of Catalan history. Signage is in Catalan, Spanish and English.

Mirador de Colom   Viewpoint

(Columbus Monument; ☎93 285 38 32; www.barcelonaturisme.com; Plaça del Portal de la Pau; adult/child €6/4; ☉8.30am-8.30pm; ⓜDrassanes) High above the swirl of traffic navigating the roundabout below, Christopher Columbus keeps permanent watch, pointing vaguely out to the Mediterranean from this Corinthian-style iron column built for the 1888 Universal Exhibition. Zip up 60m in a lift for a bird's-eye view back up La Rambla and across Barcelona's ports. You can also enjoy a wine tasting afterwards in the cellar underneath (€8 for lift and wine).

⊚ La Rambla & Barri Gòtic

La Catedral   Cathedral

(Map p68; ☎93 342 82 62; www.catedralbcn.org; Plaça de la Seu; donation €7 or choir €3, roof €3; ☉tourist visits 12.30-7.45pm Mon-Fri, 12.30-5.30pm Sat, 2-5.30pm Sun, hours of worship vary; ⓜJaume I) Barcelona's central place of worship presents a magnificent image. The richly decorated main facade, dotted with gargoyles and the kinds of stone intricacies you would expect of northern European Gothic, sets it quite apart from other churches in Barcelona. The facade was actually added in 1870, although the rest of the building was built between 1298 and 1460. Its other facades are sparse in decoration, and the octagonal, flat-roofed towers are a clear reminder that, even here, Catalan Gothic architectural principles prevailed.

Museu d'Història de Barcelona   Museum

(MUHBA; Map p68; ☎93 256 21 00; www.museuhistoria.bcn.cat; Plaça del Rei; adult/concession/child €7/5/free, 3-8pm Sun & 1st Sun of month free; ☉10am-7pm Tue-Sat, to 8pm Sun; ⓜJaume I) One of Barcelona's most fascinating museums takes you back through the centuries to the very foundations of Roman Barcino. You'll stroll over ruins of the old streets, sewers, laundries and wine- and fish-making factories that flourished here following the town's founding by Emperor Augustus around 10 BC. Equally impressive is the building itself, which was once part of the Palau Reial Major (Grand Royal Palace) on Plaça del Rei, among the key locations of medieval princely power in Barcelona.

Museu Frederic Marès   Museum

(Map p68; ☎93 256 35 00; www.museumares.bcn.cat; Plaça de Sant Iu 5; adult/concession/child €4.20/2.40/free, 3-8pm Sun & 1st Sun of month free; ☉10am-7pm Tue-Sat, 11am-8pm Sun; ⓜJaume I) One of the wildest collections of historical curios lies inside this vast medieval complex, once part of the royal palace of the counts of Barcelona. A rather worn coat of arms on the wall indicates that it was also, for a while, the seat of the Spanish Inquisition in Barcelona. Frederic Marès i Deulovol (1893–1991) was a rich sculptor, traveller and obsessive collector, and displays of religious art and vast varieties of antiques *objets* litter the museum.

Plaça del Rei
Square

(King's Square; Map p68; M Jaume I) Plaça del Rei is a picturesque plaza where Fernando and Isabel are thought to have received Columbus following his first New World voyage. It is the courtyard of the former Palau Reial Major, which today houses the superb Museu d'Història de Barcelona (p66).

Mercat de la Boqueria
Market

(Map p68; ✆93 318 20 17; www.boqueria.
barcelona; La Rambla 91; ⏰8am-8.30pm Mon-Sat;
M Liceu) Mercat de la Boqueria is possibly La Rambla's most interesting building, not so much for its Modernista-influenced design – it was actually built over a long period, from 1840 to 1914, on the site of the former St Joseph Monastery – but for the action of the food market within.

Palau de la Virreina
Architecture

(Map p68; La Rambla 99; M Liceu) The Palau de la Virreina is a grand 18th-century rococo mansion (with some neoclassical elements) housing an arts/entertainment information and ticket office run by the *Ajuntament* (town hall) (Casa de la Ciutat; Map p68; ✆93 402 70 00; www.bcn.cat; Plaça de Sant Jaume; ⏰10am-2pm Sun; M Jaume I) FREE. Built by Manuel d'Amat i de Junyent, the captain general of Chile (a Spanish colony that included the Peruvian silver mines of Potosí), it is a rare example of post-baroque building in Barcelona.

◉ El Raval

MACBA
Arts Centre

(Museu d'Art Contemporani de Barcelona; ✆93 412 08 10; www.macba.cat; Plaça dels Àngels 1; adult/concession/child under 14yr €10/8/free, 4-8pm Sat free; ⏰11am-7.30pm Mon & Wed-Fri, 10am-8pm Sat, 10am-3pm Sun & holidays; M Universitat) Designed by Richard Meier and opened in 1995, MACBA has become the city's foremost contemporary art centre, with captivating exhibitions for the serious art lover. The permanent collection is on the ground floor and dedicates itself to Spanish and Catalan art from the second half of the 20th century, with works by Antoni Tàpies, Joan Brossa and Miquel Barceló, among others; international

🡵 Escape the Crowds

Barcelona's popularity has surged in recent years, but there are many local *barrios* (districts) to explore away from the crowds.

Sant Andreu de Palomar The charming, village-like *barrio* of Sant Andreu de Palomar lies to the northeast of Barcelona's centre. The neighbourhood is filled with quaint squares, independent shops and cafes, and mesmerising Modernista architecture.

Horta The quaint, quiet *barrio* of Horta lies to the north of the centre and west of Sant Andreu, and brims with cute plazas and narrow streets. But the main attraction is the Parc del Laberint d'Horta – a huge green expanse that sits high up among rolling hills.

Sarrià Barcelona's upmarket *barrio* for the well-heeled is filled with luxury apartments, quiet narrow streets, picturesque squares and elegant Catalan architecture. The *barrio's* most fascinating sight is one of Gaudí's lesser-known buildings, the Bellesguard tower.

Pedralbes West of Sarrià, the Pedralbes *barrio* is characterised by wide leafy avenues and graceful mansions, backed by the green hills of the Collserola natural park. Make a stop at the Pavellons Güell, fronted by Gaudí's exquisite Dragon Gate with intricate curls of wrought iron.

Parc del Laberint d'Horta
GO/SHUTTERSTOCK ©

artists, such as Paul Klee, Bruce Nauman and John Cage, are also represented.

Central Barcelona

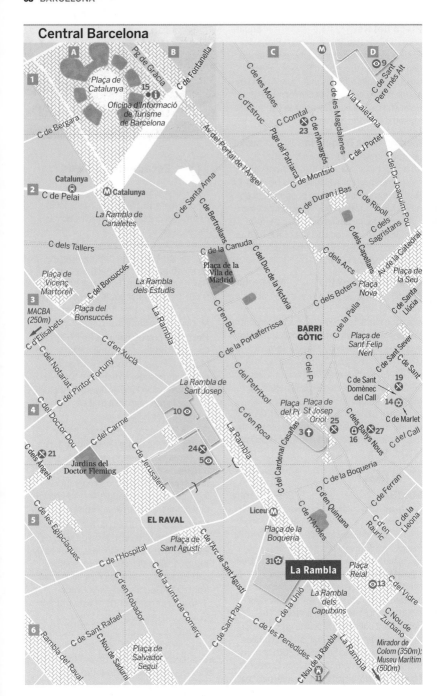

Plaça de Catalunya

15
Oficina d'Informació de Turisme de Barcelona

Pg de Gràcia

C de Fontanella

C de les Moles

C d'Estruc

C Comtal

C de n'Amargós
23

C de les Magdalenes

C de J Portet

C del Dr Joaquim Pou

C de Sant Pere més Alt
9

Via Laietana

Catalunya
C de Bergara

Av del Portal de l'Àngel

Ptge del Patriarca

C de Montsió

C de Duran i Bas

C de Ripoll

C dels Sagristans

Catalunya
C de Pelai

La Rambla de Canaletes

C de Santa Anna

C de Bertrellans

C de la Canuda

C del Duc de la Victoria

C dels Capellans

C dels Arcs

Av de la Catedral

Plaça de la Seu

C dels Tallers

Plaça de Vicenç Martorell

C del Bonsuccés

La Rambla dels Estudis

Plaça de la Vila de Madrid

C dels Boters

Plaça Nova

Plaça de Santa Llúcia

MACBA (250m)

Plaça del Bonsuccés

C d'Elisabets

La Rambla

C d'en Bot

C de la Portaferrissa

C de la Palla

BARRI GÒTIC

Plaça de Sant Felip Neri

C de Sant Sever

C del Notariat

C d'en Xuclà

C del Pintor Fortuny

La Rambla de Sant Josep

C del Petritxol

C del Pi

C de Sant Domènec del Call
14

19

C de Marlet

C del Doctor Dou

C del Carme

C d'en Roca

Plaça del Pi

Plaça de St Josep Oriol
25
3

C dels Banys Nous
16 27

C del Call

10

24
5

C de Jerusalem

La Rambla

C del Cardenal Casañas

Jardins del Doctor Fleming

C dels Àngels
21

C de les Egipcíaques

C de la Boqueria

C de Ferran

C de la Leona

EL RAVAL

Liceu

Plaça de la Boqueria

C d'en Quintana

C d'en Rauric

C de l'Hospital

Plaça de Sant Agustí

C de l'Arc de Sant Agustí

31

La Rambla

Plaça Reial
13

C del Vidre

C d'en Robador

C de la Junta de Comerç

La Rambla dels Caputxins

C Nou de Zurbano

Rambla del Raval

C de Sant Rafael

C Nou de Sadurní

Plaça de Salvador Seguí

C de Sant Pau

C de les Penedies

C de la Unió

C Nou de la Rambla

La Rambla

Mirador de Colom (350m); Museu Marítim (500m)

11

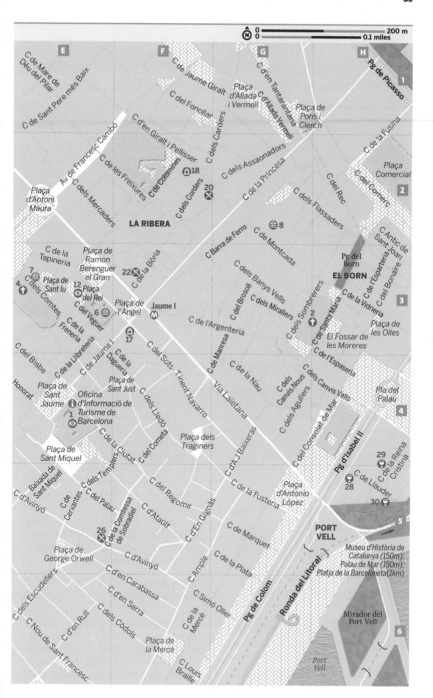

Central Barcelona

Palau Güell
Palace

(Map p68; ☑93 472 57 75; www.palauguell.cat; Carrer Nou de la Rambla 3-5; adult/concession/child under 10yr incl audio guide €12/9/free, 1st Sun of month free; ☺10am-8pm Tue-Sun Apr-Oct, to 5.30pm Nov-Mar; Ⓜ Drassanes) Palau Güell is a magnificent example of the early days of Gaudí's fevered architectural imagination. The extraordinary neo-Gothic mansion, one of the few major buildings of that era raised in Ciutat Vella (Old City), gives an insight into its maker's prodigious genius.

◉ La Ribera

Basílica de Santa Maria del Mar
Church

(Map p68; ☑93 310 23 90; www.santamaria delmarbarcelona.org; Plaça de Santa Maria; guided tour €10 1-5pm; ☺9am-8.30pm Mon-Sat, from 10am-8pm Sun; Ⓜ Jaume I) At the southwestern end of Passeig del Born stands the apse of Barcelona's finest Catalan Gothic church, Santa Maria del Mar (Our Lady of the Sea). Built in the 14th century with record-breaking alacrity for the time (it took just 54 years), the church is remarkable for its architectural harmony and simplicity.

Museu Picasso
Museum

(Map p68; ☑93 256 30 00; www.museupicasso. bcn.cat; Carrer de Montcada 15-23; adult/concession/under 16yr permanent collection €14/7.50/free, temporary exhibit €7.50/4.50/free, 6-9.30pm Thu & 1st Sun of month free; ☺9am-7pm Tue, Wed & Fri-Sun, to 9.30pm Thu; Ⓜ Jaume I) The setting alone, in five contiguous medieval stone mansions, makes the Museu Picasso unique (and worth the queues). The pretty courtyards, galleries and staircases preserved in the first three of these buildings are as delightful as the collection inside. While the collection concentrates on Pablo Picasso's formative years – potentially disappointing for those hoping for a feast of his better-known later works – there is enough material from subsequent periods to give you a thorough impression of the artist's versatility and genius.

Palau de la Música Catalana
Architecture

(Map p68; ☑93 295 72 00; www.palaumusica. cat; Carrer de Palau de la Música 4-6; adult/concession/under 10yr €20/11/free; ☺guided tours 10am-3.30pm Sep-Jun, to 6pm Easter & Jul, 9am-6pm Aug; Ⓜ Urquinaona) This concert hall is a high point of Barcelona's Modernista architecture, a symphony in tile, brick, sculpted stone and stained glass. Built by Domènech i Montaner between 1905 and 1908 for the Orfeo Català musical society, it was conceived as a temple for the Catalan Renaixença (Renaissance).

◎ L'Eixample

Casa Amatller   Architecture
(Map p72; ☑93 216 01 75; www.amatller.org; Passeig de Gràcia 41; adult/child 1hr guided tour €24/12, 40min multimedia tour €19/9.50; ⊙10am-6pm; ⓂPasseig de Gràcia) One of Puig i Cadafalch's most striking flights of Modernista fantasy, Casa Amatller combines Gothic window frames with a stepped gable borrowed from Dutch urban architecture. But the busts and reliefs of dragons, knights and other characters dripping off the main facade are pure caprice. The pillared foyer and staircase lit by stained glass are like the inside of some romantic castle. The building was renovated in 1900 for the chocolate baron and philanthropist Antoni Amatller (1851–1910).

Casa de les Punxes   Architecture
(Casa Terrades; Map p72; ☑93 018 52 42; www. casadelespunxes.com; Avinguda Diagonal 420; adult/child audiogude tour €13/10, guided tour €20/16; ⊙9am-7pm; ⓂDiagonal) Puig i Cadafalch's Casa Terrades, completed in 1905, is better known as the Casa de les Punxes (House of Spikes) because of its pointed turrets. Resembling a medieval castle, the former apartment block is the only fully detached building in L'Eixample, and was declared a national monument in 1976. Since 2017 it has been open to the public. Visits take in its stained-glass bay windows, handsome iron staircase and rooftop. Guided tours in English lasting one hour depart at 4pm.

Fundació Antoni Tàpies   Gallery
(Map p72; ☑93 487 03 15; www.fundaciotapies. org; Carrer d'Aragó 255; adult/child €7/5.60; ⊙10am-7pm Tue-Thu & Sat, to 9pm Fri, to 3pm Sun; ⓂPasseig de Gràcia) The Fundació Antoni Tàpies is both a pioneering Modernista building (completed in 1885) and the major collection of leading 20th-century Catalan artist Antoni Tàpies. Tàpies died in February 2012, aged 88; known for his esoteric work, he left behind a powerful range of paintings and a foundation intended to promote contemporary artists. Admission includes an audio guide.

ⓖ TOURS

Barcelona By Bike   Cycling
(☑671 307 325; www.barcelonabybike.com; Carrer de la Marina 13; tours from €24; ⓂCiutadella Vila Olímpica) This outfit offers various tours by bicycle, including 'The Original', a three-hour pedal that takes in a bit of Gothic Barcelona, L'Eixample (including La Sagrada Família) and the Barceloneta beachfront. Carrer de la Marina 13 is the tour meeting point; there's no office.

Runner Bean Tours   Walking
(Map p68; ☑636 108776; www.runnerbean tours.com; Plaça Reial; ⊙tours 11am & 4.30pm Mar-Sep, 11am & 3pm Oct, 11am Nov-Feb; ⓂLiceu) Runner Bean Tours offers several daily thematic tours. It's a pay-what-you-wish tour, with a collection taken at the end for the guide. The Gothic Quarter tour explores the Roman and medieval history of Barcelona, visiting highlights in the Ciutat Vella (Old City). The Gaudí tour takes in the great works of Modernista Barcelona. All tours depart from Plaça Reial.

Barcelona Walking Tours   Walking
(Map p68; ☑93 285 38 32; www.barcelona turisme.com; Plaça de Catalunya 17; ⓂCatalunya) The Oficina d'Informació de Turisme de Barcelona (p77) organises several one- to two-hour guided walking tours (available in English) exploring the Barri Gòtic (adult/child €16/free), Picasso's footsteps (€22/7) and Modernisme (€16/free). A two-hour gourmet food tour (€22/7) includes tastings. Various street-art walking and cycling tours (from €21) also take place. There is a 10% discount on most tours if you book online.

La Sagrada & L'Eixample

ⓃＮ 0 ————————— 500 m
0 ————————— 0.25 miles

[Map showing La Sagrada & L'Eixample area with streets including C de Còrsega, C de Provença, Av Diagonal, Passeig de Gràcia, Gran Via de les Corts Catalanes, and neighborhoods GRÀCIA, LA DRETA DE L'EIXAMPLE, L'ESQUERRA DE L'EIXAMPLE. Metro stops include Fontana, Diagonal, Verdaguer, Girona, Tetuan, Provença, Passeig de Gràcia. Label: La Sagrada Família. Label: Modernista Masterpieces]

La Sagrada & L'Eixample

◉ **Sights**
1 Casa Amatller...C3
2 Casa Batlló..C3
3 Casa de les Punxes....................................B2
4 Casa Lleó Morera.......................................C3
5 Fundació Antoni Tàpies B3
6 La Pedrera..B3
7 La Sagrada Família...................................D1

8 Palau del Baró Quadras............................B2
9 Palau Macaya..C2
10 Palau Montaner..C2

✖ **Eating**
11 Casa Amalia...C2
12 Entrepanes Díaz..B2
13 Tapas 24...C3

🔒 SHOPPING

Mercat de la Barceloneta   Market

(☎93 221 64 71; www.mercatdelabarceloneta.com;
Plaça del Poeta Boscà 1-2; ⊙7am-2pm Mon-Thu,
to 8pm Fri, to 3pm Sat; Ⓜ Barceloneta) Set in a
modern glass-and-steel building fronting a
long plaza in the heart of Barceloneta, this
airy market has seasonal produce and seafood stalls, as well as several places where
you can enjoy a sit-down meal. **El Guindilla**
(☎93 221 54 58; Plaça del Poeta Boscà 2; tapas
€5-11, mains €10-16; ⊙9.30am-1am Sun-Thu, to
2am Fri & Sat; Ⓜ Barceloneta) deserves special

mention for its good-value lunch specials
and outdoor seating on the plaza.

Mercat dels Encants   Market

(Fira de Bellcaire; ☎93 246 30 30; www.
encantsbcn.com; Plaça de les Glòries Catalanes;
⊙9am-8pm Mon, Wed, Fri & Sat; Ⓜ Glòries) In a
gleaming open-sided complex near Plaça de
les Glòries Catalanes, the 'Market of Charms'
is the biggest flea market in Barcelona.
Over 500 vendors ply their wares beneath
massive mirror-like panels. It's all here, from
antique furniture through to secondhand
clothes. There's a lot of junk, but you'll occasionally stumble across a *ganga* (bargain).

Artesania Catalunya   Arts & Crafts

(Map p68; 📞93 467 46 60; www.bcncrafts.
com; Carrer dels Banys Nous 11; ⏰10am-8pm
Mon-Sat, to 2pm Sun; Ⓜ Liceu) A celebration
of Catalan products, this nicely designed
store is a great place to browse for unique
gifts. You'll find jewellery with designs
inspired by Roman iconography (as well as
works that reference Gaudí and Barcelona's
Gothic era), plus pottery, wooden toys, silk
scarves, notebooks, housewares and more.

FC Botiga   Gifts & Souvenirs

(Map p68; 📞93 269 15 32; Carrer de Jaume I 18;
⏰10am-9pm; Ⓜ Jaume I) Need a Lionel Messi
football jersey, a blue and burgundy ball, or
any other football paraphernalia pertaining
to what many locals consider the greatest
team in the world? This is a convenient
spot to load up without traipsing to the
stadium.

Marsalada   Gifts & Souvenirs

(Map p68; 📞93 116 20 76; www.marsalada
design.com; Carrer de Sant Jacint 6; ⏰10am-
2pm & 4-8pm Mon-Sat; Ⓜ Jaume I) For
souvenirs with a difference, Marsalada has
hand-printed tote bags in unbleached cotton, engravings and T-shirts. Each of these
is emblazoned with a well-known Barcelona
attraction, sketched in pen and ink and
adorned with abstract colour mosaics.

⊗ EATING

⊗ Barceloneta, the Waterfront & El Poblenou

Baluard Barceloneta   Bakery €

(📞93 221 12 08; http://baluardbarceloneta.com;
Carrer del Baluard 38; items €1-3.50; ⏰8am-9pm
Mon-Sat; Ⓜ Barceloneta) Baluard has one of
the best ranges of freshly baked breads in
the city, along with filled baguettes that are
perfect for beach picnics. It also bakes a
range of tempting pastries, such as *xuiuixo*
(deep-fried custard-filled pastries from
Girona) and *bunyols* (doughnut-shaped
pastries stuffed with cheese or jam), and
tarts such as fig or wild berry.

 Shopping Strips

Avinguda del Portal de l'Àngel This
broad pedestrian avenue is lined with
high-street chains, shoe shops, bookshops and more.

Avinguda Diagonal This boulevard
is loaded with international fashion
names and design boutiques, suitably
interspersed with cafes to allow weary
shoppers to take a load off.

Carrer d'Avinyó Once a fairly squalid old
city street, Carrer d'Avinyó has morphed
into a dynamic young-fashion street.

Carrer de la Riera Baixa The place to
look for a gaggle of shops flogging pre-
loved threads.

Carrer del Consell de Cent The heart
of the private art-gallery scene in Barcelona, between Passeig de Gràcia and
Carrer de Muntaner.

Carrer del Petritxol Best for chocolate
shops and art.

Carrer del Rec Another threads
street, this one-time stream is lined
with bright, cool boutiques. Check out
Carrer del Bonaire and Carrer de l'Es-
parteria too. You'll find discount outlets
and original local designers.

Passeig de Gràcia This is Barcelona's
chic premier shopping boulevard, mostly
given over to big-name international
brands.

Avinguda del Portal de l'Àngel
MISTERVLAD/SHUTTERSTOCK ©

Bitácora
Tapas €

(☎93 319 11 10; Carrer de Balboa 1; tapas €4-12.50; ☺9am-2.30am Mon-Fri, from 10am Sat & Sun; ⓂBarceloneta) Bitácora is a neighbourhood favourite for its simple but congenial ambience and well-priced tapas plates, which come in ample portions. There's also a small hidden terrace at the back. Top picks: *ceviche de pescado* (fish ceviche), *chipirones* (baby squid) and *gambas a la plancha* (grilled prawns). Cash only, no cards.

El 58
Tapas €€

(Le cinquante huit; ☎93 601 39 03; www.face book.com/el58poblenou; Rambla del Poblenou 58; tapas €4-12; ☺1.30-11pm Tue-Sat, to 4pm Sun; ⓂPoblenou) This French-Catalan place serves imaginative, beautifully prepared tapas dishes: grilled turbot with romesco sauce and asparagus, scallop ceviche, sausage and chickpea stew, and duck magret. Solo diners can take a seat at the marble-topped front bar. The back dining room with its exposed brick walls, industrial light fixtures and local artworks is a lively place to linger over a long meal.

⊗ La Rambla & Barri Gòtic

Xurreria
Churros €

(Map p68; ☎93 318 76 91; Carrer dels Banys Nous 8; cone €1.20; ☺7am-1.30pm & 3.30-8.15pm Mon, Tue, Thu & Fri, 7am-2pm & 3.30-8.30pm Sat, 7am-2.30pm & 4.30-8.30pm Sun; ⓂJaume I) It doesn't look much from the outside, but this brightly lit takeaway joint is Barcelona's best spot for paper cones of piping-hot churros – long batter sticks fried and sprinkled with sugar and best enjoyed dunked in melted chocolate.

Venus Delicatessen
Deli €

(Map p68; ☎93 676 03 15; www.facebook.com/ venusdelicatessenbarcelona; Carrer d'Avinyó 25; tapas €3-6; ☺8.30am-1am Mon-Fri, 9.30am-1am Sat & Sun; ☏; ⓂLiceu) This sweet little deli charms you from the minute you step down from the street into its bohemian interior. Artworks line the walls, plants overhang the bar, and there's an array of bags, purses and other items for sale. Devour reliable tapas

like *bacallà salat* (dried salted cod) and ham croquettes while jazz standards play.

Cervecería Taller de Tapas
Tapas, Catalan €

(Map p68; ☎93 481 62 33; www.tallerde tapas.com; Carrer Comtal 28; mains €7-10; ☺8.30am-1am; ☏; ⓂUrquinaona) Amid white stone walls and a beamed ceiling, this buzzing, easy-going place serves a broad selection of tapas as well as changing daily specials like *cochinillo* (roast suckling pig). A smattering of global beers add to the appeal. It has a few other locations around town, including a well-placed spot with outdoor seating on **Plaça de Sant Josep Oriol** (Map p68; ☎93 301 80 20; Plaça de Sant Josep Oriol 9; mains €7-10; ☺noon-1am; ☏; ⓂLiceu).

⊗ El Raval

El Pachuco
Mexican €

(☎93 179 68 05; www.facebook.com/pachuco bcn; Carrer de Sant Pau 110; sharing plates €6-11; ☺1.30pm-2.30am; ⓂParal·lel) Get to El Pachuco early or you'll have to wait – this place is popular and rightly so. In its tiny, narrow space, exposed lightbulbs over the bar provide dim lighting, and shelves are cluttered with booze bottles and religious icons. Take a perch on a bar stool and feast on first-rate tacos, quesadillas and mezcals.

Bun Bo
Vietnamese €

(Map p68; ☎93 412 18 90; http://bunbo raval.com; Carrer dels Àngels 6; mains €8-11; ☺1pm-midnight Sun-Thu, to 1am Fri-Sat; ⓂLiceu) This long thin space is brightly decked out with blue walls, colourful lanterns and figurines, and teems with a hip-yet-friendly Raval crowd. On the menu is tasty Vietnamese fare like pho, curries and *bánh mì*. Solo diners get great spots up at the bar. There's another branch over in the Barri Gòtic.

Pinotxo Bar
Tapas €€

(Map p68; ☎93 317 17 31; www.pinotxobar.com; Mercat de la Boqueria, La Rambla 89; mains €9-17; ☺6.30am-4pm Mon-Sat; ⓂLiceu) Pinotxo is arguably La Boqueria's, and even Barcelo-

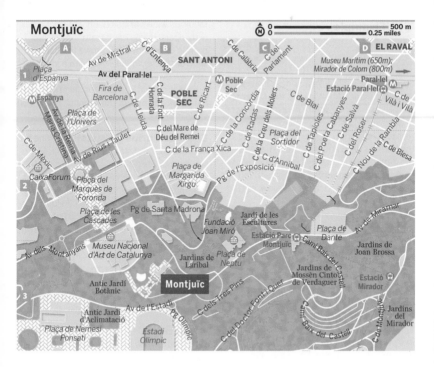

Montjuïc

na's, best tapas bar. The ever-charming owner, Juanito, might serve up chickpeas with pine nuts and raisins, a mix of potato and spinach sprinkled with salt, soft baby squid with cannellini beans, or a quivering cube of caramel-sweet pork belly.

✖ La Ribera

Cat Bar
Vegan €

(Map p68; www.catbarcat.com; Carrer de la Bòria 17; mains €6-9; ⊙1-11pm Wed-Sat, 1-5pm Sun; 🛜⌛; ⓜJaume I) This small joint may be reminiscent of a local student bar, but it serves the best vegan burgers in the city. The selection includes a spicy Mexican burger with jalapeños, a nut burger with pesto and spinach, and a hemp burger with pickles. There's also a range of artisanal vegan beers, plus a gluten-free dish of the day.

Bar del Pla
Tapas €€

(Map p68; ☑93 268 30 03; www.bardelpla. cat; Carrer de Montcada 2; mains €12-16; ⊙noon-11pm Mon-Thu, to midnight Fri & Sat; 🛜;

ⓜJaume I) A bright and occasionally rowdy place, with glorious Catalan tiling, a vaulted ceiling and bottles of wine lining the walls. At first glance, the tapas at informal Bar del Pla are traditionally Spanish, but the riffs on a theme display an assured touch. Try the ham croquettes, Wagyu burger, T-bone steak or marinated salmon with yoghurt and mustard.

Koku Kitchen
Asian €€

(☑93 269 65 36; www.kokukitchen.es; Carrer del Comerç 29; mains €9-11; ⊙1-4pm & 7.30-11.30pm; 🛜; ⓜBarceloneta) On the ground floor you'll find Koku Kitchen Buns, serving bao stuffed with beef or pork with coriander, peanuts, pickled fennel and a sake sauce, as well as dumplings and Vietnamese pho. Downstairs in the basement, sits the ramen and gyoza bar, offering some of the best steaming fragrant noodle bowls in the city.

❌ L'Eixample

Tapas 24   Tapas €

(Map p72; 📞93 488 09 77; www.carlesabellan. com; Carrer de la Diputació 269; tapas €4-12; 🕙9am-midnight; 🛜; Ⓜ Passeig de Gràcia) Hotshot chef Carles Abellán runs this basement tapas haven known for its gourmet versions of old faves. Highlights include the *bikini* (toasted ham and cheese sandwich – here the ham is cured and the truffle makes all the difference) and zesty *boquerones al limón* (lemon-marinated anchovies). You can't book, and service can be slow, but it's worth the wait.

Copasetic   Cafe €

(📞93 532 76 66; www.copaseticbarcelona. com; Carrer de la Diputació 55; mains €6-14; 🕙10.30am-midnight Tue & Wed, to 1am Thu, to 2am Fri & Sat, to 5.30pm Sun; 🛜📶; Ⓜ Rocafort) Decked out with retro furniture, Copasetic has a fun, friendly vibe. The menu holds plenty for everyone, whether your thing is eggs Benedict, wild-berry tartlets or a fat, juicy burger. There are lots of vegetarian, gluten-free and organic options, and superb (and reasonably priced) weekend brunches. Lunch *menús* (Tuesday to Friday) cost between €9.50 and €12.

Entrepanes Díaz   Sandwiches €€

(Map p72; 📞93 415 75 82; www.facebook. com/entrepanesdiaz; Carrer de Pau Claris 189; sandwiches €6-10, tapas €3-10; 🕙1pm-midnight; Ⓜ Diagonal) Gourmet sandwiches, from roast beef to suckling pig or crispy squid with squid-ink aioli, are the highlight at this sparkling old-style bar, along with sharing plates of Spanish specialities such as sea urchins and prawn fritters or blood-sausage croquettes. Service is especially charming and black and white photos of Barcelona line the walls.

🍷 DRINKING & NIGHTLIFE

Perikete   Wine Bar

(Map p68; 📞93 024 22 29; www.gruporeini. net/perikete; Carrer de Llauder 6; 🕙11am-1am; Ⓜ Barceloneta) Since opening in 2017, this fabulous wine bar has been jam-packed with locals. Hams hang from the ceilings, barrels of vermouth sit above the bar and wine bottles cram every available shelf space – over 200 varieties are available by the glass or bottle, accompanied by 50-plus tapas dishes. In the evening, the action spills into the street.

Bodega Vidrios y Cristales   Wine Bar

(Map p68; 📞93 250 45 01; www.gruposagardi. com/restaurante/bodega-vidrios-y-cristales; Passeig d'Isabel II 6; 🕙noon-4pm & 7pm-midnight Mon-Thu, noon-1am Fri-Sun; Ⓜ Barceloneta) In a history-steeped, stone-floored building dating from 1840, this atmospheric little jewel recreates a neighbourhood bodega with tins of sardines, anchovies and other delicacies lining the shelves (used in exquisite tapas dishes), house-made vermouth and a wonderful array of wines. Be prepared to stand as there are no seats (a handful of upturned wine barrels let you rest your glass).

Napar BCN   Brewery

(📞93 408 91 62; www.naparbcn.com; Carrer de la Diputació 223; 🕙noon-midnight Tue & Wed, to 1am Thu, to 2am Fri & Sat, to 11pm Sun; 🛜; Ⓜ Universitat) A standout on Barcelona's burgeoning craft-beer scene, Napar has 22 beers on tap, six of which are brewed on-site, including the IPA, pale ale and stout. There's also an accomplished list of bottled beers. It's a stunning space, with a gleaming steampunk aesthetic and a great rock and indie soundtrack. Creative food changes seasonally.

Can Paixano   Wine Bar

(Map p68; 📞93 310 08 39; www.canpaixano.com; Carrer de la Reina Cristina 7; 🕙9am-10.30pm Mon-Sat; Ⓜ Barceloneta) This lofty *cava* (sparkling wine) bar (also called La Xampanyeria) has long been run on a winning formula. The standard tipple is bubbly rosé in elegant little glasses, combined with bite-sized *bocadillos* (filled rolls) and tapas. Note that this place is usually packed to the rafters, and elbowing your way to the bar can be a struggle.

⭐ ENTERTAINMENT

Palau de la Música Catalana
Classical Music

(Map p68; 📞93 295 72 00; www.palaumusica.cat; Carrer de Palau de la Música 4-6; tickets from €18; ⏰box office 9.30am-9pm Mon-Sat, 10am-3pm Sun; Ⓜ Urquinaona) A feast for the eyes, this Modernista confection is also the city's most traditional venue for classical and choral music, although it has a wide-ranging program, including flamenco, pop and – particularly – jazz. Just being here for a performance is an experience. In the foyer, its tiled pillars all a-glitter, you can sip a pre-concert tipple.

Gran Teatre del Liceu
Theatre, Live Music

(Map p68; 📞93 485 99 00; www.liceubarcelona .cat; La Rambla 51-59; ⏰box office 11am-8pm Mon-Fri, to 6pm Sat; Ⓜ Liceu) Barcelona's grand old opera house, restored after a fire in 1994, is one of the most technologically advanced theatres in the world. To take a seat in the grand auditorium, returned to all its 19th-century glory but with the very latest in acoustics, is to be transported to another age.

ℹ INFORMATION

SAFE TRAVEL

○ Violent crime is rare in Barcelona, but petty crime (bag-snatching, pickpocketing) is a major problem.

○ Be mindful of your belongings, particularly in crowded areas.

○ Avoid walking around El Raval and the southern end of La Rambla late at night.

○ Don't wander down empty city streets at night. When in doubt, take a taxi.

○ Take nothing of value to the beach and don't leave anything unattended.

TOURIST INFORMATION

Several tourist offices operate in Barcelona. A couple of general information telephone numbers worth bearing in mind are 📞010 and 📞012. The first is for Barcelona and the other is for all Catalonia (run by the Generalitat). You sometimes strike English speakers, but for the most part operators are Catalan/ Spanish bilingual. In addition to tourist offices, information booths operate at Estació del Nord bus station and at Portal de la Pau, at the foot of the Mirador de Colom at the port end of La Rambla. Others set up at various points in the city centre in summer.

Plaça de Catalunya (Map p68; 📞93 285 38 34; www.barcelonaturisme.com; Plaça de Catalunya 17-S, underground; ⏰8.30am-9pm; Ⓜ Catalunya)

Plaça Sant Jaume (Map p68; 📞93 285 38 34; www.barcelonaturisme.com; Plaça Catalunya 17; ⏰8.30am-9pm; Ⓜ Catalunya)

Palau Robert Regional Tourist Office (Map p72; 📞93 238 80 91; http://palaurobert.gencat. cat; Passeig de Gràcia 107; ⏰9am-8pm Mon-Sat, to 2.30pm Sun; Ⓜ Diagonal) Offers a host of material on Catalonia, audiovisual resources, a bookshop and a branch of Turisme Juvenil de Catalunya (for youth travel).

ℹ GETTING AROUND

Barcelona has abundant options for getting around town. The excellent metro can get you most places, with buses and trams filling in the gaps. Taxis are the best option late at night.

Bus A hop-on, hop-off Bus Turístic, from Plaça de Catalunya, is handy for those wanting to see the city's highlights in one or two days.

Metro The most convenient option. Runs 5am to midnight Sunday to Thursday, till 2am on Friday and 24 hours on Saturday. Targeta T-10 (10-ride passes; €10.20) are the best value; otherwise, it's €2.20 per ride.

Taxi You can hail taxis on the street (try La Rambla, Via Laietana, Plaça de Catalunya and Passeig de Gràcia) or at taxi stands.

Walking Barcelona is generally best explored on foot.

PALMA DE MALLORCA, SPAIN

Palma de Mallorca at a Glance...

Palma is a stunner. Rising in honey-coloured stone from the broad waters of the Badia de Palma, this enduring city dates back to the 13th-century Christian reconquest of the island, and to the Moors, Romans and Talayotic people before that. A richly studded diadem of historical sites, Palma shelters a seemingly endless array of galleries, restaurants, craft studios and bars. Wander in any direction from the Gothic cathedral at its geographic and historical heart and you'll find medieval streets lined with aristocratic townhouses, looming baroque churches, teeming public squares and markets overflowing with all the bounty of the island.

With One Day in Port

○ Start with the colossal Gothic **Catedral de Mallorca** (p83) and **Palau de l'Almudaina** (p111). You'll spend hours meandering the Old Town's mazy lanes, and may wish to find some contemplative space at the **Jardí del Bisbe** (p89) and **Banys Àrabs** (p89).

○ Lunch at **Can Cera Gastro-Bar** (p93), within the sedate 17th-century walls of the former aristocratic mansion. Continue touring with the **Basílica de Sant Francesc** (p89) and **Es Baluard** (p109), where you can stop to snack alongside the battlements.

Best Places For...

Tapas Bar Bodega Morey (p93)

Ensaïmada (light pastry spirals dusted with icing sugar) Ca'n Joan de S'aigo (p93)

Markets Mercat de l'Olivar (p93)

Mallorcan specialities Restaurant Celler Sa Premsa (p92)

Seafood El Náutico (p94)

Previous page: Aerial view of Palma de Mallorca and Catedral de Mallorca (p82)
VULCANO/SHUTTERSTOCK ©

Palma de Mallorca Map (p90)

Cruise Port

Getting from the Port

Most cruise lines dock at **Estació Marítima**, which lies to the west of town.

Many cruise lines offer shuttle bus services to the centre of Palma. Cruise passengers can also easily get around via punctual and reliable public transportation. From Estació Marítima, the airport bus (Linea 1) departs every 15 minutes or so. One-way journeys to the centre cost €1.50. There are 29 local bus services around Palma and its bay suburbs run by EMT.

Metro is of limited use to most travellers.

Fast Facts

Currency Euro (€)

Languages Spanish, Mallorquin (a dialect of Catalan)

Money ATMs are widely available. Credit cards are accepted in most restaurants and shops.

Tourist Information Consell de Mallorca Tourist Office (p95) covers the whole island.

Visas Generally not required for stays of up to 90 days; not required for members of EU or Schengen countries. Some nationalities will need a Schengen visa.

Wi-fi There's lots of free wi-fi hotspots in Palma. Many cafes and bars have free wi-fi.

Catedral de Mallorca interior

MRKIT99/GETTY IMAGES ©

Catedral de Mallorca

Palma's vast cathedral ('La Seu' in Catalan) is the city's major architectural landmark. Aside from its sheer scale and undoubted beauty, its stunning interior features, designed by Antoni Gaudí and renowned contemporary artist Miquel Barceló, make this unlike any cathedral elsewhere in the world.

Great For...

★ Top Tip

Enter the Catedral from the north flank. You get tickets then pass into the **sacristy**, which hosts the main part of the small **Museu Capitular** (Chapter Museum).

The Interior

On passing through one of the side **chapels** into the cathedral itself, your gaze soars high to the cross vaults, supported by slender, octagonal pillars. The broad **nave** and aisles are flanked by chapels. The walls are illuminated by kaleidoscopic curtains of stained glass, including 87 windows and eight magnificent rose windows. The grandest (the **oculus maior** or 'great eye', featuring a Star of David) comprises 1115 panes of glass shimmering ruby, gold and sapphire, and is the largest Gothic rose window in the world. Visit in the morning to see the stunning effect of its coloured light and shapes reflected on the west wall. This spectacle is at its best at 8.30am on 2 February and 11 November, when the image of the main rose window appears superimposed below that of the other.

Giant organ

GIMAS/SHUTTERSTOCK ©

Explore Ashore

Take a shuttle to central Palma, which will drop you off at a convenient location near the cathedral. You can also take the airport bus (Linea 1) from Estació Marítima. It doesn't go all the way to the cathedral, so get off at La Feixina stop, from where it's around a 10- to 15-minute stroll.

❶ Need to Know

www.catedraldemallorca.org; Carrer del Palau Reial 9; adult/child €7/free; ⊘10am-6.15pm Mon-Fri Jun-Sep, to 5.15pm Apr, May & Oct, to 3.15pm Nov-Mar, 10am-2.15pm Sat year-round

The cathedral's three strikingly different **apses** show the Eucharist in three stages from left to right: institution, celebration and adoration. The left apse displays the golden wonder of the Corpus Christi altarpiece, a baroque confection (1626–41) by Jaume Blanquer devoted to the institution of the Eucharist at the Last Supper.

Other notable elements of the interior include the **giant organ**, built in 1798, and the two **pulpits**, the smaller of which was partly redone by Antoni Gaudí.

Architects & Artists

Antoni Gaudí carried out renovations from 1904 to 1914. His most important contribution was the **baldachin** that hovers over the main altar. Topped by a sculpture of Christ crucified and flanked by the Virgin Mary and St John, it looks like the gaping jaw of an oversized prehistoric shark dangling from

the ceiling of a science museum. Some 35 lamps hang from it, and what looks like a flying carpet is spread above. The genius of Barcelona Modernisme seems to have left behind an indecipherable pastiche, but then this was supposed to be a temporary version. The definitive one was never made (typical Gaudí).

Not content with this strangeness, the parish commissioned contemporary Mallorcan artist Miquel Barceló to remake the **Capella del Santíssim i Sant Pere**, in the right apse. Done in 15 tonnes of ceramics, this dreamscape representing the miracle of the loaves and fishes was unveiled in 2007. On the left, fish and other marine creatures burst from the wall; the opposite side has a jungle look, with representations of bread and fruit. In between the fish and palm fronds, standing above stacks of skulls, appears a luminous Christ, modelled on the short and stocky artist himself.

Entrance to Es Baluard

ALDORADO/SHUTTERSTOCK © ARCHITECTS: LLUÍS GARCÍA-RUIZ, JAUME GARCÍA-RUIZ, VICENTE TOMÁS AND ÁNGEL SÁNCHEZ CANTALEJO

Es Baluard

Built with flair and innovation into the shell of the Renaissance-era seaward walls, this contemporary art gallery is one of the finest on the island. Its temporary exhibitions are worth viewing, but the permanent collection – works by Miró, Barceló and Picasso – gives the gallery its cachet.

Great For...

★ Top Tip

Entry on Friday is by donation, and anyone turning up on a bike, on any day, is charged just €2.

Fortifications

The 21st-century concrete complex is cleverly built among the fortifications of a former military fortress, the old bastion of Sant Pere. The 16th-century bastion on Palma's bay forms part of the Renaissance wall that surrounded the city of Palma. Look out for the partly restored remains of an 11th-century Muslim-era tower (on your right as you arrive from Carrer de Sant Pere).

Exhibition Spaces

The ground floor houses the core of the permanent exhibition, starting with a section on Mallorcan landscapes by local and foreign artists; the big names here include Valencia's Joaquín Sorolla, Mallorca's own Miquel Barceló and Catalan Modernista artist Santiago Rusiñol.

Fortifications

Explore Ashore

Take a shuttle to central Palma, or the airport bus (Linea 1) from Estació Marítima. The bus will take you as far as La Feixina stop, from where it's about a 5-minute walk to the gallery. Plan to spend a few hours of your time here, taking in the temporary and permanent collections.

❶ Need to Know

Museu d'Art Modern i Contemporani; ☎971 90 82 00; www.esbaluard.org; Plaça de Porta de Santa Catalina 10; adult/child €6/free; ⏰10am-8pm Tue-Sat, to 3pm Sun

Also on the ground floor, and part of the permanent collection, is a room devoted to the works of Joan Miró, while on the top floor is an intriguing collection of ceramics by Pablo Picasso. Overall, it's an impressive collection that's well worth a couple of hours of your time.

Es Baluard covers a total surface of 5027 sq metres, with 2500 sq metres of exhibition space extending on to large terraces and outdoor spaces, from where you can enjoy stunning views of the Bay of Palma.

The Aljub

Es Baluard features one of the largest cisterns from the 17th century, known as the 'Aljub'. The freshwater that it stored was used to supply the Puig de Sant Pere neighbourhood, as well as ships that docked at the port. Since its inauguration, this former freshwater cistern has been used as a setting for installations of contemporary artists, and for shows and concerts.

Palau de l'Almudaina interior

TRABANTOS/SHUTTERSTOCK ©

Palau de l'Almudaina

Originally an Islamic fort, this mighty construction was converted into a residence for the Mallorcan monarchs at the end of the 13th century. The King of Spain resides here still, at least symbolically. The royal family is rarely in residence, except for the occasional ceremony.

Great For...

★ Top Tip

The Palma Pass Express (€16) covers admission to three sights including the cathedral, Es Baluard and the palace.

History

The Romans are said to have built a *castrum* (fort) here, possibly on the site of a prehistoric settlement. The Wālis (Governors) of Moorish Mallorca altered and expanded the Roman original to build their own *alcázar* (fort), before Jaume I and his successors modified it to such an extent that little of the Islamic version remains.

The Interior

The first narrow room you enter has a black-and-white ceiling, symbolising the extremes of night and day, darkness and light. You then enter a series of three grand rooms. Notice the bricked-in Gothic arches cut off in the middle. Originally these three rooms were double their present height and formed one single

Main courtyard

TRABANTOS/SHUTTERSTOCK ©

Explore Ashore

The palace is opposite the Catedral de Mallorca; a shuttle will drop you at a convenient location nearby. You can also take the airport bus (Línea 1) from Estació Marítima. Allow a few hours to wander through the series of cavernous stone-walled rooms and epic courtyards.

❶ Need to Know

https://entradas.patrimonionacional.es; Carrer del Palau Reial; adult/child €7/4, audioguide €3, guided tour €4; ☺10am-8pm Tue-Sun Apr-Sep, to 6pm Tue-Sun Oct-Mar

great hall added to the original Arab fort and known as the **Saló del Tinell** (from an Italian word, *tinello*, meaning 'place where one eats'). Once a giant banqueting and ceremonial hall, the rooms are graced by period furniture, tapestries and other curios. The following six bare rooms and terrace belonged to the original Moorish citadel.

Up the grand Royal Staircase are the **royal apartments**, a succession of lavishly appointed rooms; look up to the beautiful coffered timber *artesonado* ceilings. The centrepiece is the Saló Gòtic, the upper half of the former Saló del Tinell, where you can see where those Gothic arches wind up. Next door to the apartments is the royal **Capella de Sant'Anna**, a Gothic chapel whose entrance is a very

rare Mallorcan example of late Romanesque in rose and white marble.

The Exterior

In the main courtyard, **Patio de Armas**, troops would line up for an inspection and parade before heading out into the city. The lion fountain in its centre is one of the palace's rare Moorish remnants.

In the shadow of the Almudaina's walls, along Avinguda d'Antoni Maura, is **S'Hort del Rei** (the King's Garden).

JON DAVISON/LONELY PLANET ©

Castell de Bellver

⊙ SIGHTS

Museu Fundación
Juan March   Gallery
(📞97 171 35 15; www.march.es; Carrer de Sant
Miquel 11; ⊙10am-6.30pm Mon-Fri, 10.30am-
2pm Sat) **FREE** The Can Gallard del Canya, a
17th-century mansion overlaid with minor
Modernist touches, now houses a small
but significant collection of painting and
sculpture. The permanent exhibits – some
80 pieces held by the Fundación Juan
March – constitute a veritable who's who of
contemporary Spanish art, including Miró,
Picasso, fellow cubist Juan Gris, Dalí, and
the sculptors Eduardo Chillida and Julio
González.

Palau March   Museum
(📞971 71 11 22; www.fundacionbmarch.es; Carrer del Palau Reial 18; adult/child €4.50/free;
⊙10am-6.30pm Mon-Fri Apr-Oct, to 5pm Nov-
Mar, to 2pm Sat) This house, palatial by any
definition, was one of several residences
of the phenomenally wealthy March
family. Sculptures by 20th-century greats

including Henry Moore, Auguste Rodin,
Barbara Hepworth and Eduardo Chillida
grace the outdoor terrace. Within lie many
more artistic treasures from such lumi-
naries of Spanish art as Salvador Dalí and
Barcelona's Josep Maria Sert and Xavier
Corberó. Not to be missed are the meticulously crafted figures of an 18th-century
Neapolitan *belén* (nativity scene).

Castell de Bellver   Castle
(Bellver Castle; 📞971 73 50 65; http://castell
debellver.palma.cat; Carrer de Camilo José Cela;
adult/child €4/2, free Sun; ⊙10am-7pm Tue-Sat
Apr-Sep, to 6pm Tue-Sat Oct-Mar, to 3pm Sun)
Straddling a wooded hillside, the Castell
de Bellver is a 14th-century circular castle
(with a unique round tower), the only one
of its kind in Spain. Jaume II ordered it
built atop a hill known as Puig de Sa Mes-
quida in 1300 and it was largely completed within 10 years. Perhaps the highlight
of any visit is the spectacular views over
the woods to Palma, the Badia de Palma
and out to sea.

Basílica de Sant Francesc Church

(Plaça de Sant Francesc 7; 6-venue Spiritual Mallorca ticket €16; ⊘10am-4pm Mon-Sat Nov-Mar to 5pm Mon-Sat Apr-Oct) One of Palma's oldest churches, the Franciscan Basílica de Sant Francesc was begun in 1281 in Gothic style, while the baroque facade, with its carved postal and rose window, was completed in 1700. In the splendid Gothic cloister – a two-tiered, trapezoid affair – the elegant columns indicate it was some time in the making. Inside, the high vaulted roof is classic Gothic, while the glittering high altar is a baroque lollipop, albeit in need of a polish.

Banys Àrabs Historic Building

(Carrer de Serra 7; adult/child €2.50/free; ⊘10am-7pm Apr-Nov, to 6pm Dec-Mar) These modest baths, dating from the 10th to 12th centuries, are the single most important remaining monument to the Moorish government of the island, although all that survives are two small underground chambers, one with a domed ceiling supported by a dozen columns, some of whose capitals were recycled from demolished Roman buildings. The site may be small, but the two rooms – the caldarium (hot bath) and the tepidarium (warm bath) – evoke a poignant sense of abandonment.

Jardí del Bisbe Gardens

(Carrer de Sant Pere Nolasc 6; ⊘7am-1.30pm Mon-Sun) **FREE** A tranquil botanic garden that offers cool respite from a day's hot sightseeing, the Jardí del Bisbe is adjoined to the Palau Episcopal. Stroll among the palms, pomegranates, water lilies, thyme, artichokes and kumquat, and the orange and lemon trees, or just sit on a bench and contemplate.

🏃 TOURS

Palma City Sightseeing Bus

(📞902 10 10 81; www.city-ss.es/en/destination/palma; Passeig Marítim 19; adult/child bus €18/9, boat €12/6, bus & boat €28/14;

🏃 Escape the Crowds

You can avoid the Palma crowds if you have eight hours (or a little less) to spare. A popular destination for a cruise excursion is Valldemossa, a lovely village in a small corner of the Sierra de Tramuntana mountains, located 17km from Palma. Made famous by Frederic Chopin, who composed some of his signature works here and referred to it as the most beautiful place in the world, Valldemossa is one of the prettiest villages in Mallorca. Surrounded by forested hills and beautiful countryside, it's a favourite destination for outdoor enthusiasts. It's also home to the 13th-century monastery where Chopin lived during the winter of 1838 to 1839.

Island buses to/from Palma depart from (or near) the Estació Intermodal de Palma on Plaça d'Espanya. Bus 210 heads to Valldemossa (€1.85, 30 minutes, up to 17 daily).

Valldemossa
ANDREW MONTGOMERY/LONELY PLANET ©

⊘9.30am-10pm, reduced hours outside summer) Run by the *ajuntament* (town hall) this hop-on-hop-off bus departs from Avinguda d'Antoni Maura every 20 minutes, with commentary in various languages. It follows a circuit of the city centre, waterfront and the Castell de Bellver, and can be combined with a boat tour of the bay.

Palma de Mallorca

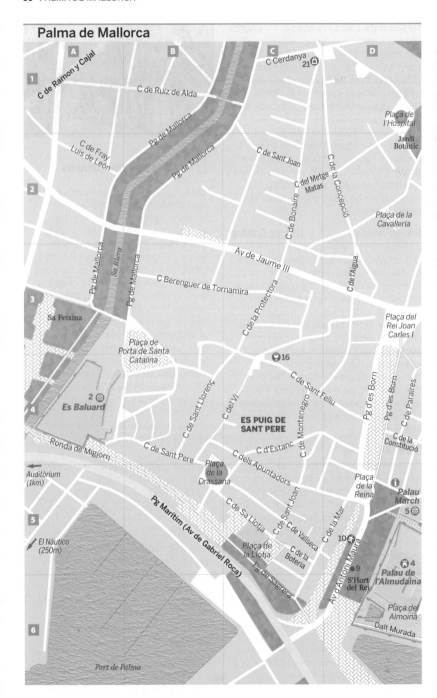

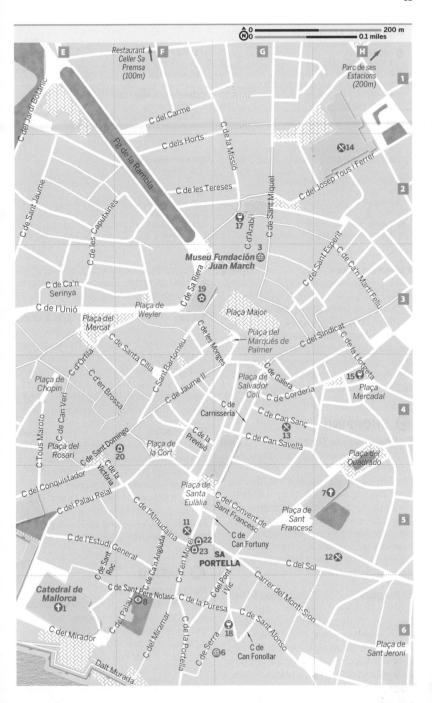

▲ 0 _____ 200 m
Ⓝ 0 _____ 0.1 miles

E   F
Restaurant
Celler Sa
Premsa
(100m)

1

G

H
Parc de ses
Estacions
(200m)

C del Jardí Botànic

C del Carme

C dels Horts

C de la Missió

Pg de la Rambla

✖14

C del Josep Tous i Ferrer

2

C de Sant Jaume

C de les Tereses

C de Sant Miquel

C de les Capuixines

17

C d'Arabí

3
Museu Fundación
Juan March

C de Sant Esperit

C de Ca'n Martí Feliu

C de Ca'n
Serinya

C de l'Unió

Plaça de
Weyler

C de Sa Riera

19

Plaça Major

3

Plaça del
Mercat

C de Santa Cília

C d'Ortila

C de les Monges

C de Sant Bartomeu

Plaça del
Marqués de
Palmer

C del Sindicat

C de la Lloreta

Plaça de
Chopin

C d'en Brossa

C de Jaume II

Plaça de
Galera

Plaça de
Salvador
Coll

C de Cordería

15

Plaça
Mercadal

4

C Tous Maroto

C de Can Veri

C de
Carnissería

C de Can Sanç

C de la
Previsió

C de Can Savellà

✖13

Plaça de
Chopin

Plaça del
Rosari

C de Sant Domingo

C de la
Victòria

20

Plaça de
la Cort

Plaça del
Quadrado

C del Conquistador

Plaça de
Santa
Eulàlia

7

C del Palau Reial

C de l'Almudaina

11
✖

C del Convent de
Sant Francesc

Plaça de
Sant
Francesc

5

C de l'Estudi General

C d'en Morei

22

C de
Can Fortuny

C de Sant Roc

C de Ca'n Angluda

23

SA
PORTELLA

12✖

C del Sol

Catedral de
Mallorca
1

C de Sant Pere Nolasc

8

C del Palau

C de la Puresa

C del Pont
i Vic

Carrer del Montí-Sion

C del Mirador

C del Miramar

C de la Portella

C de Serra

18

C de Sant Alonso

6

C de
Can Fonollar

Plaça de
Sant Jeroni

6

Dalt Murada

Palma de Mallorca

Palma on Bike Cycling

(📞971 71 80 62; www.palmaonbike.com; Avinguda d'Antoni Maura 10; city/mountain/e-bike hire per day €14/22/24; ⏰10am-2pm & 4 to 6pm) Palma on Bike has city bikes to get around Palma, as well as road bikes, rollerblades and kayaks. Rates include insurance and a helmet. It also runs Palma city tours (€25 per person; minimum two people), such as tapas (€35) and bike-and-kayak (€49) tours.

🔒 SHOPPING

Colmado Santo Domingo Food

(📞971 71 48 87; www.colmadosantodomingo. com; Carrer de Sant Domingo 1; ⏰10am-8pm Mon-Sat) It's almost impossible to manoeuvre in this narrow little shop, so crowded are its shelves with local Mallorcan food products – cheeses, honey, olives, olive oil, pâté, fig bread, balsamic vinegar and Sóller marmalade to name just a few – while *sobrassada* (spicy cured sausage) hangs from the ceiling.

El Paladar Food & Drinks

(📞971 71 74 04; www.elpaladar.es; Carrer de Bonaire 21; ⏰9am-9pm Mon-Sat) 'The Palate' is a wonderland for *jamón* (ham) lovers. The flavour of air-cured pig scents the air, mingling with the cheese, *sobrassada* and other delights on display. There's plenty of other

Mallorcan produce, including wines and canned fish, and you can perch on a stool to enjoy a glass and tasting plate.

Típika Arts & Crafts

(📞971 68 58 10; Carrer d'en Morei 7; ⏰10am-8pm Mon-Fri, to 6pm Sat, to 3pm Sun) This small shop is dedicated to promoting the craftsmanship and gastronomy of Mallorca. Here you'll find wines, olive oils, salts and liquors, as well as ceramics and other handicrafts from small family artisan businesses across the island.

Fine Books Books

(📞971 72 37 97; Carrer d'en Morei 7; ⏰10am-8pm Mon-Sat) This extraordinary collection of secondhand books, including some really valuable treasures, rambles over three floors. It's *the* place for secondhand, English-language books in Palma: if you can't find what you're looking for, Rodney will try to track it down for you.

✕ EATING

Restaurant Celler Sa Premsa Mallorcan €

(📞971 72 35 29; www.cellersapremsa.com; Plaça del Bisbe Berenguer de Palou 8; mains €9-14, menús €14; ⏰12-4pm & 7.30-11.30pm Mon-Sat) A visit to this local institution, going strong since 1958, is almost obligatory. It's a cavernous tavern filled with huge old wine barrels and faded bullfighting posters – you find plenty of these places in the Mallorcan interior but they're a dying breed here in Palma. Mallorcan specialities dominate the menu.

Bar Bodega Morey Tapas €

(⌂634 673351; Carrer d'en Morei 4; tapas €3; ⌚7.30am-4.30pm Mon-Fri) As Palma's food evolution races ahead, and the tourist dollars keep pouring in, it's reassuring to find places still giving the locals what they've long loved, at very decent prices. This whitewashed, timber-floored hole-in-the-wall just deals in classics – tortilla, *albondigas* (meatballs), *pulpo* (octopus) – but nails them without fuss. Great for a coffee or draught beer, too.

Mercat de l'Olivar Market €

(www.mercatolivar.com; Plaça de l'Olivar; ⌚7am-2.30pm Mon-Thu, to 8pm Fri, to 3pm Sat) Palma's main retail produce market is a wonderland of Mallorcan (and Spanish) comestibles. Cheese, meat, fish, vegetables and prepared dishes are just some of the delights gathered under one roof. It's a

place to linger, with cafes and tapas bars mixed among the stalls.

Ca'n Joan de S'Aigo Bakery €

(⌂971 71 07 59; www.canjoandesaigo.cat; Carrer de Can Sanç 10; pastries €1.30-3; ⌚8am-9pm) Tempting with its sweet creations since 1700, this clattering, tiled cafe is the best place for thick hot chocolate (€2) and pastries in its gloriously atmospheric, antique-strewn surrounds. The house speciality is *quart,* a feather-soft sponge cake that children love, with almond-flavoured ice cream.

Can Cera
Gastro-Bar Mediterranean €€

(⌂971 71 50 12; www.cancerahotel.com; Carrer del Convent de Sant Francesc 8; tapas €6-24; ⌚12.30-10.30pm) This restaurant spills onto a lovely inner patio at the Can Cera hotel, housed in a *palau* that dates originally to the 13th century. Dine by lantern light on tapas-sized dishes such as *frito mallorquín* (seafood fried with potato and herbs), Cantabrian anchovies, and pork ribs with honey

Colmado Santo Domingo

Palma's Patios

Few experiences in Palma beat simply milling around the backstreets of the city's Old Town, which spreads east of the cathedral. Iron gates conceal the city's *patis* (patios), the grand courtyards where nobles once received guests and horse-drawn coaches clattered to a halt. *Patis* were the intersection of public and private life, and as such they were show-pieces – polished until they gleamed and filled with flowers and plants.

There are still around 150 patrician houses with *patis* in Palma today, though most can only be observed through locked wrought-iron gates. They vary in style from Gothic to re-naissance, baroque to Modernista, but most have the same defining features: graceful arches and Ionic columns, sweeping staircases with wrought-iron balustrades and a well or cistern.

JOAN_BAUTISTA/SHUTTERSTOCK ©

and mustard. The vertical garden attracts plenty of attention from passers-by.

El Náutico Seafood €€

(☎971 72 66 00; https://tast.com/en/restaurant/el-nautico; Real Club Náutico, Plaza de San Pedro 1; mains €18-22; ⏲1pm-midnight; 👪) One of Palma's standout seafood options in the Royal Sailing Club, 'The Nautical' does hake in a variety of ways (including 'Roman-style' – with vinegar and raisins), simply grilled shellfish and other spanking-fresh marine delights. The space, with wraparound windows overlooking the marina and a decked terrace, is beautifully designed in a nautical theme.

DRINKING & NIGHTLIFE

Café L'Antiquari Bar

(☎871 57 23 13; Carrer d'Arabi 5; ⏲11.30-1am Mon-Sat) This old antique shop has been transformed into one of the most original places in Palma to nurse a drink and nibble on tapas. Curios, prints and knick-knacks adorn every corner and inch of wall space, and even the tables and chairs belong to another age. Occasionally there's music or photo exhibitions, and the coffee is excellent.

Bar Flexas Bar

(www.barflexas.com; Carrer de la Llotgeta 12; ⏲6.30pm-midnight Tue-Thu, noon to midnight Fri & Sat) A lively locals' bar with a hint of grunge, Bar Flexas took up residence long before the streets southeast of the Plaça Major became trendy and remains a great spot for a tipple far from the tourist haunts. Charmingly offbeat, it hosts art exhibitions and occasional live acts, serves good tapas and has just the right sort of attitude.

Bodega Can Rigo Bar

(☎971 41 60 07; www.bodegacanrigo.es; Carrer de Sant Feliu 16; ⏲10.30am-midnight Mon, Tue, Thu & Fri, from noon Sat, from 7pm Sun) The tapas and *pintxos* (Basque tapas) at this charismatic place, which has been going strong since 1949, are rated as some of the best in Palma. As if the intimate vibe, profusion of cosy nooks and great wine list weren't enough incitement to linger!

La Vinya de Santa Clara Wine Bar

(☎666 664330; www.lavinyadesantaclara.es; Carrer de Santa Clara 8A; ⏲1pm-midnight Mon-Sat, from 5pm Sun) With over 60 varieties by the glass, this convivial little cubby hole gives you every opportunity to get to grips with the wines of Mallorca (and beyond, if you choose). Basic tapas – cheese, *sobrassada*, empanadas and the like – keep you on your feet and socialising.

ENTERTAINMENT

Auditòrium
Live Music

(☎971 73 47 35; www.auditoriumpalma.es; Passeig Marítim 18; ⊙box office 10am-2pm & 4-9pm) This spacious, modern theatre is Palma's main stage for major performances, ranging from opera to light rock, ballet, musicals, tribute bands and gospel choirs. The Sala Mozart hosts part of the city's opera program (with the Teatre Principal), while the Orquestra Simfónica de Balears (Balearic Symphony Orchestra) are regulars from October to May.

Teatre Principal
Theatre

(☎box office 971 21 96 96; www.teatreprincipal. com/en/; Carrer de la Riera 2; ⊙box office 5-9pm Wed & Thu, 11am-2pm & 5-9pm Fri & Sat) Built in 1854 on the site of a 17th-century predecessor, destroyed by fire in 1858, rebuilt in 1860 and again restored in 2007, this is the city's prestige theatre for drama, classical music, opera and ballet. The renovation recreated the theatre's neoclassical heyday and combined it with the latest technology, resulting in great acoustics.

INFORMATION

SAFE TRAVEL

In general, Palma is a safe city. The main concern is petty theft – pickpockets and bag snatchers.

Some streets are best avoided at night, when the occasional dodgy character comes out to play; if you're alone after dark, perhaps avoid Plaça de Sant Antoni and nearby avenues, such as Avinguda de Villalonga and Avinguda d'Alexandre Rosselló. But really, the risks are very slight.

TOURIST INFORMATION

You can get lots of local city info, in English if you're lucky, by dialling ☎010.

Consell de Mallorca Tourist Office (☎971 17 39 90; www.infomallorca.net; Plaça de la Reina 2; ⊙8.30am-8pm Mon-Fri, to 3pm Sat; 🛜) Covers the whole island.

Municipal Tourist Office (☎902 102365; www. infomallorca.net; Plaça d'Espanya; ⊙9am-8pm) In one of the railway buildings off Plaça d'Espanya.

GETTING AROUND

Bicycle Cycling is a great way to explore Palma and Badia de Palma: there's a coastal bike path between Palma's port and S'Arenal, and bike lanes in the city itself, where cyclists are an accepted fact of life. There are also plenty of operators who rent out city and mountain bikes, including Palma on Bike (p92).

Bus There are 29 local bus services around Palma and its bay suburbs run by **EMT** (☎971 21 44 44; www.emtpalma.es). These include line 1 between the airport and port (€5), and line 23 serving Palma–S'Arenal–Cala Blava via Aqualand. Single-trip tickets on lines other than those to the airport and port cost €1.50, or you can buy a 10-trip card for €10.

Metro The Metro line to the city's university is of limited use. Single trips are €1.60.

Taxi A green light indicates a taxi is free to hail or you can head for one of the taxi stands in the city centre, such as those on Passeig d'es Born. Flagfall is €3.90, thereafter you pay €1 per kilometre (more on weekends and holidays). There's a minimum fare from the airport, and a supplement to visit Castell de Bellver.

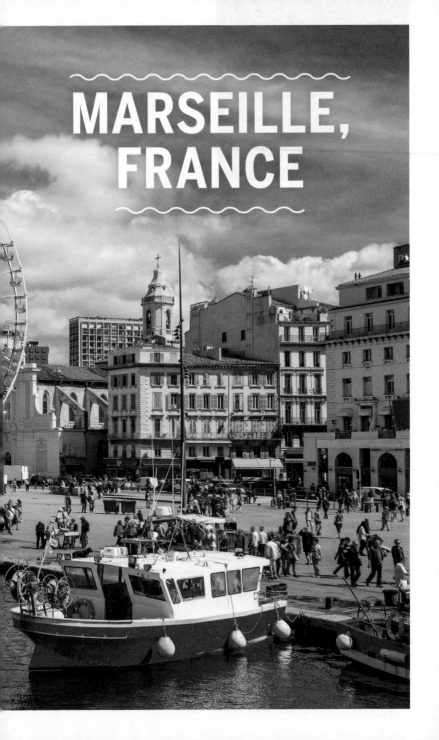

MARSEILLE, FRANCE

Marseille at a Glance...

Grit and grandeur coexist seamlessly in Marseille, an exuberantly multicultural port city with a pedigree stretching back to classical Greece and a fair claim to the mantle of France's second city. A brace of swanky new museums is just the outward sign of an optimism and self-belief that's almost palpable. Marseille's heart is the vibrant Vieux Port (old port), mast-to-mast with yachts and pleasure boats. Just uphill is the ancient Le Panier neighbourhood, the oldest section of the city. Also worth exploring is the République quarter, centred on Marseille's totemic Cathédrale de Marseille Notre Dame de la Major.

With One Day in Port

o Marvel at the Byzantine facade and opulent interior of Marseille's iconic **Basilique Notre Dame de la Garde** (p104), and its 360-degree panaroma of the city below.

o Then plunge downhill into fantastic museums such as **MUCEM** (p104) and the **Villa Méditerranée** (p104).

o Immerse yourself for the rest of the afternoon in the ambience-rich streets of Le Panier.

Best Places For...

Views Basilique Notre Dame de la Garde (p104)

Perfect pastries Le Bar à Pain (p108)

Local flavour Les Halles de la Major (p108)

Marseilles soap La Grande Savonnerie (p108)

Sweet souvenirs Four des Navettes (p105)

Marseille-Provence Airport

Marignane

Châteauneuf-les-Martigues

Tunnel du Rove

L'Estaque

Cruise Port

Rade de Marseille

Carry-le-Rouet

Port de Redonne

Le Panier

Marseille

Îles du Frioul

Château d'If

Basilique Notre Dame de la Garde

La Pointe-Rouge

Mediterranean Sea

Parc National des Calanques

Les Calanques

Les Goudes

Callelongue

Sormiou

Morgiou

Cassis

Marseille Map (p106)

Getting from the Port

The main port is the **Léon Gourret Pier** 4.5km north of the centre. From here you'll need to take a taxi, public bus (35T; departing from Gate 4) or the free city shuttle bus, which takes you as far as La Joliette. From La Joliette you can catch a tram (line T2 or T3), bus or metro (line 2) to all points within the city centre.

The free shuttle schedule varies according to the time of year and number of ships in port. Expect long queues on busy days.

Fast Facts

Currency Euro (€)

Language French

Money The main post office on rue Colbert offers currency exchange.

Visas Generally not required for stays of up to 90 days (or at all for EU nationals); some nationalities need a Schengen visa.

Tourist Information Marseille's useful tourist office (p109) has plenty of information on everything, and free wi-fi.

Wi-fi Wi-fi (pronounced 'wee-fee' in French) is available in most hotels, and at many cafes, restaurants, museums and tourist offices.

Calanque d'En-Vau

Les Calanques

*A short distance from pulsing Marseille
is the Parc National des Calanques,
where sheer cliffs interrupt small idyllic
beaches...It's easy to believe you're
miles from civilisation.*

The Marseillais cherish Les Calanques,
and come here to soak up the sun or take
a long hike. The promontories have been
protected since 1975 and shelter an extraordinary wealth of flora and fauna: 900
plant species, Bonelli's eagle, Europe's
largest lizard (the 60cm eyed lizard) and
its longest snake (the 2m Montpellier
snake).

From October to June, the best way
to see the *calanques* (inlets) – including the 500 sq km of the rugged inland
Massif des Calanques – is to hike the
many trails scented with aromatic *maquis*
(scrub). Of the many *calanques* along the
coastline, the most easily accessible are
Calanque de Sormiou and **Calanque de
Morgiou**; others require dedication and
time to reach. Marseille's tourist office

Great For...

☑ Don't Miss

Calanque de Morgiou's Nautic Bar for
seafood and dreamy views; reservations
essential.

Parc National des Calanques cliffs

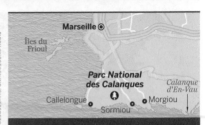

⚓

Explore Ashore

The Calanques can be reached by driving, cycling or taking a bus from from Castellane bus station. This can involve changing bus routes, depending on which Calanque you want to visit, and some walking from the nearest stop. The quickest and simplest option is to pre-book a tour.

❶ Need to Know

If you do decide to drive, be aware that roads into each *calanque* are often closed to drivers, unless you have a reservation at one of the calanque restaurants.

(p109) leads guided walks (ages eight and over).

Calanque de Morgiou

Rocky, pine-covered Cap Morgiou plunges to meet the Med at the eponymous Calanque de Morgiou – a pretty little port bobbing with fishing boats, and sheer rock faces spangled with thrill-seeking climbers.

Calanque de Sormiou

The largest *calanque* hit headlines in 1991 when diver Henri Cosquer from Cassis swam through a 150m-long passage 36m underwater into a cave to find its interior adorned with wall paintings dating from around 20,000 BC. Now named Grotte Cosquer, the cave is a protected historical monument and is closed to the public. Many more are believed to exist.

Hidden Coves

East of Calanque de Morgiou, the stone-sculptured coast brings you to three remote *calanques*: **En-Vau**, **Port-Pin** and **Port-Miou**. A steep three-hour marked trail leads from the car park (closed July to mid-September) on the **Col de la Gardiole** to En-Vau, with a pebbly beach and emerald waters encased by cliffs. The slippery and sheer descents into the *calanque* are very challenging. Its entrance is guarded by the **Doigt de Dieu** (God's Finger), a giant rock pinnacle.

Courtyard of La Vieille Charité

MYKOLASTOCK/SHUTTERSTOCK ©

Le Panier

'The Basket' is Marseille's oldest quarter – site of the original Greek settlement and nicknamed for its steep streets and buildings. Its arty ambience, cool hidden squares and sun-baked cafes make it a delight to explore.

Great For...

☑ Don't Miss

Place de Lenche and rue des Pistoles, two pretty squares ideal for soaking up local boho charm.

Lapping up local life is a big draw of this artsy neighbourhood where narrow, sun-bleached streets give way to artist workshops and bijou squares. Main street Grande Rue follows the ancient road of the Greeks to place de Lenche, location of the original Greek *agora* (marketplace).

Rebuilt after destruction in WWII, its mishmash of lanes hide artisan shops, *ateliers* (workshops), and terraced houses strung with drying washing.

Architecture & Archaeology

In the heart of the neighbourhood is **La Vieille Charité** (☑ 04 91 14 58 80; www.vieille-charite-marseille.com; 2 rue de la Charité; ☉ 10am-6pm Tue-Sun mid-Sep–mid-May, longer hours in summer; Ⓜ Joliette). This grand and gorgeous almshouse was built by Pierre Puget (1620–94), an architect and sculp-

Marseillais Soap

FREEPROD33/SHUTTERSTOCK ©

⚓

Explore Ashore

From Port Léon Gourret the easiest way to Le Panier is to take a 15-minute taxi ride. Alternatively, to go by public transport, walk 20 minutes to Littoral Gourret, and catch bus route 35 to Joliette. From here it's a 10-minute walk to La Vieille Charité.

❶ Need to Know

Ask at the tourist office (p109) about guided walks and rambles in Le Panier.

tor born just a couple of streets away, who rose to become Louis XIV's architect. With its neoclassical central chapel and elegant arcaded courtyard, it's a structure of great harmony and grace.

Entry is free, or pay to visit the **Musée d'Archéologie Méditerranéenne** (Museum of Mediterranean Archeology; ☑04 91 14 58 59; www.culture.marseille.fr; adult/child €6/free), an archaeological museum exploring Mediterranean history. Look for a famous decorated Minoan vase and a Mesopotamian enamel panel.

A second museum, the **Musée d'Arts Africains, Océaniens & Améridiens** (Museum of African, Oceanic & American Indian Art; ☑04 91 14 58 38; www.marseille.fr/node/630; adult/child €6/free), makes quite an impression with its tribal masks, pottery, shrunken heads and other artefacts.

Marseillais Soap

Soap-making in Marseille has been traced by some to the 14th century. Enter La Grande Savonnerie (p108), an artisan soap-maker on Le Panier's fringe. Shop here for the genuine Marseillais article, made with olive oil and no added perfume, and shaped into cubes. You can even have your name printed on your soap if you wish.

Another of Marseille's fine soap sellers is **72% Pétanque** (☑04 91 91 14 57; www.philippechailloux.com; 10 rue du Petit Puits; ◷10.30am-6.30pm; Ⓜ Vieux Port, Joliette), known for its unusual perfumes, such as chocolate and aniseed.

◎ SIGHTS

Marseille's galleries and museums have flourished in recent years. In addition to the many makeovers of local institutions, spectacular new facilities have been built for a number of key sites, such as MuCEM, making the buildings themselves as much of a highlight as their contents.

Basilique Notre Dame de la Garde
Basilica

(Montée de la Bonne Mère; ☑04 91 13 40 80; www. notredamedelagarde.com; rue Fort du Sanctuaire; ⊙7am-8pm Apr-Sep, to 7pm Oct-Mar; ☐60) Occupying Marseille's highest point, La Garde (154m), this opulent 19th-century Romano-Byzantine basilica is Marseille's most-visited icon. Built on the foundations of a 16th-century fort, which was itself an enlargement of a 13th-century chapel, the basilica is ornamented with coloured marble, superb Byzantine-style mosaics, and murals depicting ships sailing under the protection of La Bonne Mère (The Good Mother). The campanile supports a 9.7m-tall gilded statue of said Mother on a 12m-high pedestal, and the hilltop gives 360-degree panoramas of the city.

The basilica is a steep 1km walk from the Vieux Port; alternatively, take bus 60 or the tourist train.

Musée des Civilisations de l'Europe et de la Méditerranée
Museum

(MuCEM, Museum of European & Mediterranean Civilisations; ☑04 84 35 13 13; www.mucem.org; 7 promenade Robert Laffont; adult/child €9.50/ free; ⊙10am-8pm Wed-Mon Jul & Aug, 11am-7pm Wed-Mon May-Jun & Sep-Oct, 11am-6pm Wed-Mon Nov-Apr; ☒; Ⓜ Vieux Port, Joliette) The icon of modern Marseille, this stunning museum explores the history, culture and civilisation of the Mediterranean region through anthropological exhibits, rotating art exhibitions and film. The collection sits in a bold, contemporary building designed by Algerian-born, Marseille-educated architect Rudy Ricciotti, and Roland Carta. It is linked by a vertigo-inducing footbridge to the 13th-century **Fort**

St-Jean (Ⓜ Vieux Port), from which there are stupendous views of the Vieux Port and the surrounding sea. The fort grounds and gardens are free to explore.

The main focus of the museum is a semi-permanent exhibition ranging across the history, genealogy and culture of the Mediterranean, taking in everything from archaeological artefacts to oil paintings. It's supplemented by temporary exhibitions on subjects as niche as Marseille's love affair with football.

The history of the fort itself is explained in the Salle du Corps de Garde (guardhouse room). For a unique perspective, walk the path that twists its way between the glass wall of the J4 building and its outer lace shell, designed in high-tech black concrete to echo the fishing nets that have been cast around Marseille from its very inception.

Villa Méditerranée
Museum

(☑04 95 09 42 70; www.villa-mediterranee.org; esplanade du J4, off bd du Littoral; ⊙noon-6pm Tue-Fri, from 10am Sat & Sun; ☒; Ⓜ Vieux Port, Joliette) FREE This eye-catching white structure next to MuCEM is no ordinary 'villa'. Designed by architect Stefano Boeri in 2013, the sleek white edifice sports a spectacular cantilever overhanging an ornamental pool. Inside, a viewing gallery with glass-panelled floor (look down if you dare!), and two or three temporary multimedia exhibitions evoke aspects of the Mediterranean, be they aquatic, historical or environmental. Not unlike MuCEM, the building itself is the undisputed highlight.

La Joliette
Area

(Ⓜ Joliette, ☒ Joliette) The old maritime neighbourhood of La Joliette, moribund since the decline of the 19th-century docks, has been revitalised by bars, shops and restaurants. Ferries still depart for ports around the Med, but the long sweep of 19th-century commercial facades along Quai de la Joliette has been given an impressive scrub. Here you'll find **Marché de la Joliette** (place de la Joliette; ⊙8am-2pm Mon-Fri; Ⓜ Joliette), one of Marseille's buzziest markets, and **Les Docks** (☑04 91 44 25 28; www.lesdocks-marseille.com;

10 place de la Joliette; ⊙10am-7pm; Ⓜ️Joliette, 🚊Joliette) – once-abandoned 19th-century warehouses now filled with boutiques and galleries.

Nearby, **Les Terraces du Port** is a vast new shopping mall filled with upmarket international chains. It has a huge public terrace on level 2 with fab views of the port and coast.

TOURS

Marseille is a natural launch pad for exploring the nearby **Parc National des Calanques**. Several boat tours depart from the Vieux Port.

Croisières
Marseille Calanques   Boating

(📞04 91 58 50 58; www.croisieres-marseille-calanques.com; 1 La Canebière, Vieux Port; Ⓜ️Vieux Port) Runs 2¼-hour trips from the Vieux Port taking in six *calanques* (adult/child €23/18); 3¼-hour trips to Cassis passing 12 *calanques* (adult/child €29/22); and 1¾-hour trips around the Baie de Marseille (€10), including Château d'If (add €6).

Icard Maritime   Boating

(📞04 91 33 36 79; www.visite-des-calanques.com; quai des Belges; adult/child from €23/18; Ⓜ️Vieux Port) Runs several different trips to the *calanques* and the coastal islands, including one option that stops for a swim (€32, 3½ hours, twice daily from 18 June to 9 September).

Marseille Provence Greeters Walking

(www.marseilleprovencegreeters.com) A great idea: free walking tours led by locals, covering street art, history, food shops, football culture and lots more. Sign up in advance online and check whether your guide speaks English.

🏛️ SHOPPING

For chic shopping and large chains, stroll west of the Vieux Port to the 6th arrondissement, especially pedestrianised rue St-Ferréol.

🏛️ Château d'If

Commanding access to Marseille's Vieux Port, this broodingly photogenic **island-fortress** (📞06 03 06 25 26; www.if.monuments-nationaux.fr; Île d'If; adult/child €6/free; ⊙10am-6pm Apr-Sep, to 5pm Tue-Sun Oct-Mar) was immortalised in Alexandre Dumas' 1844 classic *The Count of Monte Cristo*. Many political prisoners were incarcerated here, including the Revolutionary hero Mirabeau and the Communards of 1871. Other than the island itself, there's not a great deal to see, but it's worth visiting just for the views of the Vieux Port. Frioul If Express runs boats (return €11, 20 minutes, up to 10 daily) from quai de la Fraternité, and also serves the **Îles du Frioul** (one/two islands return €11/16, 35 minutes, up to 21 daily).

BORIS STROUJKO/SHUTTERSTOCK ©

Maison Empereur   Homewares

(📞04 91 54 02 29; www.empereur.fr; 4 rue des Récolettes; ⊙9am-7pm Mon-Sat; 🚌2, 3) If you only have time to visit one shop in Marseille, make it this one. Run by the same family since 1827, France's oldest hardware store remains a one-stop shop for beautifully made homeware items including Opinel cutlery, Savon de Marseille soaps, wooden toy sailing boats and ceramic shaving bowls.

Four des Navettes   Food

(📞04 91 33 32 12; www.fourdesnavettes.com; 136 rue Sainte; ⊙7am-8pm Mon-Sat, 9am-1pm & 3-7.30pm Sun; Ⓜ️Vieux Port) Opened in 1781, this is the oldest bakery in Marseille; it's been passed down between three families, and it

Marseille

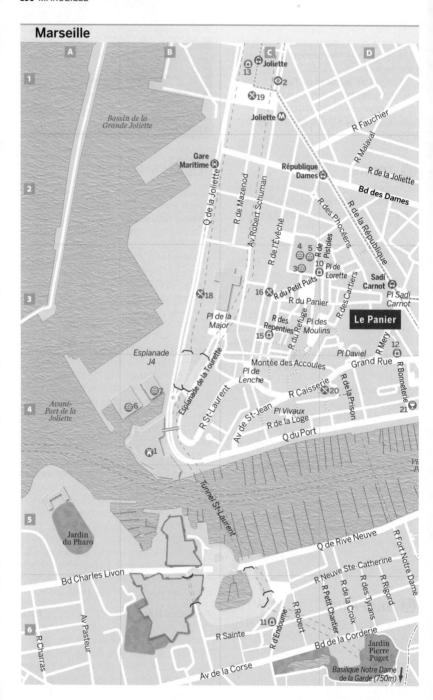

A B C D

1

Bassin de la Grande Joliette

13 Joliette
2
19
Joliette Ⓜ

Gare Maritime Ⓖ

République Dames Ⓖ

R Fauchier
R Malaval
R de la Joliette
Bd des Dames

2

Q de la Joliette
R de Mazenod
Av Robert Schuman
R de l'Evêché
R des Phocéens
R de la République

4 5 R de Pistoles
3 10 Pl de Lorette
18 16 R du Petit Puits
R du Panier
R des Cartiers

Sadi Carnot Ⓖ
Pl Sadi Carnot

3

Pl de la Major
R des Repenties
15
Pl des Moulins
R du Refuge

Le Panier

Esplanade J4

Montée des Accoules
Pl Daviel
Grand Rue
R Méry
12
R Bonneterie

Esplanade de la Tourette

Pl de Lenche
R Caisserie
20
R de la Prison
21

Avant-Port de la Joliette

6 7
R St-Laurent
Av de St-Jean
Pl Vivaux
R de la Loge
Q du Port

4

1

Tunnel St-Laurent

5

Jardin du Pharo

Q de Rive Neuve
R Fort Notre Dame

Bd Charles Livon

R Neuve Ste-Catherine
R Rigord
R de la Croix
R des Tyrans
R Petit Chantier

6

Av Pasteur
R Charras

R Sainte
R d'Endoume
11
R Robert
Bd de la Corderie

Jardin Pierre Puget

Av de la Corse

Basilique Notre Dame de la Garde (750m) ▼

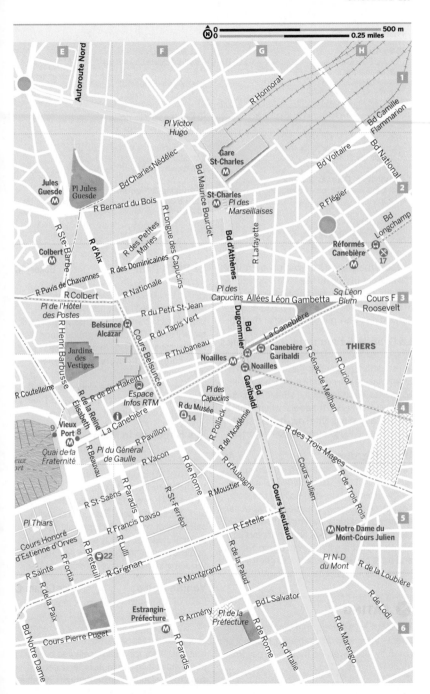

Marseille

still uses the original 18th-century oven. It is *the* address to pick up Marseille's signature biscuits, the orange-perfumed *navettes de Marseille*, as well as *calissons* (Provençal almond biscuits), nougat and other delights.

La Grande Savonnerie   Cosmetics

(☑09 50 63 80 35; www.lagrandesavonnerie.com; 36 Grande Rue; ◎9am-6pm Tue-Sun; Ⓜ Vieux Port) Soap-making is a centuries-old tradition in Marseilles, but much of the stuff for sale at the city's markets is made elsewhere. That's not the case at this little soap maker, which specialises in the genuine Marseillais article.

UndARTground   Art

(☑06 50 08 28 21; www.undartground.com; 21 rue des Repenties; ◎11am-7pm Wed-Mon; ☐49) As the street-art daubed walls of this concept store and gallery suggest, it showcases the work of local underground artists. As well as posters by eBoy and prints by Oaï of Life, expect anything from urban T-shirts and thick coffee table books to ghetto blaster pillow cases designed by AK-LH.

✖ EATING

The Vieux Port and surrounding pedestrian streets teem with cafe terraces, but choose carefully (some rely on tourists to pay too much for average food).

Le Bar à Pain   Bakery €

(☑06 45 17 37 33; 18 cours Joseph Thierry; lunch €4-5; ◎8am-8pm Tue-Fri, to 6pm Sat; ☐Canebière) Selling arguably the best baguettes in the city, this charming organic bakery in the Chapitre neighbourhood also rustles together tasty midday snacks like flaky courgette tarts and toasty tomato pizzas, all to be enjoyed on their suntrap of a terrace. The coffee is excellent too, and don't leave without trying a Ti Coco, their rum-laden coconut ball.

Les Halles de la Major   Market €

(☑04 91 45 80 10; www.leshallesdelamajor.com; 12 quai de la Tourette; mains €12-20; ◎9am-7pm; ☐82) This upscale food market inside the newly renovated vaults of La Major Cathedral is great for foodies, self-caterers and simple browsers. Each stall serves a selection of small plated specialities such as local cheeses, freshly shucked oysters and Provençal 'tapas'. There's seating, a terrace and lovely views across the water.

Vanille Noire   Ice Cream €

(☑07 77 33 68 19; www.vanillenoire.com; 13 rue Caisserie; ice cream €2; ◎12.30pm-6.45pm; Ⓜ Vieux Port) There are plenty of ice-cream shops around Marseille, but there's only one that sells black ice cream (coloured by vanilla pods, which lend a unique, bittersweet, custardy flavour). There are around 30 other flavours of ice cream and sorbet to try, all made on-site with organic ingredients. Go for the pastis (aniseed aperitif) or lavender to keep it Provençal.

🍷 DRINKING & NIGHTLIFE

In the best tradition of Mediterranean cities, Marseille embraces the cafe-lounger lifestyle. Near the Vieux Port, head to place Thiars and cours Honoré d'Estienne d'Orves for cafes that bask in the sun by day and buzz into the night, and Le Panier is an ideal place to while away an afternoon soaking up the area's boho charms.

La Caravelle   Bar
(📞04 91 90 36 64; www.lacaravelle-marseille. com; 34 quai du Port; ⏰7am-2am; 🛜; Ⓜ Vieux Port) On the 1st floor of Hôtel Bellevue, this lovely little bar is styled with rich wood and leather, with a zinc bar and yellowing murals that hint of its 1920s pedigree. If it's sunny, snag a coveted spot on the portside terrace, and sip a pastis as you watch the throng below. On Friday there's live jazz from 9pm.

La Part des Anges   Wine Bar
(📞04 91 33 55 70; www.lapartdesanges.com; 33 rue Sainte; ⏰9am-2am Mon-Sat, 9am-1pm & 6pm-2am Sun; Ⓜ Vieux Port) This fabulously convivial wine bar is named after the alcohol that evaporates through a barrel during wine or whisky fermentation: the 'angels' share'. Take your pick of dozens of wines by the glass, listed by region on a blackboard behind the bar, or buy a bottle to take away. Steak, pasta and other wine-friendly ballast is available.

🎭 ENTERTAINMENT

La Friche La Belle de Mai   Arts Centre
(📞04 95 04 95 04; www.lafriche.org; 41 rue Jobin; ⏰ticket kiosk 11am-6pm Mon, to 7pm Tue-Sat, from 12.30pm Sun; 🚌49, 52) This 45,000-sq-metre former tobacco factory is now a vibrant arts centre with a theatre, cinema, bar, bookshop, artists' workshops, multimedia displays, skateboard ramps, electro- and world-music parties and much more. Check the program online. The on-site restaurant, **Les Grandes**

Tables (📞04 95 04 95 85; www.lesgrandestables. com; 41 rue Jobin, La Friche La Belle de Mai; mains €16; ⏰noon-2pm Sun-Wed, noon-2pm & 8-10pm Thu-Sat; 🚌49, 52), is a great bet for interesting, locally sourced food.

ℹ️ INFORMATION

DISCOUNT CARDS
The **Marseille City Pass** (www.resamarseille. com; 24/48/72hr €26/33/41) covers admission to city museums and public transport, and includes a guided city tour plus other discounts. Buy it online or at the tourist office.

TOURIST INFORMATION
Tourist Office (📞08 26 50 05 00, box office 04 91 13 89 16; www.marseille-tourisme.com; 11 La Canebière; ⏰9am-6pm; Ⓜ Vieux Port) Marseille's useful tourist office has plenty of information on everything, including guided city tours (by foot, bus, electric tourist train or boat) and trips to Les Calanques. There's free wi-fi too.

Marseille Expos (www.marseilleexpos.com) This arts organisation distributes an excellent map of current galleries. Its website lists what's on.

🚉 GETTING AROUND

Cycling With the **Le Vélo** (English-language helpline 📞01 30 79 29 13; www.levelo-mpm.fr) bike-share scheme, you can pick up and drop off bikes from 100-plus stations across the city and along the coastal road to the beaches.

Driving You'll regret renting a car in Marseille – car parks and on-street parking are very expensive, and the traffic can be horrendous. If you're driving to Les Calanques (p107), most major car-rental firms have offices in or close to the train station.

Metro Marseille has two metro lines (Métro 1 and Métro 2), two tram lines (yellow and green) and an extensive bus network. Bus, metro or tram tickets (one/10 trips €1.70/14) are available from machines in the metro, at tram stops and on buses.

Bus Most buses start in front of the **Espace Infos RTM** (📞04 91 91 92 10; www.rtm.fr; 6 rue des Fabres; ⏰8.30am-6pm Mon-Fri; Ⓜ Vieux Port), where you can obtain information and tickets.

CANNES, FRANCE

Cannes at a Glance...

Glamorous Cannes sets camera flashes popping at its film festival in May, when stars pose in tuxes and full-length gowns on the red carpet. But the glitz doesn't end there. Throughout the year, as you walk among the designer bars, couture shops and palaces of La Croisette, the wealth and glamour of this city cannot fail to impress. Admiring Ferraris and Porsches and celebrity-spotting on the chic sunlounger-striped beaches and liner-sized yachts moored at the port are perennial Cannes pastimes.

With One Day in Port

○ Stroll along **La Croisette** (p114), people-watching and soaking up the atmosphere. You can also swim at one of the beaches.

○ Explore **Le Suquet** (p116) and make your way up the hill for great views and to see the medieval castle and 17th-century church.

○ If you're in Cannes on the right day, take a **tour** (p117) of the Palais des Festivals.

○ **Cruise** (p117) to the Corniche d'Or, where you can take in views of both Cannes itself and the Estérel mountains.

Best Places For...

Local produce & quick bites Marché Forville (p119)

Sandwiches PhilCat (p119)

Coffee Armani Caffè (p121)

Cheese Fromagerie Ceneri (p119)

Chocolate JP Paci (p119)

Wine L'Epicurieux (p121)

Previous page: Vieux Port (p117)
IR STONE/SHUTTERSTOCK ©

N 0 ——— 2 km
0 ——— 1 miles

Le Musée
Bonnard

Le Cannet

Vallauris

Golfe-
Juan

Cannes-
La Bocca

Cannes

La Croisette

*Vieux
Port*

*Golfe
Juan*

*Golfe de
Napoule*

Île Ste-Marguerite

Mediterranean Sea

Cannes Map (p118)

Getting from the Port

Cannes is primarily a tender port, so you'll be loaded onto a smaller vessel, which should take you to Vieux Port (p117).

It's a short, five- to 10-minute walk from Vieux Port to the Palais des Festivals (p116), which marks the beginning of La Croisette. Most main sights and restaurants are clustered around the waterfront and Vieux Port area.

Buses serving both Cannes and the surrounding region depart near the waterfront. Mistral Location (p121) – also located at Vieux Port – rents out bicycles and scooters.

Fast Facts

Currency Euro (€)

Language French

Money ATMs at most train stations and on every second street corner in towns and cities. Visa, MasterCard and Amex widely accepted.

Visas Generally not required for stays of up to 90 days (or at all for EU nationals); some nationalities need a Schengen visa.

Tourist information Cannes Tourist Office (p121) runs guided walking and themed tours in English.

Wi-fi The tourist office at the Palais des Festivals has free wi-fi.

Hotel Martinez

LONGJON/SHUTTERSTOCK ©

La Croisette

*The multi-starred hotels and couture shops lining the iconic **bd de la Croisette** (aka La Croisette) may be the preserve of the rich and famous, but anyone can enjoy strolling the glamorous, palm-shaded promenade.*

Great For...

☑ **Don't Miss**

Admiring the views of the Baie de Cannes and nearby Estérel mountains.

Architectural Gems

Along La Croisette you'll find seafront hotel palaces, dazzling in all their stunning architectural glory. Legendary addresses include the **Martinez** and the **Carlton InterContinental**, with twin cupolas modelled on the breasts of courtesan La Belle Otéro.

There's also **La Malmaison** (☎04 97 06 44 90, 04 97 06 45 21; www.cannes.com/fr/culture/centre-d-art-la-malmaison.html; 47 bd de la Croisette; ⊘10am-7pm daily Jul-Sep, 10am-1pm & 2-6pm Tue-Sun Oct-Apr, closed May & Jun), a seaside pavilion in the former games and tea room of Cannes' grandest hotel of the 1860s, the Grand Hôtel. Modern art exhibitions fill part of La Malmaison today; admission price varies depending on the exhibit.

Beach off La Croisette

PACK-SHOT/SHUTTERSTOCK ©

⚓ Explore Ashore

It's a short, five- to 10-minute walk from the port to the beginning of La Croisette. The boulevard winds around the shoreline for about 2km, so you can take your time strolling. If you fancy sunbathing or taking a dip, there are plenty of public and private beaches off La Croisette.

★ Top Tip

Mondays are generally quieter in Cannes, although some museums and restaurants are closed.

Beaches off La Croisette

Cannes is blessed with sandy beaches, although much of the bd de la Croisette stretch is taken up by private enterprises, leaving just a small strip of free sand near the Palais des Festivals for the bathing general public. This area can be found between La Plage Barrière Le Majestic Cannes restaurant and the end of Promenade Robert Favre le Bret. No umbrellas or sun lounges are provided, but you can park your towel and claim a spot.

Private beaches include family-friendly **Plage Vegaluna** (📞04 93 43 67 05; www. vegaluna.com; La Croisette; sunloungers €15-25; ⏰9.30am-7pm; 👶) and Hôtel Martinez's **Z Plage** (📞04 93 90 12 34; 73 bd de la Croisette; ⏰9.30am-6pm Apr-Sep, to 7pm Jul & Aug), where you can expect to pay €60 in July and August for the front-row blue

sunloungers. Other rows will set you back at least €45; booking ahead is advised. Most private beaches have restaurants, which are particularly delightful on warm sunny days, although you pay for the privilege of eating *les pieds dans l'eau* (on the waterfront).

Building a Brand New Beach

Cannes is currently undertaking its largest urban renewal project since 1960 – and the city's beaches are the lucky beneficiaries! In phase one of the project, barges hauled in boatloads of new sand (95,000 cu metres to be exact), effectively doubling the average width of Plage de la Croisette to 40m and protecting it from erosion.

Phases two and three, scheduled for completion by 2022, call for further beautification of public spaces, and include widening pedestrian walkways and bike lanes.

EGROY/SHUTTERSTOCK ©

Musée Bonnard

⊙ SIGHTS

Whether Cannes' soul has survived its celebrity-playground status is up for debate, but there's still enough natural beauty to make exploring worthwhile: the harbour, the bay, the clutch of offshore islands and the old quarter, Le Suquet, all spring into life on a sunny day.

Palais des Festivals
et des Congrès   Landmark

(Festival & Congress Palace; 1 bd de la Croisette; guided tour adult/child €6/free) Posing for a selfie on the 22 steps leading up to the main entrance of this concrete bunker – unlikely host to the world's most glamorous film festival – at the western end of La Croisette is an essential Cannes experience. Afterwards, wander along the **Allée des Étoiles du Cinéma**, a footpath of 46 celebrity hand imprints in the pavement; it begins with the hands of Meryl Streep in front of the tourist office.

The only way to enter the festival building and walk into the auditorium, tread the stage and learn about cinema's premier event is with a Palais des Festivals guided tour organised by the Cannes tourist office. Check

dates and get booking instructions on the tourist office website.

Le Suquet   Historic Site

Follow rue St-Antoine and snake your way up through the narrow streets of Le Suquet, Cannes' oldest district. Up top you'll find the site of Cannes' medieval castle, place de la Castre, flanked by the 17th-century Église Notre-Dame de l'Esperance. Climb the adjacent ramparts for great views of the bay.

Musée Bonnard   Museum

(⌚04 93 94 06 06; www.museebonnard.fr; 16 bd Sadi Carnot, Le Cannet; adult/child €5/3.50; ⊙10am-6pm Tue-Sun Sep-Jun, to 8pm Jul & Aug) Easily recognisable by their intense, vivacious colours, the works of neo-impressionist painter Pierre Bonnard (1867–1947) form the backbone of the colourful permanent collection at this lesser-known art museum. Housed in a restored belle-époque villa with a striking contemporary extension, the museum is in the hillside suburb of Le Cannet, about 3km north of downtown Cannes.

Bonnard arrived in Le Cannet fresh from Paris in 1910 and lived in a seafront villa with his wife, Martha, until his death in 1947. It was during this period that Bonnard painted his most important works, including several landscapes of St-Tropez, Antibes and other Riviera resorts.

Take city bus 1, operated by Palmbus (p121), from Cannes' train station to the Mairie du Cannet stop (€1.50, 15 minutes).

Vieux Port   Port
(Old Port) The celebrity yachts that line the port are here to remind you of Cannes' celebrity status, lest you forget it.

Hôtel de Ville   Landmark
Dating to 1876, Cannes' imposing four-storey town hall is one of the city's most prominent landmarks. Look for it along the waterfront between the Palais des Festivals and Le Suquet.

TOURS

Palais des Festivals
Guided Tour   Walking
(☑04 92 99 84 22; www.cannes-destination.com/guided-tour/visit-palais-festival-cannes; adult/child €6/free) This 1½-hour tourist-office-run tour takes place two or three times per month, on an irregular schedule that depends on the Palais' current lineup of festivals, trade shows and other events. There are generally no tours in May. To check dates, reserve a spot and ask about English-language tours, visit the tourist office's website, ring the office, or e-mail tourisme@palaisdesfestivals.com.

Trans Côte d'Azur Cruises   Boating
(☑04 92 98 71 30; www.trans-cote-azur.com; quai Max Laubeuf) From June to September this boat company offers all-day cruises to St-Tropez (adult/child return €50/40) and Monaco (€54/40). However, timing might be too tight for these cruises, which typically return to Cannes just before 6pm. Instead there are shorter, two-hour cruise options which include the Corniche d'Or (€27/18), where you can take in the dramatic contrasts of the Estérel's red cliffs, green forests and intense azure waters.

 Starring at Cannes

For 12 days in May, all eyes turn to Cannes, centre of the cinematic universe, where 33,000 producers, distributors, directors, publicists, stars and hangers-on descend to buy, sell or promote more than 2000 films. As the premier film event of the year, the **Festival de Cannes** (www.festival-cannes.com; ☺May) attracts around 4000 journalists from all over the world. At the centre of the whirlwind is the colossal, 60,000-sq-metre Palais des Festivals, where the official selections are screened.

The inaugural festival was scheduled for 1 September 1939, in response to Mussolini's fascist-propaganda film festival in Venice, but Hitler's invasion of Poland brought the festival to an abrupt end. It restarted in 1946 – and the rest is history. Over the years the festival split into 'in competition' and 'out of competition' sections. The goal of 'in competition' films is the prestigious Palme d'Or, awarded to the festival's best film as chosen by the jury and its president.

Tickets to the film festival are off limits to average Joes. What you can get are same-day free tickets to selected individual films, usually after their first screening. Availability is limited, and all arrangements must be made through **Cannes Cinéma** (☑04 97 06 45 15; www.cannes-cinema.com; 10 av de Vallauris; ☺10am-noon & 2-4pm).

Billboard on the Palais des Festivals

Cannes

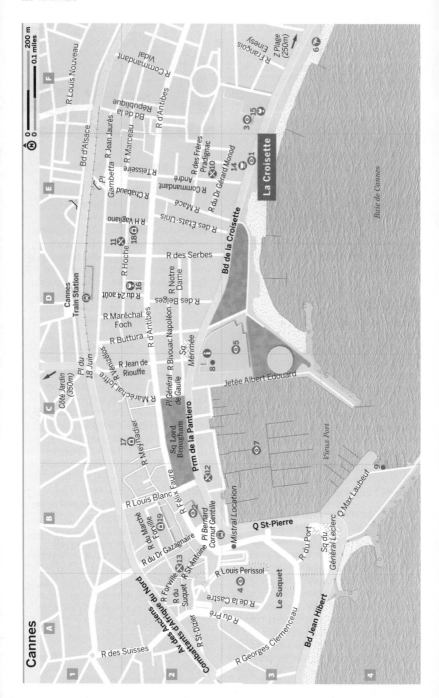

R Louis Nouveau

R Commandant Vidal

R François Einesy

Z Plage (250m)

R Louis Nouveau

Bd d'Alsace

Bd de la République

R d'Antibes

R Jean Jaurès

Pl Gambetta

R Marceau

R Teisseire

R des Frères Pradignac

3 ⊙ 15 ⓘ

R Chabaud

R Commandant André

R du Dr Gérard Monod

14 ⓘ ⊙ 1

R H Vagliano

R Macé

10 ⊗

R des États-Unis

La Croisette

11 ⊗

18 ⓘ

R Hoche

R des Serbes

Bd de la Croisette

Côté Jardin (350m)

Cannes Train Station ⓡ

R du 24 août

16 ⊙ ⊙

R des Belges

R Notre Dame

R Maréchal Foch

R Buttura

R d'Antibes

Sq Mérimée

R Meynadier

Pl du 18 Juin

R Maréchal Joffie

R des Ventolaies

R Général de Gaulle

R Bivouac Napoléon

⊙ 5

ⓘ 8 ●

Baie de Cannes

17 ⓘ

Sq Lord Brougham

Prm de la Pantiero

⊙ 7

Jetée Albert Edouard

R Louis Blanc

R Félix Faure

12 ⊗

R du Marché Forville

19 ⓘ

Pl Bernard Cornut Gentille

Mistral Location ●

Q St-Pierre

Vieux Port

R du Dr Gazagnaire

R St-Antoine

13 ⊗

R du Suquet

R St-Dizier

R Forville

R Louis Perissol

⊙ 4

R de la Castre

Le Suquet

R du Port

Sq du Général Leclerc

Q Max Laubeuf

● 9

Av des Anciens Combattants d'Afrique du Nord

R du Pré

R Georges Clemenceau

Bd Jean Hibert

R des Suisses

N

0 ⸺⸺⸺ 200 m
0 ⸺⸺⸺ 0.1 miles

Cannes

🔒 SHOPPING

Fromagerie Ceneri　　Cheese
(☑04 93 39 63 68; www.fromagerie-ceneri.com; 22 rue Meynadier; ☺10am-6pm Mon, 8am-7pm Tue-Sat, 8.30am-12.30pm Sun) With cowbells strung from the wooden ceiling, and a stunning array of cheeses, this is the best place to shop for dairy products in Cannes. A master *fromager-affineur* (cheesemonger and ripener) in business since 1968, Ceneri is a rare and precious breed on the Riviera. Its selection of *chèvre* (goat's cheese) from Provence is second to none.

It also has a top-notch selection of cheese from elsewhere in France.

JP Paci　　Chocolate
(☑04 93 39 47 94; www.paci-chocolatier.com; 28 rue Hoche; ☺9.30am-7pm Mon-Sat) Artisan *chocolatier* Jean-Patrice Paci crafts perfectly formed rounds of Camembert cheese, ravioli squares, red roses, tool boxes and flower pots out of chocolate – to uncanny perfection.

Marché Forville　　Market
(11 rue du Marché Forville; ☺7.30am-1pm Tue-Fri, to 2pm Sat & Sun) For local culture, head to Cannes' busy food market, a couple of blocks back from the port. In the biz since 1934, it is one of the most important markets in the region and the supplier of choice for restaurants – and for your beach picnic! On Monday the food stalls are replaced by an all-day *brocante* (flea market).

✖ EATING

In addition to the La Croisette private beach restaurants, several streets just inland, such as rue Hoche, are filled with restaurants and bistros. Cheaper eats can be found in and around Cannes' atmospheric food market, Marché Forville.

PhilCat　　Sandwiches €
(☑04 93 38 43 42; promenade de la Pantiéro; sandwiches & salads €3.50-5.50; ☺7am-7pm mid-Mar–Oct; 🖉) Phillipe and Catherine's prefab cabin on the waterfront is a perfect lunch spot. This is fast-food, Cannes-style – giant salads, toasted panini and the best *pan bagna* (€5.30; a gargantuan bun filled with tuna, onion, red pepper, lettuce and tomato, and dripping in olive oil) on the Riviera. The 'super' version (€5.50) throws anchovies into the mix.

Côté Jardin　　Bistro €
(☑04 93 38 60 28; www.facebook.com/pg/cotejardinbychristopheferre; 12 ave St-Louis; plats du jour €12-14, other mains €12-22; ☺noon-2pm & 7-9.30pm Tue-Sat) Craving a break from Cannes' glitz and grandiosity? This down-to-earth bistro on a residential backstreet is the perfect antidote. Enjoy superb-value *plats du jour* (dishes of the day) in an enclosed garden overhung with flowering trees, the menu changing based on what chef Christian Ferré finds at the market: Provençal beef stew, chicken curry, codfish aïoli...all updated daily on the Facebook page.

Armani Caffè

Bobo Bistro — Mediterranean €€

(☎04 93 99 97 33; www.facebook.com/
BoboBistroCannes; 21 rue du Commandant
André; pizzas €14-20, mains €18-31; ☺noon-
11pm) Predictably, it's a 'bobo' (bourgeois
bohemian) crowd that gathers at this achingly cool bistro in Cannes' fashionable
Carré d'Or. Decor is stylishly retro, with
attention-grabbing objets d'art including a
tableau of dozens of spindles of coloured yarn. Cuisine is local, seasonal and
invariably organic: artichoke salad, tuna
carpaccio with passion fruit, roasted cod
with mash *fait masion* (home-made).

Le Grain de Sel — Bistro €€

(☎04 93 38 83 65; www.legraindesel-cannes.
com; 25 rue Hoche; lunch menus €19, mains
€24-32; ☺noon-2pm Mon-Sat, 7-10pm Tue-
Sat) Vietnamese-born, French-trained
chef Nhut Nguyen is at the helm of this
delightful new bistro on Cannes' pedestrianised restaurant row. The high-ceilinged
interior dining room, done up with modern
lighting and faux bookshelves, creates a
relaxed backdrop for inventive offerings
such as shrimp tempura with Provençal
zucchini fritters or roast lamb with herbes
de Provence, parsnip mousse, dates and
candied lemon.

Table 22 — Modern European €€€

(Mantel; ☎04 93 39 13 10; www.restaurant-
mantel.com; 22 rue St-Antoine; menus €39-65,
mains €35-46; ☺noon-2pm Wed-Sun, 7.30-
10pm daily) Discover why Noël Mantel is the
hotshot of the Cannois gastronomic scene
at his refined restaurant. Service is stellar
and the seasonally inspired cuisine divine
– Mantel's food maximises local ingredients but isn't afraid to experiment with
unusual flavours and cooking techniques.
Spot the classic film stars on the walls,
from Cary Grant to Alfred Hitchcock.

🍷 DRINKING & NIGHTLIFE

Bars around the Carré d'Or (Golden Sq) –
bordered by rue Commandant André, rue
des Frères Pradignac, rue du Batéguier
and rue du Dr Gérard Monod – tend to be
young, trendy and busy. Beach and hotel
bars are more upmarket. Download the
free **Cannes Agenda** app (www.cannes.

com/fr/mairie/espace-communication/
le-mois-a-cannes.html) for listings.

L'Epicurieux   Wine Bar
(☑04 93 99 93 94; 6 rue des Frères Casanova;
☉10am-10pm Mon-Thu, to 11pm Fri & Sat) A
cosy little spot for a glass or two of a local
vintage – the wine list here is great, with
hand-picked choices from local *domaines*
(areas) including Côtes de Provence
and Côtes du Rhône. Bistro snacks and
live bands at weekends make it doubly
attractive.

JW Grill   Lounge
(☑04 92 99 70 92; 50 bd de la Croisette;
☉10am-2am) This dazzling white lounge
bar on the ground floor of the Marriott
hotel is possibly the most beautiful on the
Croisette, with designer sofas facing out to
sea. Come dusk, indulge in an €18 glass of
Champagne and revel in the chic five-star
location.

Armani Caffè   Cafe
(☑04 93 99 44 05; www.armani.com/restau-
rant/us/restaurant/armani-caffe-cannes; 42
bd de la Croisette; ☉8.30am-7pm Mon-Sat)
The alfresco cafe of Italian fashion design
house Armani is predictably chic, stylish
and full of panache. Sit beneath taupe
parasols in a prettily manicured garden
and enjoy the comings and goings of La
Croisette over a chilled glass of prosecco
(€10). Salads, pasta and panini too.

ℹ INFORMATION

Tourist Office (☑04 92 99 84 22; www.
cannes-destination.fr; 1 bd de la Croisette;
☉9am-7pm Mar-Oct, to 8pm Jul & Aug, 10am-
6pm Nov-Feb; ☏) Runs the informative 'Once
Upon a Time: Cannes' guided walking tour (€6)
in English at 9.15am (June to September) or
2.30pm (October to May) every Monday, as
well as a host of fun themed tours (in English);
see the website for details.

ℹ GETTING AROUND

Cycling Bicycles and scooters can be rented at
Mistral Location (☑06 20 33 87 64, 04 93 39
33 60; www.mistral-location.com; 4 rue Georges
Clémenceau) for €20/30 per day.

Bus Local buses serving Cannes and the surrounding region are operated by **Palmbus** (☑08
25 82 55 99; www.palmbus.fr) from a separate
bus station (place Bernard Cornut Gentille) near
the waterfront.

From bus stops in front of Cannes' train station,
Lignes d'Azur runs express services to Nice (bus
200; €1.50, 1¾ hours, every 15 minutes), Nice-
Côte d'Azur airport (bus 210; one way/return
€22/33, 50 minutes, half-hourly), Mougins (bus
600; €1.50, 25 minutes, every 20 minutes) and
Grasse (bus 600; €1.50, one hour).

NICE & VILLEFRANCHE-SUR-MER, FRANCE

In this Chapter

Nice & Villefranche-sur-Mer at a Glance...

With its mix of real-city grit, old-world opulence, year-round sunshine, vibrant street life and stunning seaside location, no place in France compares with Nice. Neighbouring Villefranche-sur-Mer offers a vision of small-town Mediterranean life that's totally unexpected so close to Nice. The 14th-century Old Town, with its tiny, evocatively named streets broken by twisting staircases and glimpses of the sea, is a delight to amble through. And thanks to its deep harbour, it's a prime port of call for cruise ships.

With One Day in Port

o Explore the evocative and lively Vieux Nice (Old Town; p126), which has its origins in the 17th century and is absolutely packed with great markets, bistros, boutiques and bars.

o Whether you come ashore here or not, take time to acquaint yourself with tiny Villefranche-sur-Mer, rather than immediately departing for nearby Nice.

Best Places For...

Architecture Promenade des Anglais, Nice (p128)

Markets Vieux Nice (p126)

Local cuisine Chez Palmyre, Nice (p129) and Les Garçons, Villefranche-sur-Mer (p133)

Bistro Bar des Oiseaux, Nice (p129)

Ice cream Fenocchio, Nice (p129)

Wine bar La Part des Anges, Nice (p131)

Gourmet food Moulin à Huile d'Olive Alziari, Nice (p128)

Sweets Maison Auer, Nice (p128)

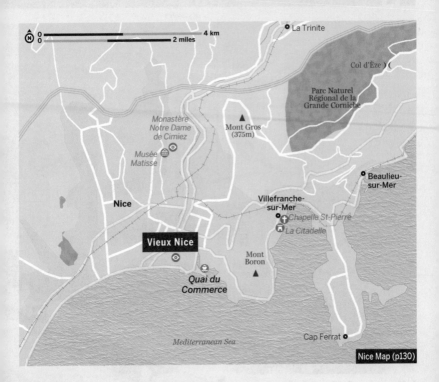

Nice Map (p130)

Getting from the Ports

Smaller vessels are likely to dock in Nice, at **Quai du Commerce**, from where it's about a 2.5km walk to the city centre. You can also pick up a bus (or a sight-seeing bus) to the city centre, or walk up Rue Cassini to get a tram from Place Garibaldi near the edge of Vieux Nice.

Larger ships tend to dock in the bay off **Villefranche-sur-Mer** and then tender passengers ashore – then you're already basically in the centre of town. The two ports are well connected to each other by bus and train (seven minutes).

Fast Facts

Currency Euro (€)

Language French

Money ATMs widely available. Credit cards accepted in most hotels and restaurants.

Visas Generally not required for stays of up to 90 days (or at all for EU nationals); some nationalities need a Schengen visa.

Tourist Information There's a helpful tourist office on Promenade des Anglais in Nice.

Wi-fi Free access is widely available throughout the city, at hotels, cafes and other public spaces.

Cours Saleya

ROSTISLAV GLINSKY/SHUTTERSTOCK ©

Vieux Nice

*Tucked into a pedestrian-friendly triangle is Nice's **oldest neighbourhood**, where the layout of narrow streets has barely changed since the 1700s. Now packed with markets, bars, bistros and boutiques, the area is a joy to wander around in.*

Great For...

☑ Don't Miss

A slice of *socca* (chickpea-flour pancake) on the raucous pavement terrace at Chez René Socca (p132).

Cours Saleya

No experience epitomises the Vieux Nice lifestyle like a trip to the market. Every morning, a massive **food market** (cours Saleya; ◷6am-1.30pm Tue-Sun) fills much of the Cours Saleya square, featuring stalls laden with fruit and vegetables, olives marinated a dozen different ways, every herb and spice known under the Provençal sun – no market is a finer reflection of local Niçois life. An adjoining **flower market** (cours Saleya; ◷6am-5.30pm Tue-Sat, 6.30am-1.30pm Sun) is worth a meander for its fragrant bucketfuls of blooms. Monday ushers in a **flea market** (Marché à la Brocante; cours Saleya; ◷7am-6pm Mon) instead, selling furniture and trinkets of all kinds (don't be afraid to bargain).

⚓

Explore Ashore

You can walk from the port terminal to Vieux Nice in about 20 minutes, or catch a bus (🚌1 to Opéra-Vielle Ville/ Cathédrale-Vieille Ville). From 2019 you will also be able to take the new 🚌2. You'll have plenty of time for soaking up the atmosphere, lunching and exploring – including checking out the castle ruins.

★ Top Tip

Themed walking tours in English depart from the **Centre du Patrimoine** (📞04 92 00 41 90; www.nice.fr/fr/culture/patrimoine; 14 rue Jules Gilly; tours adult/child €5/free; ⊘9am-1pm & 2-5pm Mon-Thu, to 3.45pm Fri).

Lofty Lookout

From Vieux Nice, staircases wind up to the **Colline du Château** (Castle Hill; ⊘8.30am-8pm Apr-Sep, to 6pm Oct-Mar) FREE, or you can take the free **lift** (Ascenseur du Château; rue des Ponchettes; ⊘9am-8pm Jun-Aug, to 7pm Apr, May & Sep, 10am-6pm Oct-Mar). Formerly a military outpost and today a city park, the hilltop affords panoramic vistas of the Promenade des Anglais from the **Tour Bellanda**. Stroll over to the **Cascade du Casteu** (an artificial 18th-century waterfall), or wander among the cypresses and ornate tombstones of the 18th-century **Cimitière du Château**.

Baroque Splendour

Baroque aficionados will adore architectural gems **Cathédrale Ste-Réparate** (📞04 93 92 01 35; place Rossetti; ⊘2-6pm Mon, 9am-noon & 2-6pm Tue-Sun), honouring the city's patron saint; and exuberant **Chapelle de la Miséricorde** (📞04 92 00 41 90; cours Saleya; ⊘2.30-5pm Tue Sep-Jun), a chapel from 1740 renowned for its exceptionally rich architecture.

Cafe Culture

Lounging on an Old Town cafe terrace, watching the world go by over a glass of pastis or a post-beach cocktail, is a national pastime in Nice. No place in Vieux Nice offers better people-watching than the beach-facing tables on the streetside deck and upstairs terrace of **La Movida** (📞04 93 80 48 04; www.movidanice.com; 41 quai des États-Unis; ⊘10am-2am). **Les Distilleries Idéales** (📞04 93 62 10 66; www.facebook.com/ldinice; 24 rue de la Préfecture; ⊘9am-12.30am) has beers on tap, local wine by the glass, and a little balcony.

Nice

◉ SIGHTS

Promenade des Anglais   Architecture

(🖳8, 52, 62) The most famous stretch of seafront in Nice – if not France – is this vast paved promenade, which gets its name from the English expat patrons who paid for it in 1822. It runs for the whole 4km sweep of the Baie des Anges with a dedicated lane for cyclists and skaters; if you fancy joining them, you can rent skates, scooters and bikes from **Roller Station** (🖉04 93 62 99 05; www. roller-station.fr; 49 quai des États-Unis; skates, boards & scooters per hour/day €5/15, bicycles €5/18; ☺9am-8pm Jul & Aug, 10am-7pm May, Jun, Sep & Oct, to 6pm Nov-Apr).

Musée Matisse   Gallery

(🖉04 93 81 08 08; www.musee-matisse-nice.org; 164 av des Arènes de Cimiez; museum pass 24hr/7 days €10/20; ☺10am-6pm Wed-Mon late Jun–mid-Oct, from 11am rest of year; 🚌15, 17, 20, 22 to Arènes/Musée Matisse) This museum, 2km north of the city centre in the leafy Cimiez quarter, houses a fascinating assortment of works by Matisse, including oil paintings, drawings, sculptures, tapestries and Matisse's famous paper cut-outs. The permanent collection is displayed in a red-ochre 17th-century Genoese villa in an olive grove. Temporary exhibitions are in the futuristic basement building. Matisse is buried in the **Monastère Notre Dame de Cimiez** (place du Monastère; ☺8.30am-12.30pm & 2.30-6.30pm; 🚌15, 17, 20, 22 to Arènes/Musée Matisse) cemetery, across the park from the museum.

🛍 SHOPPING

Maison Auer   Food

(🖉04 93 85 77 98; www.maison-auer.com; 7 rue St-François de Paule; ☺9am-6pm Tue-Sat) With its gilded counters and mirrors, this opulent shop – run by the same family for five generations – looks more like a 19th-century boutique than a sweets shop, but this is where discerning Niçois have been buying their *fruits confits* (crystallised fruit) and *amandes chocolatées* (chocolate-covered almonds) since 1820.

Friperie Caprice   Vintage

(🖉09 83 48 05 43; www.facebook.com/Caprice-VintageShop; 12 rue Droite; ☺2-7pm Mon, 11am-1.30pm & 2.30-7pm Tue-Sat) Nice's favourite vintage shop is a treasure trove of clothing, jewellery and accessories spanning much of the 20th century; what really sets it apart is the generous advice and assistance of amiable owner Madame Caprice, who knows every piece in the shop.

La Boutique du Flacon   Perfume

(www.laboutiqueduflacon.com; 22 rue Benoît Bunico; ☺11am-6pm) Take a trip back in time at this unique shop specialising in vintage perfume bottles with belle-époque-style spray pumps. English-speaking artist-owner Sarah Bartlett also sells crystalware, handbags, Murano jewellery, and floral essences from Grasse, France's perfume capital.

Moulin à Huile d'Olive Alziari   Food

(🖉04 93 62 94 03; www.alziari.com.fr; 14 rue St-François de Paule; ☺9am-7pm Mon-Sat, from 10am Sun) Superb (but expensive) hand-pressed olive oil, fresh from the mill on the outskirts of Nice. It comes in several flavours of differing fruitiness. The shop also sells delicious tapenades, jams, honeys and other goodies.

Cave Rivoli   Wine

(🖉04 93 91 09 16; www.caverivoli.com; 6 rue de Rivoli; ☺10am-1pm & 2.30-8pm Mon-Sat, 9am-1pm Sun; 🚌7, 9, 22, 27, 59, 70 to Rivoli) This shop in the stylish Carré d'Or district carries a wide selection of French wines, including the locally produced Bellet AOC.

Le Fromage   Cheese

(🖉09 51 00 19 22; www.lefromage.fr; 25 rue de la Préfecture; ☺8am-1pm & 4-7pm Tue-Sat, 8am-1pm Sun) Owner Laurent Viterbo presides over a cornucopia of locally produced cheeses – including sheep-, goat- and cow-milk varieties – at this favourite Vieux Nice *fromagerie* (cheese shop).

✖ EATING

Chez Palmyre   French €

(📞04 93 85 72 32; 5 rue Droite; 3-course menu €18; ⏰noon-1.30pm & 7-9.30pm Mon, Tue, Thu & Fri) Look no further for authentic Niçois cooking than this packed, cramped, convivial little space in the heart of the Old Town. The menu is very meat-heavy, with plenty of tripe, veal, pot-cooked chicken and the like, true to the traditional tastes of Provençal cuisine. It's a bargain, and understandably popular. Book well ahead, even for lunch.

La Rossettisserie   French €

(📞04 93 76 18 80; www.larossettisserie.com; 8 rue Mascoïnat; mains €17-20; ⏰noon-2pm & 7-10pm Mon-Sat) Roast meat is the order of the day here: make your choice from beef, chicken, veal or lamb, and pair it with a choice of mashed or sautéed potatoes, ratatouille or salad. Simple and sumptuous, with cosy, rustic decor and a delightful vaulted cellar.

Chez Pipo   French €

(📞04 93 55 88 82; www.chezpipo.fr; 13 rue Bavastro; socca €2.90; ⏰11.30am-2.30pm & 5.30-10pm Wed-Sun; 🚌1 to Garibaldi, 2 to Port Lympia) Everyone says the best *socca* can be found in the Old Town, but don't believe them – this place near Port Lympia has been in the biz since 1923 and, for our money, knocks *socca*-shaped spots off anywhere else in Nice.

Socca d'Or   Fast Food €

(📞04 93 56 52 93; www.restaurant-soccador-nice. fr; 45 rue Bonaparte; socca €3; ⏰11am-2pm & 6-10pm Mon, Tue & Thu-Sat; 🚌1 to Garibaldi, 2 to Port Lympia) Locals swear by the authentic Niçois specialities served at this low-key neighbourhood eatery: *pan bagnat* (southern France's iconic tuna sandwich) on fresh homemade bread, *tourte de blette sucrée* (sweet Swiss-chard tart), *pissaladière*, salade niçoise and, of course, the restaurant's famous namesake, *socca*.

Fenocchio   Ice Cream €

(📞04 93 80 72 52; www.fenocchio.fr; 2 place Rossetti; 1/2 scoops €2.50/4; ⏰9am-midnight Mar-Nov) There's no shortage of ice-cream

🏖 Beaches

Officially there are 25 named beaches strung out along the Baie des Anges, some of which are free, others of which are reserved solely for paying clientele. All are pebbly, so sensitive behinds might opt for one of the private beaches (€15 to €25 per day), which come with sun-loungers and comfy mattresses.

Free cold-water showers, lifeguards and first-aid posts are available most of the way along the bay, including on the public beaches; there are also a few public toilets for which you have to pay a small charge. Most beaches also offer activities, from beach volleyball to jet skis and pedalos.

Baie des Anges beach
EQROY/SHUTTERSTOCK ©

sellers in the Old Town, but this *maître glacier* (master ice-cream maker) has been king of the scoops since 1966. The array of flavours is mind-boggling – olive, tomato, fig, beer, lavender and violet to name a few. Dither too long over the 70-plus flavours and you'll never make it to the front of the queue.

Bar des Oiseaux   French €€

(📞04 93 80 27 33; 5 rue St-Vincent; 3-course lunch menu €20, dinner menus from €30; ⏰noon-1.45pm & 7.15-9.45pm Tue-Sat) Hidden down a narrow backstreet, this Old Town classic has been in business since 1961, serving as a popular nightclub before reincarnating itself as a restaurant (some of its original saucy murals have survived the transition). Nowadays it's a lively bistro serving superb traditional French

Nice

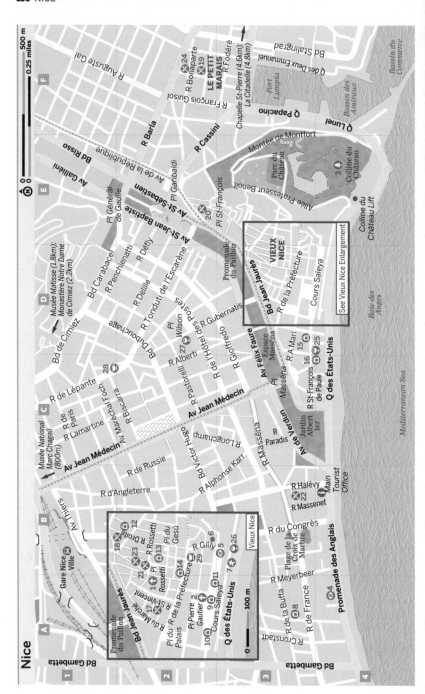

Nice

cuisine spiced up with modern twists. The weekday lunch special offers phenomenal value. Book ahead.

La Femme du Boulanger   Bistro €€

(📞04 89 03 43 03; www.facebook.com/femmeduboulanger; 3 rue Raffali; mains €20-25, tartines €16-22; ⊙9am-3pm & 7-11pm; 🚌8, 52, 62 to Massenet) This back-alley gem with pavement seating is a vision of French bistro bliss. Mains like duck *à l'orange,* honey-balsamic glazed lamb shank, or perfect *steak au poivre* (peppered steak) with *gratin dauphinois* (cheesy potatoes) and perfectly tender veggies are followed up with raspberry clafoutis, tiramisu and other scrumptious desserts. Tartines on wood-fired homemade bread are the other house speciality.

🍷 DRINKING & NIGHTLIFE

La Ronronnerie   Cafe

(📞09 51 51 26 50; www.laronronnerie.fr; 4 rue de Lépante; ⊙11.30am-6pm Tue-Sat; 🚌4 to Sasserno) Kitties rule the roost at this one-of-a-kind cafe, a must for cat-lovers. Five free-range felines roam about the tables, seeking the right lap to sit in, yawning and stretching on plush pedestals or climbing the tree branch overhead. Meanwhile, humans sip hot beverages and nibble on bagels and cake. It's squeaky clean, without a flea in sight.

La Part des Anges   Wine Bar

(📞04 93 62 69 80; www.lapartdesanges-nice.com; 17 rue Gubernatis; ⊙10am-8.30pm Mon-Thu, to midnight Fri & Sat; 🚌7, 9 to Pastorelli or Wilson) The focus at this classy wine shop and bar is organic wines – a few are sold by the glass, but the best selection is available by the bottle, served with homemade tapenades and charcuterie platters. The name means 'the Angel's Share', referring to the alcohol that evaporates as wines age. There are only a few tables, so arrive early or reserve ahead.

El Merkado   Bar

(📞04 93 62 30 88; www.el-merkado.com; 12 rue St-François de Paule; ⊙11am-1.30am Oct-Apr, 10am-2.30am May-Sep) Footsteps from cours Saleya, this hip tapas bar (strapline: 'In Sangria We Trust') struts its vintage stuff on the ground floor of a quintessential Niçois town house. Lounging on its pavement terrace or a sofa with an after-beach cocktail is the thing to do here.

ⓘ INFORMATION

Tourist Office (📞04 92 14 46 14; www.nicetourisme.com; 5 Promenade des Anglais; ⊙9am-7pm Jun-Sep, to 6pm Mon-Sat Oct-May; 📶; 🚌8, 52, 62 to Massenet) Nice's main tourist office on Promenade des Anglais provides a wealth of resources, including maps, bro-

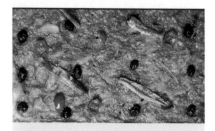

🍽 Niçois Specialities

Niçois specialities include *socca* (a savoury, griddle-fried pancake made from chickpea flour and olive oil, sprinkled with a liberal dose of black pepper), *petits farcis* (stuffed vegetables), *pissaladière* (Niçoise pizza, consisting of an onion tart topped with black olives and anchovies) and the many vegetable *beignets* (fritters). Try them at **Chez René Socca** (☑04 93 92 05 73; 2 rue Miralhéti; small plates €3-6; ⊙9am-9pm Tue-Sun, to 10.30pm Jul & Aug, closed Nov; 🐾) or Chez Pipo.

Pissaladière
RIVER THOMPSON/LONELY PLANET ©

chures, information about attractions and help booking accommodation.

ℹ GETTING AROUND

Bus Buses and trams in Nice are run by Lignes d'Azur. Tickets cost just €1.50 and include one connection, including intercity buses within the Alpes-Maritimes *département*. Buses are particularly handy for getting to the Musée Matisse.

Buses typically run every 10 to 15 minutes between 6am and 9pm. Tickets can be purchased at machines on the platform or on board. All tickets (including passes) must be validated at the beginning of each ride by inserting them into the machines provided on board.

Train SNCF long-haul trains provide near instantaneous service to suburbs east of Nice such as Villefranche-sur-Mer (eight minutes).

Tram Nice's sleek tram system (http://tramway.nice.fr) is great for getting across town. The original line charts a parabolic course through the city centre, connecting Nice-Ville train station with Vieux Nice and Le Port-Garibaldi to the southeast and Libération to the north. There are services every four to five minutes between 7am and 8pm (less frequent on Sundays). Nice's second tram line, scheduled for completion in 2019, runs east–west between the airport and the port, adding 20 new stations to the system.

Single-ride tickets cost €1.50 and can be purchased from machines at any tram stop. All tickets (and passes) must be validated at the beginning of each ride by inserting them into the machines provided on board.

Villefranche-sur-Mer

◎ SIGHTS

Chapelle St-Pierre
Church

(1 quai Courbet; €3; ⊙10am-noon & 3-7pm Wed-Mon Apr-Sep, 9.30am-12.30pm & 2-6pm Wed-Sun Oct-Mar) Villefranche was a favourite of Jean Cocteau (1889–1963), who sought solace here in 1924 after the death of his companion Raymond Radiguet. Several years later, Cocteau convinced locals to let him paint the neglected, 14th-century Chapelle St-Pierre, which he transformed into a mirage of mystical frescoes. Scenes from St Peter's life are interspersed with references to Cocteau's cinematic work (notably the drivers from *Orpheus*) and friends (Francine Weisweiller, whose Villa Santo Sospir in St-Jean-Cap-Ferrat Cocteau also decorated).

La Citadelle
Fortress

(Fort St-Elme; ☑04 93 76 33 27; place Emmanuel Philibert; ⊙10am-noon & 2-5.30pm Oct & Dec-May, 10am-noon & 3-6.30pm Jun-Sep, closed Sun morning & Nov) 🆓 Villefranche's imposing citadel is worth visiting for its impressive architecture. Built by the duke of Savoy between 1554 and 1559 to defend the gulf, its walls today shelter the town hall, well-combed public gardens and several free museums. The **Musée Volti** displays voluptuous bronzes by Villefranche sculptor Antoniucci Volti; the **Musée Goetz-Boumeester** features modern art in the citadel's former living quarters; and the **Collection Roux** comprises several

VALERY ROKHIN/SHUTTERSTOCK ©

La Citadelle

hundred ceramic figurines depicting life in medieval and Renaissance times.

❌ EATING

La Grignotière   Brasserie €
(☑04 93 76 79 83; 3 rue Poilu; pizzas €11-14, mains €15-23; ⊙noon-2pm & 7.30-9.30pm; 🖼) For a cheap and cheerful fill, there is no finer address along the coast than La Grignotière, known far and wide for its generous portions of grilled fish and veg, lasagne, pizza and other crowd-pleasers. Decor is old-fashioned and nothing to rave about, but the place is charming and unpretentious. It has a few tables on the pedestrian street.

Les Garçons   Mediterranean €€
(☑04 93 76 62 40; 18 rue du Poilu; mains €21-28; ⊙noon-2pm & 7.30-10.30pm Thu-Tue) Gourmets in the know flock to this stylish address, buried in Villefranche's rabbit warren of ancient Old Town backstreets. In summer, tables sprawl elegantly across a bijou stone square. Cuisine is creative, local and driven by the market and local fishers' catch. Red tuna tartare with avocado is a delicious staple.

ℹ️ INFORMATION

Tourist Office (☑04 93 01 73 68; www.ville franche-sur-mer.com; Jardins François Binon; ⊙9am-6.30pm Jul & Aug, 9am-noon & 2-5pm Mon-Sat Sep-Jun) From April to September the tourist office runs Friday-morning guided tours (€5, 1½ hours) of the citadel museums and Old Town. It also has information on family workshops (adult/child €5/3) held in the citadel museums.

ℹ️ GETTING AROUND

BUS

Bus 81, operated by Lignes d'Azur (www.lignes dazur.com), runs from Nice's Promenade des Arts stop (just north of Vieux Nice) to Villefranche every 20 to 25 minutes (€1.50, 10 minutes).

TRAIN

Villefranche-sur-Mer is on the coastal train line between Nice (€1.90, seven minutes) and Monaco (€3.10, 15 minutes).

MONACO & MONTE CARLO

Monaco & Monte Carlo at a Glance...

Squeezed into just 200 hectares, Monaco might be the world's second-smallest country (only the Vatican is smaller), but what it lacks in size it makes up for in attitude. World-famous Monte Carlo is an ode to concrete and glass, dominated by high-rise hotels, super yachts and apartment blocks. In dramatic contrast, the rocky outcrop known as Le Rocher, jutting out on the south side of the port, is crowned by a rather charming Old Town, home to the principality's royal palace.

With One Day in Port

○ Start by hopping across the harbour and heading straight to the **Casino de Monte Carlo** (p138). Admire the lavish interiors of the private gaming salons and the views from the terraces before making your way to Monaco's impressively situated **Musée Océano-graphique** (p142).

○ Work back from here, ticking off Monaco's royal residence, the **Palais Princier** (p146), Grace Kelly's tomb in the **Cathédrale** (p146), and then wandering back down through the winding streets of **Le Rocher** (p146) and the **Jardin Exotique** (p146) to the marina.

Best Places For...

The high life Casino de Monte Carlo (p138)

Local Life Marché de la Condamine (p147)

Family fun Musée Océanographique (p142)

Ice Cream Pierre Geronimi (p147)

Souvenir tipples L'Orangerie (p146)

Bd Guynemer

Bd d'Italie

Bd du Larvotto

FRANCE

Route de la Moyenne Corniche

Av de la République

Bd des Moulins

Larvotto

Beausoleil

Monte Carlo

Gare de Monaco

Bd Princesse Charlotte

Casino de Monte Carlo

Av d'Ostende

Mediterranean Sea

Bd du Jardin Exotique

Port de Monaco

Cruise Port

La Condamine

Bd Charles III

Monaco Ville

Musée Océanographique de Monaco

Port de Fontvieille

Fontvieille

Parc Fontvieille

Monaco Map (p148)

1 km
0.5 miles

Getting from the Port

Monaco's **Bateau Bus** (water taxi) cuts across the harbour from the cruise terminal to the waterfront on the Casino side. Back round to Le Rocher, with the Oceanographic Museum and Palace, is about a 25-minute walk. Alternatively, bus routes 1 and 2 run from the Casino around to Monaco Ville.

There are a number of lifts and escalators installed to help you navigate Monaco's steeply tiered streets (and help you appreciate the views all the more).

Fast Facts

Currency Euro (€)

Language French

Money ATMs are widely available.

Tourist Information There's a helpful office just above the Casino.

Visas Generally not required for stays of up to 90 days (or at all for EU nationals); some nationalities need a Schengen visa.

Wi-fi Monaco Telecom (www.monaco-telecom.mc) offers a network of more than 30 public wi-fi sites.

BORIS STROUJKO/SHUTTERSTOCK ©

Casino de Monte Carlo

The very emblem of Monaco, the cornerstone of the Riviera's glitzy allure, this belle-époque beauty still works its magic on all who venture near. Whether you're a seasoned gambler, a nostalgic James Bond fan or a curious onlooker, Monte Carlo's casino will make a lasting impression.

Great For...

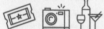

☑ Don't Miss

Come in early to see the opulent décor of the exclusive *salons privés* (private lounges).

Peeping inside Monte Carlo's legendary marble-and-gold casino is a Monaco essential. The building, open to visitors every morning, including the exclusive *salons privés*, is Europe's most lavish example of belle-époque architecture. Prince Charles III spearheaded the casino's development and in 1866, three years after its inauguration, the name 'Monte Carlo' – Ligurian for 'Mount Charles', in honour of the prince – was coined.

Les Salons

Blackjack, English and European roulette, *punto banco* (baccarat), Texas hold'em poker and *trente et quarante* (thirty and forty) entertain in the main gaming room, Salle Europe, while slot machines prevail in the Salles Renaissance and Amérique, the other two *salons ordinaires* that are open to

HORIZON IMAGES/MOTION ALAMY STOCK PHOTO ©

⚓ Explore Ashore

Hop aboard Monaco's Bateau Bus across the harbour, from where it's a 15-minute walk along Avenue JF Kennedy and Avenue d'Ostende to the Casino forecourt. Many of the Casino's *salon privés* are only open to tourists in the morning, so head here first.

❶ Need to Know

☎ 98 06 21 21; www.casinomontecarlo.com; place du Casino; morning visit incl audioguide adult/child Oct-Apr €14/10, May-Sep €17/12, salons ordinaires gaming Oct-Apr €14, May-Sep €17; ⊙ visits 9am-1pm, gaming 2pm-late

the general public for gambling. The *salons privés*, which are accessible for gambling only to frequent clients of the casino, offer all of the same table games in a more exclusive setting, without the slot machines. In the *salons super-privés*, where the James Bondesque pros play, tailor-made games are permitted and the sky is truly the limit.

Salle Europe

The Salle Europe is the oldest part of the casino and its main gaming room. *Trente et quarante* and European roulette continue to be played here, as they have been since 1865. Enormous Bohemian glass chandeliers, each weighing 150kg, hang from an ornate circular glass ceiling supported by onyx columns banded with bronze. The bull's-eye windows around

the room originally served as security observation points.

Salle Médecin

Also known as Salle Empire because of its extravagant Empire-style decor, Monégasque architect François Médecin's gaming room was designed to accommodate the casino's biggest gamblers, and it remains one of the casino's more exclusive *salons privés*, with one part still hidden from prying eyes as a *super-privé* room.

A popular filming location, it appears in the movies *Never Say Never Again* and *Golden Eye*, where James Bond himself can be seen striding across the room. The attached veranda has stunning views of the Bay of Roquebrune-Cap-Martin.

Monte Carlo Casino

TIMELINE

1863 Charles III inaugurates the first Casino on Plateau des Spélugues. The ❶ **atrium** is a small room with a wooden podium from which an orchestra entertains while punters purchase entrance tickets.

1864 Hôtel de Paris opens and the area becomes known as the 'Golden Square'.

1865 Construction of ❷ **Salle Europe**. Cathedral-like, it is lined with onyx columns and lit by eight Bohemian crystal chandeliers weighing 150kg each.

1868 The steam train arrives in Monaco and ❸ **Café de Paris** is completed.

1878–79 Gambling moves to Hôtel de Paris while Charles Garnier is charged with building a new casino with a miniature replica of the Paris Opera House, ❹ **Salle Garnier**.

1890 The advent of electricity casts a glow on architect Jules Touzet's newly added ❺ **gaming rooms** for high rollers.

1903 Inspired by female gamblers, Henri Schmit decorates ❻ **Salle Blanche** with caryatids and the painting *Les Grâces Florentines*.

1904 Smoking is banned in the gaming rooms and ❼ **Salon Rose**, a new smoking room, is added.

1910 ❽ **Salle Médecin**, immense and grand, hosts the high-spending Private Circle.

1966 Celebrations mark 100 years of uninterrupted gambling despite two world wars.

TOP TIPS

➡ After 2pm when gaming begins, admission is strictly for 18 years and over. Rooms beyond the Salle Europe are closed to the general public. Photo ID is obligatory.

➡ Don't wear trainers. A jacket for men is not obligatory (but is recommended) in the gaming rooms.

➡ In the main room, the minimum bet is €5/25 for roulette/blackjack.

➡ In the *salons privés*, there is no maximum bet.

HORIZON IMAGES/MOTION/ALAMY STOCK PHOTO ©

Atrium
The casino's 'lobby', so to speak, is paved in marble and lined with 28 Ionic columns, which support a balustraded gallery canopied with an engraved glass ceiling.

Hôtel de Paris

HÔTEL DE PARIS

Notice the horse's shiny leg (and testicles) on the lobby's statue of Louis XIV on horseback? Legend has it that rubbing them brings good luck in the casino.

Salon Rose
Smoking was banned in the gaming rooms following a fraud involving a croupier letting his ash fall on the floor. The Salon Rose (Pink Room; today a restaurant) was therefore opened in 1903 for smokers – the gaze of Gallelli's famous cigarillo-smoking ladies follows you around the room.

Salle Garnier
Taking eight months to build and two years to restore (2004–06), the opera's original statuary is rehabilitated using original moulds saved by the creator's grandson. Individual air-con and heating vents are installed beneath each of the 525 seats.

DEA/G. DAGLI ORTI/GETTY IMAGES ©

Salle Europe

The oldest part of the casino, where they continue to play *trente-et-quarante* and European roulette, which have been played here since 1865. Tip: the bull's-eye windows around the room originally served as security observation points.

Café de Paris

With the arrival of Diaghilev as director of the Monte Carlo Opera in 1911, Café de Paris becomes the go-to address for artists and gamblers. It retains the same high-glamour ambience today. Tip: snag a seat on the terrace and people-watch.

LABORANT/SHUTTERSTOCK ©

EDUCATION IMAGES/UIG VIA GETTY IMAGES ©

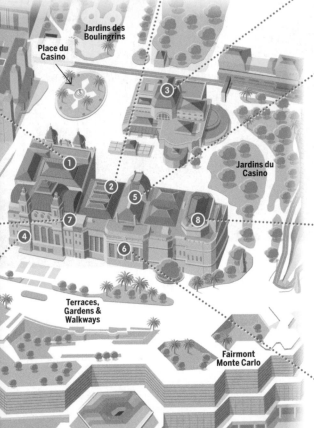

Jardins des Boulingrins

Place du Casino

③

Jardins du Casino

①

② ⑤

⑦ ⑧

④ ⑥

Terraces, Gardens & Walkways

Fairmont Monte Carlo

Hexagrace Mosaic

Salles Touzet

This vast partitioned hall, 21m by 24m, is decorated in the most lavish style: oak, Tonkin mahogany and oriental jasper panelling are offset by vast canvases, Marseille bronzes, Italian mosaics, sculptural reliefs and stained-glass windows.

Salle Médecin

Also known as Salle Empire because of its extravagant Empire-style decor, Monégasque architect François Médecin's gaming room was originally intended for the casino's biggest gamblers. Part of it still remains hidden from prying eyes as a Super Privé room.

Salle Blanche

Today a superb bar-lounge, the Salle Blanche (White Room) opens onto an outdoor gaming terrace. The caryatids on the ceiling were modelled on fashionable courtesans such as La Belle Otéro, who placed her first bet here aged 18.

BEST VIEWS

Wander behind the casino through manicured gardens and gaze across Victor Vasarely's vibrant op-art mosaic, *Hexagrace,* to views of the harbour and the sea.

MICHEL DAGNINO - MUSÉE OCEANOGRAPHIQUE DE MONACO ©

Musée Oceanographique de Monaco

Housed in a dazzling Baroque Revival building built into an 85m cliff above the Mediterranean, Monaco's Musée Oceanographique is a delight, not only for its audacious architecture but for its unique history and superb collections.

Great For...

☑ Don't Miss

The shark lagoon in the two-storey central aquarium and a 2.8-ton whale skeleton suspended in mid-air.

History

Stuck dramatically to the edge of a cliff since 1910, the world-renowned Musée Océanographique de Monaco was founded by Prince Albert I (1848–1922), a devoted marine scientist whose trips from the Mediterranean to the Arctic in the late 1800s yielded many new discoveries and a host of specimens. Having celebrated its centenary in 2010, the museum boasts one of Europe's oldest aquariums.

Highlights

Its centrepiece is the aquarium with a 6m-deep lagoon, where sharks patrol on one side while colourful small fry like the bluespine unicornfish and the blackspotted rubberlip swim merrily about on the

Explore Ashore

From the terminal, a winding route past the Palais Princier is about 25 minutes' walk. You'll need two hours to see all of the museum, before heading to the Palais Princier on the combined ticket. From the Casino de Monte Carlo, take Monaco city bus 1 or 2 to the Le Rocher stop.

❶ Need to Know

☑ 93 15 36 00; www.oceano.mc; av St-Martin; adult/child high season €16/12, low season €11/7; ☺ 9.30am-8pm Jul & Aug, 10am-7pm Apr-Jun & Sep, to 6pm Oct-Mar

other. Upstairs, two huge colonnaded rooms retrace the history of oceanography and marine biology (and Prince Albert's contribution to the field) through photographs, old equipment, numerous specimens and interactive displays.

In all there are around 90 tanks in the aquarium, containing a dazzling 450 Mediterranean and tropical species sustained by 250,000L of freshly pumped sea water per day. School holidays usher in free hourly light shows in the Salle de la Baleine (Whale Skeleton Room) and feel-the-fish sessions in the kid-friendly tactile basin, where you can handle starfishes, sea urchins and baby sharks (40 minutes, €6); tickets for the latter are sold at the entrance.

In 2019, a new outdoor turtle tank opened, allowing the public to observe marine turtles while marine biologists work to rehabilitate injured animals.

Don't miss the sweeping views of Monaco and the Med from the rooftop terrace and cafe. Save a few cents by buying a combined ticket covering same-day admission to both the Palais Princier and the Musée Océanographique; both sights sell it.

Monte Carlo Casino to Monaco-Ville

Monaco's sights are concentrated in two main zones. The old clifftop town of Le Rocher is where you'll find the prince's palace, the oceanographic museum and the cathedral. North across the port is Monaco's second centre of gravity, the Casino de Monte Carlo.

Start Casino de Monte Carlo
Distance 2km
Duration Two hours

2 Follow the Grand Prix route down to the waterfront and the **Stade Nautique Rainier III**.

4 Watch the 11.55am changing of the guard at the historic **Palais Princier** (p146).

3 Climb the zigzag streets into Monaco's steeply perched medieval town, **Le Rocher** (p146).

5 Pay your respects at the tomb of Grace Kelly in the **Cathédrale de Monaco** (p146).

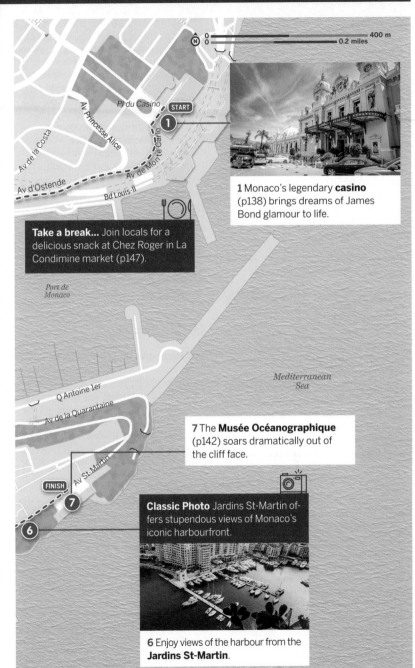

0 — 400 m
0 — 0.2 miles

Pl du Casino **START**
1

Av Princesse Alice
Av de la Costa
Av d'Ostende
Av de Monte Carlo
Av de Monte Carlo
Bd Louis-II

1 Monaco's legendary **casino** (p138) brings dreams of James Bond glamour to life.

Take a break... Join locals for a delicious snack at Chez Roger in La Condimine market (p147).

Port de Monaco

Mediterranean Sea

Q Antoine 1er
Av de la Quarantaine

7 The **Musée Océanographique** (p142) soars dramatically out of the cliff face.

Av St-Martin
FINISH
7
6

Classic Photo Jardins St-Martin offers stupendous views of Monaco's iconic harbourfront.

6 Enjoy views of the harbour from the **Jardins St-Martin**.

⊙ SIGHTS

Le Rocher
Historic Site

Monaco Ville, also called Le Rocher, is the only part of Monaco to have retained its original Old Town, complete with small, windy medieval lanes. The Old Town thrusts skywards on a pistol-shaped rock, its strategic location – which became the stronghold of the Grimaldi dynasty – overlooking the sea. There are various staircases up to Le Rocher; the best route up is via Rampe Major, which starts from place d'Armes near the port.

On your way up, look out for the statue of the late Prince Rainier looking down on his beloved Monaco, created by Dutch artist Kees Verkade in 2013.

Jardin Exotique
Gardens

(✆93 15 29 80; www.jardin-exotique.mc; 62 bd du Jardin Exotique; adult/child €7.20/3.80; ⊙9am-7pm mid-May–mid-Sep, to 6pm rest of year) Home to the world's largest succulent and cactus collection, from small echinocereus to 10m-tall African candelabras, the gardens tumble down the slopes of Moneghetti through a maze of paths, stairs and bridges. Views of the principality are spectacular. Admission includes the **Musée d'Anthropologie**, which displays prehistoric remains unearthed in Monaco, and a 35-minute guided tour of the **Grotte de l'Observatoire**. The prehistoric, stalactite- and stalagmite-laced cave is the only one in Europe where the temperature rises as you descend.

Bus 2 links Jardin Exotique with the town centre.

Palais Princier de Monaco
Palace

(✆93 25 18 31; www.palais.mc; place du Palais; adult/child €8/4, incl Collection de Voitures Anciennes car museum €11.50/5, incl Musée Océanographique €19/11; ⊙10am-6pm Apr-Jun & Sep–mid-Oct, to 7pm Jul & Aug) Built as a fortress atop Le Rocher in the 13th century, this palace is the private residence of the Grimaldi family. It is protected by the blue-helmeted, white-socked Carabiniers du Prince; changing of the guard takes place daily at 11.55am, when crowds gather outside the gates to watch.

Most of the palace is off limits, but you can get a glimpse of royal life on a tour of the glittering **state apartments**, where you can see some of the lavish furniture and priceless artworks collected by the family over the centuries. It's a good idea to buy tickets online in advance to avoid queuing.

Combined tickets including Monaco's oceanographic museum (p109) or the Prince's **classic car collection** (Monaco Top Cars Collection; ✆92 05 28 56; www.mtcc.mc; Terrasses de Fontvieille; adult/child €6.50/3, incl Palais Princier de Monaco €11.50/5; ⊙10am-6pm) are also available.

Cathédrale de Monaco
Cathedral

(4 rue Colonel Bellando de Castro; ⊙8.30am-6.45pm) FREE An adoring crowd continually shuffles past Prince Rainier's and Princess Grace's flower-adorned graves, located inside the cathedral choir of Monaco's 1875 Romanesque-Byzantine cathedral.

ⓐ SHOPPING

Les Pavillons de Monte Carlo
Mall

(allées des Boulingrins, place du Casino) The five giant snow-white 'pebbles' that sprang up on the lawns of **Jardins des Boulingrins** in 2014 are a temporary home to the luxury boutiques previously housed in the now-demolished **Sporting d'Hiver**. In 2019, they were due to relocate to the spiffy new **Monaco 1** building, just downhill on place du Casino's southwest corner.

Among the high-end boutiques you'll find here are Chanel, McQueen, Sonia Rykiel and Dior.

L'Orangerie
Drinks

(✆99 90 43 38; www.orangerie.mc; 9 rue de la Turbie; ⊙9.30am-12.30pm & 2.30-5.30pm Mon-Fri) The brainchild of expatriate Dubliner Philip Culazzo, l'Orangerie is an artisanal liqueur made with bitter oranges harvested from the citrus trees lining some of Monaco's streets. Grab a taste and bring home a bottle from this cute-as-a-button, bright orange boutique.

Office des Émissions de Timbres-Poste
Gifts & Souvenirs

(☑98 98 41 41; www.oetp-monaco.com; 23 av Albert II; ☺9am-5pm Mon-Fri) Collectors – and anyone else smitten with the quirky allure of stamps issued in the world's second-smallest country – should stop in at this official government office, which sells a wide variety of Monaco stamps, both past and present.

 EATING

Marché de la Condamine
Market €

(www.facebook.com/marche.condamine; 15 place d'Armes; ☺7am-3pm Mon-Sat, to 2pm Sun) For tasty, excellent-value fare around shared tables, hit Monaco's fabulous food court, tucked beneath the arches behind the open-air place d'Armes market. Rock-bottom budget faves include fresh pasta from **Maison des Pâtes** (☑93 50 95 77; Marché de la Condamine, 15 place d'Armes; pasta €6.40-12; ☺7am-3.30pm) and traditional Niçois *socca* from **Chez Roger** (☑93 50 80 20; Marché de la Condamine, 15 place d'Armes; socca €3; ☺10am-3pm); there's also pizza and seafood from **Le Comptoir**, truffle cuisine from **Truffle Bistrot**, a deli, a cafe, a cheesemonger and more.

Pierre Geronimi
Ice Cream €

(☑97 98 69 11; www.glacespierregeronimi.com; 36 bd d'Italie; 1/2/3 scoops €3.80/6/8; ☺8am-7pm Mon-Sat Oct-Apr, 7.30am-7.30pm Mon-Sat & 10am-6pm Sun May-Sep) A bit of a locals' secret: Monaco's best ice creams and sorbets, made by its eponymous Corsican *maître glacier*. The flavours are exciting – try chestnut flour, beetroot, matcha tea or honey and pine nut – and for the ultimate indulgence, ask for it to be served cocktail-style in a glass *verrine*. He also creates delicious ice-cream cakes and patisseries.

Le Loga
International €€

(☑93 30 87 72; www.loga.mc; 25 bd des Moulins; lunch menus €15-22, dinner menu €38, mains €16-42; ☺8am-11pm Mon, Tue & Thu-Sat, 8am-7pm Wed) On the main drag above the casino, Loga really shines on weekdays, when its wine-inclusive lunch *menus* are

 Shopping Tip

Monaco's streets drip with couture and designer shops; many congregate in Monte Carlo on av des Beaux Arts and av de Monte Carlo. For vaguely more mainstream (read: less expensive) fashion boutiques, try **Le Métropole** (☑93 50 15 36; www.metropoleshopping-montecarlo.com; 17 av des Spélugues; ☺10am-7.30pm Mon-Sat).

Le Métropole
FRIMUFILMS/SHUTTERSTOCK ©

among the best deals in Monaco. Specialities include steaks, meal-sized salads and exquisite homemade gnocchi, along with other Italian fare.

U Cavagnetu
Mediterranean €€

(☑97 98 20 40; www.facebook.com/cavagnetu.monaco; 14 rue Comte Félix Gastaldi; plat du jour €16.50, menu €27.50; ☺11am-10pm) The crush of tourist-oriented restaurants in the narrow streets of Le Rocher may make you want to run screaming, but U Cavagnetu is worth sticking around for. The tasty line-up of authentic Monégasque treats includes *barbajuans* (deep-fried ravioli), *beignets de courgettes* (zucchini fritters) and *poulpe à la monégasque* (octopus stewed with tomatoes, onion, garlic, parsley and wine).

 DRINKING & NIGHTLIFE

Café de Paris
Cafe

(☑98 06 76 23; www.facebook.com/cafedeparis-montecarlo; place du Casino; ☺8am-2am) The *grande dame* of Monaco's cafes (founded in 1882), it's perfect for *un petit café* and

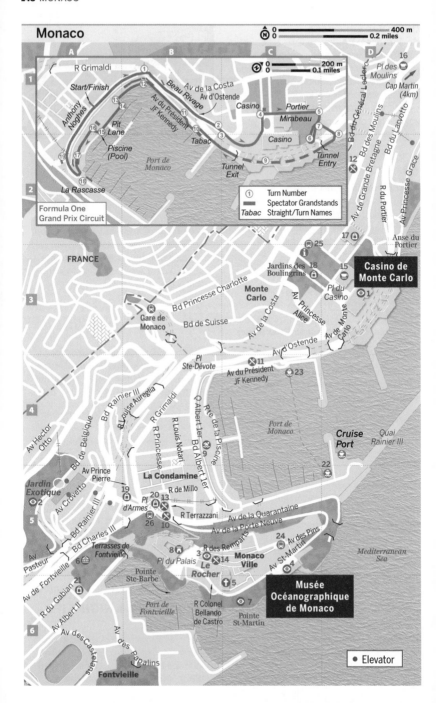

Monaco

0 — 400 m
0 — 0.2 miles

0 — 200 m
0 — 0.1 miles

Formula One Grand Prix Circuit

R Grimaldi
Start/Finish
Anthony Noghes
Beau Rivage
Av de la Costa
Av d'Ostende
Av du Président JF Kennedy
Casino
Portier
Mirabeau
Pit Lane
Piscine (Pool)
Tabac
Casino
Tunnel Entry
Port de Monaco
Tunnel Exit
La Rascasse

① Turn Number
▬ Spectator Grandstands
Tabac Straight/Turn Names

FRANCE

Bd du Général Leclerc
Pl des Moulins
Cap Martin (4km)
Bd des Moulins
Bd du Lanvotto

Bd de Grande Bretagne
Av de Grande Bretagne
R du Portier
Av Princesse Grace

Anse du Portier

25
Jardins des Boulingrins
18
15
Casino de Monte Carlo
Monte Carlo
Bd Princesse Charlotte
Gare de Monaco
Bd de Suisse
Av de la Costa
Av Princesse Alice
Pl du Casino
1
Av de Monte Carlo
Av d'Ostende

Pl Ste-Dévote
Av du Président JF Kennedy
11
23

Bd Rainier III
R Louise Auregia
R Grimaldi
R Princesse
R Louis Notari
Q Albert 1er
Bd Albert 1er
Rte de la Piscine
Port de Monaco
Cruise Port
Quai Rainier III

Av Hector Otto
Bd de Belgique

22

Av Prince Pierre
La Condamine
R de Millo
19
20 13
Pl d'Armes
26
10
R Terrazzani
Av de la Quarantaine
Av de la Porte Neuve
24
Av des Pins

Jardin Exotique
2
Av Crovetto
Bd Rainier III
Bd Charles III
Terrasses de Fontvieille
6
Pl du Palais
8
3
14
R des Remparts
Monaco Ville
Av St-Martin
Mediterranean Sea

Av Pasteur
Av de Fontvieille
Pointe Ste-Barbe
Le Rocher
5
Musée Océanographique de Monaco

21
R du Gabian
Av Albert II
Port de Fontvieille
R Colonel Bellando de Castro
Pointe St-Martin
7

Av des Castelans
Av des Papalins
Fontvieille

● Elevator

Monaco

a spot of people-watching. Everything is chronically overpriced, and the waiters can be horrendously snooty, but it's the price you pay for a front-row view of Monte Carlo's razzamatazz.

Le Teashop Teahouse
(⏧97 77 47 47; www.leteashop.com; place des Moulins; ⏰9am-7pm Mon-Sat) This super-stylish tea bar is all the rage with Monaco's ladies who lunch. There are more than 130 loose-leaf teas to choose from, served classically in a china pot, as a frothy latte or Asian-style with bubbles. The homemade cakes are too good to resist.

 INFORMATION

Tourist Office (⏧92 16 61 16; www.visitmonaco.com; 2a bd des Moulins; ⏰9am-7pm Mon-Sat, 11am-1pm Sun) Get maps and info – along with your semi-official Monaco passport stamp – at this helpful office just above the casino. From mid-June through mid-September, it also runs a tourist information kiosk down by the Port de la Condamine.

🛈 **GETTING AROUND**

Boat The solar-powered **Bateau Bus** (http://monaco-navigation.com/bateau-bus-tarif-monaco.html; quai des États-Unis) sails back and forth across the harbour between **Monaco Ville** (quai Antoine 1er) and **Monte Carlo** (quai des États-Unis). Boats make the four-minute crossing every 20 minutes from 8am to 7.50pm; buy tickets on board (€2) or from machines at the docks (€1.50).

Bus Monaco's urban bus system (www.cam.mc) has six lines. Tickets cost €1.50 if purchased from machines at bus stops, €2 on board (day ticket €5.50). Lines 1, 2, 4 and 6 are especially useful for visitors, along with the Bus de Nuit. Key stops are at **place d'Armes**, **Monaco Ville** and **Monte-Carlo Tourisme**.

After 9.20pm the Bus de Nuit (9.30pm to 12.30am) follows one big loop around town; service is extended to 4am on Friday and Saturday.

Taxi Call **Taxis Monaco** (⏧93 15 01 01; www.taximonaco.com; ⏰24h).

GENOA,
ITALY

Genoa at a Glance...

Italy's largest sea port is indefatigably contradictory, full at once of grandeur, squalor, sparkling light and deep shade. But a weighty architectural heritage speaks of its former glory – the Most Serene Republic of Genoa ruled over the Mediterranean waves during the 12th and 13th centuries – and history feels alive here. Nowhere is this more true than in its extensive Old City, an often confronting reminder of pre-modern life with its twisting maze of narrow caruggi (streets), largely intact. Emerge blinking from this thrillingly dank heart to Via Garibaldi and the splendid Enlightenment-era gold-leaf halls of the Unesco-listed Palazzi dei Rolli.

With One Day in Port

• Genoa's port is right near the heart of the city. Begin by wandering past the **Galata Museo del Mare** (p158) to the **Palazzo Reale** (p158), the finest of the Palazzi dei Rolli.

• Then head south and into the Old City; spend some time wandering the *caruggi* and check out its churches and art galleries, as well as its bars, shops and cafes.

• Grab a quick meal at **La Botega Del Gusto** (p159), then head back via the Porto Antico.

Best Places For...

Focaccia Pane e Tulipani (p159)
Wine Enoteca Pesce (p161)
Gelati Gelateria Profumo (p159)
Fashion Galleria Mazzini (p159)
Plazas Piazza de Ferrari (p156)

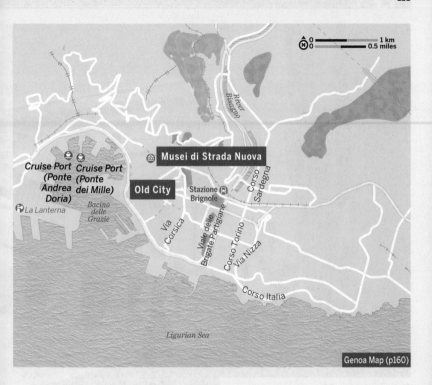

Genoa Map (p160)

Getting from the Port

Most cruise ships use the 1930s **Ponte dei Mille** terminal – an attraction in itself – although some use the **Ponte Andrea Doria** nearby.

Many of Genoa's major sights are within a 15-minute walk of the port, although the steep cobbled streets away from the seafront could slow you down if you venture that way. You can be within the walls of the Old City within 15 minutes by foot. Genoa also has an extensive bus system and a small metro system, both of which connect the port to the Old City.

Fast Facts

Currency Euro (€)

Language Italian

Money ATMs can be found throughout the city.

Tourist Information There is a helpful office in the historic centre.

Visas Generally not required for stays of up to 90 days (or at all for EU nationals); some nationalities need a Schengen visa.

Wi-fi There are public wi-fi hotspots, but to use them you must register online using a credit card or an Italian mobile number. An easier option is to head to a cafe or bar offering free wi-fi.

Palazzo Doria-Tursi on Via Garibaldi

Musei di Strada Nuova

The Musei di Strada Nuova is comprised of three palazzi – Rosso, Bianco and Doria-Tursi. Between them, they hold the city's finest collection of old masters.

Via Garibaldi

Skirting the northern edge of the Old City limits, pedestrianised Via Garibaldi (formerly Strada Nuova) was planned by Galeazzo Alessi in the 16th century. It quickly became the most sought-after quarter, lined with the palaces of Genoa's wealthiest citizens. Whether you visit the actual museums or not, the street is a must to wander. Buy tickets to the Musei di Strada Nuova at the bookshop inside Palazzo Doria-Tursi.

Palazzo Rosso

Lavishly frescoed rooms in **Palazzo Rosso** (Via Garibaldi 18) provide the backdrop for several portraits by Van Dyck of the local Brignole-Sale family.

Great For...

☑ **Don't Miss**

The Franco Albini Apartment on the third floor of Palazzo Rosso.

Palazzo Rosso

Explore Ashore

You can walk to the Musei di Strada Nuova from the port in about 20 minutes, or catch one of several buses (five minutes). Allow at least a couple of hours to explore all three *palazzi*.

❶ Need to Know

Palazzi dei Rolli; ☎010 557 21 93; www.museidigenova.it; Via Garibaldi; combined ticket adult/reduced €9/7; ⏱9am-7pm Tue-Fri, 10am-7.30pm Sat & Sun summer, to 6.30pm winter

Other standouts include Guido Reni's *San Sebastiano* and Guercino's *La morte di Cleopatra* (The Death of Cleopatra), as well as works by Veronese, Dürer and Bernardo Strozzi.

Palazzo Bianco

Flemish, Spanish and Italian artists feature at **Palazzo Bianco** (Via Garibaldi 11), the second of this triumvirate of palazzi. Rubens' *Venere e Marte* (Venus and Mars) and Van Dyck's *Vertumna e Pomona* are among the highlights, which also include works by Hans Memling, Filippino Lippi and Murillo, as well as 15th-century religious icons. Beyond the art itself, architect Franco Albini's mid-century refit is particularly lovely here.

Palazzo Doria-Tursi

This **palace** (Via Garibaldi 9) features a small but absorbing collection of legendary violinist Niccolò Paganini's personal effects. In the Sala Paganiniana, pride of place goes to his Canone violin, made in Cremona in 1743. One lucky musician gets to play the maestro's violin during October's Paganiniana festival. Other artefacts on show include letters, musical scores and his travelling chess set. The palace has also housed Genoa's town hall since 1848.

Piazza de Ferrari

BORYANA MANZUROVA/SHUTTERSTOCK ©

Old City

The heart of medieval Genoa is famed for its caruggi (narrow lanes). Looking up at the washing pegged on lines everywhere, it becomes obvious that these dark, cave-like laneways and blind alleys are still largely residential, although the number of fashionable bars, shops and cafes continues to grow.

Great For...

☑ **Don't Miss**

Primo Piano, a beautiful historical gallery that runs a program of modern and contemporary shows.

The Old City is bounded by ancient city gates **Porta dei Vacca** (Via del Campo) and **Porta Soprana** (Via di Porta Soprana), and the streets of Via Cairoli, Via Garibaldi and Via XXV Aprile.

Piazza de Ferrari

Genoa's fountain-embellished main **piazza** is ringed by magnificent buildings that include the art-nouveau **Palazzo della Borsa** (Piazza de Ferrari), which was once the country's stock exchange, and the hybrid neoclassical-modernist **Teatro Carlo Felice** (☎010 538 12 24; www.carlofelice.it; Passo Eugenio Montale 4), bombed in WWII and not fully rebuilt until 1991.

Once the seat of the independent republic, the grand **Palazzo Ducale** (www.palazzoducale.genova.it; Piazza Giacomo Matteotti 9; price varies by exhibition; ⊘hours vary) was

Porta Soprana

OLENA Z/SHUTTERSTOCK ©

⚓

Explore Ashore

You could easily spend three or four hours wandering the *caruggi* if you choose. It takes about half an hour to walk from the port to Piazza de Ferrari in the heart of the Old City, or five minutes on the metro from Principe station (opposite the port) to Piazza de Ferrari.

❶ Need to Know

Parts of the caruggi can feel somewhat unnerving, especially after dark. Although it's not particularly dangerous, do take care in the zone west of Via San Luca and south to Piazza Banchi, where most street prostitution and accompanying vice concentrates.

built in the Mannerist style in the 1590s and was largely refurbished after a fire in the 1770s. Today it hosts high-profile temporary art exhibitions, several smaller galleries and occasional markets in its lofty atrium. The palazzo also has a bookshop and cafe.

Churches

Genoa's zebra-striped Gothic-Romanesque **Cattedrale di San Lorenzo** (Piazza San Lorenzo; ⊘8am-noon & 3-7pm) owes its continued existence to the poor quality of a British WWII bomb that failed to ignite here in 1941; it still sits on the right side of the nave like an innocuous museum piece. The cathedral, fronted by three arched portals, twisting columns and crouching lions, was first consecrated in 1118. The two bell towers and cupolas were added in the 16th century.

Half-hidden behind the cathedral, but emulating it in its ecclesial brilliance, is the **Chiesa del Gesù** (Piazza Giacomo Matteotti; ⊘4.30-7pm), a former Jesuit church dating from 1597 that has an intricate and lavish interior. The wonderfully frescoed walls and ceiling are anchored by two works by the great Dutch artist Rubens – *Circoncisione* (Circumcision) hangs over the main altar, and *Miracoli di Sant'Ignazio* is displayed in a side chapel.

🍽 Pesto Genovese

It would be criminal to come to Genoa and not try pesto genovese. The city's famous pasta sauce – a pounded mix of basil, pine nuts, olive oil and sometimes garlic – really does taste, and look, better here than anywhere else, a result of the basil that's used (the leaves of very young plants are plucked daily from hothouses on city hillsides), as well as techniques honed through generations.

SUSAN WRIGHT/LONELY PLANET ©

◉ SIGHTS

Palazzo Reale   Palace

(☑010 271 02 36; www.palazzorealegenova.be-niculturali.it; Via Balbi 10; adult/reduced €6/2; ⊙9am-2pm Tue-Fri, to 7pm Wed & Thu, 1.30-7pm Sat & Sun) If you only get the chance to visit one of the Palazzi dei Rolli (group of palaces belonging to the city's most eminent families), make it this one. A former residence of the Savoy dynasty, it has terraced gardens, exquisite furnishings, a fine collection of 17th-century art and a gilded Hall of Mirrors that is worth the entry fee alone.

Santa Maria di Castello   Abbey

(☑ 347 9956740; www.santamariadicastello.it; Salita di Santa Maria di Castello 15; ⊙10-1pm & 3-6pm) Built on the site of the original settlement, and sheltering under the 11th-century Embriaci Tower, this Romanesque church and convent, itself built before AD 900, is an extraordinary and little-visited historic site. Its walls are covered with treasures that were commissioned by the noble families of Genoa from the earliest use of the church,

though some of the notable frescoes also date to the 16th and 17th century. Private tours, by coin donation, are possible.

La Lanterna   Lighthouse

(☑010 407 65 83; www.lanternadigenova.it; Via alla Lanterna; admission €6; ⊙2.30-6.30pm Sat & Sun) The port may have changed radically since its '90s rebirth, but its emblematic sentinel hasn't moved an inch since 1543. Genoa's lighthouse is one of the world's oldest and tallest – and it still works, beaming its light over 50km to warn ships and tankers. Visitors can climb its first 172 steps and ponder exhibits in an adjacent museum of lamps, lenses and related history.

Casa della Famiglia Colombo   Museum

(www.coopculture.it; Piazza Dante; adult/reduced €5/3; ⊙9am-1pm & 2-5pm Mon-Fri, 9am-1pm Sat) Not the only house claiming to be the birthplace of the navigator Christopher Columbus (Calvi in Corsica is another contender), this one probably has the most merit, as various documents inside testify. Curiously, it stands just outside the Old City walls, in the shadow of the Porta Soprana gate (built in 1155).

Galleria Nazionale   Gallery

(www.palazzospinola.beniculturali.it; Piazza Superiore di Pellicceria 1; adult/reduced €6/3; ⊙8.30am-7.30pm Tue-Sat) This gallery's paintings are wonderfully displayed over four floors of the 16th-century **Palazzo Spinola**, once owned by the Spinola family, one of Genoa's most formidable dynasties. The main focus is Italian and Flemish Renaissance art of the so-called Ligurian School (look out for Van Dyck, Rubens and Strozzi), but it's also worth visiting to gape at the decorative architecture.

Galata Museo del Mare   Museum

(www.galatamuseodelmare.it; Calata de Mari 1; adult/reduced/child €13/11/8; ⊙10am-7.30pm, closed Mon Nov-Feb) Genoa was rivalled only by Barcelona and Venice as a medieval and Renaissance maritime power, so its 'museum of the sea' is, unsurprisingly, one of its most relevant and interesting. High-tech exhibits trace the history of seafaring, from

Genoa's reign as Europe's greatest dockyard to the ages of sail and steam.

🔒 SHOPPING

Heading southwest, elegant Via Roma, adjacent to the glass-covered **Galleria Mazzini**, is Genoa's designer shopping street. It links Piazza Corvetto with Piazza de Ferrari. The Old City's lanes are full of all kinds of traditional shops as well as many new independent fashion, vintage and homewares boutiques.

Via Garibaldi 12　　　　Homewares

(📞010 253 03 65; www.viagaribaldi12.com; Via Garibaldi 12; ⏰10am-2pm & 3.30-7pm Tue-Sat) Even if you're not in the market for designer homewares, it's worth trotting up the noble stairs just to be reminded how splendid a city Genoa can be. There's an incredibly canny collection of contemporary furniture and objects, as well as 'interventions' by contemporary artists such as Damian Hirst and Sterling Ruby, with works occasionally loaned from New York's Gagosian gallery.

Mimì e Cocò　　　Children's Clothing

(📞010 403 32 97; www.mimi-coco.it; Piazza del Ferro 21; ⏰4-7.30pm Mon, 11.30am-7.30pm Tue-Sat) A wonderful find in a country increasingly dominated by big-budget labels, everything here is handmade in Genoa. Smocks, shirts, shorts, cardigans and playsuits for babies to five-year-olds are crafted from natural fibres, and their simple, traditional cuts also have a very contemporary appeal.

✖ EATING

La Botega Del Gusto　　　Ligurian €

(Vico Superiore del Ferro 3; dishes €4-8.50; ⏰11.30am-5pm Mon-Thu, to 10pm Fri & Sat) Genovese fast food done in the most authentic – and moreish – of ways can be had at this backstreet hole in the wall. Come for a quick and easy plate of *pansotti* (pasta filled with wild greens), pesto pasta, quiche-like spinach-and-artichoke *torta*, baked rabbit or steamed salt cod.

🍽 Sweet Treats

For gelato, **Gelateria San Luca** (Via San Luca 88; cones from €2; ⏰11.30am-7.30pm) has a selection of beautiful traditional gelato flavours complemented by a creative menu of semifreddo-filled cups, ice-cream sandwiches and chocolate-coated popsicles. If it's chocolate you're after, try **Pietro Romanengo fu Stefano** (www.romanengo.com; Via Soziglia 74r; ⏰9am-7.15pm Mon-Sat), a historic shop (established 1780) that specialises in candied flowers and floral waters.

And if you can't choose? Head to the twin establishments of **Gelateria Profumo** (www.villa1827.it; Via del Portello 2; cones from €2.20; ⏰noon-7.30pm Tue-Sat) – where the *panera* (a Genovese blend of coffee and cream), creamy Sorento lemon and bitter orange flavours are standouts – and **Pasticceria Profumo** (www.villa1827.it; Via del Portello 2; ⏰9am-1pm & 3.30-7.30pm Tue-Sat).

Pietro Romanengo fu Stefano
ANGEL VILLALBA/GETTY IMAGES ©

Pane e Tulipani　　　Bakery €

(📞010 817 88 41; Via dei Macelli di Soziglia 75; pizza €6.50; ⏰6am-7.30pm Mon-Sat) Hectic times rule at this poetically named bakery: everyone wants what they're selling. Drop by any time for one of their several varieties of focaccia or make a Saturday date when there are two drops (10.30am and 3.30pm) of half-price pizza margherita, a steal at €6.50. Their kamut loaves and breads from other ancient grains are also worth trying.

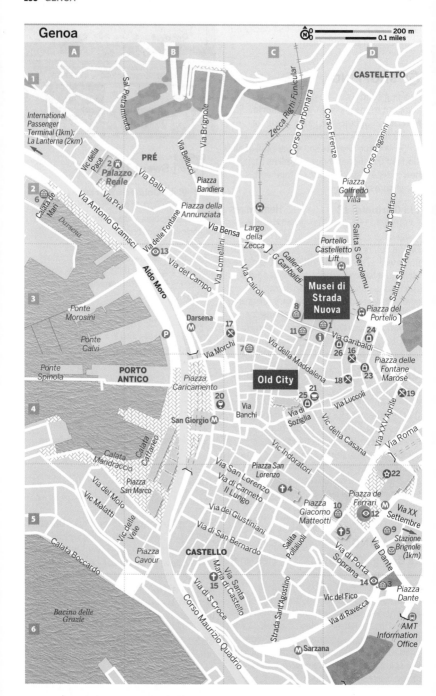

Genoa

CASTELETTO

International
Passenger
Terminal (1km);
La Lanterna (2km)

PRÉ

2 Palazzo
Reale

Piazza
Bandiera

Piazza della
Annunziata

Largo
della
Zecca

Piazza
Golfredo
Villa

Portello
Castelletto
Lift

Galleria
G Garibaldi

Via delle Fontane

Via Bensa

Via Lomellini

Via del Campo

Via Cairoli

Via della Maddalena

Musei di
Strada
Nuova

Piazza del
Portello

Ponte
Morosini

Ponte
Calvi

Darsena

Ponte
Spinola

PORTO
ANTICO

Piazza
Caricamento

Via
Banchi

San Giorgio

Old City

Piazza delle
Fontane
Marose

Via Luccoli

Via di
Soziglia

Vic della Casana

Via XXV Aprile

Via Roma

Calata
Mandraccio

Calata
Cattaneo

Vic Indoratori

Via San
Lorenzo

Via di Canneto
Il Lungo

Piazza San
Lorenzo

Piazza
Giacomo
Matteotti

Piazza de
Ferrari

Via XX
Settembre

Stazione
Brignole
(1km)

Via del Molo

Vic Malatti

Vic delle
Vele

Piazza
San Marco

Via dei Giustiniani

Via di San Bernardo

Salita
Pollaiuoli

Via Dante

Calata Boccardo

Piazza
Cavour

CASTELLO

Santa
Maria
di Castello

15

Via di S Croce

Strada Sant'Agostino

Via di Porta
Soprana

Vic del Fico

Via di Ravecca

Piazza
Dante

AMT
Information
Office

Bacino delle
Grazie

Corso Maurizio Quadrio

Sarzana

Genoa

Trattoria Da Maria   Trattoria €

(☏010 58 10 80; Vico Testadoro 14r; meals €10-18; ☺11.45am-3pm Mon-Sat, 7-9.30pm Thu & Fri) Brace yourself for lunchtime mayhem. This is a totally authentic, if well touristed, workers' trattoria and there's much squeezing into tiny tables, shouted orders and a fast and furious succession of plates plonked on tables. A daily hand-scrawled menu is a roll call of elemental favourites that keep all comers full and happy, along with the jugs of ridiculously cheap wine.

DRINKING & NIGHTLIFE

Enoteca Pesce   Wine Bar

(Via Sottoripa; ☺8.30am-7.30pm Mon-Sat) Tiny wine bars dot Genoa's Old City, although this one, under the arches by the port, is particularly characteristic and full of colourful locals. They are serious about their wine, though glasses hover around the €2 mark so it's a good place to get to know Liguria's unusual grapes.

Fratelli Klainguti   Cafe

(Via di Soziglia; ☺7.30am-7.30pm) Pre-dating cappuccinos, Klainguti opened in 1828 and its Mittel European charms, and presumably its strudel and pastries, had Verdi and

Garibaldi coming back for more. Waiters in bow ties toil under an impressive chandelier and the decor is a fabulous, if tatty, mid-century historical pastiche.

ℹ INFORMATION

Ospedale San Martino (☏010 55 51; Largo Rosanna Benci 10) Hospital.

Police Station (☏010 5 36 61; Via Armando Diaz 2)

Main Post Office (Via Dante 4; ☺ 8.30am-7pm Mon-Fri, to 12.30pm Sat)

Tourist Office (☏010 557 29 03; www.visit-genoa.it; Via Garibaldi 12r; ☺9am-6.20pm) Runs walking tours (€14).

GETTING AROUND

Bus AMT (www.amt.genova.it) operates buses throughout the city and there is an **AMT information office** (Via d'Annunzio 8; ☺7.15am-6pm Mon-Fri, 7am-7pm Sat & Sun) at the bus terminal. Bus line 383 links Stazione Brignole with Piazza de Ferrari and Stazione Principe. A ticket valid for 90 minutes costs €1.50.

Train & Metro Bus tickets can be used on mainline trains within the city limits, as well as on the metro (www.genovametro.com).

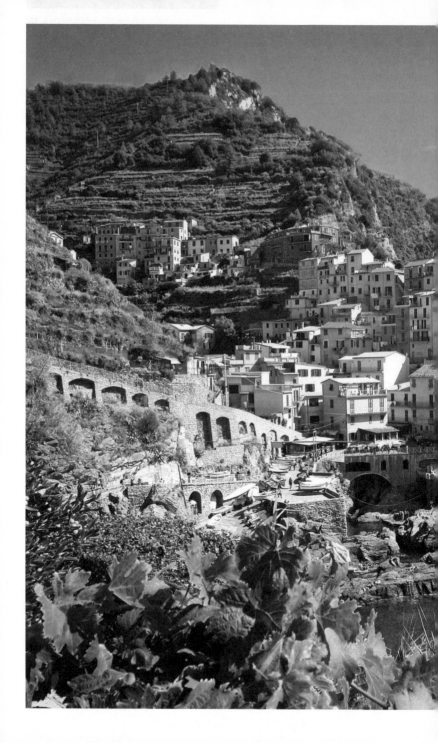

CINQUE TERRE & LA SPEZIA, ITALY

Cinque Terre & La Spezia at a Glance...

Set amid some of the most dramatic coastal scenery on the planet, these five ingeniously constructed fishing villages can bolster the most jaded of spirits. A Unesco World Heritage Site since 1997, Cinque Terre isn't the undiscovered Eden it once was but it still retains its magic. Rooted in antiquity, Cinque Terre's villages date from the early medieval period. Sinuous paths traverse seemingly impregnable cliffsides, while a 19th-century railway line cuts through a series of coastal tunnels ferrying the footsore from village to village.

With One Day in Port

- Packing a lot into a day is made easy with frequent train services. Head first to Manarola and snap a classic photo from the **Punta Bonfiglio** (p170).

- Hop on the train or ferry to Vernazza, and explore **Castello Doria** (p171), then have a classic seafood lunch at **Gianni Franzi** (p172). You can continue to **Corniglia** (p171) or **Monterosso** (p171) from here, and then return by train to La Spezia.

- Alternatively, spend your day exploring just a couple of places, or take the time for a **sanctuary walk** (p166).

Best Places For...

Panoramic Views Belvedere di Santa Maria (p171)

Hiking Manarola to Santuario della Madonna delle Salute (p167)

Romantic Adventures Grotta di Byron (p168)

Gelato Cinque Terre Gelateria Creperia (p172)

Previous page: Manarola village (p170)
©JOE8211943/BUDGET TRAVEL

Getting from the Port

Cruise ships dock at Molo Giuseppe
Garibaldi in **La Spezia**. To get to the
train station it's a 2.4km (not picturesque) walk, so getting a taxi is
recommended.

Around 40 trains per day shuttle between La Spezia and the Cinque Terre's
five villages; seven minutes to Riomaggiore, and a couple of minutes between
the other towns. The Cinque Terre Treno
Card (one/two days €16/29) gives you
unlimited train travel within the region.

Visitors will first encounter the town
of La Spezia, then the Cinque Terre
villages in the following order: Riomaggiore, Manarola, Corniglia, Vernazza and
Monterosso.

Fast Facts

Currency Euro (€)

Language Italian

Money Many places accept credit and
debit cards. ATMs can be found at some
railway stations or main

Tourist Information Cinque Terre The
Tourist Information Office (p173) and
Cinque Terre Park Office (p173) can be
found in the train station.

Visas Generally not required for stays of
up to 90 days (or at all for EU nationals);
some nationalities need a Schengen visa.

Wi-fi Wi-fi is scarce. The Cinque Terre
card offers free wi-fi at hotspots.

View from the Santuario della Madonna di Soviore trail

POOGIE/SHUTTERSTOCK ©

Walking in the Cinque Terre

With its spectacular scenery, terraced slopes and network of ancient trails, the Cinque Terre offers superlative walking. Routes cater to all levels, ranging from simple 20-minute strolls to daunting hillside hikes.

Great For...

ℹ Need to Know

A Cinque Terre trekking card is needed to access walking trails in the region.

Sanctuary Walks

Each of the Cinque Terre's villages is associated with a sanctuary perched high on the cliffsides above the azure Mediterranean. Reaching these religious retreats used to be part of a Catholic penance, but are far more enjoyable these days.

Monterosso to Santuario della Madonna di Soviore

From Via Roma, follow trail 9 up through forest and past the ruins of an old hexagonal chapel to an ancient paved mule-path that leads to Soviore, Liguria's oldest sanctuary. Here you'll find a bar, a restaurant and, on a clear day, views as far as Corsica.

Vernazza to Santuario della Madonna di Reggio

From underneath Vernazza's railway bridge, follow trail 8 up numerous flights of steps

Explore Ashore

From La Spezia train station, trains run between the five Cinque Terre villages (7-21 minutes). Devote at least an hour to wandering each village – more if you're aiming to complete a sanctuary walk, or spend some time lazing on beaches.

★ Top Tip

Check www.parconazionale5terre.it for trail details, news, online maps and to purchase your Cinque Terre Hiking Card.

and past 14 sculpted Stations of the Cross to this 11th-century chapel with a Romanesque facade.

Corniglia to Santuario della Madonna delle Grazie

This sanctuary can be approached from either Corniglia (on trail 7b) or Vernazza (trail 7), though the latter is better. Branch off the Sentiero Azzurro and ascend the spectacular Sella Comeneco to the village of San Bernardino, where you'll find the church with its adored image of Madonna and child above the altar.

Manarola to Santuario della Madonna delle Salute

The pick of all the sanctuary walks is this breathtaking traverse (trail 6) through Cinque Terre's finest vineyards to a diminutive Romanesque-meets-Gothic chapel in the tiny village of Volastra.

Riomaggiore to Santuario della Madonna di Montenero

Trail 3 ascends from the top of the village, up steps and past walled gardens to a restored 18th-century chapel that sits atop an astounding lookout next to the park's new cycling centre.

Sentiero Azzurro

Marked No 2 on maps, the **Sentiero Azzurro** (Blue Trail; admission with Cinque Terre trekking card), a narrow and precipitous 12km-long old mule-path which once linked all five villages by foot, is now the Cinque Terre's blue-ribbon hike. The trail dates to the early days of the Republic of Genoa in the 12th and 13th centuries and, until the opening of the railway line in 1874, it was the only practical means of getting from village to village.

At the time of writing, the path between Riomaggiore (the famed via dell'Amore) and Manarola, and the one between Manarola and Corniglia were both closed due to landslide damage.

PHOTOGRAPHY BY DEB SNELSON/GETTY IMAGES ©

Porto Venere

Perched on the dreamy Golfo dei Poeti's western promontory, the historic fishing port's sinuous seven- and eight-storey harbourfront houses form an almost impregnable citadel around the muscular Castello Doria.

Great For...

☑ Don't Miss

The view of the cliff faces from the ferry as it rounds the cape from La Spezia.

Romans to Romantics

The Romans built Portus Veneris as a base en route from Gaul to Spain. In later years the Byzantines, Lombards, Genovese and Napoleonic army all passed through here and made the most of its spectacular natural defences. Its appeal is, however, not just strategic: its beauty captivated poet Byron, who famously swam from the now-collapsed Grotta Arpaia's rocky cove to San Terenzo to visit fellow poet Percy Shelley.

Grotta di Byron

At the end of the quay, a Cinque Terre panorama unfolds from the rocky terraces of **Grotta di Byron**, formerly known as Grotta Arpaia, but renamed after the poet's epic swim. Despite the cave's collapse, the rocky

Chiesa di San Pietro

BENNYMARTY/GETTY IMAGES ©

Explore Ashore

Daily buses run from La Spezia's Piazza Domenico Chiodo to Portovenere (35 minutes); a taxi (€35) takes about 25 minutes. From late March to October, **Consorzio Maritimo Turistico Cinque Terre Golfo dei Poeti** (☎ 0187 73 29 87; www.navigazionegolfodeipoeti.it) sails between Porto Venere and the Cinque Terre villages.

ⓘ Need to Know

The **tourist office** (www.prolocoporto venere.it; Piazza Bastreri 7; ☺10am-noon & 3-8pm Jun-Aug, to 6pm Thu-Tue Sep-May) sells maps and walking guides in English.

terraces remain stunningly beautiful and suitably dishevelled and affecting.

To add to the frisson, know that traces of a pagan temple dedicated to Venus (hence a suggestion to the name 'Venere') have been uncovered here, as well as inside the black-and-white-marble **Chiesa di San Pietro**. Just off the promontory, you can see the tiny islands of Palmaria, Tino and Tinetto.

Chiesa di San Pietro

This stunning wind- and wave-lashed church, built in 1198 in Gothic style, stands on the ruins of a 5th-century pal-aeo-Christian church, with its extant floor still partially visible. Before its Christiani-sation, it was a Roman temple dedicated to the goddess Venus, born from the foam of the sea, from whom Porto Venere takes its name.

Castello Doria

No one knows when the original castle was built, though the current structure – a formidable example of Genoese military architecture – dates from the 16th century. A highly strategic citadel in its time, it once stood on the front line in Genoa's maritime feud with Pisa. There are magnificent views from its ornate terraced gardens.

Taking a Break

A half-dozen or so restaurants line Calata Doria, by the sea. Inland, Porto Venere's main Old Town street, Via Cappellini, has several tasty choices. **Anciua** (☎331 7719605; Via Cappellini 40; snacks from €6; ☺10am-7pm) is the perfect spot to pick up the makings of a picnic.

ALIAKSANDR ANTANOVICH/SHUTTERSTOCK ©

Castello Doria at the top of Vernazza village

⊙ SIGHTS

⊙ La Spezia

Port town La Spezia is worthy of at least a wander if you have spare time – the winding streets of the Old Town are hugely atmospheric.

Museo Amedeo Lia   Museum

(http://museolia.spezianet.it; Via Prione 234; adult/reduced €7/4.50, with temporary exhibition €10/7; ⊙10am-6pm Tue-Sun) This fine-arts museum in a restored 17th-century friary is La Spezia's star cultural attraction. The collection spans from the 13th to 18th centuries and includes paintings by masters such as Tintoretto, Montagna, Titian and Pietro Lorenzetti. Also on show are Roman bronzes and ecclesiastical treasures, such as Limoges crucifixes and illuminated musical manuscripts.

⊙ Riomaggiore

Cinque Terre's easternmost village, Riomaggiore is the largest of the five and acts as its unofficial HQ. Its peeling pastel buildings march down a steep ravine to a tiny harbour and glow romantically at sunset.

Fossola Beach   Beach

This small pebbly beach is immediately southeast of Riomaggiore marina. It's rugged and delightfully secluded. Swimmers should be wary of currents here.

⊙ Manarola

Bequeathed with more grapevines than any other Cinque Terre village, Manarola is famous for its sweet Sciacchetrà wine. It's also awash with priceless medieval relics, supporting claims that it is the oldest of the five.

Punta Bonfiglio   Viewpoint

Manarola's prized viewpoint is on a rocky promontory on the path out of town towards Corniglia where walkers stop for classic photos of the village. A rest area, including a kids' playground, has been constructed here and there's also a bar just below. Nearby are the ruins of an old chapel once used as a shelter by local farmers.

Piazzale Papa Innocenzo IV   Piazza

At the northern end of Via Discovolo, you'll come upon this small piazza dominated by a bell tower that was once used as a defensive lookout. Opposite, the **Chiesa di San Lorenzo** dates from 1338 and houses a 15th-century polyptych. If you're geared up for a steep walk, from nearby Via Rollandi you can follow a path that leads through vineyards to the top of the mountain.

◎ Corniglia

Corniglia is the 'quiet' middle village that sits atop a 100m-high rocky promontory surrounded by vineyards. It is the only Cinque Terre settlement with no direct sea access, although steep steps lead down to a rocky cove. Narrow alleys and colourfully painted four-storey houses characterise the ancient core.

Belvedere di Santa Maria   Viewpoint

Enjoy dazzling 180-degree sea views at this heart-stopping lookout in hilltop Corniglia. To find it, follow Via Fieschi through the village until you eventually reach the clifftop balcony.

La Torre   Viewpoint

This atmospheric medieval lookout is reached by a stairway that leads up from the diminutive main square, Piazza Taragio.

◎ Vernazza

Vernazza's small harbour – the only secure landing point on the Cinque Terre coast – guards what is perhaps the quaintest, and steepest, of the five villages.

Castello Doria   Castle

(€1.50; ⏲10am-7pm summer, to 6pm winter) This castle, the oldest surviving fortification in the Cinque Terre, commands superb views. Dating to around 1000, it's now largely a ruin except for the circular tower in the centre of the esplanade. To get there, head up the steep, narrow staircase by the harbour.

⌐⊐ Escape the Crowds

Consider visiting the villages out of order: the majority of visitors do each stop in order along the train line, so changing up your itinerary could help escape some of the crowds at peak times.

The 6th Village: Don't miss a chance to explore Porto Venere, which absorbs crowds better than it's smaller companions. It's also accessible by ferry, for a change of perspective.

Take the bus: If you don't fancy the crush of the train in high season, the Explora 5 Terre bus service (http://www.explora5terre.it/; day pass €18.50) offers an aircondioned alternative, and can also provide audioguides to accompany the trip.

Porto Venere harbour

◎ Monterosso

The most accessible village by car and the only Cinque Terre settlement to sport a proper stretch of beach, the westernmost Monterosso is the least quintessential of the quintet.

Convento dei Cappuccini   Church

(Salita San Cristoforo) Monterosso's most interesting church and convent complex is set on the hill that divides the Old Town from the newer Fegina quarter. The striped church, the **Chiesa di San Francesco**, dates from 1623 and has a painting attributed to Van Dyck (*Crocifissione*) to the left of the altar. The convent welcomes casual visitors but also has a program of spiritual retreats and workshops.

 Via dell'Amore

This beautiful coastal path that links Riomaggiore to Manarola in a leisurely 20-minute stroll was Cinque Terre's most popular until rockslides caused its closure in 2012. The first 200m of the path, from Manarola's train station to Bar Via dell'Amore, has reopened and is worth the brief stroll it allows. It's uncertain when the rest will be completed (predictions are for around 2021), but if it is open when you visit, definitely take the time to walk its beautiful length.

MARTINA BADINI/SHUTTERSTOCK ©

 EATING

 La Spezia

Vicolo Intherno Modern Italian €€

(☑0187 150 9698; www.vicolointherno.it; Via della Canonica 20; meals €28-36; ☺noon-3pm & 7pm-midnight Tue-Sat) 🍴 Take a seat around chunky wooden tables beneath beamed ceilings at this buzzing Slow Food–affiliated restaurant and wash down the *torte di verdure* (Ligurian vegetable pie), stockfish or roast beef with local vintages.

Riomaggiore

Dau Cila Seafood €€

(☑0187 76 00 32; www.ristorantedaucila.com; Via San Giacomo 65; meals €40-45; ☺12.30-3pm & 7-10.30pm) Perched within pebble-lobbing distance of Riomaggiore's harbour, Dau Cila is a smart, kitsch-free zone, and specialises in classic seafood and hyper-local wines.

Pair the best Cinque Terre whites with cold plates such as smoked tuna with apples and lemon, or lemon-marinated anchovies.

 Manarola

Cinque Terre Gelateria Creperia Gelato €

(Via Discovolo, Manarola; ☺11am-8pm) In the running for the title of Cinque Terre's best ice-cream joint.

Il Porticciolo Seafood €€

(☑0187 92 00 83; www.ilporticciolo5terre.it; Via Renato Birolli 92; meals €28-37; ☺11.30am-11pm) One of several restaurants lining the main route down to the harbour, this is a popular spot for an alfresco seafood feast. Expect seaside bustle and a fishy menu featuring classic crowd-pleasers such as spaghetti with mussels and crispy fried squid.

 Vernazza

Gianni Franzi Seafood €€

(☑0187 82 10 03; www.giannifranzi.it; Piazza Matteotti 5; meals €22-35; ☺mid-Mar–early Jan) Traditional Cinque Terre seafood (mussels, seafood, ravioli and lemon anchovies) has been served up in this harbourside trattoria since the 1960s. When it comes to seafood this fresh, if it's not broken, don't fix it.

Gambero Rosso Seafood €€

(☑0187 81 22 65; www.ristorantegambero-rosso.net; Piazza Marconi 7; meals €35-45; ☺noon-3pm & 7-10pm Fri-Wed) If you've been subsisting on focaccia, Gambero's house specials – *tegame di Vernazza* (anchovies with baked potatoes and tomatoes), skewered baby octopus or stuffed mussels – will really hit the spot. Bookings recommended.

 Monterosso

Ristorante Belvedere Seafood €€

(☑0187 81 70 33; www.ristorante-belvedere.it; Piazza Garibaldi 38; meals €30; ☺noon-2.30pm & 6.30-10pm Wed-Mon) With tables overlooking the beach, this unpretentious seafood restaurant is a good place to try the local bounty. Start with *penne con scampi* (pasta tubes with scampi) before diving into *zuppa di pesce* (fish soup). Or partake of the speciality, the amphora Belvedere, where lobsters, mussels, clams, octopus and swordfish are stewed in a herb-scented broth in traditional earthenware.

DRINKING & NIGHTLIFE
La Spezia
Odioilvino   Wine Bar
(392 2141825; www.facebook.com/Odioil vino; Via Daniele Manin 11; ⊙12.30-3.30pm & 6-11.30pm) A dark, bohemian, elegantly di-shevelled wine bar on a pretty street in the pedestrian centre, Odioilvino is a fine place to relax with locals over a French or local wine. Small plates such as a fish tartare or octopus salad are on offer, too.

Riomaggiore
La Conchiglia   Bar
(0187 92 09 47; Via San Giacomo 149; ⊙8am-midnight) A fantastic find: down-to-earth, friendly and unflustered staff; a fantastic well-priced local wine list; waterfront positions and a menu of big, healthy salads, *panini* and burgers if you've missed lunch or dinner service elsewhere. The shaded waterfront terrace upstairs is a delight.

Corniglia
La Scuna   Bar
(347 7997527; Via Fieschi 185; ⊙9am-1am late-March–Nov) Vinyl, beer *and* a panoramic terrace? This bastion of hipsterdom comes as a surprise in this most traditional of regions but the welcome is warm and the beers on tap are both cold and a cut way above bottled Peroni.

Vernazza
Burgus Bar   Wine Bar
(Piazza Marconi 4; ⊙7am-1am) A charming little hole-in-the-wall, with only a couple

of ringside benches looking over Piazza Marconi to the little beach, this neigh-bourhood bar serves up glasses of the fragrant, ethereal mix of local Albarola, Bosco and Vermentino grapes that is Cinque Terre DOC. They also do break-fast pastries, sandwiches and *aperitivo (pre-dinner drinks)*, and stock a range of local produce to take away.

INFORMATION
All Cinque Terre park information offices and train stations sell the Cinque Terre card (one/two days €7.50/14.50, children under four free), which is required for access to the hiking trails.

Cinque Terre Park Office (0187 74 35 00; La Spezia train station; ⊙7am-8pm) Inside La Spezia's train station.

Parco Nazionale Offices (www.parconazionale 5terre.it; ⊙8am-8pm summer, 8.30am-12.30pm & 1-5.30pm winter) Offices in the train stations of all five villages and La Spezia station; has comprehensive information about hiking-trail closures.

Tourist Office (www.myspezia.it; La Spezia Central Station; ⊙9am-1pm)

GETTING AROUND
From late March to October, **Consorzio Marit-timo Turistico Cinque Terre Golfo dei Poeti** (0187 73 29 87; www.navigazionegolfo deipoeti.it) sails between Porto Venere and the Cinque Terre villages (€18 to €22 one way, €26 including all stops, or €35 for an all-day unlimited ticket.)

Between 6.30am and 10pm, one to three trains an hour trundle along the coast between Genoa and La Spezia, stopping at each of Cinque Terre's villages. Unlimited travel between Levan-to and La Spezia is covered by the **Cinque Terre Treno Card** (https://card.parconazionale5terre. it/en; adult one/two/three day €16/29/41), or you can buy a €4 ticket for travel between any two villages.

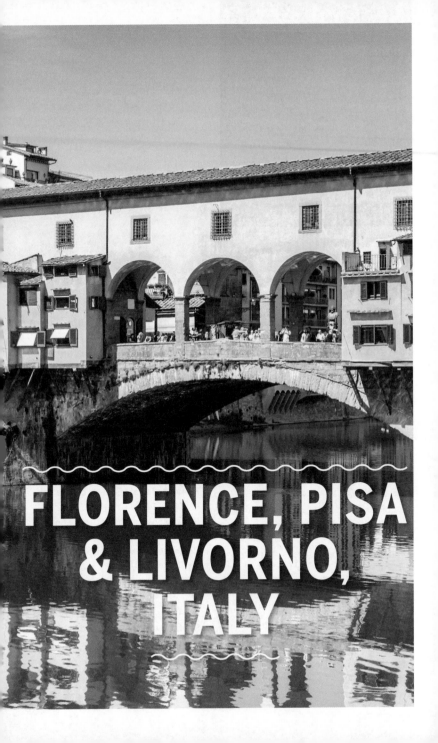

FLORENCE, PISA & LIVORNO, ITALY

In this Chapter

Florence, Pisa & Livorno at a Glance...

Icons including Florence's Duomo, Uffizi Gallery and Galleria dell'Accademia (home to Michelangelo's David), and Pisa's Leaning Tower, all live up to their hype, and both cities showcase extraordinary art and architecture. Florence is known for its world-class food, wine and shopping, too. Proud possessor of a colourful history and cosmopolitan heritage, the port city of Livorno (Leghorn in English) in Tuscany is linked with Florence and Pisa by train. Widely acknowledged as one of the most rewarding stops on Mediterranean cruise itineraries, Tuscany never fails to deliver on its promise.

With One Day in Port

• Head to Florence to marvel at its exquisite Renaissance art and architecture, focusing on the area around the **Duomo** (p178).

• Instead of Florence, choose to make your way to Pisa, home of the magnificent **Piazza dei Miracoli** (p182) with its world-famous **Leaning Tower** (p182).

• Stay in Livorno to promenade on the seafront **Terrazza Mascagni** (p195), make a pilgrimage to the fascinating **Santuario della Madonna di Montenero** (p195) and feast on delectable seafood dishes.

Best Places For...

Renaissance art Galleria degli Uffizi, Florence (p186)

Renaissance architecture Duomo, Florence (p178)

Coffee with a view Caffè Rivoire, Florence (p192)

Architectural icons Leaning Tower, Pisa (p182)

Gelato Gelateria De' Coltelli, Pisa (p193)

Seafood cuisine La Barrocciaia, Livorno (p195)

Previous page: Ponte Vecchio (p187)

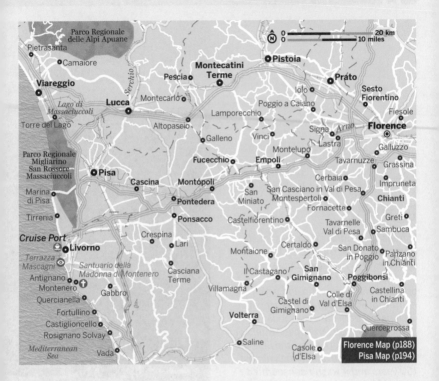

Getting from the Port

Large cruise ships dock at the industrial piers in **Livorno Port**; some smaller cruise ships dock in the old Medici Port (Porto Mediceo).

From the port, it's only a few kilometres to the main railway station, where frequent trains depart for both Florence (€9.90, 1¼ hours) and Pisa (€2.60, 20 minutes). A taxi between the port and railway station will cost around €20.

Fast Facts

Currency Euro (€)

Language Italian

Money ATMs can be found throughout Livorno, Pisa and Florence. There's a currency exchange at Via Cogorano 18, near Piazza Grande in Livorno.

Tourist information There are tourist offices in Livorno (p195), Pisa (p194) and Florence (p192).

Visas Generally not required for stays of up to 90 days (or at all for EU nationals); some nationalities need a Schengen visa.

Wi-fi Many bars, cafes and fast-food outlets have free wi-fi.

Duomo

Florence's Duomo is the city's most iconic landmark. Capped by Filippo Brunelleschi's red-tiled cupola, it's a staggering construction, and its breathtaking pink, white and green marble facade and graceful campanile (bell tower) dominate the medieval cityscape. Sienese architect Arnolfo di Cambio began working on the building in 1296, but construction took almost 150 years and it wasn't consecrated until 1436.

Great For...

ⓘ Need to Know

Cattedrale di Santa Maria del Fiore; ☏055 230 28 85; www.museumflorence.com; Piazza del Duomo; ☺10am-5pm Mon-Wed & Fri, to 4.30pm Thu & Sat, 1.30-4.45pm Sun; **FREE**

Explore Ashore

The Duomo is only a short walk from Stazione di Santa Maria Novella. After exiting the station, walk southeast along Via de' Panzani and its continuation Via de' Cerretani to access Piazza del Duomo. You'll need at least two hours to visit all of the buildings in the Duomo group.

Facade

The neo-Gothic facade was designed in the 19th century by architect Emilio de Fabris to replace the uncompleted original, torn down in the 16th century. The oldest and most clearly Gothic part of the cathedral is its south flank, pierced by the Porta dei Canonici (Canons' Door), a mid-14th-century High Gothic creation (you enter here to climb up inside the dome).

Dome

One of the finest masterpieces of the Renaissance, the **cupola** (Brunelleschi's Dome; adult/ reduced incl baptistry, campanile, crypt & museum €18/3; ⊙8.30am-7pm Mon-Fri, to 5pm Sat, 1-4pm Sun) is a feat of engineering that cannot be fully appreciated without climbing its 463 interior stone steps. It was built between 1420 and 1436 to a design by Filippo Brunelleschi, and is a staggering 91m high and 45.5m wide.

Taking inspiration from Rome's Pantheon, Brunelleschi arrived at an innovative engineering solution of a distinctive octagonal shape of inner and outer concentric domes resting on the drum of the cathedral, allowing artisans to build from the ground up without needing a wooden support frame. Over four million bricks were used in the construction, all of them laid in consecutive rings in horizontal courses using a vertical herringbone pattern.

The climb up the spiral staircase is relatively steep. Pause when you reach the balustrade at the base of the dome for the aerial view of the octagonal *coro* (choir) in the cathedral below and the seven round stained-glass windows (by Donatello, Andrea del Castagno, Paolo Uccello and Lorenzo Ghiberti) that pierce the octagonal drum.

Cupola interior

Reservations are required to climb the cupola. Book online or at the ticket office at Piazza San Giovanni 7, opposite the Baptistry's northern entrance.

Interior

The sparse decoration of the cathedral's vast interior, 155m long and 90m wide, comes as a surprise – most of its artistic treasures have been removed over the centuries according to the vagaries of ecclesiastical fashion. The interior is also unexpectedly secular in places: down the left aisle two immense frescoes of equestrian statues portray two *condottieri* (mercenaries).

Between the left (north) arm of the transept and the apse is the Sagrestia delle Messe (Mass Sacristy), its panelling a marvel of inlaid wood carved by Benedetto and Giuliano da Maiano. The fine bronze doors were executed by Luca della Robbia – his only known work in the material. Above the doorway is his glazed terracotta *Resurrezione* (Resurrection).

A stairway near the main entrance of the cathedral leads down to the Cripta Santa Reparata (crypt), where excavations between 1965 and 1974 unearthed parts of the 5th-century Chiesa di Santa Reparata that originally stood on the site.

☑ Don't Miss

The adjoining 11th-century **Battistero** (Baptistry; Piazza di San Giovanni; adult/reduced incl campanile, cupola, crypt & museum €15/3; ⊙8.15-10.15am & 11.15am-7.30pm Mon-Fri, 8.15am-6.30pm Sat, 8.15am-1.30pm Sun), an octagonal structure with gilded bronze doors.

Campanile

The 414-step climb up the cathedral's 85m-tall **campanile** (bell tower; adult/reduced incl baptistry, cupola, crypt & museum €18/3; ⊙8.15am-7pm), begun by Giotto in 1334, rewards with a staggering city panorama. The first tier of bas-reliefs around the base of its elaborate Gothic facade are copies of those carved by Pisano depicting the Creation of Man and the *attività umane* (arts and industries). Those on the second tier depict the planets, the cardinal virtues, the arts and the seven sacraments. The sculpted Prophets and Sibyls in the upper-storey niches are copies of works by Donatello and others.

What's Nearby

The **Museo dell'Opera del Duomo** (Cathedral Museum; Piazza del Duomo 9; adult/reduced incl campanile, cupola, baptistry & crypt €15/3; ⊙9am-7pm) is home to treasures including Michelangelo's *La Pietà* and Ghiberti's 15th-century *Porta del Paradiso* (Doors of Paradise).

CATARINA BELOVA/SHUTTERSTOCK ©

✕ Take a Break

Historic cafe Gilli (p192) on nearby Piazza della Repubblica is a popular spot for coffee or an *aperitivo*.

Battistero

Pisa's Piazza dei Miracoli

Pisans claim that Piazza dei Miracoli is among the world's most beautiful squares. Its walled lawns provide a photogenic setting for the impressive Duomo (Cathedral), but most eyes are drawn to the world-famous Leaning Tower.

Great For...

☑ Don't Miss

Triumph of Death, a 14th-century fresco in the Camposanto on the piazza's northern edge.

Leaning Tower

Torre Pendente (☎050 83 50 11; www.opa pisa.it; Piazza dei Miracoli; €18; ⊙8.30am-10pm Jul & Aug, 9am-8pm Apr-Jun & Sep-Oct, 9am-7pm Nov, Dec & Mar, to 6pm Jan & Feb) lives up to its name, leaning a startling 3.9 degrees. The 56m-high tower, officially the Duomo's campanile, took almost 200 years to build, but was already listing when it was unveiled in 1372. Over time, the tilt, caused by a layer of weak subsoil, worsened until it was finally halted by a major stabilisation project in the 1990s.

Building began in 1173 under the supervision of architect Bonanno Pisano, but his plans came a cropper almost immediately. Only three of the tower's seven tiers had been built when he was forced to abandon construction after it started leaning. Work resumed in 1272, with artisans and masons

Torre Pendente (Leaning Tower)

Piazza dei Miracoli

⚓

Explore Ashore

Piazza dei Miracoli is a 1.8km walk from Stazione Centrale. After exiting the station, walk north to Piazza Vittorio Emanuele II and then northwest along Via Francesco Crispi and Via Roma. Alternatively, take the LAM Rossa (Red) bus from the train station (direction Park Pietrasantina). You'll need at least 90 minutes for your visit.

❶ Need to Know

Campo dei Miracoli; ☏ 050 83 50 11; www.opapisa.it

attempting to bolster the foundations but failing miserably. They kept going, compensating for the lean by gradually building straight up from the lower storeys.

Access to the Leaning Tower is limited to groups of 45 (visitors must be over eight years old). Book tickets in advance online.

Duomo

Pisa's magnificent Romanesque **Duomo** (Duomo di Santa Maria Assunta; ⊙10am-8pm Apr-Oct, to 7pm Nov, Dec & Mar, to 6pm Jan & Feb) **FREE** was begun in 1064 and consecrated in 1118. Its striking tiered exterior, with cladding of green-and-cream marble bands, gives on to a vast columned interior capped by a gold wooden ceiling. The elliptical dome, the first of its kind in Europe, was added in 1380. The cathedral, which served as a blueprint for subsequent Romanesque churches in Tuscany, was Europe's largest when it was completed.

Admission is free via a fixed-time pass issued by the ticket offices in the piazza or with a ticket from another Piazza dei Miracoli sight. Eighty visitors are admitted every 30 minutes.

Battistero

Construction of the cupcake-style **Battistero** (Battistero di San Giovanni; €5, with Camposanto & Museo €8, child under 11 yr free; ⊙8am-8pm Apr-Nov, 9am-7pm Dec-Mar, to 5pm Jan & Feb) began in 1152. More than a century later, the building was remodelled and continued by Nicola and Giovanni Pisano and finally completed in the 14th century. Climb to the Upper Gallery to hear the custodian demonstrate the double dome's remarkable acoustics and echo effects.

The Heart of Florence

Every visitor to Florence spends time navigating the cobbled medieval lanes that run between Via de' Tornabuoni and Via del Proconsolo, but few explore them thoroughly.

Start Piazza della Repubblica
Distance 2km
Duration Two hours

4 Head past the market and along Via Porta Rossa to **Palazzo Davanzati** with its magnificent studded doors and fascinating museum.

6 Wander down the narrow **Via del Parione** to spy out old mansions and artisans' workshops.

5 Hidden behind the unassuming facade of the **Basilica di Santa Trinita** are some of the city's finest 15th-century frescoes.

Classic Photo The River Arno and the Ponte Vecchio.

7 Finish with a sundowner and spectacular Ponte Vecchio views at **Le Volpi e l'Uva**, which is just over the Arno.

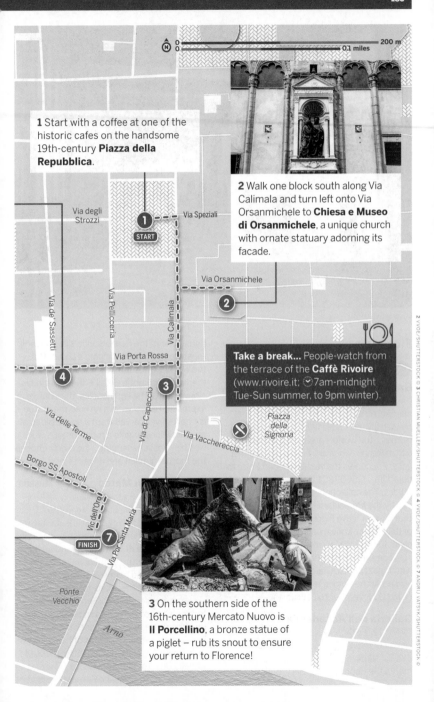

1 Start with a coffee at one of the historic cafes on the handsome 19th-century **Piazza della Repubblica**.

2 Walk one block south along Via Calimala and turn left onto Via Orsanmichele to **Chiesa e Museo di Orsanmichele**, a unique church with ornate statuary adorning its facade.

Via degli Strozzi

Via Speziali

START

Via Orsanmichele

Via de' Sassetti

Via Pellicceria

Via Calimala

2

Via Porta Rossa

Take a break... People-watch from the terrace of the **Caffè Rivoire** (www.rivoire.it; ⏰7am-midnight Tue-Sun summer, to 9pm winter).

4

Via delle Terme

Via di Capaccio

3

Piazza della Signoria

Via Vaccereccia

Borgo SS Apostoli

Vic dell'Oro

Via Por Santa Maria

FINISH **7**

Ponte Vecchio

Arno

3 On the southern side of the 16th-century Mercato Nuovo is **Il Porcellino**, a bronze statue of a piglet – rub its snout to ensure your return to Florence!

2 WOE/SHUTTERSTOCK © 3 CHRISTIAN MUELLER/SHUTTERSTOCK © 4 WOE/SHUTTERSTOCK © 7 ANDRII VATSYK/SHUTTERSTOCK ©

Galleria degli Uffizi

Florence

◉ SIGHTS

Galleria degli Uffizi   Gallery
(Uffizi Gallery; ✆055 29 48 83; www.uffizi.it; Piazzale degli Uffizi 6; adult/reduced Mar-Oct €20/10,
Nov-Feb €12/6; ⊙8.15am-6.50pm Tue-Sun)
Home to the world's greatest collection of
Italian Renaissance art, Florence's premier
gallery occupies the vast U-shaped Palazzo
degli Uffizi (1560–80), built as government
offices. The collection, bequeathed to the
city by the Medici family in 1743 on condition
that it never leave Florence, contains some
of Italy's best-known paintings, including a
room full of Botticelli masterpieces.

A combined ticket (valid three days)
with Palazzo Pitti, Giardino di Boboli and
Museo Archeologico is available for €38/21
(€18/11 November to February).

Galleria dell'Accademia   Gallery
(✆055 238 86 09; www.galleriaaccademiafirenze.
beniculturali.it; Via Ricasoli 60; adult/reduced
€12/6; ⊙8.15am-6.50pm Tue-Sun) A queue
marks the door to this gallery, built to
house one of the Renaissance's most iconic
masterpieces, Michelangelo's *David*. But
the world's most famous statue is worth
the wait. The subtle detail – the veins in his
sinewy arms, the leg muscles, the change in
expression as you move around the statue –
is impressive. Carved from a single block of
marble, Michelangelo's most famous work
was his most challenging – he didn't choose
the marble himself and it was veined.

Museo di San Marco   Museum
(✆055 238 86 08; Piazza San Marco 3; adult/re-
duced €4/2; ⊙8.15am-1.50pm Mon-Fri, to 4.50pm
Sat & Sun, closed 1st, 3rd & 5th Sun, 2nd & 4th Mon
of month) At the heart of Florence's university
area sits **Chiesa di San Marco** and an adjoining 15th-century Dominican monastery
where both gifted painter Fra' Angelico (c
1395–1455) and the sharp-tongued Savon-
arola piously served God. Today the monastery, aka one of Florence's most spiritually
uplifting museums, showcases the work of
Fra' Angelico. After centuries of being known
as 'Il Beato Angelico' (literally 'The Blessed
Angelic One') or simply 'Il Beato' (The
Blessed), the Renaissance's most blessed

religious painter was made a saint by Pope John Paul II in 1984.

Museo delle Cappelle Medicee · Mausoleum

(Medici Chapels; ☑055 238 86 02; www.bargello musei.beniculturali.it/musei/2/medicee; Piazza Madonna degli Aldobrandini 6; adult/reduced €8/4; ⊙8.15am-2pm, closed 2nd & 4th Sun, 1st, 3rd & 5th Mon of month) Nowhere is Medici conceit expressed so explicitly as in the Medici Chapels. Adorned with granite, marble, semi-precious stones and some of Michelangelo's most beautiful sculptures, it is the burial place of 49 dynasty members. Francesco I lies in the dark, imposing **Cappella dei Principi** (Chapel of Princes) alongside Ferdinando I and II and Cosimo I, II and III. Lorenzo il Magnifico is buried in the graceful **Sagrestia Nuova** (New Sacristy), which was Michelangelo's first architectural work.

Basilica di Santa Maria Novella · Basilica

(☑055 21 92 57; www.smn.it; Piazza di Santa Maria Novella 18; adult/reduced €7.50/5; ⊙9am-7pm Mon-Thu, 11am-7pm Fri, 9am-6.30pm Sat, noon-6.30pm Sun Jul & Aug, shorter hours rest of year) The striking green-and-white marble facade of 13th- to 15th-century Basilica di Santa Maria Novella fronts an entire monastical complex, comprising romantic church cloisters and a frescoed chapel. The basilica itself is a treasure chest of artistic masterpieces, climaxing with frescoes by Domenico Ghirlandaio. The lower section of the basilica's striped marbled facade is transitional from Romanesque to Gothic; the upper section and the main doorway (1456–70) were designed by Leon Battista Alberti. Book in advance online to avoid queues.

Museo di Palazzo Davanzati · Museum

(☑055 064 94 60; www.bargellomusei.beni culturali.it; Via Porta Rossa 13; adult/reduced €6/3; ⊙8.15am-2pm Mon-Fri, 1.15-7pm Sat & Sun) Home to the wealthy Davanzati merchant family from 1578, this 14th-century *palazzo* (mansion) with a wonderful central loggia gives you a view into precisely how Florentine nobles lived in the 16th century. Spot the

⌂⟶ Escape the Crowds: Florence

Cross the historic **Ponte Vecchio**, built in 1345 and the only Florentine bridge to survive destruction at the hands of retreating German forces in 1944, to access the Oltrarno ('Over the Arno') neighbourhood, home to two magnificent and often crowd-free gardens: **Giardino di Boboli** (☑055 29 48 83; www. uffizi.it/en/boboli-garden; Piazza dei Pitti; adult/reduced incl Giardino Bardini & Museo delle Porcellane Mar-Oct €10/2, Nov-Feb €6/2; ⊙8.15am-6.50pm summer, reduced hours winter, closed 1st & last Mon of month) Laid out in the mid-16th century, this large landscaped garden behind Palazzo Pitti offers beautiful views over the Florentine countryside from its upper, southern limit. Within the lower reaches of the gardens, don't miss the fantastical shell- and gem-encrusted Grotta del Buontalenti.

Villa e Giardino Bardini (☑055 2006 6233; www.villabardini.it; Costa San Giorgio 2, Via de' Bardi 1r; adult/reduced villa €10/5, gardens €6/3, gardens with Giardino di Boboli ticket free; ⊙villa 10am-7pm Tue-Sun, gardens 8.15am-7.30pm summer, shorter hours winter, closed 1st & last Mon of month) This 17th-century villa and garden was named for antiquarian art collector Stefano Bardini (1836–1922), who bought it in 1913 and restored its medieval garden. It has all the features of a quintessential Tuscan garden, including artificial grottoes, an orangery, marble statues and fountains.

Giardino di Boboli

Florence

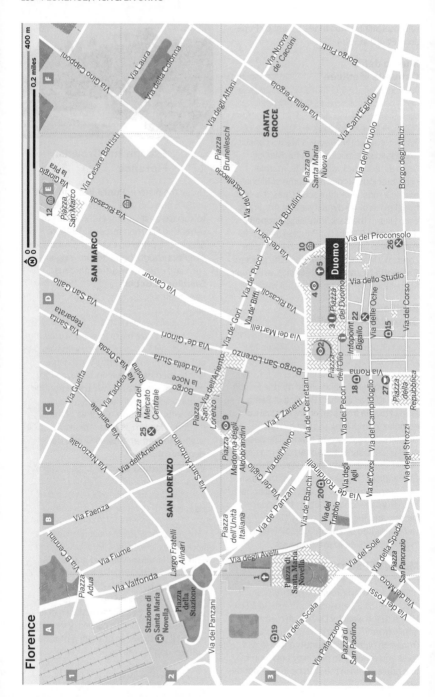

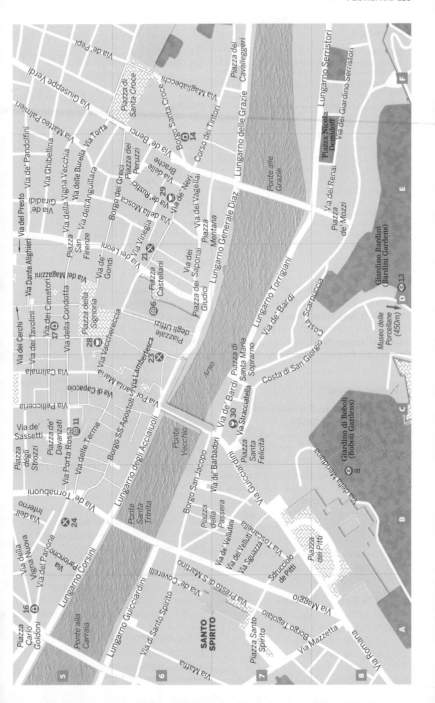

Florence

carved faces of the original owners on the pillars in the inner courtyard, and don't miss the 1st-floor **Sala Madornale** (Reception Room) with its painted wooden ceiling, exotic **Sala dei Pappagalli** (Parrot Room) and **Camera dei Pavoni** (Peacock Bedroom).

🅐 SHOPPING

Officina Profumo-Farmaceutica di Santa Maria Novella Gifts

(📞055 21 62 76; www.smnovella.it; Via della Scala 16; ⊙9am-8pm) In business since 1612, this exquisite perfumery-pharmacy began life when Santa Maria Novella's Dominican friars began to concoct cures and sweet-smelling unguents using medicinal herbs cultivated in the monastery garden. The shop, with an interior from 1848, sells fragrances, skincare products, ancient herbal remedies and preparations for everything from relief of heavy legs to improving skin elasticity, memory and mental energy.

Luisa Via Roma Fashion & Accessories

(📞055 906 41 16; www.luisaviaroma.com; Via Roma 19-21r; ⊙10.30am-7.30pm Mon-Sat, from 11am Sun) The flagship store of this historic boutique (think: small 1930s boutique selling straw hats) turned luxury online retailer is a must for the fashion-forward.

Eye-catching window displays woo the digital generation with giant screens, while seasonal themes transform the interior maze of rooms into an exotic Garden of Eden. Shop here for lesser-known designers as well as popular luxury fashion labels.

Pre- or post-shop, hobnob with the city's fashionista set over fair-trade coffee, organic cuisine and creative cold-press juices in Luisa's chic 1st-floor cafe-bar **Floret** (📞055 29 59 24; www.floret-bar.com; salads & bowls €12-16; ⊙10.30am-7.30pm Mon-Sat, from 11am Sun; 🛜) 🍴.

Benheart Fashion & Accessories

(www.benheart.it; Via dei Calzaivoli 78; ⊙10am-7.30pm) This flagship store of local superstar Ben, a Florentine-based fashion designer who set up the business with schoolmate Matteo after undergoing a heart transplant, is irresistible. The pair swore that if Ben survived, they'd go it alone – which they did, with huge success. For real-McCoy handcrafted leather designs – casual shoes, jackets and belts for men and women – there is no finer address.

Around €200 is the price you pay for a pair of double-lined shoes with soft buffalo leather, stitched before being dyed with natural pigments. Find smaller Benheart boutiques around the corner on **Via dei Cimatori** (☑055 046 26 38; Via dei Cimatori 25r; ☺10am-7.30pm) and in **Santa Maria Novella** (☑055 239 94 83; Via della Vigna Nuova 95-97r; ☺9am-8pm).

Aquaflor
Cosmetics

(☑055 234 34 71; www.aquaflorexperience.com; Borgo Santa Croce 6; ☺10am-1pm & 2-7pm) This elegant Santa Croce perfumery in a vaulted 15th-century *palazzo* exudes romance and exoticism. Artisan scents are crafted here with tremendous care and precision by master perfumer Sileno Cheloni, who works with precious essences from all over the world, including Florentine iris. Organic soaps, cosmetics and body-care products make equally lovely gifts to take back home.

Should you dream of creating your very own special perfume, count around €1500 for a three-hour bespoke workshop.

Richard Ginori
Homewares

(☑055 21 00 41; www.richardginori1735.com; Via de' Rondinelli 17r; ☺10am-7pm Mon-Wed, 10am-7.30pm Thu-Sat, noon-7pm Sun) The maze of beautiful period rooms at this elegant porcelain shop is well worth exploring. Showcasing tableware produced by Richard Ginori, a Tuscan company established in 1735, the showroom is one of the city's most beautiful retail spaces: think original parquet flooring, moulded ceilings, papered walls and an 18th-century glass conservatory filled with plants.

🍴 EATING

'Ino
Sandwiches €

(☑055 21 45 14; www.inofirenze.com; Via dei Georgofili 3r-7r; panini €6-10; ☺noon-4.30pm) 🍃 Artisan ingredients sourced locally and mixed creatively by passionate gourmet Alessandro Frassica are the secret behind this sandwich bar near the Uffizi. Create your own *panino* combo; pick from dozens of house specials; or go for an enticingly topped bruschetta – in the company of a glass of Tuscan wine or craft beer.

Trattoria Le Mossacce
Trattoria €

(☑055 29 43 61; www.trattorialemossacce. it; Via del Proconsolo 55r; meals €20; ☺noon-2.30pm & 7-9.30pm Mon-Fri) Strung with legs of ham and garlic garlands, this old-world trattoria lives up to its vintage promise of a warm *benvenuto* (welcome) and fabulous home cooking every Tuscan *nonna* would approve of. A family address, it has been the pride and joy of the Fantoni-Mannucci family for the last 50-odd years and their *bistecca alla fiorentina* (T-bone steak) is among the best in town.

Grom
Gelato €

(☑055 21 61 58; www.grom.it; Via del Campanile 2; cones & tubs €2.60-5.50; ☺10am-midnight Sun-Fri, to 1am Sat summer, 10.30am-10.30pm winter) Rain, hail or shine, queues run halfway down the street at this sweet address that many say makes some of the best gelato in the city. Ingredients are organic and its tasty hot chocolate is a delicious winter-warmer.

Mercato Centrale
Food Hall €

(☑055 239 97 98; www.mercatocentrale.it; Piazza del Mercato Centrale 4; dishes €5-15; ☺market 7am-3pm Mon-Fri, to 5pm Sat, food hall 8am-midnight; 🛜) Wander the maze of stalls rammed with fresh produce at Florence's oldest and largest food market, on the ground floor of an iron-and-glass structure designed by architect Giuseppe Mengoni in 1874. Head to the 1st floor's buzzing, thoroughly contemporary food hall with dedicated cookery school and artisan stalls cooking steaks, burgers, tripe *panini*, vegetarian dishes, pizza, gelato, pastries and pasta.

Mariano
Sandwiches €

(☑055 21 40 67; Via del Parione 19r; panini €3.50-6; ☺8am-3pm & 5-7.30pm Mon-Fri, 8am-3pm Sat) A local favourite for its simplicity and correct prices, around since 1973. From sunrise to sunset, this brick-vaulted, 13th-century cellar gently buzzes with Florentines propped at the counter sipping coffee or wine or eating salads and *panini*. Come here for a coffee-and-pastry breakfast, light lunch, an *aperitivo* (pre-dinner drink) with cheese or salami tasting platter (€13 to €17), or a *panino* to eat on the move.

Look for the green neon *'pizzicheria'* up high on the outside facade and the discrete *'alimentari'* sign above the entrance.

All'Antico Vinaio   Osteria €

(📞349 3719947, 055 238 27 23; www.allantico vinaio.com; Via de' Neri 65r; tasting platters €10-30; ⏱10am-4pm & 6-11pm Tue-Sat, noon-3.30pm Sun) The crowd spills out the door of this noisy Florentine thoroughbred, pride and joy of the Mazzanti family since 1991. Push your way to the tables at the back to taste cheese and salami in situ (reservations recommended). Or join the queue at the deli counter for a well-stuffed focaccia wrapped in waxed paper to take away – the quality is outstanding. Pour yourself a glass of wine while you wait.

🍷 DRINKING & NIGHTLIFE

Le Volpi e l'Uva   Wine Bar

(📞055 239 81 32; www.levolpieluva.com; Piazza dei Rossi 1; ⏱11am-9pm summer, 11am-9pm Mon-Sat winter) This humble wine bar remains as appealing as the day it opened in 1992. Its food and wine pairings are first class – taste and buy boutique wines by small Italian producers, matched perfectly with cheeses, cold meats and the finest crostini in town; the warm, melt-in-your-mouth *lardo di Cinta Sienese* (wafer-thin slices of aromatic pork fat) is absolutely extraordinary.

Wine-tasting classes too – or simply work your way through the impressive 50-odd different wines available by the glass (€4.50 to €9).

Ditta Artigianale   Cafe

(📞055 274 15 41; www.dittaartigianale.it; Via de' Neri 32r; ⏱8am-10pm Mon-Thu, to midnight Fri, 9am-midnight Sat, to 11pm Sun; 🛜) With industrial decor and a laid-back vibe, this ingenious coffee roastery is a perfect place to hang at any time of day. The creation of three-times Italian barista champion Francesco Sanapo, it's famed

for its first-class coffee and outstanding gin cocktails. If you're yearning for a flat white, cold brew tonic or cappuccino made with almond milk, come here.

Caffè Rivoire   Cafe

(📞055 21 44 12; www.rivoire.it; Piazza della Signoria 4; ⏱7am-midnight Tue-Sun summer, to 9pm winter) This golden oldie with an unbeatable people-watching terrace has produced some of the city's most exquisite chocolate since 1872 (sadly only available in winter). Black-jacketed bartenders with ties set the formal tone. Save several euros by joining the local Florentine crowd standing at the bar rather than sitting down at a table.

Caffè Gilli   Cafe

(📞055 21 38 96; www.gilli.it; Piazza della Repubblica 39r; ⏱7.30am-1am) Popular with locals who sip coffee standing up at the long marble bar, this is the most famous of the historic cafes on the city's old Roman forum. Gilli has been serving delectable cakes, chocolates, fruit tartlets and *mille-foglie* (lighter-than-light vanilla or custard slice) since 1733. It moved to this square in 1910 and has a beautifully preserved art nouveau interior.

Don't be surprised to pay three times as much for a drink sitting down – inside or in the conservatory-style, glassed-in terrace with prime square view – rather than at the bar; a cappuccino costs €1.40 standing up and €5.50 when served at a table.

ℹ️ INFORMATION

Infopoint Bigallo (📞055 28 84 96; www.firen-zeturismo.it; Piazza San Giovanni 1; ⏱9am-7pm Mon-Sat, to 2pm Sun) Tourist information by the Duomo.

ℹ️ GETTING AROUND

Florence is best navigated on foot: most major sights are within easy walking distance. Bicycles can be rented from the stands in front of Stazione di Santa Maria Novella.

Pisa

⊙ SIGHTS

Camposanto   Cemetery

(☑050 83 50 11; www.opapisa.it; Piazza dei Mira-coli; €5, combination ticket with Battistero or Mu-seo delle Sinopie €7, Battistero & Museo €8, child under 11 years free; ⊗8am-8pm Apr-Nov, 9am-7pm Dec-Mar, to 5pm Jan & Feb) Soil shipped from Calvary during the Crusades is said to lie within the white walls of this hauntingly beautiful, final resting place for many prom-inent Pisans, arranged around a garden in a cloistered quadrangle. During WWII, Allied artillery destroyed many of the cloisters' frescoes, but a couple were salvaged and are now displayed in the **Sala Affreschi** (Frescoes Room). Most notable is the Triumph of Death (1336–41), a remarkable illustration of Hell attributed to 14th-century painter Buonamico Buffalmacco.

Museo Nazionale di San Matteo   Museum

(☑050 54 18 65; Piazza San Matteo in Soarta 1; adult/reduced €5/2.50; ⊗8.30am-7pm Tue-Sat, to 1pm Sun) This inspiring repository of me-dieval masterpieces sits in a 13th-century Benedictine convent on the Arno's northern waterfront boulevard. The museum's collec-tion of paintings from the Tuscan school (c 12th to 14th centuries) is notable, with works by Lippo Memmi, Taddeo Gaddi, Gentile da Fabriano and Ghirlandaio. Don't miss Masaccio's St Paul, Fra' Angelico's Madonna of Humility and Simone Martini's Polyptych of Saint Catherine.

⊗ EATING

Gelateria De' Coltelli   Gelato €

(☑345 4811903; www.decoltelli.it; Lungarno Pacinotti 23; cones/tubs €2.50-4; ⊗11am-8.30pm Sun-Thu, to 10.30pm Fri & Sat Mar-May & Sep-Nov, to 11.30pm Sun-Thu, to midnight Fri & Sat Jun-Aug) Follow the crowd to this world-class gelateria across from the river, famed for its sensational artisanal, organic and 100% natural gelato. Flavours are as zesty and appealing as its bright-orange

⇱ Escape the Crowds: Pisa

Away from the crowded heavyweights of Piazza dei Miracoli, along the Arno river banks, a far more tranquil Pisa can be discovered. Splendid *palazzi*, painted a multitude of hues, line the southern *lungarno* (riverside embankment) near the waterside, triple-spired **Chiesa di Santa Maria della Spina** (Lungarno Gam-bacorti; ⊗10am-1pm Mon, 3-7pm Tue-Thu, 10am-1pm & 3-7pm Fri-Sun), an exquisite Pisan-Gothic church encrusted with tabernacles and statues. It was built between 1230 and 1233 to house a reliquary of a *spina* (thorn) from Christ's crown.

Chiesa di Santa Maria della Spina
STEVE ALLEN/SHUTTERSTOCK ©

interior. The hard part is choosing: ginger, ricotta cheese with pine nuts and honey, candied chestnuts, almond with candied lemon peel, cashew with Maldon salt, kiwi, or ricotta with candied orange peel and chocolate chips.

Pizzeria Il Montino   Pizza €

(☑050 59 86 95; Vicolo del Monte 1; pizza €6-8.50, foccacine €2.50-5, cecina €2; ⊗11am-3pm & 5.30-10.30pm Mon-Sat) There's nothing fancy about this down-to-earth pizzeria, an icon among Pisans, students and sophisticates alike. Take away or order at the bar then grab a table, inside or out, and munch on house specialities such as *cecina* (chickpea pizza), *castagnaccio* (chestnut cake) and *spuma* (sweet, nonalcoholic drink). Or go for a *focaccine* (small flat roll) filled with salami, pancetta or *porchetta* (suckling pig).

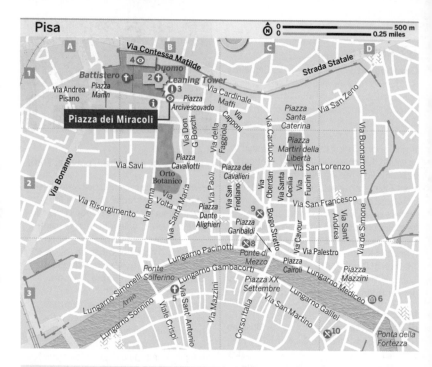

Pisa

◎ Top Sights
1 Battistero	B1
2 Duomo	B1
3 Leaning Tower	B1

◎ Sights
4 Camposanto	B1
5 Chiesa di Santa Maria della Spina	B3

6 Museo Nazionale di San Matteo	D3
7 Piazza dei Miracoli	B1

⊗ Eating
8 Gelateria De' Coltelli	C3
9 Pizzeria Il Montino	C2
10 Ristorante Galileo	D3

Ristorante Galileo   Tuscan €€
(⌧050 2 82 87; www.ristorantegalileo.com; Via
San Martino 6-8; meals €28-35, fast lunch deal
€10; ⊗12.30-2.30pm & 7.30-11pm) For good,
honest, unpretentious Tuscan cooking,
nothing beats this classical old-timer. From
the cork-covered wine list to the complimentary plate of warm homemade focaccia
and huge platters of tempting *cantuccini*
(almond-studded biscuits), Galileo makes
you feel welcome. Fresh pasta is strictly
hand- and homemade, and most veggies

are plucked fresh that morning from the
restaurant's garden.

ⓘ INFORMATION

Tourist Office (⌧050 55 01 00; www.turismo.
pisa.it/en; Piazza dei Miracoli 7; ⊗9.30am-5.30pm)
Provides city information, free maps and various
services including guided tours, bicycle rental
(per hour/day €3/15) and a computer terminal to
check train times and sign up for city bike-sharing
scheme Ciclopi. Also sells public transport tickets.

GETTING AROUND

Pisa is easy to explore by foot. Alternatively, you can pedal around town on a silver bicycle courtesy of Pisan bike-sharing scheme Cicopli (www.ciclopi.eu). Pick-up/drop-off at 25 stations dotted around the city, including at Pisa Centrale train station and Piazza Manin (adjoining Piazza dei Miracoli). Tickets on the LAM Rossa bus are valid for 70 minutes and cost €2.50 when purchased on the bus (€1.50 if purchased from a newsstand or tobacconist).

Livorno

SIGHTS

Terrazza Mascagni Street
(Viale Italia; ⊘24hr) FREE No trip to Livorno is complete without a stroll along this seafront terrace with its dramatic black-and-white chessboard-style pavement. When it was built in the 1920s, it was called Terrazza Ciano after the leader of the Livorno fascist movement; it now bears the name of Livorno-born opera composer Pietro Mascagni (1863–1945).

**Santuario della Madonna
di Montenero** Christian Site
(✆0586 57 96 27; www.santuariomontenero. org; Piazza di Montenero 9; ⊘6.30am-12.30pm & 2.30-7pm summer, to 6pm winter) The story goes like this: in 1345, the Virgin Mary appeared to a shepherd, who led her to black mountain *(monte nero),* a haven of brigands. Needless to say, the brigands immediately saw the error of their ways and built a chapel on the mountain. Soon pilgrims arrived and the chapel was extended in stages; it reached its present form in 1774. Rooms and corridors surrounding the church house a fascinating collection of 20,000 historic ex-votos thanking the Virgin for miracles.

The best time to visit is on 8 September, for the Festa del Madonna. To get here by public transport, take the LAM Rosso bus (direction: Montenero) and get off at the last stop, Piazza delle Carrozze in Montenero Basso. From there, take the historic funicular

(€1.50, on board €2.50, valid 70 minutes, every 10 to 20 minutes) up to the sanctuary.

EATING

La Barrocciaia Osteria €
(✆0586 88 26 37; www.labarrocciaia.it; Piazza Cavallotti 13; meals €25, panini €5.50-8; ⊘noon-3pm & 6-11pm Tue-Sat, 6-11pm Sun) Locals speak of La Barrocciaia with great fondness – partly because of a homely interior that's alive with banter, but also because of its simple but flavour-packed food. Stews fluctuate between wild boar and *cacciucco* (mixed seafood stew), there's always a choice of *mare* (sea) or *terra* (land) antipasti and it's perfectly acceptable to drop in for a simple *panino* and glass of wine.

Gelateria Popolare 2 Gelato €
(✆0586 26 03 54; www.gelateriapopolare2.it; Via Carlo Meyer 11; gelato €2.50-4; ⊘8am-midnight summer, 8am-8pm Tue-Sun winter;) Many locals stop at this local institution for a sugar hit after enjoying a late-afternoon *passeggiata* (stroll) on the Terrazza Mascagni, and we strongly recommend you do the same. Made fresh each day, its gelato is undoubtedly the best in town. Also serves crepes, frappès and hot chocolate (the latter in winter only).

INFORMATION

Tourist Office (✆0586 89 42 36; www.comune.livorno.it/portaleturismo; Via Pieroni 18; ⊘9am-4pm Apr-Oct, to 3pm Nov-Mar) Hands out free maps and books boat tours.

GETTING AROUND

Cruise companies usually provide bus shuttles from the cruise terminal to the centre of town. LAM Blu buses operated by CTT Nord travel between the city centre (Via Grande) and Livorno Centrale train station, and also along the seafront (€1.50, on board €2.50, valid for 70 minutes).

ROME, ITALY

In this Chapter

Rome at a Glance...

A heady mix of evocative ruins, awe-inspiring art and vibrant street life, Italy's hot-blooded capital is one of the world's most romantic and exciting cities. A visit here will give you the opportunity to sample its famed dolce vita lifestyle, be charmed by its wealth of Renaissance and baroque architecture, and marvel at monumental ruins and exquisite ancient art. Called caput mundi (capital of the world) in the glory days of the empire, Rome can still lay claim to this title in a cultural sense and offers every visitor diversions and delights galore.

With One Day in Port

○ Kick off your day in the heart of the ancient city, visiting the **Roman Forum** (p208), **Colosseum** (p200) and (if time allows) the **Palatino** (p211).

○ Enjoy lunch in Monti or the *centro storico*, then wander through **Piazza Navona** (p218), and throw a coin into the **Trevi Fountain** (p219).

○ Make your way to **Piazza di Spagna & the Spanish Steps** (p219). Do some shopping in the streets nearby before capping off your day with an *aperitivo* (pre-dinner drink).

Best Places For...

Shopping Tridente (p221)

Coffee Caffè Sant'Eustachio (p228)

Ancient art Museo Nazionale Romano: Palazzo Massimo alle Terme (p218)

Pizza by the Slice Bonci Pizzarium (p227)

Gelato Gelateria del Teatro (p226)

Afternoon cocktails Il Palazzetto (p229)

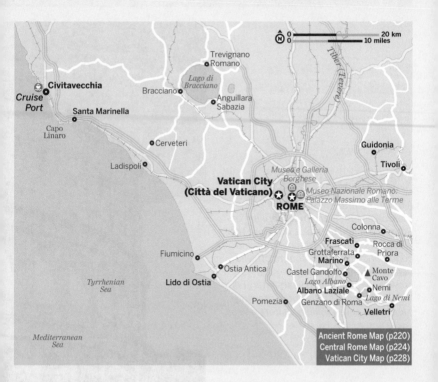

Getting from the Port

Cruise ships dock at **Civitavecchia**, about 80km north of central Rome.

There is a train station about 700m from the port entrance from where half-hourly trains travel to Rome's Stazione Termini (€4.60 to €16, 45 minutes to 1½ hours). From Stazione Termini, metro line A stops at Piazza di Spagna and St Peter's Basilica; metro line B stops at the Colosseum and Roman Forum.

Fast Facts

Currency Euro (€)

Language Italian

Money ATMS can be found throughout the city; there is a currency exchange booth at Stazione Termini in Rome.

Tourist information There are tourist offices in Stazione Termini (p229) and at the Imperial Forums (p229).

Visas Not required for EU citizens. Nationals of Australia, Brazil, Canada, Japan, New Zealand and the USA do not need visas for visits of up to 90 days.

Wi-fi Public paid wi-fi hotspots across town are run by WiFimetropolitano (www.cittametropolitanaroma.gov.it/wifimetropolitano).

Colosseum

A monument to raw, merciless power, the Colosseum is the most thrilling of Rome's ancient sights. It was here that gladiators met in mortal combat and condemned prisoners fought off wild beasts in front of baying, bloodthirsty crowds. Two thousand years later it is Italy's top tourist attraction, drawing more than seven million visitors a year.

Great For...

❶ Need to Know

Colosseo; ☎ 06 3996 7700; www.parcocolosseo.it; Piazza del Colosseo; adult/reduced incl Roman Forum & Palatino €12/7.50, SUPER ticket €18/13.50; ⊗ 8.30am-1hr before sunset; Ⓜ Colosseo

Explore Ashore

The Colosseum is easily accessed by metro from Stazione Termini station (Line B; direction Laurentina). A taxi from the station will cost around €8. You'll need at least 45 minutes to explore; longer if you have booked a tour.

Built by Vespasian (r AD 69–79), the arena was inaugurated in AD 80, eight years after it had been commissioned. To mark the occasion, Vespasian's son and successor Titus (r AD 79–81) staged games that lasted 100 days and nights, during which 5000 animals were slaughtered. Trajan (r AD 98–117) later topped this, holding a marathon 117-day killing spree involving 9000 gladiators and 10,000 animals.

Although the 50,000-seat arena was Rome's most fearsome, it wasn't the biggest – the Circo Massimo could hold up to 250,000 people. The name Colosseum, when introduced in medieval times, was a reference not to its size but to the Colosso di Nerone, a giant statue of Nero that stood nearby.

With the fall of the Roman Empire in the 5th century, the Colosseum was abandoned and gradually became overgrown. In the Middle Ages it served as a fortress for two of the city's warrior families, the Frangipani and the Annibaldi. During the Renaissance and baroque periods, it was plundered of its precious travertine, and the marble was used to make huge palaces.

Recently, pollution and vibrations caused by traffic and the metro have taken a toll. Between 2014 and 2016 it was given a major clean-up as part of an ongoing €25-million restoration project, its first in 2000 years.

Exterior

The outer walls have three levels of arches, framed by Ionic, Doric and Corinthian columns. These were originally covered in travertine, and marble statues filled the niches on the 2nd and 3rd storeys. The upper level, punctuated with windows and

slender Corinthian pilasters, had supports for 240 masts that held up a huge canvas awning over the arena, shielding spectators from sun and rain. The 80 entrance arches, known as *vomitoria,* allowed the spectators to enter and be seated in a matter of minutes.

Arena

The stadium originally had a wooden floor covered in sand – *harena* in Latin, hence the word 'arena' – to prevent combatants from slipping and to soak up spilt blood.

Stands

The *cavea,* for spectator seating, was divided into three tiers: magistrates and senior officials sat in the lowest tier, wealthy citizens in the middle, and the plebeians in the highest tier. Women (except for Vestal Virgins) were relegated to the cheapest sections at the top. Tickets were numbered and spectators assigned a seat in a specific sector – in 2015, restorers uncovered traces of red numerals on the arches, indicating how the sectors were numbered. The podium, a broad terrace in front of the tiers of seats, was reserved for the emperor, senators and VIPs.

Hypogeum

Accessed from the floor of the arena, this subterranean complex served as the stadium's backstage area. Here stage sets were prepared and combatants, both human and animal, would gather before showtime. Gladiators entered from the nearby Ludus Magnus (gladiator school) via an underground corridor, while a second tunnel, the Passaggio di Commodo, allowed the emperor to arrive without having to pass through the crowds.

To hoist people, animals and scenery up to the arena, the hypogeum was equipped with a sophisticated network of 80 winch-operated lifts, all controlled by a single pulley system.

> ### ★ Top Tip
>
> Beat the queues by buying your ticket at the Palatino, about 250m away at Via di San Gregorio 30. And if you want to visit the Belvedere (top three tiers) and the hypogeum's tunnels, book online in advance at www.coopculture.it.

BY PIOTR JACZEWSKI/GETTY IMAGES ©

> ### ✕ Take a Break
>
> Avoid the rip-off restaurants in the immediate vicinity. Instead push on to the area east of the Colosseum to casual **Cafè Cafè** (☏06 7045 1303; www.cafe-cafebistrot.it; Via dei Santi Quattro 44; meals €15-20; ☽9.30am-8.30pm Wed-Mon, to 4pm Tue; ☐Via di San Giovanni in Laterano).

ELIJAH LOVKOFF/SHUTTERSTOCK ©

St Peter's Basilica

In a city of outstanding churches, none can hold a candle to St Peter's Basilica. Italy's largest, richest and most spectacular basilica, it's a powerful testimony to the artistic genius of Michelangelo and Bernini.

Great For...

Don't Miss

Climbing the (numerous, steep and tiring, but worth it) steps of the dome for views over Rome.

The original church, commissioned by Emperor Constantine, was built around 349 on the site where St Peter is said to have been buried between AD 64 and 67. Like many medieval churches, it eventually fell into disrepair and it wasn't until the mid-15th century that efforts were made to restore it, first by Pope Nicholas V and then, rather more successfully, by Julius II.

In 1506 construction began on a design by Bramante, but building ground to a halt when the architect died in 1514. In 1547 Michelangelo stepped in to take on the project. He simplified Bramante's plans and drew up designs for what was to become his greatest architectural achievement: the dome. Sadly, Michelangelo didn't live to see the basilica built – architects Giacomo della Porta and Domenico Fontana completed the dome to his design and Carlo Maderno

Michaelangelo's *Pietà*

SERGIO BERTINO/SHUTTERSTOCK ©

⚓ Explore Ashore

St Peter's is easily accessed by metro from Stazione Termini (Line A; direction Battistini). A taxi will cost around €15. You'll need at least 45 minutes to visit.

ℹ Need to Know

Basilica di San Pietro; ☎06 6988 3731; www. vatican.va; St Peter's Sq; ⊘7am-7pm Apr-Sep, to 6pm Oct-Mar; ⎙Piazza del Risorgimento, ⓂOttaviano-San Pietro; `FREE`

designed the monumental facade. The basilica was finally consecrated in 1626.

Strict dress codes are enforced: no shorts, miniskirts or bare shoulders.

Facade

Built between 1608 and 1612, Maderno's immense facade is 48m high and 115m wide. Eight 27m-high columns support the upper attic on which 13 statues stand representing Christ the Redeemer, St John the Baptist and 11 of the apostles. The central balcony, the **Loggia della Benedizione**, is where the pope stands to deliver his *Urbi et Orbi* blessing at Christmas and Easter.

Interior

At the beginning of the right aisle is Michelangelo's hauntingly beautiful *Pietà*. Sculpted when the artist was 25, it's the

only work he ever signed; his signature is etched into the sash across the Madonna's breast. On a pillar just beyond the *Pietà*, Carlo Fontana's gilt and bronze **monument to Queen Christina of Sweden** commemorates the Swedish monarch who converted to Catholicism in 1655.

Moving on, you'll come to the **Cappella di San Sebastiano**, home of Pope John Paul II's tomb, and the **Cappella del Santissimo Sacramento**, a sumptuously decorated baroque chapel with works by Borromini, Bernini and Pietro da Cortona. Beyond the chapel, the grandiose **monument to Gregory XIII** sits near the roped-off **Cappella Gregoriana**, built by Gregory XIII from designs by Michelangelo.

Much of the right transept is closed off, but you can make out the **monument to Clement XIII**, one of Canova's most famous works.

Dominating the centre of the basilica is Bernini's 29m-high **baldachin**. Supported by four spiral columns and made with bronze taken from the Pantheon, it stands over the **papal altar**, which itself stands over St Peter's original grave. Above the baldachin, Michelangelo's **dome** soars to a height of 119m. It's supported by four massive stone **piers** named after the saints whose statues adorn the Bernini-designed niches – Longinus, Helena, Veronica and Andrew.

At the base of the **Pier of St Longinus** is Arnolfo di Cambio's much-loved 13th-century bronze **statue of St Peter**, whose right foot has been worn down by centuries of caresses.

Dominating the tribune behind the altar is Bernini's extraordinary **Cattedra di San Pietro**, centred on a wooden seat once thought to have been St Peter's, but in fact dating to the 9th century. To the right of the throne, Bernini's **monument to Urban VIII**

depicts the pope flanked by the figures of Charity and Justice.

In the roped-off left transept, the **Cappella della Madonna della Colonna** takes its name from the Madonna that stares out from Giacomo della Porta's marble altar. To its right, above the **tomb of St Leo the Great**, is a fine relief by Alessandro Algardi. Under the next arch is Bernini's **monument to Alexander VII**.

Near the head of the left aisle are the so-called **Stuart monuments**. On the right is the monument to Clementina Sobieska, wife of James Stuart, by Filippo Barigioni, and on the left is Canova's vaguely erotic monument to the last three members of the Stuart clan, the pretenders to the English throne who died in exile in Rome.

Dome of Saint Peter's Basilica

Dome

From the **dome** (with/without lift €10/8; ⊘8am-6pm Apr-Sep, to 5pm Oct-Mar) entrance, you can walk the 551 steps to the top or take a small lift halfway and then follow on foot for the last 320 steps. Either way, it's a long, steep climb. But you'll be rewarded with stunning views from a perch 120m above St Peter's Square.

Free Tours

Free English-language tours of the basilica are run by seminarians from the Pontifical North American College (www.pnac.org), usually departing 2.15pm Monday, Wednesday and Friday from the Ufficio Pellegrini e Turisti. No tickets necessary, but check the website to verify tour dates.

BILL PERRY/SHUTTERSTOCK ©

Museo Storico Artistico

Accessed from the left nave, the **Museo Storico Artistico** (Tesoro, Treasury; ☎06 6988 1840; €5 incl audio guide; ⊘9am-6.10pm Apr-Sep, to 5.10pm Oct-Mar, last entrance 30min before closing) sparkles with sacred relics. Highlights include a tabernacle by Donatello and the 6th-century *Crux Vaticana*.

Vatican Grottoes

Extending beneath the basilica, the **Vatican Grottoes** (⊘8am-5pm Apr-Sep, to 4pm Oct-Mar) FREE contain the tombs and sarcophagi of numerous popes, as well as several columns from the original 4th-century basilica. The entrance is in the Pier of St Andrew.

St Peter's Tomb

Excavations beneath the basilica uncovered part of the original church and what archaeologists believe is the **Tomb of St Peter** (☎06 6988 5318; www.scavi.va; €13). The excavations can only be visited by guided tour; book online well in advance.

What's Nearby?

Laid out between 1656 and 1667 to a design by Gian Lorenzo Bernini, when seen from above **St Peter's Square** resembles a giant keyhole with two semicircular colonnades, each consisting of four rows of Doric columns, encircling a giant ellipse that straightens out to funnel believers into the basilica. Bernini described the colonnades as representing 'the motherly arms of the church'.

★ Local Knowledge

Near the main entrance, a red floor disc marks the spot where Charlemagne and later Holy Roman emperors were crowned by the pope.

VIACHESLAV LOPATIN/SHUTTERSTOCK ©

Roman Forum

The Roman Forum was ancient Rome's showpiece centre, a grandiose district of temples, basilicas and vibrant public spaces. Nowadays, it's a collection of impressive, if sketchily labelled, ruins that can leave you drained and confused. But there's something wonderfully compelling about walking in the footsteps of Julius Caesar and other legendary figures of Roman history.

Originally an Etruscan burial ground, the Forum was first developed in the 7th century BC, growing over time to become the social, political and commercial hub of the Roman Empire. But like many of ancient Rome's great urban developments, it fell into disrepair after the fall of the Roman Empire until eventually it was used as pasture land. In the Middle Ages it was known as the Campo Vaccino ('Cow Field') and extensively plundered for its stone and marble. The area was systematically excavated in the 18th and 19th centuries, and excavations continue to this day.

Via Sacra to Campidoglio

Entering the Forum from Largo della Salara Vecchia – you can also enter directly from the Palatino or via an entrance near

Great For...

☑ **Don't Miss**

The frescoed Chiesa di Santa Maria Antiqua (p210).

⚓

Explore Ashore

The Roman Forum is easily accessed by metro from Stazione Termini station (Line B; direction Laurentina; Colosseo stop). A taxi from the station costs around €8. You'll need at least 45 minutes to explore.

❶ Need to Know

Foro Romano; ☏06 3996 7700; www.parcocolosseo.it; Largo della Salara Vecchia, Piazza di Santa Maria Nova; adult/reduced incl Colosseum & Palatino €12/7.50, SUPER ticket €18/13.50; ◷8.30am-1hr before sunset; SUPER ticket sites Tue, Thu, Sat & afternoon Sun only; 🚍Via dei Fori Imperiali

---

the Arco di Tito – you'll see the **Tempio di Antonino e Faustina** ahead to your left. Erected in AD 141, this was transformed into a church in the 8th century, the Chiesa di San Lorenzo in Miranda. To your right, the 179 BC **Basilica Fulvia Aemilia** was a 100m-long public hall with a two-storey porticoed facade.

At the end of the path, you'll come to **Via Sacra**, the Forum's main thoroughfare, and the **Tempio di Giulio Cesare**, which stands on the spot where Julius Caesar was cremated after his assassination in 44 BC.

Heading right up Via Sacra brings you to the **Curia**, the original seat of the Roman Senate, though what you see today is a reconstruction of how it looked in the reign of Diocletian (r 284–305). At the

end of Via Sacra, the **Arco di Settimio Severo** (Arch of Septimius Severus) was built in AD 203 to commemorate the Roman victory over the Parthians. Close by, the **Colonna di Foca** (Column of Phocus) rises above what was once the Forum's main square, **Piazza del Foro**.

The eight granite columns that rise behind the Colonna are all that survive of the **Tempio di Saturno** (Temple of Saturn), an important temple that doubled as the state treasury. Behind it are (from north to south): the ruins of the **Tempio della Concordia** (Temple of Concord), the **Tempio di Vespasiano** (Temple of Vespasian and Titus) and the **Portico degli Dei Consenti**.

Tempio di Castore e Polluce & Casa delle Vestali

From the path that runs parallel to Via Sacra, you'll pass the stubby ruins of the **Basilica Giulia**. At the end of the basilica, three columns remain from the 5th-century-BC **Tempio di Castore e Polluce** (Temple of Castor and Pollux).

Nearby, the 6th-century **Chiesa di Santa Maria Antiqua** (SUPER ticket adult/reduced €18/13.50; ☺9am-6.30pm Tue, Thu & Sat, from 2pm Sun summer, 9am-3.30pm Tue, Thu & Sat, from 2pm Sun winter) is the oldest church in the Forum, a veritable treasure trove of early Christian art. Accessible from in front of the church is the **Rampa imperiale** (Domitian's Ramp; SUPER ticket adult/reduced €18/13.50; ☺9am-6.30pm Tue, Thu & Sat, from 2pm Sun summer, 9am-3.30pm Tue, Thu & Sat, from 2pm Sun winter), a passageway that linked the Forum to the Palatine.

Back towards Via Sacra is the **Casa delle Vestali** (House of the Vestal Virgins), home of the virgins who tended the flame in the adjoining **Tempio di Vesta**.

Via Sacra Towards the Colosseum

Heading up Via Sacra past the **Tempio di Romolo** (Temple of Romulus; SUPER ticket adult/reduced €18/13.50; ☺9am-6.30pm Tue, Thu & Sat, from 2pm Sun summer, 9am-3.30pm Tue, Thu & Sat, from 2pm Sun winter), you'll come to the **Basilica di Massenzio** (Basilica di Costantino), the largest building on the forum.

Beyond the basilica, the **Arco di Tito** (Arch of Titus) was built in AD 81 to cele-

Tempio di Romolo & Basilica di Massenzio

brate the victories of Titus, Domitian's brother, against rebels in Jerusalem.

What's Nearby?

The area surrounding the Roman Forum is littered with forums and monuments dating from ancient times, including the sprawl of ruins over the road from the Roman Forum that is known collectively as the **Imperial Forums** (Fori Imperiali; ☑ 06 06 08; Piazza Santa Maria di Loreto; adult/reduced €4/3, free 1st Sun of month Oct-Mar; ☺ by reservation). Constructed between 42 BC and AD 112, they include the **Mercati di Traiano** (Trajan's Markets), accessible through the **Museo dei Fori**

✕ Take a Break

Alongside its views of the Colonna di Traiano, Terre e Domus (p223) offers regional dishes and Lazio wines.

VIACHESLAV LOPATIN/SHUTTERSTOCK ©

Imperiali (☑ 06 06 08; www.mercatiditraiano.it; Via IV Novembre 94; adult/reduced incl exhibition €11.50/9.50; ☺ 9.30am-7.30pm; ▣ Via IV Novembre), and the magnificent **Colonna Traiana** (Trajan's Column).

Sandwiched between the Roman Forum and the Circo Massimo, the **Palatino** (Palatine Hill; ☑ 06 3996 7700; www.parcocolosseo.it; Via di San Gregorio 30, Piazza di Santa Maria Nova; adult/reduced incl Colosseum & Roman Forum €12/7.50, SUPER ticket €18/13.50; ☺ 8.30am-1hr before sunset, some SUPER ticket sites Mon, Wed, Fri & morning Sun only; Ⓜ Colosseo) is one of Rome's most spectacular sights, an atmospheric area of towering pine trees, majestic ruins and unforgettable views. This is where Romulus supposedly founded the city in 753 BC and Rome's emperors lived in palatial luxury. Look out for the **stadio** (stadium) and the ruins of the **Domus Flavia** (imperial palace), and don't miss the grandstand views over the Roman Forum from the Orti Farnesiani.

Roman Forum

A HISTORICAL TOUR

In ancient times, a forum was a market place, civic centre and religious complex all rolled into one, and the greatest of all was the Roman Forum (Foro Romano). Situated between the Palatino (Palatine Hill), ancient Rome's most exclusive neighbourhood, and the Campidoglio (Capitoline Hill), it was the city's busy, bustling centre. On any given day it teemed with activity. Senators debated affairs of state in the ❶ **Curia**, shoppers thronged the squares and traffic-free streets and crowds gathered under the ❷ **Colonna di Foca** to listen to politicians holding forth from the ❷ **Rostri**. Elsewhere, lawyers worked the courts in basilicas including the ❸ **Basilica di Massenzio**, while the Vestal Virgins quietly went about their business in the ❹ **Casa delle Vestali**.

Special occasions were also celebrated in the Forum: religious holidays were marked with ceremonies at temples such as ❺ **Tempio di Saturno** and ❻ **Tempio di Castore e Polluce**, and military victories were honoured with dramatic processions up Via Sacra and the building of monumental arches like ❼ **Arco di Settimio Severo** and ❽ **Arco di Tito**.

The ruins you see today are impressive but they can be confusing without a clear picture of what the Forum once looked like. This spread shows the Forum in its heyday, complete with temples, civic buildings and towering monuments to heroes of the Roman Empire.

TOP TIPS

➡ Get grandstand views of the Forum from the Palatino and Campidoglio.

➡ Visit first thing in the morning or late afternoon; crowds are worst between 11am and 2pm.

➡ In summer it gets hot in the Forum and there's little shade, so take a hat and plenty of water.

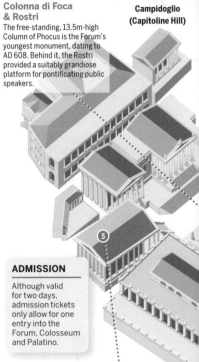

Colonna di Foca & Rostri
The free-standing, 13.5m-high Column of Phocus is the Forum's youngest monument, dating to AD 608. Behind it, the Rostri provided a suitably grandiose platform for pontificating public speakers.

Campidoglio (Capitoline Hill)

ADMISSION

Although valid for two days, admission tickets only allow for one entry into the Forum, Colosseum and Palatino.

Tempio di Saturno
Ancient Rome's Fort Knox, the Temple of Saturn was the city treasury. In Caesar's day it housed 13 tonnes of gold, 114 tonnes of silver and 30 million sestertii worth of silver coins.

IASCIC/SHUTTERSTOCK©

VIACHESLAV LOPATIN/SHUTTERSTOCK ©

Tempio di Castore e Polluce
Only three columns of the Temple of Castor and Pollux remain. The temple was dedicated to the Heavenly Twins after they supposedly led the Romans to victory over the Latin League in 496 BC.

Arco di Settimio Severo

One of the Forum's signature monuments, this imposing triumphal arch commemorates the military victories of Septimius Severus. Relief panels depict his campaigns against the Parthians.

Curia

This big barn-like building was the official seat of the Roman Senate. Most of what you see is a reconstruction, but the interior marble floor dates to the 3rd-century reign of Diocletian.

Basilica di Massenzio

Marvel at the scale of this vast 4th-century basilica. In its original form the central hall was divided into enormous naves; now only part of the northern nave survives.

Via Sacra

Tempio di Giulio Cesare

JULIUS CAESAR

Julius Caesar was cremated on the site where the Tempio di Giulio Cesare now stands.

Arco di Tito

Said to be the inspiration for the Arc de Triomphe in Paris, the well-preserved Arch of Titus was built by the emperor Domitian to honour his elder brother Titus.

Casa delle Vestali

White statues line the grassy atrium of what was once the luxurious 50-room home of the Vestal Virgins. The virgins played an important role in Roman religion, serving the goddess Vesta.

Centro Storico Piazzas

Rome's *centro storico* boasts some of the city's most celebrated piazzas, and several lovely but lesser-known squares. Each has its own character, but together they encapsulate much of the city's beauty, history and drama.

Start Piazza Colonna
Distance 1.5km
Duration 3½ hours

Classic Photo Piazza della Rotonda with the Pantheon in the background.

4 It's a short walk along Via del Seminario to Piazza della Rotonda, where the **Pantheon** (p218) needs no introduction.

5 Piazza Navona (p218) is Rome's great showpiece square, where you can compare the two giants of Roman baroque – Gian Lorenzo Bernini and Francesco Borromini.

Corso del Rinascimento

Via della Dogana Vecchia

Piazza della Rotonda

Salita dei Crescenzi

Piazza Navona

Via degli Staderari

Via della Rotonda

Piazza Sant'Eustachio

Via del Canestrari

Via della Cuccagna

Piazza di San Pantaleo

Via Monterone

Via dei Cappellari

Corso Vittorio Emanuele II

Via del Monserrato

Via dei Baullari

Via dei Giubbonari

Lgt dei Tebaldi

Tiber

FINISH

Take a break... Those in the know head to **Forno Roscioli** (p226) for some of Rome's best pizza by the slice.

7 Just beyond the Campo, the more sober **Piazza Farnese** is overshadowed by the austere facade of the Renaissance **Palazzo Farnese**.

0
200 m
0
0.1 miles
N
START
Piazza di Montecitorio
Via di Pietra
Via dei Pastini
Via del Caravita
Via del Seminario
Via di Sant'Ignazio
Via della Minerva
Via del Corso
1
2
3

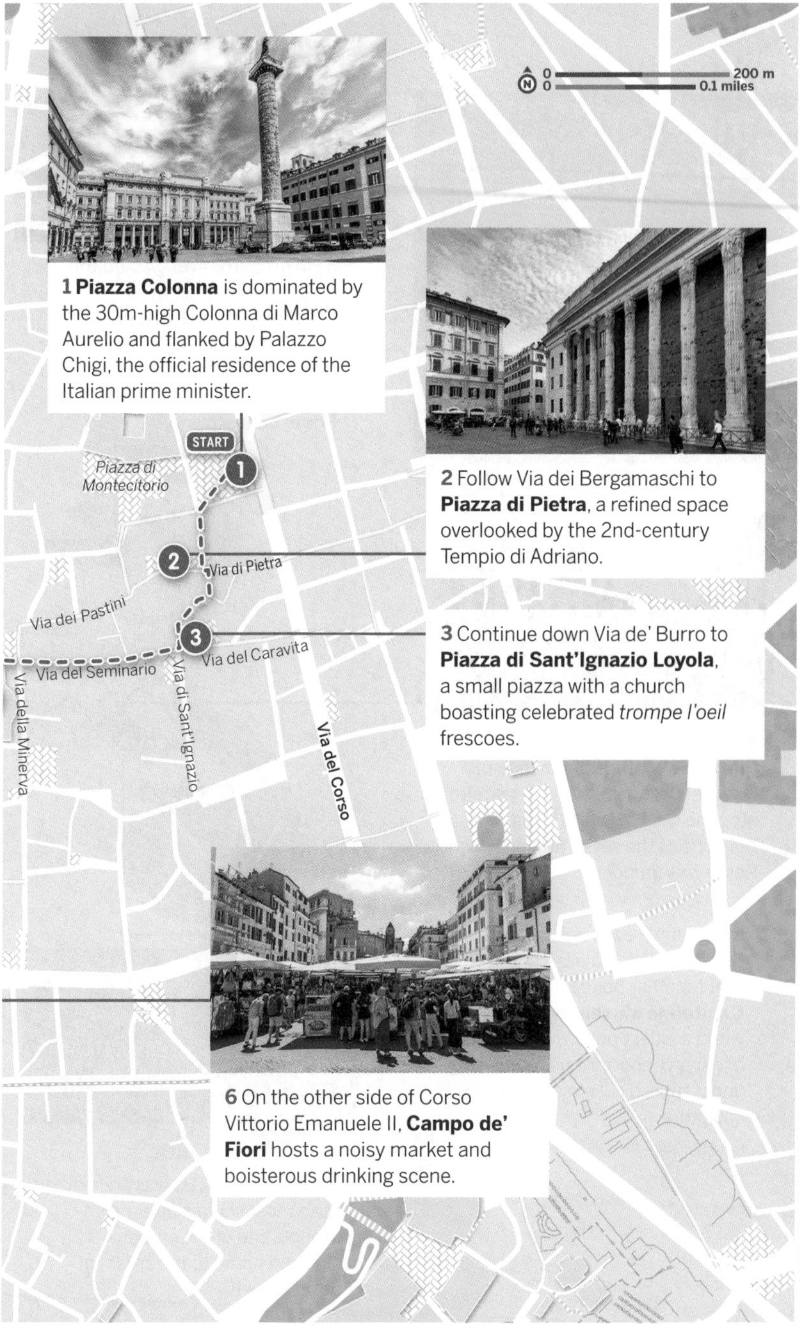

1 Piazza Colonna is dominated by the 30m-high Colonna di Marco Aurelio and flanked by Palazzo Chigi, the official residence of the Italian prime minister.

2 Follow Via dei Bergamaschi to **Piazza di Pietra**, a refined space overlooked by the 2nd-century Tempio di Adriano.

3 Continue down Via de' Burro to **Piazza di Sant'Ignazio Loyola**, a small piazza with a church boasting celebrated *trompe l'oeil* frescoes.

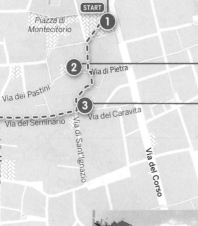

6 On the other side of Corso Vittorio Emanuele II, **Campo de' Fiori** hosts a noisy market and boisterous drinking scene.

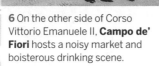

1 BRIAN KINNEY/SHUTTERSTOCK © 2 LASZLO SZIRTESI/SHUTTERSTOCK © 4 KAMIRA/SHUTTERSTOCK © 5 GIVAGA/SHUTTERSTOCK © 6 CHRISTIAN MUELLER/SHUTTERSTOCK ©

Emperors' Footsteps

Follow in the footsteps of an ancient Roman on this whistle-stop tour of the city's most famous ruins.

Start Colosseum
Distance 1.5km
Duration Four hours

6 No emperor ever walked the massive mountain of white marble that is **Vittoriano**, but it's worth stopping off to take the panoramic lift to the top, from where you can see the whole of Rome beneath you.

4 The Michelangelo-designed **Piazza del Campidoglio**, one of Rome's most beautiful piazzas, sits atop the Campidoglio (Capitoline Hill), one of the seven hills on which Rome was founded.

5 Flanking Piazza del Campidoglio are two stately *palazzi* (mansions) that together house the **Capitoline Museums**. These, the world's oldest public museums, boast an important picture gallery and a superb collection of classical sculpture.

Take a break... Hidden away in the Capitoline Museums but accessible by its own entrance, the **Terrazza Caffarelli** (📞06 6919 0564; 🕘9.30am-7pm) is a convenient spot for a coffee with magical views.

2 The **Palatino** (p211) was ancient Rome's most sought-after neighbourhood, site of the emperor's palace and home to the cream of imperial society.

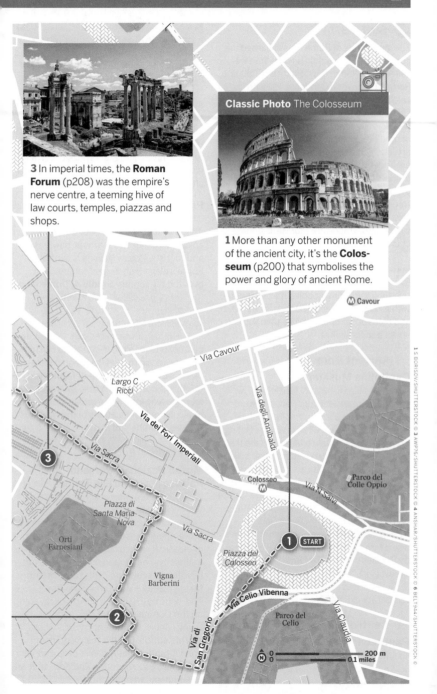

3 In imperial times, the **Roman Forum** (p208) was the empire's nerve centre, a teeming hive of law courts, temples, piazzas and shops.

Classic Photo The Colosseum

1 More than any other monument of the ancient city, it's the **Colosseum** (p200) that symbolises the power and glory of ancient Rome.

Ⓜ Cavour

Via Cavour

Largo C
Ricci

Via dei Fori Imperiali

Via degli Annibaldi

Via Sacra

3

Piazza di
Santa Maria
Nova

Via Sacra

Colosseo
Ⓜ

Parco del
Colle Oppio

Via N Salvi

Orti
Farnesiani

1 START

Vigna
Barberini

Piazza del
Colosseo

2

Via Celio Vibenna

Via di San Gregorio

Parco del
Celio

Via Claudia

Ⓝ 0 _____ 200 m
0 _____ 0.1 miles

◎ SIGHTS

The great icons of Rome's classical age are concentrated in a tightly packed area we call Ancient Rome: the Colosseum, Palatino, Roman Forum and Capitoline Hill with its celebrated museums are all here, within easy walking distance of each other. Northwest lies the *centro storico* with its labyrinth of medieval lanes, animated piazzas and art-laden churches. Immediately northeast are Tridente, Trevi and Quirinale, where tourists flock to admire the iconic Spanish Steps and Trevi Fountain. East of these three neighbourhoods lies Esquilino, the area around Rome's central train station, where some important museums and churches are located.

Across the Tiber River is Vatican City, home to the Vatican Museums and St Peter's Basilica. To its south, on the same side of the river, is Trastevere, a cobbled maze peppered with exquisite churches, Renaissance *palazzi* and more photo opportunities than you can shake a selfie stick at.

◎ Ancient Rome

Capitoline Museums   Museum

(Map p220; Musei Capitolini; ☑06 06 08; www. museicapitolini.org; Piazza del Campidoglio 1; adult/reduced €11.50/9.50; ☺9.30am-7.30pm, last admission 6.30pm; ☒Piazza Venezia) Dating from 1471, the Capitoline Museums are the world's oldest public museums. Their collection of classical sculpture is one of Italy's finest, boasting works such as the iconic *Lupa Capitolina* (Capitoline Wolf), a life-size bronze of a she-wolf suckling Romulus and Remus, and the *Galata morente* (Dying Gaul), a moving depiction of a dying warrior. There's also a formidable gallery with masterpieces by the likes of Titian, Tintoretto, Rubens and Caravaggio.

Ticket prices increase when there's a temporary exhibition on.

◎ Centro Storico

Pantheon   Church

(Map p225; www.pantheonroma.com; Piazza della Rotonda; ☺8.30am-7.30pm Mon-Sat, 9am-6pm Sun; ☒Largo di Torre Argentina) **FREE** A striking 2000-year-old temple, now a church, the Pantheon is the best preserved of Rome's ancient monuments and one of the most influential buildings in the Western world. Built by Hadrian over Marcus Agrippa's earlier 27 BC temple, it has stood since around AD 125, and while its greying, pockmarked exterior might look its age, it's still a unique and exhilarating experience to pass through its vast bronze doors and gaze up at the largest unreinforced concrete dome ever built.

Piazza Navona   Piazza

(Map p225; ☒Corso del Rinascimento) With its showy fountains, baroque *palazzi* and colourful cast of street artists, hawkers and tourists, Piazza Navona is central Rome's elegant showcase square. Built over the 1st-century **Stadio di Domiziano** (Domitian's Stadium; ☑06 6880 5311; www. stadiodomiziano.com; Via di Tor Sanguigna 3; adult/reduced €8/6; ☺10am-6.30pm Sun-Fri, to 7.30pm Sat), it was paved over in the 15th century and for almost 300 years hosted the city's main market. Its grand centrepiece is Bernini's **Fontana dei Quattro Fiumi** (Fountain of the Four Rivers), a flamboyant fountain featuring an Egyptian obelisk and muscular personifications of the rivers Nile, Ganges, Danube and Plate.

◎ Monti & Esquilino

Museo Nazionale Romano: Palazzo Massimo alle Terme   Museum

(☑06 3996 7700; www.coopculture.it; Largo di Villa Peretti 1; adult/reduced €10/5; ☺9am-7.45pm Tue-Sun; ☒Termini) One of Rome's pre-eminent museums, this treasure trove of classical art is a must-see when you're in the city. The ground and 1st floors are devoted to sculpture, with some breathtaking pieces – don't miss *The Boxer*, a 2nd-century-BC Greek bronze excavated on the Quirinal Hill in 1885, and the *Dying Niobid*, a 4th-century-BC Greek marble statue. But it's the magnificent and vibrantly coloured Villa Livia and Villa Farnesia frescoes on the 2nd floor that are the undisputed highlights.

◎ Tridente & Trevi

Piazza di Spagna & the Spanish Steps
Piazza

(Map p224; Ⓜ Spagna) A magnet for visitors since the 18th century, the Spanish Steps (Scalinata della Trinità dei Monti) provide a perfect people-watching perch. The 135 gleaming steps rise from Piazza di Spagna to the landmark **Chiesa della Trinità dei Monti** (☑06 679 41 79; http://trinitadeimonti. net/it/chiesa/; Piazza Trinità dei Monti 3; ◷10.15am-8pm Tue-Thu, noon-9pm Fri, 9.15am-8pm Sat, 9am-8pm Sun).

Piazza di Spagna was named after the Spanish Embassy to the Holy See, although the staircase, designed by the Italian Francesco de Sanctis, was built in 1725 with money bequeathed by a French diplomat.

Trevi Fountain
Fountain

(Map p224; Fontana di Trevi; Piazza di Trevi; Ⓜ Barberini) The Fontana di Trevi, scene of movie star Anita Ekberg's late-night dip in *La Dolce Vita,* is a flamboyant baroque ensemble of mythical figures and wild horses taking up the entire side of the 17th-century Palazzo Poli. After a Fendi-sponsored restoration finished in 2015, the fountain gleams brighter than it has for years. The tradition is to toss a coin into the water, thus ensuring that you'll return to Rome – on average about €3000 is thrown in every day.

◎ Vatican City, Borgo & Prati

Vatican Museums
Museum

(Map p228; Musei Vaticani; ☑06 6988 4676; www. museivaticani.va; Viale Vaticano; adult/reduced €17/8; ◷9am-6pm Mon-Sat, to 2pm last Sun of month, last entry 2hr before closing; ☐Piazza del Risorgimento, ⓂOttaviano-San Pietro) Founded by Pope Julius II in the early 16th century and enlarged by successive pontiffs, the Vatican Museums boast one of the world's greatest art collections. Exhibits, which are displayed along about 7km of halls and corridors, range from Egyptian mummies and Etruscan bronzes to ancient busts, old masters and modern paintings. Highlights include the spectacular collection of classical statuary in the **Museo Pio-Clementino**,

a suite of rooms frescoed by Raphael, and the Michelangelo-painted **Sistine Chapel**.

⊙ TOURS

A Friend in Rome
Tours

(☑340 5019201; www.afriendinrome.it) Silvia Prosperi and her team offer a range of private tours covering the Vatican and main historic centre, plus areas outside the capital. They can also organise kid-friendly tours, food-and-wine itineraries, vintage-car drives and horse rides along Via Appia Antica. Rates start at €165 for a basic three-hour tour (up to eight people); add €55 for every additional hour.

Roman Guy
Tours

(☑342 8761859; https://theromanguy.com) A professional setup that organises a wide

Ancient Rome

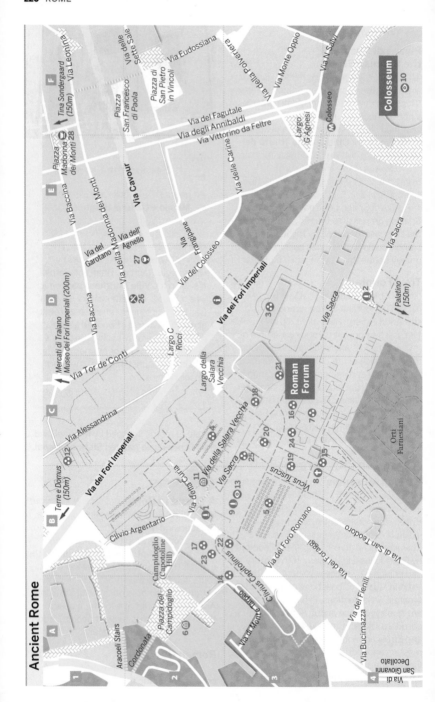

Ancient Rome

range of group and private tours. Packages, led by English-speaking experts, include skip-the-line visits to the Vatican Museums and St Peter's Basilica (€60), tours of the Colosseum and Roman Forum (€65), and foodie tours of Trastevere (€90 including dinner). Day trips to Florence and Pompeii are also available.

Open Bus Vatican & Rome Bus

(www.operaromanapellegrinaggi.org/it/roma-cristiana/open-bus-vatican-rome; tour €12, 24/48hr ticket €25/28) The Vatican-sponsored Opera Romana Pellegrinaggi runs a hop-on, hop-off bus departing from Piazza Pia and Termini. Stops are situated near main sights, including St Peter's Basilica, Piazza Navona and the Colosseum. Tickets are available on board, online or at the info point just off St Peter's Square.

🔒 SHOPPING

Tridente is queen of Rome shopping. Main street Via del Corso and the streets surrounding it are lined cheek by jowl with beautiful boutiques selling everything from savvy street wear and haute-couture fashion to handmade paper stationery, artisan jewellery, perfume, homewares and food. Specialist streets include quaint Via Margutta for antiques; Via dei Condotti for designer fashion; and Via della Pugna for small, independent boutiques.

🔒 Centro Storico

Ibiz – Artigianato in Cuoio Fashion & Accessories

(Map p225; 🗹 06 6830 7297; www.ibizroma.it; Via dei Chiavari 39; ⊙10am-7.30pm Mon-Sat; 🚌Corso Vittorio Emanuele II) In her diminutive family workshop, Elisa Nepi and her team craft beautiful butter-soft leather wallets, bags, belts, keyrings and sandals, in elegant designs and myriad colours. You can pick up a belt for about €35, while for a shoulder bag you should bank on around €145.

Bartolucci Toys

(Map p225; 🗹 06 6919 0894; www.bartolucci. com; Via dei Pastini 98; ⊙10am-10pm; 🚌Via del Corso) It's difficult to resist going into this magical toyshop where everything is carved out of wood. By the main entrance, a Pinocchio pedals his bike robotically, perhaps dreaming of the full-size motorbike parked nearby, while inside there are all manner of ticking clocks, rocking horses, planes and more Pinocchios than you're likely to see in your whole life.

Marta Ray Shoes

(Map p228; 🗹 06 6880 2641; www.martaray.it; Via dei Coronari 121; ⊙10am-8pm; 🚌Via Zanardelli)

Women's ballet flats, and elegant, everyday bags in rainbow colours and super-soft leather, are the hallmarks of the Rome-born Marta Ray brand. At this store, one of three in town, you'll find a selection of trademark ballerinas as well as ankle boots and an attractive line in modern, beautifully designed handbags.

You'll find branch stores at Via della Reginella 4 in the Jewish Ghetto and Via del Moro 6 in Trastevere.

Calzoleria Petrocchi
Shoes

(Map p228; ☑06 687 62 89; www.calzoleria-petrocchi.it; Vicolo Sugarelli 2; ☉7am-1pm & 2-5.30pm Mon-Fri, 8am-1pm Sat, by appointment Sun; ☐Corso Vittorio Emanuele II) This historic shoemaker has been hand-crafting leather shoes for well-heeled Romans and film icons such as Audrey Hepburn and Robert De Niro since 1946. Choose from the ready-to-wear collection or design a bespoke pair of your own: head artisan Marco Cecchi personally takes clients' measurements and customises shoes based on their selection of leather and style.

🅐 Monti & Esquilino

Perlei
Jewellery

(☑06 4891 3862; www.perlei.com; Via del Boschetto 35; ☉10am-8pm Mon-Sat, 11am-2pm & 3-7pm Sun; ⓜCavour) Pieces of avant-garde body jewellery catch the eye in the window of this tiny artisan jeweller on Monti's best shopping street. Inside, handmade pieces by Tammar Edelman and Elinor Avni will appeal to those with a modernist aesthetic – their graceful arcs, sinuous strands and architectural arrangements are elegant and eye-catching.

There's a second store at Via di Ripetta 10, near Piazza del Popolo.

Tina Sondergaard
Fashion & Accessories

(☑06 8365 57 61; www.facebook.com/tina.sonder gaard.rome; Via del Boschetto 1d; ☉10.30am-7.30pm Mon-Sat, closed Aug; ⓜCavour) Sublimely cut and whimsically retro-esque, Tina Sondergaard's handmade creations for women are a hit with the local fashion cognoscenti. Styles change by the week

rather than the season, femininity is the leitmotif, and you can have adjustments made (included in the price). Everything is remarkably well priced considering the quality of the fabrics and workmanship.

There's a second shop at Via del Pellegrino 83, near the Campo de' Fiori.

🅐 Tridente & Trevi

Bomba
Clothing

(☑06 361 28 81; www.cristinabomba.com; Via dell'Oca 39; ☉11am-7.30pm Tue-Sat, from 3.30pm Mon; ⓜFlaminia) Opened by designer Cristina Bomba over four decades ago, this gorgeous boutique is now operated by her fashion-designing children Caterina (womenswear) and Michele (menswear). Using the highest-quality fabrics, their creations are tailored in the next-door atelier (peek through the front window); woollens are produced at a factory just outside the city. Pricey but oh-so-worth-it.

Chiara Baschieri
Clothing

(☑333 6364851; www.chiarabaschieri.it; Via Margutta, cnr Vicolo Orto di Napoli; ☉11am-7pm Tue-Sat; ⓜSpagna) One of Rome's most impressive independent designers, Chiara Baschieri produces classic, meticulously tailored clothing featuring exquisite fabrics. Her style has echoes of 1960s Givenchy – if Audrey Hepburn had ever stopped by, Chiara would no doubt have gained another fan.

Fausto Santini
Shoes

(Map p224; ☑06 678 41 14; www.faustosantini.com; Via Frattina 120; ☉10am-7.30pm Mon-Sat, 11am-7pm Sun; ⓜSpagna) Rome's best-known shoe designer, Fausto Santini is famous for his beguilingly simple, architectural shoe designs, with beautiful boots and shoes made from butter-soft leather. Colours are beautiful, and the quality is impeccable.

Gente
Fashion & Accessories

(☑06 320 76 71; www.genteroma.com; Via del Babuino 77; ☉10.30am-7.30pm Mon-Fri, to 8pm Sat, 11.30am-7.30pm Sun; ⓜSpagna) This multi-label boutique was the first in Rome to bring all the big-name luxury designers

Craftsman at Bartolucci's toyshop (p221)

under one roof and its vast emporium-styled space remains an essential stop for every serious fashionista. Its men's store is across the road, at Via Babuino 185. A second women's store on Via Frattina focuses on accessories.

Flumen Profumi
Perfume

(Map p224; ☎06 6830 7635; www.flumenprofumi. com; Via della Fontanella di Borghese 41; ⊙11am-2pm & 3.30-7.30pm; ☐Via del Corso) Unique 'made in Rome' scents are what this artisan perfumery is all about. Natural perfumes are oil-based, contain four to eight base notes and evoke *la dolce vita* – Incantro fuses pomegranate with white flower, while Ritrovarsi Ancora is a nostalgic fragrance evocative of long, lazy, family meals around a countryside table (smell the fig!).

🅐 Vatican City, Borgo & Prati

Il Sellaio
Fashion & Accessories

(Map p228; ☎06 321 17 19; www.serafinipel-letteria.it; Via Caio Mario 14; ⊙9.30am-7.30pm Mon-Fri, 9.30am-1pm & 3.30-7.30pm Sat; Ⓜ Ottaviano-San Pietro) During the 1960s

Ferruccio Serafini was one of Rome's most sought-after artisans, making handmade leather shoes and bags for the likes of Liz Taylor and Marlon Brando. Nowadays, his daughter Francesca runs the family shop where you can pick up beautiful hand-stitched bags, belts and accessories. Have designs made to order or get your leather handbags and luggage reconditioned.

🅧 EATING

🅧 Ancient Rome

Terre e Domus
Lazio €€

(Map p220; ☎06 6994 0273; Via Foro Traiano 82-4; meals €30-40; ⊙9am-midnight Mon & Wed-Sat, from 10am Sun; ☐Via dei Fori Imperiali) Staffed by young graduates from a local *scuola alberghiera* (catering college), this luminous modern restaurant is the best option in the touristy Forum area. With minimal decor and large windows overlooking the Colonna Traiana, it's a relaxed spot to sit down to rustic local staples, all made with locally sourced ingredients, and a glass or two of regional wine.

Central Rome

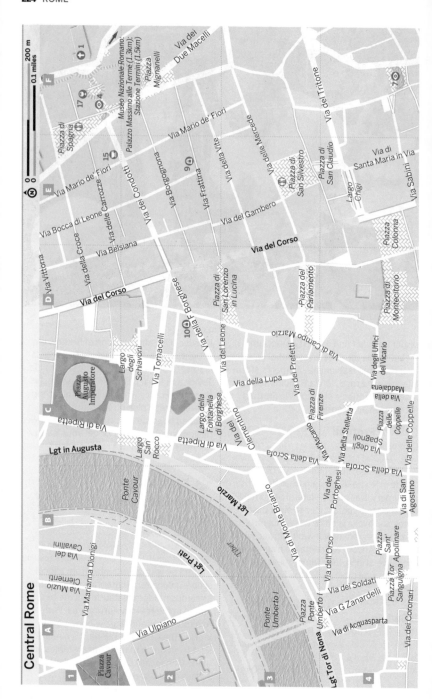

200 m
0.1 miles

Via Muzio Clementi
Via Marianna Dionigi
Piazza Cavour
Via del Cavallini
Via Ulpiano
Lgt Prati
Ponte Cavour
Lgt in Augusta
Via di Ripetta
Piazza Augusto Imperatore
Largo degli Schiavoni
Largo San Rocco
Via Tomacelli
Via di Ripetta
Tevere
Lgt Marzio
Ponte Umberto I
Piazza Ponte Umberto I
Via di Monte Brianzo
Lgt Tor di Nona
Via dell'Orso
Via dei Soldati
Via G Zanardelli
Via di Acquasparta
Piazza Tor Sanguigna
Piazza Sant' Apollinare
Via di San Agostino
Via dei Coronari
Via dei Portoghesi
Piazza di Firenze
Via degli Spagnoli
Via della Stelletta
Via della Scrofa
Via dei Prefetti
Via della Lupa
Via di Campo Marzio
Via degli Uffici del Vicario
Via della Maddalena
Piazza delle Coppelle
Via delle Coppelle
Piazza del Parlamento
Piazza di Montecitorio
Piazza Colonna
Via del Corso
Piazza di San Lorenzo in Lucina
Via del Leone
Via della F Borghese
Largo della Fontanella di Borghese
Via del Clementino
Via della Scrofa
Via Vittoria
Via del Corso
Via della Croce
Via Belsiana
Via Bocca di Leone
Via Mario de' Fiori
Via delle Carrozze
Via del Condotti
Via Borgognona
Via Frattina
Via della Vite
Via Mario de' Fiori
Via del Gambero
Via delle Mercede
Piazza di San Silvestro
Piazza di San Claudio
Largo Chigi
Via del Tritone
Via di Santa Maria in Via
Via Sabini
Piazza di Spagna
Via dei Due Macelli
Piazza Mignanelli
Museo Nazionale Romano: Palazzo Massimo alle Terme (1.3km); Stazione Termini (1.5km)

1
4
17
15
9
10
7

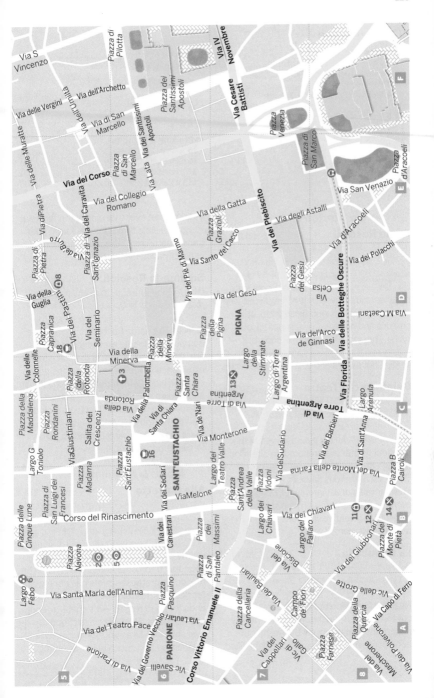

Central Rome

Centro Storico

Forno Roscioli
Bakery €

(Map p225; ☏06 686 40 45; www.anticoforno
roscioli.it; Via dei Chiavari 34; pizza slices from €2,
snacks €2.50; ⊙7am-8pm Mon-Sat, 8.30am-7pm
Sun; 🚇Via Arenula) This is one of Rome's top
bakeries, much loved by lunching locals who
crowd here for luscious sliced pizza, prize
pastries and hunger-sating *supplì* (risotto
balls). The pizza margherita is superb, if
messy to eat, and there's also a counter
serving hot pastas and vegetable side dishes.

Gelateria del Teatro
Gelato €

(Map p228; ☏06 4547 4880; www.gelateria-
delteatro.it; Via dei Coronari 65; gelato from €3;
⊙11am-8pm winter, 10am-10.30pm summer;
🚇Via Zanardelli) All the gelato served at this
excellent gelateria is prepared on-site – look
through the window and you'll see how.
There are numerous flavours, all made from
premium seasonal ingredients, ranging from
evergreen favourites such as pistachio and
hazelnut to inventive creations like rosemary,
honey and lemon.

La Ciambella
Italian €€

(Map p225; ☏06 683 29 30; www.la-ciambella.
it; Via dell'Arco della Ciambella 20; meals €35-45;
⊙noon-11pm Tue-Sun; 🚇Largo di Torre Argentina)
Near the Pantheon but as yet largely undiscovered by the tourist hordes, this friendly
restaurant beats much of the neighbourhood competition. Its handsome, light-filled

interior is set over the ruins of the Terme di
Agrippa, visible through transparent floor
panels, setting an attractive stage for interesting, imaginative food.

Salumeria Roscioli
Ristorante €€€

(Map p225; ☏06 687 52 87; www.salumeria-
roscioli.com; Via dei Giubbonari 21; meals €55;
⊙12.30-4pm & 7pm-midnight Mon-Sat; 🚇Via
Arenula) The name Roscioli has long been
a byword for foodie excellence in Rome,
and this deli-restaurant is the place to
experience it. Tables are set alongside the
counter, laden with mouth-watering Italian
and foreign delicacies, and in a small bot-
tle-lined space behind. The food, including
traditional Roman pastas, is top-notch and
there are some truly outstanding wines.
Reservations essential.

⊗ Monti & Esquilino

Alle Carrette
Pizza €

(Map p220; ☏06 679 27 70; www.facebook.com/
allecarrette; Via della Madonna dei Monti 95;
pizza €5.50-9; ⊙11.30am-4pm & 7pm-midnight;
Ⓜ Cavour) Authentic pizza, super-thin and
swiftly cooked in a wood-burning oven, is
what this traditional Roman pizzeria on one
of Monti's prettiest streets has done well
for decades. Romans pile in here at weekends for good reason – it's cheap, friendly
and delicious. All of the classic toppings are
available, as well as gourmet choices such
as anchovy and zucchini flower (yum!).

Tridente & Trevi

Colline Emiliane
Italian €€

(📞06 481 75 38; www.collineemiliane.com; Via degli Avignonesi 22; meals €45; ⏱12.45-2.45pm & 7.30-10.45pm Tue-Sat, 12.45-2.45pm Sun; ⓂBarberini) Serving sensational regional cuisine from Emilia-Romagna, this restaurant has been operated by the Latini family since 1931; the current owners are Paola (dessert queen) and Anna (watch her making pasta each morning in the glassed-off lab). Our three recommendations when eating here: start with the *antipasti della casa* (€26 for two persons), progress to pasta and don't scrimp on dessert.

Il Margutta
Vegetarian €€

(📞06 3265 0577; www.ilmargutta.bio; Via Margutta 118; lunch buffet weekdays/weekends €15/25, meals €35; ⏱8.30am-11.30pm; 🍴; ⓂSpagna) This chic art-gallery-bar-restaurant is packed at lunchtime with Romans feasting on its good-value, eat-as-much-as-you-can buffet deal. Everything on its menu is organic, and the evening menu is particularly creative – vegetables and pulses combined and presented with care and flair. Among the various tasting menus is a vegan option.

Vatican City, Borgo & Prati

Bonci Pizzarium
Pizza €

(📞06 3974 5416; www.bonci.it; Via della Meloria 43; pizza slices €5; ⏱11am-10pm Mon-Sat, from noon Sun; ⓂCipro) Pizzarium, the takeaway of Gabriele Bonci, Rome's acclaimed pizza emperor, serves Rome's best sliced pizza, bar none. Scissor-cut squares of soft, springy base are topped with original combinations of seasonal ingredients and served for immediate consumption. Often jammed, there are only a couple of benches and stools for the tourist hordes; head across to the plaza at the metro station for a seat.

Cotto Crudo
Sandwiches €

(Map p228; 📞06 6476 0954; www.cottocrudo.it; Borgo Pio 46; panini/mains from €4.50/7; ⏱10am-4.30pm & 6.30-9pm Mon-Wed, to 10pm Thu-Sat, to 8pm Sun; 🛜; 🚇Piazza del Risorgimento, ⓂOtta-

🍽 Roman Cuisine

Like most Italian cuisines, the *cucina romana* (Roman cooking) was born of careful use of local ingredients – making use of the cheaper cuts of meat, like *guanciale* (pig's cheek), and greens that could be gathered wild from the fields.

There are a few classic Roman pasta dishes that almost every trattoria and restaurant in Rome serves. These carb-laden comfort foods are seemingly simple, yet notoriously difficult to prepare well. Iconic Roman dishes include carbonara (pasta with *guanciale,* egg and salty *pecorino romano;* sheep's milk cheese), *alla gricia* (with *guanciale* and onions), *amatriciana* (invented when a chef from Amatrice added tomatoes to *alla gricia*) and *cacio e pepe* (with *pecorino romano* and black pepper).

Other Roman specialities include *baccalà con i ceci* (salted cod with chickpeas), *trippa alla Romana* (tripe stewed in tomato sauce and topped with *pecorino*), *saltimbocca alla Romana* (pan-fried veal escalopes wrapped with prosciutto and sage and finished in white wine) and *coda alla vaccinara* (oxtail stew, cooked with tomato sauce, celery, clove and bitter chocolate).

Carbonara at Salumeria Roscioli

viano-San Pietro) Among the tourist traps on Borgo Pio, the main drag through what's left of the medieval Borgo neighbourhood, this hole-in-the-wall sandwich shop is ideal for a Vatican pit stop. Specialising in produce

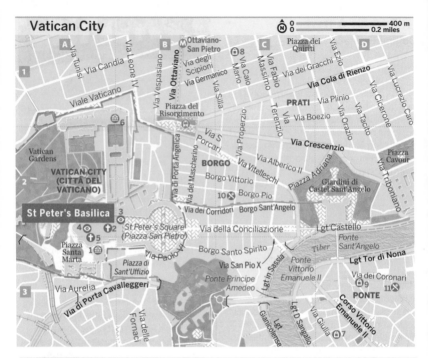

Vatican City

from Emilia-Romagna, it serves *panini* laden with delectable fillings such as aged Parma ham, *mortadella* (pork cold cut; aka high-end baloney) and *culatella* (a type of salami), plus cheeses and vegetables.

 DRINKING & NIGHTLIFE

🚇 Ancient Rome

Cavour 313   Wine Bar
(Map p220; 📞06 678 54 96; www.cavour313.it; Via Cavour 313; ⏰12.30-2.45pm daily & 6-11.30pm Mon-Thu, to midnight Fri & Sat, 7-11pm Sun, closed Aug; Ⓜ Cavour) Cavour 313 is a historic wine

bar, a snug, wood-panelled retreat frequented by everyone from tourists to actors and politicians. It serves a selection of cold cuts and cheeses, as well as daily specials, but the headline act is the wine – with over 1000 mainly Italian labels to choose from, you're sure to find something to tickle your palate.

🚇 Centro Storico

Caffè Sant'Eustachio   Coffee
(Map p225; 📞06 6880 2048; www.santeustachi-oilcaffe.it; Piazza Sant'Eustachio 82; ⏰7.30am-1am Sun-Thu, to 1.30am Fri, to 2am Sat; 🚌Corso del Rinascimento) Always busy, this workaday

cafe near the Pantheon is reckoned by many to serve the best coffee in town. To make it, the bartenders sneakily beat the first drops of an espresso with several teaspoons of sugar to create a frothy paste to which they add the rest of the coffee. The result is superbly smooth.

La Casa del Caffè Tazza d'Oro   Coffee

(Map p225; ✆06 678 97 92; www.tazzadorocof-feeshop.com; Via degli Orfani 84-86; ⏰7am-8pm Mon-Sat, 10.30am-7.30pm Sun; ☐Via del Corso) A busy cafe with burnished 1940s fittings, this is one of Rome's best coffee houses. Its position near the Pantheon makes it touristy but its coffees are brilliant – the espresso hits the mark every time and there's a range of delicious *caffè* concoctions, including *granita di caffè*, a crushed-ice coffee served with whipped cream.

Monti & Esquilino
La Bottega del Caffè   Cafe

(Map p220; ✆06 474 15 78; Piazza Madonna dei Monti 5; ⏰8am-2am; ☎; MCavour) On one of Rome's prettiest squares in Monti, La Bottega del Caffè – named after a comedy by Carlo Goldoni – is the hotspot in Monti for lingering over excellent coffee, drinks, snacks and lunch or dinner. Heaters in winter ensure balmy al fresco action year-round.

Tridente & Trevi
Antico Caffè Greco   Cafe

(Map p224; ✆06 679 17 00; www.facebook.com/AnticoCaffeGreco; Via dei Condotti 86; ⏰9am-9pm; MSpagna) Rome's oldest cafe, open since 1760, is still working the look with the utmost elegance: waiters in black tails and bow tie or frilly white pinnies, scarlet flock walls and age-spotted gilt mirrors. Prices reflect this amazing heritage: pay €9 for a cappuccino sitting down or join locals for the same (€2.50) standing at the bar.

Il Palazzetto   Cocktail Bar

(Map p224; ✆06 6993 4560; Vicolo del Bottino 8; ⏰noon-6pm winter, 4pm-midnight summer, closed in bad weather; MSpagna) No terrace proffers such a fine view of the Spanish Steps over an expertly shaken cocktail.

Ride the lift up from the discreet entrance on narrow Vicolo del Bottino or look for stairs leading to the bar from the top of the steps. Given everything is al fresco, the bar is only open in warm, dry weather.

INFORMATION

Stazione Termini Tourist Information (✆06 06 08; www.turismoroma.it; Via Giovanni Giolitti 34; ⏰8am-6.45pm; MTermini) Located inside the station next to the Mercato Centrale, not far from the car-rental and left-luggage desks. Pick up city maps and reserve city tours at this efficient tourist office.

Fori Imperiali Tourist Information (Via dei Fori Imperiali; ⏰9.30am-7pm, to 8pm Jul & Aug; ☐Via dei Fori Imperiali) Can provide maps, leaflets and a toilet (€1).

GETTING AROUND

Public transport options include buses, trams, metro and a suburban train network. Walking is the best way of getting around the *centro storico*. The main transport hub is Stazione Termini.

Tickets These come in various forms and are valid on all buses, trams and metro lines. Children under 10 travel free. A BIT (single ticket; €1.50) is valid for 100 minutes and can be used on all forms of transport but only once on the metro. A Roma 24-hour ticket costs €7 and can be used on all forms of transport. Buy tickets from the little bus next to the ATAC Information Booth in front of Stazione Termini.

Bus Services are plentiful but not particularly reliable – you're better off taking the metro or a taxi.

Metro The metro network is limited but reasonably efficient. Two main lines serve the centre, A (orange) and B (blue), crossing at Stazione Termini. Take line A for the Trevi Fountain (Barberini), Spanish Steps (Spagna) and St Peter's (Ottaviano–San Pietro).Take line B for the Colosseum (Colosseo) and Roman Forum.

Taxi Official licensed taxis are white with a taxi sign on the roof and Roma Capitale written on the front door along with the taxi's licence number. Always go with the metered fare, never an arranged price.

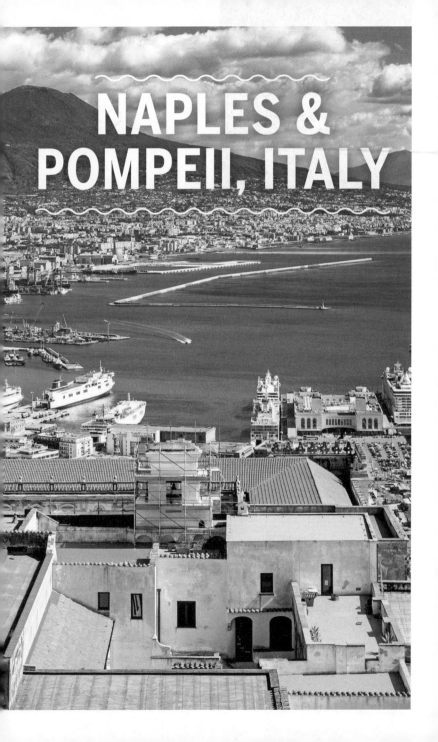

NAPLES &
POMPEII, ITALY

Naples & Pompeii at a Glance...

Italy's third-largest city is one of its oldest, most artistic and most delicious. Naples' centro storico (historic centre) is a Unesco World Heritage Site and its archaeological treasures are among the world's most impressive. Then there's the food: blessed with rich volcanic soils, a bountiful sea and centuries of culinary know-how, the Naples region is one of Italy's epicurean heavyweights. An easy day trip from Naples, you'll find Europe's most compelling archaeological site at the ruins of ancient Pompeii.

With One Day in Port

o Catch the first train out to **Pompeii** (p240) and spend the morning among the ruins before heading back to Naples for lunch at **Salumeria** (p252), a restaurant with a modern twist on traditional recipes.

o Head north to **Museo Archeologico Nazionale** (p234), a treasure chest of ancient art, propaganda and classical sculpture.

o Spend the rest of the afternoon wandering the backstreets to find Naples' hidden **artisan studios**.

Best Places For...

Classical and fine art Museo Archeologico Nazionale (p236)

Eating L'Altro Loco (p253)

Subterranean secrets Catacombe di San Gennaro (p238)

Artisan studios Lello Esposito (p249)

Coffee Caffè Gambrinus (p253)

Previous page: View of Naples and Mount Vesuvius
MARIIA GOLOVIANKO/SHUTTERSTOCK ©

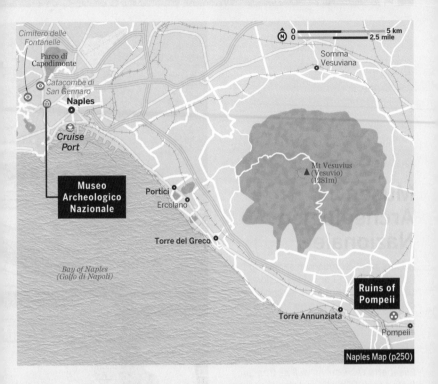

Naples Map (p250)

Getting from the Port

ANM (www.anm.it) operates city buses in Naples. There's no central bus station, but most buses pass through Piazza Garibaldi. Bus 154 runs from the port area to Chiaia along Via Volta, Via Vespucci, Via Marina, Via Depretis, Via Acton, Via Morelli and Piazza Vittoria.

Fast Facts

Currency Euro (€)

Language Italian

Money ATMs are widely available, including at major train stations and at the airport. Credit cards are accepted in most hotels and restaurants.

Tourist information There's a tourist office in the *centro storico* and another opposite Teatro San Carlo.

Visas Generally not required for stays of up to 90 days (or at all for EU nationals); some nationalities need a Schengen visa.

Wi-fi Free wi-fi is common. Many hotels, restaurants, cafes and bars offer it free, though signal strength can vary.

Museo Archeologico Nazionale

Naples' premier museum serves up one of the world's finest collections of Graeco-Roman artefacts. Originally a cavalry barracks and later the seat of the city's university, the museum was established by the Bourbon king Charles VII in the late 18th century to house the antiquities he inherited from his mother, Elisabetta Farnese, as well as treasures looted from Pompeii and Herculaneum.

Great For...

☑ Don't Miss

Toro Farnese, La battaglia di Alessandro contro Dario and *Farnese Atlante.*

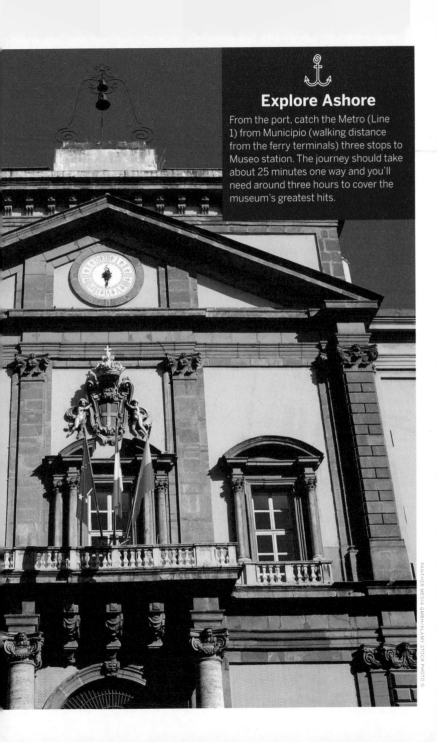

⚓

Explore Ashore

From the port, catch the Metro (Line 1) from Municipio (walking distance from the ferry terminals) three stops to Museo station. The journey should take about 25 minutes one way and you'll need around three hours to cover the museum's greatest hits.

Before tackling the **collection** (☏848 800288; www.museoarcheologiconapoli.it; Piazza Museo Nazionale 19; adult/reduced €15/7.50; ⊙9am-7.30pm Wed-Mon; Ⓜ Museo, Piazza Cavour), consider investing in the *National Archaeological Museum of Naples* (€12), published by Electa. It's also worth calling ahead to ensure that the galleries you want to see are open, as staff shortages often mean that sections of the museum close for part of the day.

Farnese Collection

The basement houses the Borgia collection of Egyptian relics and epigraphs (closed indefinitely on our last visit). The ground-floor Farnese collection of colossal Greek and Roman sculptures features the celebrated *Toro Farnese* (Farnese Bull) and a muscle-bound *Ercole* (Hercules).

Sculpted in the early 3rd century AD and noted in the writings of Pliny, the *Toro Farnese*, probably a Roman copy of a Greek original, depicts the humiliating death of Dirce, Queen of Thebes. According to Greek mythology she was tied to a wild bull by Zeto and Amphion as punishment for her treatment of their mother Antiope, the first wife of King Lykos of Thebes. Carved from a single colossal block of marble, the sculpture was discovered in 1545 near the Baths of Caracalla in Rome and restored by Michelangelo, before eventually being shipped to Naples in 1787.

Ercole was discovered in the same Roman excavations, albeit without his legs. A pair of substitute limbs was made by Guglielmo della Porta, but when the originals turned up at a later dig, the Bourbons had them fitted onto the torso.

Farnese Atlante

Mosaics

If you're short on time, take in the *Toro* and *Ercole* before heading straight to the mezzanine floor, home to an exquisite collection of mosaics, mostly from Pompeii. Of the series taken from the Casa del Fauno, it's *La battaglia di Alessandro contro Dario* (The Battle of Alexander against Darius) that really stands out. The best-known depiction of Alexander the Great, the 20-sq-metre mosaic was probably made by Alexandrian craftsmen working in Italy around the end of the 2nd century BC. Other intriguing mosaics include a cat killing a duck and a collection of Nile animals.

MICHAEL BROOKS/ALAMY STOCK PHOTO ©

Gabinetto Segreto

Beyond the mosaics, the Gabinetto Segreto (Secret Chamber) contains a small but much-studied collection of ancient erotica. Pan is caught in the act with a nanny goat in the collection's most famous piece – a small and surprisingly sophisticated statue taken from the Villa dei Papiri in Herculaneum. You'll also find a series of nine paintings depicting erotic positions – a menu for brothel patrons.

Sala Meridiana

Originally the royal library, the enormous Sala Meridiana (Great Hall of the Sundial) on the 1st floor is home to the *Farnese Atlante,* a statue of Atlas carrying a globe on his shoulders, as well as various paintings from the Farnese collection. Look up and you'll find Pietro Bardellino's riotously colourful 1781 fresco depicting the (short-lived) triumph of Ferdinand IV of Bourbon and Marie Caroline of Austria in Rome.

The rest of the 1st floor is largely devoted to fascinating discoveries from Pompeii, Herculaneum, Boscoreale, Stabiae and Cuma. Among them are whimsical wall frescoes from the Villa di Agrippa Postumus and the Casa di Meleagro, extraordinary bronzes from the Villa dei Papiri, as well as ceramics, glassware, engraved coppers and Greek funerary vases.

✕ Take a Break
Head down to boho Piazza Bellini for drinks at **Spazio Nea** (✆ 081 45 13 58; www.spazionea.it; Via Costantinopoli 53; ☉ 9am-2am, to 3am Fri & Sat; 🛜; Ⓜ Dante).

Catacombe di San Gennaro

Subterranean Naples

Lurking beneath Naples' loud and greasy streets is one of the world's most thrilling urban wonderlands, a silent, mostly undiscovered sprawl of Greek-era grottoes, paleo-Christian burial chambers, catacombs and ancient ruins.

Great For...

☑ **Don't Miss**

The skulls in the Cimitero delle Fontanelle.

Catacombe di San Gennaro

Naples' oldest and most sacred **catacomb** (☏081 744 37 14; www.catacombedinapoli.it; Via Capodimonte 13; adult/reduced €9/6; ⊘1hr tours hourly 10am-5pm Mon-Sat, to 2pm Sun; 🚌R4, 178 to Via Capodimonte) became a Christian pilgrimage site when San Gennaro's body was interred here in the 5th century. Experience an evocative otherworld of tombs, corridors and broad vestibules, and treasures including 2nd-century Christian frescoes, 5th-century mosaics and the oldest known portrait of San Gennaro.

Cimitero delle Fontanelle

First used during the 1656 plague, the ghoulish **Fontanelle Cemetery** (☏081 1925 6964; www.cimiterofontanelle.com; Via Fontanelle 80; ⊘10am-5pm; 🚌C51 to Via Fontanelle, Ⓜ Materdei) **FREE** became Naples' main burial site during

Detail in the Cimitero delle Fontanelle

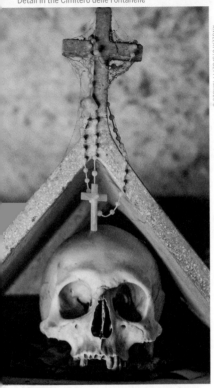

ANGELAFOTO/GETTY IMAGES ©

Explore Ashore

Catacombe di San Gennaro and Cimitero delle Fontanelle are accessible by bus. Galleria Borbonica is a 20 minute walk southwest from the port. Complesso Monumentale di San Lorenzo Maggiore can be reached by metro from the ferry terminals.

❶ Need to Know

For more on Naples' underground wonders check out www.napoliun plugged.com/locations-category/ subterranean-naples.

the 1837 cholera epidemic. At the end of the 19th century it was a hotspot for the anime *pezzentelle* (poor souls) cult, in which locals adopted skulls and prayed for their souls. Take a tour with the **Cooperativa Sociale Onlus 'La Paranza'** (🕿 081 744 37 14; www. catacombedinapoli.it; Via Capodimonte 13; ⏱ information point 10am-5pm Mon-Sat, to 2pm Sun; 🚌 R4, 178 to Via Capodimonte).

Galleria Borbonica

Conceived by Ferdinand II in 1853 to link the Palazzo Reale to the barracks and the sea, the never-completed **Bourbon Tunnel** (🕿 366 2484151, 081 764 58 08; www.galleria-borbonica.com; Vico del Grottone 4; 1hr standard tour adult/reduced €10/5; ⏱ standard tour 10am, noon, 3pm & 5pm Fri-Sun; 🚌 R2 to Via San Carlo, Ⓜ Chiaia-Monte di Dio) is part of the 17th-century Carmignano Aqueduct system,

itself incorporating 16th-century cisterns. An air-raid shelter and military hospital during WWII, this underground labyrinth rekindles the past with evocative wartime artefacts.

Complesso Monumentale di San Lorenzo Maggiore

Architecture and history buffs shouldn't miss this richly layered religious **complex** (🕿 081 211 08 60; www.laneapolissotterrata. it; Via dei Tribunali 316; church free, museum & excavations guided tour adult/reduced €10/7.50; ⏱ church 8am-7pm, excavations & museum 9.30am-5.30pm; Ⓜ Dante). Aside from Ferdinando Sanfelice's petite facade, the Cappella al Rosario and the Cappellone di Sant'Antonio, its baroque makeover was stripped away last century to reveal its austere, Gothic elegance. Beneath the basilica, a sprawl of extraordinary **ruins** will transport you back two millennia.

Ruins of Pompeii

Around 30 minutes by train from Naples, you'll find Europe's most compelling archaeological site: the ruins of Pompeii. Sprawling and haunting, the site is a remarkably well-preserved slice of ancient life. Here you can walk down Roman streets and snoop around millennia-old houses, temples, shops, cafes, amphitheatres and even a brothel.

Great For...

Naples
Bagnoli
Marechiaro
Portici
Ercolano
Torre del Greco
Somma Vesuviana
Mt Vesuvius (Vesuvio) (1281m)
San Gennaro Vesuviano
Terzigno
Ruins of Pompeii
Bay of Naples (Golfo di Napoli)
Torre Annunziata
Pompeii

ℹ Need to Know

☏081 857 53 47; www.pompeiisites.org; adult/reduced €15/7.50; ⊙9am-7.30pm Mon-Fri Apr-Oct, 9am-5.30pm Mon-Fri Nov-Mar; from 8.30am Sat & Sun year round ⊠Circumvesuviana to Pompei Scavi-Villa dei Misteri)

Explore Ashore

To reach the *scavi* (excavations) by Circumvesuviana train (€2.80 from Naples), alight at Pompei–Scavi-Villa dei Misteri station, located beside the main entrance at Porta Marina. If driving from Naples, head southeast on the A3, using the Pompei exit and follow the signs to Pompei Scavi. Car parks (about €5 all day) are clearly marked and vigorously touted. Allow at least three or four hours here, longer if you want to go into detail.

Visiting the Site

Much of the site's value lies in the fact that the city wasn't blown away by Vesuvius in AD 79, but buried beneath a layer of lapilli (burning fragments of pumice stone). The remains first came to light in 1594, but systematic exploration didn't begin until 1748. Since then 44 of Pompeii's original 66 hectares have been excavated.

Foro

A huge grassy rectangle flanked by lime-stone columns, the *foro* (forum) was ancient Pompeii's main piazza, as well as the site of gladiatorial battles before the *anfiteatro* (amphitheatre)was constructed. The buildings surrounding the forum are testament to its role as the city's hub of civic, commercial, political and religious activity.

Lupanare

Ancient Pompeii's only dedicated brothel, Lupanare is a tiny two-storey building with five rooms on each floor. Its collection of raunchy frescoes was a menu of sorts for clients. The walls in the rooms are carved with graffiti – including declarations of love and hope written by the brothel workers – in various languages.

Teatro Grande

The 2nd-century-BC Teatro Grande was a huge 5000-seat theatre carved into the lava mass on which Pompeii was built.

Anfiteatro

Gladiatorial battles thrilled up to 20,000 spectators at the grassy *anfiteatro*. Built in

Ruins of a villa in Pompeii

70 BC, it's the oldest known Roman amphitheatre in existence.

Casa del Fauno

Covering an entire *insula* (city block) and boasting two atria at its front end, Pompeii's largest private house, Casa del Fauno (House of the Faun), is named after the delicate bronze statue in the *impluvium* (rain tank). It was here that early excavators found Pompeii's greatest

LAURADIBI/SHUTTERSTOCK ©

mosaics, most of which are now in Naples' Museo Archeologico Nazionale. Valuable on-site survivors include a beautiful, geometrically patterned marble floor.

Villa dei Misteri

This restored, 90-room villa is one of the most complete structures left standing. The **Dionysiac frieze**, the most important fresco on-site, spans the walls of the large dining room. One of the biggest, most arresting paintings from the ancient world, it depicts the initiation of a bride-to-be into the cult of Dionysus, the Greek god of wine.

Body Casts

The body casts in the Granai del Foro (Forum Granary), made in the late 19th century by pouring plaster into the hollows left by disintegrated bodies, are one of the most haunting sights at Pompeii. Among the casts is a pregnant slave; the belt around her waist would have displayed the name of her owner.

Tours

You'll almost certainly be approached by a guide outside the *scavi* (excavations) ticket office: note that authorised guides wear identification tags. If considering a guided tour of the ruins, reputable tour operators include **Yellowsudmarine Tours** (☎329 1010328; www.yellowsudmarine.com; 2hr Pompeii guided tour €150, plus entrance fee) and **Walks of Italy** (www.walksofitaly.com; 3hr Pompeii guided tour per person €59).

Tragedy in Pompeii

24 AUGUST AD 79

8am Buildings including the ❶ **Terme Suburbane** and the ❷ **Foro** are still undergoing repair after an earthquake in AD 63 caused significant damage to the city. Despite violent earth tremors overnight, residents have little idea of the catastrophe that lies ahead.

Midday Peckish locals pour into the ❸ **Thermopolium di Vetutius Placidus**. The lustful slip into the ❹ **Lupanare**, and gladiators practise for the evening's planned games at the ❺ **Anfiteatro**. A massive boom heralds the eruption. Shocked onlookers witness a dark cloud of volcanic matter shoot some 14km above the crater.

3pm–5pm Lapilli (burning pumice stone) rains down on Pompeii. Terrified locals begin to flee; others take shelter. Within two hours, the plume is 25km high and the sky has darkened. Roofs collapse under the weight of the debris, burying those inside.

25 AUGUST AD 79

Midnight Mudflows bury the town of Herculaneum. Lapilli and ash continue to rain down on Pompeii, bursting through buildings and suffocating those taking refuge within.

4am–8am Ash and gas avalanches hit Herculaneum. Subsequent surges smother Pompeii, killing all remaining residents, including those in the ❻ **Orto dei Fuggiaschi**. The volcanic 'blanket' will safeguard frescoed treasures like the ❼ **Casa del Menandro** and ❽ **Villa dei Misteri** for almost two millennia.

Villa dei Misteri
Home to the world-famous *Dionysiac Frieze* fresco. Other highlights at this villa include *trompe l'oeil* wall decorations in the *cubiculum* (bedroom) and Egyptian-themed artwork in the *tablinum* (reception).

Villa di Diomede

Casa del Poeta Tragico
Porta Ercolano
Casa del Fauno

Tempio di Apollo
Basilica

Porta Marina

Terme del Foro

Macellum

Teatro Grande

Quadriportico dei Teatri
Porta di Stabia
Teatro Piccolo

Foro
An ancient Times Square of sorts, the forum sits at the intersection of Pompeii's main streets and was closed to traffic in the 1st century AD. The plinths on the southern edge featured statues of the imperial family.

TOP TIPS

➡ Visit in the afternoon.
➡ Allow three hours.
➡ Wear comfortable shoes and a hat.
➡ Bring drinking water.
➡ Don't use flash photography.

Lupanare

The prostitutes at this brothel were often slaves of Greek or Asian origin. Mattresses once covered the stone beds and the names engraved in the walls are possibly those of the workers and their clients.

POROJNICU STELIAN / SHUTTERSTOCK ©

Thermopolium di Vetutius Placidus

The counter at this ancient snack bar once held urns filled with hot food. The *lararium* (household shrine) on the back wall depicts Dionysus (the god of wine) and Mercury (the god of profit and commerce).

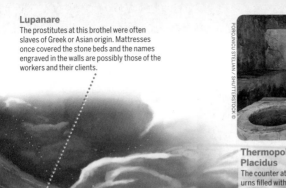

Casa dei Vettii

Porta del Vesuvio

EYEWITNESS ACCOUNT

Pliny the Younger (AD 61–c 112) gives a gripping, first-hand account of the catastrophe in his letters to Tacitus (AD 56–117).

Porta di Nola

Casa della Venere in Conchiglia

Porta di Sarno

③

⑦

Grande Palestra

⑤

⑥

Tempio di Iside

Orto dei Fuggiaschi

The Garden of the Fugitives showcases the plaster moulds of 13 locals seeking refuge during Vesuvius' eruption – the largest number of victims found in any one area. The huddled bodies make for a moving scene.

EDELLA / GETTY IMAGES ©

Casa del Menandro

This dwelling most likely belonged to the family of Poppaea Sabina, Nero's second wife. A room to the left of the atrium features Trojan War paintings and a polychrome mosaic of pygmies rowing down the Nile.

Anfiteatro

Magistrates, local senators and the games' sponsors and organisers enjoyed front-row seating at this veteran amphitheatre, home to gladiatorial battles and the odd riot. The parapet circling the stadium featured paintings of combat, victory celebrations and hunting scenes.

Centro Storico Wander

The *centro storico* is the loud, pounding heart of Naples, a dizzying rush of bellowing baristas, cultish shrines and operatic *palazzi* (mansions). Take a deep breath and dive in.

Start Port'Alba
Distance 1.8km
Duration 2 ½ hours

1 Begin at the old city gate of **Port'Alba**, inaugurated in 1625 by the Spanish viceroy of Naples, Antonio Alvárez.

2 Drop into erudite bookshop **Colonnese** (☎081 45 98 58; https://colonnese.it; ⊗10am-7.30pm; MDante) to browse vintage Neapolitan prints and postcards.

3 Slip into the **Chiesa di San Pietro a Maiella** to admire Mattia Preti's baroque paintings in the coffered wooden ceiling.

Classic Photo Cappella Sansevero

4 View Giuseppe Sanmartino's inimitable *Veiled Christ* sculpture inside the **Cappella Sansevero** (p248)

⊗N 0 ⊢————————————┤ 200 m
    0 ⊢————————————┤ 0.1 miles

M Piazza
  Cavour

Take a break... Pizzeria Gino Sorbillo (☎081 44 66 43; www. sorbillo.it; ⊙ noon-3.30pm & 7-11.30pm Mon-Sat; pizzas from €4; Ⓜ Dante), a cult-status pizzeria, is besieged by hungry hordes.

Via Duomo

Vico dei Gerolomini

Vico Giganti

FINISH **7**

Via dei Tribunali

7 At Via Duomo, turn left to reach Naples' **Duomo** (p248), home to spectacular baroque interiors and the oldest baptistry in Western Europe.

Vico Cinquesanti

Piazza San Gaetano

Via dei Tribunali

6

Via Atri

Vico Giuseppe Maffei

Via San Gregorio Armeno

5

Via Francesco de Sanctis

Vico S Nicola al Nilo

Via Nilo

Vico SS Filippo e Giacomo

Via G Paladino

Via San Biagio dei Librai

6 The Gothic simplicity of the **Basilica di San Lorenzo Maggiore** (p247) is worth a peek before turning right into bustling Via San Gregorio Armeno.

Piazzetta Nilo

Piazza San Domenico Maggiore

Vico S Severino

Ⓜ Duomo

5 Adjoining a blissful cloister, the show-stopping **Chiesa e Chiostro di San Gregorio Armeno** is on Via San Gregorio Armeno.

1 LAURADIBI/SHUTTERSTOCK © 4 NATIONAL GEOGRAPHIC IMAGE COLLECTION/ALAMY STOCK PHOTO © 5 DINOPH/SHUTTERSTOCK © 6 DINOPH/SHUTTERSTOCK © 7 ELEVATIONUS/SHUTTERSTOCK ©

⊙ SIGHTS

◎ Centro Storico

Cappella Sansevero   Chapel

(☏081 551 84 70; www.museosansevero.it; Via
Francesco de Sanctis 19; adult/reduced €7/5;
☺9am-7pm Wed-Mon; MDante) It's in this
Masonic-inspired baroque chapel that you'll
find Giuseppe Sanmartino's incredible
sculpture, *Cristo velato* (Veiled Christ), its
marble veil so realistic that it's tempting to
try to lift it and view Christ underneath. It's
one of several artistic wonders that include
Francesco Queirolo's sculpture *Disinganno*
(Disillusion), Antonio Corradini's *Pudicizia*
(Modesty) and riotously colourful frescoes
by Francesco Maria Russo, the latter un-
touched since their creation in 1749.

Complesso Monumentale
di Santa Chiara   Basilica

(☏081 551 66 73; www.monasterodisantachiara.
it; Via Santa Chiara 49c; basilica free, Complesso
Monumentale adult/reduced €6/4.50; ☺basilica
7.30am-1pm & 4.30-8pm, Complesso Monumentale 9.30am-5.30pm Mon-Sat, 10am-2.30pm Sun;
MDante) Vast, Gothic and cleverly deceptive,
the mighty **Basilica di Santa Chiara** stands
at the heart of this tranquil monastery complex. The church was severely damaged in
WWII: what you see today is a 20th-century
recreation of Gagliardo Primario's 14th-
century original. Adjoining it are the basilica's **cloisters**, adorned with brightly coloured 17th-century majolica tiles and frescoes.

Duomo   Cathedral

(☏081 44 90 97; Via Duomo 149; cathedral/
baptistry free/€2; ☺cathedral 8.30am-1.30pm
& 2.30-7.30pm Mon-Sat, 8.30am-1.30pm & 4.30-
7.30pm Sun, baptistry 8.30am-12.30pm & 3.30-
6.30pm Mon-Sat, 8.30am-1pm Sun, Cappella di
San Gennaro 8.30am-1pm & 3-6.30pm Mon-Sat,
8.30am-1pm & 4.30-7pm Sun; ☒147, 182, 184 to
Via Foria, MPiazza Cavour) Whether you go for
Giovanni Lanfranco's fresco in the Cappella
di San Gennaro (Chapel of St Janarius), the
4th-century mosaics in the baptistry or the
thrice-annual miracle of San Gennaro, do
not miss Naples' cathedral. Kick-started by
Charles I of Anjou in 1272 and consecrated

in 1315, it was largely destroyed in a 1456
earthquake. It has had copious nips and
tucks over the subsequent centuries.

◎ Toledo, Quartieri Spagnoli &
Santa Lucia

Palazzo Reale   Palace

(Royal Palace; ☏081 40 05 47; www.coopculture.
it; Piazza del Plebiscito 1; adult/reduced €6/3;
☺9am-8pm Thu-Tue; ☒R2 to Via San Carlo,
MMunicipio) Envisaged as a 16th-century
monument to Spanish glory (Naples was
under Spanish rule at the time), the magnificent Palazzo Reale is home to the **Museo del
Palazzo Reale**, a rich and eclectic collection
of baroque and neoclassical furnishings, porcelain, tapestries, sculpture and paintings,
spread across the palace's royal apartments.

Gallerie d'Italia –
Palazzo Zevallos Stigliano   Gallery

(☏081 42 50 11; www.palazzozevallos.com; Via
Toledo 185; adult/reduced €5/3; ☺10am-7pm
Tue-Fri, to 8pm Sat & Sun; MMunicipio) Built for a
Spanish merchant in the 17th century and re-
configured in belle-époque style by architect
Luigi Platania in the early 20th century, Palazzo Zevallos Stigliano houses a compact yet
stunning collection of Neapolitan and Italian
art spanning the 17th to early 20th centuries.
Star attraction is Caravaggio's mesmerising swansong, *The Martyrdom of St Ursula*
(1610). Completed weeks before the artist's
lonely death, the painting depicts a vengeful
king of the Huns piercing the heart of his
unwilling virgin-bride-to-be, Ursula.

Teatro San Carlo   Theatre

(☏081 797 24 68; www.teatrosancarlo.it; Via
San Carlo 98; guided tour adult/reduced €7/5;
☺guided tours 10.30am, 11.30am, 12.30pm,
2.30pm, 3.30pm & 4.30pm daily; ☒R2 to Via San
Carlo, MMunicipio) An evening at Italy's largest
opera house is magical. If you can't make it
to a performance, consider taking one of the
45-minute guided tours of the venue. Tours
usually take in the foyers, elegant main hall
and royal box (the best seat in the house)
and tickets can be purchased at the theatre
up to 15 minutes before each tour begins.

😊 COURSES

Eating well is a Neapolitan obsession, and the city's cornucopia of speciality food stores, markets and time-tested eateries may well ignite a desire to delve into Naples' culinary traditions and secrets. If so, **Toffini Academy** (☎081 66 53 36; http://toffini.it/ Corsi; Via Martucci 35; 3hr cooking course from €60; 🚌627 to Via Crispi, Ⓜ Piazza Amedeo) offers single-session cooking lessons in an intimate, contemporary setting. Courses are available in Italian and English.

😊 TOURS

Guided tours can be an excellent way to explore Naples from a different, often intimate angle. Fans of Elena Ferrante's Neapolitan novels can relive scenes from the best-selling books on a **Looking for Lila** (☎389 8463510; www.lookingforlila.com; 5hr tour for 2 people €250) tour, while food lovers can taste-test their way around the *centro storico* on a **Culinary Backstreets** (https://culinarybackstreets.com/culinary-walks/naples; 5½hr tour adult/7-12yr US€135/67.50) walking tour. If you're keen on street art, **Napoli Paint Stories** (☎333 6290673; www.facebook.com/Napoli-Paint-Stories-826714954052903; tour adult/reduced €15/12; ⊙varies, usually Sat & Sun) runs walking tours of the city's booming street-art scene, while the Galleria Borbonica (p239), **Napoli Sotterranea** (Underground Naples; ☎081 29 69 44; www.napolisotterranea.org; Piazza San Gaetano 68; adult/reduced €10/8; ⊙English tours 10am, noon, 2pm, 4pm & 6pm; Ⓜ Dante) and Complesso Monumentale di San Lorenzo Maggiore (p239) all run guided tours of the ancient vestiges that lurk beneath the city's streets.

For something altogether more active, **Kayak Napoli** (☎338 2109978, 331 9874271; www.kayaknapoli.com; Bagno Sirena, Via Posillipo 357; tours €25-30; 🚌140 to Via Posillipo) 🍃 offers kayaking and SUP tours of Naples' beautiful, historic coastline. For families with young children and those who can't walk far, hop-on, hop-off bus tours by **City Sightseeing Napoli** (☎081 551 72 79; www.city-sightseeing.it/

👍 Secret Artisan Studios

Down dark streets, behind unmarked doors and in unsuspecting courtyards, artisan studios litter the *centro storico*. Dive into the city's idiosyncratic arts scene at the following locations:
Lello Esposito (☎081 551 41 71, 335 5874189; www.lelloesposito.com; Piazza San Domenico Maggiore 9; Ⓟ; Ⓜ Dante) Dividing his time between Naples and New York, the infectiously charming Lello Esposito (who speaks very little English) creates large-scale sculptures and installations that explore and transform the city's folklore, from giant eggs with San Gennaro heads to bound Pulcinellas. It's a good idea to call or email ahead.
Officina D'Arti Grafiche di Carmine Cervone (☎081 29 54 83; www.facebook.com/OfficinaDartiGraficheDiCarmineCervone; Via Anticaglia 12; ⊙9am-7.30pm Mon-Sat; Ⓜ Piazza Cavour, Museo) Lovers of print and typography shouldn't miss Carmine's one-of-a-kind printing workshop, crammed with rare vintage machinery, including a late-19th-century linotype machine.
MAC Ceramics (☎333 6031376; www.facebook.com/bottegadiceramica; Via Nilo 12; ⊙10am-7pm Mon-Sat; Ⓜ Dante) Antimo De Santis and his partner Marina Pascali are the talents behind this pocket-sized ceramics showroom. Everything from the playful espresso cups to the ceramic air balloons are made from scratch and by hand, without an industrial mould in sight.

A Pulcinella by Lello Esposito
ANTONIO GRAVANTE/SHUTTERSTOCK ©

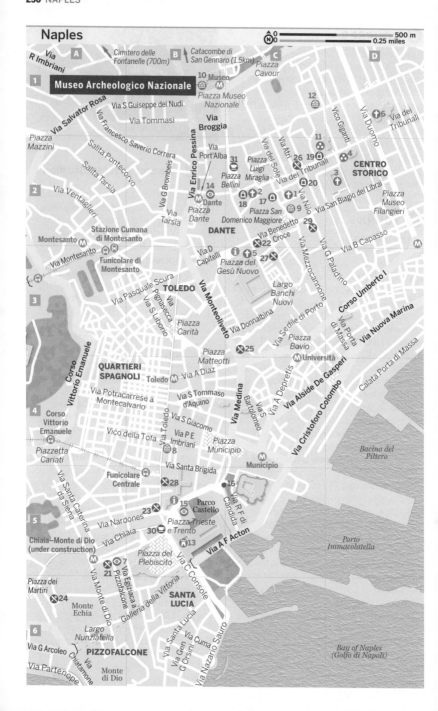

Naples

0 N

0 — 500 m
— 0.25 miles

Via R Imbriani

A

Cimitero delle Fontanelle (700m)

B

Catacombe di San Gennaro (1.5km)

C

Piazza Cavour

D

1

Museo Archeologico Nazionale

10 Museo

Piazza Museo Nazionale

12

Via S Guiseppe dei Nudi

Via Tommasi

Via Salvator Rosa

Via Francesco Saverio Correra

Via Broggia

Vico Giganti

Via Duomo

6 Via dei Tribunali

Piazza Mazzini

Salita Pontecorvo

Salita Tarsia

Via G Brombeis

Via Enrico Pessina

Via Port'Alba

31

Via Atri

Via del Sole

Via dei Tribunali

11

26 19

CENTRO STORICO

2

Via Ventaglieri

Via Tarsia

14

Piazza Luigi Miraglia

Piazza Bellini

2

17

18

Piazza San Domenico Maggiore

20

1

3

Via San Biagio dei Librai

Piazza Museo Filangieri

M Dante

Piazza Dante

9

DANTE

29

Via Nilo

Via B Capasso

Montesanto M

Stazione Cumana di Montesanto

Funicolare di Montesanto

Via Montesanto

Via D Capitelli

Via Benedetto Croce

22

Via Mezzocannone

Via G Paladino

M

Corso Umberto I

3

Via Pasquale Scura

TOLEDO

5

27

Piazza del Gesù Nuovo

Largo Banchi Nuovi

Via Pignasecca

Via S Liborio

Via Monteoliveto

Via Donnalbina

Via Sedile di Porto

Via Porta di Massa

Via Nuova Marina

Piazza Carità

Calata Porta di Massa

4

Corso Vittorio Emanuele

QUARTIERI SPAGNOLI

Toledo M

Via A Diaz

Piazza Matteotti

25

Piazza Bovio

Università M

Corso Vittorio Emanuele

Via Potracarrese a Montecalvario

Via S Tommaso d'Aquino

Via S Giacomo

Via Medina

Via S Bartolomeo

Via A Depretis

Via Alside De Gasperi

Via Cristoforo Colombo

Bacino del Piltero

Piazzetta Cariati

Vico della Tofa

Via Toledo

Via P E Imbriani

8

Piazza Municipio

Funicolare Centrale

Via Santa Brigida

Municipio M

16

Via R F di Candida

5

Via Santa Caterina da Siena

28

23

15

Parco Castello

Via Nardones

Piazza Trieste e Trento

Porto Immacolatella

Chiaia–Monte di Dio (under construction)

Via Chiaia

30

13

Via A F Acton

Piazza del Plebiscito

Via C Console

Piazza dei Martiri

24

M

7

21

Via Monte di Dio

Via Egiziaca a Pizzofalcone

Galleria della Vittoria

SANTA LUCIA

6

Via G Arcoleo

Monte Echia

Largo Nunziatella

PIZZOFALCONE

Via Santa Lucia

Via Gen G Orsini

Via Cuma

Via Nazario Sauro

Bay of Naples (Golfo di Napoli)

Via Chiatamone

Via Partenope

Monte di Dio

Naples

en/naples; adult/reduced €23/11.50) are a handy means of getting around the main sights.

🔒 SHOPPING

Shopping in Naples is a highly idiosyncratic experience, dominated by specialist, family-heirloom businesses. Neapolitan folklore inspires its many artisans, who create everything from ceramic bowls and *pastori*, to leather goods and sculptural jewellery. The city also has a long, proud sartorial tradition, and its handmade leather gloves and luxe bespoke suits and shirts are coveted the world over.

Bottega 21   Fashion & Accessories
(☎081 033 55 42; www.bottegaventuno.it; Vico San Domenico Maggiore 21; ☺9.30am-8pm Mon-Sat) Top-notch Tuscan leather and traditional, handcrafted methods translate into coveted, contemporary leather goods at Bottega 21. Block colours and clean, simple designs underline the range, which includes stylish totes, handbags, backpacks and duffel bags, as well as wallets and coin purses, unisex belts, gloves, sandals, tobacco pouches and, occasionally, notebook covers.

La Scarabattola   Arts & Crafts
(☎081 29 17 35; www.lascarabattola.it; Via dei Tribunali 50; ☺10.30am-2pm & 3.30-7.30pm Mon-Fri, 10am-8pm Sat; Ⓜ Dante) Not only do La Scarabattola's handmade sculptures of *magi* (wise men), devils and Neapolitan folk figures constitute Jerusalem's official Christmas crèche, but the artisanal studio's fans also include fashion designer Stefano Gabbana and Spanish royalty. Figurines aside, sleek ceramic creations (like Pulcinella-inspired place-card holders) inject Neapolitan folklore with refreshing contemporary style.

Gay Odin   Chocolate
(☎081 551 34 91; www.gay-odin.it; Via Toledo 427; ☺9.30am-8pm Mon-Sat, 10am-2pm Sun; Ⓜ Dante) One of several branches around town, Gay Odin is famous for its delectable artisanal chocolates.

✖ EATING

Naples is one of Italy's gastronomic darlings, and the bonus of a bayside setting makes for some seriously memorable meals. While white linen, candlelight and

Teatro San Carlo interior (p248)

€50 bills are readily available, some of the best bites await in the city's spit-and-sawdust trattorias, where two courses and house wine can cost under €20.

⊗ Centro Storico

'O Sfizio   Neapolitan €
(☎081 1895 8824; Via Santa Maria la Nova 50; panini €3.50-5, dishes €4-5; ⊙7am-7pm Mon-Sat; 🚌R4 to Via Monteoliveto, Ⓜ Università, Toledo) It's not atmosphere that draws fans to humble 'O Sfizio, a bargain-priced takeaway by a traffic-ridden thoroughfare. It's the *parmigiana di melanzana* that's so good that many locals vote it above their own mothers' versions. 'O Sfizio's iteration is simply gorgeous, never oily or heavy yet generously laden with *parmigiano reggiano*, mozzarella and slightly crisp aubergine.

Tandem   Neapolitan €
(☎081 1900 2468; Via G Paladino 51; meals €19; ⊙12.30-3.30pm & 7-11.30pm; 🛜; Ⓜ Dante) *Ragù* (a rich tomato-and-meat sauce) might be a Sunday-lunch staple in Naples, but laid-back Tandem serves it up all week long. Whether you're tucking into *rigatoni*

al ragù or a *ragù* fondue, expect rich, fragrant goodness that could make your *nonna* weep. Complete with vegetarian options, it's a small, simple spot with a cult following, so head in early or (on weekends) book.

Salumeria   Neapolitan €€
(☎081 1936 4649; www.salumeriaupnea.it; Via San Giovanni Maggiore Pignatelli 34/35; sandwiches from €5.50, charcuterie platters from €8.50, meals around €30; ⊙12.30-5pm & 7.15pm-midnight Thu-Tue; 🛜; Ⓜ Dante) Small producers, local ingredients and contemporary takes on provincial Campanian recipes drive bistro-inspired Salumeria. Nibble on quality charcuterie and cheeses or fill up on artisanal *panini*, hamburgers or Salumeria's sublime *ragù napoletano* (*ragù* slow-cooked over two days). Even the ketchup here is made in-house, using DOP Piennolo tomatoes from Vesuvius.

⊗ Toledo & Quartieri Spagnoli

Sfogliatella Mary   Pastries €
(sfogliatelle €1.80; ⊙8am-8.30pm Tue-Sun; 🚌R2 to Via San Carlo, Ⓜ Municipio) At the Via Toledo

entrance to Galleria Umberto I, this tiny takeaway vendor is widely considered the queen of the *sfogliatella* (sweetened ricotta pastry). Usually still warm from the oven, it's available in *riccia* (filo-style pastry) and *frolla* (shortcrust pastry) forms, both defined by a perfect balance of textures and flavours.

Il Gelato Mennella
Gelato €

(📞081 40 44 58; www.pasticceriamennella.it; Via Toledo 110; gelato from €2.50; ⊙10am-11.30pm Mon-Fri, to 1am Sat & Sun; 🚌R2 to Via San Carlo, Ⓜ Municipio) Could it be ingredients like prized Campanian *nocciole* (hazelnuts) from Giffoni and Sicilian pistachios from Bronte? Perhaps it's the absence of artificial nasties? Whatever the secret, Mennella scoops out smashing gelato, bursting with real, vivid flavours and velvety texture. The waffle cones are made fresh on-site and a number system means no queue jumping!

⊗ Santa Lucia & Chiaia

Da Ettore
Neapolitan €€

(📞081 764 35 78; Via Gennaro Serra 39; meals €25; ⊙1-3pm & 8-10pm Tue-Sat, 1-3pm Sun; 🛜; 🚌R2 to Via San Carlo, Ⓜ Chiaia-Monte di Dio) This homey, eight-table trattoria has an epic reputation. Scan the walls for famous fans like comedy great Totò, and a framed passage from crime writer Massimo Siviero, who mentions Ettore in one of his tales. The draw is solid regional cooking, which includes one of the best *spaghetti alle vongole* (spaghetti with clams) in town. Book two days ahead for Sunday lunch.

L'Altro Loco
Italian €€€

(📞081 764 17 22; Vicoletto Cappella Vecchia 4/5; meals €55; ⊙8-11.30pm Mon-Sat Jun & Jul, 1-3.30pm Sat & Sun, 8-11.30pm Mon-Sat Sep-May, closed Aug; 🚌E6 to Piazza dei Martiri) It might be a little overpriced, but few Neapolitan restaurants match the sophisticated ambience of this softly lit fine-diner, its booths peopled by well-tailored professionals and Loren lookalikes. The focus is on freshness, lightness and subtlety, from the vibrant *insalatina di astici e gamberi* (lobster-and-shrimp salad) to the

standout tempura-style *baccalà* (salted cod) stuffed with *provola* (provolone) and *friarielli* (bitter greens).

🍷 DRINKING & NIGHTLIFE

Caffè Gambrinus
Cafe

(📞081 41 75 82; www.grancaffegambrinus.com; Via Chiaia 1-2; ⊙7am-1am Sun-Fri, to 2am Sat; 🚌R2 to Via San Carlo, Ⓜ Municipio) Gambrinus is Naples' oldest and most venerable cafe, serving superlative Neapolitan coffee under flouncy chandeliers. Oscar Wilde knocked back a few here and Mussolini had some rooms shut to keep out left-wing intellectuals. Sit-down prices are steep, but the *aperitivo* (pre-dinner drink) nibbles are decent and sipping a *spritz* (a type of cocktail made with Prosecco) or a luscious *cioccolata calda* (hot chocolate) in its belle-époque rooms is something worth savouring.

ℹ️ INFORMATION

Tourist Information Office (📞081 551 27 01; www.inaples.it; Piazza del Gesù Nuovo 7; ⊙9am-5pm Mon-Sat, to 1pm Sun; Ⓜ Dante) In the *centro storico*.

Tourist Information Office (📞081 40 23 94; www.inaples.it; Via San Carlo 9; ⊙9am-5pm Mon-Sat, to 1pm Sun; 🚌R2 to Via San Carlo, Ⓜ Municipio) At Galleria Umberto I, directly opposite Teatro San Carlo.

ℹ️ GETTING AROUND

Naples' city centre is relatively compact and best explored on foot. The city is also serviced by an affordable network of buses, funiculars and both metro and suburban trains. Metro Line 1 connects Napoli Centrale to Piazza Municipio (for hydrofoil and ferry terminals), Via Toledo, the edges of the *centro storico* and Vomero. Line 2 runs to Chiaia, Mergellina and Pozzuoli. Circumvesuviana trains are handy for Pompeii and numerous archaeological sites, including Ercolano (Herculaneum) and Oplontis.

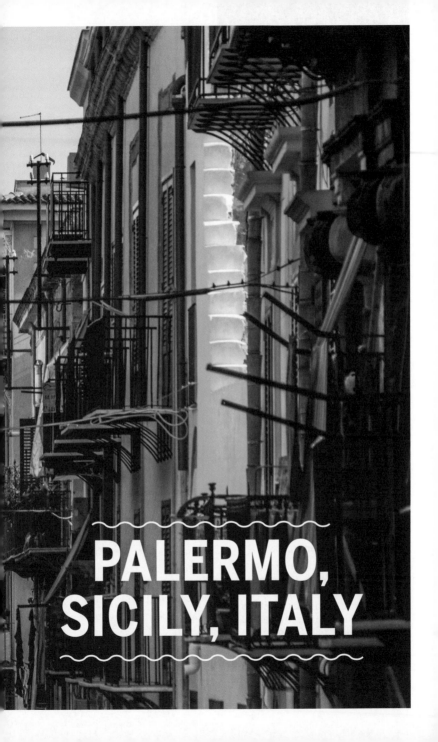

PALERMO,
SICILY, ITALY

Palermo at a Glance...

For millennia at the crossroads of civilisations, Palermo delivers a heady, heavily spiced mix of Byzantine mosaics, Arabesque domes and frescoed cupolas. This is a city at the edge of Europe and at the centre of the ancient world. A place where souk-like markets rub against baroque churches, where date palms frame Gothic palaces and where the blue-eyed and fair have bronze-skinned cousins. Despite its noisy streets, Sicily's largest city is a shy beast, rewarding the inquisitive with citrus-filled cloisters, stucco-laced chapels and vintage stores filled with the threads of faded aristocrats.

With One Day in Port

o Begin with Palermo's crown jewel, **Palazzo dei Normanni** (p258), where the mosaics of King Roger's royal bedroom are only a prelude to his magnificent **Cappella Palatina** (p258).

o In the afternoon, visit the commanding Arab-Norman **Cattedrale di Palermo** (p260), then head east to fountain-studded **Piazza Pretoria** (p265). Tackle centuries of art at **Galleria Regionale della Sicilia** (p264) or join the ancients at Palermo's **Museo Archeologico Regionale** (p264).

o Cap the riches of the day with dinner at **Bisso Bistrot** (p268).

Best Places For...

Street food Francu U Vastiddaru (p268)

Sweet treats Pasticceria Fratelli Magrì (p268)

Markets Mercato di Ballarò (p264)

Wine Enoteca Buonivini (p269)

Sicilian food Trattoria al Vecchio Club Rosanero (p268)

Previous page: Palermo street and the Church of San Matteo
MATEJ KASTELIC/500PX ©

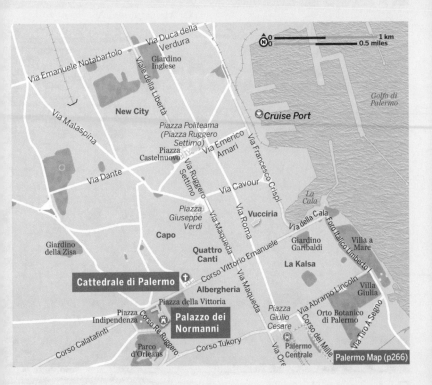

N
0 — 1 km
0 — 0.5 miles

Via Duca della Verdura

Via Emanuele Notabartolo

Giardino Inglese

Viale della Libertà

Via Malaspina

New City

Golfo di Palermo

⚓ **Cruise Port**

Piazza Politeama (Piazza Ruggero Settimo)

Piazza Castelnuovo

Via Emerico Amari

Via Francesco Crispi

Via Dante

Via Ruggero Settimo

Via Cavour

La Cala

Piazza Giuseppe Verdi

Capo

Via Maqueda

Via Roma

Vucciria

Via della Cala

Foro Italico Umberto I

Quattro Canti

Giardino Garibaldi

Villa a Mare

Giardino della Zisa

Corso Vittorio Emanuele

La Kalsa

🕀 **Cattedrale di Palermo**

Albergheria

Via Maqueda

Villa Giulia

Piazza della Vittoria

Piazza Giulio Cesare

Via Abramo Lincoln

Orto Botanico di Palermo

Via Tito A. Segno

Piazza Indipendenza

Corso Re Ruggero

Ⓐ **Palazzo dei Normanni**

Corso Calatafimi

Parco d'Orleans

Corso Tukory

Via dei Mille

Via Oreto

Palermo Centrale

Palermo Map (p266)

Getting from the Port

Cruise ships dock at the **Stazione Marittima**, which can be slightly overwhelming. Be prepared for a busy crowd of taxis and hawkers waiting outside the terminal.

From the port it's 1.8km (about a 25-minute walk) to the heart of the old city at the Quattro Canti (p264). If catching a taxi, use only official, white licensed taxis and check that the meter is reset and running before you depart.

Once in the old city, walking is the best way to explore. Palermo's orange, white and blue city buses are frequent, but often overcrowded and slow.

Fast Facts

Currency Euro (€)

Language Italian

Money ATMs widely available. Credit cards accepted in most hotels and restaurants.

Tourist information The main branch of Palermo's city-run information booths is on Piazza Bellini.

Visas Generally not required for stays of up to three months.

Wi-fi Free wi-fi is available at many restaurants, cafes and bars. The city also hosts numerous free wi-fi hotspots.

Ceiling of the Cappella Palatina

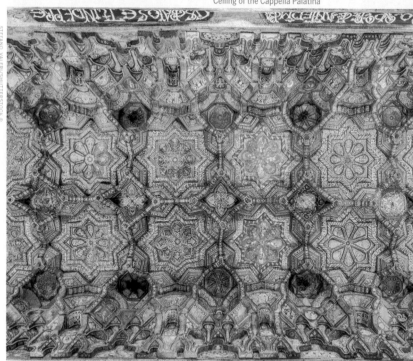

STEFANO_VALERI/SHUTTERSTOCK ©

Palazzo dei Normanni

This austere palace, once the seat of a magnificent court, today houses Sicily's parliament. In addition to political haggling, the palace holds Palermo's greatest treasure, the Cappella Palatina. Designed by Norman King Roger II in 1130, this mosaic-clad chapel swarms with figures in glittering gold.

Great For...

☑ **Don't Miss**

The incredible Cappella Palatina, a masterpiece of Arab craftsmanship.

This venerable palace dates to the 9th century but owes its current look (and name) to a major 12th-century Norman makeover, during which spectacular mosaics were added to its **Royal Apartments** and priceless jewel of a chapel, the **Cappella Palatina**.

Queues are likely and you'll be refused entry if you're wearing shorts, a short skirt or a low-cut top. The top level houses Sicily's regional parliament and the Royal Apartments, including mosaic-lined **Sala dei Venti**, and **Sala di Ruggero II**, King Roger's magnificent 12th-century bedroom. These latter attractions are only open from Friday to Monday.

Cappella Palatina

This extraordinary **chapel** (Palatine Chapel; ⊗8.15am-5.40pm Mon-Sat, 8.15-9.45am &

Palazzo dei Normanni exterior

KIEVVICTOR/SHUTTERSTOCK ©

Explore Ashore

The palace is about 1km west of the Quattro Canti. It's possible to walk here, but you might want to take a taxi back to the port. Or catch a cruise shuttle, which will take you to the historic centre. Expect to spend at least an hour at the palace and a few more at the chapel.

❶ Need to Know

Palazzo Reale; ☑091 626 28 33; www.federicosecondo.org; Piazza Indipendenza 1; adult/reduced incl exhibition Fri-Mon €12/10, Tue-Thu €10/8; ◷8.15am-5.40pm Mon-Sat, to 1pm Sun

11am-1pm Sun) is Palermo's top tourist attraction. Located on the mid-level of Palazzo dei Normanni's three-tiered loggia, its glittering gold mosaics are complemented by inlaid marble floors and a wooden *muqarnas* ceiling, a decorative device resembling stalactites that is unique in a Christian church.

The chapel's well-lit interior is simply breathtaking. Every centimetre is inlaid with precious stones, giving the space a lustrous quality. The exquisite mosaics were mainly the work of Byzantine Greek artisans brought to Palermo by Roger II in 1140 especially for this project. They capture expressions, detail and movement with extraordinary grace and delicacy, and sometimes with enormous power – most notably in the depiction of Christ the Pantocrator and angels on the dome. The bulk of

the mosaics recount tales of the Old Testament, though other scenes recall Palermo's pivotal role in the Crusades. Some mosaics are later (less-assured) additions, for instance the Virgin and saints in the main apse under Christ the Pantocrator.

Don't miss the painted wooden ceiling featuring *muqarnas*, a masterpiece of Arabic-style honeycomb carving reflecting Norman Sicily's cultural complexity (and, many speculate, a sign of Roger II's secret identity as a Muslim). The walls are decorated with handsome marble inlay that displays a clear Islamic aesthetic, and the carved marble in the floor is stunning: marble was as precious as any gemstone in the 12th century, so the floor's value at the time of its construction is almost immeasurable by today's standards.

S-F/SHUTTERSTOCK ©

Cattedrale di Palermo

A feast of geometric patterns, ziggurat crenellations, maiolica cupolas and blind arches, Palermo's cathedral has suffered aesthetically from multiple reworkings over the centuries, but remains a prime example of Sicily's unique Arab-Norman architectural style.

Great For...

☑ **Don't Miss**

The panoramic views from the roof of the cathedral.

History

Construction began in 1184 at the behest of Palermo's archbishop, Walter of the Mill (Gualtiero Offamiglio), an Englishman who was tutor to William II. Walter held great power and had unlimited funds at his disposal, but with the building of the magnificent cathedral at Monreale he felt his power diminishing. His solution was to order the construction of an equally magnificent cathedral in Palermo. This was erected on the location of a 9th-century mosque (itself built on a former chapel); a detail from the mosque's original decor is visible at the southern porch, where a column is inscribed with a passage from the Quran. The cathedral's proportions and grandeur became a statement of the power struggle between Church and throne, a potentially dangerous situation that was

Explore Ashore

The cathedral is within walking distance (about 30 minutes) of the cruise port area. Alternatively, take a taxi or a shuttle bus (offered by the cruise line) into the historic centre. From here, it's a short stroll to the cathedral. Allow at least two hours for your visit.

❶ Need to Know

329 3977513; www.cattedrale.palermo. it; Corso Vittorio Emanuele; cathedral free, royal tombs €1.50, treasury & crypt €3, roof €5, all-inclusive ticket adult/reduced €8/4; ⏰7am-7pm Mon-Sat, 8am-1pm & 4-7pm Sun

tempered by Walter's death in 1191, which prevented him from seeing (and boasting about) the finished building.

The Exterior

Since then the cathedral has been much altered, sometimes with great success (as in Antonio Gambara's 15th-century three-arched portico that became a masterpiece of Catalan Gothic architecture), and sometimes less so (as in Ferdinando Fuga's clumsy dome, added between 1781 and 1801). Thankfully, the eastern exterior is still adorned with the exotic interlacing designs of Walter's original cathedral. The southwestern facade was laid in the 13th and 14th centuries, and is a beautiful example of local craftsmanship in the Gothic style. The cathedral's entrance is fronted by a statue of Santa Rosalia, one

of Palermo's patron saints, and a beautiful painted intarsia decoration above the arches depicts the tree of life in a complex Islamic-style geometric composition of 12 roundels, thought to date to 1296.

The Interior

To the left as you enter the cathedral, the Monumental Area harbours royal Norman tombs containing the remains of two of Sicily's greatest rulers: Roger II (rear left) and Frederick II of Hohenstaufen (front left), as well as Henry VI and William II. The treasury houses a small collection of Norman-era jewels and religious relics. Most extraordinary is the fabulous 13th-century crown of Constance of Aragon, made by local craftsmen in fine gold filigree and encrusted with gems. More bizarre treasures include the tooth and ashes of Santa Rosalia.

Historic Palermo

Dense but compact, central Palermo is best explored on foot. This tour covers some of the city's most enticing assets, from dazzling Byzantine mosaics and Arab-Norman domes, to baroque stuccowork and millennia-old treasures.

Start Cappella Palatina
Distance 4.2km
Duration Six to seven hours

6 Continue north on Via Alessandro Paternostro to Corso Vittorio Emanuele. Head up Via Roma and end your saunter at the nearby **Museo Archeologico Regionale** (p264).

3 Continue further east to **Quattro Canti** (p264), Palermo's most beautiful junction that divides the city's four historic neighbourhoods.

2 Head east through the Mannerist-style city gate of **Porta Nuova** to the architectural fusion that is the **Cattedrale di Palermo** (p260).

Take a break... Stop in at **Bisso Bistrot** (p268) if you're feeling peckish or thirsty.

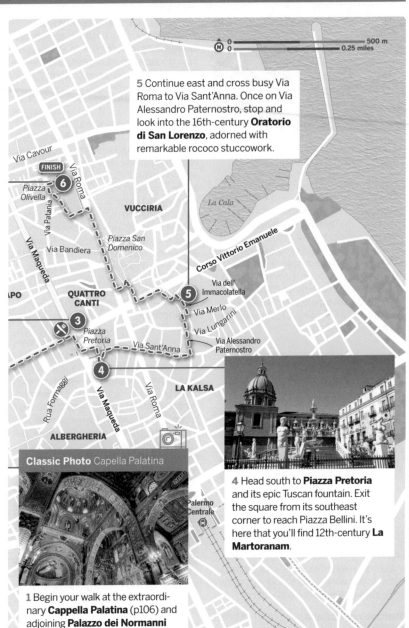

5 Continue east and cross busy Via Roma to Via Sant'Anna. Once on Via Alessandro Paternostro, stop and look into the 16th-century **Oratorio di San Lorenzo**, adorned with remarkable rococo stuccowork.

0 500 m
0 0.25 miles

Via Cavour

FINISH

Piazza Olivella

Via Roma

Via Patania

Via Maqueda

Via Bandiera

VUCCIRIA

La Cala

Piazza San Domenico

Corso Vittorio Emanuele

APO

QUATTRO CANTI

Via dell' Immacolatella

Via Merlo

Via Lungarini

Piazza Pretoria

Via Sant'Anna

Via Alessandro Paternostro

LA KALSA

R.ua Formaggi

Via Maqueda

Via Roma

ALBERGHERIA

Palermo Centrale

Classic Photo Capella Palatina

4 Head south to **Piazza Pretoria** and its epic Tuscan fountain. Exit the square from its southeast corner to reach Piazza Bellini. It's here that you'll find 12th-century **La Martoranam**.

1 Begin your walk at the extraordinary **Cappella Palatina** (p106) and adjoining **Palazzo dei Normanni** (p258).

1 ELESI/SHUTTERSTOCK © 2 MAEKFOTO/SHUTTERSTOCK © 4 LATATIM/SHUTTERSTOCK © 6 ANTON KUDELIN/SHUTTERSTOCK ©

 Quattro Canti

Officially titled Piazza Vigliena, the elegant intersection of Corso Vittorio Emanuele and Via Maqueda is better known as the **Quattro Canti**. Marking the epicentre of the old city, the junction is framed by a perfect circle of curvilinear facades that disappear up to the blue vault of the sky in a clever display of perspective. Each facade lights up in turn throughout the course of the day, landing it the nickname Il Teatro del Sole (Theatre of the Sun).

PAOLO QUERCI/SHUTTERSTOCK ©

◎ SIGHTS

Galleria Regionale della Sicilia
Museum

(Palazzo Abatellis; ☑091 623 00 11; www.regione. sicilia.it/beniculturali/palazzoabatellis; Via Alloro 4; adult/reduced €8/4; ⊙9am-6pm Tue-Fri, to 1pm Sat & Sun) Housed in the stately 15th-century Palazzo Abatellis, this art museum – widely regarded as Palermo's best – showcases works by Sicilian artists from the Middle Ages to the 18th century. One of its greatest treasures is *Trionfo della Morte* (Triumph of Death), a magnificent fresco (artist unknown) in which Death is represented as a demonic skeleton mounted on a wasted horse, brandishing a wicked-looking scythe while leaping over his hapless victims.

Mercato di Ballarò
Market

(Via Ballarò 1; ⊙7.30am-8.30pm) Snaking for several city blocks southeast of Palazzo dei Normanni is Palermo's busiest street market, which throbs with activity well into the early evening. It's a fascinating mix of noises, smells and street life, and the cheapest place for everything from Chinese padded bras to fresh produce, fish, meat, olives and cheese – smile nicely for *un assaggio* (a taste).

Teatro Massimo
Theatre

(☑box office 091 605 35 80; www.teatromassimo. it; Piazza Giuseppe Verdi; guided tours adult/ reduced €8/5; ⊙9.30am-6pm) Taking over 20 years to complete, Palermo's neoclassical opera house is the largest in Italy and the second-largest in Europe. The closing scene of *The Godfather: Part III,* with its visually arresting juxtaposition of high culture, crime, drama and death, was filmed here and the building's richly decorated interiors are nothing short of spectacular. Guided 30-minute tours are offered throughout the day in English, Italian, French, Spanish and German.

Museo Archeologico Regionale
Museum

(☑091 611 68 07; www.regione.sicilia.it/ bbccaa/salinas; Piazza Olivella 24; €3; ⊙9am-6pm Tue-Sat, to 1.30pm Sun) Situated in a Renaissance monastery, this splendid, wheelchair-accessible museum houses some of Sicily's most valuable Greek and Roman artefacts, including the museum's crown jewel, a series of original decorative friezes from the temples at Selinunte. Other important finds in the museum's collection include Phoenician sarcophagi from the 5th century BC, Greek carvings from Himera, the Hellenistic Ariete di bronzo di Siracusa (Bronze Ram of Syracuse), Etruscan mirrors and the largest collection of ancient anchors in the world.

Chiesa di San Giuseppe dei Teatini
Church

(Corso Vittorio Emanuele; ⊙7am-noon & 4-8pm Mon-Sat, 7am-1pm & 5-8.30pm Sun) In the southwestern corner of the Quattro Canti is the 17th-century Chiesa di San Giuseppe dei Teatini, topped by an elegant cupola designed by Giuseppe Mariani and flanked by the two lower orders of Paolo Amato's unfinished campanile. Significantly restored after suffering damage in WWII, its monumental baroque interior includes Filippo Tancredi's scenes from the life of St Gaetano capping the nave and Flemish painter Guglielmo Borremans' *Triumph of St Andrea Avellino* gracing the dome.

La Martorana
Church

(Chiesa di Santa Maria dell'Ammiraglio; Piazza Bellini 3; adult/reduced €2/1; ⏱9.30am-1pm & 3.30-5.30pm Mon-Sat, 9-10.30am Sun) On the southern side of Piazza Bellini, this luminously beautiful 12th-century church was endowed by King Roger's Syrian emir, George of Antioch, and was originally planned as a mosque. Delicate Fatimid pillars support a domed cupola depicting Christ enthroned amid his archangels. The interior is best appreciated in the morning, when sunlight illuminates the magnificent Byzantine mosaics.

Museo dell'Inquisizione
Museum

(Palazzo Chiaramonte-Steri; ☎091 2389 3788; Piazza Marina 61; adult/reduced €8/5; ⏱10am-6pm Tue-Sun) Housed in the lower floors and basements of 14th-century Palazzo Chiaramonte Steri, this fascinating museum explores the legacy of the Inquisition in Palermo. Thousands of 'heretics' were detained here between 1601 and 1782; the honeycomb of former cells has been painstakingly restored to reveal multiple layers of their graffiti and artwork (religious and otherwise). Visits are by one-hour guided tour only, conducted in English and Italian and departing roughly every 40 to 60 minutes from the ticket desk.

Fontana Pretoria
Square

(Piazza Pretoria) Fringed by imposing churches and buildings, Piazza Pretoria is dominated by the over-the-top Fontana Pretoria, one of Palermo's major landmarks. The fountain's tiered basins ripple out in concentric circles, crowded with nude nymphs, tritons and leaping river gods. Such flagrant nudity proved a bit much for Sicilian churchgoers, who prudishly dubbed it the Fontana della Vergogna (Fountain of Shame).

 Street Markets

Palermo's historical ties with the Islamic world and its proximity to North Africa reverberate in the noisy street life of the city's ancient centre, and nowhere is this stronger than in its markets.

The Mercato di Ballarò is filled with stalls peddling household goods, clothes and foodstuffs of every possible description – this is where many Palermitans do their daily shop. The **Mercato del Capo** (Via Sant'Agostino; ⏱7am-8pm Mon, Tue, Thu-Sat, to 1pm Wed & Sun), which extends through the tangle of lanes and alleyways of the Albergheria and Capo quarters is the most atmospheric of all. Here, meat carcasses sway from huge metal hooks, glistening tuna and swordfish are expertly dismembered, and anchovies are filleted. Long and orderly lines of stalls display pungent cheeses, tubs of plump olives and a huge array of fruits and vegetables. Palermo's best-loved flea market, **Mercatino Antiquariato Piazza Marina** (⏱7am-1pm Sun), takes over Piazza Marina and surrounding streets every Sunday morning. Head early for the best finds.

The markets are busiest in the morning. Remember: keep an eye on your belongings while exploring.

Fruit stall at Mercato di Ballarò
GARY YIM/SHUTTERSTOCK ©

Oratorio di San Domenico
Chapel

(www.ilgeniodipalermo.com; Via dei Bambinai 2; €4, incl Oratorio di Santa Cita €6; ⏱9am-6pm) Dominating this small chapel is Anthony van Dyck's fantastic blue-and-red altarpiece, *The Virgin of the Rosary with St Dominic*

Palermo

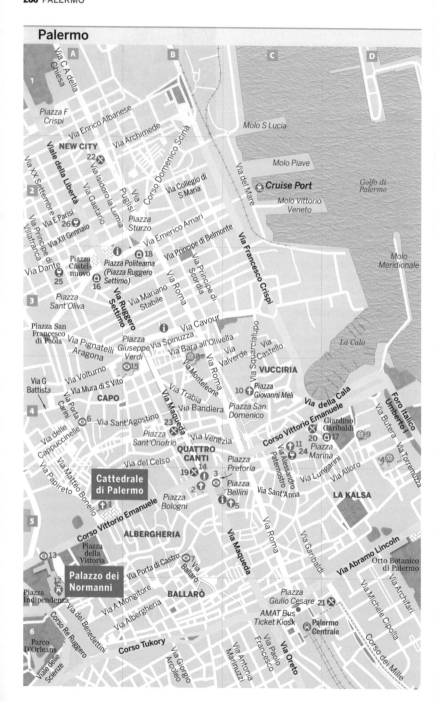

Via C A della Chiesa

Piazza F Crispi

Via Enrico Albanese

Molo S Lucia

NEW CITY

Via Archimede

22

Via Isidoro la Lumia

Corso Domenico Scina

Via Puglisi

Via Collegio di S Maria

Molo Piave

Via del Mare

Cruise Port

Molo Vittorio Veneto

Golfo di Palermo

Viale della Libertà

Via XX Settembre

Via Villafranca

Via Gaetario

Piazza Sturzo

Via E Parisi

26

Via XII Gennaio

Via Emerico Amari

Via Principe di Belmonte

Molo Meridionale

Via Principe di Villafranca

Via Dante

Piazza Castelnuovo

18

Piazza Politeama (Piazza Ruggero Settimo)

16

Via Principe di Scordia

Via Francesco Crispi

25

Piazza Sant'Oliva

Via Ruggero Settimo

Via Mariano Stabile

Via Roma

Piazza San Francesco di Paola

Via Cavour

La Cala

Via Pignatelli Aragona

Piazza Giuseppe Verdi

Via Spinuzza

Via Bara all'Olivella

Via Valverde

Via Castello

Via Squarcialupo

VUCCIRIA

Via G Battista

Via Volturno

15

Via Mura di S Vito

Via Monteleone

Via Roma

Via Porta Carini

CAPO

6

Via Sant'Agostino

Via Trabia

Via Bandiera

10

Piazza Giovanni Meli

Via della Cala

Via Maqueda

Piazza San Domenico

Corso Vittorio Emanuele

Foro Italico I Umberto

Via Butera

Via delle Cappuccinelle

23

Piazza Sant'Onofrio

Via Venezia

Giardino Garibaldi

20

17

9

Via Matteo Bonello

Via Papireto

Via del Celso

QUATTRO CANTI

19

14

3

Piazza Pretoria

11

24

Piazza Marina

Via Alloro

Via Alessandro Paternostro

Via Lungarini

Via Torremuzza

Cattedrale di Palermo

2

1

Piazza Bologni

Piazza Bellini

5

Piazza Sant'Anna

LA KALSA

Corso Vittorio Emanuele

13

Piazza della Vittoria

ALBERGHERIA

Via Maqueda

Via Roma

Via Garibaldi

Via Abramo Lincoln

Orto Botanico di Palermo

Palazzo dei Normanni

12

Via Porta di Castro

7

Via Ballarò

BALLARÒ

Via A Mongitore

Via Alberghria

Piazza Indipendenza

Piazza Giulio Cesare

21

Via Michele Cipolla

Via Archirafi

Corso Re Ruggero

Via de Benedettini

AMAT Bus Ticket Kiosk

Palermo Centrale

Parco D'Orleans

Viale delle Scienze

Corso Tukory

Via Giorgio Arcoleo

Via Antonia Marinuzzi

Via Paolo Francesco

Via Oreto

Corso dei Mille

Palermo

and the Patronesses of Palermo. Van Dyck completed the work in Genoa in 1628, after leaving Palermo in fear of the plague. Also gracing the chapel are Giacomo Serpotta's amazingly elaborate stuccoes (1710–17), vivacious and whirling with figures. Serpotta's name meant 'lizard' or 'small snake', and he often included these signature reptiles in his work; see if you can find one!

ACTIVITIES

Palermo Street Food
Walking

(www.palermostreetfood.com; 3hr tour per person €30) Led by an enthusiastic group of young Palermitans, these walking tours offer insight into Palermo's celebrated street food as well as its architecture and art. Tours are conducted in the morning and evening, the morning option including an exploration of historic produce markets. Book tours at least 48 hours in advance.

Streaty
Walking

(www.streaty.com; 3hr tour per person adult/ child €39/15) These walking tours make a grand circuit of the city's street-food stalls, as well as offering glimpses into the city's history and traditions. The morning tour runs year-round, while the evening tour

operates from June to September. Participants are given a street food 'passport', allowing you to keep track of the places you've visited.

Vegetarians can be catered for if requested in advance when booking.

SHOPPING

Bottega dei Sapori e dei Saperi della Legalità
Food & Drinks

(☑091 32 20 23; Piazza Castelnuovo 13; ⊙10am-1pm & 4.30-7.30pm Mon-Sat) For edible souvenirs with a dollop of social consciousness, consider buying some wine, olive oil, pasta, couscous or marmalade – all grown on lands confiscated from the Mafia – at this unique store. It's run by the Libera Terra organisation, famous for its outspoken resistance to the Mafia's influence in Sicilian society.

Siculamente
Clothing

(www.siculamente.it; Via Emerico Amari 136; ⊙9.30am-1.30pm & 4-8pm) Wear a little Sicilian slang with one of the T-shirts, hats or bags sold at this cool little shop. All bear captions in local dialect, from pithy Sicilian proverbs to cheeky, humorous or political statements. The store's online catalogue provides

 Palermo's Street Food

Bangkok, Mexico City, Marrakesh, Palermo: clued-in gastronomes around the world know that Sicily's capital is one of the world's street-food capitals. The mystery is simply how Palermo is not the obesity capital of Europe, given just how much noshing goes on! Palermitans are at it all the time: when they're shopping, commuting, discussing business, romancing...basically at any time of the day. What they're devouring is the *buffitieri* – little hot snacks prepared at stalls and designed for eating on the spot.

Typical *buffitieri*
ALVARO GERMAN VILELA/SHUTTERSTOCK ©

translations into English and Italian to help your friends decipher exactly what kind of statement you're trying to make.

⊗ EATING

Trattoria al Vecchio Club Rosanero
Sicilian €

(☏349 4096880; Vicolo Caldomai 18; mains €3-12; ☉1-3.30pm Mon-Sat & 8-11pm Thu-Sat; ☏) A veritable shrine to the city's football team (*rosa nero* refers to the team's colours of pink and black), cavernous Vecchio Club scores goals with its bargain-priced, flavour-packed grub. Fish and seafood are the real fortes here; if it's on the menu, order the *caponata e pesce spada* (sweet-and-sour vegetable salad with swordfish). Head in early to avoid a wait.

Pasticceria Fratelli Magrì
Pastries €

(☏091 58 47 88; www.pasticceriamagri.com; Via Isidoro Carini 42; pastries from €2; ☉7am-9pm

Mon-Sun) This third-generation pastry shop remains one of Palermo's best. Defy your dentist with made-from-scratch staples like *cassata* (a concoction of sponge cake, cream, marzipan, chocolate and candied fruit) or *cannoli* (pastry shells with a sweet filling of ricotta or custard), or tuck into less-obvious classics like *patata* (sponge-based pastry with custard, marzipan and almond paste) and *torta savoia,* a decadent, multilayered Sicilian cake made using dark chocolate and hazelnuts. The shop also serves coffee.

Bisso Bistrot
Bistro €

(☏328 1314595; http://bissobistrot.it; Via Maqueda 172; mains €5-9; ☉9am-11pm Mon-Sat) Frescoed walls, exposed ceiling beams and reasonably priced appetisers, *primi* (first courses) and *secondi* (main courses) greet diners at this swinging, smart-casual bistro. Located at the northwest corner of the Quattro Canti, its fabulous edible offerings cover all bases, from morning *cornetti* (croissants) to lunch and dinner meat, fish and pasta dishes (the latter are especially good). Solo diners will appreciate the front bar seating.

Francu U Vastiddaru
Street Food €

(Corso Vittorio Emanuele 102; sandwiches €1.50-4; ☉9am-1am) Palermitan street food doesn't get any better or cheaper than the delicious *panini* hawked from this hole-in-the-wall sandwich shop just off Piazza Marina. Options range from the classic *panino triplo* (with chickpea fritters, potato croquettes and eggplant) to the owner's trademark *panino vastiddaru* (with roast pork, salami, Emmental cheese and spicy mushrooms).

Gelateria Ciccio Adelfio
Gelato €

(☏091 616 15 37; Corso dei Mille 73; gelato from €1; ☉7am-midnight) A quick walk from Stazione Centrale, this veteran gelateria is one of Palermo's best. Forget the cup and cone: go local and have your ice cream sandwiched in a brioche (€2). From classic flavours like pistachio, *torrone* (nougat) or *cannoli*, to more daring concoctions like Mars (Ciccio's icy take on the chocolate bar), the gelato here is fresh, velvety and an utter bargain.

🍷 DRINKING & NIGHTLIFE

Enoteca Buonivini   Wine Bar

(☎091 784 70 54; Via Dante 8; ⊙9.30am-1.30pm & 4pm-midnight Mon-Sat) Thirsty suits flock to this bustling, urbane *enoteca* (wine bar), complete with bar seating, courtyard and a generous selection of wines by the glass. There's no shortage of interesting local drops, not to mention artisan cheese and charcuterie boards, beautiful pasta dishes and grilled meats. When you're done, scan the shelves for harder-to-find craft spirits (Australian gin, anyone?) and Sicilian gourmet pantry essentials.

Pizzo & Pizzo   Wine Bar

(☎091 601 45 44; Via XII Gennaio 1; ⊙12.30-3.30pm & 7-11.30pm Mon-Sat; 🛜) Divided into a wine bar-cum-restaurant and next-door deli-bistro, Pizzo & Pizzo is a great place for *aperitivi* (pre-dinner drinks), with complimentary morsels like cucumber topped with ricotta mousse, spicy orange marmalade, mustard seed and pistachio. The convivial, neighbourly vibe and array of cheeses, cured meats and smoked fish might just convince you to stick around for dinner.

Botteghe Colletti   Bar

(☎327 9259307; Via Alessandro Paternostro; ⊙6.30pm-2.30am) Red theatrical curtains, old wooden cabinets and flickering candles in old gin bottles: this snug bar pulls a mixed-aged crowd of artists, students and general bohemians, clutching drinks, nibbling on *aperitivo* bites and spilling out onto the atmospheric street. Order a smoked Negroni, strike up a conversation or while away the hours with a game of chess.

ⓘ INFORMATION

SAFE TRAVEL

Contrary to stereotypes, Palermo is a relatively safe city with low rates of violent crime. That said, it pays to follow a few basic rules.

• Wear your handbag across your body and away from the street to avoid moped-riding thieves from snatching it.

• Be aware of your possessions in crowded areas, especially city buses and markets.

• Avoid poorly lit and deserted streets at night, especially those around the train station and the Kalsa district.

TOURIST INFORMATION

Municipal Tourist Office (☎091 740 80 21; http://turismo.comune.palermo.it; Piazza Bellini; ⊙8.45am-6.15pm Mon-Fri, from 9.45am Sat) The main branch of Palermo's city-run information booths. Other locations include **Piazza Ruggero Settimo** (Teatro Politeama Garibaldi; ⊙8.30am-1.30pm Mon-Fri), **Via Cavour** (⊙8.30am-6.30pm Mon-Fri, 9am-7pm Sun), the Port of Palermo and Mondello, though these are only intermittently staffed, with unpredictable hours.

🛈 GETTING AROUND

Bus Palermo's orange, white and blue city buses, operated by **AMAT** (☎848 800817, 091 35 01 11; www.amat.pa.it), are frequent but often overcrowded and slow. The free map handed out at Palermo tourist offices details the major bus lines; most stop at the train station.

Tickets, valid for 90 minutes, cost €1.40 and can be pre-purchased from *tabaccherie* (tobacconists) or the AMAT bus booth on Piazza Giulio Cesare just outside Palermo Centrale train station, or €1.80 on board the bus. A day pass costs €3.50. Once you board the bus, ensure to validate your ticket in the machine.

Taxis Taxis are expensive in Palermo, and heavy traffic can make matters worse. Official taxis should have a *tassametro* (meter), which records the fare; check for this before embarking. Hailing a passing taxi on the street is not customary; rather, you'll need to phone ahead for a taxi or wait at one of the taxi ranks at major travel hubs such as the train station, Piazza Politeama, Teatro Massimo and Piazza Independenza.

Walking The best way to experience central Palermo's atmosphere and architecture is on foot. Palermo's port is a 10-minute walk from Piazza Politeama, heart of the new city. From here, local buses whiz down Via Roma and Via Maqueda to Palermo Centrale, where trains serve destinations in Sicily and on the mainland.

CAGLIARI, SARDINIA, ITALY

Cagliari at a Glance...

The best way to arrive in Sardinia's historic capital is by sea, the city rising in a helter-skelter of golden-hued palazzi (mansions), domes and facades up to the rocky centrepiece, Il Castello. Although Tunisia is closer than Rome, Cagliari is the most Italian of Sardinia's cities. Vespas buzz down tree-fringed boulevards and locals hang out at busy cafes in the seafront Marina district. Cagliari wears its history on its sleeve and everywhere you go you will come across traces of its rich past: ancient Roman ruins, museums filled with prehistoric artefacts, centuries-old churches and elegant palazzi.

With One Day in Port

o Exploring **Il Castello** (p274) is a must, for the views if nothing else.

o You could while away the rest of the day at the **cathedral** (p275) and **archaeological museum** (p276), before exploring the rest of the city.

o Or head just east of town to buzzing **Poetto beach** (p281).

Best Places For...

Coffee Caffè Svizzero (p285)

Swimming Poetto beach (p281)

An aperitif Caffè Libarium Nostrum (p277)

Gelati Gocce di Gelato e Cioccolato (p285)

History Nora (p278)

Views Torre dell'Elefante (p274)

Wandering around Il Castello (p274)

Cagliari Map (p282)

Getting from the Port

Cagliari's cruise ships dock at the **main port**, just off Via Roma, at the southwestern edge of the city.

It's approximately 1.5km from ship to city – an easy walk – although the port offers a free shuttle from the ship to Piazza Matteotti, where you'll find the main bus station, the train station and a taxi rank.

Fast Facts

Currency Euro (€)

Languages Sardinian (Sardo), Italian

Money Banks and ATMs are widely available, particularly around the port and train station.

Restaurants Most close between 2.30pm and 7.30pm.

Tourist Information The island's main tourist office is near the cruise terminal.

Visas Generally not required for stays of up to 90 days (or at all for EU nationals); some nationalities need a Schengen visa.

Wi-fi Free wi-fi is available in many cafes and restaurants.

Cattedrale di Santa Maria

Il Castello

This hilltop citadel is Cagliari's most iconic image. Its domes, towers and palazzi, once home to the city's aristocracy, rise above the sturdy ramparts built by the Pisans and Aragonese.

Great For...

☑ Don't Miss

Exploring the narrow medieval lanes of Cagliari's hilltop citadel, and emerging to find view after dramatic view.

Uncovering the Castello

Inside the battlements, the old medieval city reveals itself, with university, cathedral, museums and Pisan palaces all wedged into a jigsaw of narrow high-walled alleys.

Sleepy though it may seem, the area harbours a number of boutiques, bars and cafes popular with visitors, students and hipsters.

Two Towers

One of only two Pisan towers still standing, the **Torre dell'Elefante** (www.benicultural icagliari.it; Via Santa Croce, cnr Via Università; adult/reduced €3/2; ☺10am-7pm summer, 9am-5pm winter) was built in 1307 as a defence against the Aragonese. Named after the sculpted elephant by the vicious-looking portcullis, the 42m-high tower became something of a horror show, thanks to the

Elephant sculpture on the Torre dell'Elefante

TRAVELNERD/SHUTTERSTOCK ©

⚓

Explore Ashore

Spend anything from an hour to a full day exploring the Castello. It's a steep 2km walk up from the port or take the elevator at the bottom of the Scalette di Santa Chiara behind Piazza Yenne. Bus 7 circles from Piazza Yenne up to Il Castello and back (daily €3.30).

★ Top Tip

The walls are best admired (and photographed) from afar – good spots include the Roman amphitheatre (p281) and Bonaria (p283).

severed heads used by the city's Spanish rulers to adorn it. The crenellated storey was added in 1852 and used as a prison for political detainees. Climb to the top for far-reaching views over the city's rooftops to the sea.

Rising above the skyline by the Castello's northeastern gate, the 36m-high **Torre di San Pancrazio** (www.beniculturalicagliari. it; Piazza Indipendenza; adult/reduced €3/2) is the twin of Elefante. Completed in 1305, it was built on the city's highest point and commands expansive views of the Golfo di Cagliari.

Cattedrale di Santa Maria

Cagliari's graceful 13th-century **cathedral** (☏070 864 93 88; www.duomodicagliari.it; Piazza Palazzo 4; ⊘8am-noon & 4-8pm Mon-Sat, 8am-1pm & 4.30-8.30pm Sun) stands proudly on Piazza Palazzo. Except for the square-based bell tower, little remains of the original Gothic structure: the clean Pisan-Romanesque facade is an imitation, added between 1933 and 1938. Inside, the once-Gothic church has all but disappeared beneath a rich icing of baroque decor, the result of a radical late-17th-century makeover. Bright frescoes adorn the ceilings, and the side chapels spill over with exuberant sculptural whirls.

The third chapel on the right, the Cappella di San Michele, is perhaps the most baroque of all, with its ornate sculptural depiction of a serene-looking St Michael casting devils into hell.

At the central door, note the two stone pulpits, sculpted by Guglielmo Agnelli between 1158 and 1162. They originally formed a single unit, which stood in Pisa's Duomo until donated to Cagliari in 1312. It was split by the meddlesome Domenico Spotorno, the architect behind the 17th-century baroque facelift, and the big stone lions that originally formed its base were removed to the altar where they now stand.

Beneath the altar is the Santuario dei Martiri (Sanctuary of Martyrs), the only one of several underground rooms open to the public. It is an impressive sight with its sculptural decoration and intricate carvings.

Palazzo Viceregio

Just steps from the cathedral, this pale lime **palazzo** (Piazza Palazzo 2; €1.50; ⊘10am-6.30pm Tue-Sun) was once home to the city's Spanish and Savoy viceroys. Today it serves as the provincial assembly and stages regular exhibitions and summer music concerts. You can visit several richly decorated rooms culminating in the Sala del Consiglio.

Museo Archeologico Nazionale

Of the four museums at the Cittadella dei Musei, this is the undoubted star. Sardinia's premier **archaeological museum** (☑070 6051 8245; http://museoarcheocagliari.benic-ulturali.it; Piazza Arsenale; adult/reduced €7/2, incl Pinacoteca Nazionale €9/4.50; ⊘9am-8pm Tue-Sun) showcases artefacts spanning thousands of years, from the early Neolithic, through the Bronze and Iron Ages to the Phoenician and Roman eras. Highlights include a series of colossal figures known as the Giganti di Monte Prama and a superb collection of *bronzetti* (bronze figurines) which, in the absence of any written records, are a vital source of information about Sardinia's mysterious Nuragic culture. In all, about 400 Nuragic bronzes have been discovered, many in sites of religious importance.

Palazzo Viceregio

The Giganti di Monte Prama, on the 3rd floor, are 2m-high sculptures that are the only Nuragic stone statues to have been discovered in Sardinia, and are among the oldest examples of their type in the Mediterranean. They date to the 8th and 9th centuries BC.

Pinacoteca Nazionale

Cagliari's principal **gallery** (☏070 65 69 91; www.pinacoteca.cagliari.beniculturali.it; Piazza Arsenale; adult/reduced €4/2, incl Museo Archeologico Nazionale €9/4.50; ☺9am-8pm Tue-Sun) showcases a prized collection of 15th- to 17th-century art. Many of the best works are *retablos* (grand altarpieces), painted by Catalan and Genoese artists. Of those by known Sardinian painters, the four 16th-century works by Pietro Cavaro, father of the so-called Stampace school and arguably Sardinia's most important artist, are outstanding.

Also represented is the painter's father, Lorenzo, and son Michele. Another Sardinian artist of note is Francesco Pinna, whose 17th-century *Pala di Sant'Orsola* hangs here. These images tend to show the influence of Spain and Italy, rather than illuminating the Sardinian condition. However, there is a brief line-up of 19th- and early-20th-century Sardinian painters, such as Giovanni Marghinotti and Giuseppe Sciuti.

Views of City & Sea

The vast neoclassical **Bastione di Saint Remy**, comprising a gallery space, monumental stairway and panoramic terrace, was built into the city's medieval walls between 1899 and 1902. The highlight is the elegant Umberto I terrace, which commands sweeping views over Cagliari's jumbled rooftops to the sea and distant mountains.

To reach the terrace, try the stairway on Piazza Costituzione or take the elevator from the Giardino Sotto Le Mure.

> **★ Did You Know?**
>
> The neighbourhood is known to locals as Su Casteddu, a term also used to describe the whole city.

VALERY ROKHIN/SHUTTERSTOCK ©

> **✕ Take a Break**
>
> Offering some of the best views in town, modish bar **Caffè Libarium Nostrum** (☏346 5220212; Via Santa Croce 33; ☺7.30am-2am Tue-Sun) has panoramic seating on top of the medieval ramparts.

Ruins of a patrician villa

PECOLD/SHUTTERSTOCK ©

Nora

Nora's ruins are all that remain of what was once one of Sardinia's most powerful cities. Highlights of the site include a Roman theatre and an ancient baths complex. The site is accessible by guided tour only. They are excellent and begin every 30 minutes.

Great For...

☑ Don't Miss

Pick up supplies for lunch. Nora is in a quiet spot, with few eating options nearby (the nearest being in Pula).

History

Founded by Phoenicians in the 8th century BC, Nora later became an important Punic centre, and in the 3rd century AD, the island's Roman capital. It was eventually abandoned in the 8th century as the threat of Arab raids became too much for its nervous citizens.

Highlights

Upon entry, you pass a single melancholy column. This is all that's left of a temple dedicated to Tanit, the Carthaginian Venus, who was once worshipped here. Beyond this is a small 2nd-century Roman theatre facing the sea.

Towards the west are the substantial remains of the Terme al Mare (Baths by the Sea). Four columns (a tetrastyle) stand at the heart of what was a patrician

Floor mosaic

PECOLD/SHUTTERSTOCK ©

Explore Ashore

Nora is near the town of Pula, some 32km southwest of Cagliari. From Cagliari there are hourly buses to Pula (€3.30, one hour), and shuttle buses (10 minutes, approximately hourly) between Nora and Piazza Municipio in Pula. Allow at least four hours for the whole excursion if on public transport.

❶ Need to Know

☑070 920 91 38; http://nora.beniculturali. unipd.it; adult/reduced €7.50/4.50; ⊙10.30am-7pm Apr-Sep, 10.30am-5.30pm Oct, 10am-4pm Nov–mid-Feb, 8.30am-5pm mid-Feb–Mar

villa; the surrounding rooms retain their mosaic floor decoration. More remnants of mosaics can be seen at a temple complex towards the tip of the promontory.

Overlooking the ruins, the Torre del Coltellazzo is a 17th-century watchtower set on the site of the Phoenician city's acropolis.

Take a Break

In Pula, you'll have no trouble finding somewhere to eat. The main area is Piazza del Popolo and the streets fanning from it. The pick of Pula's lunch spots is **S'Incontru** (☑070 920 81 28; www.sincontru.it; Piazza del Popolo 69; meals €15-30; ⊙noon-4.30pm & 7pm-midnight), with wood-fired pizzas, grilled steaks and seafood pasta.

What's Nearby

Make a quiet, peaceful day of it with a post-tour swim at **Spiaggia di Nora**, a pleasant, clean beach with calm, clear waters and a view of the ruins and watchtower.

On the western side of the Nora promontory, 1km from the ruins, you can often spy pink flamingos stalking around the **Laguna di Nora** (☑070 920 95 44; www.lagunadinora.it; adult/reduced €8/6, excursions €25/15; ⊙visitor centre 10am-8pm Jun-Aug, to 7pm Sep). The visitor centre has a small aquarium and displays dedicated to whales and dolphins. There are also nature trails to wander.

Be sure you allow enough time to return to the port.

◉ SIGHTS

Cagliari's key sights are concentrated in four central districts: Il Castello, Stampace, Marina and Villanova.

Bordered by Largo Carlo Felice to the west and seafront Via Roma, the characterful Marina district is a joy to explore on foot, not so much for its sights, of which there are few, but for the atmosphere of its dark, narrow lanes crammed with artisan shops, cafes and trattorias.

To the west, high up the hill, is Stampace, where you'll find a number of important churches, a botanic garden and a rocky Roman amphitheatre.

Extending east of Marina, the 19th-century Villanova district boasts some of the city's most picturesque streets – the area around Piazza San Domenico is particularly alluring – as well as wide traffic-clogged roads and imposing piazzas. Its star sight is the hard-to-miss Santuario & Basilica di Nostra Signora di Bonaria.

Museo del Tesoro e Area Archeologica di Sant'Eulalia   Museum

(☏391 4694189; www.mutseu.org; Vico del Collegio 2; adult/reduced €5/2.50; ⊙ 9.30am-4pm Tue-Sun Nov-Mar, 9.30am-6pm Tue-Sun Apr-Oct) In the heart of the Marina district, this museum contains a rich collection of religious art, as well as an archaeological area beneath the adjacent **Chiesa di Sant' Eulalia**. The main drawcard is a 13m section of excavated Roman road (constructed between the 1st and 2nd centuries AD), which archaeologists think would have connected with the nearby port.

Chiesa di Santo Sepolcro   Church

(Piazza del Santo Sepolcro 5; ⊙10am-noon & 5-7pm) The most astonishing feature of this church is an enormous 17th-century gilded wooden altarpiece housing a figure of the Virgin Mary. From the church, stairs lead down to the crypt, a creepy grotto consisting of two cave-like rooms gouged out of bare rock. In one you'll find a skull and crossbones on the wall.

Piazza Yenne   Piazza

The focal point of the Marina district, and indeed of central Cagliari, is Piazza Yenne. The small square is adorned with a statue of **King Carlo Felice** to mark the beginning of the SS131 cross-island highway, the project for which the monarch is best remembered.

Cripta di Santa Restituta   Crypt

(☏070 667 01 68; Via Sant'Efisio 14; adult/reduced €2/1; ⊙10am-1pm) This crypt has been in use since pre-Christian times. It's a huge, eerie, natural cavern where the echo of leaking water drip-drips. Originally a place of pagan worship, it became the home of the martyr Restituta in the 5th century and a reference point for Cagliari's early Christians. The Orthodox Christians then took it over – you can still see remnants of their frescoes – until the 13th century, when it was abandoned.

The nearby **Chiesa di Sant'Anna** (Piazza Santa Restituta; ⊙7.30-10.30am & 5-8pm Tue-Sun), rising grandly above a wide staircase, is more impressive outside than in. It was largely destroyed by bombing in 1943 but painstakingly rebuilt.

Chiesa di San Michele   Church

(Via Ospedale 2; ⊙8-11am & 7-8.30pm Mon-Sat, 9am-noon & 7-9pm Sun) Although consecrated in 1538, this Jesuit church is best known for its lavish 18th-century decor, considered the finest example of baroque styling in Sardinia. The spectacle starts outside with the ebullient triple-arched facade and continues through the vast colonnaded atrium into the magnificent octagonal interior. Here six heavily decorated chapels radiate from the centre, capped by a grand, brightly frescoed dome. Also of note is the sacristy, with its vivid frescoes and intricate inlaid wood.

Before you go inside, take a minute to admire the massive four-columned pulpit in the atrium, built and named in honour of the Spanish emperor Carlos V.

Orto Botanico Gardens

(Botanic Gardens; ☏070 675 35 08; www.
ccb-sardegna.it; Viale Sant'Ignazio da Laconi 11;
adult/reduced €4/2; ⏱9am-6pm Tue-Sun summer, to 2pm winter) Established in 1858, the
Orto Botanico is one of Italy's most famous
botanic gardens. Today it extends over
5 hectares and nurtures 2000 species of
flora. Leafy arches lead to trickling fountains
and gardens bristling with palm trees, cacti
and ficus trees with huge snaking roots.

Specimens from as far afield as Asia,
Australia, Africa and the Americas sidle up
to the local carob trees and oaks. Littering
the gardens are a Punic cistern, a Roman
quarry and an aqueduct.

Anfiteatro Romano Archaeological Site

(Viale Sant'Ignazio da Laconi) Cagliari's most
significant Roman monument is this
2nd-century amphitheatre. The structure
is carved into the rocky flank of the Buon
Cammino hill, near the northern entrance
to Il Castello. Over the centuries much of
the original theatre has been cannibalised
for building material, but enough survives
to stir the imagination.

Galleria Comunale d'Arte Gallery

(☏070 677 75 98; www.museicivicicagliari.it; Giardini Pubblici; adult/reduced €6/2.50; ⏱10am-
8pm Tue-Sun Jun-Aug, 10am-6pm Tue-Sun
Sep-May) Housed in a neoclassical villa in
the Giardini Pubblici (Public Gardens) north
of the Castello, this terrific gallery focuses
on modern and contemporary art. Works
by many of Sardinia's top artists are on
show, alongside paintings and sculptures
from the Collezione Ingrao, a formidable
collection of 20th-century Italian art.

Once you have finished in the gallery, visit the gardens, which command sweeping
views over Cagliari's modern skyline.

Exmà Cultural Centre

(☏070 66 63 99; www.exmacagliari.com; Via
San Lucifero 71; admission varies, typically €3-5;
⏱10am-1pm & 4-9pm Tue-Sun summer, 9am-1pm
& 4-8pm Tue-Sun winter) Housed in Cagliari's
18th-century *mattatoio* (abattoir) – hence
the sculpted cow's head over the entrance

Poetto Beach & the Wetlands

Fabulous **Poetto beach** is one of the
longest stretches of sand in Italy and an
integral part of Cagliari's city life. The
strip is lined with bars, snack joints and
restaurants, known locally as *chioschi*
(kiosks), many of which rent out beach
gear – prices start at around €15 for an
umbrella and two sunloungers.

The southern end of the beach is
the most popular, with its picturesque
Marina Piccola. Looming over the marina
is the craggy Promontorio di Sant' Elia,
known as the Sella del Diavola (Devil's
Saddle). According to local legend, the
headland was the scene of an epic battle
between Lucifer and the Archangel
Michael, in which Satan was thrown off
his horse and his saddle fell into the sea.
Although much of the headland is now
owned by the military and closed to the
public, you can access it via a scenic
walking path.

Poetto is an easy bus ride from
the city centre. Hop on bus PF or PQ
from Piazza Matteotti. On the way
there, consider detouring to the **Parco
Naturale Regionale Molentargius**
(www.parcomolentargius.it; ⏱6.30am-9pm
summer, 7am-6pm winter), reed-fringed
wetlands that attract nesting, migrant
and wintering birds in their thousands.
You may spot pink flamingos, purple
herons, little egrets, marsh harriers,
sandwich terns and black-winged stilts
from the observation points.

Poetto beach
STEFANO GARAU/SHUTTERSTOCK ©

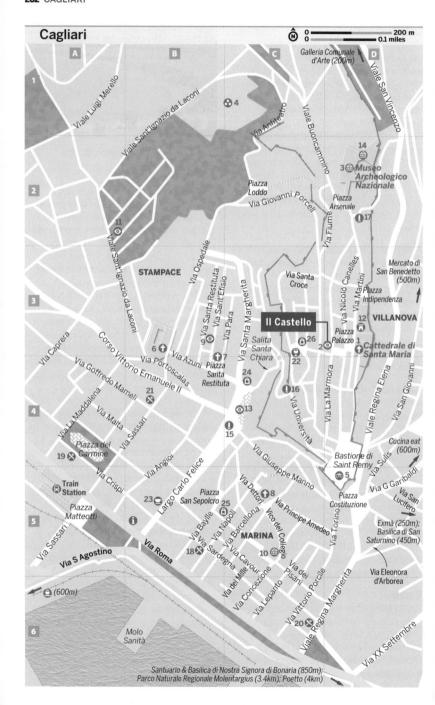

Cagliari

0   200 m
0   0.1 miles

Galleria Comunale
d'Arte (200m)

Viale San Vincenzo

Viale Luigi Merello

Viale Sant'Ignazio da Laconi

Via Anfiteatro

Viale Buoncammino

14

3 Museo
Archeologico
Nazionale

Piazza
Loddo

Via Giovanni Porcell

Piazza
Arsenale

17

Via Flume

Viale Sant'Ignazio da Laconi

11

STAMPACE

Via Ospedale

Via Santa Restituta

Via Sant'Efisio

Via Para

Via Santa Margherita

Via Santa
Croce

Via Nicolò Canelles

Via Martini

Mercato di
San Benedetto
(500m)

Piazza
Indipendenza

12 VILLANOVA

Il Castello

Piazza
Palazzo

1 Cattedrale di
Santa Maria

Via Caprera

Corso Vittorio Emanuele II

Via Goffredo Mameli

6

Via Azuni

Via Portoscalas

9

7

Piazza
Santa
Restituta

Salita
Santa
Chiara

26

2

22

Via La Marmora

Via Regina Elena

Via San Giovanni

21

24

16

13

15

Via Università

Via La Maddalena

Via Malta

Via Sassari

Piazza del
Carmine

19

Via Crispi

Via Angioi

Largo Carlo Felice

Via Giuseppe Manno

Bastione di
Saint Remy

5

Cucina eat
(600m)

Via Sulis

Via G Garibaldi

Via San Lucifero

Train
Station

Piazza
Matteotti

23

Piazza
San Sepolcro

25

Via Dettori

8

Via Principe Amedeo

Piazza
Costituzione

Piazza
Sassari

Via S Agostino

Via Roma

18

Via Baylle

Via Barcellona

Via Napoli

Via Sardegna

Via Cavour

MARINA

Vico del Collegio

10

Via dei
Pisani

Via Torino

Exmà (250m);
Basilica di San
Saturnino (450m)

(600m)

Molo
Sanità

Via del Mille

Via Concezione

Via Lepanto

20

Via Vittorio Porcile

Viale Regina Margherita

Via Eleonora
d'Arborea

Via XX Settembre

Santuario & Basilica di Nostra Signora di Bonaria (850m);
Parco Naturale Regionale Molentargius (3.4km); Poetto (4km)

Cagliari

⊚ Top Sights
1 Cattedrale di Santa Maria.........................D3
2 Il Castello D3
3 Museo Archeologico Nazionale D2

⊚ Sights
4 Anfiteatro Romano....................................C1
5 Bastione di Saint Remy.............................D5
6 Chiesa di San Michele...............................B3
7 Chiesa di Sant'Anna B4
8 Chiesa di Santo Sepolcro C5
9 Cripta di Santa Restituta B3
10 Museo del Tesoro e Area
    Archeologica di Sant'Eulalia...................C5
11 Orto Botanico...A2
12 Palazzo Viceregio D3
13 Piazza Yenne C4
14 Pinacoteca Nazionale...............................D2

15 Statue of Carlo Felice C4
16 Torre dell'Elefante....................................C4
17 Torre di San Pancrazio.............................D2

⊗ Eating
18 Antica Cagliari B5
19 Gocce di Gelato e Cioccolato...................A4
20 Luigi Pomata...C6
21 Ristorante Ammentos...............................B4

⊙ Drinking & Nightlife
22 Caffè Libarium Nostrum C3
23 Caffè Svizzero...B5

⊙ Shopping
24 Antica Enoteca Cagliaritana C4
25 Loredana Mandas B5
26 Sorelle Piredda...C3

and around the internal courtyard – Exmà is a delightful cultural centre. Check the website for details of its varied program of events, performances, concerts and exhibitions.

Basilica di San Saturnino   Basilica

(Piazza San Cosimo; ⊙9am-7pm Sat & 1st Sun of month) One of the oldest churches in Sardinia, the Basilica di San Saturnino is a striking example of Paleo-Christian architecture. Based on a Greek-cross pattern, the domed basilica was built over a Roman necropolis in the 5th century, on the site where Saturninus, a much-revered local martyr, was buried. According to legend, Saturninus was beheaded in AD 304 during emperor Diocletian's anti-Christian pogroms.

Santuario & Basilica di Nostra Signora di Bonaria   Church

(⏹070 30 17 47; Piazza Bonaria 2; donations welcome; ⊙6.30-11.45am & 4.30-8pm summer, 6.30-11.45am & 4-7pm winter) Crowning the Bonaria hill, around 1km southeast of Via Roma, this religious complex is a hugely popular pilgrimage site. Devotees come from all over the world to visit the 14th-century Gothic church sanctuary and pray to Nostra Signora di Bonaria, a statue of the Virgin Mary and Christ that supposedly saved a ship's crew during a storm. To the right of the sanctuary, the towering neoclassical

basilica still acts as a landmark to returning sailors. Construction started on this in 1704 but the money ran out and it wasn't officially completed until 1926.

The historic seat of the Mercedari order of monks, the sanctuary was originally part of a fortified compound built by the Aragonese. The Spaniards arrived in Cagliari in 1323 intent on wresting the city from the Pisans, but when they saw what they were up against, they set up camp on the fresh mountain slopes of Montixeddu, which over time came to be known as Bonaria for its clean air – from the Italian *buon'aria* meaning 'good air'. A three-year siege ensued, during which the camp grew to become a fortress with its own church.

Little remains of the fortress, apart from its Gothic portal, a truncated bell tower, which initially served as a watchtower, and the church. Above the church altar hangs a tiny 15th-century ivory ship, whose movements are said to indicate the wind direction in the Golfo degli Angeli.

The sanctuary's **museum** is accessible through the small cloister, with the mummified corpses of four plague-ridden Aragonese nobles whose bodies were found miraculously preserved inside the church.

Buses 30 and 31 run along the seafront to near the sanctuary.

 Lunch on the Go

For a delicious packed lunch go into one of the neighbourhood *salumerie* (delicatessens) and ask for a thick cut of *pecorino sardo* (Sardinian *pecorino* cheese) and a slice or two of prosciutto (ham) in a freshly baked *panino* (bread roll). Or, stock up on picnic goodies at the Mercato di San Benedetto.

Deli at the Mercato di San Benedetto
PAOLO CERTO/SHUTTERSTOCK ©

🔒 SHOPPING

Cagliari has a refreshing absence of overtly touristy souvenir shops, although they do exist. Style-conscious shoppers will find plenty to browse on Via Giuseppe Manno and Via Giuseppe Garibaldi. Nearby Via Sulis is another good area with several fashion boutiques and jewellery stores. You'll also find various artisanal shops tucked away, particularly in the Marina district. Sunday is best for flea market and antique finds.

Mercato di San Benedetto　　Market
(Via San Francesco Cocco Ortu; ⊙7am-2pm Mon-Sat) Cagliari's historic morning food market is exactly what a thriving market should be – busy, noisy and packed with fresh, fabulous produce: fish, salami, heavy clusters of grapes, *pecorino* the size of wagon wheels, steaks, sushi, you name it.

Antica Enoteca Cagliaritana　Wine
(☑070 67 05 32; www.enotecacagliaritana.it; Piazza Yenne 8; ⊙9am-1.15pm & 4.30-8.15pm Mon-Sat) Wine buffs will enjoy exploring

the racks at this specialist wine shop on Piazza Yenne. The emphasis is on Sardinian wines but you'll also come across Italian and international labels, as well as spirits, liqueurs and champagnes. You can have orders sent anywhere in the world except the US (customs difficulties, apparently).

Sorelle Piredda　Fashion & Accessories
(☑334 2157266, 349 5500528; www.sardegna
artigianato.com/it/artigiano/sorelle-piredda;
Piazza San Giuseppe 4; ⊙10am-7.30pm Mon-Sat)
For haute couture with history, search out this oh-so-stylish Castello boutique. The shop itself is a sight, set over a Punic cistern and ancient Roman streets, but it's the imaginative designs of the Piredda sisters that steal the limelight: slinky evening dresses, capes and intricate shawls inspired by ancient Sardinian motifs and traditional island costumes.

Loredana Mandas　Jewellery
(☑070 66 76 48; www.loredanamandas.com;
Via Sicilia 31; ⊙9.30am-1pm & 5-8.30pm
Mon-Sat summer, 9.30am-1pm & 4.30-8pm
Mon-Sat winter) For something very special, seek out this jewellery workshop where artisan Loredana Mandas creates the exquisite gold filigree for which Sardinia is so famous. Her designs, which often incorporate precious or semi-precious gemstones, cost from around €220 to €2000 plus.

✴ EATING

It's not difficult to eat well in Cagliari. The city offers everything from classy fine-dining restaurants to humble neighbourhood trattorias, pizzerias, bars and takeaways. Marina is chock-full of places, some of which are obviously touristy but many that are not and are popular with locals. Other good eat streets include Via Sassari and Corso Vittorio Emanuele.

Luigi Pomata　Seafood €€
(☑070 67 20 58; www.luigipomata.com; Viale Regina Margherita 14; mains restaurant €20-30, bistrot €15; ⊙1-3pm & 8-11pm Mon-Sat) There's

always a buzz at chef Luigi Pomata's minimalist seafood restaurant, with pared-down decor and chefs skilfully preparing super-fresh sushi. For a more casual eating experience, try the Pomata Bistrot, beneath the main restaurant, where you can dine on dishes such as stuffed squid with broccoli cream in a tranquil, relaxed setting.

Antica Cagliari   Sardinian €€
(070 734 01 98; www.anticacagliari.it; Via Sardegna 49; mains €10-25; 12.30-3pm & 7.30-11.30pm) A cut above most restaurants in the Marina district, this vaulted restaurant always has a good buzz. Diners come for its traditional seafood, which stars in dishes such as spaghetti *vongole e bottarga* (with clams and mullet roe) and sea bass cooked with Vermentino white wine, olives and laurel. Reserve ahead for one of the few outdoor tables.

Ristorante Ammentos   Sardinian €€
(070 65 10 75; Via Sassari 120; fixed-price menu €15-30; 1-3pm & 8-11pm Wed-Mon) Dine on authentic southern Sardinian fare in rustic surrounds at this traditional old-school trattoria. *Malloreddus* (typical Sardinian gnocchi) with Gorgonzola cheese is a delicious lead to succulent meat dishes such as wild pork and sausages.

Gocce di Gelato e Cioccolato   Gelato €
(Piazza del Carmine 21; gelato €1.70-4.50; noon-10pm Mon-Fri, to 11pm Sat, 10.30am-1.30pm & 4.30-10pm Sun, longer hours summer) Stop by for divine handmade gelati, desserts (try the millefeuille), spice-infused pralines and truffles.

🍷 DRINKING & NIGHTLIFE

Cucina eat   Wine Bar
(070 099 10 98; www.shopcucina.it; Piazza Galileo Galilei 1; 10.30am-11.30pm Mon-Sat) A bookshop, a bar, a bistro? Cucina eat is pretty much all of these, with its central bar and ceiling-high shelves stocked with wines, olive oils, cookbooks and kitchen

gadgets, all of which are available to buy. Cool and relaxed, it's a fine spot to wind down with a bottle of wine and a light meal (around €20 to €25).

Caffè Svizzero   Cafe
(070 65 37 84; Largo Carlo Felice 6; 7am-9pm Mon-Sat) At the bottom of Largo Carlo Felice, this Liberty-style place has been a stalwart of Cagliari cafe society since the early 20th century. Anything from tea to cappuccinos and cocktails is on offer in its polished wood and brick-vaulted interior.

ℹ INFORMATION

Banks and ATMs are widely available, particularly around the port and train station, on Largo Carlo Felice and Corso Vittorio Emanuele.

Tourist office (070 677 81 73; www.cagliari turismo.it; Via Roma 145, Palazzo Civico; 9am-8pm Apr-Oct, 10am-1pm daily & 2-6pm Mon-Sat Nov-Mar) Helpful English-speaking staff can provide city information and maps. The office is just inside Palazzo Civico's main entrance, on the right.

ℹ GETTING AROUND

Bus Routes by **CTM** (Consorzio Trasporti e Mobilità; 800 078870; www.ctmcagliari.it) cover the city and surrounding area. You might use the buses to reach a handful of out-of-the-way sights, and they come in handy for Poetto beach. An all-day ticket costs €3.30.

Taxi There are taxi ranks at **Piazza Matteotti** (Via Sassari), **Piazza Repubblica** and on **Largo Carlo Felice** (Piazza Yenne). Otherwise you can call the radio taxi firms **Radio Taxi 4 Mori** (070 40 01 01; www.cagliaritaxi.com) and **Rossoblù** (070 66 55; www.radiotaxirossoblu.com).

Walking The centre of Cagliari is small enough to explore on foot. The walk up to Il Castello is tough, but there's an elevator at the bottom of the Scalette di Santa Chiara behind Piazza Yenne.

VALLETTA,
MALTA

In This Chapter

Valletta at a Glance...

Valletta is Malta's Lilliputian capital, built by the Knights of St John on a peninsula that's only 1km by 600m. It may be small, but it's packed full of sights; when Unesco named Valletta a World Heritage site, it described it as 'one of the most concentrated historic areas in the world'. The Renzo Piano–designed City Gate, Parliament Building and Opera House have changed the cityscape and galvanised it into life. These sights, along with Valletta's status as European Capital of Culture for 2018, have seen the city reborn, with new museums, restored golden-stone fortresses, and new bars and restaurants.

With One Day in Port

○ Start the day with coffee at **Lot Sixty One** (p303) or **No 43** (p303) before wandering Valletta's history-loaded streets.

○ Be sure to visit major attractions evoking the island's illustrious history: **St John's Co-Cathedral** (p292), the **Grand Master's Palace** (p294) and the **National Museum of Archaeology** (p298).

○ Admire Valletta's recent contemporary additions at **MUŻA** (p299) and Renzo Piano's **Parliament Building** (p299) and **City Gate** (p299), before taking in astounding Grand Harbour views from **Upper Barrakka Gardens** (p298).

Best Places For...

Traditional Maltese cuisine Noni (p303)

Ftira Nenu the Artisan Baker (p303)

Coffee Lot Sixty One (p303)

Quick eats No 43 (p303)

Souvenirs Artisans Centre (p302)

Previous page: Valletta skyline
ANTON ZELENOV/GETTY IMAGES ©

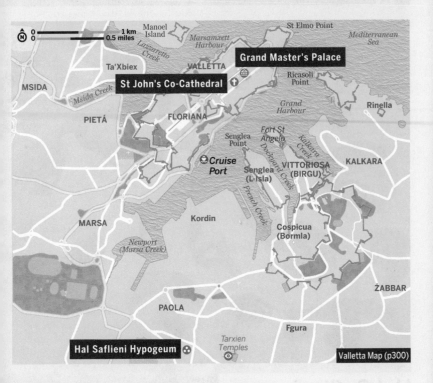

Map labels: Manoel Island, St Elmo Point, Mediterranean Sea, Marsamxett Harbour, Lazzaretto Creek, **Grand Master's Palace**, Ta'Xbiex, VALLETTA, Ricasoli Point, **St John's Co-Cathedral**, MSIDA, Msida Creek, Grand Harbour, Rinella, PIETÁ, FLORIANA, Senglea Point, Fort St Angelo, Kalkara Creek, Dockyard Creek, VITTORIOSA (BIRGU), KALKARA, ⚓ **Cruise Port**, Senglea (L-Isla), French Creek, MARSA, Kordin, Cospicua (Bormla), Newport (Marsa Creek), ŻABBAR, PAOLA, Fgura, Tarxien Temples, **Hal Saflieni Hypogeum**, Valletta Map (p300)

Getting from the Port

The Upper Barrakka Lift (p302) connects Valletta to the **Sea Passenger Terminal** at the Valletta Waterfront. There are also regular buses, as well as stops for the hop-on, hop-off services.

There's a taxi information kiosk on Valletta Waterfront where you can organise and pay the set rate for your taxi journey upfront. The cheapest fare (to an address in Valletta or Floriana) is €12.

Fast Facts

Currency Euro (€)

Languages Malti, English

Money ATMs are widespread. Some smaller restaurants only accept cash.

Tourist information The Tourist Office (p303) provides plenty of maps, walking trail pamphlets and brochures.

Visas Malta is in the Schengen area. Visas are not required for citizens of EU and EEA countries. Other nationalities should check www.identitymalta.com/schengen.

Wi-fi Many bars and cafes offer wi-fi access, and there are also free public hotspots in Valletta's main plazas (www.mca.org.mt/wifi-hotspots).

Model layout of the Hal Saflieni Hypogeum

Hal Saflieni Hypogeum

The Hal Saflieni Hypogeum is one of the country's most important prehistoric sites. Around 5000 years old, the mysterious subterranean burial chambers inspire awe and provide a unique insight into life and death across the millennia.

Great For...

☑ Don't Miss

The fascinating audiovisual presentation about the site.

The Hypogeum (from the Greek, meaning 'underground') is a subterranean necropolis, discovered during building work in 1902. To visit is to step into a mysterious and silent world. Its halls, chambers and passages, immaculately hewn out of the rock, cover some 500 sq metres; it is thought to date from around 3600 to 3000 BC, and an estimated 7000 bodies may have been interred here.

The ancient workers mimicked built masonry in carving out these underground chambers, and exploited the rock's natural weaknesses and strengths to carve out the spaces by hand and create a safe underground structure. Carbon dioxide exhaled by visiting tourists did serious damage to the delicate limestone walls of the burial chambers, and it was closed to the public for 10 years up to mid-2000. It

Explore Ashore

The Hal Saflieni Hypogeum lies in Paola, 6km south of Valletta. Several buses depart from the Floriani A stop on Triq Sant' Anna (a 15-minute stroll from port), including 1, 2, 3, 82 and 84 (15 to 20 minutes, frequent), and stop at Pjazza Paola, a five-minute walk from the Hypogeum. Allow one to two hours here.

❶ Need to Know

📞2180 5019; www.heritagemalta.org; Triq iċ-Ċimiterju; adult/child €35/15, audiovisual only adult/child €5/3.50; ☺9am-5pm, 50min tours on the hour, last tour 4pm

has been restored with Unesco funding; the microclimate is now strictly controlled and visitor numbers to the site are limited (10 per tour and eight tours per day).

A 20-minute audiovisual presentation is also available at the Hypogeum. This does not need to be booked in advance but does not include access to the Hypogeum itself.

Note that prebooking online is essential; try to book around three months before your visit. For health and safety reasons, children under the age of six cannot visit the Hypogeum.

What's Nearby?

The **Tarxien Temples** (📞2169 5578; www.heritagemalta.org; Triq it-Templi Neolitiċi; adult/child €6/3; ☺9am-5pm), pronounced 'tar-sheen', are hidden up a backstreet several blocks east of the Hypogeum. These megalithic structures were excavated in 1914 and are thought to date from between 3600 and 2500 BC. There are four linked structures, built with massive stone blocks up to 3m by 1m by 1m in size, decorated with spiral patterns, pitting and animal reliefs.

The large statue of a broad-hipped female figure was found in the right-hand niche of the first temple, and a copy remains in situ. In 2015 works took place to add a visitor centre and erect a cover to protect the temples.

The temples are a 10-minute walk from the Hypogeum.

St John's Co-Cathedral

The austere exterior of Valletta's magnificent cathedral is no preparation for the frenzy of baroque gold and lavish decoration in its interior, making it Malta's most impressive church.

Great For...

☑ Don't Miss

Caravaggio's *Beheading of St John the Baptist* in the Oratory – the largest work ever produced by the artist.

The Cathedral

St John's Co-Cathedral was designed by architect Girolamo Cassar, and built between 1573 and 1578, taking over from the Church of St Lawrence in Vittoriosa as the place where the Knights of St John would gather for communal worship. The interior was revamped in the 17th century in exuberant Maltese baroque style – an astounding surprise after the plain facade.

Every wall, pillar and rib of the long, low nave is encrusted with rich ornamentation, giving the effect of a dusty gold brocade. The floor is an iridescent patchwork quilt of marble tomb slabs, and the vault dances with paintings by Mattia Preti depicting events from the life of St John the Baptist.

The cathedral has eight chapels allocated to the various langues (divisions, based on nationality), including the Chapel of Germa-

FREISEIN/SHUTTERSTOCK ©

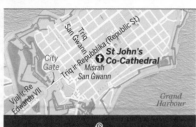

⚓

Explore Ashore

Take bus 130 to stop Valletta 18, then catch bus 133 from stop Valletta 1A to Gang, where it's a two-minute walk to the cathedral (19-minute journey all up). Or it's a 17-minute walk to the cathedral via the Upper Barrakka Lift (p302). Allow two hours to explore the cathedral.

❶ Need to Know

☑2122 0536; www.stjohnscocathedral. com; Triq ir-Repubblika; adult/child €10/free; ⊙9.30am-4.30pm Mon-Fri, to 12.30pm Sat

ny, the Chapel of Castille, Leon & Portugal and the sumptuous Chapel of Aragon. The **Chapel of the Holy Relics** guards a wooden figure of St John, said to be from the galley in which the Knights departed from Rhodes in 1523. The altar is dominated by the *Baptism of Christ* by Giuseppe Mazzuoli. The austere **Chapel of France**, with a Preti altarpiece of St Paul, houses lavish funerary monuments, including those of Grand Masters Adrien de Wignacourt and Fra Emmanuel de Rohan-Polduc. Preti's painting, *The Mystic Marriage of St Catherine,* hangs in the exquisite baroque **Chapel of Italy**, overlooking a bust of Grand Master Gregorio Carafa.

The **Oratory** was built in 1603 as a plain, unadorned building for novices, and later redecorated by Preti. It contains Caravaggio's menacing *Beheading of St John the Baptist* (c 1608) and his *St Jerome,* full of quiet power and pathos.

St John's was raised to a status equal to that of St Paul's Cathedral in Mdina – the official seat of the Archbishop of Malta – by a papal decree of 1816, hence the term 'co-cathedral'.

Visitors should dress appropriately for a house of worship. Stiletto heels are not permitted, to protect the marble floor.

The Museum

Scheduled to reopen in 2020 after an extensive and impressive remodelling, the Cathedral Museum houses the beautiful 16th-century Graduals of L-Isle Adam, illuminated choral books and a magnificent collection of 17th-century Flemish tapestries based on drawings by Rubens. A new feature is an excellent exhibition on the life and times of Caravaggio.

State Rooms

RYZHKOV SERGEY/SHUTTERSTOCK ©

Grand Master's Palace

Once the residence of the Grand Masters of the Knights of St John, the 16th-century Grand Master's Palace conceals a sumptuous interior behind a stern exterior.

Great For...

☑ **Don't Miss**

The 5000 suits of armour in the Armoury.

From Malta's independence until 2015 the building was the seat of Malta's parliament.

The Armoury

The Armoury is housed in what was once the Grand Master's stables. Originally, the armour and weapons belonging to the Knights were stored at the Palace Armoury; when a Knight died, they became the property of the Order. The collection of more than 5000 suits of 16th- to 18th-century armour is all that remains of an original 25,000 – Napoleon's light-fingered activities, overenthusiastic housekeeping by the British and general neglect put paid to the rest.

Some of the most interesting pieces are the breastplate worn by la Valette, the beautifully damascened suit made for Alof de Wignacourt, the captured Turkish Sipahi

The Armoury Corridor

RYZHKOV SERGEY/SHUTTERSTOCK ©

⚓

Explore Ashore

Take bus 130 to stop Valletta 18, then catch bus 133 from stop Valletta 1A to Nawfragju, where it's a two-minute walk to the palace (20-minute journey all up). It's a 20-minute stroll via the Upper Barrakka Lift (p302).

❶ Need to Know

www.heritagemalta.org; Pjazza San Ġorġ; adult/child incl Palace State Apartments, Armoury & audio guide €10/5; ⊘Armoury 9am-5pm, State Apartments 10am-4pm Fri-Wed

(cavalry) armour, and reinforced armour with bullet marks. There are also displays of some beautiful weapons, including crossbows, muskets, swords and pistols.

State Rooms & Halls

In the **State Apartments**, five rooms are usually open to the public, although one-off exhibitions – and the fact that the palace remains the official residence of the Maltese president – may mean some rooms are closed. The long **Armoury Corridor**, decorated with trompe l'œil painting, scenes of naval battles and the portraits and escutcheons of various Grand Masters, leads to the **Council Chamber** on the left. It is hung with 17th-century Gobelins tapestries gifted to the Order in 1710 by Grand Master Ramon

de Perellos, featuring exotic scenes of Africa, India, the Caribbean and Brazil.

Beyond lie the **State Dining Room** and the **Supreme Council Hall**, where the Supreme Council of Order met. It is decorated with a frieze depicting events from the Great Siege of 1565, while the minstrels' gallery bears paintings showing scenes from the Book of Genesis. At the far end of the hall a door gives access to the **Hall of the Ambassadors**, or Red State Room, where the Grand Master would receive important visitors, and where the Maltese president still receives foreign envoys. It contains portraits of the French kings Louis XIV, Louis XV and Louis XVI, the Russian Empress Catherine the Great and several Grand Masters. The neighbouring **Pages' Room**, or Yellow State Room (despite the abundance of greenish tones), was used by the Grand Master's 16 attendants.

Highlights of Valletta

This walk explores some of Valletta's backstreets, and affords some great views.

Start City Gate
Distance 2.25km
Duration One hour

Take a Break... High-end bistro **Noni** (p303) combines traditional Maltese and Mediterranean flavours.

4 The **National Museum of Archaeology** (p298) is housed in the Auberge de Provence; highlights include the 'fat ladies' statues from Ħaġar Qim.

2 Renzo Piano's 2015 **Parliament Building** (p299) is simultaneously architecturally bold and in sync with centuries of history.

Marsamxett Harbour

Triq Nofs in-Nhar

Triq Melita

Triq Papa Piju V

Pjazza Kastilja

Triq San Ġwann

Triq ir-Repubblika (Republic St)

Misraħ ir-Repubblika

Triq il-Merkanti (Merchant's St)

START

1 The Renzo Piano–designed **City Gate** (p299) is an inspiring new structure channelling the heritage of Valletta's original 1633 city entrance.

3 The Auberge d'Italie (1574) now houses **MUŻA** (p299), Malta's new National Community Art Museum.

5 St John's Co-Cathedral (p292) is the most important church of the Knights of St John and is filled with glorious baroque excesses.

Triq il-Fontana

Triq l-Isqaf l-Qadim (Hospital St)

Triq il-Merkanti (Merchant's St)

Triq San Nikola (St Nicholas St)

Triq San Duminiku

Triq San Kristofru

Triq l-Arcisqof

Triq il-Mediterran

FINISH 7

Triq il-Levant

Triq Santa Barbara

Grand Harbour

6 History from the Great Siege through to the Cold War's end is covered in the **National War Museum** (p298) in Fort St Elmo.

Classic Photo Across the Grand Harbour towards Fort St Angelo.

7 The **Lower Barrakka Gardens** contain a little Doric temple commemorating Sir Alexander Ball, the naval captain who took Malta from the French in 1800.

Upper Barrakka Gardens

PITK/SHUTTERSTOCKS ©

⦿ SIGHTS

National Museum of Archaeology · Museum

(☏2122 1623; www.heritagemalta.org; Triq ir-Repubblika; adult/child €5/2.50; ☺9am-6pm Mar-Dec, to 5pm Jan & Feb) The National Museum of Archaeology is housed in the impressive Auberge de Provence. Exhibits include delicate stone tools dating from 5200 BC, Phoenician amulets and an amazing temple model from Ta' Ħaġrat – a prehistoric architectural maquette. More impressive still are the beautifully modelled prehistoric figurines that were found locally. Best is the **Sleeping Lady**, found at the Hypogeum (p107), which is around 5000 years old. It shows a recumbent woman with her head propped on one arm, apparently deep in slumber.

Upper Barrakka Gardens · Park

(⛲) These colonnaded gardens perched high above Grand Harbour were created in the late 16th century as a relaxing haven for the Knights from the nearby Auberge d'Italie. They provide a shady retreat from the bustle of the city, and the balcony has one of the best views in Malta.

The terrace below is occupied by the **Saluting Battery** (☏2180 0992; www.salutingbattery.com; adult/child incl audio guide €3/1; ☺10am-5pm, guided tours 11am, 12.15pm & 3pm), where a cannon once fired salutes to visiting naval vessels.

Fort St Elmo & National War Museum · Fortress, Museum

(☏2123 3088; www.heritagemalta.org; adult/child €10/5.50; ☺9am-6pm Mon-Sat, noon-6pm Sun Apr-Sep, 9am-5pm Oct-Mar) Guarding Marsamxett and Grand Harbours is Fort St Elmo, named after the patron saint of mariners. The fort was built by the Knights in 1552 in just four months to guard the harbours on either side of the Sceberras Peninsula, and bore the brunt of Turkish arms during 1565's Great Siege. After restoration, the fort reopened in 2015, and now contains the National War Museum, which covers Malta's wartime history, including the Great Siege and the country's ordeal during WWII.

MUŻA · Museum

(Auberge d'Italie; ☏2122 5769; www.muza.
heritagemalta.org; Auberge d'Italie; ⊙9am-5pm)
MUŻA is a 2018 incarnation of Malta's Museum of Fine Arts, which closed in a previous
location in 2016. Sited in the Auberge d'Italie,
a 16th-century building once housing Italian
members of the Knights of St John, MUŻA
combines highlights from the former museum, including historic maps and paintings,
with an interactive 21st-century approach to
community art and storytelling.

City Gate · Monument

The Renzo Piano–designed City Gate
forms part of the architect's dramatic and
harmonious development. It echoes the
dimensions of the original 1633 entrance,
rather than the 1960s gate that it replaced,
allowing passers-by to have the sensation
of crossing a real bridge, and giving them
views of the ditch and fortifications. The
architecture is pared down and stark,
and the gate is framed by a pair of metal
blades, each 25m high, designed to look like
knights' sabres.

Parliament Building · Notable Building

Renzo Piano's breathtaking Parliament
Building was completed in 2014. Its design
includes two massive volumes of stone that
look suspended in air, but are supported by
stilts. The blocks have been machine-cut
to lighten their appearance, while reducing
solar radiation and letting in daylight.
Covering the rooftop are 600 sq metres of
photovoltaic panels, which generate most
of the energy required to heat the building
in winter and cool it in summer.

Church of
St Paul's Shipwreck · Church

(Triq San Pawl, enter from Triq Santa Luċija;
donations welcome; ⊙9.30am-noon & 3.30-6pm
Mon-Sat, 10.45-11.45am & 4-6pm Sun) **FREE** In AD
60 St Paul was shipwrecked on Malta and
brought Christianity to the population. This
church has a 19th-century facade, but the interior dates from the 16th century. It houses
many treasures, including a gilded statue of
St Paul, carved in Rome in the 1650s, carried

 Caravaggio in Malta

The Italian painter Michelangelo Merisi
(1571–1610) is better known by the
name of his home town, Caravaggio, in
northern Italy. His realist depictions of
religious subjects and dramatic use of
light shocked and revolutionised the
16th-century art world.

He made his name in Rome with a
series of controversial works, but was
also notorious for his volatility and
violence. Numerous brawls culminated
in Caravaggio murdering a man during
an argument over a tennis game. He fled
Rome and went into hiding in Naples for
several months. Then, towards the end of
1607, he moved to Malta.

Here, Caravaggio was welcomed as
a famous artist and produced several
works for the Knights of St John, including the famous *Beheading of St John
the Baptist* for the Oratory of St John's
Co-Cathedral (p109). In July 1608 he was
admitted into the Order as a Knight of
Justice, but only two months later he was
arrested for an unspecified crime, and
imprisoned in Fort St Angelo.

He escaped to Sicily, but was
expelled from the Order and spent the
next two years on the run. He created
some of his finest paintings – ever
darker and more twisted – during this
period. He died in Italy; the cause of
his death remains unknown.

Caravaggio's *Beheading of Saint John the Baptist*
VLADIMIR ZHOGA/SHUTTERSTOCKS ©

shoulder-high through the streets of Valletta
on the saint's feast day (10 February).

Valletta

Marsamxett Harbour

Triq San Bastjan

Misrah l-Indipendenza

Pool

Triq il-Punent

St Salvatore Bastion

Triq it-Teatru l-Antik (Old Theatre St)

Triq iz-Zekka

Triq Santa Lucija

Triq Marsamxett

Misrah Mattia Preti

18

Triq I-Assedju il-Kbir

St Andrew's Bastion

Triq San Patriżju

Triq l-Ifran (Old Bakery St)

Triq San Marku

Triq San Andrija

St Michael's Bastion

Triq l-Inginieri

Triq MA Vassalli

Triq Melita

Triq San Gwann

Misrah l-Assedju l-Kbir

Misrah ir-Repubblika

14 ✕

Triq iz-Zekka

Triq il-Mithna

Great Ditch

St John's Co-Cathedral

Triq Nofs in-Nhar (South St)

National Museum of Archaeology 🏛 3

20

ⓘ 4

Misrah San Gwann

Hastings Gardens

St John's Cavalier

St John's Bastion

Triq San Gwann Kavalier

Triq il-Papa Piju V

Triq ir-Repubblika (Republic St)

Triq San Zakkarija

Misrah il-Helsien

10

21

Triq il-Merkanti (Merchant's St)

22

Triq il-Papa Piju V

11

7

Valletta Bus Station

ⓘ

Triq Melita

Pjazza Kastilja

Triq il-Batterija

Triq SantʼAnton

St James Bastion

Upper Barrakka Gardens

5

Vjal ir-Re Edwardu VII

Triq Nelson

Great Ditch

13

12

8

Lascaris Bastion

St James Ditch

Glormu Cassar Av

Pjazza San Publiju

Herbert Ganado Gardens

Valletta Waterfront (Pinto Wharf) (600m)

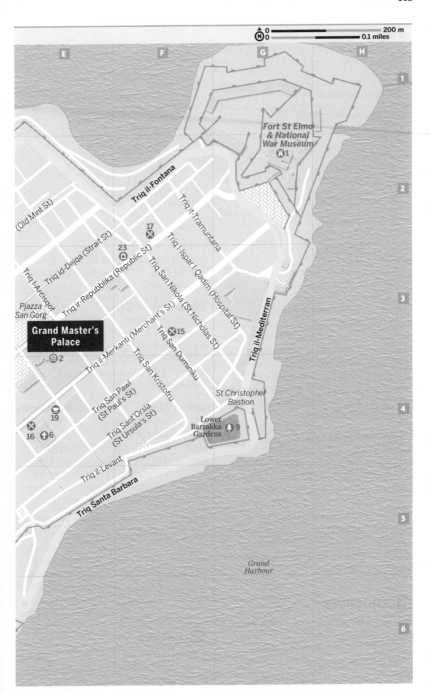

N

0 ——————— 200 m
0 ——————— 0.1 miles

E   F   G   H

1

Fort St Elmo
& National
War Museum
⌖1

2

Triq il-Fontana

(Old Mint St)

Triq it-Tramuntana

17
⊗

23
⌂

Triq id-Dejqa (Strait St)

Triq ir-Repubblika (Republic St)

Triq San Nikola (St Nicholas St)

Triq l-Ispar l-Qadim (Hospital St)

Triq l-Arcisqof

Pjazza
San Gorg

3

Grand Master's
Palace

⌂2

Triq il-Merkanti (Merchant's St)

Triq San Duminiku

⊗15

Triq il-Mediterran

St Christopher
Bastion

4

⊗   ⌂
19

16 ⓘ6

Triq San Pawl
(St Paul's St)

Triq San Kristofru

Triq Sant'Orsla
(St Ursula's St)

Lower
Barrakka
Gardens

♟9

Triq il-Levant

5

Triq Santa Barbara

Grand
Harbour

6

Valletta

Lascaris War Rooms   Museum

(☎2123 4717; www.lascariswarrooms.com; Lascaris Ditch; adult/child/family €12/5/25; ⊙10am-5pm) A mechanically ventilated underground tunnel complex that lies 40m beneath the Upper Barrakka Gardens (p298), this housed Britain's top-secret command in Malta during WWII and remained in use until 1977. Restored in 2009, the rooms are laid out as they would have been, and provide a fascinating behind-the-scenes glimpse. Get here by going to the Saluting Battery in the Upper Barrakka Gardens.

Upper Barrakka Lift   Lift

Between 1905 and 1973 there was a lift between the Grand Harbour and the Upper Barrakka Gardens (p298). In 2012, it was finally replaced by the marvellous panoramic lift that now connects Upper Barrakka Gardens with the Lascaris Ditch, a short walk from Valletta Waterfront. It's 58m high and can carry 21 passengers. Pay on the way up (€1), but not on the way down; if you have a ferry ticket, it's free.

🔒 SHOPPING

Artisans Centre   Arts & Crafts

(☎2122 1563; 288 Triq ir-Repubblika; ⊙9am-7pm Mon-Fri, to 6pm Sat) Good selection of ceramics, silver and glass from both Malta and Gozo. Especially popular are traditional Maltese brass door knockers. Designs include lions (for protection) and dolphins (for prosperity).

Silversmith's Shop   Jewellery

(218 Triq ir-Repubblika; ⊙9am-5pm Mon-Fri, to 3pm Sat, to 1pm Sun) Fine filigree work is the speciality at this traditional workshop that's been in the same family since 1972. Current artisan Matthew Borg is the son of the original owner.

Mdina Glass   Arts & Crafts

(☎2141 5786; www.mdinaglass.com.mt; 14 Triq il-Merkanti; ⊙10am-7pm Mon-Fri, to 4pm Sat) Mdina Glass features hand-blown glass produced by craft workshops near Mdina, in a range of styles and colours from traditional to decidedly modern – vases, bowls, paperweights, collectables and more.

Ċekċik   Clothing

(☎7940 2108; www.cekcik.com.mt; 15 Triq Melita; ⊙10am-6pm Mon-Fri, to 3pm Sat) Named after the Malti word for 'knick-knack', Ċekċik features contemporary Maltese T-shirts, tote bags and screen prints amid its otherwise global selection of ethnically inspired items.

⊗ EATING

Caffe Cordina   Cafe €

(☎2123 4385; www.caffecordina.com; 244 Triq ir-Repubblika; mains €8.25-16; ⊙8am-7pm

Mon-Sat, to 3pm Sun) Cordina was established in 1837 and is now a local institution. You have the choice of waiter service at the sun-shaded tables in the square or inside, or joining the locals at the zinc counter inside for a quick caffeine hit.

No 43 Cafe €

(☑2703 2294; www.facebook.com/no43valletta; 43 Triq il-Merkanti; snacks & salads €3-6; ☺8am-5pm Mon-Sat; 🍴) 🌿 Salad specials, plump sandwiches and toasted chicken wraps all feature at this compact Australian-owned cafe. Fruit salad with Greek yoghurt and cold-pressed juices are both healthy options, and some of Valletta's best coffee is served with genuine Down Under charm and friendliness. Apparently, the Aussie owner's Maltese mum came from just up the road in Floriana.

Nenu the Artisan Baker Maltese €€

(☑2258 1535; www.nenuthebaker.com; 143 Triq San Duminiku; mains €10-13; ☺11.45am-2.30pm Tue-Sun, 6-11.30pm Tue-Sat) Often the answer when you ask a local, 'What's the best place to try *ftira*?', Nenu's decades-old wood-fired oven turns out a dizzying selection of Malta's traditional pizza-like, baked flatbreads. Olives, capers, cheeses and meats all feature. The menu also strays deliciously into other Maltese classics.

Noni Mediterranean €€€

(☑2122 1441; www.noni.com.mt; 211 Triq ir-Repubblika; mains €19-26; ☺6-10pm Mon-Sat, noon-2.30pm Thu-Sat) 🌿 Descend into Noni's stylish stone-lined basement space and be surprised by modern spins on traditional Maltese and Mediterranean flavours. Dishes are prepared with a light touch and could include a silky smooth parfait of rabbit liver, or wonderfully tender slow-cooked octopus with Israeli couscous. An excellent wine list and craft beers from Malta and Belgium are other tasty diversions.

Rubino Mediterranean €€€

(☑2122 4656; www.rubinomalta.com; 53 Triq l-If-ran; mains €17-24; ☺noon-2.30pm Mon-Fri, 7.30-10.30pm Tue-Sat) White-tableclothed Rubino is a classy place that earns rave reviews

for its seasonal dishes such as spaghetti with sea urchins or sea-bass *involtini* (rolls) stuffed with pine nuts and mint. The velvety risotto is particularly renowned. Leave room for dessert – the house speciality is *cassata siciliana* (sponge cake soaked in liqueur, layered with ricotta cheese). Over-fives only.

🍸 DRINKING & NIGHTLIFE

Lot Sixty One Cafe

(☑7984 1561; www.lotsixtyonecoffee.com.mt; Triq it-Teatru l-Antik; ☺8am-5pm Mon-Thu, 8am-8pm Fri, 9am-5pm Sat & Sun) 🌿 Lot Sixty One's modern take on a Valletta coffee house includes organic and fair-trade beans roasted locally, and a sweet selection of snacks including muffins, brownies and bliss balls. It's very popular for takeout coffee with locals, but it's worth securing a table on wildly sloping Old Theatre St for a more leisurely experience.

ℹ️ INFORMATION

Tourist Information Office (☑2122 0193; www.visitmalta.com; 28 Triq Melita; ☺9am-5pm Mon-Sat, to 1pm Sun & public holidays) Helpful tourist office with plenty of maps, walking trail pamphlets and brochures. There's also a smaller kiosk near the **bus station** (Vjal Nelson) and the entrance to the City Gate; its opening hours are flexible (based on availability of staff), but it's usually open during July and August.

ℹ️ GETTING AROUND

BUS

Bus 133 is a circular bus route that zips half-hourly around Valletta's city walls, calling at Castille, Marsamxett and Floriana. As well as being a good way to get around, this route offers some great views.

TAXI

There's a taxi rank just outside City Gate (p299), and, within the city walls, **Smart Cabs** (☑7741 4177; 3 people within city perimeter/to cruise-ship terminal €5/8) electric taxis can be picked up outside St John's Co-Cathedral (p109). Taxis also wait near the Castille Hotel outside the pedestrian entrance to the Upper Barrakka Gardens (p298).

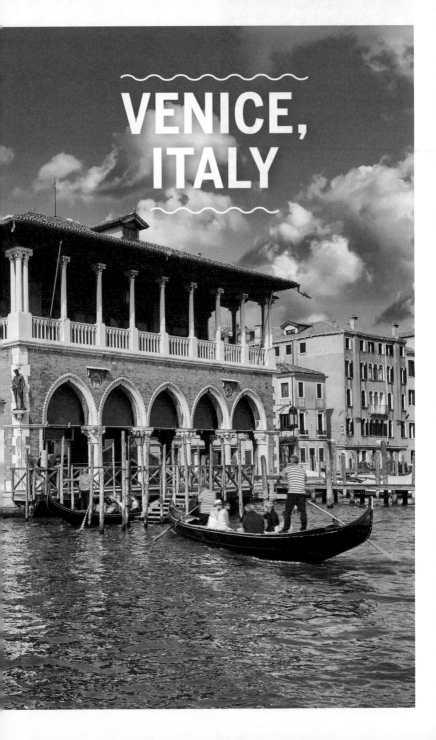

VENICE, ITALY

Venice at a Glance...

Imagine the audacity of building a city of marble palaces on a lagoon. Rather than surrendering to acque alte (high tides) like others might, Venetians flooded the world with vivid painting, baroque music, modern opera, spice-route cuisine, bohemian-chic fashions and a Grand Canal's worth of spritz: the signature Prosecco and Aperol cocktail. Today, cutting-edge architects and billionaire benefactors are spicing up the art scene, musicians are rocking out 18th-century instruments and backstreet osterie (taverns) are winning a slow food following. The people who made walking on water look easy are well into their next act.

With One Day in Port

○ Begin your day in the Palazzo Ducale (p321), then break for espresso at the baroque counter of Grancaffè Quadri (p326) before admiring the Byzantine blitz of golden mosaics inside Basilica di San Marco (p310).

○ Browse boutique-lined backstreets to Museo Fortuny, the palace fashion house whose gowns freed women from corsets.

○ Pause atop wooden Ponte dell'Accademia (p309) for Grand Canal photo ops, then surrender to timeless drama that no camera can convey inside Gallerie dell'Accademia (p312).

Best Places For...

Gelato Suso (p324)

Cicheti Cantine del Vino già Schiavi (p324)

Classic Venetian cuisine Osteria Boccadoro (p326)

Coffee Caffè Florian (p326)

Wine Cantina Do Spade (p326)

Glass ElleElle (p322)

Carnevale masks Ca' Macana Atelier (p323)

Previous page: Fish market on Grand Canal, Venice
YASONYA/SHUTTERSTOCK ©

0 — 1 km
0 — 0.5 miles

Sacca Serenella
Murano
Canale delle Sacche
Canale delle Navi
Canale delle Navi
Fondamente Nuove
Isola di San Michele
Laguna Veneta
CANNAREGIO The Ghetto
Isola del Tronchetto
Stazione di Santa Lucia (Ferrovia)
SANTA CROCE
Grand Canal
Cruise Port
Stazione Merci
SAN POLO RIALTO
Grand Canal
Basilica di San Marco
Santa Marta
SANTA MARTA
San Basilio Terminal
SAN MARCO CASTELLO LA TANA
Isola di San Pietro
Arsenale
Gallerie dell'Accademia
Canale di Fusina
DORSODURO
Canale di San Marco
Giardini Pubblici
SANT'ELENA
SACCA FISOLA
Canale della Giudecca
Chiesa di San Giorgio Maggiore
Isola di Sant'Elena
GIUDECCA
Isola della Giudecca

Central Venice Map (p318)

Getting from the Port

Venice's main cruise ship terminal, **Venezia Terminal Passeggeri**, formerly the Stazione Marittima, has seven quays, and is located at the western end of Santa Croce between the Isola del Tronchetto and Piazzale Roma. It is connected to Piazzale Roma by monorail, although most cruise ships offer free shuttles. To reach other parts of Venice, take the *vaporetto* (small passenger ferry) or a water taxi.

Some ships dock at the **Terminal San Basilio**, where *vaporetti* connect to the rest of Venice.

Fast Facts

Currency Euro (€)

Languages Italian and Venetian (dialect)

Money ATMs are widely available and credit cards accepted at most places. To change money you'll need to present your ID.

Visas Not required for EU citizens. Nationals of Australia, Brazil, Canada, Japan, New Zealand and the USA do not need visas for visits of up to 90 days.

Wi-fi Wi-fi access is increasingly available in cafes.

Ponte di Rialto

ELENA ODAREEVA/SHUTTERSTOCK ©

Grand Canal

Never was a thoroughfare so aptly named as the Grand Canal. Snaking through the heart of the city, Venice's signature waterway is flanked by a magnificent array of Gothic, Moorish, Renaissance and rococo palaces.

Great For...

☑ Don't Miss

The Ponte di Rialto, the Palazzo Grassi and the iconic Basilica di Santa Maria della Salute.

For most people, a trip down the Grand Canal starts near the train station, near the Ponte di Calatrava. Designed by avant-garde Spanish architect Santiago Calatrava in 2008, it's one of the few modern structures you'll see in central Venice.

Leaving the bridge in your wake, on your left you'll pass the arcaded, 15th-century Gothic facade of the **Ca' d'Oro** (☎041 522 23 49; www.cadoro.org; Calle di Ca' d'Oro 3932; adult/reduced €11/5.50; ⊙8.15am-2pm Mon, to 7.15pm Tue-Sun, 2nd fl 10am-6pm Tue-Sun; 🚤Ca' d'Oro), now home to an art museum.

Ponte di Rialto & Around

A short way on, the **Ponte di Rialto** (🚤Rialto) is the oldest of the four bridges that cross the canal. Built in the late 16th century to a monumental design by Antonio da Ponte, it links the *sestieri (districts)* of San Marco and San Polo, and forms a popular

Gallerie dell'Accademia (p113)

Stazione di
Santa Lucia
(Ferrovia)

Grand Canal

Stazione
Merci

Ponte di Rialto

Palazzo
Grassi

Palazzo
Ducale

Ponte
dell'Accademia

Basilica di Santa
Maria della Salute

⚓ Explore Ashore

From Piazzale Roma take *vaporetti* 1 or
2. It takes around 40 minutes to reach
Piazza San Marco.

★ Top Tip

Jump off at Rialto and search out Al
Mercà (p325) for a cosy drink.

ademia), whose simple design seems out of
place amid Venice's fairy-tale architecture.
Nearby, the Gallerie dell'Accademia (p312)
is Venice's premier art gallery and the Peggy Guggenheim (p317) impresses with its
collection of celebrated modern paintings.

vantage point for photographers. Nearby,
local shoppers crowd to the **Rialto Market**
(Rialto Mercato; 🖉041 296 06 58; Campo de la
Pescaria; ⊗7am-2pm; 🚤Rialto Mercato).

Palazzo Grassi

Clean, geometric **Palazzo Grassi** (🖉041
200 10 57; www.palazzograssi.it; Campo
San Samuele 3231; adult/reduced incl Punta
della Dogana €18/15; ⊗10am-7pm Wed-Mon
mid-Mar–Nov; 🚤San Samuele) comes into
view on the first bend after the Rialto. A
noble 18th-century palace, it now houses
show-stopping contemporary art. Over
the water, spy out the sumptuous Ca'
Rezzonico (p317).

Ponte dell'Accademia & Around

A couple of ferry stops further down is
the wooden **Ponte dell'Accademia** (btwn
Campo di San Vidal & Campo della Carità; 🚤Acc-

Basilica di Santa Maria della Salute

The imperious dome of the basilica (p320)
has overlooked the canal's entrance since
the 17th century. Impressive both outside
and in, it harbours a number of important
works by Titian.

St Mark's & Palazzo Ducale

At the mouth of the canal, disembark for
Piazza San Marco (🚤San Marco). Dominating the waterside is Palazzo Ducale (p321),
the historic residence of the Venetian
doges.

Basilica di San Marco

With its profusion of spires and domes, lavish marble-work and 8500 sq metres of luminous mosaics, Venice's signature basilica is an unforgettable sight.

The original basilica, founded in the 9th century to house the corpse of St Mark after wily Venetian merchants smuggled it out of Egypt in a barrel of pork fat, burnt down in 932. It was rebuilt in Venice's cosmopolitan image, with Byzantine domes, a Greek cross layout and walls clad in marble from Syria, Egypt and Palestine.

Exterior & Portals

The front of St Mark's ripples and crests like a wave, its five niched portals capped with shimmering mosaics and frothy stonework arches. The oldest mosaic (1270) is in the lunette above the far-left portal, depicting St Mark's stolen body arriving at the basilica. The theme is echoed in three of the other lunettes, including one showing turbaned officials recoiling from the hamper of pork fat.

Great For...

☑ **Don't Miss**

Loggia dei Cavalli, where reproductions of the four bronze horses gallop off the balcony over Piazza San Marco.

PHILLIP MINNIS/SHUTTERSTOCK ©

Basilica di San Marco

Piazza San Marco

Piazzetta San Marco

Giardini Ex Reali

Canale di San Marco

⚓ Explore Ashore

Vaporetti 1 and 2 connect Piazalle Roma to the two main San Marco piers (Vallaresso and Giardinetti), which are a short walk to the basilica. *Vaporetto* 2 links the San Basilio Terminal with San Marco. Allow around an hour to admire the glittering basilica, but factor in long queues in peak season.

❶ Need to Know

St Mark's Basilica; ☏041 270 83 11; www.basilicasanmarco.it; Piazza San Marco; ⊙9.30am-5pm Mon-Sat, 2-5pm Sun summer, to 4.30pm Sun winter; 🚤San Marco; **FREE**

Mosaics

Blinking is natural upon your first glimpse of the basilica's glittering ceiling mosaics, many made with 24-carat gold leaf. Just inside the vestibule are the basilica's oldest mosaics: Apostles with the Madonna, standing sentry by the main door for more than 950 years. Inside the church proper, three golden domes vie for your attention. The Pentecost Cupola shows the Holy Spirit, represented by a dove, shooting tongues of flame onto the heads of the surrounding saints. In the central 13th-century Ascension Cupola, angels swirl around the central figure of Christ hovering among the stars.

Pala d'Oro

Tucked behind the main altar (€2), this stupendous golden screen is studded with 2000 emeralds, amethysts, sapphires, rubies, pearls and other gemstones. But the most priceless treasures here are biblical figures in vibrant cloisonné, begun in Constantinople in AD 976 and elaborated by Venetian goldsmiths in 1209.

Tesoro & Museum

Holy bones and booty from the Crusades fill the Tesoro (Treasury; €3); while ducal treasures on show in the **museum** (☏041 270 83 11; adult/reduced €5/2.50; ⊙9.45am-4.45pm) would put a king's ransom to shame. A highlight is the Quadriga of St Mark's, a group of four bronze horses originally plundered from Constantinople and later carted off to Paris by Napoleon before being returned to the basilica and installed in the 1st-floor gallery.

Gallerie dell'Accademia

Housed in the former Santa Maria della Carità convent complex, the Gallerie dell'Accademia traces the development of Venetian art from the 14th to 18th centuries, with works by Bellini, Titian, Tintoretto, Veronese and Canaletto.

Great For...

☑ Don't Miss

Bellini's *Miracle of the Reliquary of the Cross at San Lorenzo Bridge* and Titian's *Presentation of the Virgin.*

At the time of writing, the gallery was in the midst of a lengthy restoration and several rooms were closed. An attempt has been made to move some of the most famous works to spaces usually used for temporary exhibitions, but don't be surprised if some of the masterpieces described here are not on view or are not where we've said they'll be.

Early Works

The grand gallery you enter upstairs features vivid early works that show Venice's precocious flair for colour and drama. Case in point: Jacobello Alberegno's *Apocalypse Polyptych* (Room 1) shows the Whore of Babylon riding a hydra, babbling rivers of blood from her mouth.

Rooms 2–23

UFO arrivals seem imminent in the eerie skies of Carpaccio's *Crucifixion and*

Ceiling of the Sala dell'Albergo

MARK EDWARD HARRIS/GETTY IMAGES ©

Explore Ashore

The Accademia *vaporetto* stop is located in front of the gallery. It's served by line 1 and 2, which connect to the cruise ports. Allow 1½ hours for a proper visit and be sure to book timed tickets in advance online (booking fee €1.50) to skip the lengthy queue.

❶ Need to Know

☑ 041 522 22 47; www.gallerieaccademia. it; Campo de la Carità 1050; adult/reduced €12/2; ⏱ 8.15am-2pm Mon, to 7.15pm Tue-Sun; 🚤 Accademia

Glorification of the Ten Thousand Martyrs of Mount Ararat (Room 2), which offers an intense contrast to Giovanni Bellini's quietly elegant *Madonna and Child between St Catherine and Mary Magdalene* (Room 4).

At the time of writing, Room 15 was being used to display gallery highlights that were usually displayed in Room 10 (under restoration). Tintoretto's *St Mark Rescues a Saracen* (1562) is an action-packed blockbuster, with fearless Venetian merchants and an improbably muscular, long-armed saint rescuing a turbaned sailor. In the same room, Titian's 1576 *Pietà* was possibly finished posthumously by Palma il Giovane, but notice the smears of paint Titian applied with his bare hands and the column-base self-portrait, foreshadowing Titian's own funeral monument.

Room 20 contains Gentile Bellini's *Miracle of the Reliquary of the Cross at San Lorenzo Bridge,* thronged with cosmopolitan crowds. The original convent chapel (Room 23) is a serene showstopper fronted by a Bellini altarpiece. Sharing the space is Giorgione's *La tempesta* (The Storm).

Sala dell'Albergo

The Accademia's grand finale is the newly restored Sala dell'Albergo (Room 24), with a lavishly carved ceiling, Antonio Vivarini's wrap-around 1441–50 masterpiece of fluffy-bearded saints, and Titian's touching 1534–39 *Presentation of the Virgin*. Here, a tiny Madonna trudges up an intimidating staircase while a distinctly Venetian crowd points to her example – yet few of the pearl-clad merchants offer alms to the destitute mother, or even feed the begging dog.

San Marco Royal Tour

Dogi and dignitaries had the run of San Marco for centuries, and now it's your turn. Follow this royal tour that ends with your own palace intrigue.

Start Piazzatta San Marco
Distance 2.5km
Duration 1-1¼ hours

5 La Fenice (p316) was faithfully reconstructed in 1996 after an arson attack.

Take a Break... Pause for a coffee at 18th-century **Caffè Florian** (p326).

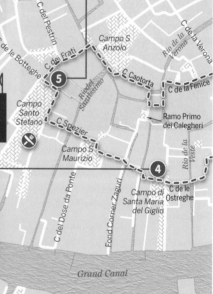

4 The bell tower of 15th-century **Chiesa di Santo Stefano** (p317) leans 2m, as though it's had one *spritz* too many. The church's brick facade features marble Gothic portals by Bartolomeo Bon.

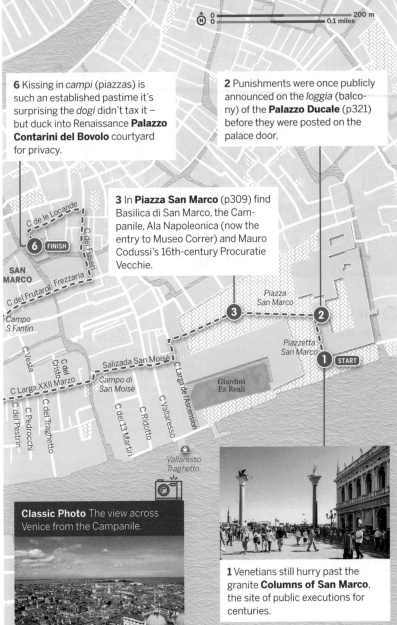

6 Kissing in *campi* (piazzas) is such an established pastime it's surprising the *dogi* didn't tax it – but duck into Renaissance **Palazzo Contarini del Bovolo** courtyard for privacy.

2 Punishments were once publicly announced on the *loggia* (balcony) of the **Palazzo Ducale** (p321) before they were posted on the palace door.

3 In **Piazza San Marco** (p309) find Basilica di San Marco, the Campanile, Ala Napoleonica (now the entry to Museo Correr) and Mauro Codussi's 16th-century Procuratie Vecchie.

C de le Locande

C del Fuseri

6 FINISH

SAN MARCO

Frezzaria

C del Frutarol

Campo S Fantin

C Veste

C del Cristo

Salizada San Moisè

C Larga de l'Ascension

Piazza San Marco

3

2

Piazzetta San Marco

1 START

C Larga XXII Marzo

Campo di San Moisè

C del Traghetto

C dei 13 Martiri

C Ridotto

C Vallaresso

Giardini Ex Reali

C del Pedrocchi

C del Pestrin

Vallaresso Traghetto

Classic Photo The view across Venice from the Campanile.

1 Venetians still hurry past the granite **Columns of San Marco**, the site of public executions for centuries.

0 200 m
0 0.1 miles

Museo Correr

◎ SIGHTS
◎ San Marco

Museo Correr   Museum
(☏041 240 52 11; www.correr.visitmuve.
it; Piazza San Marco 52; adult/reduced incl
Palazzo Ducale €20/13, with Museum Pass free;
☽10am-7pm Apr-Oct, to 5pm Nov-Mar; 🚊San
Marco) Napoleon pulled down an ancient
church to build his royal digs over Piazza
San Marco, and then filled them with the
riches of the doges while taking some
of Venice's finest heirlooms to France
as trophies. When he lost Venice to the
Austrians, Empress Sissi remodelled the
palace, adding ceiling frescoes, silk cladding and brocade curtains. It's now open
to the public and full of many of Venice's
reclaimed treasures, including ancient
maps, statues, cameos and four centuries
of artistic masterpieces.

Museo Fortuny   Museum
(☏041 520 09 95; www.fortuny.visitmuve.it;
Campo San Beneto 3958; adult/reduced €10/8;
☽10am-6pm Wed-Mon; 🚊Sant'Angelo) Find design inspiration at the palatial home studio
of art nouveau designer Mariano Fortuny y
Madrazo (1871–1949), whose uncorseted
Delphi-goddess frocks set the standard for
bohemian chic. The 1st-floor salon walls are
eclectic mood boards: Fortuny fashions and
Isfahan tapestries, family portraits and artfully peeling plaster. Interesting temporary
exhibitions spread from the basement to
the attic, the best of which use the general
ambience of grand decay to great effect.

La Fenice   Theatre
(☏041 78 66 54; www.teatrolafenice.it; Campo
San Fantin 1965; ☽9.30am-6pm; 🚊Giglio) Once
its dominion over the high seas ended,
Venice discovered the power of the high Cs,
opening La Fenice in 1792. Rossini, Doni-
zetti and Bellini staged operas here; Verdi
premiered *Rigoletto* and *La Traviata;* and international greats Stravinsky, Prokofiev and
Britten composed for the house, making La
Fenice the envy of Europe. From January
to July and September to October, opera
season is in full swing. If you can't attend a
performance (tickets €25-250), it's possible
to explore the theatre with an audio guide
(adult/reduced €11/7).

Chiesa di Santo Stefano   Church

(☑041 522 50 61; www.chorusvenezia.org; Campo Santo Stefano; museum €3, with Chorus Pass free; ⊗10.30am-4.30pm Mon-Sat, to 7pm Sun; 🛥Sant'Angelo) **FREE** The freestanding bell tower, visible from the square behind, leans disconcertingly, but this brick Gothic church has stood tall since the 13th century. Credit for shipshape splendour goes to Bartolomeo Bon for the marble entry portal and to Venetian shipbuilders, who constructed the vast wooden *carena di nave* (ship's keel) ceiling that resembles an upturned Noah's ark.

◎ Dorsoduro

Ca' Rezzonico   Museum

(Museum of 18th-Century Venice; ☑041 241 01 00; www.visitmuve.it; Fondamenta Rezzonico 3136; adult/reduced €10/7.50, or with Museum Pass free; ⊗10am-5pm Wed-Mon; 🛥Ca' Rezzonico) Baroque dreams come true at this Baldassare Longhena–designed Grand Canal *palazzo* (mansion), where a marble staircase leads to a vast gilded **ballroom** and sumptuous salons filled with period furniture, paintings, porcelain and mesmerising ceiling frescoes, four of which were painted by Giambattista Tiepolo. The building was largely stripped of its finery when the Rezzonico family departed in 1810, but this was put right after the city acquired it in 1935, and refurnished it with pieces salvaged from other decaying palaces.

Peggy Guggenheim Collection   Museum

(☑041 240 54 11; www.guggenheim-venice.it; Calle San Cristoforo 701; adult/reduced €15/9; ⊗10am-6pm Wed-Mon; 🛥Accademia) After losing her father on the *Titanic,* heiress Peggy Guggenheim became one of the great collectors of the 20th century. Her palatial canalside home, Palazzo Venier dei Leoni, showcases her stockpile of surrealist, futurist and abstract expressionist art, with works by up to 200 artists, including her ex-husband Max Ernst, Jackson Pollock (among her many rumoured lovers), Pablo Picasso and Salvador Dalí.

🖝 Escape the Crowds

In high season (June to September) the crowds along the Riva degli Schiavoni and in Piazza San Marco can be overwhelming, but venture further afield and you'll be surprised by world-class attractions in areas undisturbed by mass tourism.

Galleria Giorgio Franchetti alla Ca' d'Oro (☑041 522 23 49; www.cadoro. org; Calle di Ca' d'Oro 3932; adult/reduced €8.50/2; ⊗8.15am-2pm Mon, to 7.15pm Tue-Sun, 2nd fl 10am-6pm Tue-Sun; 🛥Ca'd'Oro) A stunning gallery stuffed with masterpieces, housed in one of the most beautiful buildings on the Grand Canal. Don't miss the views from the 1st-floor galleries.

Ca' Pesaro (☑041 72 11 27; www.capesaro. visitmuve.it; Fondamenta de Ca' Pesaro 2076; adult/reduced €10/7.50, with Museum Pass free; ⊗10am-5pm Tue-Sun; 🛥San Stae) Venice's modern art museum includes works by Matisse, Rodin, Chagall, Kandinsky, Lichtenstein and Wildt.

Ocean Space (Chiesa di San Lorenzo; www. tba21.org; Campo San Lorenzo 5069; ⊗11am-7pm Tue-Sun; 🛥San Zaccaria) A new academy combining art and science, with cross-disciplinary shows tackling the subject of climate change in the fantastic restored shell of Chiesa di San Lorenzo.

Palazzo Grimani (☑041 520 03 45; www. palazzogrimani.org ; Ramo Grimani 4858; adult/reduced €5/2, incl Ca' D'Oro €10/4; 🛥San Zaccaria) Discover Cardinal Grimani's impressive Graeco-Roman statuary collection, in this frescoed palace hidden down an easy-to-miss alley.

Galleria Giorgio Franchetti alla Ca' d'Oro

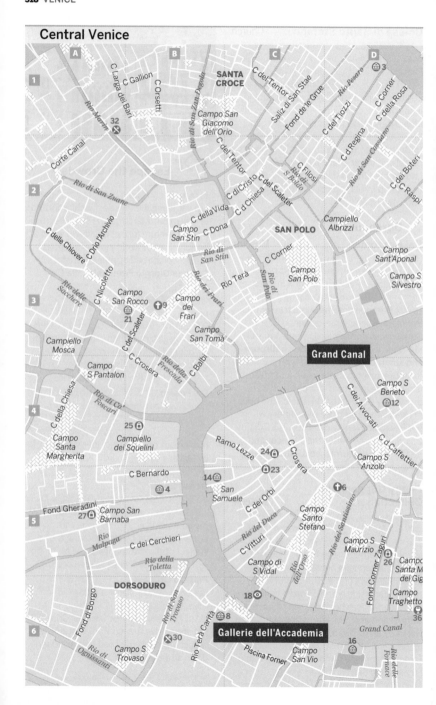

Central Venice

SANTA CROCE

Campo San Giacomo dell'Orio

SAN POLO

Campiello Albrizzi

Campo Sant'Aponal

Campo S Silvestro

Campo San Polo

Campo San Stin

Campo dei Frari

Campo San Tomà

Grand Canal

Campiello Mosca

Campo S Pantalon

Campo Santa Margherita

Campiello dei Squelini

Campo S Beneto

Campo S Anzolo

Ramo Lezze

San Samuele

Campo Santo Stefano

Campo S Maurizio

Campo Santa M del Gig

Campo Traghetto

Campo San Barnaba

C Bernardo

DORSODURO

Campo di S Vidal

Gallerie dell'Accademia

Grand Canal

Campo S Trovaso

Piscina Forner

Campo San Vio

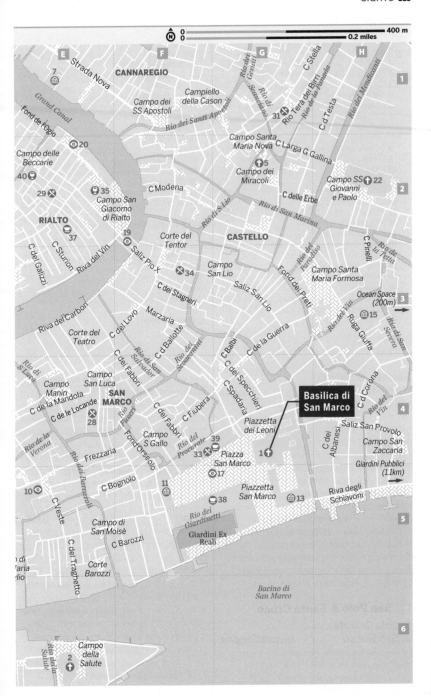

400 m
0.2 miles

CANNAREGIO

Strada Nova

7

Grand Canal

Fond de l'Ogio

Campo delle
Beccarie

40

29

RIALTO

37

C del Galizzi

C del Sturion

Riva del Vin

Riva del Carbon

Rio di S Luca

Campo dei
SS Apostoli

Campiello
della Cason

Rio dei Santi Apostoli

Campo Santa
Maria Nova

Campo dei
Miracoli

5

C Modena

C delle Erbe

Campo San
Giacomo
di Rialto

35

19

Saliz Pio X

Corte del
Tentor

34

Campo
San Lio

C dei Stagneri

Marzaria

Corte del
Teatro

C del Loyo

C d Ballotte

Rio di San
Salvador

C dei Fabbri

C de la Mandola

Campo
San Luca

**SAN
MARCO**

C de le Locande

28

Campo
Manin

Rio di la
Verona

Rio dei Barcaroli

10

C Veste

Frezzaria

C Bognolo

Fond Orseolo

Campo
S Gallo

C dei Fabbri

C Fiubera

Campo di
San Moisè

C Barozzi

Rio dei
Giardinetti

Giardini Ex
Reali

Corte
Barozzi

C del Traghetto

Rio di
Maria
dio

Rio della
Salute

Campo
della
Salute

2

Rio dei
Gesuiti

Rio di
Scudaziana

C Stella

31

Rio dei Biri

Rio de la Panada

C d Testa

Rio dei Mendicanti

C Larga G Gallina

Campo SS
Giovanni
e Paolo

22

Rio di San Lio

Rio di San Marina

CASTELLO

C delle Erbe

Rio del
Paradiso

Fond dei Preti

Campo Santa
Maria Formosa

C Pinelli

Rio de
la Tetta

Rio di San
Severa

Ocean Space
(200m)

15

Ruga
Giuffa

Saliz San Lio

C de la Guerra

C Balbi

C C dei Specchieri

C Spadaria

C dei
Spechieri

Basilica di
San Marco

Piazzetta
dei Leoni

1

39

33

Piazza
San Marco

17

11

38

Piazzetta
San Marco

13

C dei
Albanesi

Saliz San Provolo

Campo San
Zaccaria

Giardini Pubblici
(1.1km)

Riva degli
Schiavoni

C d Corona

Rio del
Vin

Bacino di
San Marco

Central Venice

Basilica di Santa Maria della Salute
Basilica

(Our Lady of Health Basilica; www.basilicasalute-venezia.it; Campo de la Salute 1; sacristy adult/reduced €4/2; ⊙9.30am-noon & 3-5.30pm; ⛴Salute) **FREE** Baldassare Longhena's magnificent basilica is prominently positioned near the entrance to the Grand Canal, its white stones, exuberant statuary and high domes gleaming spectacularly under the sun. The church makes good on an official appeal by the Venetian Senate directly to the Madonna in 1630, after 80,000 Venetians had been killed by plague. The Senate promised the Madonna a church in exchange for her intervention on behalf of Venice – no expense or effort spared.

◎ San Polo & Santa Croce

Scuola Grande di San Rocco
Historic Building

(⛘041 523 48 64; www.scuolagrandesanrocco.org; Campo San Rocco 3052; adult/reduced €10/8; ⊙9.30am-5.30pm; ⛴San Tomà) Every-

one wanted the commission to paint this building dedicated to St Roch, patron saint of the plague-stricken, so Tintoretto cheated: instead of producing sketches like rival Veronese, he gifted a splendid ceiling panel of the saint, knowing it couldn't be refused, or matched by other artists. This painting still crowns the **Sala dell'Albergo**, upstairs, and Tintoretto's work completely covers the walls and ceilings of all the main halls.

I Frari
Basilica

(Basilica di Santa Maria Gloriosa dei Frari; ⛘041 272 86 18; www.basilicadeifrari.it; Campo dei Frari 3072, San Polo; adult/reduced €3/1.50, with Chorus Pass free; ⊙9am-6pm Mon-Sat, 1-6pm Sun; ⛴San Tomà) A soaring Gothic church, the Friary's assets include marquetry choir stalls, Canova's pyramid mausoleum, Bellini's achingly sweet *Madonna with Child* triptych in the sacristy, and Longhena's creepy Doge Pesaro funereal monument. Upstaging them all, however, is Titian's 1518 *Assunta* (Assumption) altarpiece, in which a radiant red-cloaked Madonna reaches heavenward, steps onto a cloud and escapes this mortal coil. Titian himself – lost to the plague in 1576 at the age of 94 – has his memorial here.

◎ Cannaregio

Chiesa di Santa Maria dei Miracoli   Church

(Campo dei Miracoli 6074; adult/reduced €3/1.50, with Chorus Pass free; ⊙10.30am-4.30pm Mon-Sat; ⛴Fondamente Nove) This magnificent church was built between 1481 and 1489 to house Nicolò di Pietro's Madonna icon after the painting began to miraculously weep in its outdoor shrine. Aided by public fundraising, Pietro and Tullio Lombardo's design used marble scavenged from slag heaps in San Marco and favoured the human scale of radically new Renaissance architecture in place of the grandiose Gothic status quo.

The Ghetto   Jewish Site

(⛴Guglie) In medieval times this part of Cannaregio housed a *getto* (foundry), but it was as the designated Jewish quarter from the 16th to 19th centuries that the word acquired a whole new meaning. In accordance with the Venetian Republic's 1516 decree, by day Jewish lenders, doctors and clothing merchants were permitted to attend to Venice's commercial interests, but at night and on Christian holidays they were locked within the gated island of the **Ghetto Nuovo** (New Foundry).

◎ Castello

Zanipolo   Basilica

(Basilica di San Giovanni e Paolo; ☎041 523 59 13; www.basilicasantigiovanniepaolo.it; Campo Zanipolo; adult/reduced €3.50/1.50; ⊙9am-6pm Mon-Sat, noon-6pm Sun; ⛴Ospedale) Commenced in 1333 but not finished until the 1430s, this vast church is similar in style and scope to the Franciscan Frari in San Polo, which was being raised at the same time. Both oversized structures feature red-brick facades with high-contrast detailing in white stone. After its completion,

🏛 Palazzo Ducale

Holding pride of place on the waterfront, this pretty Gothic **palace** (Ducal Palace; ☎041 271 59 11; www.palazzoducale.visitmuve.it; Piazzetta San Marco 1; adult/reduced incl Museo Correr €20/13, with Museum Pass free; ⊙8.30am-7pm summer, to 5.30pm winter; ⛴San Zaccaria) is an unlikely setting for the political and administrative seat of a great republic, but an exquisitely Venetian one. Beyond its dainty colonnades and geometrically patterned facade of white Istrian stone and pale pink Veronese marble lie grand rooms of state, the doge's private apartments and a large complex of council chambers, courts and prisons.

A standard ticket allows you access to the grand central **courtyard**, a display of historic masonry (**Museo dell'Opera**) on the ground floor and a circuit of the main part of the palace that leads through the state rooms, armoury, prisons and institutional rooms. The **Doge's Apartments** are now used for temporary art exhibitions, which are ticketed separately (around €10 extra). Further rooms, too small for the masses, can be visited on the 1¼-hour **Secret Itineraries Tour** (☎041 4273 0892; adult/reduced €20/14; ⊙tours in English 9.55am, 10.45am & 11.35am).

JAVEN/SHUTTERSTOCK ©

Zanipolo quickly became the go-to church for ducal funerals and inside you'll find 25 of their lavish tombs, plus works by Bellini, Lorenzetti and Veronese.

Worth a Detour: Murano

Venetians have been working in glass since the 10th century, but due to the fire hazards of glass-blowing, the industry was moved to the island of Murano in the 13th century. Woe betide the glass-blower with wanderlust: trade secrets were so jealously guarded that any glass worker who left the city was guilty of treason and subject to assassination. Today, glass artisans ply their trade at workshops all over the island, with shops selling their expensive wares lining the Fondamenta dei Vetrai.

Nason Moretti has been making modernist magic happen in glass since the 1950s, and the third-generation glass designers are in fine form at **ElleElle** (☑041 527 48 66; www.elleellemurano.com; Fondamenta Manin 52, Murano; ⏱10.30am-6pm; ⛴Faro). Everything is signed, including an exquisite (and expensive) range of hand-blown drinking glasses, jugs, bowls, vases, tealight holders, decanters and lamps.

Mind-boggling miniatures are the trademarks of glass-blower **Cesare Toffolo** (☑041 73 64 60; www.toffolo.com; Fondamenta dei Vetrai 37, Murano; ⏱10am-6pm; ⛴Colonna), but you'll also find some dramatic departures: chiselled cobalt-blue vases, glossy black candlesticks that look like minarets, and drinking glasses so fine that they seem to be made out of air.

Murano is less than 10 minutes from Fondamente Nove by *vaporetto*.

Traditional glass-blowing in Murano

Giardini Pubblici Gardens

(Riva dei Partigiani; ⛴Giardini) Begun under Napoleon as the city's first public green space, these leafy gardens are now the main home of the Biennale. Around half of the gardens is open to the public all year round; the rest is given over to the permanent **Biennale pavilions**, each representing a different country. Many of them are attractions in their own right, from Carlo Scarpa's daring 1954 raw-concrete-and-glass Venezuelan Pavilion to Denton Corker Marshall's 2015 Australian Pavilion in black granite.

◎ Isola di San Giorgio Maggiore

Chiesa di San Maggiore Church

(St George's Church; ☑041 522 78 27; www.abbaziasangiorgio.it; Isola di San Giorgio Maggiore; bell tower adult/reduced €6/4; ⏱9am-6pm; ⛴San Giorgio Maggiore) FREE Begun in 1565 and completed in 1610, this dazzling Benedictine abbey church owes more to ancient Roman temples than the bombastic baroque of Palladio's day. Inside is a generously proportioned nave, with high windows distributing filtered sunshine. Two of Tintoretto's masterworks flank the altar, and a lift whisks visitors up the 60m-high bell tower for stirring panoramas – a great alternative to queuing at San Marco's Campanile.

◉ TOURS

See Venice Cultural

(☑349 0848303; www.seevenice.it; tours per hr €75) Intimate and insightful cultural tours are offered by Venetian native Luisella Romeo, whose love and enthusiasm for the city is as infectious as her knowledge is deep. She covers all the grand-slam sights, as well as offering off-the-beaten path itineraries, guided tours of contemporary art museums, visits to artisan studios, design shops and musical venues, which expand visitors' Venetian experiences.

Context Travel Cultural

(☑800 6916036; www.contexttravel.com; group tours from €85;) Context offers scholarly tours for the curious minded. Groups are small and subjects range from politics to art, history and ecology. Families should try the Art Tour, Lion Hunt, Daily Life in Venice and, for older kids, the Science and Secrets of the Lagoon – led by a marine biologist.

🔒 SHOPPING
🔒 San Marco
Chiarastella Cattana   Homewares
(📞041 522 43 69; www.chiarastellacattana. com; Salizada San Samuele 3216; ⏰11am-7pm Mon-Sat; 🚤San Samuele) Transform any home with these locally woven, strikingly original Venetian linens. Whimsical cushions feature chubby purple rhinoceroses and grumpy scarlet elephants straight out of Pietro Longhi paintings, and hand-tasselled jacquard hand towels will dry your guests in style. Decorators and design aficionados should save an afternoon to consider dizzying woven-to-order napkin and curtain options.

Guadagni   Design
(📞041 522 16 64; www.guadagnidesign.it; Salizada San Samuele 3336; ⏰11am-1pm & 3-7pm Tue-Sat; 🚤San Samuele) This interior design store has sumptuous fabrics, contemporary design products and sleek fittings and furnishings for sale. The charming owner, Carla Canazza Guadagni, will happily explain the designers and pieces on show.

Poli Distillerie   Alcohol
(📞041 866 01 04; www.grappa.com; Campiello Feltrina 2511b; ⏰10am-7pm; 🚤Santa Maria del Giglio) This grappa store positively gleams, thanks to its copper-chrome fittings. The Poli family has been distilling grappa since 1898, and the friendly sales team can guide you through the variety on offer.

🔒 Dorsoduro
Paolo Olbi   Arts & Crafts
(📞041 523 76 55; www.olbi.atspace.com; Calle Foscari 3253; ⏰10.30am-12.40pm & 3.30-7.30pm Mar-Dec, 3.30-7.30pm Jan & Feb; 🚤San Tomà) Thoughts worth committing to paper

deserve Paolo Olbi's keepsake books, albums and stationery, whose fans include Hollywood actors and NYC mayors (ask to see the guestbook). Ordinary journals can't compare to Olbi originals, handmade with heavyweight paper and bound with exquisite leather bindings. The watercolour postcards of Venice make for beautiful, bargain souvenirs.

Signor Blum   Toys
(📞041 522 63 67; www.signorblum.com; Campo San Barnaba 2840; ⏰10am-1.30pm & 2.30-7.30pm Mon-Sat; 🚤Ca' Rezzonico) Kids may have to drag adults away from the 2D wooden puzzles of the Rialto Bridge and grinning wooden duckies before these clever handmade toys induce acute cases of nostalgia. Mobiles made of colourful carved gondola prows would seem equally at home in an arty foyer and a nursery. And did we mention the Venice-themed clocks?

🔒 Cannaregio
Codex Venezia   Art
(📞041 524 61 82; www.codexvenezia.it; Fondamenta degli Ormesini 2799; ⏰9.30am-12.30pm & 4-7.30pm Mon-Fri, 9.30am-12.30pm Sat; 🚤San Marcuola) Nelson Kishi's studio contains wonderful prints and original works, mainly in ink on paper, many of them depicting Venetian scenes. Kishi's delicate and intricate cityscapes capture the beauty and bustle of Venice, all packed into this tiny art space.

Nicolao Atelier   Clothing
(📞041 520 70 51; www.nicolao.com; Fondamenta de la Misericordia 2590; ⏰9.30am-1pm & 2-6pm Mon-Fri; 🚤San Marcuola) If you're wondering where Cinderella goes to find the perfect ball gown or Prince Charming his tights, look no further than this fairy-tale wonderland. An exquisite handmade Carnevale outfit will set you back €250 to €300 – and that's just to hire. Out of season the store does brisk business catering to theatres, opera houses and films worldwide.

Entrance to Ca' Macana Atelier (p323)

Ca' Macana Atelier   Arts & Crafts

(☎041 71 86 55; www.camacanaatelier.blogspot.
it; Rio Terà San Leonardo 1374; ⊙9am-8pm; ⍾San
Marcuola) Resist buying inferior mass-
produced Carnevale masks until you've
checked out the traditionally made papier-
mâché and leather masks at this long-estab-
lished shop and workshop. The steampunk
range is exactly as creepy as you'd hope.

EATING

San Marco

Suso   Gelato €

(☎348 5646545; www.gelatovenezia.it; Calle de
la Bissa 5453; scoops €1.60; ⊙10am-midnight;
⍾Rialto) ✿ Suso's gelati are locally made
and free of artificial colours. Indulge in rich,
original seasonal flavours such as marsca-
pone cream with fig sauce and walnuts.
Gluten-free cones are available.

Ai Mercanti   Italian €€

(☎041 523 82 69; www.aimercanti.it; Calle
Fuseri 4346a; meals €35-40; ⊙11.30am-3pm
& 7-10pm Tue-Sat, 7-11pm Mon; ⍾Rialto) With
its pumpkin-coloured walls, gleaming
golden fixtures and jet-black tables and
chairs, Ai Mercanti effortlessly conjures
up a romantic mood. No wonder diners
whisper over glasses of wine selected
from the vast list before tucking into modern bistro-style dishes. Although there's
a focus on seafood and secondary cuts of
meat, there are some wonderful vegetarian options as well.

Ristorante Quadri   Italian €€€

(☎041 522 21 05; www.alajmo.it; Piazza San
Marco 121; meals €140-225; ⊙12.30-2.30pm &
7.30-10.30pm Tue-Sun; ⍾San Marco) When it
comes to Venetian glamour, nothing beats
this historic Michelin-starred restaurant
overlooking Piazza San Marco. A small
swarm of servers greets you as you're
shown to your table in a room decked out
with silk damask, gilt, painted beams and
Murano chandeliers. Dishes are precise
and delicious, deftly incorporating Venetian touches into an inventive modern
Italian menu.

Dorsoduro

Cantine del Vino già Schiavi — Venetian €

(041 523 00 34; www.cantinaschiavi.com; Fondamenta Priuli 992; cicheti €1.50; 8.30am-8.30pm Mon-Sat; Zattere) It may look like a wine shop and function as a bar, but this legendary canalside spot also serves the best *cicheti* (Venetian tapas) on this side of the Grand Canal. Choose from the impressive counter selection or ask for a filled-to-order roll. Chaos cheerfully prevails, with an eclectic cast of locals propping up the bar.

Osteria Bakán — Italian €€

(041 564 76 58; Corte Maggiore 2314a; meals €36-44; 8am-3pm & 6-10pm Wed-Mon; Santa Marta) A strange mix of local drinking den and surprisingly adventurous restaurant, Bakán has bucketloads of atmosphere – with old beams and soft jazz inside, and tables on a tucked-away courtyard. The homemade pasta is excellent, or you could opt for the likes of *guance di vitello* (veal cheeks) or ginger prawns with pilaf rice.

San Polo & Santa Croce

Osteria Trefanti — Venetian €€

(041 520 17 89; www.osteriatrefanti.it; Fondamenta del Rio Marin o dei Garzoti 888; meals €40-45; noon-2.30pm & 7-10.30pm Tue-Sun; ; Riva de Biasio) La Serenissima's spice trade lives on at simple, elegant Trefanti, where gnocchi might get an intriguing kick from cinnamon, and turbot is flavoured with almond and coconut. Seafood is the focus; try the 'doge's fettucine', with mussels, scampi and clams. Furnished with recycled copper lamps, the space is small and deservedly popular – so book ahead.

Cannaregio

Pasticceria Dal Mas — Bakery €

(041 71 51 01; www.dalmaspasticceria.it; Rio Terà Lista di Spagna 150; pastries €1.30-6.50; 7am-9pm; ; Ferrovia) This historic Venetian bakery-cafe sparkles with mirrors, marble and metal trim, fitting for the pastries displayed within. Despite the perpetual morning crush, the efficient team

Cicheti

Cicheti are some of the best culinary finds in Italy, served at lunch and from around 6pm to 8pm with sensational Veneto wines. *Cicheti* range from basic bar snacks (spicy meatballs) to inventive small plates: think white Bassano asparagus and plump lagoon shrimp wrapped in pancetta at **All'Arco** (041 520 56 66; Calle de l'Ochialer 436; cicheti €2-2.50; 9am-2.30pm Mon-Sat; Rialto Mercato); wild boar salami at **Vino Vero** (041 275 00 44; www.facebook.com/vinoverovenezia; Fondamenta de la Misericordia 2497; noon-midnight Tue-Sun, from 5pm Mon; San Marcuola); or bite-sized bread rolls crammed with tuna, chicory and horseradish at **Al Mercà** (346 8340660; Campo Cesare Battisti già de la Bella Vienna 213; 10am-2.30pm & 6-8pm Mon-Thu, to 9.30pm Fri & Sat; Rialto Mercato).

Prices start at €1 for meatballs and range from €3 to €6 for gourmet fantasias, typically devoured standing up or on stools at the bar. Filling *cicheti* such as *crostini* and *panini* cost €1.50 to €6.

Venice's *cicheti* hotspots include:

Cannaregio Along Fondamenta degli Ormesini and off Strada Nova.

San Polo & Santa Croce Around the Rialto Market and Ruga Ravano.

Castello Via Garibaldi and Calle Lunga Santa Maria Formosa.

San Marco Around Campo San Bartolomeo, Campo Santo Stefano and Campo della Guerra.

PFEIFFER/SHUTTERSTOCK ©

Cafes

To line your stomach with coffee and pastry before your next *giro d'ombra*, check out Venice's legendary cafe-bars, and skip milky cappuccino for a stronger *macchiatone* (espresso with a 'big stain' of hot milk). For local flavour, try the **Torrefazione Cannaregio** (☑041 71 63 71; www.torrefazionecannaregio.it; Fondamenta dei Ormesini 2804; ☺7am-7.30pm Mon-Sat, 9am-6pm Sun; ⚓Guglie) *noxea*: coffee beans roasted with hazelnuts. House-roasted speciality blends are also the order of the day at **Caffè del Doge** (☑041 522 77 87; www.caffedeldoge.com; Calle dei Cinque 609; ☺7am-7pm; ⚓San Silvestro).

Historic baroque cafes around Piazza San Marco like **Caffè Florian** (☑041 520 56 41; www.caffeflorian.com; Piazza San Marco 57; ☺9am-11pm; ⚓San Marco) and **Grancaffè Quadri** (☑041 522 21 05; www.alajmo.it; Piazza San Marco 121; ☺9am-midnight; ⚓San Marco) serve coffee and hot chocolate with live orchestras – though your heart might beat a different rhythm once you get the bill. Hint: **Caffè Lavena** (☑041 522 40 70; www.lavena.it; Piazza San Marco 133/134; ☺9.30am-11pm; ⚓San Marco) offers a €1.50 espresso at the counter.

Hot chocolate from Caffè Florian
MARK READ/LONELY PLANET ©

dispenses top-notch coffee and *cornetti* (croissants) with admirable equanimity. Come mid-morning for mouth-watering, still-warm quiches. The hot chocolate is also exceptional – hardly surprising given the sibling chocolate shop next door.

Osteria Boccadoro   Venetian €€€
(☑041 521 10 21; www.boccadorovenezia.it; Campiello Widmann 5405a; meals €40-55; ☺noon-3pm & 7-11pm Tue-Sun; ⚓Fondamente Nove) The sweetly singing birds in this *campo* (square) are probably angling for your leftovers, but they don't stand a chance. Chef-owner Luciano and son Simone's creative *crudi* (raw seafood) are two-bite delights, and cloud-like gnocchi and homemade pasta are gone too soon. Fish is sourced from the lagoon or the Adriatic and vegetables come from the restaurant's kitchen garden.

🍷 DRINKING & NIGHTLIFE

Cantina Do Spade   Wine Bar
(☑041 521 05 83; www.cantinadospade.com; Sotoportego de le Do Spade 860; ☺10am-3pm & 6-10pm Wed-Mon, 6-10pm Tue; 📶; ⚓Rialto Mercato) Famously mentioned in Casanova's memoirs, cosy 'Two Spades' was founded in 1488 and continues to keep Venice in good spirits with its bargain Tri-Veneto and Istrian wines, and young, laid-back management. Come early for market-fresh *fritture* (fried battered seafood) and grilled squid, or linger with satisfying, sit-down dishes like *bigoli in salsa* (pasta in anchovy and onion sauce).

Bar Longhi   Cocktail Bar
(☑041 79 47 81; www.hotelgrittipalacevenice.com; Campo di Santa Maria del Giglio 2467; ☺11am-1am; ⚓Giglio) Gritti Palace's beautiful Bar Longhi may be pricey, but if you consider your surrounds – Fortuny fabrics, an intarsia marble bar, 18th-century mirrors and million-dollar Piero Longhi paintings – the price of a signature orange martini starts to seem reasonable. In summer you'll have to choose between the twinkling interior and a spectacular Grand Canal terrace.

ℹ️ INFORMATION

Vènezia Unica (☑041 24 24; www.veneziaunica.it) runs tourist information services in Venice. It provides information on sights, itineraries, transport, special events and exhibitions. Discount passes can be prebooked online.

GETTING AROUND

VAPORETTO

ACTV (Azienda del Consorzio Trasporti Veneziano; ☏041 272 21 11; http://actv.avmspa.it/en) runs all public transport in Venice, including the waterborne small passenger ferries. Although the service is efficient and punctual, boats on main lines get full fast and can be overcrowded during Carnevale and in peak season. One-way tickets cost €7.50, with a 24-hour unlimited travel pass available for €20. Tickets and passes are available dockside from ACTV ticket booths and ticket vending machines, or from tobacconists.

Inter-island ferry services to Murano, Torcello, the Lido and other lagoon islands are usually provided on larger *motonave*.

Vaporetto stops can be confusing, so check the signs at the landing dock to make sure you're at the right stop for the direction you want. At major stops like Ferrovia, Piazzale Roma, San Marco and Zattere, there are often two separate docks for the same *vaporetto* line, heading in opposite directions. The cluster of stops near Piazza San Marco is especially tricky. If your boat doesn't stop right in front of Piazza San Marco, don't panic: it will probably stop at San Zaccaria, just past the Palazzo Ducale.

To plan itineraries, check schedules and buy tickets download the useful vaporetto app **daAaB**. If you purchase tickets through the app, you can then scan your phone at the barriers in place of a ticket.

GONDOLA

A gondola ride offers a view of Venice that is anything but pedestrian. Official daytime rates are €80 for 40 minutes (€100 for 40 minutes from 7pm to 8am), not including songs or tips. Additional time is charged in 20-minute increments (day/night €40/50). You may negotiate a price break in overcast weather or around noon. Agree on a price, time limit and singing in advance to avoid unexpected surcharges.

Gondolas cluster at *stazi* (stops) along the Grand Canal and near major monuments and tourist hotspots, but you can also book a pickup by calling **Ente Gondola** (☏041 528 50 75; www.gondolavenezia.it).

Supported by the Gondoliers Association, **Gondolas 4 All** (☏328 2431382; www.gondolas4all.com; Fondamente Cossetti; per 30min €80; ☒Piazzale Roma) offers gondola rides to wheelchair users in a specially adapted gondola. Embarkation is from a wheelchair-accessible pier at Piazzale Roma.

WATER TAXI

Licensed water taxis are a costly way to get around Venice, though they may prove handy when you're late to be somewhere. Fares can be metered or negotiated in advance. Official rates start at €15 plus €2 per minute. There's a €10 surcharge for night trips (10pm to 6am) and a €10 surcharge for each extra passenger above the first four. Tipping isn't required.

Make sure your water taxi has the yellow strip with the licence number displayed. There are official water-taxi ranks in front of **Piazzale Roma** (Fondamente Cossetti) and at Tronchetto.

Even if you're in a hurry, don't encourage your taxi driver to speed through Venice – this kicks up *motoschiaffi* (motorboat wakes) that expose Venice's ancient foundations to degradation and rot.

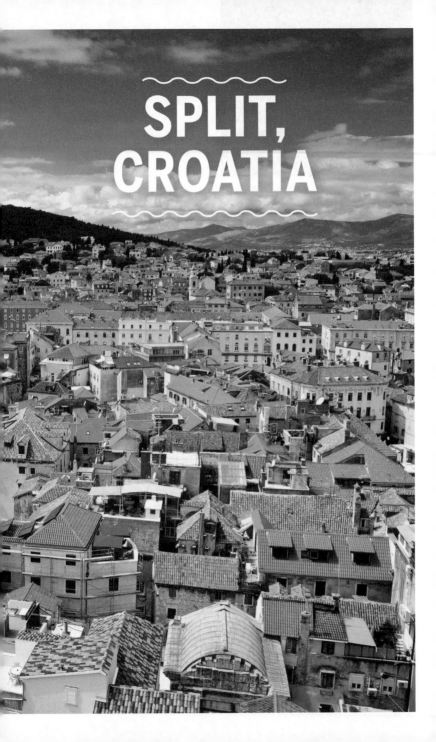

SPLIT,
CROATIA

In this chapter

Split at a Glance...

Croatia's second-largest city, Split is a great place to see Dalmatian life as it's really lived. Always buzzing, this exuberant city has just the right balance between tradition and modernity. Step inside Diocletian's Palace (one of the world's most impressive Roman monuments) and you'll see dozens of bars, restaurants and shops thriving amid the atmospheric old walls. To top it off, Split has a unique setting. Its dramatic coastal mountains act as the perfect backdrop to the turquoise waters of the Adriatic and help divert attention from the high-rise apartment blocks that fill its suburbs.

With One Day in Port

○ To stretch your legs and avoid the early crowds at Diocletian's Palace, climb up the stone stairs to **Marjan Forest Park** (p342) to enjoy a drink and the views over the city at **Vidilica** (p345) cafe.

○ Next, explore **Diocletian's Palace** (p332), visiting the peristil, cathedral, vestibule and substructure, and calling into **Split City Museum** (p340).

○ Finish your day with a coffee or **cocktail** on the Riva waterfront promenade.

Best Places For...

Traditional food Villa Spiza (p344)

Seafood Konoba Fetivi (p344)

Ice cream Luka (p344)

Atmosphere Marcvs Marvlvs Spalatensis (p345)

Wine and cheese Paradox (p345)

Split Map (p341)

Getting from the Port

Cruise ships dock at the southernmost berths in **Split's city harbour**.

It's just a 1km stroll along the waterfront from here to Diocletian's Palace and the old town. Taxis line up at the harbour, but because the ride to the old town is so short, some might not be willing to drive it.

Fast Facts

Currency Kuna (KN)

Language Croatian

Money You can change money at travel agencies or at any post office. There are ATMs around the bus and train stations and throughout the city.

Tourist information Tourist offices on Peristil square in Diocletian's Palace and on the Riva waterfront promenade.

Visas Generally not required for stays of up to 90 days, with some exceptions.

Wi-fi There's free wi-fi at many cafes and bars in the inner city.

NIYAZZ/SHUTTERSTOCK ©

Diocletian's Palace

In a prime harbourside location, this extraordinary complex is one of the world's most imposing ancient Roman structures. Don't expect a palace or museum, though – the labyrinthine streets are packed with people, bars, shops and restaurants.

Great For...

☑ Don't Miss

The octagonal Cathedral of St Domnius (p334), which was built as a mausoleum for Diocletian.

Walls & Gates

Built as a combined imperial residence, military fortress and fortified town, the **palace** measures 215m from north to south and 180m east to west, altogether covering 38,700 sq metres. Although the original structure has been added to continuously over the millennia, the alterations have only served to increase the allure of this fascinating site.

Diocletian – the first Roman emperor to abdicate voluntarily – commissioned this magnificent palace to be completed in time for his retirement in AD 305. It was built from lustrous white stone transported from the island of Brač, and construction lasted 10 years. Diocletian spared no expense, importing marble from Italy and Greece, and columns and 12 sphinxes from Egypt.

Sphinx imported from Egypt

YKD/SHUTTERSTOCK ©

⚓ Explore Ashore

It's just a 1km stroll along the waterfront to Diocletian's Palace. Set aside at least two hours to explore within the palace walls.

★ Top Tip

It's worth paying for entry to the **Split Ethnographic Museum** (Etnografski muzej Split; ☎021-344 161; www.etnografski-muzej-split.hr; Iza Vestibula 4; adult/child 20/10KN; ☺9.30am-8pm Mon-Sat, to 1pm Sun Jun-Sep, 9.30am-6pm Mon-Fri, 10am-2pm Sat & Sun Oct, 9.30am-4pm Mon-Fri, to 2pm Sat Nov-May) to access the terrace and take in the views.

Each wall has a gate at its centre that's named after a metal: the elaborate northern **Golden Gate** (Zlatna Vrata; Dioklecijanova bb), the southern **Bronze Gate** (Brončana Vrata; Obala hrvatskog narodnog preporoda bb), the eastern **Silver Gate** (Srebrna Vrata) and the western **Iron Gate** (Željezna Vrata). Between the eastern and western gates there's a straight road (Krešimirova, also known as Decumanus), which separated the imperial residence on the southern side, with its state rooms and temples, from the northern side, once used by soldiers and servants.

Bronze Gate & Substructure

Although it's easy to lose sight of the palace amid the bustle of Split's waterfront promenade, take time to step back and look up. The original arches and columns of the palace wall can be easily discerned above

the shops and restaurants. It would have presented a magnificent face to the sea, with the water lapping at the base of the walls. It's not hard to see why Diocletian built his imperial apartments on this south-facing side of the palace, gazing directly out over the water.

The unassuming Bronze Gate once opened straight from the water into the palace basements, enabling goods to be unloaded directly from ships and stored here. Now this former tradesman's entrance is the main way into the palace from the Riva.

While the central part of the **substructure** (Supstrukcije Dioklecijanove palače; www.mgst.net; Obala hrvatskog narodnog preporoda bb; adult/child 42/22KN; ☺8.30am-9pm Apr-Sep, to 5pm Sun Oct, 9am-5pm Mon-Sat, to 2pm Sun Nov-Apr) is now a major thoroughfare lined with souvenir stalls, entry to the chambers on either side is ticketed. Mostly empty save the odd sarcophagus or bit of column, the basement rooms and corridors exude a haunting timelessness that is worth the price of admission. For fans of *Game of Thrones,* here be dragons – Daenerys Targaryen keeps her scaly brood here when she's in Meereen.

Peristil & Vestibule

From the substructure, stairs lead up to the ceremonial heart of the palace, a picturesque colonnaded ancient Roman courtyard (or peristyle; **peristil** in Croatian). In summer you are almost guaranteed to see a pair of strapping local lads dressed as legionaries adding to the scene. Sitting between the columns near the cathedral is

a black-granite Egyptian sphinx, dating from the 15th century BC.

At the southern end of the peristyle, above the basement stairs, is the **vestibule** (Peristil bb) `FREE` – a grand and cavernous domed room, open to the sky, which was once the formal entrance to the imperial apartments.

Cathedral of St Domnius

Dominating one side of the peristyle, Split's octagonal **cathedral** (Katedrala sv Duje; Peristil bb; cathedral/belfry 35/20KN; ⏰8am-8pm Jun-Sep, 7am-noon & 5-7pm May & Oct, 7am-noon Nov-Feb, 8am-5pm Mar & Apr) is one of the best-preserved ancient Roman buildings still standing today. It was built as a mausoleum for Diocletian, who was interred here in AD 311. As emperor, he was the last famous persecutor of the Christians, but his victims got the last laugh. In

Vestibule of Diocletian's Palace

the 5th century Diocletian's sarcophagus was destroyed and his tomb converted into a church dedicated to an early bishop, martyred in Salona's amphitheatre in AD 304.

The exterior is still encircled by an original colonnade of 24 columns. A much later addition, the tall Romanesque **bell tower**, was constructed between the 13th and 16th centuries and reconstructed in 1908 after it collapsed. Tickets are sold separately for those eager to climb up for views over the old town's rooftops. You'll need a head for heights, as the steep stone stairs quickly give way to flimsy metal ones suspended over the internal void.

NENSI BERAM/SHUTTERSTOCK ©

Inside the cathedral, the domed interior has two rows of Corinthian columns and a frieze running high up on the walls that, surprisingly, still includes images of the emperor and his wife. To the left of the main altar is the **altar of St Anastasius** (Sveti Staš; 1448), carved by Juraj Dalmatinac. It features a relief of *The Flagellation of Christ* that is considered one of the finest sculptural works of its time in Dalmatia.

The **choir** is furnished with 13th-century Romanesque seats, the oldest of their kind in Dalmatia. Other highlights include a 13th-century **pulpit**; the **right-hand altar**, carved by Bonino da Milano in 1427; and the **vault** above the high altar, decorated with murals by Dujam Vušković. Take a look at the remarkable scenes from the life of Christ on the wooden **entrance doors**. Carved by Andrija Buvina in the 13th century, the images are presented in 28 squares, 14 on each side, and recall the fashion of Romanesque miniatures of the time.

Temple of Jupiter

Now the cathedral's baptistery, this wonderfully intact building was originally an ancient Roman **temple** (Jupiterov hram; 10KN, free with cathedral ticket; ⊘8am-7pm Mon-Sat, 12.30-6.30pm Sun May-Oct, to 5pm Nov-Apr) dedicated to the king of the gods. It still has its original barrel-vaulted ceiling and decorative frieze, although a striking bronze statue of St John the Baptist by Ivan Meštrović now fills the spot where Jupiter once stood. The font is made from 13th-century carved stones recycled from the cathedral's rood screen. Of the columns that once supported a porch, only one remains. The black-granite sphinx guarding the entrance was defaced (literally) by early Christians, who considered it a pagan icon.

✕ **Take a Break**

Tucked into the ground floor of a 15th-century Gothic house in the northern part of the palace, Marcvs Marvlvs Spalatensis (p345) is a great place for wine and a snack.

Klis Fortress

This imposing fortress spreads along a limestone bluff above the valley leading into Split. Its long and narrow form (304m by 53m) derives from constant extensions over the course of millennia.

Great For...

☑ **Don't Miss**

The view from the top of the fortress down over Split and the offshore islands in the Adriatic Sea.

Walls & Gates

There are three gates to pass through before you reach the inner part of the fortress. The ticket office is located in the main gate at the lower end of the complex, built by the Austrians in the 1820s. From here a path twists up to the second gate, which was the main entrance in the Middle Ages – although its current form is also courtesy of the Austrians. The last gate, also medieval, is reached by a set of stone steps at the far end of the fort. Its current appearance is from a Venetian reconstruction in 1763.

Historical Displays

A series of highly informative but very wordy panels detailing Klis' long and complicated history are displayed in a 17th-century Venetian-built armoury in

TATIANA POPOVA/SHUTTERSTOCK ©

Klis Fortress

Sućurac · Klis

Adriatic Sea · Solin

Split · Stobreč

⚓

Explore Ashore

Klis is 12km northeast of Split's city centre. A taxi from the harbour takes 20 to 30 minutes, depending on traffic. City bus 22 takes roughly 45 minutes and departs every couple of hours on weekdays from the **Croatian National Theatre** (Hrvatsko narodno kazalište Split; ☏021-306 908; www.hnk-split.hr; Trg Gaje Bulata 1). You'll want around 45 minutes at the fortress.

ⓘ Need to Know

Tvrđava Klis; ☏021-240 578; www.tvrda-vaklis.com; Klis bb; adult/child 40/15KN; ⊙9.30am-4pm

---

the inner part of the fortress. In a nutshell, it goes like this: founded by the Illyrians in the 2nd century BC; taken by the Romans; became a stronghold of medieval Croatian duke Trpimir; resisted attacks for 25 years before falling to the Turks in 1537; briefly retaken in 1596 before returning to Turkish control; fell to the Venetians in 1648.

The room also contains a collection of 17th- to 19th-century muskets, swords and armour, and a mock-up of the sort of garb worn by the Uskoks, the local warriors who defended the castle from the Turks.

St Vitus' Church & Upper Fortress Views

At the heart of the upper fortress is a simple, square church topped with a dome, dedicated to St Vitus (Sv Vid). During the Turkish period it was converted into a mosque.

The views from the entire fortress are remarkable, but no less so than at the very top, taking in all of the sprawling city of Split and the islands beyond.

Game of Thrones Exhibition

For fans of HBO's fantasy series *Game of Thrones,* Klis Fortress is Meereen – the city where Daenerys Targaryen had all those nasty slave-masters crucified in season four. If you're having trouble visualising Klis in its *GoT* guise, there's a display of stills from the show in an 18th-century gunpowder chamber in the top part of the fortress.

Explore the Emperor's Palace

This atmospheric walk will take you right into the heart of Diocletian's Palace, where Roman monuments sit side-by-side with some of the city's coolest bars.

Start Grgur Ninski statue
Distance 500m
Duration One hour

6 Snake through the maze of streets lined with medieval buildings housing some of Split's best bars to the high arches of the **Iron Gate** (p333).

7 Pass through to **Narodni trg**, which has been Split's main civic square since medieval times.

5 Take the stairs up into the well-preserved **vestibule** (p334), a domed room, open to the sky, once the formal entrance to the emperor's personal quarters.

Narodni Trg

FINISH

7

Bosanska

6

Krešimirova

Maruliceva

Obala Hrvatskog Narodnog Preporoda (Riva)

Split Harbour

N 0 ——————————— 100 m

1 Begin outside Diocletian's Palace at the imposing **statue of Grgur Ninski** (p340); rub his toe for good luck.

2 Take the stairs down to the grand **Golden Gate** (p333), the main processional entrance into the palace.

Classic Photo Peristil

3 Walk along Dioklecijanova to the **peristil** (p334), the ceremonial court at the approach to the imperial apartments.

Take a Break... Grab a cushion right on the Peristil's steps at **Luxor** (p345).

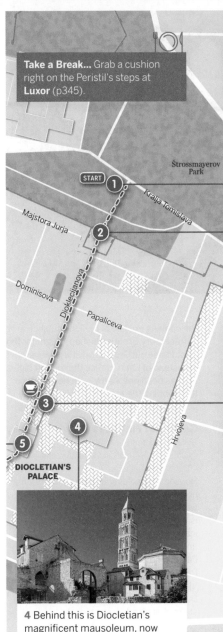

Štrossmayerov Park

START (1)

Kralja Tomislava

Majstora Jurja

(2)

Dominisova

Dioklecijanova

Papaliceva

Hrvojeva

(3)

(4)

(5)

DIOCLETIAN'S PALACE

4 Behind this is Diocletian's magnificent mausoleum, now the **Cathedral of St Domnius** (p334).

1 STEVE ESTVANIK/SHUTTERSTOCK © 3 KIRK FISHER/SHUTTERSTOCK © 4 PIOTRBB/SHUTTERSTOCK © 6 CORTYN/SHUTTERSTOCK © 7 APEXPHOTOS/GETTY IMAGES ©

MICHAEL PASCHOS/SHUTTERSTOCK ©

Split City Museum

◎ SIGHTS

The frenetic waterfront promenade, commonly known as the Riva, is your best central reference point in Split. To the east is buzzy Bačvice beach and to the west is the wooded Marjan Hill.

Split City Museum
Museum

(Muzej grada Splita; ☑021-360 171; www.mgst. net; Papalićeva 1; adult/child 22/12KN; ⊙8.30am-9pm Apr-Sep, 9am-5pm Tue-Sat, to 2pm Sun Oct-Mar) Built by Juraj Dalmatinac in the 15th century for one of the many noblemen who lived within the old town, the Large Papalić Palace is considered a fine example of late-Gothic style, with an elaborately carved entrance gate that proclaimed the importance of its original inhabitants. The interior has been thoroughly restored to house this museum, which has interesting displays on Diocletian's Palace (p332) and on the development of the city.

Grgur Ninski statue
Statue

(Kralja Tomislava bb) Sculpted by Ivan Meštrović, this gargantuan statue is one of the defining images of Split. Its subject, a 10th-century Croatian bishop, fought for the right to use old Croatian in liturgical services instead of Latin. Notice that his left big toe has been polished to a shine – it's said that rubbing the toe brings good luck and guarantees that you'll come back to Split.

Gallery of Fine Arts
Gallery

(Galerija umjetnina Split; ☑021-350 110; www. galum.hr; Kralja Tomislava 15; adult/child 40/20KN; ⊙10am-6pm Tue-Fri, to 2pm Sat & Sun) Housed in a building that was the city's first hospital (1792), this gallery exhibits 400 works of art spanning 700 years. Upstairs is the permanent collection – a chronological journey that starts with religious icons and continues with works by the likes of Paolo Veneziano, Albrecht Dürer and Guido Reni, alongside the work of locals such as Vlaho Bukovac, Ivan Meštrović and Cata Dujšin-Ribar. The temporary exhibits downstairs change every few months.

Archaeological Museum
Museum

(Arheološki muzej; ☑021-329 340; www. armus.hr; Zrinsko-Frankopanska 25; adult/

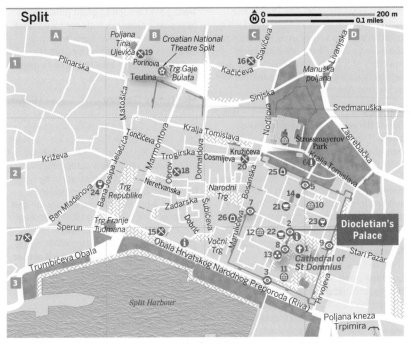

Split

◉ Top Sights

1 Cathedral of St Domnius	C3
2 Diocletian's Palace	C3

◉ Sights

3 Bronze Gate	C3
Diocletian's Palace Substructure	(see 3)
4 Gallery of Fine Arts	C2
5 Golden Gate	D2
6 Grgur Ninski statue	D2
7 Iron Gate	C2
8 Peristil	C3
9 Silver Gate	D3
10 Split City Museum	D2
11 Split Ethnographic Museum	C3
12 Temple of Jupiter	C3
13 Vestibule	C3

◉ Activities, Courses & Tours

14 Split Walking Tours	C2

◆ Eating

15 Brasserie on 7	B3
16 Gušt	C1
17 Konoba Fetivi	A3
18 Kruščić	B2
19 Luka	B1
20 Villa Spiza	C2

◯ Drinking & Nightlife

21 D16	C2
22 Luxor	C3
23 Marcvs Marvlvs Spalatensis	D2
24 Paradox	A2

◯ Shopping

Diocletian's Cellars	(see 3)
25 Studio Naranča	C2
26 Uje	C2

child 20/10KN; ⊙9am-2pm & 4-8pm Mon-Sat Jun-Sep, closed Sat afternoon & Sun Oct-May) A treasure trove of classical sculpture and mosaics is displayed at this excellent mu-

seum, a short walk north of the town centre. Most of the vast collection originated from the ancient Roman settlements of Split and neighbouring **Salona** (☎021-213

358; Don Frane Bulića bb, Solin; adult/child 30/15KN; ⊙9am-7pm Mon-Sat, to 2pm Sun), and there's also some Greek pottery from the island of Vis. There are displays of jewellery and coins, and a room filled with artefacts dating from the Palaeolithic Age to the Iron Age.

Bačvice — Beach

Sandy Bačvice is Split's most popular beach. There's a lot of concrete and it's perpetually crowded, but it offers a good taste of everyday Split life. Locals come here during the day to swim, sunbathe and drink coffee; a younger crowd returns in the evening for the bars and clubs. There are showers and changing rooms at both ends of the beach.

Marjan Forest Park — Park

(Park-šuma Marjan; www.marjan-parksuma.hr) Looming up to 178m over Split's western fringes, this nature reserve occupies a big space in Split's psyche. The views over the city and surrounding islands are extraordinary, and the shady paths provide a welcome reprieve from both the heat and the summertime tourist throngs.

Trails pass through fragrant pine forests to scenic lookouts, a 16th-century Jewish cemetery, medieval chapels and cave dwellings once inhabited by Christian hermits. Climbers take to the cliffs near the end of the peninsula.

Meštrović Gallery — Gallery

(Galerija Meštrović; ☑021-340 800; www. mestrovic.hr; Šetalište Ivana Meštrovića 46; adult/child 40/20KN; ⊙9am-7pm Tue-Sun May-Sep, to 4pm Tue-Sun Oct-Apr) At this stellar art museum you'll see a comprehensive, well-arranged collection of works by Ivan Meštrović, Croatia's premier modern sculptor, who built the grand mansion as a personal residence in the 1930s. Although Meštrović intended to retire here, he emigrated to the USA soon after WWII. Admission includes entry to the nearby **Kaštilac** (☑021-340 800; Šetalište Ivana Meštrovića 39; adult/child 40/20KN, with Meštrović Gallery free; ⊙9am-7pm Tue-Sun May-Oct; 9am-4pm Tue-Sat, 10am-3pm Sun Nov-Apr), a fortress housing other Meštrović works.

From left: Bačvice; Grgur Ninski statue (p340), sculpted by Ivan Meštrović; Marjan Forest Park; Meštrović Gallery

ANDRAS_CSONTOS/SHUTTERSTOCK ©

HUANG ZHENG/SHUTTERSTOCK ©

ⓖ TOURS

Split Walking Tours   Tours

(☏ 099 82 15 383; www.splitwalkingtour.com; Dioklecijanova 3) Leads walking tours in English, Spanish, Italian, German and French, departing from the Golden Gate at set times during the day (check the website). Options include the 75-minute Diocletian's Palace Tour (100KN) and the two-hour Split Walking Tour (160KN), which includes the palace and the medieval part of town. It also offers kayaking, diving, cycling tours, boat trips and excursions.

ⓐ SHOPPING

Uje   Food & Drinks

(☏ 021-342 719; www.uje.hr; Marulićeva 1; ⏱ 8am-8.30pm Mon-Fri, to 2pm Sat) For a little place, Uje stocks a large range of top-quality Croatian olive oil, along with locally made jam, pasta sauce, *rakija* (grappa), wine, soap and wooden products.

Diocletian's Cellars   Market

(Obala hrvatskog narodnog preporoda bb; ⏱ 9am-9pm) The main passage through the basement of Diocletian's Palace is lined with stalls selling jewellery, gifts made from Brač stone, scarves, T-shirts, handmade soap and prints. For a touristy souvenir strip, the quality's actually pretty good.

Studio Naranča   Design

(☏ 021-344 118; www.studionaranca.com; Majstora Jurja 5; ⏱ 10am-7pm Mon-Sat, to 2pm Sun May-Sep) Showcasing the work of local artist Pavo Majić, 'Studio Orange' sells original art and very cool T-shirts, tote bags and postcards featuring his designs.

ⓧ EATING

Dozens of restaurants are clustered around the Riva, the old town and the Veli Varoš neighbourhood to the west.

Kruščić   Bakery €

(☏ 099 26 12 345; www.facebook.com/Kruscic. Split; Obrov 6; items 6-15KN; ⏱ 8am-2pm) Split's best bakery serves delicious bread, pastries and pizza slices. The focus is more savoury than sweet, although you'll find sweet things, too.

ALEX RINKUS/SHUTTERSTOCK ©

JOHN ELK III/ALAMY STOCK PHOTO ©

JOHN KISS/ALAMY STOCK PHOTO ©

Luxor cafe-bar

Luka
Sweets €

(Svačićeva 2; items 8-12KN; ⊙8.30am-11pm Mon-Sat, 10am-11pm Sun; 🛜) Little Luka is as sweet as they come, serving muffins, cakes and coffee to locals on one of the inner city's least touristy squares. In summer there are queues out the door for the homemade ice cream.

Gušt
Pizza €

(📱021-486 333; www.pizzeria-gust.hr; Slavićeva 1; pizzas 40-62KN; ⊙9am-11pm Mon-Sat) Split's diehard pizza fans swear by this joint – it's cheap and very local, serving delicious pizza with Neapolitan-style chewy bases. The stone and brick walls make it a cosy retreat in winter.

Villa Spiza
Dalmatian €€

(Kružićeva 3; mains 50-100KN; ⊙noon-midnight Mon-Sat) A locals' favourite, just outside the walls of Diocletian's Palace, this low-key joint offers daily-changing, great-quality Dalmatian mainstays – calamari, risotto, veal – at reasonable prices. The restaurant is split into two spaces across from one another in the same street.

Konoba Fetivi
Dalmatian, Seafood €€

(📱021-355 152; www.facebook.com/KonobaFetivi; Tomića stine 4; mains 70-95KN; ⊙noon-11pm Tue-Sun) Informal and family-run, with a TV screening sports in the corner, Fetivi feels more like a tavern than most that bear the *konoba* name. However, that doesn't detract from the food, which is first rate. Seafood is the focus here. The cuttlefish stew with polenta is highly recommended, but the whole fish is wonderfully fresh, too.

Brasserie on 7
Modern European €€€

(📱021-278 233; www.brasserieon7.com; Obala hrvatskog narodnog preporoda 7; mains breakfast 68-94KN, lunch 88-150KN, dinner 105-240KN; ⊙7.30am-11.30pm Apr-Sep, 8am-4pm Oct-Mar) The best of the Riva eateries; this waterfront brasserie's outdoor tables are the perfect vantage point for watching the passing parade. Start the day with a cooked breakfast, end it with a cocktail, and fill the hours in between with a light lunch, a more substantial dinner, or wine and a cheese platter. The service is excellent, too.

DRINKING & NIGHTLIFE

Marcvs Marvlvs
Spalatensis
Wine Bar

(www.facebook.com/marvlvs; Papalićeva 4; ⏲11am-midnight Jun-Aug, to 11pm Mon-Sat Sep-May; 🛜) Fittingly, the 15th-century Gothic home of the 'Dante of Croatia', Marko Marulić, now houses this wonderful little 'library jazz bar' made up of small rooms crammed with books and frequented by ageless bohemians, tortured poets and wistful academics. Cheese, chess, cards and cigars are all on offer, and there's often live music.

Paradox
Wine Bar

(📞021-787 778; www.paradox.hr; Bana Josipa Jelačića 3; ⏲8am-midnight; 🛜) This stylish wine and cheese bar has a fantastic rooftop terrace, a massive selection of Croatian wines (more than 120, including 40 by the glass) and a variety of local cheeses to go with them. The clued-up staff members really know their stuff, and there's live music most weekends.

Luxor
Cafe

(📞021-341 082; www.facebook.com/Lvxor1700; Peristil bb; ⏲8am-midnight; 🛜) Touristy, yes, but this cafe-bar is a great place to have coffee and cake right in the ceremonial heart of Diocletian's Palace. Cushions are laid out on the steps and there's live music nightly.

D16
Cafe

(📞091 79 00 705; www.d16coffee.com; Dominisova 16; ⏲7am-7pm Mon-Sat, 9am-7pm Sun; 🛜) D16's baristas are serious about coffee and they've got the beards to prove it. Hidden away in the back lanes of Diocletian's Palace, this hip little speciality roaster is your best bet for a superbly executed flat white, cold brew or espresso with almond milk. Just be prepared to pay double the price you'd pay at a local-style cafe.

Vidilica
Cafe, Bar

(Nazorov Prilaz 1; ⏲8am-midnight; 🛜) It's worth the climb up the stone stairs through the ancient Veli Varoš quarter for a drink on the terrace of this hilltop cafe with glorious city, harbour and mountain views.

 Klapa Your Hands!

Few visitors to Dalmatia will leave without at some point being mesmerised by the dulcet tones of a *klapa* song. This a cappella tradition involves a bunch of burly men in a circle, singing tear-jerkers about love, betrayal, patriotism, death, beauty and other life-affirming subjects in honeyed multi-tonal harmonies.

Traditional *klapa* singers
CPIFBG13/SHUTTERSTOCK ©

INFORMATION

Split's **tourist information offices** (⏲8am-9pm Jun-Sep, 8am-8pm Mon-Sat, to 5pm Sun Apr, May & Oct, 9am-4pm Mon-Fri, to 2pm Sat Nov-Mar) **are on Peristil** (📞021-345 606; www.visitsplit.com; Peristil bb) square in Diocletian's Palace and on the **Riva** (📞021-360 066; Obala hrvatskog narodnog preporoda 9) waterfront promenade.

ⓘ GETTING AROUND

Bus Operating local buses, **Promet Split** (📞021-407 888; www.promet-split.hr) has an extensive network throughout Split (per journey 11KN) and to Klis (13KN). You can buy tickets on the bus, but if you buy from a kiosk, a two-journey (ie return, known as a 'duplo') central-zone ticket costs only 17KN. Buses run about every 15 minutes from 5.30am to 11.30pm.

Taxis line up in front of the exit from the city harbour's international area.

Walking Split's old town is small and close to the harbour, so you can explore most places on foot.

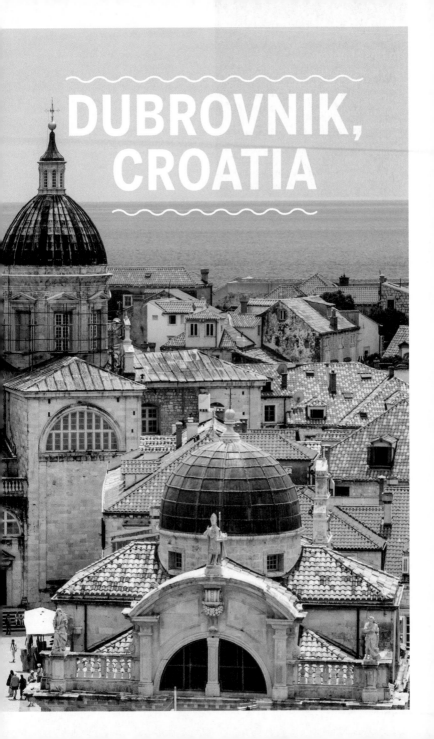

DUBROVNIK, CROATIA

Dubrovnik at a Glance...

Whether you're visiting Dubrovnik for the first time or the hundredth, the sense of awe never fails to descend when you set eyes on the beauty of the old town. Indeed, it's hard to imagine anyone becoming jaded by the city's limestone streets, baroque buildings and the endless shimmer of the Adriatic, or failing to be inspired by a walk along the ancient city walls. Marvel at the interplay of light on the old stone buildings, exhaust yourself climbing up and down narrow lanes, then plunge into the azure sea.

With One Day in Port

○ Head up **Mt Srđ** (p355) for a great overview of the city and its surroundings. Next take a walk along the **city walls** (p350) to get a closer view of the city's terracotta rooftops.

○ Spend the rest of the day wandering the marbled streets of the **Old Town** (p356) and calling into whichever church, palace or museum takes your fancy.

○ When it starts to bake, head to **D'vino** (p365) to sample some local wines, or take a dip in the **Adriatic**.

Best Places For...

Ice cream Peppino's (p363)

Seafood Proto (p364)

Traditional food Konoba Ribar (p364)

Seafront location Bard Mala Buža (p365)

Wine D'vino (p365)

Previous page: Dubrovnik's Old City
ANDREY OMELYANCHUK/500PX ©

Getting from the Port

Most large ships dock at the terminal in **Gruž**, 3km northwest of the old town. Most offer a shuttle service to Pile Gate in the old town. Some smaller ships dock by the old town and take guests into the Old Harbour by tender.

The not-especially-scenic walk between Gruž and the old town takes 40 minutes. A taxi takes 10 to 15 minutes in normal traffic. Buses 1a and 1b take around 15 minutes from the bus station (p365) in Gruž to Pile Gate.

Fast Facts

Currency Kuna (KN)

Language Croatian

Money There are plenty of ATM machines around (called '*bankomat*' locally); debit and credit cards widely accepted.

Tourist information Tourist offices at the cruise terminal in Gruž and just outside Pile Gate near the Old Town.

Visas Generally not required for stays of up to 90 days, with some exceptions.

Wi-fi Most restaurants, cafes, bars and city buses have free wi-fi, as does Obala Stjepana Radića, right outside the port.

City walls with a view of Lokrum Island

City Walls & Forts

No visit to Dubrovnik would be complete without a walk around the spectacular city walls, the finest in the world and the city's main claim to fame.

Great For...

☑ Don't Miss

The sublime view over the old town and the shimmering Adriatic from the top of the walls.

Walking the Walls

There are entrances to the walls from near the Pile Gate (p358), the **Ploče Gate** (Vrata od Ploča) and the **Maritime Museum** (Pomorski muzej; ☎020-323 904; www.dumus.hr; Tvrđava Sv Ivana; multimuseum pass adult/child 120/25KN; ◷9am-6pm Tue-Sun Apr-Oct, to 4pm Nov-Mar). The Pile Gate entrance tends to be the busiest, and entering from the Ploče side means getting the steepest climbs out of the way first (you're required to walk in an anticlockwise direction).

Starting from the Ploče Gate entrance, you'll quickly reach **St Luke's Tower** (1467), facing the Old Harbour and **Fort Revelin**. The northern, landward section of wall is the highest, reaching a peak at rounded **Fort Minčeta** at the city's northwestern corner. Completed in 1464 to designs by

Ploče Gate

ANAMARIA MEJIA/SHUTTERSTOCK ©

Explore Ashore

Most ships offer a shuttle service from the port to Pile Gate. Set aside an hour and a half to walk the 2km-long walls, so you have plenty of time to enjoy the views. Fort Lawrence is a 10- to 15-minute walk from Pile Gate and you need 15 to 20 minutes to visit.

❶ Need to Know

Gradske zidine; ☎020-638 800; www.wallsofdubrovnik.com; adult/child 200/50KN; ☉8am-6.30pm Apr-Oct, 9am-3pm Nov-Mar

History of the Walls

The first set of walls to enclose the city was built in the 9th century. In the middle of the 14th century the 1.5m-thick defences were fortified with 15 square forts. The threat of attacks from the Turks in the 15th century prompted the city to strengthen the existing forts and add new ones, so that the entire old town was contained within a stone barrier 2km long and up to 25m high. The walls are thicker on the land side – up to 6m – and range from 1.5m to 3m on the sea side.

Guided Tours

Dubrovnik Walks (p362) runs excellent English-language guided walks departing from near the Pile Gate. The two-hour 'Walls & Wars' tour is 190KN. No reservations necessary.

Juraj Dalmatinac, the battlements provide remarkable views over the rooftops.

From here it's mainly downhill as you pass over Pile Gate and then narrow to single file as you climb towards **Fort Bokar**. The seaward stretch of the walls passes a couple of cafe-bars and souvenir stores, before terminating at **Fort St John** at the entrance to Dubrovnik's Old Harbour.

Fort Lawrence

St Blaise gazes down from the walls of this large, freestanding **fortress** (Tvrđava Lovrjenac; www.citywallsdubrovnik.hr; Pile; 50KN, free with city walls ticket; ☉8am-6.30pm Apr-Oct, 9am-3pm Nov-Mar), constructed atop a 37m-high promontory adjacent to the old town to guard the city's western approach from invasion. The battlements offer wonderful views over the old town.

Trsteno Arboretum

OLDSKOOLDESIGN/SHUTTERSTOCK ©

Game of Thrones Locations

Dubrovnik is like a fantasy world for many, but fans of Game of Thrones have more reason to indulge in flights of fancy than most, as much of the immensely popular TV series was filmed here.

Great For...

☑ **Don't Miss**

The city walls, which have often featured in the TV series, particularly during the siege of King's Landing.

Dubrovnik features prominently in the series, standing in for the cities of King's Landing and Qarth.

City Walls, Fort Lawrence & Gradac Park

Tyrion Lannister commanded the defence of King's Landing from the seaward-facing walls (p350) during the Battle of the Blackwater. **Fort Minčeta** (Tvrđava Minčeta) stood in for the exterior of Qarth's House of Undying.

Fort Lawrence (p351) is King's Landing's famous Red Keep and both the interior and the exterior will be familiar. Cersei fare-welled her daughter Myrcella from the little harbour beneath the fort. Nearby **Gradac Park** (Don Frana Bulića bb, Pile) was the site of the Purple Wedding feast, where King Joffrey finally got his comeuppance.

Fort Lawrence (p351)

MITZY/SHUTTERSTOCK ©

Explore Ashore

Most ships offer a shuttle service from the port to Pile Gate. You need around three hours to tour the old town locations on foot (including the City Walls, Fort Lawrence and Gradac Park). It's a 30-minute bus ride each way to Trsteno Arboretum, and you need at least half an hour to explore. Allow at least an hour and a half to visit Lokrum Island, including the boat rides.

★ Top Tip

Both Dubrovnik Day Tours (p362) and Dubrovnik Walks (p362) offer *Game of Thrones* tours.

Trsteno Arboretum

The Red Keep gardens, where the Tyrells endlessly chatted and plotted during seasons three and four, are at the **Trsteno Arboretum** (☑020-751 019; adult/child 50/30KN; ☉7am-7pm May-Oct, 8am-4pm Nov-Apr), 14km northwest of Dubrovnik. The oldest of their kind in Croatia, the gardens have a Renaissance layout, with a set of geometric shapes made with plants and bushes, citrus orchards, a maze, a palm collection and a pond. Catch bus 12, 15, 22 or 35 from Dubrovnik's bus station.

Lokrum Island

The reception for Daenerys in Qarth was held in the **Benedictine monastery** cloister on the lush island of Lokrum (p361), a 10-minute boat ride from Dubrovnik's Old Harbour. There's a *Game of Thrones* exhibition and a reproduction Iron Throne.

Locations in the Old Town

The grand atrium of the Rector's Palace (p359) featured as the palace of the Spice King of Qarth – they didn't even bother moving the statue!

The stairs on **Uz Jezuite** connecting the St Ignatius of Loyola Church to Gundulić Sq were the starting point for Cersei Lannister's memorable naked penitential walk, which continued down **Stradun**.

Sv Dominika street and staircase outside the Dominican Monastery (p358) were used for various King's Landing market scenes.

The exterior of the **Ethnographic Museum** (Etnografski muzej; ☑020-323 056; www.dumus.hr; Od Rupa 3; adult/child multimuseum pass 120/25KN; ☉9am-4pm Wed-Mon) was used as Littlefinger's brothel.

Srđ Hill

The incredible views from the top of this 412m-high hill take in all of Dubrovnik and Lokrum, with the Elafiti Islands filling the horizon.

Great For...

☑ Don't Miss

The view from the top – Dubrovnik's old town looks like a scale model of itself or an illustration on a page from here.

Dubrovnik during the Homeland War

Set inside the crumbling Napoleonic Fort Imperial (completed in 1812) near the cable-car terminus, this permanent **exhibition** (Dubrovnik u Domovinskom ratu; ☎020-324 856; Fort Imperial, Srđ; adult/child 30/15KN; ⊗8am-10pm; P) is dedicated to the siege of Dubrovnik during the 1990s 'Homeland War'. By retaining control of the fort, the local defenders ensured that the city wasn't captured. Though understandably one-sided and overly wordy, the displays provide in-depth coverage of events, including video footage.

Way of the Cross

This route starts on the highway, above the old town, and terminates at Fort Imperial. Lined with 14 highly stylised brass

⚓ Explore Ashore

Most people spend 30 minutes to an hour at the top of Srđ hill. Bus 8 links the bus station in Gruž with the cable car in 20 minutes. From Pile Gate it's a 10-minute walk to the cable car.

★ Top Tip
Save yourself a steep walk take a taxi from the port to the top of the hill.

reliefs illustrating the 14 Stations of the Cross, the hike up Srđ takes roughly an hour (allow 40 minutes for the return leg).

Wear good shoes, as the path is comprised of potentially treacherous loose rock. There is no shade along the way, so pack ample water, a hat and sunscreen, and skip the hike altogether in peak summer heat.

Buggy Safari

Departing near the upper cable-car terminus, **Buggy Safari** (✆098 16 69 730; www. buggydubrovnik.com; cable-car terminus, Srđ; 1-/2-people trip 400/600KN; ⊙Mar-Nov) offers trips in souped-up quad bikes through the mountainous nether regions of Srđ, visiting forts and a farm. Expect to come back caked in mud and dust.

Cable Car

Built in 1969, and the first of its kind in the Adriatic, Dubrovnik's cable car whisks you from just north of the city walls to the top of **Srđ** (Srđ bb) in under four minutes. The city end has the best views.

The large **cross** adjacent to the upper-terminus building, originally erected in 1935, was sculpted from the island of Brač's famous white stone. The terminus building houses a restaurant, souvenir shop, toilets and a viewing platform.

As of when this book was going to print, the cable car was temporarily closed. It is unclear when it is due to reopen. See www.dubrovnikcablecar.com for updates.

When open, there can be a long queue for the cable car (sometimes over 30 minutes).

Walking Within the Walls

This walk will guide you through the scenic streets and squares of Dubrovnik's Old Town, past palaces, churches and the beautiful Old Harbour.

Start Pile Gate
Distance 1.2km
Duration One hour

1 Head through the **Pile Gate** (p358) to the beginning of Placa (aka Stradun), Dubrovnik's marbled main street.

6 Head down Od Puča, the main shopping strip, and cut through the market on busy **Gundulićeva poljana**.

7 At the far end, head up the Jesuit Stairs to **St Ignatius of Loyola Church** (p359).

Adriatic Sea

Take a Break... Finish your walk at Buža (p365) bar.

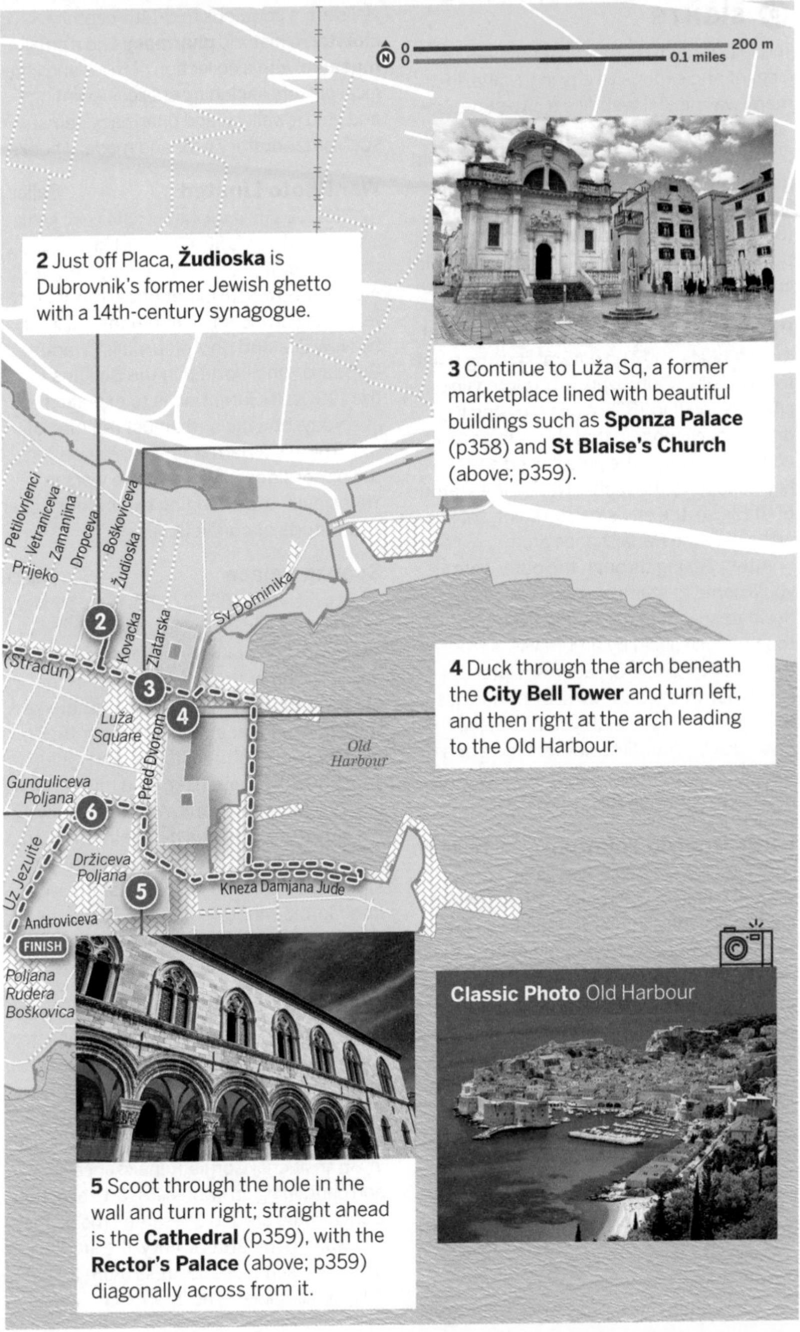

2 Just off Placa, **Žudioska** is Dubrovnik's former Jewish ghetto with a 14th-century synagogue.

3 Continue to Luža Sq, a former marketplace lined with beautiful buildings such as **Sponza Palace** (p358) and **St Blaise's Church** (above; p359).

4 Duck through the arch beneath the **City Bell Tower** and turn left, and then right at the arch leading to the Old Harbour.

Classic Photo Old Harbour

5 Scoot through the hole in the wall and turn right; straight ahead is the **Cathedral** (p359), with the **Rector's Palace** (above; p359) diagonally across from it.

Map labels: Petilovrijenci, Vetraniceva, Zamanjina, Boškoviceva, Prijeko, Dropceva, Žudioska, Kovacka, Zlatarska, Sv Dominika, (Stradun), Luža Square, Pred Dvorom, Old Harbour, Gunduliceva Poljana, Uz Jezuite, Držiceva Poljana, Androviceva, FINISH, Poljana Rudera Boškovica, Kneza Damjana Jude

200 m
0.1 miles

◉ SIGHTS

Today Dubrovnik is the most prosperous, elegant and expensive city in Croatia. In many ways it still feels like a city-state, isolated from the rest of the nation by geography and history. It's become such a tourism magnet that there's even talk of having to limit visitor numbers in the car-free old town – the main thoroughfares can get impossibly crowded, especially when multiple cruise ships arrive at the same time.

Pile Gate   Gate

(Gradska vrata Pile) The natural starting point to any visit to Dubrovnik is this imposing city gate, built in 1537. While crossing the drawbridge, imagine that this was once lifted every evening, the gate closed and the key handed to the rector. Notice the statue of St Blaise, the city's patron saint, set in a niche over the Renaissance arch.

After passing through the outer gate you'll come to stairs and a ramp leading down to an inner gate dating from 1460, topped once again by a St Blaise statue, this one by leading Croatian sculptor Ivan Meštrović (1883–1962). As you pass through the Gothic arch you'll immediately be struck by your first view of Placa, or as it's commonly known, Stradun, Dubrovnik's pedestrian promenade.

Large Onofrio Fountain   Fountain

(Velika Onofrijeva fontana; Poljana Paska Miličevića) One of Dubrovnik's most famous landmarks, this circular fountain was built in 1438 as part of a water-supply system that involved bringing water from a spring 12km away. Originally the fountain was adorned with sculptures, but it was heavily damaged in the 1667 earthquake and only 16 carved masks remain, with their mouths dribbling drinkable water into a drainage pool. Its sibling, the ornate **Little Onofrio Fountain**, is in Luža Sq at the other end of Stradun.

Franciscan Monastery
& Museum   Christian Monastery

(Franjevački samostan i muzej; ☎020-321 410; Placa 2; 30KN; ⊙9am-6pm Apr-Oct, to 2pm Nov-Mar) Within this monastery's solid stone walls are a gorgeous mid-14th-century **cloister**, a historic **pharmacy** and a small **museum** with a collection of relics and liturgical objects, including chalices, paintings and gold jewellery, and pharmacy items such as laboratory gear and medical books.

War Photo Limited   Gallery

(☎020-322 166; www.warphotoltd.com; Antuninska 6; adult/child 50/40KN; ⊙10am-10pm May-Sep, to 4pm Wed-Mon Apr & Oct) An immensely powerful experience, this gallery features compelling exhibitions curated by New Zealand photojournalist Wade Goddard, who worked in the Balkans in the 1990s. Its intention is to expose the everyday, horrific and unjust realities of war. There's a permanent exhibition on the upper floor devoted to the wars in Yugoslavia; the changing exhibitions cover a multitude of conflicts.

Sponza Palace   Palace

(Palača Sponza; ☎020-321 031; Placa bb; May-Oct free, Nov-Apr 25KN; ⊙archives display & cloister 10am-10pm May-Oct, cloister 10am-3pm Nov-Apr) One of the few buildings in the old town to survive the 1667 earthquake, the Sponza Palace was built from 1516 to 1522 as a customs house, and it has subsequently been used as a mint, treasury, armoury and bank. Architecturally, it's a mixture of styles beginning with an exquisite Renaissance portico resting on six Corinthian columns. The 1st floor has late-Gothic windows and the 2nd-floor windows are in a Renaissance style, with an alcove containing a statue of St Blaise.

Dominican Monastery
& Museum   Christian Monastery

(Dominikanski samostan i muzej; ☎020-321 423; www.dominicanmuseum.hr; Sv Dominika 4; adult/child 30/20KN; ⊙9am-5pm) This imposing structure is an architectural highlight, built in a transitional Gothic-Renaissance style and containing an impressive art collection. Constructed around the same time as the city walls in the 14th century, the stark exterior resembles a fortress more than a religious complex. The interior contains a graceful 15th-century **cloister** constructed by local artisans after the designs of the Florentine architect Maso di Bartolomeo.

St Blaise's Church
Church

(Crkva Sv Vlahe; Luža Sq; ⊙8am-noon & 4-5pm Mon-Sat, 7am-1pm Sun) Dedicated to the city's patron saint, this exceptionally beautiful church was built in 1715 in the ornate baroque style. The interior is notable for its marble altars and a 15th-century silver gilt statue of St Blaise (within the high altar), who is holding a scale model of pre-earthquake Dubrovnik. Note also the stained-glass windows designed by local artist Ivo Dulčić in 1971.

Rector's Palace
Palace

(Knežev dvor; 🖉020-321 497; www.dumus. hr; Pred Dvorom 3; adult/child 80/25KN, incl in multimuseum pass adult/child 120/25KN; ⊙9am-6pm Apr-Oct, to 4pm Nov-Mar) Built in the late 15th century for the elected rector who governed Dubrovnik, this Gothic-Renaissance palace contains the rector's office and private chambers, public halls, administrative offices and a dungeon. During his one-month term the rector was unable to leave the building without the permission of the senate. Today the palace has been turned into the **Cultural History Museum**, with artfully restored rooms, portraits, coats of arms and coins, evoking the glorious history of Ragusa.

Cathedral of the Assumption
Cathedral

(Katedrala Marijina Uznesenja; Držićeva poljana; treasury 20KN; ⊙8am-5pm Mon-Sat, 11am-5pm Sun Easter-Oct, 9am-noon & 4-5pm Mon-Sat Nov-Easter) Built on the site of a 7th-century basilica, Dubrovnik's original cathedral was enlarged in the 12th century, supposedly funded by a gift from England's King Richard I, the Lionheart, who was saved from a shipwreck on the nearby island of Lokrum. Soon after the first cathedral was destroyed in the 1667 earthquake, work began on this, its baroque replacement, which was finished in 1713.

🔝 Escape the Crowds

Dubrovnik is an extremely popular destination and it can be very crowded during the summer high season (May to September), particularly in July and August.

Pile Gate is the most popular entrance to the old town, so consider starting your visit at Ploče Gate (p350) instead. It's also better to use one of the other entrances to access the City Walls (p350), such as at **Fort St John** (Tvrđava sv Ivana; City Walls) or Ploče Gate. The most crowded parts of the wall walk are Fort Minčeta and the spot directly above LargOnofrio Fountain, which offers a perfect view straight along Stradun.

In the old town, the worst crowds are on the central flat streets, such as Stradun, Od Puča and Prijeko. To find a quieter area, often all it takes is climbing a flight of stairs.

The Franciscan Monastery can get busy with tour groups, particularly in the morning. The Dominican Monastery is a less-crowded alternative.

There are often waits of over half an hour to take the cable car up Srđ hill, particularly later in the day. Consider taking a taxi. Drivers offer panoramic tours, including photo stops at multiple viewpoints, and can drop you off by one of the city gates at the end.

Fort St John

Dubrovnik

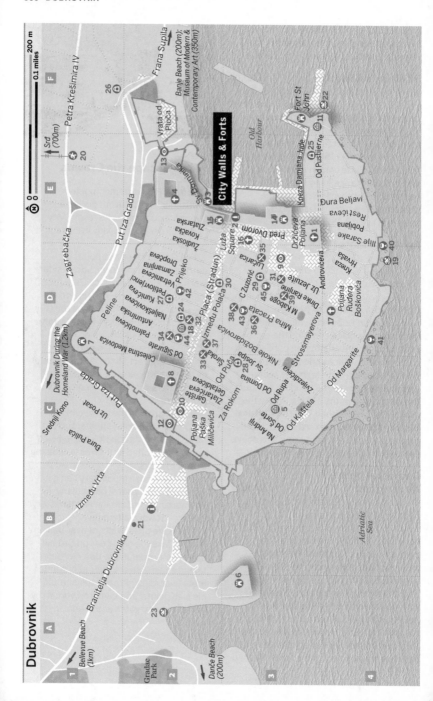

City Walls & Forts

200 m
0.1 miles

Srd
(700m)
Frana Supila

Banje Beach (200m);
Museum of Modern &
Contemporary Art (350m)

Petra Krešimira IV

Vrata od
Ploča

Bellevue Beach
(1km)

Gradac
Park

Dance Beach
(200m)

Branitelja Dubrovnika

Dubrovnik During the
Homeland War (1.2km)

Put Iza Grada

Srednji Kono

Uz Posat

Đura Pulića

Izmedu Vrta

Zagrebačka

Peline

Celestina Medovica

Palmotićeva

Antuninska

Naljeskovićeva

Kunićeva

Prijeko

Žudioska

Kovačka

Zlatarska

Boškovićeva

Zamanjina

Vetranićeva

Petilovrijenci

Dropčeva

Od Sigurate

Izmedu Polaca

Plača (Stradun)

Luža
Square

Pred Dvorom

Lučarica

Uz Jezuite

C Zuzorić

M Kaboge

Dinka Ranjine

Miha Pracata

Nikole Božidarevića

Od Puča

Sv Josipa

Od Domina

Od Rupa

Za Rokom

Garište

Gundulićeva

Zlatarićeva

Stroza

Za Rokom

Poljana
Paška
Miličevića

Zvijezdićeva

Strossmayerova

Androvićeva

Držićeva
Poljana

Ilije Sarake
Poljana
Restićeva

Đura Beljavi

Od Margarite

Na Andriji

Od Šorte

Od Kaštela

Adriatic
Sea

Old
Harbour

Kneza Damjana Jude

Od Pustijerne

Fort St
John

Kneza
Hrvaša

Poljana
Ruđera
Boškovića

Dubrovnik

St Ignatius of Loyola Church
Church

(Crkva Sv Ignacija Lojolskoga; ☎020-323 500; Poljana Ruđera Boškovića 6; ⊙7am-7pm) Dramatically poised at the top of a broad flight of stairs, this Jesuit church was built in the baroque style between 1699 and 1725. Inside, magnificent frescoes display scenes from the life of St Ignatius, founder of the Society of Jesus. Abutting the church is the former Jesuit Collegium Ragusinum, today the Diocesan Classical high school.

Museum of Modern Art
Gallery

(Umjetnička galerija; ☎020-426 590; www. ugdubrovnik.hr; Frana Supila 23, Ploče; with multi-museum pass adult/child 120/25KN; ⊙9am-8pm Tue-Sun) Spread over three floors of a significant modernist building east of the old town, this excellent gallery showcases Croatian artists, particularly painter Vlaho Bukovac from nearby Cavtat. Head up to the sculpture terrace for excellent views.

Lokrum
Island

(☎020-311 738; www.lokrum.hr; adult/child incl boat 150/25KN; ⊙Apr-Nov) Lush Lokrum is a beautiful, forested island full of holm oaks, black ash, pines and olive trees, only a 10-minute ferry ride from Dubrovnik's Old Harbour. It's a popular swimming spot, although the beaches are rocky. Boats leave roughly hourly in summer (half-hourly in July and August). The public boat ticket price includes the entrance fee, but if you arrive with another boat, you're required to pay 120KN at the information centre on the island.

The island's main hub is its large medieval **Benedictine monastery**, which houses a restaurant and a display on the island's history and Game of Thrones, which was partly filmed on Lokrum. This is your chance to pose imperiously on a reproduction of the Iron Throne. The monastery has a pretty cloister garden and a significant botanical garden, featuring giant agaves and palms from South Africa

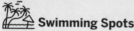 **Swimming Spots**

If you want to cool off, there are plenty of places for a swim. **Banje Beach** (www.banjebeach.com; Frana Supila 10, Ploče) is the closest beach to the old town, just east of Ploče Gate, but it can get very crowded. Other options include swimming off the rocks at the base of the city walls at **Porporela** or **Buža**, or heading to one of the bays west of the old town, such as **Šulić Bay** (Od Tabakerije 11, Pile), **Danče Beach** (Don Frana Bulića bb, Pile) or **Bellevue Beach** (Montovjerna). Lokrum Island is also a popular place to swim.

Banje Beach
GORAN JAKUS/SHUTTERSTOCK ©

and Brazil. Near the centre of the island is circular **Fort Royal**, commenced during the French occupation in the early 19th century but mainly used by the Austrians. Head up to the roof for views over the old town.

To reach the **nudist beach**, head left from the ferry and follow the signs marked FKK; the rocks at its far end are Dubrovnik's de facto gay beach. Another popular place for a swim is the small saltwater lake known as the **Dead Sea**.

Make sure you check what time the last boat to the mainland departs. The last boat of the day is always very busy, so it's a good idea to get to the dock with plenty of time to spare. Smoking is not permitted anywhere on the island.

🎫 TOURS

Dubrovnik Day Tours
Tours

(📱098 17 51 775; www.dubrovnikdaytours. net) Private day trips (prices on enquiry) led by licensed guides to as far away as Korčula, Split, Kotor, Budva, Mostar and Sarajevo, as well as sightseeing and *Game of Thrones* tours around Dubrovnik. It also offers tailored small-group tours targeted to cruise passengers and marketed as Dubrovnik Shore Tours (www. dubrovnikshoretours.net).

Dubrovnik Walks
Walking

(📱095 80 64 526; www.dubrovnikwalks.com; Brsalje 8, Pile; ☉Mar-Dec) Excellent English-language guided walks departing from near the Pile Gate, including 90-minute old-town (120KN) and *Game of Thrones* (150KN) tours, and a two-hour 'Walls & Wars' tour (130KN); no reservations necessary between April and October. It also offers 2½-hour sea-kayaking tours (day/sunset 230/250KN).

🛍 SHOPPING

Kawa
Gifts & Souvenirs

(📱091 89 67 509; www.kawa.life; Hvarska 2, Ploče; ☉10am-8pm) Selling 'wonderful items made by Croatians', this very cool design store sells everything from wines and craft beers to jewellery, clothing, homewares and even its own line of products under the Happy Čevapi label. Superb service rounds off the experience.

Uje
Food & Drinks

(📱020-321 532; www.uje.hr; Placa 5; ☉11am-6pm Jan-Mar, 9am-9pm Apr, May & Oct-Dec, 9am-11pm Jun-Sep) Uje specialises in olive oils, along with a wide range of other locally produced epicurean delights, including some excellent jams, pickled capers, local herbs and spices, figs in honey, chocolate, wine and *rakija* (grappa). There's another **branch** (📱020-324 865; Od Puča 2; ☉9am-9pm Sep-Jun, to midnight Jul & Aug) around the corner.

Medusa · Gifts & Souvenirs

(📞020-322 004; www.medusa.hr; Prijeko 18; 🕒9am-10pm Apr-Oct, 10am-5pm Nov-Mar) This self-described 'charming shop for charming people' sells locally produced soaps, flavoured salt, *rakija*, neckties, objects made from Brač stone, art prints, chocolate and toiletries.

Terra Croatica Dubrovnik · Gifts & Souvenirs

(📞020-323 209; www.facebook.com/terra croatica.dubrovnik; Od Puča 17; 🕒9am-9pm) A welcome interlude in a streak of shops with cheesy souvenirs and *Game of Thrones* paraphernalia, Terra Croatica wears its Authentically Croatian Souvenir certification proudly. Pop in for gift-sized foodie treats like olive oils, wines, truffles and gourmet chocolates, but also for handmade ceramics, stone mortars, cosmetics and Dalmatian cookbooks.

Craft & Stones · Gifts & Souvenirs

(📞095 72 14 442; www.facebook.com/ dubrovnikwithlove; Od Pustjerne bb; 🕒8am-8pm daily Jun-Sep, 9am-5pm Mon-Sat Mar-May & Oct) This little treasure-trove is a dream come true for a local stonemason-artisan couple. Pero carves local limestone into salt and pepper shakers, candle holders and sculptures while Lena designs extra-cool totes and T-shirts that capture local sayings or particular states of mind. Find them in a picturesque alley leading up to the Maritime Museum.

Clara Stones Jewellery · Jewellery

(📞020-321 706; www.clarastones.com; Nalješkovićeva 8; 🕒9.30am-10pm Apr-Oct, to 4pm Nov-Mar) Split across two spaces facing each other across the lane, Clara Stones is all about appreciation of red Adriatic coral. The bold jewellery designs often feature it in the rough, and a casual presentation in the workshop gives insight into the controlled harvesting and tedious processing of what is the region's signature treasure.

EATING

There are some very average restaurants in Dubrovnik and prices are the highest in Croatia, so choose carefully. That said, there are some great eateries scattered around.

Dolce Vita · Sweets €

(Nalješkovićeva 1a; ice cream/pancakes from 11/22KN; 🕒11am-midnight) Over a dozen different kinds of sumptuous, creamy gelati are on offer at this sweet spot. Alternatively, choose from a substantial menu of cakes and pancakes. You'll have no trouble finding it, as its bright orange chairs and lanterns picturing an ice-cream cone pop out from a narrow side street just off Stradun.

Fast Food Republic · Fast Food €

(www.facebook.com/RepublicDubrovnik; Široka 4; mains 39-100KN; 🕒10am-midnight; 📶) Owned and operated by a friendly young crew, this little burger bar serves a tasty selection of burgers, sandwiches, pizza slices and hot dogs. For a local twist, try an octopus burger.

Peppino's · Ice Cream €

(www.peppinos.premis.hr; Od Puča 9; scoops from 14KN; 🕒11am-midnight) With over 20 tempting varieties of thick, delicious gelato on offer, this artisanal ice-cream shop serves everything from your standard chocolate to funky remakes based on popular candy or cakes. The premium ice cream has an even richer flavour, and gluten-free scoops are also available.

Buffet Kamenice · Dalmatian €

(📞020-323 682; Gundulićeva Poljana 8; mains 45-88KN; 🕒8am-10pm) Known for a simple menu of Dalmatian specialties, Kamenice's signature dishes include squid risotto, mussels in *buzara* (white wine) sauce, as well as fried 'small fish' and calamari to die for. But as the name translates to 'oysters', start your meal with some fresh Ston oysters. The restaurant is easily spotted by its blue-and-white-striped chairs on Gundulićeva poljana.

PAUL PRESCOTT/SHUTTERSTOCK ©

Proto

Pupo Dalmatian €€€
(☎020-323 555; www.pupodubrovnik.com; Miha Pracata 8; mains 75-160KN; ⊙noon-midnight; 📶) Tucked away in an old-town alley, Pupo is a good choice for seafood but remains especially loved for its sweets. Leave room for a slice of Dubrovnik almond cake, or skip around the corner to its sister patisserie, Pupica, for coffee and cake.

Oliva Pizzeria Pizza €€
(☎020-324 594; www.pizza-oliva.com; Lučarica 5; mains 74-105KN; ⊙10am-11pm; 📶🌱) There are a few pasta dishes on the menu, but this attractive little restaurant is really all about pizza. And the pizza is worthy of the attention. Grab a seat on the street and tuck in.

Nishta Vegan €€
(☎020-322 088; www.nishtarestaurant.com; Prijeko bb; mains 98-108KN; ⊙11.30am-11.30pm Mon-Sat; 🌱) The popularity of this tiny old-town restaurant is testament not just to the paucity of options for vegetarians and vegans in Croatia, but also to the imaginative and beautifully presented food produced within. Each day of the week has its own menu with cooked and raw options.

Proto Seafood €€€
(☎020-323 234; www.esculaprestaurants.com; Široka 1; mains 225-356KN; ⊙10.30am-11pm) This elegant place is known for its fresh fish and bags of old-town atmosphere. To say it's 'long-standing' is an understatement – it opened its doors in 1886 and has served the likes of Edward VIII and Wallis Simpson. The menu showcases Dalmatian and Istrian cuisine, including fresh pasta, grilled fish and a few token meat dishes.

Restaurant Dubrovnik European €€€
(☎020-324 810; www.restorandubrovnik.com; Marojice Kaboge 5; mains 110-230KN; ⊙noon-midnight; 📶) One of Dubrovnik's most upmarket restaurants has a wonderfully unstuffy setting, occupying a covered rooftop terrace hidden among the venerable stone buildings of the old town. A strong French influence pervades a menu full of decadent and rich dishes, such as confit duck and perfectly cooked steak.

🍸 DRINKING & NIGHTLIFE

Bard Mala Buža
Bar

(Iza Mira 14; ⊘9am-3am May-Oct) The more upmarket and slick of two cliff bars pressed up against the seaward side of the city walls. This one is lower on the rocks and has a shaded terrace where you can lose a day happily, mesmerised by the Adriatic vistas.

D'vino
Wine Bar

(☑020-321 130; www.dvino.net; Palmotićeva 4a; ⊘9am-midnight Mar-Nov; 🛜) If you're interested in sampling top-notch Croatian wine, this convivial bar is the place to go. As well as a large and varied wine list, it offers tasting flights presented by cool and knowledgeable staff (three wines from 55KN) plus savoury breakfasts, snacks and platters. Sit outside for the authentic old-town-alley ambience, but check out the whimsical wall inscriptions inside.

Buža
Bar

(off Od Margarite; ⊘8am-2am Jun-Aug, to midnight Sep-May) Finding this ramshackle bar-on-a-cliff feels like a real discovery as you duck and dive around the city walls and finally see the entrance tunnel. However, Buža's no secret – it gets insanely busy, especially around sunset. Wait for a space on one of the concrete platforms, grab a cool drink in a plastic cup and enjoy the vibe and views.

Dubrovnik Beer Factory
Craft Beer

(www.facebook.com/dubrovnikbeerfactory; Miha Pracata 6; ⊘9am-1am; 🛜) The name might mislead you: this isn't, in fact, a brewery, but the selection of Croatian craft beer is good enough to justify the tag. Still, with huge murals, vaulted ceilings, historic stone details and a large beer garden tucked away in the back, the setting remains the true drawcard. It also serves food and hosts live music.

Razonoda
Wine Bar

(☑020-326 225; www.thepucicpalace.com; Od Puča 1; ⊘noon-midnight Mar-Oct, from 6pm Nov-Feb; 🛜) Dark wood and moody lighting make this a refined option for wine and tapas. The lengthy wine list (more than 70 available by the glass) is best navigated with the assistance of the professional and knowledgeable staff.

Buzz Bar
Bar

(☑020-321 025; www.thebuzzbar.wixsite.com/buzz; Prijeko 21; ⊘8am-2am; 🛜) Appropriately named, this buzzy little bar is rocky and relaxed, with craft beer and cocktails the main poisons – aside from those being exhaled by the recalcitrant smokers in the corner.

ℹ️ INFORMATION

If you want to get through all the essential sights of Dubrovnik in one day, it's well worth buying the **Dubrovnik Card** (190KN). If you were already planning on walking the city walls (admission 150KN) and buying a museum pass (120KN), the Dubrovnik Card makes a lot of sense. It also scores you free rides on buses and discounts at various restaurants and shops. The card can be purchased online at a discounted rate (www.dubrovnikcard. com), or at tourist offices and museums.

Dubrovnik's tourist board has offices in **Pile** (☑020-312 011; www.tzdubrovnik.hr; Brsalje 5; ⊘8am-8pm) and **Gruž** (☑020-417 983; www. tzdubrovnik.hr; Obala Pape Ivana Pavla II 1; ⊘8am-8pm Jun-Oct, 8am-3pm Mon-Fri, to 1pm Sat Nov-Mar, 8am-8pm Mon-Fri, to 2pm Sat & Sun Apr & May) that dispense maps, information and advice.

ℹ️ GETTING AROUND

Dubrovnik's walled old town is pedestrianised, so you'll need to explore on foot.

Boat The public boat to Lokrum departs from the big pier in the old town harbour. Tickets are sold at stalls in front of the boats. Connections depend on the weather, but typically depart on an hourly schedule, increasing in frequency in the peak season.

Bus Dubrovnik has a superb bus service; buses run frequently and generally on time. The fare is 15KN if you buy from the driver and 12KN if you buy a ticket at a *tisak* (news stand). Timetables are available at www.libertasdubrovnik.hr. To get to the old town from Gruž bus station, take bus 1a, 1b, 3 or 8.

Taxi You will find taxis lined up inside the international area of Gruž port, near the berths.

KOTOR, MONTENEGRO

Kotor at a Glance...

Wedged between brooding mountains and a moody corner of the bay, achingly atmospheric Kotor (Котор) is perfectly at one with its setting. Hemmed in by staunch walls snaking improbably up the surrounding slopes, the town is a medieval maze of museums, churches, cafe-strewn squares and Venetian palaces and pillories. Its cobblestones ring with the sound of children racing to school in centuries-old buildings, lines of laundry flutter from wrought-iron balconies, and hundreds of cats – the descendants of seafaring felines – loll in marble laneways. Budva and the beaches of Perast are just short trips away.

With One Day in Port

o Spend a couple of hours getting lost and found again in the maze of Kotor's winding streets. Don't miss clambering up the **ancient town walls** (p370) for out-of-this-world views of the bay.

o If you have time, it's worth exploring outside the city walls, too – spend some time cycling or kayaking around the bay; visit pretty **Perast** (p379), just a 20-minute bus ride away;

o Alternatively, take half the day to explore the old town of medieval seaside resort, **Budva** (p372).

Best Places For...

Coffee or cocktails Letrika (p381)

Views City Walls (p370)

Architecture St Tryphon's Cathedral (p377)

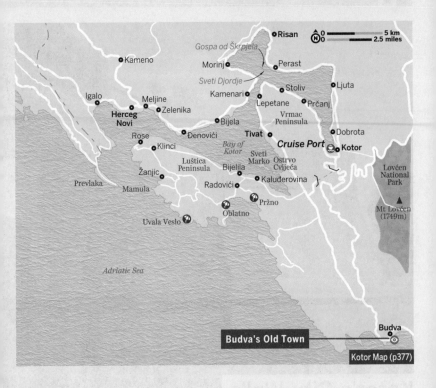

Risan

Gospa od Škrpjela

Kameno

Morinj

Perast

Sveti Djordje

Stoliv

Ljuta

Igalo

Meljine

Kamenari

Prčanj

Zelenika

Lepetane

Herceg
Novi

Bijela

Vrmac
Peninsula

Rose

Đenovići

Tivat

Dobrota

Bay of
Kotor

Cruise Port

Kotor

Klinci

Lovćen
National
Park

Luštica
Peninsula

Sveti
Marko

Ostrvo
Cvijeća

Žanjic

Bijelila

Prevlaka

Mamula

Radovići

Kaluđerovina

Mt Lovćen
(1749m)

Pržno

Oblatno

Uvala Veslo

Adriatic Sea

Budva

Budva's Old Town

Kotor Map (p377)

0   5 km
N 0   2.5 miles

Getting from the Port

You can be within the city's walls within minutes of getting off the ship. The **Sea Gate** is the nearest of the Old Town's main gates to the dock and the tourist office is right beside it.

Budva is a 25-minute taxi ride or 40-minute bus trip from the port in Kotor.

There are buses to Perast every 30 minutes, or a taxi will get you there in about 15 minutes. Water taxis are another option during summer.

Fast Facts

Currency Euro (€)

Language Montenegrin

Money You'll find a choice of banks with ATMs on the main square, Trg od Oružja.

Visas Not required for citizens of European countries, Turkey, Israel, Singapore, South Korea, Japan, Australia, New Zealand, Canada and the USA. In most cases this allows a stay of up to 90 days.

Wi-fi Many bars and cafes offer wi-fi, and there are often free hotspots in tourist areas.

KULEABRA/SHUTTERSTOCK ©

Kotor's City Walls

The climb along the city's fortified walls will definitely get your heart rate up, but the views from St John's Fortress at the top are entirely worth the effort. Come nightfall, the spectacularly lit-up walls glow as serenely as a halo. Some cruise lines will offer an organised walk, but you can be your own guide on this classic Kotor experience.

Great For...

☑ **Don't Miss**

The spectacular views from St John's Fortress.

History of Kotor

It's thought that Kotor began as Acruvium, part of the Roman province of Dalmatia. Its present look owes much to nearly 400 years of Venetian rule, when it was known as Cattaro. In 1813 it briefly joined with Montenegro for the first time, but the Great Powers decided to hand it back to Austria, under whose control it remained until after WWI. There's a strong history of Catholic and Orthodox cooperation in the area.

Walking the City Walls

It may not be as impressive as Dubrovnik's or as shiny as Budva's, but Kotor's Old Town feels much more lived-in and ever

The winged lion of St Mark

Explore Ashore

Give yourself two hours for a round-trip. This includes time for breaks to catch your breath and photos. There are entry points near the River Gate and behind Trg od Salate – less than a 10-minute walk from the port.

❶ Need to Know

€8; ⊘24hr, fees apply 8am-8pm May-Sep

The Climb to St John's

The energetic can make a 1200m ascent up the fortifications via 1350 steps to a height of 260m above sea level. At the top, you'll reach **St John's Fortress** (also known as the Castle of San Giovanni or St Ivan). It's worth the climb – the views of the bay, town and looming Mt Lovćen from St John's are glorious.

Pace Yourself

Take water, wear sensible shoes and pace yourself. The steps can be narrow and steep. When tackling the walls in summer, avoid the heat of the day if you can and don't scrimp on water.

Those less physically inclined can still appreciate the sight of the snaking, surreal walls – they're visible from all over Kotor.

so dramatic. The way it seems to grow out of the sheer grey mountains surrounding it adds a thrill of foreboding to the experience – as if they could at any point choose to squeeze the little town in a rocky embrace. A walk along the city walls lets you take it all in.

The city's fortifications started to head up St John's Hill in the 9th century and by the 14th century a protective loop was completed, which continued to be added to right up until the 19th century. The walls are fiercely guarded by the winged lion of St Mark (Venetian symbol of power) – you'll see it stamped into the ancient stone like a grand seal of approval.

Entrance to the citadela

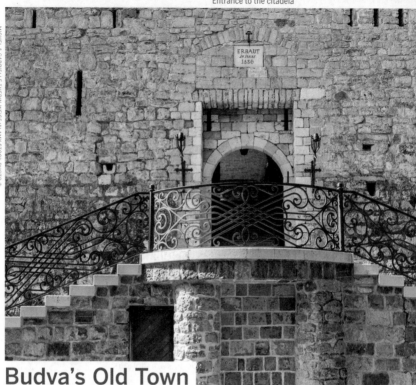

Budva's Old Town

Budva's walled Old Town (Stari Grad) rises from the Adriatic like a miniature, less frantic Dubrovnik. There's an atmosphere of romance and a typically Mediterranean love of life palpable around every corner.

You can while away the hours exploring the labyrinth of narrow cobbled streets, visiting tiny churches and charming galleries, drinking in al fresco cafe-bars, snacking on pizza and being inspired by the gorgeous sea views from the citadela. If you have more time, there's a beach on either side.

Much of the Old Town was ruined by two earthquakes in 1979, but it has since been completely rebuilt and now houses more shops, bars and restaurants than residences.

Town Walls

A walkway about 1m wide leads around the landward walls of the Stari Grad, offering views across the rooftops and down onto some beautiful hidden gardens. Admission only seems to be charged in the height of summer; at other times it's either free or locked. The entrance is near the citadela.

Great For...

☑ **Don't Miss**

Taking a walk to the little beach immediately south of the Old Town for a photo of the naked dancer statue.

View of the Old Town from the citadela

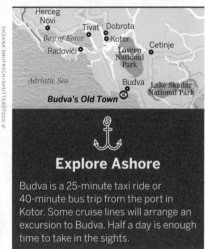

Budva's Old Town

⚓ Explore Ashore

Budva is a 25-minute taxi ride or 40-minute bus trip from the port in Kotor. Some cruise lines will arrange an excursion to Budva. Half a day is enough time to take in the sights.

❶ Need to Know

Entry to the town walls is €2; ⊘10am-8pm

The largest of the churches is Catholic **St John the Baptist's Church** (Crkva Sv Ivana Krstitelja). A side chapel houses the Madonna of Budva – a 12th-century icon venerated by Catholic and Orthodox Budvans alike.

Ričardova Glava

Immediately south of the Old Town, this little beach has the ancient walls as an impressive backdrop. Wander around the headland and you'll come to a statue of a naked dancer, one of Budva's most-photographed landmarks. Carry on and you'll find the quiet, double-bayed Mogren Beach.

'The Montenegrin Miami'

Though Budva has been settled since the 5th century BC, you'll be hard-pressed finding much – outside of the Old Town – that isn't shiny and relatively new. Development has run rampant here, and not all of it appears to be particularly well thought out. In the height of the season, Budva's sands are blanketed with package holidaymakers from Russia and Ukraine, while the nouveau riche park their multimillion-dollar yachts in the town's guarded marina. That said, Budva has a hectic charm all of its own.

Citadela

The **citadela** (€3.50; ⊘9am-midnight May-Oct, to 5pm Nov-Apr) at the Old Town's seaward end offers striking views, a restaurant and a library full of model ships, rare tomes and maps displayed safely behind glass. It's thought to be built on the site of the Greek acropolis, but the present incarnation dates from the 19th-century Austrian occupation.

Trg između crkava

Literally the 'square between the churches', this open area below the citadela provides a visual reminder of the once-cosy relationship between Orthodox and Catholic Christians in this area.

Beautiful frescoes cover the walls and ceiling of **Holy Trinity Church** (Crkva Sv Trojice; ⊘8am-10pm Jun-Sep, 8am-noon & 4-7pm Oct-May), in the centre of the square.

Kotor's Old Town

Spend some time in the maze of the Old Town's winding streets. Cruise ships dock right by the city walls.

Start Sea Gate
Distance 850m
Duration 30 minutes

3 Walk left across the square and then take the first lane to the right. You'll pass the Catholic **St Claire's Franciscan Church** and Orthodox **St Nicholas' Church**.

Škurda River

Trg Sv Luke

START

Trg od Oružja

Jadranski Put

Bay of Kotor

1 Start at the **Sea Gate**, the main entrance to the Old Town. Look for the stone relief of the Madonna and Child flanked by St Tryphon and St Bernard.

2 The gate opens onto the Old Town's largest square, Armoury Sq, where you'll see the **clock tower**.

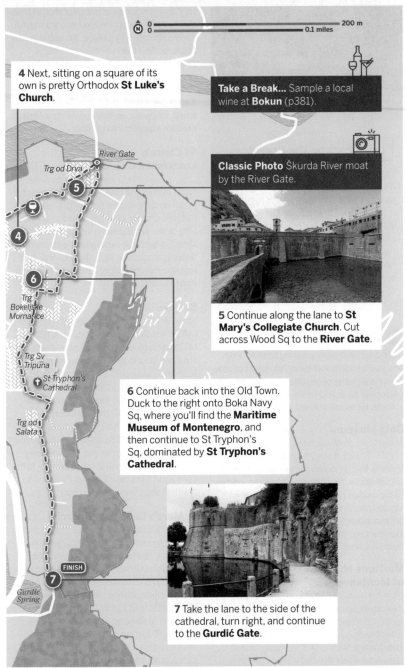

4 Next, sitting on a square of its own is pretty Orthodox **St Luke's Church**.

Take a Break... Sample a local wine at **Bokun** (p381).

Classic Photo Škurda River moat by the River Gate.

River Gate

Trg od Drva

5 Continue along the lane to **St Mary's Collegiate Church**. Cut across Wood Sq to the **River Gate**.

Trg Bokeljske Mornarice

Trg Sv Tripuna

St Tryphon's Cathedral

6 Continue back into the Old Town. Duck to the right onto Boka Navy Sq, where you'll find the **Maritime Museum of Montenegro**, and then continue to St Tryphon's Sq, dominated by **St Tryphon's Cathedral**.

Trg od Salata

FINISH

Gurdić Spring

7 Take the lane to the side of the cathedral, turn right, and continue to the **Gurdić Gate**.

Escape the Crowds

Tiny Kotor can quickly fill with visitors. It's well worth getting a little lost in the streets of the Old Town away from the main square. Try the River Gate, tucked in the slightly quieter northern corner of town, beside the park-like Trg od Drva (Wood Sq), for views and Kotor cats. Spend part of your day exploring the quieter islands of Perast (p379).

Trg od Drva
RNDMS/SHUTTERSTOCK ©

◉ SIGHTS

Spend some time wandering the Old Town and you'll soon know every nook and cranny. There are plenty of old churches to pop into, palaces to ogle, and many coffees and/or *vinos* to be drunk in Kotor's shady squares.

Cats Museum   Museum
(www.catsmuseum.org; Trg od Kina; adult/child €1/50c; ☺10am-6pm) Crazy cat people and those with a fondness for whimsical vintage art will adore this charming museum, home to thousands of moggie-themed postcards, lithographs, prints, jewellery and beautiful antique advertisements. The small admission fee goes towards taking care of Kotor's famous felines.

Maritime Museum of Montenegro   Museum
(Pomorski muzej Crne Gore; ☎032-304 720; www.museummaritimum.com; Trg Bokeljske Mornarice; adult/child €4/1; ☺9am-8pm Mon-Sat, 10am-4pm Sun Jul & Aug, 8am-6pm Mon-Sat, 9am-1pm Sun May, Jun & Sep, 9am-5pm Mon-Fri, to noon Sat & Sun Oct-Apr) Kotor's proud history as a naval power is celebrated in three storeys of displays housed in a wonderful early-18th-century palace. An audio guide helps explain the collection of photographs, paintings, uniforms, exquisitely decorated weapons and models of ships.

Just outside the museum, look out for the **Karampana Well** and its ornate wrought-iron fence; for centuries, this tiny well provided all of Kotor's fresh drinking water.

St Claire's Franciscan Church   Church
(Franjevačka crkva Sv Klare; near Trg Sv Luke) Aside from a fine rose window there's not much ornamentation on the facade of this Catholic church, built between the 14th and 17th centuries. But head inside for the full Venetian baroque experience, with cherubs floating around the high altar holding aloft realistic-looking draperies carved entirely from marble.

St Luke's Church   Church
(Crkva Sv Luke; Trg Sv Luke) Sweet little St Luke's speaks volumes about the history of Croat-Serb relations in Kotor. It was constructed in 1195 as a Catholic church, but from 1657 until 1812 Catholic and Orthodox altars stood side by side, with each faith taking turns to hold services here. It was then gifted to the Orthodox Church.

Fragments of 12th-century frescoes still survive, along with two wonderfully painted iconostases: one from the 17th-century in the main church and one from the 18th century in the side chapel of St Spiridon, another saint venerated by both faiths.

St Mary's Collegiate Church   Church
(Crkva Sv Marije Koleđate; Trg od Drva) Built in 1221 on the site of a 6th-century basilica, this Catholic church is distinguished by impressive 20th-century bronze doors covered in bas-reliefs, the remains of frescoes, a particularly gruesome larger-than-life crucifix, and a glass coffin containing the body of Blessed Osanna of Cattaro (1493–1565). She was what is known as an anchoress, choosing to be walled into a small cell attached to a church so as to devote her life to prayer.

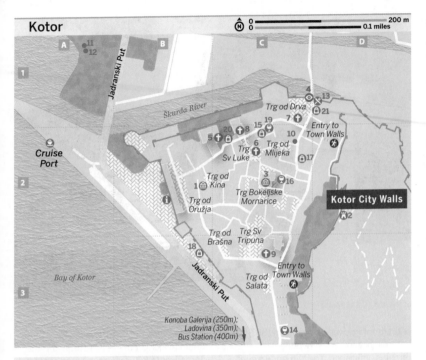

Kotor

St Nicholas' Church Church

(Crkva Sv Nikole; Trg Sv Luke) Breathe in the smell of incense and beeswax in this Orthodox church, built in 1909 and adorned with four huge canvasses depicting the gospel writers, a gift from Russia in 1998. The silence, the iconostasis with its silver bas-relief panels, the dark wood against bare grey walls, the filtered light through the dome and the simple stained glass conspire to create a mystical atmosphere.

St Tryphon's Cathedral Church

(Katedrale Sv Tripuna; Trg Sv Tripuna; church & museum €2.50; ◷9am-8pm Apr-Oct, to 5pm Nov, Dec & Mar, to 1pm Jan & Feb) Kotor's most impressive building, this Catholic cathedral was consecrated in 1166 but reconstructed after several earthquakes. When the

St Tryphon's Cathedral (p377)

entire frontage was destroyed in 1667, the baroque bell towers were added; the left one remains unfinished. The cathedral's gently hued interior is a masterpiece of Roman-esque architecture with slender Corinthian columns alternating with pillars of pink stone, thrusting upwards to support a series of vaulted roofs. Look for the remains of Byzantine-style frescoes in the arches.

The gilded-silver bas-relief altar screen is considered Kotor's most valuable treasure.

Upstairs is a **Sacral Art Museum**, filled with paintings, vestments and a spooky wooden crucifix dating from 1288. Behind the grill in the reliquary chapel are assorted body parts of saints, including St Tryphon himself. The early martyr's importance to both the Catholic and Orthodox churches makes him a fitting patron for the city.

🄯 TOURS

Adventure Montenegro　　Outdoors
(☏069-049 733; www.adventuremontenegro.com; Trg od Mlijeka) Rent a kayak and explore the bay on your own terms (per day single/

double kayak €20/25). It also offers three-hour kayaking tours (€35), rafting on the Tara River (€80), five-hour speedboat tours of the bay (€280 for up to six people), and a range of sightseeing tours for cruise-boat passengers.

Kotor Bay Tours　　Tours
(☏069-152 015; www.kotorbaytours.com; Park Slobode) This well-organised group offers tonnes of tours and activities, including kayak and cycle trips. Gourmands won't want to miss their 'All about Mussels' tour (€50), which combines a Kotor and Perast tour with hours of eating and drinking at a local mussel farm.

Kotor Open Tour　　Bus
(☏067-333 977; www.hoponhopoff.me; adult/child €20/10; ⊙departs every 30min 9am-5pm) On sunny days during summer, these open-top, hop-on, hop-off sightseeing buses ply the busy road between Kotor, Perast and Risan, showing off the hotspots and providing histories and explanations via multilanguage audio guides. The ticket lasts all day and includes a Kotor walking tour and

admission to museums in Perast and Risan. At peak times the traffic can crawl.

Montenegro Submarine   Boating

(☑069-576 355; www.montenegrosubmarine. me; Park Slobode; ☺9am-8pm Mar-Nov) Want to find out if Kotor Bay is as beautiful down below as it is on top? Hop aboard this really-quite-adorable bright-red semi-submersible (adult/child €12/8) and find out; there's above-water seating as well. The company also offers speedboat tours to Perast and Gospa od Škrpjela island (€20/10) and to the Blue Cave (€30/15).

🔒 SHOPPING

There are almost as many antique and souvenir shops as there are cats in the Old Town.

Cats of Kotor   Gifts & Souvenirs

(☑069-249 783; www.catsofkotor.com; near Trg od Mlijeka; ☺9am-9pm) Though you can't bundle them into your backpack (tempting as it may be), you can bring home the cats of Kotor in the form of beautiful, locally made handicrafts with a feline flavour. Part gallery, part boutique, this quirky shop sells everything from cat-themed jewellery and clothes to original artworks.

Efesya Souvenir   Gifts & Souvenirs

(☑063-469 624; www.efesyasouvenir.com; near Trg od Mlijeka; ☺9am-7pm) The best of a crop of Turkish shops to spring up in recent years, Efesya sells colourful glass lamps, ceramics, scarves, bags and even chess sets.

Kotor Bazaar   Market

(near Trg Sv Luke; ☺9am-10pm) Recently opened in the long-abandoned cloister of a Dominican Monastery, this little market has stalls selling T-shirts, souvenirs and religious icons. In the back corner there's a little medieval 'museum', where for €3 you can pose with replica weapons and armour, or try your hand with a bow and arrow.

 Perast

Looking like a chunk of Venice that has floated down the Adriatic and anchored itself onto the Bay of Kotor, Perast (Пераст) hums with melancholy memories of the days when it was rich and powerful. Despite having only one main street, this tiny town boasts 16 churches and 17 formerly grand *palazzi* (mansions). Some are enigmatic ruins sprouting bougainvillea and wild fig, while others are caught up in the whirl-wind of renovation that has hit the town.

The town slopes down from the high-way to a narrow waterfront road (Obala Marka Martinovića) that runs along its length. At its heart is **St Nicholas' Church** (Crkva Sv Nikole; Obala Marka Mar-tinovića bb; treasury €1; ☺8am-6pm), set on a small square lined with date palms and the bronze busts of famous citizens.

Perast's most famous landmarks are two peculiarly picturesque islands with equally peculiar histories – **Gospa od Škrpjela** (Our-Lady-of-the-Rock Island; ☺church 9am-7pm Jul & Aug, to 5pm Apr-Jun & Sep-Nov, to 3pm Dec-Mar) and **Sveti Djordje** (St George's Island).

There's no bus station, but buses to and from Kotor (€1.50, 25 minutes) stop at least every 30 minutes on the main road at the top of town. Water tax-is zoom around the bay during summer and call into all ports, including Perast. Regular taxis from Kotor to Perast cost around €15.

Perast shoreline

From left: Kotor Bazaar (p379); City Market; Seafood platter from the Bay of Kotor

Secondhand Shop — Clothing

(Trg od Drva) If you feel like ditching your duds after a long, sweaty day of kicking along the cobblestones (or just love a bargain), this Old Town op-shop is overflowing with top-quality threads.

City Market — Market

(Gradska pijaca; Jadranski Put; ⊘7am-2pm) Self-caterers can stock up at this food market under the town walls. The vendors are happy to give out free samples of everything, from local *pršut* (prosciutto) and cheese to olives and strawberries. On summer evenings, stalls spring up selling clothes, jewellery and souvenirs.

🍴 EATING

There are dozens of restaurants, bakeries and takeaway joints on Kotor's cobbled lanes. Most restaurants stick to the tried-and-true Montenegrin seafood theme. For the sweet-toothed, look out for the cherry-filled strudel.

Ladovina — Montenegrin, Dalmatian €€

(☑063-422 472; www.ladovina.me; Njegoševa 209; mains €9-20; ⊘8am-1am) Tucked away in the Škaljari neighbourhood, south of the Old Town, this relaxed cafe-restaurant has tables beneath an open-sided pagoda under a canopy of trees. The menu includes veal, lamb and octopus claypots, and a mix of seafood and meat grills. There's a terrific selection of wine by the glass and craft beer. Save room for the Kotor cream pie.

Bastion — Montenegrin, Seafood €€

(☑032-322 116; www.bastion123.com; Trg od Drva; mains €8-22; ⊘10am-midnight) At a slight remove from the frenetic heart of the Old Town, Bastion offers a mixture of fresh seafood and traditional meaty grills. If the weather's being well behaved, grab a table outside.

Konoba Galerija — Montenegrin, Seafood €€

(☑032-322 125; www.restorangalerija.com; Šuranj bb; mains €9-22; ⊘11am-11pm) This bustling place on the waterfront excels

in both meat and seafood, as well as fast and attentive service (along the coast, you'll find these things are often mutually exclusive). Try the prawns or mixed seafood in *buzara* sauce, a deceptively simple – yet sublime – blend of olive oil, wine, garlic and mild spices.

🍸 DRINKING & NIGHTLIFE

Kotor is full of cafe-bars that spill onto its squares and fill them with the buzz of conversation. Take your pick.

Letrika   Cocktail Bar
(www.facebook.com/artbarletrika; near Trg Bokeljske Mornarice; ⏰8am-1am) By day, Letrika is a quiet place for a sneaky drink, with a steampunk aesthetic and side-alley location. On summer nights, DJs set up outside and the lane gets jammed with hip young things dancing and sipping cocktails.

Bokun   Wine Bar
(www.facebook.com/BOKUNWINEBAR; near Trg Sv Luke; ⏰8am-1am May-Oct, to 11pm Nov-Apr; 🛜) This evocative little nook is an ideal place

to sample local wines (and perfectly paired meats and cheeses), all to the accompaniment of live music on weekends (think jazz, soul and samba).

Bandiera   Bar
(www.facebook.com/bandiera.kotor; 29 Novembar bb; ⏰8am-1am; 🛜) This cluttered, cavernous old-school bar is a top hang-out, where laid-back conversations and rock music take precedence over texting and techno.

ℹ️ INFORMATION

Tourist Information Booth (📞032-325 951; www.tokotor.me; Jadranski Put; ⏰8am-8pm Apr-Oct, to 6pm Nov-Mar) Stocks free maps and brochures, and can help with contacts for private accommodation.

ℹ️ GETTING AROUND

Bus The bus station (📞032-325 809; www.auto buskastanicakotor.me; Škaljari bb; ⏰6am-8pm) is to the south of town, just off the road leading to the tunnel. The bus to Budva is €4 and takes 40 minutes.

CORFU, GREECE

In This Chapter

Corfu at a Glance...

Corfu, the idyllic refuge where the shipwrecked Odysseus was soothed and sent on his way home, continues to welcome weary travellers with its lush scenery, bountiful produce and pristine beaches. Since the 8th century BC the island the Greeks call Kerkyra has been prized for its untamed beauty and strategic location. Ancient armies fought to possess it, while in the early days of modern Greece it was a beacon of learning. Vestiges of the past range from Corfu Town's Venetian architecture to British legacies, such as cricket and ginger beer.

With One Day in Port

• The Old Town's most eye-catching feature is the grand French-built **Liston** (p390) arcade, facing the Old Fort across the lawns of the **Spianada** (p390), and lined with packed cafes.

• At its northern end, the neoclassical **Palace of St Michael & St George** (p388) contains the excellent Corfu **Museum of Asian Art** (p388).

• Head inland and you can lose yourself for a happy hour or two amid the maze-like alleyways, seeking out sumptuous Orthodox churches or cosy cafes as the mood takes you.

Best Places For...

Traditional Greek food To Tavernaki tis Marinas (p393)

Art galleries Corfu Museum of Asian Art (p388)

Beaches Vidos Island (p390)

Spice shopping Sweet'n'Spicy Bahar (p391)

History Palaio Frourio (p386)

Previous page: Corfu Town
SLAVICA STAJIC/500PX ©

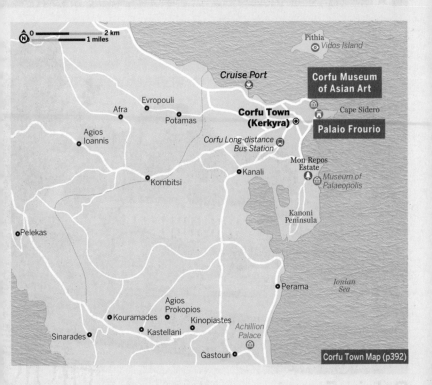

On the map:
- Pithia
- Vidos Island
- Cruise Port
- Corfu Museum of Asian Art
- Evropouli
- Afra
- Potamas
- Corfu Town (Kerkyra)
- Cape Sidero
- Palaio Frourio
- Agios Ioannis
- Corfu Long-distance Bus Station
- Mon Repos Estate
- Kanali
- Museum of Palaeopolis
- Kombitsi
- Kanoni Peninsula
- Pelekas
- Perama
- Ionian Sea
- Agios Prokopios
- Kouramades
- Kinopiastes
- Achillion Palace
- Sinarades
- Kastellani
- Gastouri
- Corfu Town Map (p392)

Scale: 0 — 2 km / 1 miles

Getting from the Port

Corfu Town is home to the island's main ferry port. Corfu Town is at the centre of an efficient network of local buses, and you can get pretty much anywhere on the island from the long-distance bus station in the New Town. Buy tickets at kiosks (or sometimes on board).

Fast Facts

Currency Euro (€)

Language Greek

Money ATMS are located in almost all tourist areas. Credit cards (MasterCard and Visa) are widely accepted.

Visas Citizens of Australia, New Zealand, Canada, the UK and the US do not need a visa to enter Greece for stays up to three months (90 days).

Wi-fi Some hotels, cafes and restaurants have wi-fi access.

ELBE24/SHUTTERSTOCK ©

Palaio Frourio

The rocky headland that juts east from Corfu Town is topped by the Venetian-built 14th-century Palaio Frourio. Before that, already enclosed within massive stone walls, it cradled the entire Byzantine city. A solitary bridge crosses its seawater moat.

Only parts of this huge site, which also holds later structures from the British era, are accessible to visitors; wander up to the lighthouse on the larger of the two hills for superb views.

A gatehouse contains the small Byzantine Collection of Corfu, while the temple-like Church of St George stands on a large terrace to the south.

Byzantine Collection of Corfu

This **gallery** (incl in Palaio Frourio ticket; ⊗9am-4pm Tue-Sun Jun-Oct, 8am-4pm Tue-Sun Nov-May) occupies one room of a former gatehouse within the Old Fort. While it's not to be confused with the superior Antivouniotissa Museum, it does display some attractive frescoes and simple mosaics, while panels describe the early history of Christianity on Corfu.

Great For...

☑ **Don't Miss**

The colossal Church of St George on the outskirts of Palaio Frourio.

Church of St George

Explore Ashore

Local bus 15 (€1.70, hourly starting at 7.20am Monday to Friday, eight daily Saturday, four daily Sunday) connects the New Port with Plateia G Theotoki (Plateia San Rocco) in the New Town. From there it's a 15-minute walk to the fort.

❶ Need to Know

Old Fort; ☎26610 48310; https://ecotourism-greece.com/attractions/old-fortress-corfu-town/; adult/concession €6/3; ⊗8am-8pm Apr-Oct, 8.30am-3pm Nov-Mar

Church of St George

A dazzling white edifice resembling an ancient Greek temple dominates a sweeping flat platform on the southern flanks of the Palaio Frourio. Visible from far along the coast, it's actually a **church** (incl in Palaio Frourio ticket; ⊗8am-8pm Apr-Oct, 8.30am-3pm Nov-Mar), built by the British in 1840 for the local Anglican community. Now Orthodox, it hosts just two services per year, plus occasional concerts and exhibitions.

Take a Break

Make the most of your paid admission to the Old Fort by lingering over a sunset beer (or winter-morning hot chocolate) at **Palaio Frourio Café** (☎26610 42279; www.corfuoldfortress.com; ⊗10am-late; 🛜), a huge terrace cafe enjoying sweeping sea views beside the temple-like Church of St George. It also serves snacks and salads.

Palace of St Michael & St George

TATIANA DYUBANOVA/SHUTTERSTOCK ©

Corfu Museum of Asian Art

Home to stunning artefacts ranging from prehistoric bronzes to works in onyx and ivory, this excellent museum occupies the central portions of the Palace of St Michael & St George.

Great For...

☑ Don't Miss

Centuries of Corfiot art at Municipal Art Gallery I.

Beyond the northern end of the Spianada, the smart Regency-style **Palace of St Michael & St George** (adult/concession €6/3; ⊙8am-8pm Apr-Oct, 9am-4pm Tue-Sun Nov-Mar) was built by the British from 1819 to house the High Commissioner and the Ionian Parliament. It's now home to the prestigious **Corfu Museum of Asian Art** (the entry fee covers both this museum and the palace). Two municipal art galleries I, (entry €3) and II (free entry), are housed in one annex, and its small formal gardens make a pleasant refuge.

In the Corfu Museum of Asian Art, one gallery provides a chronological overview of Chinese ceramics, while showcasing remarkable jade carvings and snuff bottles. The India section opens with Alexander the Great, 'When Greece Met India', and displays fascinating Graeco-Buddhist figures. The Japanese section incorporates

Kollanti, The God of War figurine

TIM GRAHAM/ALAMY STOCK PHOTO ©

Corfu Museum of Asian Art

Arseniou

Donzelot

Nikiforou Theotoki

Kapodistriou

Agoniston Polytechniou

⚓ Explore Ashore

Local bus 15 (€1.70, hourly starting at 7.20am Monday to Friday, eight daily Saturday, four daily Sunday) connects the New Port with Plateia G Theotoki (Plateia San Rocco) in the New Town. From there it's a 15-minute walk to the museum.

❶ Need to Know

📞26610 30443; www.matk.gr; Palace of St Michael & St George; adult/child incl palace entry €6/3; ⊗8am-8pm Apr-Oct, 9am-4pm Tue-Sun Nov-Mar

magnificent samurai armour, Noh masks and superb woodblock prints.

The areas where the palace's original sumptuous decor remain most visible – such as the Throne Room with its elaborate *trompe l'oeil* murals – host temporary exhibitions.

Municipal Art Gallery I

Make the effort to find this **gallery** (📞26610 48690; www.artcorfu.com; €3; ⊗10am-4pm Tue-Sun) – it's entered from the exterior on the palace's eastern side. You'll be rewarded with a handful of high-quality Byzantine icons, including 16th-century works by the Cretan Damaskinos, plus a more extensive array of canvases by Corfiot painters. Look out for the Italian-influenced 19th-century father and son artists, Spyridon and Pavos Prossalendis.

Municipal Art Gallery II

At the eastern (seaward) end of the front terrace of the Palace of St Michael & St George, the **Modern Art Gallery** (📞26610 48690; ⊗9am-4pm Tue-Sun) **FREE** holds some fabulous exhibitions in a beautifully refurbished space – it's definitely worth dropping by to see what's on.

Take a Break

Stop for a bite to eat at **En Plo** (📞26610 81813; www.enplocorfu.com; Gate of St Nicholas, Faliraki; mains €13-20; ⊗9.30am-11.30pm; 🛜), down at sea level and a three-minute walk from the museum. The views are magnificent.

SIGHTS

Achillion Palace
Historic Building

(☎26610 56245; www.achillion-corfu.gr; Gastouri; adult/concession €8/6; ⊗8am-8pm Apr-Nov, to 4pm Dec-Mar) Set atop a steep coastal hill 12km south of Corfu Town, the Achillion Palace was built during the 1890s as a summer palace for Austria's empress Elizabeth, the niece of King Otto of Greece. The palace's two principal features are its intricately decorated central staircase, rising in geometrical flights, and its sweeping garden terraces, which command eye-popping views.

There's surprisingly little to see inside, other than mementoes of Elizabeth, who was assassinated in Genoa in 1898, and of the German kaiser Wilhelm II, who bought the palace in 1907 and added the namesake statue of Achilles Triumphant.

It's well worth getting an audio guide; the descriptions of various statues, paintings and background are excellent for context. They are free, but you need to hand over official government ID of some kind. You can use the guides for up to 50 minutes only.

Bus N-10 runs to the Achillion from Corfu Town (€1.70, 20 minutes).

Liston
Architecture

Corfu Town owes the elegant, photogenic Liston, the arcade that lines the northern half of the Spianada, to neither the Venetians nor the British, but to the French. Designed during the brief Napoleonic occupation of Corfu (1807–14), its harmonious four-storey houses were modelled on Paris' then-new rue de Rivoli. A procession of grand, see-and-be-seen cafes sprawls under the arcade, open to both the Spianada and to Kapadistriou around the back.

Mon Repos Estate
Park

(Kanoni Peninsula; ⊗8am-3pm Tue-Sun) **FREE** This park-like wooded estate 2km around the bay south of the Old Town was the site of Corfu's most important ancient settlement, Palaeopolis. More recently, in 1921, the secluded neoclassical villa that now holds the **Museum of Palaeopolis** (☎26610 41369; adult/concession €4/2; ⊗8am-3pm Tue-Sun) was the birthplace of Prince Philip, husband of Britain's Queen Elizabeth II. Footpaths lead through the woods to ancient ruins, including those of a Doric temple atop a small coastal cliff.

It takes half an hour to walk to Mon Repos from town, or you can catch bus 2a from the Spianada (€1.70, every 20 minutes). Bring a picnic and plenty of water; there are no shops nearby.

Antivouniotissa Museum
Museum

(Byzantine Museum; ☎26610 38313; www.antivouniotissamuseum.gr; off Arseniou; adult/concession €4/2; ⊗8am-3pm Tue-Sun) Home to an outstanding collection of Byzantine and post-Byzantine icons and artefacts, the exquisite, timber-roofed Church of Our Lady of Antivouniotissa doubles as both church and museum. It stands atop a short, broad stairway that climbs from shore-front Arseniou, and frames views out towards wooded Vidos Island.

Belying the plain facade, the ornate and intricately decorated interior holds treasures dating from the 15th century onwards.

Vidos Island
Island

Hourly boats from the Old Port make the 10-minute crossing to tiny, thickly wooded Vidos Island (€5 return), immediately offshore. There's a taverna at the jetty, but the big attraction is to walk the 600m across the island to reach a couple of lovely beaches on its northern shore.

Church of Agios Spyridon
Church

(Agios Spyridonos; ⊗8am-9pm) Pilgrims and day trippers alike throng this Old Town landmark. As well as magnificent frescoes, the small 16th-century basilica holds the remains of Corfu's patron saint, Spyridon, a 4th-century Cypriot shepherd. His body, brought here from Constantinople in 1453, lies in an elaborate silver casket, and is paraded through the town on festival days.

Spianada
Park

The Spianada, the park adjoining the Old Town, was cleared by the Venetians to allow a clear line of fire from the Old Fort. During the 19th century the British laid out a cricket pitch on the lawns of its northern portion, which still hosts occasional matches today.

Paved avenues lead across its more formal southern half to a bandstand and other monuments. Horse-drawn carriages tout for passengers along the central road, also a base for buses and taxis.

🟢 ACTIVITIES

All sorts of tours can help you explore in and around Corfu Town, whether on foot with **Corfu Walking Tours** (☑69328 94466, 69458 94450; www.corfuwalkingtours.com; €64-75), by bus with **Ichnos Excursions** (☑26610 21300; www.toursincorfu.gr; Ethnikis Antistaseos 2; per 4 people from €250), or in the **toy-train** (€8) and **horse-drawn carriage** (Dousmani) tours that start from the Spianada.

Corfu Taxi Tours (☑69455 80996; www.corfutaxitours.com) are aimed primarily at giving cruise passengers a quick overview of the island – the outfit claims it can show you the best of Corfu in five hours. The tours are customised to suit the interests of each specific small group. The entire island has excellent walking. You can organise a day's guided hiking with **Corfu Walks & Hikes** (www.walking-corfu.blogspot.co.uk).

🔒 SHOPPING

The Old Town is crammed with shopping opportunities. The heaviest concentration of souvenir shops, which sell everything from 'evil eye' amulets and olive-wood carvings to pashminas and perfume, is along narrow Filarmonikis between the two main churches, while N Theotoki is good for idiosyncratic boutiques.

Sweet'n'Spicy Bahar   Spices
(☑26610 33848; www.sweetnspicy.gr; Agias Sofias 12; ☺9.45am-2pm) Gloriously aromatic spice and condiment shop, run by an ever-so-enthusiastic Greek-Canadian-Lebanese woman with a palpable love for devising her own enticing mixes of Greek and imported spices.

Icon Gallery   Arts & Crafts
(☑26614 00928; www.iconcraft.gr; Guilford 52; ☺10am-10.30pm Mon-Sat; 🤶) True to its name, this tasteful hole-in-the-wall boutique sells stunning icons, handmade by an artists' co-op, as well as fine heraldic art and antiques.

Papagiorgis   Food & Drinks
(☑26610 39474; www.papagiorgis.gr; N Theotoki 32; ☺9am-midnight) Irresistible old-fashioned patisserie that's an Old Town landmark thanks to its 40 different flavours of ice cream, plus a mouth-watering array of homemade tarts, biscuits and honey.

To Ploio   Jewellery
(☑26610 39068; www.toploio.gr; N Theotoki 109; ☺10am-7pm) While specialising in hand-crafted contemporary jewellery that's both elegant and playful, this eye-catching Old Town boutique also sells souvenir wooden ships as well as prints and postcards.

🍴 EATING & DRINKING

Corfiot cuisine shows the delicious influences of many cultures, especially Italian. Delectable Corfiot bites are considered 'spicy' to mainlander Greeks. These include *sofrito* (a traditional veal dish), *pastitsadha* (traditional meat and pasta dish from Corfu) and *tsigareli* (cabbage or wild greens in a spicy tomato-based sauce).

Pane & Souvlaki   Grill €
(☑26610 20100; www.panesouvlaki.com; Guilford 77; mains €6-13.50; ☺noon-1am) Arguably the Old Town's best-value budget option (the locals rave), with outdoor tables on the Town Hall square, this quick-fire restaurant does exactly what its name suggests, serving up three skewers of chicken or pork with chunky chips, dipping sauce and warm pitta in individual metal trays. The salads and burgers are good, too.

Rosy's Bakery   Bakery €
(☑26615 51412; www.facebook.com/RosysBakery CorfuGreece; Paleologlou 71; sweets & pastries from €2; ☺10am-11.30pm; 🤶) Ultra- friendly bakery-cafe that's a real home away from

Corfu Town

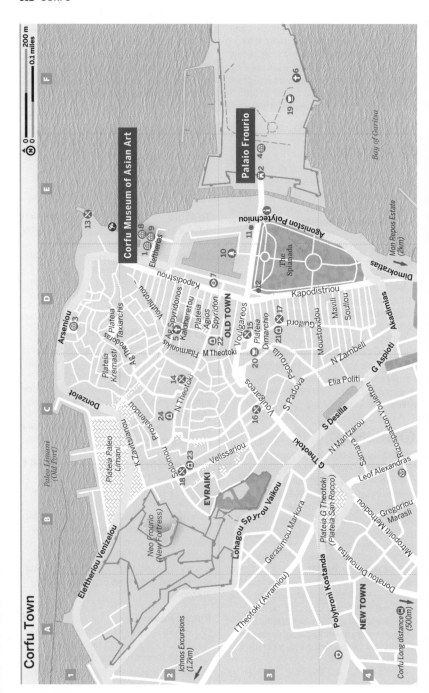

Corfu Museum of Asian Art

Palaio Frourio

Corfu Town

home. It serves luscious, creamy cakes, succulent pastries, local yoghurt with kumquats and good coffee. There's another, takeaway-only branch further down the lane.

Starenio   Bakery €
(🖉26610 47370; www.facebook.com/starenio bakery; Guilford 59; sweets & pastries from €2; ☺8am-8pm Mon-Sat) A magical little bakery, dripping with bougainvillea, where in-the-know locals linger at tables on the sloping pedestrian street to savour cakes, coffee, pastries, and delicious fresh pies with vegetarian fillings such as mushrooms or nettles.

To Tavernaki
tis Marinas   Taverna €€
(🖉26611 00792; Velissariou 35; mains €8-15; ☺noon-11.30pm) The stone walls, hardwood floors and cheerful staff lift the ambience of this taverna. Check the daily specials or choose anything from *mousakas* (baked layers of aubergine or courgette, minced meat and potatoes topped with cheese sauce) or sardines-in-the-oven to steak. Accompany it all with a dram of ouzo or *tsipouro* (distilled spirit similar to raki).

It's bit tricky to find: it's nestled between Agias Sofias and Velissariou.

Estiatorio Bellissimo   Greek €€
(🖉26610 41112; Plateia Limonia; mains €8-18; ☺10am-midnight) The Old Town holds few

nicer spots for an al fresco evening than this casual but stylish restaurant that spreads across a peaceful pedestrian square. As well as steaks and seafood, it serves Corfiot specialities such as *pastitsadha kokora* – chicken in red sauce, 'with a lot of cheese' – plus crepes and salads.

Piccolo Espresso Bar   Coffee
(🖉26610 81747; www.facebook.com/piccolo. corfu; Plateia Dimarchio 17; ☺8am-2am; 🛜) Stylish little espresso cafe, on the Town Hall square, where the soothing, dazzling white courtyard is also ideal for a late-night drink.

❶ INFORMATION

Municipal Tourist Kiosk (www.corfu.gr; Spianada; ☺8am-4pm Mon-Fri Mar-Nov) Helps with transport and things to do around Corfu.

Post Office (Leoforos Alexandras 26; ☺7.30am-8.30pm Mon-Fri)

Tourist Police (🖉26610 29168; I Andreadi 1) In the New Town, off Plateia G Theotoki (Plateia San Rocco).

❶ GETTING AROUND

The streets and alleyways of Corfu Town are compact enough to wander around as you explore the sights, shops, cafes and restaurants.

HANIA, GREECE

In This Chapter

Hania at a Glance...

Hania (also spelled Chania) is Crete's most evocative city, with its pretty Venetian quarter, criss-crossed by narrow lanes, culminating in a magnificent harbour. Remnants of Venetian and Turkish architecture abound, with old townhouses now transformed into atmospheric restaurants and boutique hotels. Though all this beauty means the old town is crowded in summer, it's still a great place to unwind. The Venetian Harbour is super for a stroll and a coffee, while indie boutiques and an entire lane (Skrydlof) dedicated to leather products provide great shopping.

With One Day in Port

○ Spend an hour or three ambling the waterfront promenade of the **Venetian Harbour** (p398), then dive into the labyrinthine lanes of the old town for a spot of **shopping** (p402).

○ After perusing a raft of antiquities at the engrossing **Hania Archaeological Museum** (p400), head to **Nea Hora Beach** (p402) for an afternoon of leisure.

Best Places For...

Coffee Pallas (p405)

Flaky Cretan pastries Bougatsa Iordanis (p403)

Al fresco cocktails Sinagogi (p403)

Deli treats Miden Agan (p402)

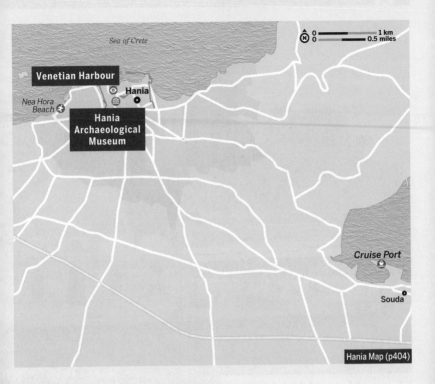

Hania Map (p404)

Getting from the Port

Hania's port is at **Souda**, 7km southeast of town (and the site of a NATO base).

The port is linked to town by bus (€2, or €2.50 if bought aboard) and taxi (around €12). Hania buses, operated by Chania Urban Buses (http://chaniabus.gr), meet each boat.

Fast Facts

Currency Euro (€)

Language Greek

Money ATMs can be found in the old town on Halidon.

Tourist information There's a tourist office in the town hall.

Visas Citizens of Australia, New Zealand, Canada, the UK and the US do not need a visa to enter Greece for stays up to three months (90 days).

Wi-fi Free wi-fi is widely available in public spaces, including the harbour, around the central market and at Plateia 1866, as well as at most hotels, restaurants, cafes and bars.

Mosque of Kioutsouk Hasan

KAVALENKAVA/SHUTTERSTOCK ©

Venetian Harbour

With its waterfront promenade and pastel-coloured townhouses, there are few places where Hania's historic charm and grandeur is more palpable than in the old Venetian Harbour.

Great For...

☑ **Don't Miss**

Views of the harbour and lighthouse from atop the Firkas Fortress.

Hania, along with the rest of Crete, was claimed by the rising power of Venice following the Fourth Crusade (1204), and the city was renamed La Canea. After briefly losing the city to their Genoese rivals in 1266, the Venetians wrested it back in 1290. They constructed massive fortifications to protect the city, making it a key strategic hub in their Mediterranean trading empire for three-and-a-half centuries.

Today the harbourfront is where tourists and locals stroll, gossip and people-watch as the sparkling sea swirls between the imposing Firkas Fortress, a peachy portside mosque and a striking lighthouse.

Firkas Fortress

The **Firkas Fortress** (⏱8am-2pm Mon-Fri) at the western tip of the harbour heads the best-preserved section of the Venetians'

Firkas Fortress

KAVALENKAVA/SHUTTERSTOCK ©

Sea of Crete

Akti Kanari **Venetian Harbour** Akti Koundourioti

Pireos

Halidon

Kypou

El Venizelou

Explore Ashore

Frequent local buses from Souda port stop near the *agora* market hall, a 10-minute walk (via shopping streets and past cafes) to the port. Allow three to four hours to stroll the waterfront and delve into the Maritime Museum of Crete.

✕ Take a Break

Stop for a buzz-inducing coffee at Pallas (p405) to fuel a jaunt to the lighthouse.

---

massive fortifications, built to protect the city from marauding pirates and invading Turks. The Turks invaded anyway, in 1645, and Hania was captured by the Ottoman Empire after a two-month siege. The Turks made it the seat of the Turkish Pasha until they were forced out in 1898. While in residence, the Turks turned the hulking fortress into a barracks and a prison. Today, parts of it house the **Maritime Museum of Crete** (☏ 28210 91875; www.mar-mus-crete.gr; Akti Koundourioti; adult/concession €3/2; ⓦ 9am-5pm Mon-Sat, 10am-6pm Sun May-Oct, 9am-3.45pm Mon-Sat Nov-Apr), which celebrates Crete's nautical tradition with model ships, naval instruments, paintings, photographs, maps and memorabilia. One room is dedicated to historical sea battles, while upstairs there's thorough documentation on the WWII-era Battle of Crete.

Mosque of Kioutsouk Hasan

On the eastern side of the Venetian Harbour, this **ex-mosque** (Mosque of the Janissaries) `FREE` is one of the prettiest and most dominant vestiges from the Turkish period. It was built in 1645, making it the oldest Ottoman building in town.

Hania Lighthouse

The **lighthouse** `FREE` at the mouth of the Venetian Harbour is one of Hania's landmark buildings. The stone tower rises 21m above a stone base and was built in the 16th century by the Venetians, although it underwent various changes over the years. It's a nice walk out here with photogenic views of the waterfront.

MILAN GONDA/SHUTTERSTOCK ©

Hania Archaeological Museum

The setting, in the beautifully restored 16th-century Venetian Church of San Francisco, is reason enough to visit this fine collection of artefacts ranging from Neolithic to Roman times.

Great For...

☑ **Don't Miss**

The museum's display of antediluvian copper, bronze and silver coins.

Museum Collection

The discovery of clay tablets with Linear B script during ongoing excavations on **Kastelli Hill** (cnr Kanevaro & Kantanoleon; ☺excavations usually 8am-3pm Mon-Fri) to the east of the Venetian Harbour has led archaeologists to conclude that present-day Hania sits atop an important Minoan city and palace site called Ancient Kydonia. The finest among the unearthed artefacts are displayed in Hania's archaeological museum, alongside pieces from other ancient Minoan and Roman sites.

Late-Minoan sarcophagi catch the eye as much as a large glass case with an entire herd of clay bulls (used to worship Poseidon). Other standouts include Roman floor mosaics, Hellenistic gold jewellery, clay tablets with Linear A and Linear B

MILAN GONDA/SHUTTERSTOCK ©

⚓

Explore Ashore

The archaeological museum is small but fascinating, and a great addition to an exploration of Hania's Venetian Harbour (p398). Allow at least an hour to view the exhibits and mosaics.

❶ Need to Know

☎28210 90334; http://chaniamuseum. culture.gr; Halidon 28; adult/concession/child €4/2/free; ⊙8.30am-8pm Wed-Mon Apr-Oct, to 4pm Wed-Mon Nov-Mar

script, and a marble sculpture of Roman emperor Hadrian.

Also particularly impressive are the statue of Diana and, in the pretty courtyard, a marble fountain decorated with lions' heads, a vestige of the Venetian tradition. A Turkish fountain is a relic from the building's days as a mosque. To the north of the church, three small rooms display choice finds from a private collection of Minoan pottery, jewellery and clay models.

Museum Building

The construction date of the church itself is unknown, but it is thought to be well over 400 years old. The building served as a mosque under the Turks, a movie theatre in 1913, and a munitions depot for the Germans during WWII.

What's Nearby?

Hania's interesting **Folklore Museum** (☎28210 90816; Halidon 46b; adult/child €2/free; ⊙9am-6pm Mon-Fri) contains a selection of crafts including weavings with traditional designs, local paintings, as well as several rooms of a traditional Cretan house. Find the entrance inside the courtyard and upstairs. Just down the road, the **modern art gallery** (☎28210 92294; www. pinakothiki-chania.gr; Halidon 98-102; adult/child €2/free; ⊙10am-2pm & 6-9pm Mon-Sat) evokes the interior of a boat and presents temporary exhibitions of contemporary works by local and national artists on three elegant, well-lit floors.

Permanent Collection of Ancient & Traditional Shipbuilding

◎ SIGHTS

Byzantine & Post-Byzantine Collection   Museum

(☎28210 96046; Theotokopoulou 78; adult/concession/child €2/1/free; ⊗8am-3pm Tue-Sun) In the impressively restored Venetian Church of San Salvatore, this small but fascinating collection of artefacts, icons, jewellery and coins spans the period from AD 62 to 1913. Highlights include a segment of a mosaic floor for an early-Christian basilica, an icon of St George slaying the dragon and a panel, recently attributed to El Greco.

Permanent Collection of Ancient & Traditional Shipbuilding   Museum

(☎28210 91875; Neorio Moro, Akti Defkaliona; adult/child €2/1; ⊗9am-5pm Mon-Sat, 10am-6pm Sun mid-Apr–Oct) The *Minoa*, a painstaking replica of a Minoan ship that sailed from Crete to Athens for the 2004 Olympics ceremonies, now permanently docks in a converted Venetian shipyard (*neoria*). Tools used in its making and photographs from the epic journey bring to life this amazing feat.

Nea Hora Beach   Beach

(Akti Papanikoli) Hania's in-town beach is only a 10-minute walk west of the Venetian Harbour. The 500m-long yellow-sand strip is backed by tavernas, small markets and holiday apartment rentals. Fairly shallow, it's good for kids and popular with locals on weekends.

🔒 SHOPPING

Hania offers top shopping, especially in the backstreets. Theotokopoulou is lined with souvenir and handicraft shops. Skrydlof offers a vast array of local and imported sandals, belts and bags. Find some of the most authentic crafts in the Splantzia quarter, along Chatzimichali Daliani and Daskalogianni. The **agora** (Covered Market; Chatzimichali Giannari; ⊗8am-2pm Mon, Wed & Sat, 8am-9pm Tue, Thu & Fri; 🚻) is touristy but still worth a wander.

Miden Agan   Food & Drinks

(☎28210 27068; www.midenaganshop.gr; Daskalogianni 70; ⊗10am-5pm Mon-Wed & Sat, to 9pm Thu & Fri) Food-and-wine lovers are spoiled for choice at this excellent shop, which stocks more than 800 Greek wines, as well as its own wine and liquors. There's a variety of beautifully packaged local traditional gourmet deli foods, including olive oil and honey and its own line of spoon sweets (try the white pumpkin).

Roka Carpets   Arts & Crafts

(☑28210 74736; Zambeliou 61; ☉11am-9pm Mon-Sat) This is one of the few places in Crete where you can buy genuine, hand-woven goods (note, though, they are not antiques). Amiable Mihalis Manousakis and his wife weave wondrous rugs on a 400-year-old loom, using methods that have remained essentially unchanged since Minoan times.

Sifis Stavroulakis   Jewellery

(☑28210 50335; www.sifisjewellery.gr; Chatzimichali Daliani 54; ☉9am-2pm & 6-10pm Apr-Oct, 9am-2pm Nov-Mar) Beautiful naturalistic jewellery made with semi-precious stones and metals create floral and human forms in this small shopfront and jeweller's workshop.

Georgina
Skalidi   Fashion & Accessories

(☑28215 01705; www.georginaskalidi.com; Chatzimichali Daliani 58; ☉11am-2pm & 6-10pm Mon-Sat) This internationally distributed local designer creates wonderful contemporary leather bags, jewellery and accessories.

Exantas Art Space   Crafts, Books

(☑28210 95920; Zambeliou & Moschon; ☉10am-2pm & 6-11pm) This high-concept store has great postcards with old photos and engravings, handmade gifts and games, Cretan music as well as a good range of travel, coffee-table and art books.

EATING

Hania has some of the finest restaurants in Crete. These can be found inland from the Venetian Harbour.

Bougatsa Iordanis   Cretan €

(☑28210 88855; www.iordanis.gr; Apokoronou 24; bougatsa €3; ☉6am-2.30pm Mon-Sat, to 1.30pm Sun; ⊕) Locals start salivating at the mere

 Sit Back & Relax

If you need a coffee or an afternoon raki (distilled spirit), the cafe-bars around the Venetian Harbour are nice places to sit, but charge top euro. For a more local vibe, head to Plateia 1821 in the Splantzia quarter, the interior streets near Potie, or to alt-flavoured Sarpidona on the eastern end of the harbour.

Sinagogi (☑28210 95242; Parodos Kondylaki 15; ☉noon-5am May-Oct; ☎) Housed in a roofless Venetian building on a small lane next to the synagogue, this popular summer-only lounge bar has eclectic decor and is a laid-back place to relax and take it all in.

Kleidi (☑28210 52974; Plateia 1821; ☉9am-late; ☎) The shaded plaza tables here invite lingering over an iced coffee. There's no written sign, just the image of a keyhole (*kleidi* means key).

Splantzia Quarter

mention of this little bakery-cafe dedicated to making the finest *bougatsa* since 1924. The flaky treat, filled with sweet or savoury cheese, is cooked fresh in enormous slabs and carved up in front of your eyes. Pair it with a coffee and you're set for the morning. There's nothing else on the menu!

Kouzina EPE   Cretan €

(☑28210 42391; www.facebook.com/kouzina epe; Daskalogianni 25; mezhedes €4-9.50; ☉noon-7.30pm Mon-Sat) This cheery lunch spot gets contemporary designer flair from the cement floor, country-white tables and groovy lighting. It hands down wins

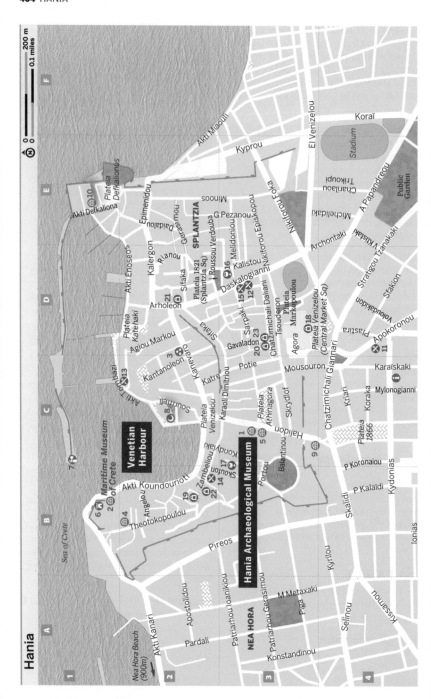

Hania

Sea of Crete

Nea Hora Beach
(900m)

Maritime Museum
of Crete

**Venetian
Harbour**

Hania Archaeological Museum

NEA HORA

SPLANTZIA

Stadium

Koraï

Public
Garden

Plateia
Defkalionos

Akti Defkaliona

Akti Miaouli

Kyprou

El Venizelou

A Papandreou

Charilaou
Trikoupi

Michelidaki

Nikiforou Foka

Minoos

G Pezanou

Archontaki

Vlastaki

Stratigou Tzanakaki

Roussou Verdouba

Kalistou

Nikiforou Episkopou

Plateia Markopoulou

Plateia Venizelou
(Central Market Sq)

Stakion

Plastira

Apokoronou

Voloudakion

Daskalogianni

Sarpaki

Chatzimichali Daliani

Tsouderon

Agora

Karaïskaki

Mylonogianni

Plateia
1866

Kriari

Plateia Koraka

Chatzimichali Giannari

Mousouron

Skrydlof

Plateia
Athinagora

Potie

Gavaladon

Kanevaro

Katre

Karaoli Dimitriou

Haldon

Balantinou

Portou

P Koronaiou

P Kalaïdi

Skalidi

Kyriou

Ionias

Kissamou

Selinou

Konstandinou

M Metaxaki

Piga

Patriarhou Gerasimou

Patriarhou Ioannikiou

Apostolidou

Pardali

Akti Kanari

Pireos

Akti Koundourioti

Theotokopoulou

Angelou

Zambeliou

Skouton

Kondylaki

Plateia
Venizelou

Sourmeli

Kantanoleon

Akti Tombazi

Plateia
Katehaki

Agiou Markou

Arholeon

Sifaka

Sfaka

Plateia 1821
(Splantzia Sq)

Melidoniou

Kalergon

RIanou

Daidalou

Gerasimou

Epimenidou

Akti Enoseos

Hania

the area's 'local favourite', by serving great value, delicious blackboard-listed *mayirefta* (ready-cooked meals) prepared by the owner; you can inspect what you're about to eat in the open kitchen.

Pallas International €€
(☏28210 45688; www.pallaschania.gr; Akti Tombazi 15; mains €8-16; ☺8am-4am; ☏) This much buzzed-about hipster cafe-bar has a sweet location in an impeccably renovated former customs house from 1830 right in the Venetian Harbour. Grab a high chair, sofa or table to linger over the three-tiered breakfast, a crisp salad for lunch or a juicy steak dinner – or pop by just for coffee or cocktails.

To Maridaki Seafood €€
(☏28210 08880; www.tomaridaki.gr; Daskalogianni 33; mezedhes €4-14; ☺noon-midnight Mon-Sat) This modern seafood *mezedhopoleio* (restaurant specialising in mezedhes) is often packed with chatty locals. Dishes straddle the line between tradition and innovation with to-die-for mussels *saganaki* and delicious house white wine. The complimentary panna cotta is a worthy finish.

Tamam Restaurant Mediterranean €€
(☏28210 96080; www.tamamrestaurant.com; Zambeliou 49; mains €8-13; ☺noon-12.30am;) This convivial taverna in a converted Turkish bathhouse has captured people's attention since 1982 with strong-flavoured Cretan dishes that often incorporate Middle Eastern spices and touches. The boneless lamb in tomato sauce with raisins and mint is a winner. Tables spill out onto the narrow alleyway.

ⓘ INFORMATION

Banks cluster around Plateia Markopoulou in the new city, but there are also ATMs in the old town on Halidon.

Alpha Bank (cnr Halidon & Skalidi)

National Bank of Greece (cnr Tzanakaki & Giannari)

TOURIST INFORMATION

Municipal Tourist Office (☏28213 36155; chania@ofcrete.gr; Kydonias 29; ☺8.30am-2.30pm Mon-Fri) Modest selection of brochures, maps and transport timetables at the town hall. Open some Saturdays.

ⓘ GETTING AROUND

Hania town is best navigated on foot, since most of it is pedestrianised.

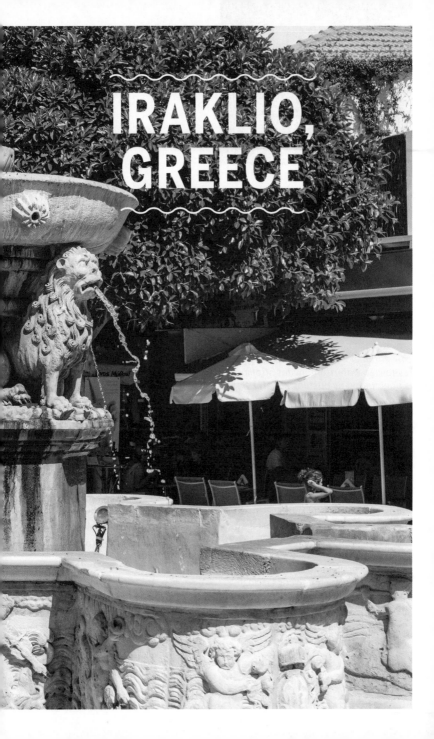

IRAKLIO, GREECE

Iraklio at a Glance...

Crete's capital city, Iraklio (also called Heraklion), is the island's economic and administrative hub. It's also home to Crete's blockbuster sights: the must-see Heraklion Archaeological Museum and the nearby Palace of Knossos, which both provide fascinating windows into Crete's ancient past. Though not pretty in a conventional way, Iraklio definitely grows on you if you take the time to explore. A revitalised waterfront invites strolling and the newly pedestrianised historic centre is punctuated by bustling squares flanked by buildings from the time when Christopher Columbus first set sail.

With One Day in Port

○ Make a beeline for **Knossos** (p410), arriving before 10am if possible, to explore the site's main features in relative peace, moving on to the less popular corners when it gets busy.

○ Then gear up for thousands of years of history and spend several fascinating hours at the **Heraklion Archaeological Museum** (p416).

○ Follow it up with a post-culture hot chocolate at **Utopia** (p420).

Best Places For...

Coffee Miniatoura (p421)

Sweet pastries Phyllo Sofies (p420)

Picnic supplies Iraklio Market (p420)

Cretan dishes Peskesi (p420)

Previous page: Morosini Fountain (p419)

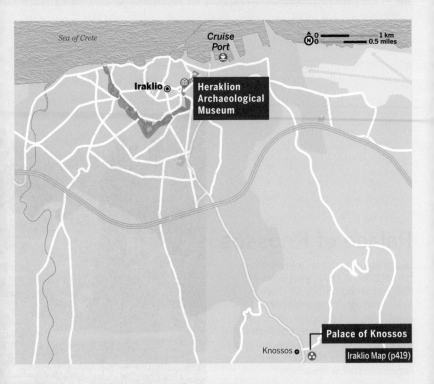

Getting from the Port

The ferry port is 500m to the east of Koules Fortress and the old harbour; the local bus terminal is outside the port entrance. The city centre is within walking distance of the cruise port. You can also flag down a taxi (or phone for one on ☎2814 003084).

Fast Facts

Currency Euro (€)

Language Greek

Money Banks with ATMs are plentiful, especially along 25 Avgoustou.

Tourist information Stop by the tourist office on Plateia Venizelou for maps and brochures.

Visas Citizens of Australia, New Zealand, Canada, the UK and the US do not need a visa to enter Greece for stays up to three months (90 days).

Wi-fi There are a number of free municipal wi-fi hotspots in town; most cafes and bars also have free wi-fi.

Palace of Knossos

Rub shoulders with the ghosts of the Minoans at the largest Bronze Age archaeological site on Crete. Incorporating an immense palace, courtyards, private apartments, baths, lively frescoes and more, the Palace of Knossos – once the grand capital of Minoan Crete – is now the island's most famous historical attraction.

Great For...

Palace of Knossos

❶ Need to Know

☎2810 231940; http://odysseus.culture.gr; Knossos; adult/concession €15/8, incl Heraklion Archaeological Museum €16/8; ⏱8am-8pm Apr-Aug, to 5pm Sep-Mar; 🅿; 🚌2

Explore Ashore

The palace is located 5km south of Iraklio. City bus 2 runs from the city centre – from Bus Station A or from outside Hotel Capsis Astoria – every 15 minutes. Tickets cost €1.50 if purchased from a kiosk or vending machine and €2.50 from the bus driver. Allow up to two hours to get your bearings and explore the site.

History & Excavation

Knossos' first palace (1900 BC) was destroyed by an earthquake around 1700 BC and rebuilt to a grander and more sophisticated design. It was partially destroyed again between 1500 and 1450 BC, and inhabited for another 50 years before burning down.

The complex comprised domestic quarters, public reception rooms, shrines, workshops, treasuries and storerooms, all flanking a paved central courtyard.

Excavation of the site started in 1878 with Cretan archaeologist Minos Kalokerinos, and continued from 1900 with British archaeologist Sir Arthur Evans. Evans was so enthralled by his discoveries that he spent 35 years and £250,000 of his own money excavating and reconstructing sections of the palace. Although controversial in expert circles – with many archaeologists believing that Evans sacrificed accuracy to his overly vivid imagination – his reconstructions help casual visitors visualise what the palace might have looked like in its heyday.

The first treasure to be unearthed in the flat-topped mound called Kefala was a fresco of a Minoan man, followed by the discovery of the Throne Room. The archaeological world was stunned that a civilisation of this maturity and sophistication had existed in Europe at the same time as the great pharaohs of Egypt. Over the course of the excavations, Evans unearthed remains of a Neolithic civilisation beneath the remains of the Bronze Age Minoan palace. He also discovered some 3000 clay tablets containing Linear A and Linear B script and wrote his own definitive description of his work at Knossos in a four-volume opus called *The*

Frescoes on the South Portico (p414)

Palace of Minos. Evans received many honours for his work and was knighted in 1911.

Highlights

Throne Room

Behind an antechamber, this beautifully proportioned room is separated by a pillar from a sunken basin that may have been used for purification rituals preceding ceremonies held in the presence of the king. The ruler may have been seated on the alabaster chair ('throne') to the right with followers squatting on the stone benches lining the walls that are decorated with frescoes of plants and griffins.

> **★ Top Tip**
>
> Bring water, sunscreen and a hat, as the site can get very hot in summer. Comfortable shoes are also a must.

Queen's Megaron

With its painted pillars and playful dolphin fresco on the far wall, Evans believed this pretty space in the residential eastern wing was the queen's bedroom, complete with adjacent 'bathroom'.

Hall of the Double Axes

This is a spacious double room, possibly where the ruler both slept and carried out court duties. It takes its name from the double axe marks *(labrys)* on its light well, a symbol sacred to the Minoans and the origin of the word 'labyrinth'.

Magazine of the Giant Pithoi

Covered storerooms in the east wing hold giant clay jars decorated with ornamental reliefs that once held oil, wine and other staples.

Drainage System

Remnants of a drainage channel and underground clay pipes show that the Minoans had developed a sophisticated water supply and sewage system.

Guided Tours

Optional guided tours last about 1½ hours and leave from the little kiosk past the ticket booth. Most tours are in English, though other languages are available too. Prices vary according to group numbers (€10 per person in a group with an eight-person minimum). Private tours cost €100 with a maximum of six people.

> **✕ Take a Break**
>
> Grab a cab (10 minutes) to **Elia & Diosmos** (☑2810 731283; www.olivemint. gr; Dimokratias 263, Skalani; mains €8-13; ☉11am-midnight Tue-Sun; ☎) ✐ in the nearby Iraklio Wine Country for flavour-intense Cretan dishes.

> **☑ Don't Miss**
>
> The delightful dolphin-and-fish fresco in the Queen's Megaron (bedroom).

Palace of Knossos

THE HIGHLIGHTS IN TWO HOURS

The Palace of Knossos is Crete's busiest tourist attraction, and for good reason. A spin around the partially and imaginatively reconstructed complex (shown here as it was thought to be at its peak) delivers an eye-opening glimpse into the remarkably sophisticated society of the Minoans, who dominated southern Europe some 4000 years ago.

From the ticket booth, follow the marked trail to the ❶ **North Entrance** where the Charging Bull fresco gives you a first taste of Minoan artistry. Continue to the Central Court and join the queue waiting to glimpse the mystical ❷ **Throne Room**, which probably hosted religious rituals. Turn right as you exit and follow the stairs up to the so-called Piano Nobile, where replicas of the palace's most famous artworks conveniently cluster in the ❸ **Fresco Room**. Walk the length of the Piano Nobile, pausing to look at the clay storage vessels in the West Magazine. Circle back and descend to the ❹ **South Portico**, beautifully decorated with the Cup Bearer fresco. Make your way back to the Central Court and head to the palace's eastern wing to admire the architecture of the ❺ **Grand Staircase** that led to what Sir Arthur Evans imagined to be the royal family's private quarters. For a closer look at some rooms, walk to the south end of the courtyard, stopping for a peek at the ❻ **Prince of the Lilies Fresco**, and head down to the lower floor. A highlight here is the ❼ **Queen's Megaron** (Evans imagined this was the Queen's chambers), playfully adorned with a fresco of frolicking dolphins. Stay on the lower level and make your way to the ❽ **Giant Pithoi**, huge clay jars used for storage.

South Portico
Fine frescoes, most famously the Cup Bearer, embellish this palace entrance anchored by a massive open staircase leading to the Piano Nobile. The Horns of Consecration recreated nearby once topped the entire south facade.

Fresco Room
Take in sweeping views of the palace grounds from the west wing's upper floor, the Piano Nobile, before studying copies of the palace's most famous artworks in its Fresco Room.

West Court

West Magazines

❹ Horns of Consecration

FOOD TIP

Save your appetite for a meal in the nearby Iraklio Wine Country, amid sun-baked slopes and lush valleys. It's just south of Knossos.

Prince of the Lilies Fresco
One of Knossos' most beloved frescoes was controversially cobbled together from various fragments and shows a young man adorned in lilies and peacock feathers.

PLANNING

To beat the crowds and avoid the heat, arrive before 10am. Budget one or two hours to explore the site thoroughly.

Throne Room

Sir Arthur Evans, who began excavating the Palace of Knossos in 1900, imagined the mythical King Minos himself holding court seated on the alabaster throne of this beautifully proportioned room. However, the lustral basin and griffin frescoes suggest a religious purpose, possibly under a priestess.

North Entrance

Bulls held a special status in Minoan society, as evidenced by the famous relief fresco of a charging beast gracing the columned west bastion of the north palace, which harboured workshops and storage rooms.

Grand Staircase

The royal apartments in the eastern wing were accessed via this monumental staircase sporting four flights of gypsum steps supported by columns. The lower two flights are original. It's closed to the public.

Piano Nobile

③

②

①

⑤

Central Court

Royal Apartments

⑧

⑥

⑦

Giant Pithoi

These massive clay jars are rare remnants from the Old Palace period and were used to store wine, oil and grain. The jars were transported by slinging ropes through a series of handles.

Queen's Megaron

The queen's room is among the prettiest in the residential eastern wing thanks to the playful Dolphin Fresco. The adjacent bathroom (with clay tub) and toilet are evidence of a sophisticated drainage system.

Minoan pottery

PECOLD/SHUTTERSTOCK ©

Heraklion Archaeological Museum

Housed in a revamped 1930s Bauhaus building, this extraordinary museum showcases artefacts spanning 5500 years from Neolithic to Roman times, including a Minoan collection of unparalleled richness.

The museum's treasure trove includes pottery, jewellery and sarcophagi, plus famous frescoes from the sites of Knossos, Tylissos, Amnissos and Agia Triada. The pieces are grouped into comprehensive themes, such as settlements, trade, death and religion, bringing to life both the day-to-day functioning and long-term progression of societies on Crete and beyond.

Ground-Floor Highlights

Starting on the ground floor, Rooms I to III focus on the Neolithic period to the Middle Bronze Age (6000 BC to 1700 BC), showing life in the first settlements in Crete and around Knossos. The undisputed eye-catcher in Room III is the elaborately embellished Kamares tableware of red, black and white clay, including a 'royal dinner service' from Phaestos.

Great For...

☑ Don't Miss

The vibrant Minoan frescoes on the museum's 1st floor.

Stone bull's head

MILAN GONDA/SHUTTERSTOCK ©

Explore Ashore

It's a 20-minute stroll from the cruise port passenger station to the museum. Allow at least two hours for this extraordinary collection, if necessary taking a break in the on-site cafe.

❶ Need to Know

www.heraklionmuseum.gr; Xanthoudidou 2; adult/reduced/child €10/5/free, combined ticket with Palace of Knossos adult/reduced €16/8; ⊙8am-8pm Mon & Wed-Sun, 10am-8pm Tue mid-Apr-Oct, 8am-4pm Nov-mid-Apr

Rooms IV to VI illustrate life in the Late Bronze Age (1700 BC to 1450 BC), when Minoan culture reached its zenith. One of the most significant exhibits is the Phaistos disc, a stunning clay piece embossed with 45 signs, which has never been deciphered.

Rooms VII and VIII reveal the importance of Minoan religion and ideology with cult objects and figurines. In Room VIII, the snake goddesses and stone bull's head (inlaid with seashell and crystal) are two stunning ceremonial items from Knossos. In Room X, look for the extraordinary boar's helmet and gold-handled swords.

Rooms XI and XII highlight settlements, sanctuaries and graves of the Late Bronze Age. The remarkable sarcophagus from Agia Triada (Room XII) is presumed to be that of a ruler, given its honorific fresco-style scenes.

First-Floor Highlights

Room XIII showcases Minoan frescoes (1800 BC to 1350 BC), including Evans' famous (or infamous) recreations. Famous works include the Prince of the Lilies, the Ladies in Blue, the Cupbearer, La Parisienne and the Dolphin Fresco.

Rooms XV to XIX focus on the Geometric and Archaic periods (10th to 6th century BC), the transition to the Iron Age and formation of the first Greek cities.

Rooms XX to XXII move to the Classical, Hellenistic and Roman periods (5th to 4th century BC), where utensils, figurines, stunning mosaic floors and amphorae set the scene for the foundation of the autonomous Greek city-states, followed by civil wars and, finally, the Roman period.

Ground Floor (Part II)

Rooms XXVI and XXVII (7th to 4th century BC) house the sculpture collection.

Venetian cannon in Koules Fortress

◎ SIGHTS

Koules Fortress   Fortress

(Rocca al Mare; http://koules.efah.gr; Venetian
Harbour; adult/reduced €2/1; ⊗8am-8pm
May-Sep, to 4pm Nov-Apr) After six years of
restoration, Iraklio's symbol, the 16th-
century fortress called Rocca al Mare by
the Venetians, reopened in August 2016
with a brand-new exhibit. It tells the story
of the building, zeroes in on milestones in
city history and displays ancient amphorae, Venetian cannons and other finds
recovered from shipwrecks around Dia
island by Jacques Cousteau in 1976. The
presentation is insightful and atmospheric
thanks to muted light filtering in through
the old cannon holes.

Visits conclude on the rooftop with panoramic views over the sea and the city.

Historical Museum
of Crete   Museum

(www.historical-museum.gr; Sofokli Venizelou
27; adult/reduced €5/3; ⊗9am-5pm Mon-Sat,
10.30am-3pm Sun Apr-Oct, 9am-3.30pm Mon-
Sat, 10.30am-3.30pm Sun Nov-Mar) If you're
wondering what Crete's been up to for the
past, say, 1700 years, a spin around this
engagingly curated museum is in order.
Exhibits hopscotch from the Byzantine to
the Venetian and Turkish periods, culminating with WWII. Quality English labelling,
interactive stations throughout and audio
guides (€3) in five languages greatly
enhance the experience.

The Venetian era gets special emphasis
and even a huge model of the city circa
1650 prior to the Turkish occupation.
Start in the introductory room, which
charts the major phases of history
through maps, books, artefacts and images. First-floor highlights include the only
two **El Greco paintings** in Crete (1569's
The Baptism of Christ and 1570's *View of
Mt Sinai and the Monastery of St Catherine*), 13th- and 14th-century frescoes,
exquisite Venetian gold jewellery and em-
broidered vestments. A historical exhibit
charts Crete's road to independence from
the Turks in the early 20th century. The
most interesting rooms on the 2nd floor
are the recreated study of Cretan-born
author **Nikos Kazantzakis** and those

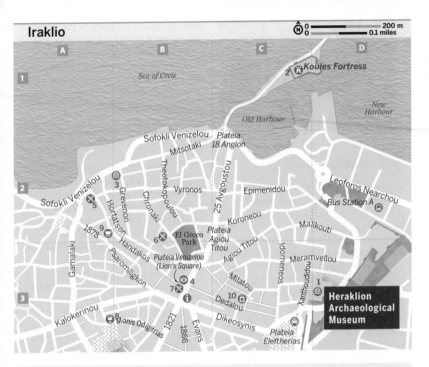

Iraklio

dramatically detailing aspects of the WWII **Battle of Crete** in 1941, including the Cretan resistance and the role of the Allied Secret Service. The top floor features an outstanding **folklore collection**.

Morosini Fountain   Fountain
(Lion Fountain; Plateia Venizelou) Four water-spouting lions make up this charming fountain, which is the most beloved Venetian vestige around town. Built in 1628 by Francesco Morosini, it once supplied Iraklio with fresh water. Flanked by bustling cafes and fast-food joints, it's a fun spot to spend an hour resting and people-watching.

◉ SHOPPING

Iraklio has some good shopping along 25 Avgostou, Dedalou and Handakos. The side streets and the main thoroughfare Kalokerinou have mostly shops catering to local needs.

Iraklio Market

An Iraklio institution, if slightly touristy these days, this busy narrow **market** (Odus 1866; ⊙hours vary) along Odos 1866 (1866 St) is one of the best in Crete and has everything you need to put together a delicious picnic. Stock up on the freshest fruit and vegetables, creamy cheeses, honey, succulent olives, fresh breads and whatever else grabs your fancy. There are also plenty of other stalls selling pungent herbs, leather goods, hats, jewellery and some souvenirs. Cap off a spree with a coffee at one of the quaint *kafeneia* (coffee houses).

Fruit and vegetable stall in Iraklio Market
EFESENKO/SHUTTERSTOCK ©

Aerakis Music   Music
(☏2810 225758; www.aerakis.net; Koraï Sq 14; ⊙9am-9pm Mon-Fri, to 5pm Sat) An Iraklio landmark since 1974, this little shop stocks an expertly curated selection of Cretan and Greek music, from old and rare recordings to the latest releases, many on its own record labels, Cretan Musical Workshop and Seistron.

There's also a small selection of musical instruments, books and Cretan products like knives and woven bags. All can also be ordered online.

✖ EATING
Phyllo Sofies   Cafe €
(www.phyllosophies.gr; Plateia Venizelou 33; mains €3.50-12.50; ⊙6am-midnight; 🛜) With

tables sprawling out towards the Morosini Fountain, this is a great place to sample *bougatsa* (creamy semolina pudding wrapped in a pastry envelope and sprinkled with cinnamon and sugar). The less-sweet version is made with *myzithra* (sheep's-milk cheese).

Peskesi   Cretan €€
(☏2810 288887; www.peskesicrete.gr; Kapetan Haralampi 6-8; mains €9-14; ⊙1pm-2am; 🛜🖉)
🖉 This foodie hotspot oozes rustic sophistication from every nook and cranny of its maze of stone rooms lidded by wood-beam ceilings. Chefs use heirloom produce and organic meats and olive oils from their own farm to revive ancient recipes in slow-cooked progressive ways. Killer dish: *kreokakavos,* a Minoan roast pork. The all-Cretan wine list is tops, too.

It's located in a tiny lane off the northwest corner of El Greco Park. Book ahead – this is Irakilo's best.

Parasties   Greek €€
(☏2810 225009; www.parastiescrete.gr; Handakos 81; mains €9-43; ⊙noon-1am; 🛜)
Parasties' owner Haris is genuine about serving great-quality local produce and top Cretan wines. And his passion shows in his gourmet menu of inventively updated traditional fare, including a daily special. Grab a seat under an annex with a bar, in the roomy dining area or on the side patio with sea views.

Decor is stylish and you can watch the chef toss her snails and other delights in the open kitchen.

🍷 DRINKING & NIGHTLIFE
Utopia   Cafe
(www.facebook.com/OutopiaCafeBeerOutopia; Handakos 51; ⊙9am-2am; 🛜) The Aztecs called it the 'elixir of the gods' and if you too worship at the cocoa altar, make a beeline to this been-here-forever cafe for the best hot chocolate in town (14 varieties, none of which are translated – go for hazelnut praline). Add a side of decadence

Peskesi

with an order of ice cream or delectable pastry or skip the sweet stuff altogether and order from the extensive beer menu.

Miniatoura
Bar

(www.facebook.com/miniatoura.cafe; 11 Monis Odigitrias; drinks from €4; ☻7am-2pm; 🛜) This cosy spot serves serious Brazilian- and Indian-sourced espresso out of its Italian-made La Marzocco machine and offers a shaded patio across the street from the Museum of Christian Art and Agios Minas Cathedral.

❶ ORIENTATION

Iraklio's main sights are wedged within the historic town, hemmed in by the waterfront and the old city walls. Many of the finest buildings line up along the main thoroughfare, 25 Avgoustou, which skirts the lovely central square, Plateia Venizelou (also called Lion Sq after its landmark fountain). East of here, Koraï is the hub of

Iraklio's cafe scene, which leads towards the vast Plateia Eleftherias with the Heraklion Archaeological Museum nearby.

❶ INFORMATION

Tourist Info Point (📞2813 409777; www. heraklion.gr; Plateia Venizelou; ☻8.30am-2.30pm Mon-Fri)

❶ GETTING AROUND

Much of the historic town has been pedestrianised and is thus eminently walkable. For longer journeys there are small taxi stands all over town; the main ones are at the Regional Bus Station, on Plateia Eleftherias and at the northern end of 25 Avgoustou.

City bus 2 to Knossos leaves from near the Regional Bus Station (note: this is on the site of the old long-distance bus station; if there's confusion, local buses are blue and white).

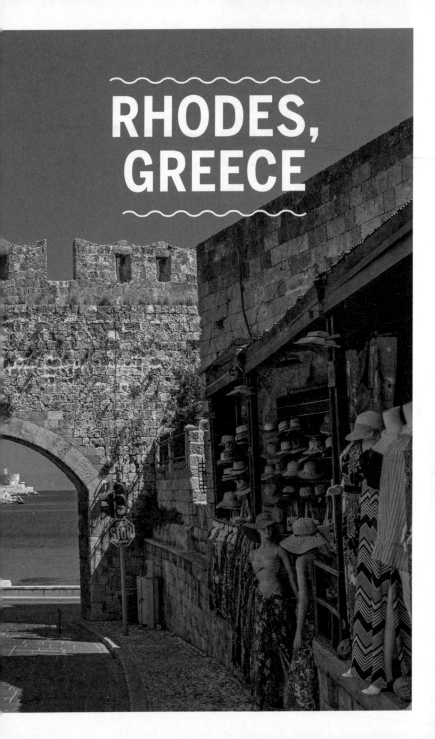

RHODES, GREECE

Rhodes at a Glance...

By far the largest and historically the most important of the Dodecanese islands, Rhodes (ro-dos) abounds in beaches, wooded valleys and ancient history. Whether you arrive in search of buzzing nightlife, languid sun worshipping, diving in crystal-clear waters or to embark on a culture-vulture journey through past civilisations, it's all here. The atmospheric Old Town of Rhodes is a maze of cobbled streets that will spirit you back to the days of the Byzantine Empire and beyond. Further south is the picture-perfect town of Lindos, a soul-warming vista of sugar-cube houses spilling down to a turquoise bay.

With One Day in Port

○ Start your day with a trip to Lindos to see the **Acropolis** (p428) before returning to Rhodes Town.

○ Enjoy local cuisine at **Taverna Kostas** (p431) and then spend the afternoon exploring the Old Town (p426).

○ Top the day off by visiting the **Archaeological Museum** (p430) and the **Palace of the Grand Master** (p430).

Best Places For...

Greek food Taverna Kostas (p431)

Baklava Old Town Corner Bakery (p431)

Seafood Meltemi (p434)

Souvenirs Rodoscope Creative Gallery (p431)

Ancient history Archaeological Museum (p430)

Rhodes Old Town Map (p432)

Getting from the Port

Cruise ships dock in the **Rhodes' Tourist Harbour** at the northern tip of the island.

From here, it's a 10-minute walk to the Old Town, which is best navigated on foot. Taxis can take you from the port to the new town, and elsewhere on the island.

Fast Facts

Currency Euro (€)

Language Greek

Money You'll find plenty of ATMs throughout Rhodes Town, including next door to the Old Town tourist office and on Plateia Kypriou in the new town.

Visas Generally not required for stays of up to 90 days; however, travellers from some nations may require a visa, so double-check with the Greek embassy.

Wi-fi Free wi-fi is available in many cafes and some restaurants.

Old Town street and Mosque of Süleyman

Rhodes Old Town

Getting lost in Rhodes' Old Town is a must. A glorious mixture of Byzantine, Turkish and Italian architecture, erected atop far more ancient and largely unidentifiable remains, the Old Town is a world of its own. Officially consisting of three separate sections, casual visitors seldom notice the transition from one to the next.

Great For...

☑ Don't Miss

The magnificent Palace of the Grand Master (p430) in the northwestern corner of the Knights' Quarter.

Knights' Quarter

The Knights of St John, essentially an occupying army during the 14th and 15th centuries, transformed the northern segment of the Old Town into what is known today as the Knights' Quarter. The Knights took care to protect themselves from the local population as well as potential invaders, erecting mighty fortress-like mansions as well as a fortified palace.

Wander up the **Street of the Knights** (Ippoton; ⊙24hr), once home to the Knights themselves. They were divided into seven 'tongues' or languages, according to their place of origin – England, France, Germany, Italy, Aragon, Auvergne and Provence – and each was responsible for protecting a section of the bastion.

At the eastern end of the Street of the Knights is the 1519 **Inn of the Order of the**

Knights' Quarter

NEMO1963/SHUTTERSTOCK ©

Explore Ashore

The Old Town is a 10-minute walk from the port. Taxis cannot access most of the largely pedestrianised Old Town, so you'll be dropped at the gate nearest your destination. Allow at least half a day to take in the highlights.

★ Top Tip

There's no public access to the ramparts that encircle the Old Town, but you can descend into the moat that separates the inner and outer walls, which are now filled with lush gardens.

May-Oct) **FREE**. Founded in 1794 by Ahmed Hasuf, it houses a small number of Persian and Arabic manuscripts and a collection of Qurans handwritten on parchment.

Jewish Quarter

With its narrow streets, the ghostly quiet Jewish Quarter is often overlooked, but as recently as the 1920s there was a population of 4000 living here. Built in 1577, **Kahal Shalom Synagogue** (Polydorou 5; ☺10am-3pm Sun-Fri Apr-Oct) is Greece's oldest synagogue. Exhibits in the **Jewish Synagogue Museum** (☎22410 22364; www.rhodesjewishmuseum.org; Dosiadou; ☺10am-3pm Sun-Fri Apr-Oct) **FREE** include early-20th-century photos, intricately decorated documents and displays about the 1673 Jews deported from Rhodes to Auschwitz in 1944, of whom only 151 survived.

Tongue of Italy (Ippoton). Further along is the **Inn of France**, the most ornate and distinctive of the inns. Across the alleyway is the **Inn of Provence**, with four coats of arms forming the shape of a cross, and opposite is the **Inn of Spain**. Near the end of the avenue, St John of the Collachio was originally a knights' church with an underground passage linking it to the palace across the road.

Hora

Bearing traces of its Ottoman past is the **Hora** (Turkish Quarter), the tangle of cobbled alleyways otherwise known as the Turkish Quarter. During Turkish times, churches were converted to mosques, the most important of which is the colourful, pink-domed **Mosque of Süleyman** (Sokratous). Opposite is the 18th-century **Muslim Library** (Sokratous; ☺9.30am-3pm Mon-Sat

Main Beach and Acropolis

Acropolis of Lindos

Your first glimpse of the towering Acropolis on the cypress-silvered hill is guaranteed to steal your breath away, but at the top you'll find one of the finest views in Greece.

Great For...

☑ **Don't Miss**

The spectacular Temple to Athena Lindia.

The Acropolis

A steep footpath climbs the 116m-high rock above Lindos to reach the beautifully preserved Acropolis. First walled in the 6th century BC, the clifftop is now enclosed by battlements constructed by the Knights of St John. Once within, you're confronted by stunning ancient remains that include a **Temple to Athena Lindia** and a 20-columned **Hellenistic stoa**. Silhouetted against the deep blue sky, the stark white columns are dazzling, while the long-range coastal views are out of this world.

Be sure to pack a hat and some water, as there's no shade at the top, and take care to protect young kids from the many dangerous drop-offs. Donkey rides to the Acropolis from the village entrance only spare you around three minutes of exposed

Remains of the Acropolis

MARCELLO LANDOLFI/SHUTTERSTOCK ©

Explore Ashore

Buses to and from Rhodes' **Eastern Bus Terminal** (☏22410 27706; www. ktelrodou.gr) run every 1½ hours (€5.50). Alternatively, there a boats offering day trips to Lindos at Mandraki Harbour. A taxi will take around 50 minutes from the port. Allow an hour or two to explore the Acropolis; longer if you're also visiting the town.

ⓘ Need to Know

☏22413 65200; adult/concession/child €12/6/free; ⊙8am-7.40pm Tue-Fri, 8am-3pm Sat-Mon Apr-Oct, 8.30am-3pm Tue-Sun Nov-Mar

walking on the hillside, and you should note that animal-rights groups urge people to consider the treatment of the donkeys before deciding to take a ride.

Lindos

Lindos has been enjoying its wonderful setting for 4000 years, since the Dorians founded the first settlement at this excellent harbour and vantage point. Since then, it has been successively overlaid with Byzantine, Frankish and Turkish structures, the remains of which can be glimpsed all around.

Two magnificent beaches line the crescent harbour that curves directly below the village. The larger, logically known as **Main Beach**, is a perfect swimming spot for kids – sandy with shallow water. Follow a path north to the western tip of the bay to

reach the smaller, taverna-fringed **Pallas Beach**. Don't swim near the jetty here, which is home to sea urchins, but if it gets too crowded you can swim from the rocks beyond.

Ten minutes' walk from town on the other, western, side of the Acropolis, sheltered **St Paul's Bay** is similarly caressed by turquoise waters.

Set in a former sea captain's residence, **Kalypso** (☏22440 32135; www.kalypsolindos. com; mains €13; ⊙10am-midnight; ❄🐾) is perfect for lunch. Choose from seating on the roof terrace or inside. Sea bass, octopus, *makarounes* (homemade pasta served with fresh onions and melted local cheese) and grilled lamb chops are but a few of the delights. Try the 'Kalypso bread' with feta and tomato.

 Acropolis of Rhodes

The site of the ancient Hellenistic city of Rhodes, now known as the **Acropolis of Rhodes** (⊘24hr) FREE, stretches up the slopes of Monte Smith, 2km southwest of the Old Town. Restored structures include a tree-lined stadium from the 2nd century BC and the adjacent theatre, originally used for lectures by the Rhodes School of Rhetoric. Steps climb from there to the Temple of Pythian Apollo. Get here on city bus 5, or via a stiff half-hour hike.

Theatre of the Acropolis of Rhodes
VIVOOO/SHUTTERSTOCK ©

◉ SIGHTS

Archaeological Museum　　Museum

(☏22413 65200; Plateia Mousiou; adult/child €8/free; ⊘8am-8pm daily Apr-Oct, to 3pm Tue-Sun Nov-Mar) By far the best museum in the Dodecanese, this airy 15th-century former Knights' Hospital extends from its main building out into the beautiful gardens. Room after room holds magnificently preserved ancient treasures, excavated from all over the island and ranging across 7000 years. Highlights include the exquisite 'Aphrodite Bathing' marble statue from the 1st century BC, a pavilion displaying wall-mounted mosaics, and a reconstructed burial site from 1700 BC that held not only a helmeted warrior but also his horse.

Palace of the
Grand Master　　Historic Building

(☏22410 23359, 22413 65270; €6; ⊘8am-8pm Apr-Oct, to 3pm Nov-Mar) From the outside, the magnificent Palace of the Grand Master looks much as it did when erected by the Knights Hospitaller during the 14th century. During the 19th century, however, it was devastated by an explosion, so the interior as you see it today is an Italian reconstruction, completed in the '18th year of the Fascist Era' (1940). The dreary magisterial chambers upstairs hold haphazard looted artworks, so the most interesting section is the exhibit on ancient Rhodes downstairs.

Roloi Clock Tower　　Landmark

(Orfeos 1; €5; ⊘9am-midnight May-Oct) The best panoramic view of Rhodes is found at the top of this stunning 7th-century clock tower. Damaged by an explosion in 1856, it was rebuilt with baroque elements by Feht Pasha. The entrance fee includes one free drink on the attractive terrace below. The best times to come are early morning or late in the afternoon.

Modern Greek
Art Museum　　Gallery

(☏22410 43780; www.mgamuseum.gr; Plateia Haritou; adult/child €3/free; ⊘8am-2pm Tue-Sat, 5-8pm Fri) The main gallery of the Modern Greek Art Museum, near the New Town's northern tip, holds paintings, engravings and sculptures by Greece's greatest 20th-century artists, including Yannis Gaitis, Spiros Vasiliou and Vaso Katraki. The museum's other three sites – the Nestoridi Building and the Centre of Modern Art, both in the New Town, and the original Art Gallery, in the Old Town – are currently closed because of a lack of available funding.

⊙ TOURS

Rhodes Segway Tours　　History

(☏6983245246, 22411 12409; www.rhodes segwaytours.com; Miltiadou 8, Old Town; €59; ⊘9am-8pm;) ⚑ A sightseeing experience unlike any other, this is a brilliant way to spare your energy and see more of the Old Town. It's a little bit sci-fi, rolling soundlessly past ancient buildings on your Segway with your expert guide chatting away as if it

Archaeological Museum

was perfectly normal! Tours last two hours. Training provided. Helmets required! Also does night tours (€85).

🏠 SHOPPING

Rodoscope
Creative Gallery   Ceramics
(📞6972202138; Ippodamou 39; ⊙10am-8pm)
This tasteful boutique has a collection of one-off bracelets, beach-bum-chic jewellery, driftwood sculpture, handmade T-shirts and fine ceramics. Only the work of Rhodian artists features here. Out back there's a peaceful courtyard to admire your gifts over a cool drink from the cafe. Ask about the courses run here.

Natura Greca   Cosmetics
(📞22410 77380; www.naturagreca.com; Sokratous 78-80; ⊙9am-11pm) 🍃 A breath of organic in the artificial tittle tattle of Sokratous, this shop features natural products from around Greece, including: olive, almond and argon oil beauty products, herbs, jams, honey, sponges, soaps and hand-painted icons, plus olive wood chopping boards and bowls.

So Greek   Food & Drinks
(📞22410 36870; https://sogreek.business.site; Ipodamou; ⊙9am-11pm Mon-Sat) 🍃 The perfect pit stop for choice gifts, So Greek sells nicely packaged Greek wine, olive oil and a wide selection of homemade honey, natural cosmetics and herbs and spices.

🍴 EATING

Taverna Kostas   Greek €
(📞22410 26217; Pythagora 62; mains €7-10; ⊙10am-late; ❄) Run by grandfather Kostas, this is not only the friendliest and best-value restaurant in the Old Town but also one of the best. Forget the bare lime-washed walls and simple decor; eating here is like taking a place at the table of a friend – indeed, regulars set their own places! Serves succulent octopus salad, calamari and sea bream.

Old Town Corner Bakery   Bakery €
(📞22410 38494; Omirou 88; snacks €2-6; ⊙7am-7pm Mon-Sat, 8am-3pm Sun; 🛜) With jazz and aromatic arabica coffee drifting

Rhodes Old Town

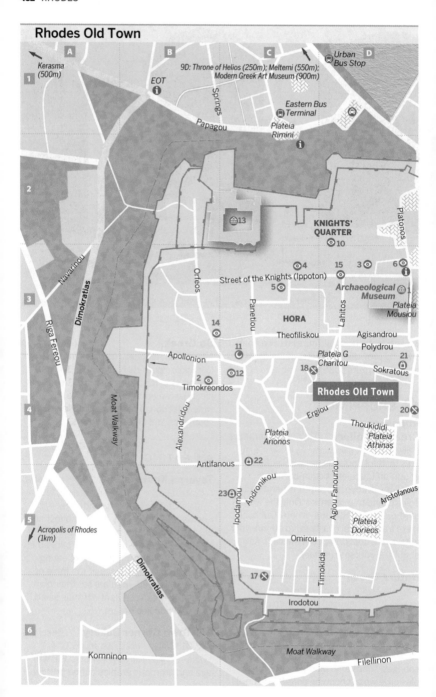

Kerasma
(500m)

9D: Throne of Helios (250m); Meltemi (550m);
Modern Greek Art Museum (900m)

Urban
Bus Stop

EOT

Springs

Papagou

Eastern Bus
Terminal

Plateia
Rimini

Platonos

🏛13

KNIGHTS'
QUARTER
⦿10

Navarinou

Dimokratias

Riga Fereou

Orfeos

Street of the Knights (Ippoton)

⦿4   15   3⦿   6⦿

5⦿

Archaeological
Museum 🏛

Panetiou

Lahitos

HORA

Plateia
Mousiou

14
⦿

Theofiliskou

Agisandrou

Polydrou

11
Ⓒ

Apollonion

Plateia G
Charitou

21

Moat Walkway

2⦿   ⦿12

Timokreondos

18

Sokratous

Rhodes Old Town

Alexandridou

Ergiou

20

Plateia
Arionos

Thoukididi
Plateia
Athinas

Antifanous

🔒22

Androniko

Aristofanous

Acropolis of Rhodes
(1km)

23🔒

Ipodamou

Agiou Fanouriou

Plateia
Dorieos

Omirou

Timokida

17

Irodotou

Dimokratias

Komninon

Moat Walkway

Filellinon

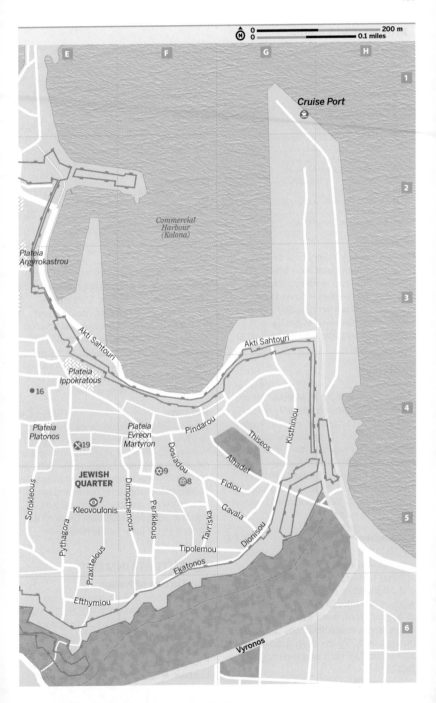

0   200 m
0   0.1 miles

E   F   G   H

Cruise Port

Commercial Harbour (Kolona)

Plateia Argyrokastrou

Akti Sahtouri

Plateia Ippokratous

Akti Sahtouri

● 16

Plateia Platonos

Plateia Evreon Martyron

Pindarou

Thiseos

Kisthiniou

⊗19

JEWISH QUARTER

Dosiadou

⊛9

🏛8

Alhadef

Fidiou

⊚7
Kleovoulonis

Sofokleous

Dimosthenous

Perikleous

Tavriska

Gavala

Dionisou

Pythagora

Praxitelous

Tipolemou

Ekatonos

Efthymiou

Vyronos

Rhodes Old Town

through this tiny bakery cafe and out onto the street where there are a few stools, this is an Old Town residents' favourite. Has amazing pastries – dawn-fresh croissants sell out very quickly – club sandwiches, baklava (filo pastry with nuts and honey), apple pie and a host of healthy juices.

To Marouli   Greek €

(☏22413 04394; Platonos 22; mains €11-13; ☺noon-10pm; ※🐾🌿) 🌿 'Marouli' means lettuce, and in this veggie-only restaurant, that's exactly what you can expect: plenty of greens. The pasta, which comes from Italy, is a safe bet (delicious; the owner is Italian). But then again, it's hard to choose between the likes of vegan Thai pineapple and fried rice, gnocchi with saffron, or mushroom and zucchini strudel with salad.

Petaladika   Greek €€

(☏22410 27319;Menakleous 8;mains €8-15; noon-late) Petaladika might look like just another tourist trap, tucked into a corner just off the main drag, but with its fresh, white, wood interior and chic tables and chairs out front, it's a hot favourite with locals, and a mainstay of the Old Town dining scene. Try the deep-fried baby squid, zucchini balls and freshly grilled fish.

Meltemi   Taverna €€

(☏22410 30480; Kountourioti 8; mains €10-15; ☺noon-late; P※🌿🍽) From the outside, Meltemi is unspectacular. Step into its nautically themed interior, however, and try to resist its seafood treasures: octopus, jumbo prawns, lobster, huge portions of calamari as well as feisty salads, all delivered with gusto. Add to this wide-screen sea views and you can see why it's one of best seafront spots in the New Town.

Kerasma   Greek €€

(☏22413 02410; www.kerasmarestaurant.com; George Leontos 4-6; mains €15; ☺noon-11.30pm Mon-Sat, 6-11.30pm Sun; ※🌿) This contemporary restaurant has an open, stylish setting and offers Greek fusion food with dishes like grilled octopus dipped in honey and beef fillet with purple gnocchi. There's also an impressive cellar of 60 different Greek wines. An injection of taste for the New Town.

🌟 ENTERTAINMENT

9D: Throne of Helios   Film

(☏22410 76850; www.throneofhelios.com; Martiou 2; adult/child €13/9; ☺11am-7pm Mon-Fri, to 10pm Sat & Sun; 🌿🍽) Journey back to the birth of Rhodes in this 3D experience. History is brought to life with the aid of hydraulic chairs, falling rain, snow and bubbles. Amazing visuals recreate the

Roloi Clock Tower (p430)

Colossus of Rhodes' construction, the citadel's creation under the Knights of St John, and more – up to the present day.

There is an additional short film after the main film (optional and extra) that's more suited to kids with its Disney-style 3D cartoon.

INFORMATION

EOT (Greek Tourist Information Office; ✆22410 44335; www.ando.gr/eot; cnr Makariou & Papagou; ⊙8.30am-2.45pm Mon-Fri) National tourism information, with brochures, maps and transport details.

Rhodes Tourism Office – New Town (✆22410 35495; www.rhodes.gr; Plateia Rimini; ⊙7.30am-3pm Mon-Fri) Conveniently poised between Mandraki Harbour and the Old Town; efficiently run with lots of free brochures and helpful staff.

Rhodes Tourism Office – Old Town (✆22410 35945; www.rhodes.gr; cnr Platonos & Ippoton; ⊙7am-3pm Mon-Fri) In an ancient building at the foot of the Street of the Knights, this helpful office supplies excellent street maps, leaflets and brochures.

GETTING AROUND

BICYCLE

Bicycles are available for rent from **Margaritis** (✆22410 37420; www.margaritisrentals.gr; l Kazouli St 17; ⊙24hr) in the New Town.

BUS

In Rhodes Town, local buses leave from the **urban bus stop** (Mandraki) on Mandraki Harbour. Bus 11 makes a circuit around the coast, up past the aquarium and on to the Acropolis. Bus 2 goes to Analipsi, bus 3 to Rodini, bus 4 to Agios Dimitrios and bus 5 to the Acropolis. Buy tickets on-board.

TAXI

Rhodes Town's main taxi rank is east of Plateia Rimini, on the northern edge of the Old Town. There are two zones on the island for taxi meters: zone one is Rhodes Town and zone two (for which rates are slightly higher) is everywhere else. Set taxi fares are posted at the rank.

You can also phone for a **taxi** (✆in Rhodes Town 22410 69800, outside Rhodes Town 22410 69600; www.rhodes-taxi.gr) or **disabled-accessible taxi** (✆22410 77079).

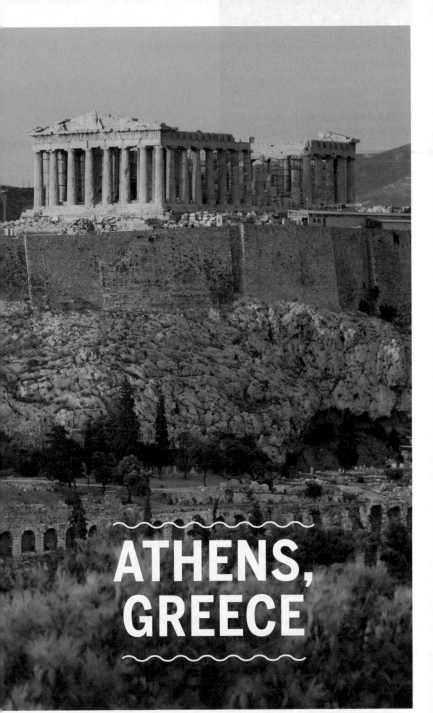

ATHENS,
GREECE

In This Chapter

Athens at a Glance...

With equal measures of grunge and grace, Athens (Αθήνα) is a heady mix of history and edginess. Cultural and social life plays out amid, around and within ancient landmarks, and the magnificent Acropolis towers over all. This temple city, built in the 5th century BC, serves as a daily reminder to Greeks of their heritage and the city's many transformations. There is crackling energy in galleries, political debates and street art. Go with an open mind, and you'll be rewarded.

With One Day in Port

○ Start by experiencing the **Acropolis** (p440), the most important ancient site in the Western world (allow at least half a day).

○ Your next stop is the **National Archaeological Museum** (p446), the highlights of which can be seen in a few hours of exploration. The **Temple of Olympian Zeus** (p450) is hard to miss. If you're pressed for time, you can see most of the temple (and Hadrian's Arch) from outside the fence.

○ Cap off your day by wandering around monument-packed **central Athens**.

Best Places For...

Local cuisine Kalderimi (p459)

Ice cream Cremino (p458)

Coffee Little Kook (p459)

Gourmet food Pantopoleion (p458)

Market Monastiraki Flea Market (p458)

Gifts and souvenirs Forget Me Not (p455)

Bar with a view Couleur Locale (p459)

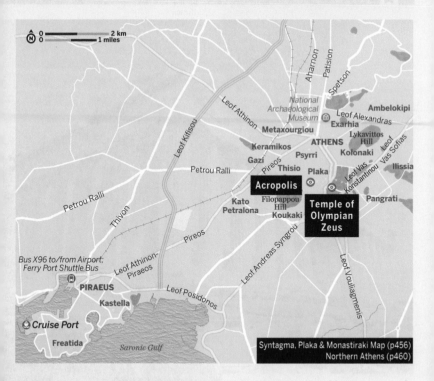

Syntagma, Plaka & Monastiraki Map (p456)
Northern Athens (p460)

Getting from the Port

Piraeus port, 10km southwest of Athens city centre, can be chaotic, but fortunately there is a free in-port shuttle bus.

The metro is the best and cheapest way to get into the city centre (€1.40 per ticket, 25 minutes). Either walk (about 20 minutes) or catch the shuttle to Piraeus metro station (green line). Taxis (€20) take around 25 minutes to the city centre. In summer, a port-to-city express bus is another option.

Fast Facts

Currency Euro (€)

Language Greek

Money There are plenty of ATMs in Athens, and credit and debit cards are widely accepted.

Visas Citizens of Australia, New Zealand, Canada, the UK and the US do not need a visa to enter Greece for stays up to three months (90 days).

Wi-fi Free wireless hotspots are at Syntagma, Thisio, Gazi and the port of Piraeus.

Acropolis

Crowned by the Parthenon, the Acropolis is visible from almost everywhere in Athens. Its marble gleams white in the midday sun and takes on a honey hue as the sun sinks. A glimpse of this magnificent sight cannot fail to exalt your spirit.

Great For...

☑ Don't Miss

The superb views from the floor-to-ceiling windows in the Acropolis Museum (p443).

Building the Acropolis

The Acropolis was first inhabited in Neolithic times (4000–3000 BC). The earliest temples were built during the Mycenaean era, in homage to the goddess Athena. People lived on the Acropolis until the late 6th century BC, but in 510 BC the Delphic oracle declared it the sole province of the gods.

After all the buildings on the Acropolis were reduced to ashes by the Persians on the eve of the Battle of Salamis (480 BC), Pericles set about his ambitious rebuilding program. He transformed the Acropolis into a city of temples, which has come to be regarded as the zenith of Classical Greece. He spared no expense – only the best materials, architects, sculptors and artists were good enough for a city dedicated to the cult of Athena. It was a showcase of lavishly coloured buildings and gargantuan

Porch of the Caryatids (p445)

DAVID BUFFINGTON/GETTY IMAGES ©

⚓ Explore Ashore

Allow at least half a day to experience the Acropolis site; a little longer if you plan to visit the Acropolis Museum. Catch the in-port shuttle to Piraeus station, then take the green line to Thissio station (15 to 20 minutes). From here it's a 10-minute scenic, uphill walk to the Acropolis' western entrance.

❶ Need to Know

Map p456; ☎210 321 4172; http://odysseus. culture.gr; adult/concession/child €20/10/ free; ⊗8am-8pm May-Sep, reduced hours in winter, last entry 30min before closing; ⓂAkropoli

statues, some of bronze, others of marble plated with gold and encrusted with precious stones.

Preserving the Site

Foreign occupation, inept renovations, visitors' footsteps, earthquakes and, more recently, acid rain and pollution have all taken their toll on the surviving monuments. In a devastating sequence of events in 1687, the Venetians opened fire on the Acropolis, attacking the Turks, who had been storing gunpowder there, and causing an explosion in the Parthenon that damaged all of the buildings. Another devastating blow was suffered in 1801, when Thomas Bruse, Earl of Elgin, spirited away a portion of the Parthenon frieze; it's still on display in London's British Museum, despite Greece's ongoing campaign for its return.

In 1987 the Acropolis became a World Heritage–listed site. Major restoration programs are ongoing. Most of the original sculptures and friezes have been moved to the Acropolis Museum, so what you see now on the hill are replicas.

Parthenon

The **Parthenon** (Map p456) is the monument that more than any other epitomises the glory of ancient Greece. It is dedicated to Athena Parthenos, the goddess embodying the power and prestige of the city. Designed by Iktinos and Kallicrates to be the pre-eminent monument of the Acropolis, and completed in time for the Great Panathenaic Festival of 438 BC, it is the largest Doric temple ever constructed in Greece, and the only one built completely of Pentelic marble (apart from the wood in its roof).

Temple of Athena Nike

Recently restored, this exquisitely proportioned tiny Pentelic marble **temple** (Map p456) was designed by Kallicrates and built around 425 BC. The internal cella housed a wooden statue of Athena as Victory (Nike), and the exterior friezes illustrated scenes from mythology, the Battle of Plataea (479 BC) and Athenians fighting Boeotians and Persians. Parts of the frieze are in the Acropolis Museum, as are some relief sculptures, including the beautiful depiction of Athena Nike fastening her sandal.

Odeon of Herodes Atticus

The path continues west from the Asclepion to the magnificent **Odeon of Herodes Atticus** (Herodeon; Map p456; ☎210 324 1807;

Ⓜ Akropoli), known as the Herodion. It was built in AD 161 by wealthy Roman Herodes Atticus in memory of his wife, Regilla. The theatre was excavated in 1857–58 and completely restored between 1950 and 1961. Performances of drama, music and dance are held here during the **Athens & Epidaurus Festival** (Hellenic Festival; ☎210 928 2900; www.greekfestival.gr; ☉ Jun-Aug).

Theatre of Dionysos

Originally, a 6th-century-BC timber theatre was built here, on the site of the Festival of the Great Dionysia. During Athens' golden age, the theatre hosted productions of the works of Aeschylus, Sophocles, Euripides and Aristophanes. Reconstructed in stone and marble between 342 and 326 BC, the **theatre** (Map p456; Dionysiou Areopagitou) held 17,000 spectators (spread over 64

Acropolis Museum

tiers, of which only about 20 survive) and an altar to Dionysos in the orchestra pit.

Propylaia

The monumental entrance to the Acropolis, the **Propylaia** (Map p456) was built by Mnesicles between 437 BC and 432 BC and consists of a central hall with two wings on either side. In ancient times its five gates were the only entrances to the 'upper city'. The middle gate opens onto the Panathenaic Way. The ceiling of the central hall

---

> **✕ Take a Break**
>
> Swing into **Dionysos** (Map p456; ☎ 210 923 1936; www.dionysoszonars.gr; Rovertou Galli 43, Makrygianni; restaurant mains €16.50-98; ☺ restaurant noon-1am, cafe 8am-1am; Ⓜ Akropoli) for coffee and excellent views of the monument.

---

was painted with gold stars on a dark-blue background. The northern wing was used as a *pinakothiki* (art gallery).

Erechtheion

The **Erechtheion** (Map p456), completed around 406 BC, was a sanctuary built on the most sacred part of the Acropolis: the spot where Poseidon struck the ground with his trident, and where Athena produced the olive tree. Named after Erechtheus, a mythical king of Athens, the temple housed the cults of Athena, Poseidon and Erechtheus. This supreme example of Ionic architecture was ingeniously built on several levels to compensate for the uneven bedrock.

Acropolis Museum

The grand **Acropolis Museum** (Map p456; ☎ 210 900 0900; www.theacropolismuseum.gr; Dionysiou Areopagitou 15, Makrygianni; adult/child €10/free; ☺ 8am-4pm Mon, to 8pm Tue-Sun, to 10pm Fri Apr-Oct, 9am-5pm Mon-Thu, to 10pm Fri, to 8pm Sat & Sun Nov-Mar; Ⓜ Akropoli) displays the surviving treasures from the temple hill, with emphasis on the Acropolis as it was in the 5th century BC, the apotheosis of Greece's artistic achievement. The museum showcases layers of history: glass floors expose subterranean ruins, and the Acropolis itself is visible through the floor-to-ceiling windows, so the masterpieces are always in context.

> **★ Top Tip**
>
> The ground on the site is uneven and can get slippery – this is not the site for heels or flip-flops.

The Acropolis

A WALKING TOUR

Cast your imagination back in time, two and a half millennia ago, and envision the majesty of the Acropolis. Its famed and hallowed monument, the Parthenon, dedicated to the goddess Athena, stood proudly over a small city, dwarfing the population with its graceful grandeur. In the Acropolis' heyday in the 5th century BC, pilgrims and priests worshipped at the temples illustrated here (most of which still stand in varying states of restoration). Many were painted brilliant colours and were abundantly adorned with sculptural masterpieces crafted from ivory, gold and semiprecious stones.

As you enter the site today, elevated on the right perches one of the Acropolis' best-restored buildings: the diminutive ❶ Temple of Athena Nike. Follow the Panathenaic Way through the Propylaia and up the slope towards the Parthenon – icon of the Western world. Its ❷ majestic columns sweep up to some of what were the finest carvings of their time: wrap-around ❸ pediments, metopes and a frieze. Stroll around the temple's exterior and take in the spectacular views over Athens and Piraeus below.

As you circle back to the centre of the site, you will encounter those renowned lovely ladies, the ❹ Caryatids of the Erechtheion. On the Erechtheion's northern face, the oft-forgotten ❺ Temple of Poseidon sits alongside ingenious ❻ Themistocles' Wall. Wander to the Erechtheion's western side to find Athena's gift to the city: ❼ the olive tree.

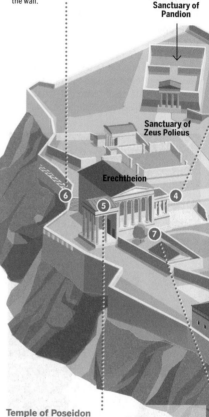

Themistocles' Wall
Crafty general Themistocles (524–459 BC) hastened to build a protective wall around the Acropolis and in so doing incorporated elements from archaic temples on the site. Look for the column drums built into the wall.

Sanctuary of Pandion

Sanctuary of Zeus Polieus

Erechtheion

Temple of Poseidon
Though he didn't win patronage of the city, Poseidon was worshipped on the northern side of the Erechtheion, which still bears the mark of his trident-strike. Imagine the finely decorated coffered porch painted in rich colours, as it was in the past.

ALEXTRAVELERPHOTOGRAPHER/GETTY IMAGES ©

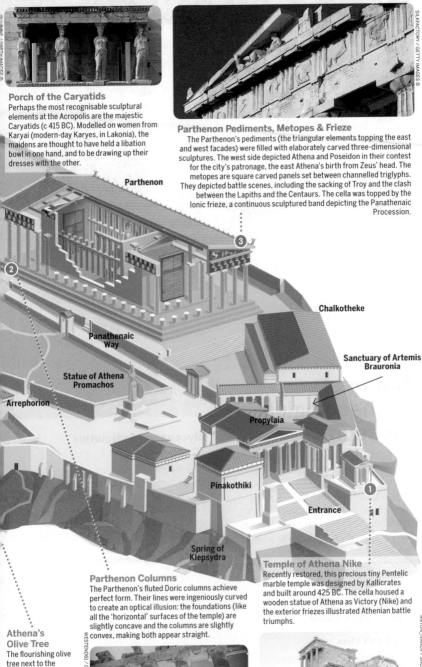

Porch of the Caryatids

Perhaps the most recognisable sculptural elements at the Acropolis are the majestic Caryatids (c 415 BC). Modelled on women from Karyai (modern-day Karyes, in Lakonia), the maidens are thought to have held a libation bowl in one hand, and to be drawing up their dresses with the other.

Parthenon Pediments, Metopes & Frieze

The Parthenon's pediments (the triangular elements topping the east and west facades) were filled with elaborately carved three-dimensional sculptures. The west side depicted Athena and Poseidon in their contest for the city's patronage, the east Athena's birth from Zeus' head. The metopes are square carved panels set between channelled triglyphs. They depicted battle scenes, including the sacking of Troy and the clash between the Lapiths and the Centaurs. The cella was topped by the Ionic frieze, a continuous sculptured band depicting the Panathenaic Procession.

Parthenon

Chalkotheke

Panathenaic Way

Statue of Athena Promachos

Sanctuary of Artemis Brauronia

Arrephorion

Propylaia

Pinakothiki

Entrance

Spring of Klepsydra

Temple of Athena Nike

Recently restored, this precious tiny Pentelic marble temple was designed by Kallicrates and built around 425 BC. The cella housed a wooden statue of Athena as Victory (Nike) and the exterior friezes illustrated Athenian battle triumphs.

Athena's Olive Tree

The flourishing olive tree next to the Erechtheion is meant to be the sacred tree that Athena produced to seize victory in the contest for Athens.

Parthenon Columns

The Parthenon's fluted Doric columns achieve perfect form. Their lines were ingeniously curved to create an optical illusion: the foundations (like all the 'horizontal' surfaces of the temple) are slightly concave and the columns are slightly convex, making both appear straight.

SILKFACTORY / GETTY IMAGES ©

WESTEND61 / GETTY IMAGES ©

ANTON_IVANOV / SHUTTERSTOCK ©

National Archaeological Museum

The National Archaeological Museum houses the world's finest collection of Greek antiquities. The enormous neoclassical building holds more than 10,000 pieces of sculpture, pottery, jewellery, frescoes and more. You likely won't see it all, but whatever you do see will be a treat.

Great For...

☑ Don't Miss

The Akrotiri Frescoes upstairs in Gallery 48.

Mycenaean Antiquities (Gallery 4)

Directly ahead as you enter the museum is the prehistoric collection, showcasing some of the most important pieces of Mycenaean, Neolithic and Cycladic art, many in solid gold. The fabulous collection of Mycenaean antiquities is the museum's tour de force.

Mask of Agamemnon

This great death mask of beaten gold is commonly known as the Mask of Agamemnon, the king who, according to legend, attacked Troy in the 12th century BC – but this is hardly certain. Heinrich Schliemann, the archaeologist who endeavoured to prove that Homer's epics were true tales, and not just myth, unearthed the mask at Mycenae in 1876. Since then, archaeologists have determined the surrounding grave

Marble figurine

⚓ Explore Ashore

The best way from the port is the metro. Walk (around 20 minutes) or catch the in-port shuttle to Piraeus station. Catch the green line to Viktoria station (around 25 minutes), from where it's a five- to 10-minute walk to the museum.

❶ Need to Know

Map p460; ☑213 214 4800; www.namuseum. gr; Patision 44, Exarhia; adult/child €10/free mid-Apr–Oct; €5/free Nov–mid-Apr; ⊙8am-8pm Wed-Mon, 12.30am-8pm Tue mid-Apr–Oct, reduced hours Nov–mid-Apr; ☐2, 3, 4, 5 or 11 to Polytechnio, Ⓜ Viktoria

items date from centuries earlier, and one researcher even asserts that Schliemann, a master of self-promotion, forged it completely.

Vaphio Cups

The exquisite Vaphio gold cups, with scenes of men taming wild bulls, are regarded as among the finest surviving examples of Mycenaean art. They were found in a tholos (Mycenaean tomb shaped like a beehive) at Vaphio, near Sparta.

Cycladic Collection (Gallery 6)

This room contains some of the superbly minimalist marble figurines of the 3rd and 2nd millennia BC that inspired modern artists such as Picasso. One splendid example measures 1.52m and dates from 2600 to 2300 BC.

Sounion Kouros (Gallery 8)

The galleries to the left of the entrance house the oldest and most significant pieces of the sculpture collection. Galleries 7 to 13 exhibit fine examples of Archaic *kouroi* (male statues) from the 7th century BC to 480 BC. The most interesting is the colossal 600 BC Sounion Kouros, which stood before the Temple of Poseidon at Sounio. Its style marks a transition point in art history, starting with the rigid lines of older Egyptian carving but also showing some of the lifelike qualities – including the so-called 'Archaic smile' – that the Greeks would perfect in later centuries.

Artemision Bronze (Gallery 15)

This room is dominated by the incredibly precise, just-larger-than-life bronze statue of Zeus or Poseidon (no one really knows which), excavated from the sea off Evia in

1928. The muscled figure, which dates from 460 BC, has an iconic bearded face and holds his arms outstretched, his right hand raised to throw what was once a lightning bolt (if Zeus) or trident (if Poseidon).

Varvakeion Athena (Gallery 20)

Admire the details on this statue of Athena, made in AD 200: the helmet topped with a sphinx and griffins, a Gorgon shield and the hand holding a small figure of winged Nike (missing its head). Now imagine it all more than 10 times larger and covered in gold – that was the legendary, now-lost colossal figure of Athena (11.5m tall) that the master sculptor Pheidias erected in front of the Parthenon in the 5th century BC. This daintier version is thought to be the best extant replica of that colossus.

Jockey of Artemision (Gallery 21)

This is another find from the shipwreck off Evia excavated in 1928. This delicately rendered bronze horse and rider dates from the 2nd century BC; only a few parts were found at first, and it was finally reassembled in 1972. Opposite the horse are several lesser-known but equally exquisite works, such as the statue of a demure nude Aphrodite struggling to hold her draped gown over herself.

Antikythera Shipwreck (Gallery 28)

Precious treasures discovered in 1900 by sponge divers off the island of Antikythera include the striking bronze Antikythera Youth, forged in the 4th century BC. His hand once held some spherical object, now

Gold jewellery from the Mycenaean Antiquities collection (p446)

lost. More mysterious is the Antikythera Mechanism, an elaborate clockwork device, now in fragments, apparently for calculating astronomical positions, as well as dates of eclipses and the Olympic games, among other events. Who made it, and when, is still unknown.

VIACHESLAV LOPATIN/SHUTTERSTOCK ©

Egyptian Galleries (Galleries 40 & 41)

Two rooms present the best of the museum's significant Egyptian collection, the only one in Greece. Dating from 5000 BC to the Roman conquest, artefacts include mummies, bronze figurines and beautifully evocative Roman-era painted portraits from caskets (so-called Fayum portraits).

Akrotiri Frescoes (Gallery 48)

Upstairs a room is devoted to the spectacular and incredibly old Minoan frescoes from a prehistoric settlement on Santorini (Thira). The frescoes were preserved when they were buried by a volcanic eruption in the late 16th century BC. The frescoes include Boxing Children and Spring, depicting red lilies and a pair of swallows kissing in mid-air. The gallery also has videos of the 1926 eruption and the Akrotiri excavation.

Pottery Collection (Gallery 55)

The superb pottery collection traces the development of pottery from the Bronze Age through the Protogeometric and Geometric periods, to the famous Attic blackfigured pottery (6th century BC), and red-figured pottery (late 5th to early 4th centuries BC). Other uniquely Athenian vessels are the Attic White Lekythoi, slender vases depicting scenes at tombs.

Panathenaic Amphorae (Gallery 56)

This room displays some of the ceramic vases presented to the winners of the Panathenaic Games. Each one contained oil from the sacred olive trees of Athens; victors might have received up to 140 of them. The vases are painted with scenes from the relevant sport and an armed Athena *promachos* (champion).

Temple of Olympian Zeus

You can't miss this marvel, smack in the centre of Athens. In terms of ground area, it is the largest temple in Greece. It was probably also one of the most drawn-out projects in history, begun in the 6th century BC and finished in AD 131.

Great For...

★ Top Tip

There is no shade: wear a hat and sunscreen and bring water.

Temple

Seven centuries after Peisistratos started, Hadrian finished the temple by placing a giant gold-and-ivory statue of Zeus inside. Then he matched it with an equally large one of himself. Maybe his pride jinxed it: the next century, the temple was destroyed when the Herulians (a Germanic tribe from near the Black Sea) sacked the city.

Columns

The temple was built with 104 Corinthian columns, each with a base diameter of 1.7m and standing 17m high. Only 15 remain, the rest having been repurposed over the centuries, so you'll have to squint to imagine the whole scope of the temple. The one fallen column was blown down in a gale in 1852.

Hadrian's Arch

COLORMAKER/SHUTTERSTOCK ©

Explore Ashore

The metro is the best (and cheapest) way to get here. Walk (around 20 minutes) or catch the in-port shuttle to Piraeus station. Take the green line to Omonia (about 20 minutes), then switch to the red line and travel to Akropoli (around five minutes). If you are rushed, you can see much of the temple from outside the gate.

ⓘ Need to Know

Olympieio; Map p456; ☏210 922 6330; http://odysseus.culture.gr; Leoforos Vasilissis Olgas; adult/student/child €6/3/free; ⊘8am-3pm Oct-Apr, to 8pm May-Sep; Ⓜ Akropoli, Syntagma

Original Temple

Hadrian's temple is built on the site of a smaller one (590–560 BC), also dedicated to the cult of Olympian Zeus. Look closely: its foundations can still be seen.

Hadrian's Arch

Just outside the temple fence, at the corner of Leoforos Vasilissis Olgas and Amalias, sits this lofty **monument** (Map p456; Ⓜ Akropoli, Syntagma) FREE, erected as thanks to Roman emperor Hadrian, probably just after the temple was consecrated. The inscriptions laud the new Roman era: the northwest frieze reads, 'This is Athens, the ancient city of Theseus', while the southeast frieze states, 'This is the city of Hadrian, and not of Theseus'.

Sanctuary of Pan

Outside the temple fence to the south, explorers can find a slip of the Ilissos River (elsewhere covered by pavement). Nearby is a rock-cut sanctuary to the god Pan, another Roman-era worship site. Look for it near a church at the corner of Ardittou and Athanasiou Diakou.

⊗ Take a Break

For a rest in shade and a light snack, head to the Zappeio Gardens' **Aegli Cafe** (☏210 336 9300; Zappeio Gardens; ⊘9am-midnight; Ⓜ Syntagma). Or walk up to Mets for a laid-back coffee at the **Odeon Cafe** (☏210 922 3414; Markou Mousourou 19, Mets; ⊘10am-2am Sun-Thu, to 3am Fri & Sat; Ⓜ Akropoli) and a spinach pie from the excellent bakery across the street.

Syntagma & Plaka to Monastiraki

Monument-packed central Athens is best explored on foot. The main civic hub – Plateia Syntagmatos – merges into the historic neighbourhoods, making for an atmospheric stroll.

Start Plateia Syntagmatos
Distance 2.5km
Duration Three hours

7 Monastiraki, a colourful, chaotic central square teeming with street vendors, leads to a shopper's or people-watcher's paradise: the **Monastiraki Flea Market** (p458).

6 Hadrian's Library (adult/child €4/free; 🕙8am-3pm) was once the most luxurious public building in the city, erected by the eponymous emperor around AD 132.

4 The 17th-century **Bath House of the Winds** (adult/child €2/free; 🕙8am-3pm Wed-Mon), a historic (but nonfunctional) *hammam* is one of the few remnants of the Ottoman Empire, and the only surviving public bath building.

Take a break... Chill out at **Klepsydra** (📞210 321 2493; Thrasyvoulou 9, 🕙9am-1am; ⓂMonastiraki), a cafe offering quiet respite in the busy downtown area.

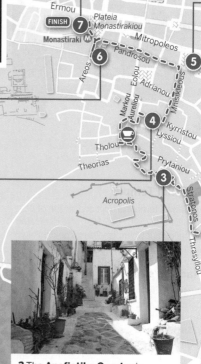

3 The **Anafiotika Quarter** is a picturesque maze of little whitewashed houses, the legacy of stonemasons brought in from Anafi to build the king's palace after Independence in 1821.

5 The expansive Plateia Mitropoleos is home to **Athens Cathedral** (⏰7am-7pm) and its smaller, more historically significant neighbour, the 12th-century **Church of Agios Eleftherios** (pictured above).

Classic Photo *Evzones* (presidential guards) in Plateia Syntagmatos.

1 Plateia Syntagmatos is home to the parliament building (watch the changing of the guards, every hour on the hour) and the Peisistratos aqueduct, unearthed during metro excavations.

2 Reliefs at the **Lysikrates Monument**, built in 334 BC, depict the battle between Dionysos and the Tyrrhenian pirates, whom the god transformed into dolphins.

Map labels:
Plateia Syntagmatos
Leof Vasilissis Sofias
Ermou
START
Syntagma
Plateia Mitropoleos
Mitropoleos
Syntagma
Xenofontos
National Gardens
PLAKA
Filellinon
Souri
Adrianou
Leof Vasilissis Amalias
Dedalou
Thespidos
Thalou
Leof Vas Olgas
Zappeio Gardens
Vyronos
Frynihou
Akropoli
Leof Andreas Syngrou

National Gardens

◉ SIGHTS

Benaki Museum
of Greek Culture   Museum
(Map p460; ☑210 367 1000; www.benaki.gr;
Koumbari 1, cnr Leoforos Vasilissis Sofias, Kolona-
ki; adult/student/child €9/7/free, 6pm-midnight
Thu free; ⊙9am-5pm Wed & Fri, to midnight Thu
& Sat, to 4pm Sun; ⓂSyntagma, Evangelismos)
Antonis Benakis, a politician's son born in
Alexandria, Egypt, in the late 19th century,
endowed what is perhaps the finest museum in Greece. Its three floors showcase
impeccable treasures from the Bronze Age
up to WWII. Especially gorgeous are the
Byzantine icons and the extensive collection of Greek regional costumes, as well as
complete sitting rooms from Macedonian
mansions, intricately carved and painted.
Benakis had such a good eye that even the
agricultural tools are beautiful.

Ancient Agora   Historic Site
(Map p456; ☑210 321 0185; http://odysseus.
culture.gr; Adrianou 24, Monastiraki; adult/
student/child €8/4/free; ⊙8am-8pm May-Oct,
to 3pm Nov-Apr; ⓂMonastiraki) The Agora

was ancient Athens' heart, the lively hub of
administrative, commercial, political and
social activity. Socrates expounded his
philosophy here, and in AD 49 St Paul came
here to win converts to Christianity. The site
today is a lush respite, with the grand **Temple of Hephaistos**, a good **museum** and
the late-10th-century Byzantine **Church
of the Holy Apostles**, trimmed in brick
patterns that mimic Arabic calligraphy. The
greenery harbours birds and lizards. Allow
about two hours to see everything.

National Gardens   Gardens
(Map p456; ☑210 721 5019; www.cityofathens.
gr; ⊙7am-dusk; ⓂSyntagma) **FREE** The
former royal gardens, designed by Queen
Amalia in 1838, are a pleasantly un-
kempt park that makes a welcome shady
refuge from summer heat and traffic.
Tucked among the trees are a cafe, a
playground, turtle and duck ponds, and a
tiny (if slightly dispiriting) zoo. The main
entrance is on Leoforos Vasilissis Sofias,
south of parliament; you can also enter
from Irodou Attikou to the east, or from
the adjacent **Zappeio Gardens** (Map p456;

Leoforos Vasilissis Amalias; Ⓜ Syntagma) FREE
to the south.

Church of Agios
Dimitrios Loumbardiaris   Church

(Map p456; www.facebook.com/agiosdimitri-
osloumpardiaris; Filopappou Hill, Thisio; Ⓜ Thissio,
Akropoli) At the foot of Filopappou Hill, this
16th-century church may not be the oldest
in Athens, but it is certainly one of the
loveliest, with a heavy timber roof, marble
floors and a permanent scent of incense. A
great 1732 fresco of St Dimitrios, astride his
horse in a pose copied from ancient images
of Alexander the Great, adorns the interior.
The churchyard, with its wooden gate and
bells, conjures Japan – a touch by modernist architect Dimitris Pikionis.

Kerameikos   Historic Site

(Map p460; ☑210 346 3552; http://odysseus.
culture.gr; Ermou 148, Kerameikos; adult/child incl
museum €8/free; ⊙8am-8pm, reduced hours in
low season; Ⓜ Thissio) This lush, tranquil site,
uncovered in 1861 during the construction of
Pireos St, is named for the potters who settled it around 3000 BC, then on the clay-rich
banks of the Iridanos River. But it's better
known as a cemetery, used through the 6th
century AD, and, ironically, the grave markers
give a sense of ancient life: numerous marble
stelae are carved with vivid portraits and familiar scenes. There is also an excellent small
museum (Ⓜ Thissio, Kerameikos) here.

🄯 SHOPPING

Forget Me Not   Gifts & Souvenirs

(Map p456; ☑210 325 3740; www.forgetmeno-
tathens.gr; Adrianou 100, Plaka; ⊙10am-10pm
May-Sep, to 8pm Oct-Apr; Ⓜ Syntagma, Monastiraki) This impeccable small store (well,
two shops, one upstairs and one down
around the corner) stocks supercool gear,
from fashion to housewares and gifts, all
by contemporary Greek designers. Great
for gift shopping – who doesn't want a
set of cheerful 'evil eye' coasters or some
Hermès-winged beach sandals?

Early Greek Philosophers

Late-5th and early-4th-century BC
philosophers introduced new modes of
thought rooted in rationality, logic and
reason: gifts that have shaped Western
philosophy ever since. These are the
big names:

Socrates (469–399 BC) Athens'
most noble citizen taught his students
to reason for themselves by asking
probing questions. He was charged
with corrupting the city's youth, then
jailed (on Filopappou Hill, according
to legend) and sentenced to death by
drinking hemlock. His legacy is a mode
of reason based on eliminating hypoth-
eses through questions – the so-called
Socratic method.

Plato (427–347 BC) Socrates' star
student documented his teacher's
thoughts in books such as *The Sympo-
sium*. Plato wrote *The Republic* to warn
Athens that unless its people respected law and leadership, and educated
its youth, it would be doomed.

Aristotle (384–322 BC) Plato's student established his own school and
worked in fields such as astronomy,
physics, zoology, ethics and politics.
Aristotle was also the personal physician to Philip II, King of Macedon, and
tutor of Alexander the Great.

Statue of Socrates
KIRILL SKOROBOGATKO/SHUTTERSTOCK ©

Syntagma, Plaka & Monastiraki

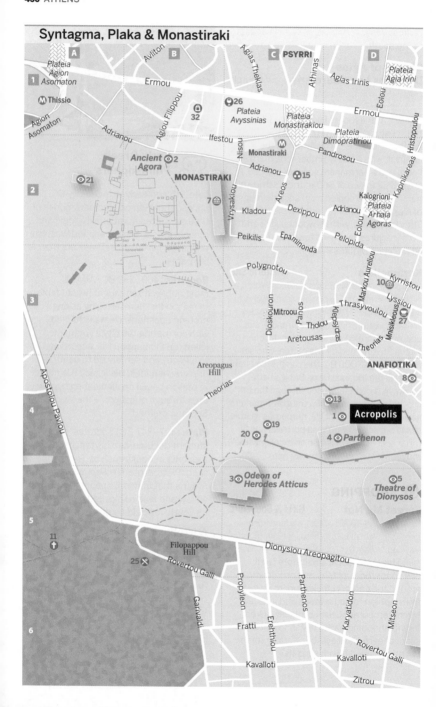

Plateia
Agion
Asomaton

Aviiton

Ermou

PSYRRI

Agias Theklas

Athinas

Agias Irinis

Plateia
Agia Irini

Eolou

Thissio

Agion
Asomaton

Adrianou

Agiou Filippou

32

26

Plateia
Avyssinias

Plateia
Monastirakiou

Ifestou

Nisou

Plateia
Dimopratiriou

Ermou

Eolou

Kapnikareas Hristopoulou

Adrianou

**Ancient
Agora**

2

MONASTIRAKI

Monastiraki

Adrianou

Pandrosou

15

Kalogrioni
Plateia
Arhaia
Agoras

21

7

Vrysakiou

Areos

Kladou

Dexippou

Adrianou

Eolou

Peikilis

Epaminonda

Pelopida

Polygnotou

Markou Aureliou

10

Kyrristou

Lyssiou

27

Dioskouron

Mitroou

Panos

Tholou

Thrasyvoulou

Klepsydras

Mnisikleous

Aretousas

Theorias

ANAFIOTIKA

Areopagus
Hill

Theorias

8

13

1

Acropolis

Apostolou Pavlou

4

19

20

4 **Parthenon**

3 **Odeon of
Herodes Atticus**

5
**Theatre of
Dionysos**

11

Filopappou
Hill

25

Rovertou Galli

Dionysiou Areopagitou

Propyleon

Parthenos

Karyatidon

Mitseon

Garivaldi

Fratti

Erehthiou

Rovertou Galli

Kavalloti

Kavalloti

Zitrou

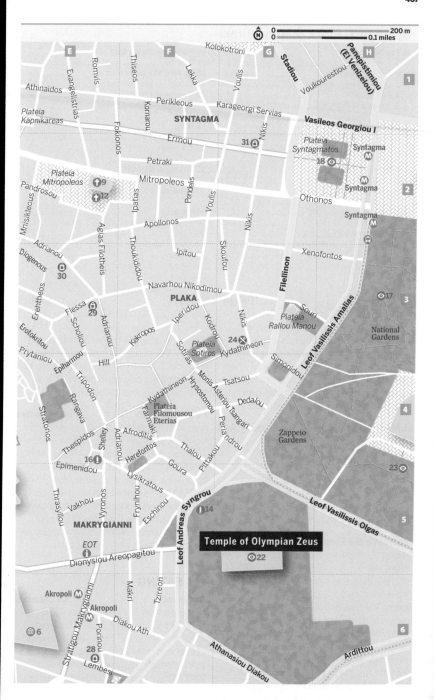

Syntagma, Plaka & Monastiraki

Flâneur   Design

(Map p456; ☑210 322 6900; Adrianou 110,
cnr Flessa, Plaka; ⊙11am-8pm; MSyntagma,
Monastiraki) This cute shop has a tightly
curated collection of souvenirs and travel
gear. Get your hand-stamped 'φλανέρ'
(that's 'flâneur' spelled in Greek) notebooks
and your feta-tin patches and pins here.
Even stocks vinyl by Greek indie bands.

El.Marneri Galerie   Jewellery, Art

(Map p456; ☑210 861 9488; www.eleni
marneri.com; Lembesi 5-7, Makrygianni;
⊙11am-8pm Tue, Thu & Fri, to 4pm Wed & Sat;
MAkropoli) Sample rotating exhibitions
of local modern art and some of the best
jewellery in the city. Handmade, unusual
and totally eye-catching.

Monastiraki Flea Market   Market

(Map p456; Plateia Avyssinias, Monastiraki;
⊙daily May-Oct, Sun-Wed & Fri Nov-Apr; MMo-
nastiraki) Ifestou is signed as the 'Athens
flea market', but this is mostly souvenir
shops. The true flea feel is on Plateia Avyssinias and in nearby small streets, where
dusty *palaiopoleia* ('old-stuff sellers') rule.
For the best rummaging, come Sunday
mornings, when the bric-a-brac explodes
out onto the pavements, including on Ast-
ingos and even across Ermou in Psyrri.

Korres   Cosmetics

(Map p456; ☑210 321 0054; www.korres.com;
Ermou 4, Syntagma; ⊙9am-9pm Mon-Fri, to 8pm
Sat; MSyntagma) Many pharmacies stock
some of this popular line of natural beauty
products, but you can get the full range at
the company's original location, where it
grew out of a homeopathic pharmacy.

Pantopoleion   Food & Drinks

(Map p460; ☑210 323 4612; www.atenco.gr; Sofokleous 1, Omonia; ⊙8am-7pm; MPanepistimio)
There are plenty of shops in Athens selling
Greek traditional foods, but this one is
notable for its scale and scope. 'Everything
for the Mediterranean diet', as the shop's
full name attests, includes Santorini capers,
boutique olive oils, Cretan rusks, jars of
preserves, and countless other edible souvenirs and Greek wines and spirits.

EATING

Cremino   Ice Cream €

(Map p456; Nikis 50a, Plaka; scoops €2.20;
⊙11.30am-6.30pm, later in spring & summer;
MSyntagma, Akropoli) The lovely proprietress
at Cremino makes gelato and sorbet that's
both intensely flavoured and incredibly
light, using cow and buffalo milk. Flavours

change daily, but look for creamy-chewy kaïmaki, a classic recipe with Chios mastic resin and orchid root.

Kalderimi — Taverna €

(Map p460; ☑210 331 0049; Plateia Agion Theodoron, cnr Skouleniou, Monastiraki; mains €6-8; ⊙11am-8pm Mon-Thu, to 10pm Fri & Sat; 🛜; Ⓜ Panepistimio) Look behind the **Church of Agii Theodori** (cnr Dragatsaniou & Agion Theodoron, Syntagma; Ⓜ Panepistimio) FREE for this taverna offering Greek food at its most authentic. Everything is freshly cooked and delicious: you can't go wrong. Hand-painted tables edge a pedestrian street, providing for a feeling of peace in one of the busiest parts of the city. (It helps that it closes just before nearby bars get rolling.)

Mavro Provato — Mezedhes €

(Black Sheep; ☑210 722 3466; www.tomauro provato.gr; Arrianou 31-33, Pangrati; dishes €6-17.50; ⊙1pm-1am Mon-Sat, until 7pm Sun; Ⓜ Evangelismos) Book ahead for this wildly popular modern *mezedhopoleio* (mezedhes restaurant) in Pangrati, where tables line the footpath and delicious small (well, small for Greece) plates are paired with regional Greek wines.

Telis — Taverna €€

(Map p460; ☑210 324 9582; Evripidou 86, Psyrri; meal with salad €13; ⊙noon-midnight Mon-Sat; Ⓜ Thissio) A fluorescent-lit beacon of good food and kind service on a grimy block, Telis has been serving up simplicity since 1978. There's no menu, just a set meal: a small mountain of charcoal-grilled pork chops atop chips, plus a side vegetable. Greek salad is optional, as is beer or rough house wine.

Seychelles — Greek €€

(Map p460; ☑210 118 3478; www.seycheles.gr; Kerameikou 49, Metaxourgio; mains €8.50-14.50; ⊙2pm-12.30am Sun-Thu, until 1am Fri & Sat; Ⓜ Metaxourgio) Gutsy, fresh food, an open kitchen, friendly service, a handwritten daily menu and rock on the soundtrack: Seychelles may be the Platonic ideal of a restaurant. Dishes can look simple – meaty pan-fried mushrooms with just a sliver of

sheep's cheese, say, or greens with fish roe – but the flavour is excellent. Go early or book ahead; it's deservedly popular.

🍷 DRINKING & NIGHTLIFE

Couleur Locale — Bar

(Map p456; ☑216 700 4917; www.couleurlo-caleathens.com; Normanou 3, Monastiraki; ⊙10am-2am Sun-Thu, to 3am Fri & Sat; Ⓜ Monastiraki) Look for the entrance to this rooftop bar down a narrow pedestrian lane, then inside the arcade. From there, an elevator goes to the 3rd floor and its lively all-day bar-restaurant. It's a go-to spot for Athenians who love a chill coffee or a louder evening, all in view of their beloved Acropolis.

Yiasemi — Cafe

(Map p456; ☑213 041 7937; www.yiasemi.gr; Mniskleous 23, Plaka; ⊙10am-3am; Ⓜ Monasti-raki) Proof that Plaka is still very much a Greek neighbourhood, despite the tourists, this cafe attracts a good mix of young Athenians, who set up for hours in the big armchairs or out on the scenic steps. It's better by day (especially for the great veg breakfast buffet) and on weeknights, when it's not overwhelmed by the scene at nearby restaurants.

Little Kook — Cafe

(Map p460; ☑210 321 4144; www.facebook.com/littlekookgr; Karaïskaki 17, Psyrri; ⊙10am-midnight Mon-Fri, from 9am Sat & Sun; 🚻; Ⓜ Monastiraki) Nominally, this place sells coffee and cake. But it's really about its dazzling decor, which conjures an odd childhood fantasy. Precisely which one depends on the season, as the theme changes regularly. Everywhere are dolls, props, paintings and table decorations. You'll know you're getting close when you see party streamers over the street. Kids will be dazzled; Instagrammers will swoon.

ℹ️ INFORMATION

Athens City Information Kiosk Acropolis

(www.thisisathens.org; Syntagma; Ⓜ Syntagma) Maps, transport information and all Athens info.

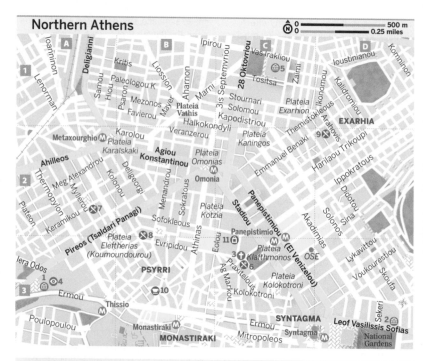

Northern Athens

Athens Contemporary Art Map (www.athens artmap.net) Download a PDF of art spaces and events; alternatively, pick up a paper copy at galleries and cafes around town.

EOT (Greek National Tourism Organisation; Map p456; ☑210 331 0347, 210 331 0716; www. visitgreece.gr; Dionysiou Areopagitou 18-20, Makrygianni; ⊙8am-8pm Mon-Fri, 10am-4pm Sat & Sun May-Sep, 9am-7pm Mon-Fri Oct-Apr; MAkropoli) Free Athens map, current site hours and bus and train information.

ℹ️ GETTING AROUND

BUS

Typical service is every 15 minutes, 5am to midnight.

In lieu of maps, use Google Maps for directions or the trip planner at the website of the bus company, **OASA** (Athens Urban Transport Organisation; ☑11185; www.oasa.gr; ⊙6.30am-11.30pm Mon-Fri, from 7.30am Sat & Sun) – click 'Telematics'. The most useful lines for tourists are trolleybuses 2, 5, 11 and 15, which run north from Syntagma past the National Archaeological Museum.

METRO

The metro works well and posted maps have clear icons and English labels. Trains operate from 5.30am to 12.30am, every four minutes during peak periods and every 10 minutes off-peak. Get information at www.stasy.gr. All stations have wheelchair access.

There are three lines: Line 1 (green, to Piraeus), Line 2 (red) and Line 3 (blue).

TAXI

Taxis are excellent value but it can be tricky getting one, especially during rush hour.

Thrust your arm out vigorously...you may still have to shout your destination to the driver to see if they are interested. Make sure the meter is on. It can be much easier to use the mobile app **Beat** (www.thebeat.co/gr) or **Taxiplon** (☑18222; www.taxiplon.gr) – you can pay in cash.

If a taxi picks you up while already carrying passengers, the fare is not shared: each person pays the fare on the meter minus any diversions to drop others (note what it's at when you get in).

Short trips around central Athens cost about €5; there are surcharges for luggage and pickups at transport hubs. Nights and holidays, the fare is about 60% higher.

TRAM

Tram (www.stasy.gr) services run from 5.30am to 1am Sunday to Thursday (every 10 minutes), and to 2.30am on Friday and Saturday (every 40 minutes). Ticket vending machines are on the platforms.

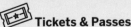 **Tickets & Passes**

The transit system uses the unified Ath. ena Ticket, a reloadable paper card available from ticket offices and machines in the metro. You can load it with a set amount of money or buy a number of rides (€1.40 each; discount when you buy five or 10) or a 24-hour/five-day travel pass for €4.50/9.

Children under six travel free; people under 18 or over 65 are technically eligible for half-fare, but you must buy the Ath.ena Ticket from a ticket office.

Swipe the card at metro turnstiles; on buses and trams, validate the ticket in the machine as you board, and keep it with you in case of spot-checks. One swipe is good for 90 minutes, including any transfers or return trips.

GEORGE TSITOURAS PHOTOS/SHUTTERSTOCK ©

WALKING

Central Athens is compact and good for strolling. From Gazi in the west to the Byzantine & Christian Museum in the east, for example, takes only about 45 minutes to walk. In summer, however, take the punishing sun into consideration.

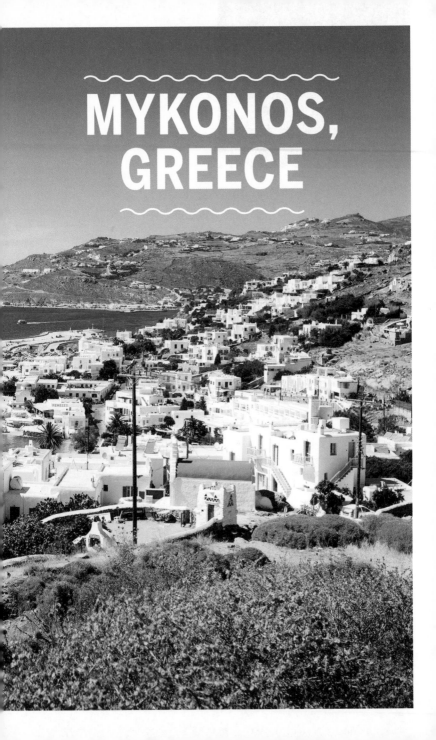

MYKONOS, GREECE

Mykonos at a Glance...

Mykonos is the great glamour island of Greece and flaunts its sizzling St-Tropez-meets-Ibiza style and party-hard reputation. Mykonos Town (aka Hora), the island's well-preserved port and capital, is a traditional whitewashed Cycladic maze, delighting in its cubist charms and its chichi cafe-bar-boutique scene. In the heart of the waterfront Little Venice quarter, tiny flower-bedecked churches jostle with glossy boutiques, and there's a cascade of bougainvillea around every corner. Mykonos is also the jumping-off point for the archaeological site of the nearby island of Delos.

With One Day in Port

○ Choose your beach, pull up a bit of sand and settle in for the day. **Agios Stefanos** (p466) is the closest to port, but some of the beaches further afield offer more breathing space.

○ Alternatively, catch the 9am boat out to the ancient sacred island of **Delos**, returning at noon for lunch at **Nikos Taverna** (p473).

○ Wander around **Little Venice** (p472) for a spot of shopping, before heading back to port.

Best Places For...

Ancient history Delos (p468)

Accessible beaches Agios Stefanos (p466)

Classic photo Windmills (p470)

Art Eliza's Art Gallery (p471)

Coffee Popolo (p473)

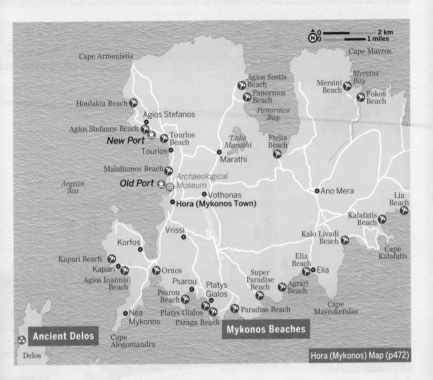

Ancient Delos

Mykonos Beaches

Hora (Mykonos) Map (p472)

Getting from the Port

Mykonos has two ferry quays: the **Old Port**, 400m north of town, where a couple of fast ferries dock, and the **New Port**, 2km north of town, where the bigger fast ferries and all conventional ferries dock.

The KTEL Mykonos bus network has two main terminals (p473) plus pick-up points at the Old and New Ports. Buses in high season run frequently; the fare is €1.60 to €2.30 depending on the distance travelled.

Fast Facts

Currency Euro (€)

Language Greek

Money There are plenty of ATMs on Mykonos that accept all major credit cards.

Visas Citizens of Australia, New Zealand, Canada, the UK and the US do not need a visa to enter Greece for stays up to three months (90 days).

Wi-fi Free wi-fi is available in many hotels, cafes and restaurants.

Paradise Beach

JEKATARINKA/SHUTTERSTOCK ©

Mykonos Beaches

Mykonos' golden-sand beaches in their formerly unspoilt state were the pride of Greece. Now most are jammed with umbrellas and backed by beach bars, but they do make for a hopping scene that draws floods of beachgoers. Moods range from the simply hectic to the outright snobby, and nudity levels vary.

Great For...

☑ Don't Miss

Agios Sostis (p467), with its gorgeous strip of white sand.

Agios Stefanos The nearest beaches to Hora were overtaken by the construction of the New Port. That leaves little Agios Stefanos (4km north of Hora), within sight of the cruise ship port. A narrow but popular curve of sand, there are plenty of tavernas behind it.

Agia Anna A tiny strip of sand in town, Agia Anna is not one of Mykonos' finest, but it is centrally located, popular with families and good for a quick dip.

Agios Ioannis About 5km southwest of Hora is the family-oriented Agios Ioannis. A sandy crescent studded with beach umbrellas, it's lapped at by shallow waters. Part of the film Shirley Valentine was filmed here. For lunch, check out Hippie Fish, a sprawling, all-white restaurant-bar on the beach. Linger over Greek and Mediterranean fare, including fresh morsels from the sushi bar.

Agios Stefanos

SAIKO3P/SHUTTERSTOCK ©

Explore Ashore

Without your own vehicle, catch buses from Hora or caïques from Ornos and Platys Gialos to further beaches. Mykonos Cruises (p471) has an online timetable of its sea-taxi services.

ⓘ Need to Know

You'll need tough wheels for out-of-the-way beaching, such as **Fokos** and **Mersini** on the northeast coast.

Psarou A long stretch of white sand and teal waters, Psarou is favoured by local cognoscenti. Just up from the beach, Nikos Gallop is an established favourite that focuses largely on the bounty of the sea, prepared Mediterranean-style.

Platys Gialos Platys Gialos is one of Mykonos' most popular beaches, lined with restaurants and with a broad stretch of white sand. This is the place to try flyboarding or rent a stand-up paddleboard or kayak. For lunch, try Nikolas Taverna, which has been run by the same family for three generations. The current proprietor, Nikolas, goes fishing for fresh catch of the day to go with the locally sourced meats and vegetables from the family farm. Solid and satisfying.

Paradise Party people should head about 1km east from Platys Gialos to famous white-sand Paradise Beach, which is not a recognised gay

beach but has an action-packed younger scene, a camping resort and nightlife that doesn't quit.

Super Paradise Down a steep access road, Super Paradise (aka Plintri or Super P) has a fully gay section (including the JackieO' beach club) and a huge eponymous club. Celebrity sightings, a crush of scantily-clad young bodies heaving to the DJs' beats, cocktails by the sea – it's got it al. Music kicks off in the afternoons and pumps until the wee hours. Numerous free shuttle buses from Hora.

Elia Mixed and gay-friendly Elia is a long, lovely stretch of sand and is the last caïque stop. Elia Mykonos, attached to the hotel of the same name, is a light and bright restaurant within toe-dipping distance of the sea. Many items on the menu hail from the sea as well, with the exception of the meaty pasta dishes.

Agios Sostis A wide, gorgeous strip of white sand that receives far fewer visitors than the south coast, Agios Sostis is fairly sheltered from the meltemi (dry northerly wind). There's a sheltered cove directly below, and a legendary taverna, Kiki's. Every day around noon, customers line up (enjoying complimentary wine spritzers in the queue) for their enormous portions of solid local food off the grill: pork chops, octopus, swordfish, feta cheese, accompanied by epic salads and served beneath a shady vine trellis on a terrace overlooking the sea.

House of Dionysos

JANKABRT/SHUTTERSTOCK ©

Ancient Delos

The mythical birthplace of twins Apollo and Artemis, splendid Ancient Delos was a shrine turned sacred treasury and commercial centre. This Unesco World Heritage Site is one of the most important archaeological sites in Greece. Cast your imagination wide to transform this sprawling ruin into the magnificent city it once was.

Great For...

☑ **Don't Miss**

The Terrace of the Lions, the most-photographed part of the Delos site.

History

The mythical birthplace of twins Apollo and Artemis, Delos was first inhabited in the 3rd millennium BC. From the 8th century BC it became a shrine to Apollo, and the oldest temples date from this era. The dominant Athenians had full control of Delos – and thus the Aegean – by the 5th century BC.

Arriving at Ancient Delos

Boats from Mykonos dock on a bay south of the tranquil **Sacred Harbour**. Licensed guides (around €10 per person) may tout for business as you disembark and can provide context to the various ruins.

While many significant finds from Delos are in Athens' National Archaeological Museum (p466), the site's **museum** (◷10am-7pm) FREE has an interesting collection, including lions from the Terrace of the Lions.

Terrace of the Lions

MILA ATKOVSKA/SHUTTERSTOCK ©

Explore Ashore

Boats for Delos (return adult/child €20/10, 30 minutes) leave Hora (Mykonos) four times daily in high season from 9am to 5pm, returning between noon and 8pm. Establish your return boat when buying tickets, either online or from the **Delos Boat Ticket Kiosk** (☑22890 28603; www.delostours.gr; adult/child return ticket €20/10).

ⓘ Need to Know

☑22890 22259; museum & site adult/concession €12/6; ☺8am-8pm Apr-Oct, to 2pm Nov-Mar

The Ruins

From the dock, follow the arrowed path past the ruins of the **South Stoa**, built after the mid-3rd century BC with 28 Doric columns, and used to house shops and workshops. Continue to the **Sanctuary of Apollo**, northeast of the harbour. The **Sacred Way** (a wide, paved path used by ancient pilgrims) enters the complex through the **Propylaia** to a compound of magnificent temples and treasuries. Three were dedicated to Apollo: **Temple of the Delians** (Great Temple), **Temple of the Athenians** and **Poros Temple**. The sanctuary also housed the classical treasuries and the **Artemision** (Sanctuary of Artemis).

North of the sanctuary is the much-photographed **Terrace of the Lions**. To the northeast, the now-empty **Sacred Lake** is where Leto gave birth to Apollo

and Artemis. Next, head south to the **Theatre Quarter**, where Delos' wealthiest inhabitants lived in houses surrounded by peristyle courtyards, with intricate, colourful mosaics. The most lavish include the **House of Dionysos**, named after its mosaic depicting the wine god riding a panther, and the **House of Cleopatra**.

The **theatre** dates from 300 BC and had a large cistern, which supplied much of the town's water. The **House of the Masks** has another mosaic of Dionysos astride a panther between two centaurs. The extraordinary mosaic at the **House of the Dolphins** incorporates lions, griffins and dolphins.

Steep **Mt Kynthos** (113m) rises to the southeast of the harbour. On clear days it has terrific views of the encircling islands, as well as monuments such as the Sanctuaries of Zeus Kynthios and Athena Kynthia, and the Temple of Hera.

◎ SIGHTS

Aegean Maritime Museum
Museum

(☎22890 22700; Enoplon Dynameon 10; adult/student €4/2; ◷10.30am-1pm & 6.30-9pm Apr-Oct) Amid the barnacle-encrusted amphorae, ye olde nautical maps and navigation instruments, there are numerous detailed models of various famous sailing ships and paddle steamers. You can also learn the difference between an Athenian trireme, a Byzantine dromon and an ancient Egyptian seagoing ship. There's an enormous Fresnel lighthouse lantern in the courtyard.

Panagia Paraportiani
Church

(Paraportianis) Mykonos' most famous church, the whitewashed, rock-like Panagia Paraportiani, comprises four small chapels – plus another on an upper storey reached by an exterior staircase. It's usually locked but the fabulously photogenic whitewashed exterior is the drawcard.

Archaeological Museum
Museum

(☎22890 22325; Agiou Stefanou; adult/child €4/free; ◷9am-4pm Tue-Sun) Peruse pottery from Delos, dating back to the 9th century BC, and grave *stelae* (pillars) and jewellery from the island of Renia (Delos' necropolis). Chief exhibits include a statue of Hercules in Parian marble.

Windmills
Landmark

(off Plateia Alefkandra) Constructed in the 16th century by the Venetians for the milling of wheat, seven of Mykonos' iconic windmills are picturesquely situated on a small hill overlooking the harbour.

✦ ACTIVITIES

There's good diving around Mykonos, with wrecks, caves and walls to explore, and scuba diving operators on Paradise Beach and Lia Beach. Kalafatis Beach and Ftelia Beach are good for windsurfing, while Platys Gialos is the place to try flyboarding or rent a stand-up paddleboard or kayak.

Panagia Paraportiani

ROMAN SIGAEV/SHUTTERSTOCK ©

Platys Gialos
Watersports — Water Sports

(6977279584; www.mykonoswatersports.gr;
Platys Gialos Beach; ⏰9am-9pm Mon-Fri) This
operator specialises in adrenalin-packed
water sports and arranges wakeboarding,
wakeskating, waterskiing and wakesurfing
sessions. It can also introduce you to the
new flyboard craze, and rent sea kayaks
and stand-up paddleboards.

GoDive Mykonos — Diving

(📱6942616102; www.godivemykonos.com; Lia
Beach; 1-/2-tank dives €80/130; ⏰9.30am-
6pm; 🅿️) This highly professional operator
is based on Lia Beach and offers a full
range of activities below the waves, from
multiday scuba safaris to night dives, PADI
courses, snorkelling trips and Bubblemak-
er inductions for kids over eight.

Mykonos On Board Sailing — Sailing

(📱6932471055; www.mykonosonboard.com)
Highly recommended private and semi-
private yachting excursions around Mykonos
and to nearby islands Delos and Rhenia.

🅖 TOURS

Mykonos Traveller — Travel Agency

(MAC; 📱6986993013; https://mykonostraveller.
com; ⏰9am-1pm & 4-9pm) Organises guided
tours, excursions, private tours and charters. Tours go to Delos (adult/child €50/25,
including the return boat trip, admission
fee and guide) and to the island of Tinos
(€70/45), to see its holy church and other
sights. Also organises a walking tour of
Hora and a bus tour around the island
(€40/25). A full-day island cruise along the
south coast (€70/40) and a 4WD safari
to isolated beaches (€65/35) are also
available.

Mykonos Cruises — Boat

(📱22890 23995; www.mykonos-cruises.gr;
⏰8am-7pm Apr-Oct) An association of sea-
taxi operators offering services to the
island's best beaches. See the timetables
online. The main departure point is Platys
Gialos, with drop-offs and pick-ups at

 Art Galleries

Eliza's Art Gallery (📱22890 24461; www.
elizasgallery.com; Mavrogenous 15; ⏰10am-
10pm) Gorgeous glass creations, quirky
lamps, jewellery and works by renowned
Naxos sculptor Yiannis Nanouris.

Art & Soul Gallery (📱22890 27244;
www.mykonosgallery.com; Mavrogenous 18;
⏰10am-11pm) Run by the Rousounelos
family for over 30 years, this gallery
is for serious collectors. On display
you'll find sculpture and paintings by
renowned Greek artists, each sold with
a certificate of authenticity.

Rarity Gallery (📱22890 25761; www.rarity
gallery.com; Kalogera 20-22; ⏰10am-midnight)
FREE This little gallery is well worth a
peek for its temporary exhibitions that
showcase paintings, sculpture and
photography by the likes of Paul Rousso,
Yigal Ozeri and George Pusenkoff.

GREECE/ALAMY STOCK PHOTO ©

Ornos, Paraga, Paradise, Super Paradise,
Agrari and Elia beaches (€20 for a day
pass). Cruises and personalised itineraries
can also be arranged.

Yummy Pedals — Mountain Biking

(📱22890 71883, 6972299282; www.yummy-
pedals.gr; 4hr tour from €50) A world away
from the beach bars, multilingual Dimitra
offers guided mountain-biking tours
through the backroads of Mykonos. The
duration and route is personalised to fit
your skill level, but may take in farms, villages and quiet beaches (with swimming
and snacking stops). Tours begin and end

Hora (Mykonos)

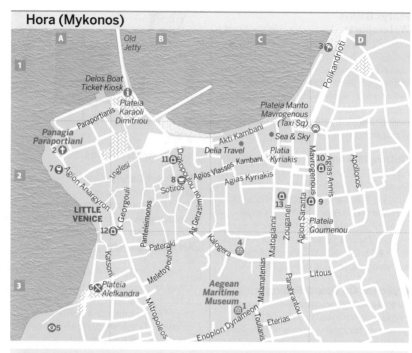

Hora (Mykonos)

at Dimitra's family's vineyard, with the option of food and wine.

Mykonos Tour & Excursions
Walking

(📞 22890 79376; www.mykonos-web.com; €69) This four-hour tour of the island takes in a couple of beaches and the monastery of Ano Mera by bus, and the highlights of Mykonos Town – Little Venice, the windmills, Paraportiani church – on foot. Knowledgeable guides.

🛍 SHOPPING

Mavrogenous St is good for art, Matogliani is best for luxe brands and excellent Greek designers, while the streets of Little Venice mix fashion with jewellery and tat. Most stores close in the winter (November to March).

Mayonaisa Darling
Jewellery

(📞 6975592478; www.mayonaisadarling.com; Drakopoulou 6; ⊙11am-midnight) Worth buying for the designer's name alone, this collection of original handmade jewellery uses hypoallergenic materials, semi-precious stones and recycled pieces, like gears from vintage clocks.

Mykonos Sandals   Shoes

(22890 22451; www.mykonos-sandals.gr; Little Venice; 10.30am-10.30pm) Come for the sunset cocktails and stay for the hand-made leather sandals, from this company established in 1948.

Olive Oil Shop   Gifts & Souvenirs

(22890 23598; Matogianni 15; 10am-midnight) Going strong for more than 20 years, this cute shop specialises in all things olive oil – soap, skincare products, the oil itself, plus olivewood kitchen implements and locally produced honey and herbs.

EATING & DRINKING

Nice n Easy   Fusion €€

(22890 25421; www.niceneasy.gr; Little Venice; mains €12-25; 9am-1am;) With a great view of Mykonos' windmills from its seafront terrace, this outpost specialises in organic fusion dishes. The chef has spent time in California, and as a result healthy options like egg-white omelettes, quinoa salad and various vegan offerings appear on the menu.

Nikos Gallop   Seafood €€

(22890 24306; www.facebook.com/nikos.gallop; Platys Gialos; mains €10-25; 11am-1am;) Just up from Platys Gialos Beach, this established favourite focuses largely on the bounty of the sea, prepared Mediterranean-style.

Popolo   Coffee

(22890 22208; www.popolomykonos.com; Drakopoulou 18; 8.30am-2.30am;) Hidden in Hora's labyrinthine depths, this tiny cafe has gained a reputation as the best place for coffee on Mykonos. Freshly cooked break-fasts, plus salads, sandwiches and juices throughout the day seal the deal.

Katerina's Bar   Cocktail Bar

(22890 23084; www.katerinaslittlevenice mykonos.com/en/; Agion Anargyron; 9am-3am;

) This bar, owned by the first female Greek naval captain, has a cool balcony and eases you into the evening's action with relaxing sounds.

INFORMATION

There is information online at www.inmykonos.com and www.mykonos.gr.

Mykonos Traveller (p471) Helpful for all things Mykonos.

Sea & Sky (22890 22853; www.seasky.gr; Akti Kambani; 8.30am-9pm) Sells ferry tickets.

Delia Travel (22890 22322; www.facebook.com/delia.travel.mykonos; Akti Kambani; 9am-9pm) Sells ferry tickets.

ⓘ GETTING AROUND

BUS

Terminal A, the **southern bus station** (www.mykonosbus.com; Fabrika Sq), known as Fabrika, serves Ornos and Agios Ioannis Beach, Platys Gialos, Paraga and Super Paradise Beaches. A regular bus connects the New Port with the southern bus station.

Terminal B, the **northern bus station** (www.mykonosbus.com), sometimes called Remezzo, is behind the OTE office and has services to Agios Stefanos via Tourlos, Ano Mera, and Kalo Livadi, Kalafatis and Elia beaches. Private transfer buses operate in summer's peak every hour (11am to 11pm) from the Old Port to Paradise Beach (via Fabrika). There are also frequent shuttles to Super Paradise Beach. Buses for Tourlos and Agios Stefanos stop at the Old and New Ports.

TAXI

Taxis (22890 23700, 22890 22400) queue at Hora's Plateia Manto Mavrogenous (Taxi Sq), bus stations and ports, but waits can be long in high season. All have meters, and the minimum fare is €3.50 (plus €0.50 per bag, €3.30 for phone booking).

Approximate fares from Hora include New Port (€6), Ornos (€12), Platys Gialos (€14), Paradise (€15), Kalafatis (€22) and Elia (€22).

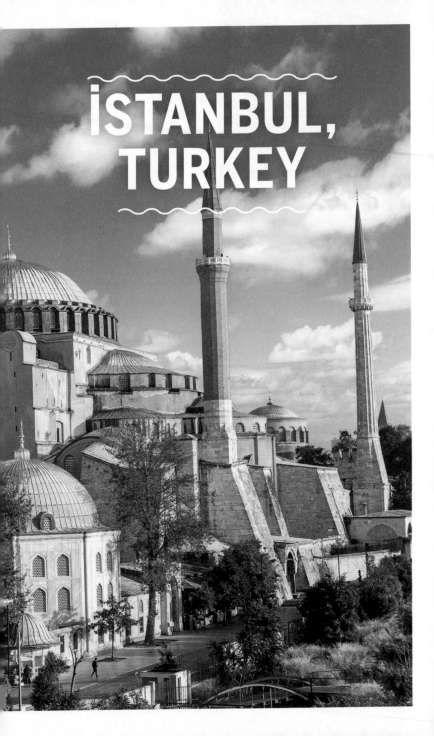

İSTANBUL, TURKEY

In This Chapter

İstanbul at a Glance...

Ask any local to describe what they love about İstanbul and they're likely to smile and say merely that there is no other place like it. Once here, you'll quickly realise what they mean. This is a destination where Byzantine churches sit next to Ottoman mosques, where traditional teahouses are as easy to find as sophisticated cocktail bars, where bustling bazaars and sleek modern boutiques compete for custom, and where it's possible to cross from Europe to Asia in a short ferry trip. With more attractions than it has minarets (and that's a lot), İstanbul is a city that is as unique as it is unforgettable.

With One Day in Port

○ Head to Sultanahmet to visit **Aya Sofya** (p478) and **Topkapı Palace** (p482).

○ Head over to the **Grand Bazaar** (p490), to enjoy some traditional Turkish food at one of the simple eateries, indulge in some shopping and then visit the most magnificent of all Ottoman mosques, the **Süleymaniye** (p491).

○ Walk through the **Spice Bazaar** (p491) and then across the Galata Bridge to bohemian Beyoğlu, the heart of the modern city.

Best Places For...

Shopping Grand Bazaar (p490)

Baklava Karaköy Güllüoğlu (p498)

Traditional bath treatments Kılıç Ali Paşa Hamamı (p494)

Tea breaks Derviş Cafe & Restaurant (p499)

Ottoman interiors Topkapı Palace (p482)

Orientalist art Pera Museum (p491)

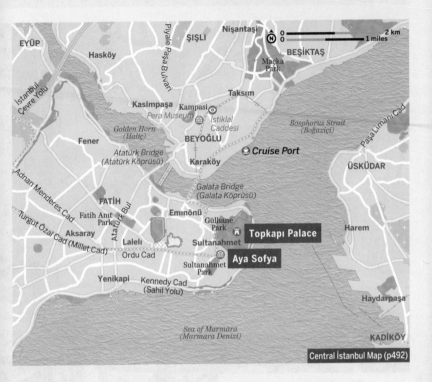

EYÜP

Hasköy

ŞIŞLI

Nişantaşi

BEŞİKTAŞ

Maçka Park

İstanbul Çevre Yolu

Piyale Paşa Bulvari

Taksım

Kasımpaşa

Kampasi

Pera Museum

İstiklal Caddesi

Golden Horn (Haliç)

Fener

BEYOĞLU

Bosphorus Strait (Boğaziçi)

Paşa Limanı Cad

ÜSKÜDAR

Atatürk Bridge (Atatürk Köprüsü)

Karaköy

⚓ Cruise Port

Adnan Menderes Cad

Galata Bridge (Galata Köprüsü)

FATİH

Fatih Anıt Park

Eminönü

Gülhane Park

Topkapı Palace

Harem

Turgut Özal Cad (Millet Cad)

Aksaray

Atatürk Bul

Laleli

Sultanahmet

Ordu Cad

Sultanahmet Park

Aya Sofya

Yenikapı

Kennedy Cad (Sahil Yolu)

Haydarpaşa

Sea of Marmara (Marmara Denizi)

KADİKÖY

2 km
1 miles

Central İstanbul Map (p492)

Getting from the Port

Cruise ships dock at the Salıpazarı docks in **Beyoğlu**.

From here you can walk through Karaköy and across the Galata Bridge to the Bazaar District, flag down a taxi in busy Meclis-i Mebusan Caddesi, or take a tram to the Old City or a tram and funicular to Beyoğlu. The Fındıklı and Tophane tram stops are both close by, but only Tophane has a ticket machine.

Fast Facts

Currency Turkish lira (₺)

Language Turkish

Money ATMS can be found throughout the city; currency exchanges in Sultanahmet and around the Grand Bazaar.

Visas Nationals of countries including Australia, Canada, India, the UK, USA and some EU countries need a visa for Turkey.

Wi-fi Most cafe chains throughout the city (Starbucks, Caffè Nero, Espresslab etc) offer free wi-fi.

Aya Sofya interior

ARTUR BOGACKI/SHUTTERSTOCK ©

Aya Sofya

Commissioned by the great Byzantine emperor Justinian and consecrated as the church of Hagia Sophia in 537, this unique building is notable for its rich history, religious importance and extraordinary beauty.

Great For...

☑ Don't Miss

The Ottoman-era Aya Sofya Tombs (p490), accessed via a gate on Babıhumayün Caddesi.

Imperial Door

The main entrance to the Nave is crowned with a striking mosaic of Christ as Pantocrator (Ruler of All). At Christ's feet an emperor (probably Leo VI) prostrates himself. The Virgin Mary is on Christ's left and to his right is the Archangel Gabriel.

Nave

Made 'transparent' by its profusion of windows and columned arcades, Aya Sofya's nave is as visually arresting as it is enormous. The chandeliers hanging low above the floor are Ottoman additions, as are the elevated kiosk where the sultan worshipped and the large 19th-century medallions inscribed with gilt Arabic letters.

Aya Sofya interior

PANOM/SHUTTERSTOCK ©

Explore Ashore

It's a short taxi or tram trip from the port to Aya Sofya Meydanı (Aya Sofya Sq), from where the Old City's major sights (Aya Sofya, Topkapı Palace, Blue Mosque, Basilica Cistern) are easily accessed by foot. You'll need at least one hour in Aya Sofya.

ⓘ Need to Know

Hagia Sophia; ☏0212-522 1750, 0212-522 0989; www.ayasofyamuzesi.gov.tr/en; Aya Sofya Meydanı 1; adult/child under 8yr ₺60/free; ⊙9am-7pm Tue-Sun mid-Apr–Oct, to 5pm Nov–mid-Apr; ☐Sultanahmet

Apse

A 9th-century mosaic of the Virgin and Christ Child in the apse is the focal point of the nave. The *minber* (pulpit) and the *mihrab* (prayer niche indicating the direction of Mecca) were added during the Ottoman period.

Dome

Aya Sofya's famous dome measures 30m in diameter and 56m in height. It is supported by 40 ribs resting on four huge pillars concealed in the interior walls (a great innovation at the time). On its completion, the Byzantine historian Procopius described it as being 'hung from heaven on a golden chain'.

Mosaics

The upstairs galleries are home to a number of exquisite Byzantine mosaics. These include a Deesis (Last Judgement) in the south gallery, which depicts Christ with the Virgin Mary on his left and John the Baptist on his right. On the other side of the south gallery are mosaics depicting the Empress Zoe, one of only three Byzantine women to rule as empress in their own right, and a family group of Emperor John Comnenus II, Empress Eirene and their son Alexius depicted with the Virgin Mary.

Downstairs, as you exit the building, be sure to look back to see a 10th-century mosaic showing the Emperor Constantine (right) offering the Virgin Mary the city of Constantinople; the Emperor Justinian (left) is offering her Hagia Sophia.

Aya Sofya

A TIMELINE

537 Emperor Justinian, depicted in one of the church's famous **❶ mosaics**, presides over the consecration of Byzantium's new basilica, Hagia Sophia (Church of the Holy Wisdom).

557 The huge **❷ dome**, damaged during an earthquake, collapses and is rebuilt.

843 The second Byzantine Iconoclastic period ends and figurative **❸ mosaics** begin to be added to the interior. These include a depiction of the Empress Zoe and her third husband, Emperor Constantine IX Monomachos.

1204 Soldiers of the Fourth Crusade led by the Doge of Venice, Enrico Dandolo, conquer and ransack Constantinople. Dandolo's **❹ tomb** is eventually erected in the church whose desecration he presided over.

1453 The city falls to the Ottomans; Mehmet II orders that Hagia Sophia be converted to a mosque and renamed Aya Sofya.

1577 Sultan Selim II is buried in a specially designed tomb, which sits alongside the **❺ tombs** of four other Ottoman Sultans in Aya Sofya's grounds.

1847–49 Sultan Abdül Mecit I orders that the building be restored and redecorated; the huge **❻ Ottoman Medallions** in the nave are added.

1935 The mosque is converted into a museum by order of Mustafa Kemal Atatürk, president of the new Turkish Republic.

2009 The face of one of the four **❼ seraphs** is uncovered during major restoration works in the nave.

2012 Restoration of the exterior walls and western upper gallery commences.

TOP TIP

Bring binoculars if you want to properly view the mosaic portraits in the apse and under the dome.

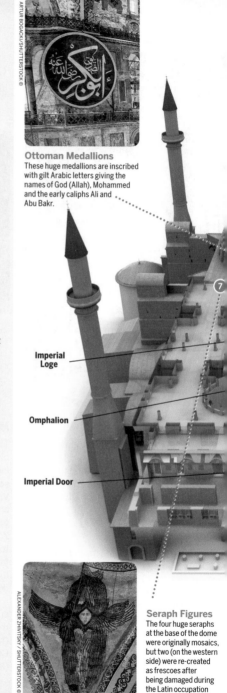

ARTUR BOGACKI/SHUTTERSTOCK ©

Ottoman Medallions
These huge medallions are inscribed with gilt Arabic letters giving the names of God (Allah), Mohammed and the early caliphs Ali and Abu Bakr.

Imperial Loge

Omphalion

Imperial Door

ALEXANDER ZHIVITSKY / SHUTTERSTOCK ©

Seraph Figures
The four huge seraphs at the base of the dome were originally mosaics, but two (on the western side) were re-created as frescoes after being damaged during the Latin occupation (1204–61).

Dome

Soaring 56m from ground level, the dome was originally covered in gold mosaics but was decorated with calligraphy during the 1847–49 restoration works overseen by Swiss-born architects Gaspard and Giuseppe Fossati.

Christ Enthroned with Empress Zoe and Constantine IX Monomachos

This mosaic portrait in the upper gallery depicts Zoe, one of only three Byzantine women to rule as empress in their own right.

BYELIKOVA OKSANA/SHUTTERSTOCK ©

Ottoman Tombs

The tombs of five Ottoman sultans and their families are located in Aya Sofya's southern corner and can be accessed via Babıhümayun Caddesi. One of these occupies the church's original Baptistry.

Aya Sofya Tombs

Former Baptistry

Muvakkithane (place where prayer hours were determined)

Exit

Ablutions Fountain

Primary School

Main Entrance

Grave of Enrico Dandolo

The Venetian doge died in 1205, only one year after he and his Crusaders had stormed the city. A 19th-century marker in the upper gallery indicates the probable location of his grave.

Constantine the Great, the Virgin Mary and Emperor Justinian

This 11th-century mosaic shows Constantine (right) offering the Virgin Mary the city of Constantinople. Justinian (left) is offering her Hagia Sophia.

STIG ALENAS / SHUTTERSTOCK ©

Gate of Salutation

NEJDET DUZEN/SHUTTERSTOCK ©

Topkapı Palace

Libidinous sultans, ambitious courtiers, beautiful concubines and scheming eunuchs lived and worked in this pavilion palace between the 15th and 19th centuries, when it was the court of the Ottoman Empire.

Great For...

☑ Don't Miss

The Marble Terrace in the Fourth Court, which overlooks the Golden Horn and offers wonderful photo opportunities.

Mehmet the Conqueror had the first stage of the palace built shortly after the Conquest in 1453, and lived here until his death in 1481. The Ottoman sultans used it as their main residence until the 19th century, when they moved to ostentatious European-style palaces on the shores of the Bosphorus.

Unlike typical European palaces, which feature one large building with outlying gardens, Topkapı is a series of pavilions, kitchens, barracks, audience chambers, kiosks and sleeping quarters built around a central enclosure. The quality of the traditional Turkish decorative arts (tiles, inlay, calligraphy etc) that were used to adorn the palace are among the best in existence.

First Court

Before you enter the Imperial Gate of Topkapı, take a look at the ornate structure

Imperial Gate

AYHAN ALTUN/GETTY IMAGES ©

Explore Ashore

It's a reasonably short taxi or tram trip from the port to Topkapı Palace. By tram, alight at either the Gülhane or Sultanahmet stop; it's a steep uphill walk from Gülhane. You'll need at least 2.5 hours here.

❶ Need to Know

Topkapı Sarayı; ☎0212-512 0480; www.topkapisarayi.gov.tr; Babıhümayun Caddesi; palace adult/child under 8yr ₺60/free, Harem adult/child under 6yr ₺35/free; ☉9am–6.45pm Wed-Mon mid-Apr–Oct, to 4.45pm Nov–mid-Apr, last entry 45min before closing; 🚊Sultanahmet

in the cobbled square just outside. This is the rococo-style **Fountain of Sultan Ahmet III**, built in 1728 by the sultan who so favoured tulips. As you pass through the Imperial Gate, you enter the First Court, known as the Court of the Janissaries or the Parade Court. On your left is the Byzantine church of Hagia Eirene, more commonly known as **Aya İrini**. The ticket office for the palace is on the right, before the gate leading to the Second Court.

Second Court

Pass through the turnstiles at the Middle Gate to access the heart of the palace. Diplomatic and government business was enacted in the ornate **Imperial Council Chamber** (Dîvân-ı Hümâyûn) on the left (west) side of the court and food for lavish banquets was once produced in the

massive **Palace Kitchens** on the right (east) side. North of the Imperial Council Chamber is the **Outer Treasury**, where an impressive collection of Ottoman and European arms and armour is displayed,

Harem

Accessed from the northwest corner of the Second Court, this complex was the private residence of the sultans and their families. It features many opulently decorated bed chambers, reception rooms, hamams and courtyards. Highlights include the **Salon of the Valide** (Sultan's mother), **Imperial Hall**, **Privy Chamber of Murat III**, **Privy Chamber of Ahmet III** and **Twin Kiosk/Apartment of the Crown Prince**. Also in this complex (and visited using the same ticket) is the **Dormitory of the Zülüflü Baltacılar**

Corps, a meticulously restored structure featuring swathes of magnificent 16th- and 17th-century İznik tiles.

Third Court

The sultan's private domain, this court was once staffed and guarded by white eunuchs. Look for the **Audience Chamber**, constructed in the 16th century but refurbished in the 18th century; important officials and foreign ambassadors were brought to this little kiosk to conduct the high business of state. Also notable are the pretty **Library of Ahmet III**, built in 1719; and the **Dormitory of the Expeditionary Force**, which now houses a rich collection of imperial robes, kaftans and uniforms. On the left (west) side of the court are the sumptuously tiled **Sacred Safekeeping Rooms**, which house

many relics of the Prophet; and the **Dormitory of the Privy Chamber**, which now houses portraits of 36 sultans.

Imperial Treasury

Located on the eastern edge of the Third Court, Topkapı's Treasury houses an incredible collection of objects made from or decorated with gold, silver, rubies, emeralds, jade, pearls and diamonds. The building itself was constructed during Mehmet the Conqueror's reign in 1460 and was used originally as reception rooms. One of the largest diamonds in the world, the teardrop-shaped Spoonmaker's Diamond, now housed here, was found in a rubbish dump and purchased by a wily street peddler for three spoons. It was closed for restoration at the time of research.

Topkapi Palace interior

Fourth Court

Pleasure pavilions occupy the palace's Fourth Court, also known as the Tulip Garden. These include the **Mecidiye Kiosk**, which was built in the 19th century; and the late-17th-century **Kiosk of Kara Mustafa Pasha** (Sofa Köşkü), which has a gilded ceiling, painted walls and delicate stained-glass windows. During the reign of Ahmet III, the Tulip Garden outside this kiosk was filled with the latest varieties of the flower.

Marble Terrace

This platform, up the stairs at the end of the Tulip Garden, has a decorative pool, three pavilions and the whimsical **İftariye Kameriyesi**, a small structure commissioned by İbrahim I in 1640 as a picturesque place to break the fast of Ramazan.

Murat IV had the **Revan Kiosk** built in 1636 after reclaiming the city of Yerevan (now in Armenia) from Persia. Soon after, he had the **Baghdad Kiosk**, one of the last examples of classical palace architecture, constructed to commemorate his victory over that city. The small **Circumcision Room** (Sünnet Odası) was used for the ritual that admits Muslim boys to manhood. Built by İbrahim I in 1640, the outer walls of this room have particularly beautiful tile panels.

✕ Take a Break

Enjoy a light lunch at Sutiş (p497), a garden cafe in the First Court.

Eavesdropping Sultans

In the Imperial Council Chamber, look for the gold grille high in the wall – the sultan sometimes listened in on council meetings through this.

Topkapı Palace

DAILY LIFE IN THE IMPERIAL COURT

A visit to this opulent palace compound, with its courtyards, harem and pavilions, offers a fascinating glimpse into the lives of the Ottoman sultans. During its heyday, royal wives and children, concubines, eunuchs and servants were among the 4000 people living within Topkapı's walls.

The sultans and their families rarely left the palace grounds, relying on courtiers and diplomats to bring them news of the outside world. Most visitors would go straight to the magnificent **❶ Imperial Council Chamber**, where the sultan's grand vizier and Dîvân (Council) regularly met to discuss affairs of state and receive foreign dignitaries. Many of these visitors brought lavish gifts and tributes to embellish the **❷ Imperial Treasury**.

After receiving any guests and meeting with the Dîvân, the grand vizier would make his way through the ornate **❸ Gate of Felicity** into the Third Court, the palace's residential quarter. Here, he would brief the sultan on the deliberations and decisions of the Dîvân in the colonnaded **❹ Audience Chamber**.

Meanwhile, day-to-day domestic chores and intrigues would be underway in the **❺ Harem** and servants would be preparing feasts in the massive **❻ Palace Kitchens**. Amid all this activity, the **❼ Marble Terrace** was a tranquil retreat where the sultan would come to relax, look out over the city and perhaps regret his sequestered lifestyle.

DON'T MISS

There are spectacular views from the terrace above the Konyalı Restaurant and also from the Marble Terrace in the Fourth Court.

Harem
The sultan, his mother and the crown prince had sumptuously decorated private apartments in the Harem. The most beautiful of these are the Twin Kiosks (pictured), which were used by the crown prince.

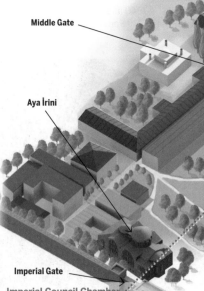

Harem Ticket Office

Middle Gate

Aya İrini

Imperial Gate

Imperial Council Chamber
This is where the Dîvân (Council) made laws, citizens presented petitions and foreign dignitaries were presented to the court. The sultan sometimes eavesdropped on proceedings through the window with the golden grille.

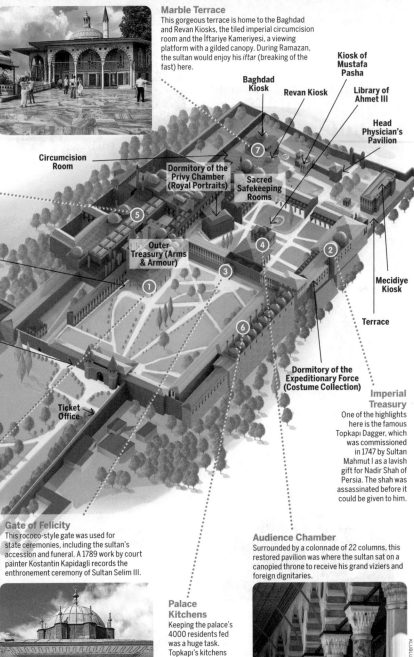

Marble Terrace
This gorgeous terrace is home to the Baghdad and Revan Kiosks, the tiled imperial circumcision room and the İftariye Kameriyesi, a viewing platform with a gilded canopy. During Ramazan, the sultan would enjoy his *iftar* (breaking of the fast) here.

Kiosk of Mustafa Pasha

Baghdad Kiosk

Revan Kiosk

Library of Ahmet III

Head Physician's Pavilion

Circumcision Room

Dormitory of the Privy Chamber (Royal Portraits)

Sacred Safekeeping Rooms

Outer Treasury (Arms & Armour)

Mecidiye Kiosk

Terrace

Dormitory of the Expeditionary Force (Costume Collection)

Ticket Office

Imperial Treasury
One of the highlights here is the famous Topkapı Dagger, which was commissioned in 1747 by Sultan Mahmut I as a lavish gift for Nadir Shah of Persia. The shah was assassinated before it could be given to him.

Gate of Felicity
This rococo-style gate was used for state ceremonies, including the sultan's accession and funeral. A 1789 work by court painter Kostantin Kapidagli records the enthronement ceremony of Sultan Selim III.

Audience Chamber
Surrounded by a colonnade of 22 columns, this restored pavilion was where the sultan sat on a canopied throne to receive his grand viziers and foreign dignitaries.

Palace Kitchens
Keeping the palace's 4000 residents fed was a huge task. Topkapı's kitchens occupied 10 domed buildings with 20 huge chimneys, and were workplace and home for 800 members of staff.

KLUBLU/SHUTTERSTOCK ©

Sultanahmet Saunter

Explore the heart of İstanbul's Old City in this walk through Sultanahmet's mosque-studded streets.

Start Aya Sofya Meydanı
Distance 2.3km
Duration two hours/ five to six hours if you visit Aya Sofya and Topkapı Palace

3 Veer left into picturesque Soğukçeşme Sokak, turn into Caferiye Sokak and then cross Alemdar Caddesi to reach the **Hippodrome**, where horse-drawn chariots raced in Byzantine times.

4 Walk down Şehit Mehmet Paşa Yokuşu and continue down Katip Sinan Camii Sokak to **Sokullu Şehit Mehmet Paşa Mosque** with its gorgeous tiled interior.

5 Veer left down Şehit Mehmet Paşa Sokak, turn left at Kadırga Limanı Caddesi and then seek out **Küçük (Little) Aya Sofya**, a Byzantine church subsequently converted into a mosque.

Divan Yolu Cad

Sultanahmet

BINBIRDIREK

Terzihane Sk

3

Dizdariye Çeşmesi Sk

Katip Sinan Camii Sk

Şehit Mehmet Paşa Yokuşu

Atmeydanı Cad

Şehit Mehmet Paşa Sk

4

Tavukhane Sk

Nakilbent Sk

Kadırga Limanı Cad

Aksakal Cad

Sıfa Hamamı Sk

Küçük Ayasofya Cami Sk

KÜÇÜK AYASOFYA

Küçük Ayasofya Cad

5

Mustafapaşa Sk

2 Head up Babıhümayun Caddesi to the Fountain of Sultan Ahmet III, an ornate rococo-style fountain outside **Topkapı Palace** (p482)

1 From the cruise terminal, take a taxi or tram to Sultanhmet. Admire the Byzantine magnificence of Aya Sofya and the adjacent Ottoman-era **Aya Sofya Tombs** (p490).

Classic Photo Blue Mosque

6 Continue east along Küçük Ayasofya Caddesi, walk up the hill at Aksakal Caddesi and then follow Nakilbent Sokak to the Arasta Bazaar, a shopping arcade built as part of the **Blue Mosque** (p490) complex.

Take a Break... The shady tables at **Derviş Cafe & Restaurant** (p499) offer splendid Blue Mosque views.

SULTANAHMET

CANKURTARAN

Fountain of Sultan Ahmet III

Aya Sofya *Meydani*

START

Sultanahmet Park

Yerebatan Cad

Alemdar Cad

Caferiye Sk

Soğukçeşme Sk

Seftali Sk

Babıhümayun Cad

Ishakpaşa Cad

Dalbasti Sk

Torun Sk

FINISH

N | 0 — 200 m
0 — 0.1 miles

⊙ SIGHTS

Most of the city's major museums and attractions are located in Sultanahmet and around the Grand Bazaar in the Old City.

◎ Sultanahmet

Blue Mosque   Mosque

(Sultanahmet Camii; ☎0212-458 4468; Hippodrome; ⊗closed to nonworshippers during 6 daily prayer times; 🚇Sultanahmet) İstanbul's most photogenic building was the grand project of Sultan Ahmet I (r 1603–17), whose tomb is located on the north side of the site facing Sultanahmet Park. The mosque's wonderfully curvaceous exterior features a cascade of domes and six slender minarets. Blue İznik tiles adorn the interior and give the building its unofficial but commonly used name.

Basilica Cistern   Historic Site

(Yerebatan Sarnıçı; ☎0212-512 1570; www.yerebatan.com; Yerebatan Caddesi; adult/child under 8yr ₺20/free; ⊗9am-5.30pm Nov–mid-Apr, to 6.30pm mid-Apr–Oct; 🚇Sultanahmet) This subterranean structure was commissioned by Emperor Justinian and built in 532. The largest surviving Byzantine cistern in İstanbul, it was constructed using 336 columns, many of which were salvaged from ruined temples and feature fine carved capitals. Its symmetry and sheer grandeur of conception are quite breathtaking, and its cavernous depths make a great retreat on summer days.

İstanbul Archaeology Museums   Museum

(İstanbul Arkeoloji Müzeleri; ☎0212-520 7740; www.istanbularkeoloji.gov.tr; Osman Hamdi Bey Yokuşu Sokak, Gülhane; adult/child under 8yr ₺30/free; ⊗9am-6pm Tue-Sun mid-Apr–Oct, 9am-4pm Tue-Sun Nov–mid-Apr; 🚇Gülhane) This superb museum showcases archaeological and artistic treasures from the Topkapı collections. Housed in three buildings, its exhibits include ancient artefacts, classical statuary and an exhibition tracing İstanbul's history. There are many highlights, but the sarcophagi from the Royal Necropolis of Sidon are particularly striking. Note that

the ticket office closes one hour before the museum's official closing time.

Museum of Turkish & Islamic Arts   Museum

(Türk ve İslam Eserleri Müzesi; ☎0212-518 1805; www.tiem.gov.tr; Atmeydanı Caddesi 46, Hippodrome; adult/child under 8yr ₺35/free; ⊗9am-4.30pm Nov–mid-Apr, to 6.30pm mid-Apr–Oct, closed Mon Nov-Mar; 🚇Sultanahmet) This Ottoman palace was built in 1524 for İbrahim Paşa, childhood friend, brother-in-law and grand vizier of Süleyman the Magnificent. Recently renovated, it has a magnificent collection of artefacts, including exquisite calligraphy and one of the world's most impressive antique carpet collections. Some large-scale carpets have been moved from the upper rooms to the **Carpet Museum** (Halı Müzesi; ☎0212-512 6993; cnr Babıhümayun Caddesi & Soğukçeşme Sokak; ₺10; ⊗9am-4pm Tue-Sun; 🚇Sultanahmet or Gülhane), but the collection remains a knockout with its palace carpets, prayer rugs and glittering artefacts such as a 17th-century Ottoman incense burner.

Aya Sofya Tombs   Tomb

(Aya Sofya Müzesi Padişah Türbeleri; ☎0212-522 1750; http://ayasofyamuzesi.gov.tr/en; Babıhümayun Caddesi; ⊗9am-5pm; 🚇Sultanahmet) **FREE** Part of the Aya Sofya complex but entered via Babıhümayun Caddesi, these tombs are the final resting places of five 16th- and 17th-century sultans – Mehmet III, Selim II, Murat III, İbrahim I and Mustafa I – most of whom are buried with members of their families. The ornate interior decoration in the tombs features the very best Ottoman tile work, calligraphy and decorative paintwork.

◎ Bazaar District

Grand Bazaar   Market

(Kapalı Çarşı, Covered Market; www.kapalicarsi.org.tr; ⊗9am-7pm Mon-Sat, last entry 6pm; 🚇Beyazıt Kapalıçarşı) The colourful and chaotic Grand Bazaar is the heart of İstanbul's Old City and has been so for centuries. Starting as a small vaulted *bedesten* (warehouse) built by order of Mehmet the Conqueror in

1461, it grew to cover a vast area as lanes between the *bedesten*, neighbouring shops and *hans* (caravanserais) were roofed and the market assumed the sprawling, labyrinthine form that it retains today.

When here, be sure to peep through doorways to discover hidden *hans*, veer down narrow lanes to watch artisans at work and wander the main thoroughfares to differentiate treasures from tourist tack. It's obligatory to drink lots of tea, compare price after price and try your hand at the art of bargaining. Allow at least three hours for your visit; some travellers spend three days!

Süleymaniye Mosque
Mosque

(Professor Sıddık Sami Onar Caddesi; ☉dawn-dusk; ⓂVezneciler) The Süleymaniye crowns one of İstanbul's seven hills and dominates the Golden Horn, providing a landmark for the entire city. Though it's not the largest of the Ottoman mosques, it is certainly one of the grandest and most beautiful. It's also unusual in that many of its original *külliye* (mosque complex) buildings have been retained and sympathetically adapted for reuse.

Spice Bazaar
Market

(Mısır Çarşısı, Egyptian Market; ☏0212-513 6597; www.misircarsisi.org; ☉8am-7pm Mon-Fri, 8am-7.30pm Sat, 9.30am-7pm Sun; ⓇEminönü) Vividly coloured spices are displayed alongside jewel-like *lokum* (Turkish delight) at this Ottoman-era marketplace, providing eye candy for the thousands of tourists and locals who make their way here every day. Stalls also sell caviar, dried herbs, honey, nuts and dried fruits. The number of stalls selling tourist trinkets increases annually, yet this remains a great place to stock up on edible souvenirs, share a few jokes with vendors and marvel at the well-preserved building.

◎ Beyoğlu
İstiklal Caddesi
Street

(Independence Ave; ⓂTaksim, Şişhane) Once called the Grand Rue de Pera but renamed İstiklal (Independence) in the early years of the Republic, Beyoğlu's premier boulevard

Mosque Etiquette

● Remove your shoes before walking on the mosque's carpet; you can leave them on shelves near the mosque door or place them in one of the plastic bags provided and carry them with you.

● Women should always cover their heads and shoulders with a shawl or scarf; both women and men should dress modestly.

● Avoid visiting mosques at prayer times – within 30 minutes of when the *ezan* (call to prayer) sounds from the mosque's minaret – and also around Friday lunch, when weekly sermons and group prayers are held.

● Speak quietly and don't photograph people who are praying.

Shoe stand in the Blue Mosque
PIT STOCK/SHUTTERSTOCK ©

is a perfect metaphor for 21st-century Turkey, being an exciting mix of modernity and tradition. Contemporary boutiques and cutting-edge cultural centres are housed in its grand 19th-century buildings, and an antique tram traverses its length alongside crowds of pedestrians making their way to the bustling cafes, bistros and bars for which Beyoğlu is known.

Pera Museum
Museum

(Pera Müzesi; ☏0212-334 9900; www.peramuseum.org; Meşrutiyet Caddesi 65, Tepebaşı; adult/student/child under 12yr ₺20/10/free; ☉10am-7pm Tue-Thu & Sat, to 10pm Fri, noon-6pm Sun; ⓂŞişhane, ⓇTünel) There's plenty to see at

Central İstanbul

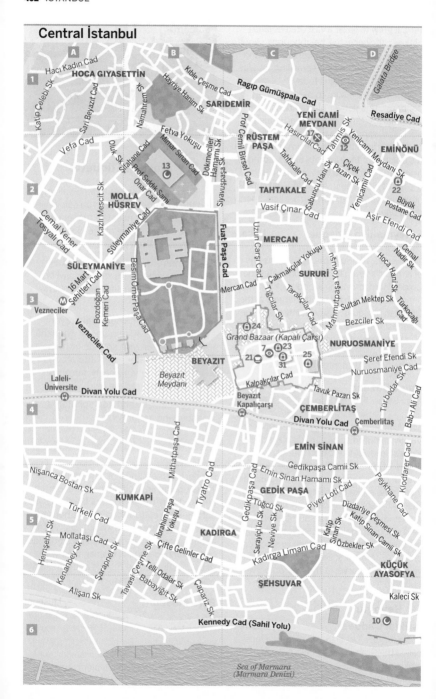

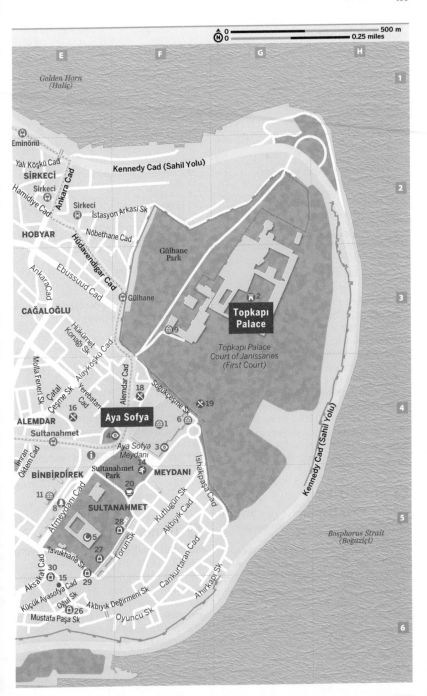

N 0 — 500 m
0 — 0.25 miles

Golden Horn
(Haliç)

Eminönü

Yalı Köşkü Cad

SİRKECİ
Sirkeci

Hamidiye Cad

Ankara Cad

Sirkeci
İstasyon Arkasi Sk

Kennedy Cad (Sahil Yolu)

HOBYAR

Hüdavendigar Cad

Nöbethane Cad

Gülhane
Park

Ankara Cad
Ebussuud Cad

CAĞALOĞLU

Gülhane

Topkapı
Palace

2

Hükümet
Konağı Sk

9

Molla Feneri Sk

Alayköşkü Cad

Yerebatan
Cad

Alemdar Cad

Topkapı Palace
Court of Janissaries
(First Court)

Çatal
Çeşme Sk

16

18

Soğukçeşme Sk

ALEMDAR

Aya Sofya

19

Sultanahmet

1

6

4

3

Aya Sofya
Meydanı

Kennedy Cad (Sahil Yolu)

İmran
Öktem Cad

BİNBİRDİREK

Sultanahmet
Park

14

MEYDANI

İshakpaşa Cad

11

8

Atmeydanı Cad

20

Bosphorus Strait
(Boğaziçi)

SULTANAHMET

28

Kutluğün Sk

Akbıyık Cad

5

27

Tavukhane Sk

Torun Sk

Cankurtaran Cad

30

15

29

Aksakal Cad

Küçük Ayasofya Cad

Oğul Sk

26

Akbıyık Değirmeni Sk

Ahırkapı Sk

Mustafa Paşa Sk

Oyuncu Sk

Central İstanbul

this impressive museum, but its major draw is undoubtedly the 2nd-floor exhibition of paintings featuring Turkish Orientalist themes. Drawn from Suna and İnan Kıraç's world-class private collection, the works provide fascinating glimpses into the Ottoman world from the 17th to 20th centuries and include the most beloved painting in the Turkish canon – Osman Hamdı Bey's *The Tortoise Trainer* (1906). Other floors host high-profile temporary exhibitions (past exhibitions have showcased Warhol, de Chirico, Picasso and Botero).

⊕ ACTIVITIES

Kılıç Ali Paşa Hamamı — Hamam

(☎0212-393 8010; http://kilicalipasahamami. com; Hamam Sokak 1, off Kemeraltı Caddesi, Tophane; traditional hamam ritual ₺270; ⊙women 8am-4pm, men 4.30-11.30pm; ⛴Tophane) It took seven years to develop a conservation plan for this 1580 Mimar Sinan–designed building and complete the meticulous restoration. Fortunately, the result was well worth waiting for. The hamam's interior is simply stunning and the place is run with total professionalism, ensuring a clean and enjoyable Turkish bath experience.

Services include a traditional hamam ritual (₺220) and massage (from ₺160).

Ayasofya Hürrem Sultan Hamamı — Hamam

(☎0212-517 3535; www.ayasofyahamami.com; Aya Sofya Meydanı 2; bath treatments €55-160, massages €100-160; ⊙8am-10pm; ⛴Sultanahmet) This meticulously restored twin hamam dating to 1556 offers the most luxurious traditional bath experience in the Old City. Designed by Mimar Sinan, it was built just across the road from Aya Sofya by order of Süleyman the Magnificent and named in honour of his wife Hürrem Sultan, commonly known as Roxelana.

⊕ TOURS

İstanbul Walks — Walking

(☎0212-516 6300, 0554 335 6622; www.istanbul-walks.com; 1st fl, Şifa Hamamı Sokak 1; tours €60-130; ⛴Sultanahmet) Specialising in cultural tourism, this company is run by history buffs and offers a large range of guided walking tours conducted by knowledgeable English-speaking guides. Tours concentrate on İstanbul's various neighbourhoods, but there are also tours of major monuments, a Turkish coffee trail, and a Bosphorus and Golden

Horn cruise by private boat. Significant discounts for children aged under seven.

🛍 SHOPPING

🔒 Sultanahmet

The best shopping in Sultanahmet is found in the Arasta Bazaar, next to the Blue Mosque.

Jennifer's Hamam — Homewares

(📞0212-516 3022; www.jennifershamam.com; Arasta Bazaar 135; ⏰8.30am-9pm Apr-Oct, to 7pm Nov-Mar; 🚋Sultanahmet) Owned by Canadian Jennifer Gaudet, this shop stocks top-quality hamam items, including towels, robes and *peştemals* (bath wraps) produced using certified organic cotton and silk on old-style shuttled looms. It also sells natural soaps and *keses* (coarse cloth mittens used for exfoliation). Prices are set; no bargaining.

Mehmet Çetinkaya Gallery — Carpets, Jewellery

(📞0212-517 6808, 0212-517 1603; www.cetinkayagallery.com; Tavukhane Sokak 5-7; ⏰9am-8pm; 🚋Sultanahmet) Mehmet Çetinkaya is one of the country's foremost experts on antique oriental carpets and kilims (pileless woven rugs). Built over a Byzantine well, his flagship store-cum-gallery stocks items of artistic and ethnographic significance, and is full of treasures including carpets, kilims, textiles and jewellery. A branch in the **Arasta Bazaar** sells textiles and antique jewellery.

Nakkaş — Carpets

(📞0212-516 5222; www.nakkasrug.com; Nakilbent Sokak 13; ⏰9am-7pm; 🚋Sultanahmet) Nakkaş sells carpets, textiles, ceramics and jewellery. Its varied collection of more than 20,000 carpets and kilims includes antique rugs, hand-woven pieces and traditional Anatolian carpets. A few have even won design awards.

🔒 Bazaar District

Epoque — Antiques

(📞0212-527 7865; Sandal Bedesten Sokak 38, Grand Bazaar; ⏰8.30am-6.15pm Mon-Sat;

♨ Visiting a Hamam

Visiting a hamam is one of İstanbul's quintessential experiences. Traditional hamams have separate sections for men and women, or have only one set of facilities and admit men and women at different times.

Bath etiquette requires that men cover their genitalia with a *peştemal* (cotton towel) at all times. Most women wear a bikini or a pair of knickers (Turks tend to do the latter). Some tourist hamams don't mind women baring all. During the bathing, everyone washes their private parts themselves, without removing the *peştemal* or underclothes.

Upon entry you will be allocated a dressing cubicle or locker and given a *peştemal* and either plastic sandals or wooden clogs. Store your clothes and don the *peştemal* and footwear. An attendant will then lead you to the *hararet* (steam room), where you wash and relax before enjoying the soap massage that forms the base of all hamam packages. During the massage you will be lathered in soapsuds, scrubbed with a *kese* (coarse cloth mitten) and doused with water. After it's finished, you can stay in the *hararet* or adjourn to the *camekan* (entrance hall), where you can rest; at some hamams you can order something to eat or drink here.

The average hamam experience takes around one hour. Tipping the attendant is appreciated but not obligatory.

Soap massage at Ayasofya Hürrem Sultan Hamamı

The Art of Bargaining

If you are keen to buy a carpet or kilim (rug) while in İstanbul, keep the following tips in mind:

- Scam artists abound in the carpet trade. Be extremely wary in all of your negotiations and dealings. Never let someone you meet on the street take you into a rug shop – these touts work on commission.

- The 'official' prices in rug shops have almost always been artificially inflated to allow for a bargaining margin, with 20% to 30% the rule of thumb.

- Never feel pressured to buy something. The tea you will almost inevitably be offered is gratis. If you choose to drink tea with the rug merchant, you don't need to buy anything in exchange.

- Before starting to bargain, decide how much you like the carpet or rug and how much you are prepared to pay for it. It's important that you stick to this. The shopkeepers here are professional bargainers and have loads of practice in talking customers into purchases against their better judgement.

Shopping for carpets in İstanbul
ROBEDERO/GETTY IMAGES ©

🏛Beyazıt-Kapalı Çarşı) Serious antique shoppers should make their way to this old-fashioned business near the bazaar's Nuruosmaniye Gate. Silver candlesticks and trays, enamelled cigarette cases, jewellery, watches and an extraordinary range of icons are on offer in the elegant shop.

The elderly owner and sales members are happy to welcome browsers.

Necef Antik & Gold · Jewellery

(☎0212-513 0372; necefantik@outlook.com; Şerifağa Sokak 123, İç Bedesten, Grand Bazaar; ⊗8.30am-6.30pm Mon-Sat; 🏛Beyazıt-Kapalı Çarşı) Owner Haluk Botasun has been hand-crafting 24-carat gold jewellery in his tiny İç Bedesten store for decades, producing attractive pieces in Byzantine and Ottoman styles. The earrings and cufflinks featuring delicate mosaics are particularly desirable.

Derviş · Textiles

(☎0212-528 7883; www.dervis.com; Halıcılar Sokak 51, Grand Bazaar; ⊗9am-7pm Mon-Sat; 🏛Beyazıt-Kapalı Çarşı) Raw cotton and silk *peştemals* share shelf space here with traditional Turkish dowry vests and engagement dresses. If these don't take your fancy, the pure olive-oil soaps and old hamam bowls are sure to step into the breach. There's another **branch** (Cebeci Han 10, Grand Bazaar; ⊗8.30am-7pm Mon-Sat; 🏛Beyazıt-Kapalı Çarşı) off Yağlıçılar Caddesi.

Ali Muhıddin Hacı Bekir · Food

(☎0212-522 8543; www.hacibekir.com.tr; Hamidiye Caddesi 33, Eminönü; ⊗7.30am-9pm; 🏛Eminönü) Many people think that this historic shop, which has been operated by members of the same family for over 200 years, is the best place in the city to buy *lokum*. Choose from *sade* (plain), *cevizli* (walnut), *fıstıklı* (pistachio), *badem* (almond) or *roze* (rose water).

🅐 Beyoğlu

Hiç · Homewares

(☎0212-251 9973; www.hiccrafts.com; Lüleci Hendek Caddesi 35, Tophane; ⊗11am-7pm Mon-Sat; 🏛Tophane) Interior designer Emel Güntaş is one of İstanbul's style icons and this recently opened contemporary crafts shop in Tophane is a favourite destination for the city's design mavens. The stock includes cushions, carpets, kilims, silk scarves, lamps, furniture, glassware, porcelain and felt crafts. Everything here is artisan-made and absolutely gorgeous.

Ali Muhıddin Hacı Bekir

Nahıl
Handicrafts, Bathware

(0212-251 9085; www.nahil.com.tr; Bekar Sokak 17, Taksim; ⊙10am-7pm Mon-Sat; MTaksim) The felting, lacework, embroidery, all-natural soaps and soft toys in this lovely shop are made by economically disadvantaged women in Turkey's rural areas. All profits are returned to them, ensuring that they and their families have better lives.

🍴 EATING

🍴 Sultanahmet

Sutiş
Turkish €

(0212-514 9494; www.sutis.com.tr; First Court, Topkapı Palace; sandwiches ₺17-21, burgers ₺28-29, desserts ₺15-17; ⊙9am-7pm Apr–mid-Sep, to 5pm mid-Sep–Mar) This branch of the popular local chain is a great place to enjoy the Sutiş signature dish – *bal kamak* (honey and clotted cream), which is wonderful slathered on *simit* (sesame-encrusted bread ring) or bread. Enjoy it with a tea, coffee or fresh fruit juice. Prices are reasonable considering the location, and the terrace seating is delightful in fine weather.

Deraliye
Turkish €€€

(☎0212-520 7778; www.deraliyerestaurant. com; Ticarethane Sokak 10; mezes ₺15-55, mains ₺28-69; ⊙11.30am-4pm & 6pm-midnight; ❄️📶; 🚇Sultanahmet) Providing a taste of the sumptuous dishes once served in the great Ottoman palaces, Deraliye offers diners the chance to order delights such as the goose kebap served to Süleyman the Magnificent or Mehmet II's favourite lamb stew. Those with less adventurous palates can opt for modern standards such as kebaps. There are whirling dervish and Ottoman music performances on weekends.

Matbah
Turkish €€€

(☎0212-514 6151; www.matbahrestaurant.com; Ottoman Hotel Imperial, Caferiye Sokak 6/1; mezes ₺14-20, mains ₺29-65; ⊙noon-10.30pm; 📶📶; 🚇Sultanahmet) One of a growing number of restaurants specialising in so-called Ottoman palace cuisine, Matbah offers dishes devised centuries ago in the royal kitchens of Constantinople. The menu changes with the season and features unusual ingredients such as goose, quail, quince and molasses.

Bazaar District

Hamdi Restaurant   Kebap €€

(0212-512 1144; www.hamdirestorant.com.tr; Kalçın Sokak 11, Eminönü; mezes ₺12-28, kebaps ₺29-50; noon-11.30pm; P ❋ ; Eminönü) One of the city's best-loved restaurants, this place near the Spice Bazaar is owned by Hamdi Arpacı, who started out as a street-food vendor in the 1960s. His tasty Urfa-style kebaps were so popular that he soon graduated from his modest stand to this building, which has views of the Old City, Golden Horn and Galata from its top-floor terrace.

Beyoğlu

Hayvore   Turkish €

(0212-245 7501; http://hayvore.com.tr/; Turnacıbaşı Sokak 4, Galatasaray; soups ₺6-10, pides ₺16-23, portions ₺10-20; 11.30am-11pm; ❋ ; Taksim) Notable *lokantas* (traditional eateries serving ready-made dishes) are few and far between in modern-day Beyoğlu, so the existence of this bustling place next to the Galatasaray Lycée is to be celebrated. Specialising in Black Sea cuisine, its delicious leafy greens, pilafs, *hamsi* (fresh anchovy) dishes, soups and pides (Turkish-style pizza) are best enjoyed at lunch – go early to score a table.

Karaköy Güllüoğlu   Sweets, Börek €

(0212-293 0910; www.karakoygulluoglu.com; Katlı Otopark, Kemankeş Caddesi, Karaköy; portion baklava ₺11-19, portion börek ₺9-9.50; 7am-midnight Mon-Thu, 7am-1am Fri-Sat, 8am-1am Sun; ; Karaköy) This much-loved *baklavacı* (baklava shop) opened in 1949 and was the first İstanbul branch of a business established in Gaziantep in the 1820s. There are other Güllüoğlu offshoots around town, but this remains the best. Pay for a *porsiyon* (portion) of whatever takes your fancy at the register, then order at the counters.

Karaköy Lokantası   Turkish €€

(0212-292 4455; www.karakoylokantasi.com; Kemankeş Caddesi 37a, Karaköy; mezes ₺10-24, lunch portions ₺13-25, mains ₺28-55; noon-4pm & 6pm-midnight Mon-Sat, 4pm-midnight Sun; ❋ ; Karaköy) Known for its gorgeous tiled interior, genial owner and bustling vibe, Karaköy Lokantası serves tasty and

Karabatak

well-priced food to its loyal local clientele. It functions as a *lokanta* during the day, but at night it morphs into a *meyhane* (tavern), with slightly higher prices. Bookings are essential for dinner.

🍷 DRINKING & NIGHTLIFE

🍷 Sultanahmet

Derviş Cafe & Restaurant   Tea Garden

(cnr Dalbastı Sokak & Kabasakal Caddesi; ⊙7am-midnight; 🚊Sultanahmet) Superbly located directly opposite the Blue Mosque, the Derviş beckons patrons with its comfortable cane chairs and shady trees. Efficient service, reasonable prices and peerless people-watching opportunities make it a great place for a leisurely çay (₺4), nargile (water pipe; ₺35), *tost* (toasted sandwich; ₺10) and a game of backgammon.

🍷 Bazaar District

Şark Kahvesi   Cafe

(Oriental Coffee Shop; ☎0212-512 1144; Yağlıkçılar Caddesi 134, Grand Bazaar; ⊙8.30am-6pm Mon-Sat; 🚊Beyazıt-Kapalı Çarşı) The Şark's arched ceiling betrays its former existence as part of a bazaar street – years ago some enterprising *kahveci* (coffeehouse owner) walled up several sides and turned it into a cafe. Located on one of the bazaar's major thoroughfares, it's popular with both stall-holders and tourists, who enjoy tea, coffee (Turkish, espresso and filter) or a cold drink.

🍷 Beyoğlu

Karabatak   Cafe €

(☎0212-243 6995; www.karabatak.com; Kara Ali Kaptan Sokak 7, Karaköy; ⊙8.30am-10.30pm Mon-Fri, 9.30am-10.30pm Sat & Sun; 🛜; 🚊Tophane) Importing dark-roasted Julius Meinl coffee from Vienna, Karabatak's baristas use it to conjure up some of Karaköy's best brews. The outside seating is hotly contested, but the quiet tables inside can be just as alluring. Choose from filter, espresso or Turkish

coffee and order a panino (sandwich) if you're hungry.

ℹ️ INFORMATION

Tourist Office – Sultanahmet (☎0212-518 1802; Hippodrome, Sultanahmet; ⊙9am-5.30pm; 🚊Sultanahmet) Helpful, conveniently located tourist office. ATMs and public toilets are found nearby.

ℹ️ GETTING AROUND

Public transport is cheap and efficient. *Jetons* (ticket tokens; ₺5) can be purchased from ticket machines or offices at some tram stops, at ferry docks and at funicular and metro stations.

Funicular A funicular called the Tünel carries passengers between Karaköy and Tünel Meydanı (Sq), at the southern end of İstiklal Caddesi. *Jetons* costs ₺4. Another funicular carries passengers from the Kabataş tram stop to Taksim Meydanı, where it connects to the metro.

Metro The M2 connects the Taksim Sq and Şişhane metro stops in Beyoğlu with the Vezneciler-İstanbul University stop near the Grand Bazaar and Süleymaniye Mosque (direction Yenıkapı).

Taxi Taxi fares are very reasonable and rates are the same during both day and night. It costs around ₺20 to travel between the port and Aya Sofya Meydanı in Sultanahmet or the Grand Bazaar. A fare from the port to Taksim Meydanı should cost around ₺15. Insist on the driver using the meter – if they demand a flat fare they are almost certainly trying to gouge you. Tips aren't obligatory – most locals round up to the nearest lira.

Tram The closest tram stops to the cruise terminals are Karaköy, Fındıklı and Tophane; *jetons* can be purchased at Karaköy and Tophane. From these stops, trams run to Sultanahmet and the Bazaar District (direction Bağcılar or Cevizlibağ) and also to Kabataş, from where a funicular carries passengers to Taksim Meydanı (Sq) at the northern end of İstiklal Caddesi. Note the tram line will be extended from Kabataş to Beşiktaş-Mecidiyeköy in the future.

Vieux Nice (p126)

In Focus

Statue of Romulus and Remus, Rome

History

Understanding Mediterranean Europe's long and often troubled history is crucial to understanding the region today. Fragments of that history can be encountered in the tumbledown remains of Roman amphitheatres and bathhouses, in the hulking bulwarks of coastal fortresses, and in the winding streets, broad boulevards and governing institutions of its many stately cities.

7000–3000 BC
For 4000 years, inhabitants of the Mediterranean region lived a simple agrarian life.

3000–1100 BC
The discovery of how to blend copper and tin into a strong alloy heralds the Bronze Age.

753 BC
According to legend, Rome is founded by twin brothers, Romulus and Remus.

Pompeii ruins (p240)

Prehistory

The first settlers arrived in Europe around two million years ago, but it wasn't until the end of the last major ice age, between 12,000 BC and 8000 BC, that humans really took hold. As the glaciers and ice sheets retreated, hunter-gatherer tribes extended their reach northwards in search of new land.

From these beginnings, pastoral communities emerged during Neolithic times (7000–3000 BC). Agriculturally sophisticated, they grew crops, bred sheep and goats, and used clay to produce pots, vases and stylised representations of idols as figures of worship.

Greeks & Romans

The civilisation of ancient Greece emerged around 2000 BC and made huge leaps forward in science, technology, architecture, philosophy and democratic principles. Indeed, many

323 BC

The death of Alexander the Great serves as a transition point between the Classical and Hellenistic eras of ancient Greek history.

1st century BC–AD 4

The Romans conquer much of Europe. The Roman Empire flourishes under Augustus and his successors.

AD 79

Mt Vesuvius showers molten rock and ash upon Pompeii and Herculaneum.

Statue of Emperor Augustus, Rome

PERSPECTIVESTOCK/SHUTTERSTOCK ©

★ First Five Roman Emperors

Augustus (27 BC–AD 14)

Tiberius (AD 14–37)

Caligula (AD 37–41)

Claudius (AD 41–54)

Nero (AD 54–68)

of the writers, thinkers and mathematicians of ancient Greece, from Pythagoras to Plato, continue to exert a profound influence today.

Indo-European migrants introduced the processing of bronze into Greece and from there began three remarkable civilisations: Cycladic, Minoan and Mycenaean. The Cycladic civilisation was a cluster of fishing and farming island communities with a sophisticated artistic temperament, while the Minoans were Europe's first advanced civilisation, named after King Minos, the mythical ruler of Crete. Using bronze, the Minoans were able to build great sea vessels and their reach extended across Asia Minor and North Africa. The jury is out on what triggered the demise of this great civilisation, but the decline of the Minoans coincided with the rise of Mycenae (1600–1100 BC), which reached its peak between 1500 and 1200 BC with mainland city-states such as Corinth, Tiryns and Mycenae.

Then came the Romans, who set about conquering most of Europe and devised the world's first republic. Initially, the Romans were a rough-and-ready lot. Rome did not bother to mint coins until 269 BC, even though the neighbouring (and later conquered or allied) Etruscans and Greeks had long had their own currencies. The Etruscans and Greeks also brought writing to the attention of the Romans, who found it useful for documents and technical affairs.

Slowly at first, then with gathering pace, Roman armies conquered the Italian peninsula. Wars with Carthage and other rivals in the east led Rome to take control of Sardinia, Sicily, Corsica, mainland Greece, Spain, most of North Africa and part of Asia Minor by 133 BC. By the second half of the 2nd century BC, Rome was the most important city in the Mediterranean, with a population of 300,000.

At its height, Roman power extended all the way from Celtic Britain to ancient Persia (Iran). By AD 100, the city of Rome was said to have had more than 1.5 million inhabitants and all the trappings of an imperial capital. The Romans' myriad achievements are almost too numerous to mention: they founded cities, raised aqueducts, constructed roads, laid sewers and built baths all over the continent, and produced a string of brilliant writers, orators, politicians, philosophers and military leaders.

100–138	395	410
The Roman Empire reaches its greatest extent during the reign of Hadrian.	The Roman Empire is split into separate western and eastern courts with competing capitals in Mediolanum and Constantinople.	The sacking of Rome by the Goths brings an end to (western) Roman dominance.

Dark Ages to Middle Ages

Rome's empire-building ambitions eventually proved too much, and a series of political troubles and military disasters resulted in the sacking of Rome (in 410) by the Goths. Although Roman emperors clung onto their eastern Byzantine empire for another thousand years, founding a new capital at Constantinople (modern day İstanbul), Rome's dominance over Western Europe was over.

After the decline of Rome, Western Europe regressed into what became known as the 'Dark Ages', an era of cultural stagnation, demographic decline and feudalism about which relatively little is documented. Meanwhile over in the Balkans, Rome's Eastern Empire carried on somewhat more illustriously as Byzantium, its size and influence ebbing and flowing until its final collapse in 1453. At its greatest extent in around 555, Byzantium included Turkey, Greece, the Balkan states, Italy and parts of North Africa.

The next few centuries were marked by a series of conflicts in which the various kingdoms of the European mainland sought to gain political and strategic control. In AD 711, the Moors – Arabs and Berbers who had converted to the Islamic religion prevailing throughout northern Africa – crossed the Straits of Gibraltar, defeating the Visigothic army. They went on to rule the Iberian Peninsula for almost 800 years, until the fall of Granada in 1492, leaving behind a flourishing architectural, scientific and academic legacy.

Meanwhile, in the late 8th century Charlemagne, King of the Franks, brought together much of Western Europe under what would become known as the Holy Roman Empire. This alliance of Christian nations sent troops to reclaim the Holy Land from Islamic control in a series of campaigns known as the Crusades.

The Renaissance

Europe's troubles rumbled on into the 14th and 15th centuries. In the wake of further conflicts and political upheavals, as well as the devastating outbreak of the Black Death, control over the Holy Roman Empire passed into the hands of the Austrian Habsburgs, a political dynasty that was to become one of the continent's dominant powers.

The Italian city-states of Genoa, Venice, Pisa and Amalfi consolidated their control over the Mediterranean, establishing trading links with much of the rest of Europe and the Far East, and embarking on some of the first journeys in search of the New World.

In the mid-15th century, a new age of artistic and philosophical development broke out across the continent. The Renaissance was an artistic and cultural movement that unapologetically tapped the philosophy and ideas of classical antiquity for inspiration. Revisiting works of Greek and Roman scribes and builders, Italian 'Renaissance Men' such as writer Francesco Petrarch, architect Filippo Brunelleschi and painter Leonardo da Vinci styled themselves as budding humanists aiming to replace the tradition and dogma of the Middle Ages with self-expression and rational thought. The Renaissance ushered in an exciting new era of exploration and discovery that gradually spread all

1347–51	**1453**	**15th century**
The Black Death rages across Europe, wiping out an estimated 45% to 50% of the continent's population.	The Christian civilisation of Byzantium (aka the Eastern Roman Empire) falls to the Ottomans.	The Italian Renaissance brings about a revolution in art, architecture and science.

★ **Best Historical Buildings**

Colosseum (p200), Italy

Pompeii (p240), Italy

City Walls & Forts (p350), Croatia

Palace of Knossos (p410), Greece

Aya Sofya (p478), Turkey

Dubrovnik city walls & fortresses (p350)

EKATERINA KUPEEVA/SHUTTERSTOCK ©

over Europe. Scientists looked up to the stars and carefully dissected the human body, artists rethought the rules of painting using realism, linear perspective and close studies of nature, and architects dusted off building methods forgotten since Roman times.

In a relatively short space of time, civilisation made a giant intellectual leap into the future. Developments were revolutionary and contagious, changing society forever. Michelangelo designed a spectacular new dome for St Peter's Basilica in Rome; Christopher Columbus, at the behest of the Spanish monarchy, set sail for the Americas; and the printing press, pioneered by Johannes Gutenberg in Germany, became the new means of mass communication.

The Reformation & the Enlightenment

While the Renaissance challenged artistic ideas, the Reformation dealt with questions of religion. Challenging Catholic 'corruption' and the divine authority of the pope, the German theologian Martin Luther established his own breakaway branch of the Church, to which he gave the name 'Protestantism', in 1517. Luther's stance was soon echoed by the English monarch Henry VIII, who cut ties with Rome in 1534 and went on to found his own (Protestant) Church of England, sowing the seeds for centuries of conflict between Catholics and Protestants.

By the early 17th century, whole nation states were embroiled in the growing religious fissure, which eventually culminated in the long and bloody Thirty Years' War (1618–48), which began as a conflict between Catholics and Protestants and eventually sucked in most of Europe's principal powers. France and Spain were key figures, although other Mediterranean countries, which remained predominantly Catholic, escaped its clutches. The war was ended by the Peace of Westphalia in 1648, and Europe entered a period of comparative stability.

The Enlightenment (sometimes known as 'The Age of Reason') is the name given to a philosophical movement that spread throughout European society during the mid- to late-17th century. It emphasised the importance of logic, reason and science over the doctrines

1517	1789	1815
Martin Luther nails his demands to the church door in Wittenberg, sparking the Reformation.	The French Revolution overthrows the Bourbon monarchy and lays down the principals of liberty, equality and fraternity.	The Congress of Vienna ends the Napoleonic wars and redraws the map of Europe.

of religion. Key figures included the philosophers Baruch Spinoza, John Locke, Immanuel Kant and Voltaire, as well as scientists such as Isaac Newton.

The Enlightenment also questioned the political status quo. Since the Middle Ages, the majority of Europe's wealth and power had been concentrated in the hands of an all-powerful elite, largely made up of monarchs and aristocrats. This stood in direct contradiction to one of the core values of the Enlightenment – equality. Many thinkers believed it was an impasse that could only be solved by revolution.

Revolution

Things came to a head in 1789 when armed mobs stormed the Bastille prison in Paris, thus kick-starting the French Revolution. The Revolution began with high ideals, inspired by its iconic slogan of *liberté, egalité, fraternité* (liberty, equality, brotherhood). Before long, things turned sour and heads began to roll. Hardline republicans seized control and de-manded retribution for centuries of oppression. Scores of aristocrats met their end under the guillotine's blade, including the French monarch Louis XVI, who was publicly executed in January 1793 in Paris' Place de la Concorde, and his queen, Marie-Antoinette, who was killed in October that year.

The Reign of Terror between September 1793 and July 1794 saw religious freedoms revoked, churches closed, cathedrals turned into 'Temples of Reason' and thousands beheaded. In the chaos, a dashing young Corsican general named Napoleon Bonaparte (1769–1821) seized his chance.

Napoleon assumed power in 1799 and in 1804 was crowned Emperor. He fought a series of campaigns across Europe, including invasions of Spain and Italy, and conquered vast swathes of territory for the French empire. Following a disastrous campaign to conquer Russia in 1812, however, his grip on power faltered and he was defeated by a coalition of British and Prussian forces at the Battle of Waterloo in 1815.

Industry, Empire & WWI

Having vanquished Napoleon, Britain emerged as Europe's predominant power. With such innovations as the steam engine, the railway and the factory, Britain unleashed the Industrial Revolution and, like many of Europe's major powers (including France, Spain, Belgium and the Austro-Hungarian Empire), set about developing its colonies across much of Africa, Australasia and the Middle and Far East.

Before long these competing empires clashed again, with predictably catastrophic con-sequences. The assassination of the heir to the Austro-Hungarian Empire, Franz Ferdinand, in 1914 led to the outbreak of the Great War, or WWI, as it came to be known. Mediterrane-an Europe's loyalties were divided in the conflict: Greece and Italy were initially neutral, but eventually sided with France and the Western Allies against Turkey and the Central Powers on the promise of land following a victory; Spain remained neutral.

1914–18	**1939–45**	**1957**
Colonial rivalry, rearmament and a complex system of alliances push Europe into WWI.	WWII rages across Europe, devastating many cities. After peace is declared, much of Eastern Europe falls under communist rule.	The European Economic Community (EEC) is formed by a collection of Western European countries.

In the Treaty of Versailles, the defeated powers of Austro-Hungary and Germany lost large areas of territory and found themselves crippled with a massive bill for reparations, sowing seeds of discontent that would be exploited a decade later by a fanatical Austrian painter by the name of Adolf Hitler.

Rise of Fascism

Hitler's rise to power was astonishingly swift. By 1933 he had become Chancellor and, as the head of the Nazi Party, assumed total control of Germany. Having spent much of the 1930s building up a formidable war machine, assisting General Franco's nationalist forces during the Spanish Civil War, Hitler annexed former German territories in Austria and parts of Czechoslovakia, before extending his reach onward into Poland in 1939.

The occupation of Poland proved the final straw. Britain, France and its Commonwealth allies declared war on Germany, which had formed its own alliance of convenience with the Axis powers of Italy (led by the fascist dictator Benito Mussolini) and Japan.

WWII

Having done a secret deal with Joseph Stalin over the Soviet Union's spheres of influence to the east, Hitler unleashed his blitzkrieg on an unsuspecting Western Europe, and within a few short months had conquered huge areas of territory forcing the French into submission and driving the British forces to a humiliating retreat at Dunkirk. Italy, initially neutral, joined the war on the side of Germany in June 1940, when it seemed almost over, invading Greece later that year in what would become the disastrous Greco-Italian War. In September 1943, Italy surrendered to the Allies, then, on 13 October, Italy switched sides and declared war on its former Axis partners.

At either ends of the Mediterranean, Spain and Turkey stayed almost completely out of WWII.

The Axis retained the upper hand until the Japanese attack on Pearl Harbor forced a reluctant USA into the war in 1941. Hitler's subsequent decision to invade the Soviet Union in 1941 proved to be a catastrophic error, resulting in devastating German losses that opened the door for the Allied invasion of Normandy in June 1944.

After several months of bitter fighting, Hitler's remaining forces were pushed back towards Berlin. Hitler committed suicide on 30 April 1945, and the Russians took the city, crushing the last pockets of German resistance.

Europe United

After WWII ended in 1945 most of Europe lay in ruins, propped up by economic aid from the Americans (through the US$12 billion Marshall Plan) or the Soviet Union (through the concurrent Molotov Plan). Following centuries of war, genocide and petty squabbles be-

1993	2002	2009
The Maastricht Treaty leads to the formation of the European Union (EU).	Twelve member states of the EU ditch their national currencies in favour of the euro.	Europe is rocked by a series of financial crises, leading to costly bailouts for Ireland, Greece, Portugal and Spain.

tween incestuous royal families, the continent appeared to have finally learned its lesson. Slowly but surely, Europe began to put its differences aside and work on forging long-term cooperation.

The formation of the European Economic Community (EEC) in 1957 began as a loose trade alliance between six nations (Belgium, France, Italy, Luxembourg, the Netherlands and West Germany). By 1992, this alliance had evolved into the European Union (EU) and when the Treaty of Maastricht came into effect in 1993 its core membership had expanded to 28 countries. Five new candidates – Turkey, North Macedonia, Montenegro, Albania and Serbia – are on the books for future membership. All except Albania and North Macedonia have started negotiations for entry.

Another key development was the implementation of the Schengen Agreement in 1995, which abolished border checks across much of mainland Europe and allowed EU citizens to travel freely throughout member states (with the notable exceptions of the UK and Ireland).

Even more momentous was the adoption of the single currency of the euro on 1 January 1999, as a cashless accounting currency; euro banknotes and coins have been used since 1 January 2002. To date, 19 countries have joined the Eurozone, while Denmark and Sweden have chosen to retain their national currencies. In future any new states joining the EU will be required to adopt the euro as a condition of entry. It's a hot topic, especially since the financial crash in countries including Greece and Spain, which required richer nations (principally, France and Germany) to bail out several of their more indebted European neighbours.

Economic Challenges & Looking Forward

Since the 2009 European debt crisis, growth throughout Mediterranean Europe has been sluggish, with many countries dipping in and out of recession. Unemployment figures across many European nations remain high, especially in Spain and Greece.

Although the euro stabilised after a series of multi-billion-euro rescue packages for Greece, Ireland, Portugal and Spain, the currency is still subject to uncertainty. In 2015, an extension of Greece's bailout was granted to avoid a Greek exit (aka 'Grexit'), and to prevent other debt-saddled countries following suit. And the European Central Bank launched massive quantitative easing (QE) measures involving money printing and bond buying, pumping over €1 trillion into the economy in an effort to resuscitate it.

Though not without its current prickly issues and localised political crises, the problems of Mediterranean Europe today seem refreshingly minor compared to the plagues, revolutions and century-long wars that afflicted the region's ancestors of yore.

2015	**2016**	**2017**
Greece defaults on loan payments. Bailout proposals with tough conditions trigger riots and Greek banks close.	Some EU borders are shut as millions of refugees and other unofficial migrants attempt to reach safe European havens.	Following a referendum in favour of quitting the EU, the UK triggers Article 50, setting in motion 'Brexit'.

Michelangelo's *David*, Galleria dell'Accademia (p186), Florence

Art & Architecture

For thousands of years great art and architecture have sprung forth from Mediterranean Europe. The region's museums and galleries are repositories of all kinds of creative treasures, from ancient Minoan frescoes to the very latest audiovisual installations. The region's architecture similarly spans time and space, moulded by the rise and fall of countless civilisations.

Art

The Ancient World

Art was a crucial part of everyday life for ancient civilisations: decorative objects were a sign of status and prestige, while statues were used to venerate and honour the dead, and monuments and temples were lavishly decorated to appease the gods.

Classical sculpture began to gather pace in Greece in the 6th century BC with the renderings of nudes in marble. Most statues were created to revere a particular god or goddess. The statues of the preceding Archaic period, known as *kouroi,* had focused on symmetry and form, but in the early 5th century BC artists sought to create expression

La Sagrada Família (p52), Barcelona

and animation. As temples demanded elaborate carvings, sculptors were called upon to create large reliefs upon them.

During the 5th century BC, the craft became yet more sophisticated, as sculptors were taught to successfully map a face and create a likeness of their subject in marble busts. Perhaps the most famous Greek sculptor was Phidias, whose reliefs upon the Parthenon depicting the Greek and Persian Wars – now known as the Parthenon Marbles – are celebrated as among the finest of the Golden Age.

In art, as in so many other realms, the ancient Romans looked to the Greeks for inspiration.

Sculpture flourished in southern Italy into the Hellenistic period. It also gained popularity in central Italy, where the art of the Etruscans was greatly refined by the contribution of Greek artisans, who arrived to trade.

In Rome, sculpture, architecture and painting flourished, first under the Republic and then the empire. But the art that was produced here during this period differed in key ways from the Greek art that influenced it. Essentially secular, it focused less on ideals of aesthetic harmony and more on accurate representation, taking sculptural portraiture to new heights of verisimilitude, as innumerable versions of Pompey, Titus and Augustus showing a similar visage attest.

Medieval Art

During the Middle Ages, the power of the Church and its importance as an artistic patron meant that the majority of medieval art dealt with religious subjects. The Old Testament, the crucifixion, the apostles and the Last Judgement were common topics. Some of the

Ancient Literary Masters

Homer Homer's classic work, the *Iliad*, written in the 8th century BC, relates in poetic epithet a mythical episode of the Trojan War. The *Odyssey* recounts the epic adventures of Odysseus on his journey home from the Trojan War.

Herodotus *The Histories*, written by Herodotus in the 5th century BC, chronicles the conflicts between the ancient Greek city-states and Persia. The work is considered to be the first narrative of historical events ever written.

Virgil Roman epic poet Virgil spent 11 years and 12 books tracking the outbound adventures and inner turmoil of Trojan hero Aeneas, from the fall of Troy to the founding of Rome. *Aeneid* was a kind of sequel to Homer's *Iliad* and *Odyssey*.

Ovid Fellow Roman Ovid's *Metamorphoses* chronicled civilisation from murky mythological beginnings to Julius Caesar, and his how-to seduction manual *Ars amatoria* (The Art of Love) inspired countless Casanovas.

finest medieval artworks are actually woven into the fabric of Mediterranean Europe's churches in the form of frescoes painted onto panels or walls.

In Greece, Byzantine church frescoes and icons depicted scenes from the life of Christ and figures of the saints. The 'Cretan school' of icon painting, influenced by the Italian Renaissance and artists fleeing to Crete after the fall of Constantinople, combined technical brilliance and dramatic richness.

Meanwhile, often regarded as just plain 'dark', the Italian Middle Ages had an artistic brilliance that's hard to ignore. Perhaps it was the sparkling hand-cut mosaic of Ravenna's Byzantine basilicas that provided the guiding light, but something inspired Giotto di Bondone (c 1266–1337) to leap out of the shadows with his daring naturalistic frescoes in Padua's Cappella degli Scrovegni and the Basilica di San Francesco in Assisi. With them he gave the world a new artistic language, and from there it was just a short step to the dawning light of the Renaissance.

The Renaissance & the Baroque

From quiet beginnings in 14th-century Florence, the Renaissance erupted across Italy before spreading across Europe. Artists such as Leonardo da Vinci (1452–1519), Michelangelo (1475–1564), Raphael (1483–1520), Titian (c 1488/90–1576) and Botticelli (1445–1510) introduced new techniques, colours and forms into the artistic lexicon, drawing inspiration from the sculptors and artists of the classical world.

Landscape and the human form gained increasing importance during the Renaissance. Michelangelo's masterpiece, *David,* is often cited as the perfect representation of the human figure (despite the fact that the artist deliberately distorted its proportions to make it more pleasing to the eye).

In the wake of the Renaissance came the great names of the baroque period, epitomised by the Italian artist Caravaggio (1571–1610), who had no sentimental attachment to classical models and no respect for 'ideal beauty'. He shocked contemporaries in his relentless search for truth and his radical, often visceral, realism. One look at his *Conversion of St Paul* and the *Crucifixion of St Peter* (1600–01), both in Rome's Basilica di Santa Maria del Popolo, or his *Le sette opere di Misericordia* (The Seven Acts of Mercy; 1607) in Naples' Pio Monte della Misericordia, and the raw emotional intensity of his work becomes clear.

Arguably the best known of all baroque artists was the sculptor Gian Lorenzo Bernini (1598–1680), who used works of religious art, such as *Ecstasy of St Theresa* in Rome's Chiesa di Santa Maria della Vittoria, to arouse feelings of exaltation and mystic transport.

While creative boundary pushing was obviously at play, the baroque was also driven by the Counter-Reformation, with much of the work commissioned in an attempt to keep hearts and minds from the clutches of the Protestant church. Baroque artists were early adopters of the sex sells mantra, depicting Catholic spirituality, rather ironically, through worldly joy, exuberant decoration and uninhibited sensuality.

Romanticism

Emerging as a proverbial Beethoven of the art world in the 18th century, Francisco de Goya (1747–1828) acted as a bridge between two distinct eras. The Spanish romantic painter is sometimes referred to as the last of the Old Masters and the first of the more enlightened modernists. His vast body of work, which spanned over 60 years, from the 1760s to the 1820s, included cartoons, court paintings, documentary realism, macabre war prints, the first nonmythical nude in Western art, and the disturbing 'black paintings', which he etched directly onto the walls of his house when he was old, deaf (like Beethoven) and battling insanity.

Inspired by Goya, romanticism reached its peak in the mid-19th century, when it became popular in Britain and France. Suddenly, clarity and dainty brushstrokes were out, and expressive colours and large heroic landscapes were in.

From Impressionism to Modernism

Although impressionism had its roots in romanticism, the movement was a radical departure from anything that had gone before. When the early impressionists, including the soon-to-be-famous Claude Monet (1840–1926), Edgar Degas (1834–1917), Pierre-Auguste Renoir (1841–1919), Alfred Sisley (1839–99) and Camille Pissarro (1830–1903), debuted their work at an exhibition in a photo studio in Paris in April 1874, they were met with bafflement and derision rather than polite applause. Tearing up the erstwhile artistic rule book, these precocious Frenchmen were proposing a revolutionary new approach to art. Experimenting with different painting techniques, the impressionists used delicate brushstrokes, dynamic colour contrasts and clever ways of capturing light to enliven their work. Above all, they were solidly anchored in the present.

The Italian equivalent of French impressionism was the Macchiaioli movement based in Florence. Its major artists were Telemaco Signorini (1835–1901) and Giovanni Fattori (1825–1908), whose socially engaged and light-infused work can be viewed in the Palazzo Pitti's Galleria d'Arte Moderna in Florence.

As impressionism grew more palatable and entered the mainstream, some of its adherents – led initially by Paul Cézanne – began pushing the envelope further to create more abstract works. The new style, dubbed post-impressionism, peaked in the mid-1880s and was characterised by the intricate pointillism of Pissarro, the swirling colours of Dutch master Vincent Van Gogh, and the vivid primitivism of Paul Gauguin.

Gauguin was a heavy influence on Pablo Picasso (1881–1973), the most famous artist of the 20th century, who practically wrote his own art history, weaving his way through a smorgasbord of stylistic shifts from his Blue Period to his Rose Period and from cubism to surrealism. Seminal works included the proto-cubist *Les Demoiselles d'Avignon* and the potent anti-war statement, *Guernica*. Picasso drew on multiple sources for his inspiration, tracking back as far as pre-Roman Iberian sculpture for artistic ideas. In turn, he inspired a whole generation of new artists to branch out and ruthlessly experiment. By the advent of modernism in the late 19th century, Europe was no longer just exporting artistic ideas, it was importing them as well. Its ever-evolving art scene had never been so fickle and fragmented.

Qur'an, Museum of Turkish & Islamic Arts (p490), İstanbul

TARIHGEZGINI/SHUTTERSTOCK ©

Modern & Contemporary Art

Art in the 20th century in Mediterranean Europe was characterised by a bewildering diversity of styles, including (but certainly not limited to) cubism (exemplified by Picasso and Georges Braque), Fauvism (Henri Matisse and André Derain) and futurism (Umberto Boccioni). The early 20th century also saw the rise of the Dada movement in France, and no piece of French art better captures its rebellious spirit than Marcel Duchamp's *Mona Lisa*, complete with moustache and goatee.

With the close of WWII, Paris' role as artistic world capital ended. The focus shifted back to southern France in the 1960s with new realists such as Arman (1928–2005) and Yves Klein (1928–62), both from Nice. In 1960 Klein famously produced *Anthropométrie de l'Époque Bleue,* a series of imprints made by naked women (covered from head to toe in blue paint) rolling around on a white canvas, in front of an orchestra of violins and an audience in evening dress.

The death of Franco in 1975 acted as a catalyst for Spanish art. New talent sprang up, and galleries enthusiastically took on anything revolutionary, contrary or cheeky. The 1970s and 1980s were a time of almost childish self-indulgence. Catalonia picked up where it had left off in the vanguard of the avant-garde, and its most celebrated modern artist and sculptor was the amazingly versatile Antoni Tàpies (1923–2012), whose often abstract, hard-to-define work ranged over countless materials and varied themes spanning left-wing politics, Zen meditation and art as alchemy.

In Italy, the 1980s saw a return to painting and sculpture in a traditional (primarily figurative) sense. Dubbed 'Transavanguardia', this movement broke with the prevailing international focus on conceptual art and was thought by some critics to signal the death of avant-garde. Artists who were part of this movement include Sandro Chia (b 1946), Mimmo Paladino (b 1948), Enzo Cucchi (b 1949) and Francesco Clemente (b 1952).

The late 20th century and 21st century to date have introduced many more artistic movements: abstract expressionism, neoplasticism, minimalism, formalism and pop art, to name a few, with street art and digital art also constantly breaking new ground.

Architecture

Classicism

Classical architecture began with the ancient Greeks but was later copied and developed by the Romans, who spread it liberally around their burgeoning empire, making it the first truly pan-European architectural movement. Many consider the harmonious temples and sun-dappled colonnades that graced Athens and Rome to be the peak of human architectural achievement. Built to last, many of these incredible buildings survive today. Some, such as the Parthenon atop the Acropolis in Athens, stand as distinguished ruins two-and-a-half thousand years after they were constructed.

Classicism emphasised symmetry, proportion and order. Greek buildings were dominated by thick, but elegant columns decorated with 'capitals' that varied in design depending on which architectural era they hailed from (Doric, Ionic or Corinthian). Rows of columns were organised into colonnades, while decoration – minimal at first, but gradually becoming more extravagant – was strategically placed on friezes and reliefs depicting warriors or gods in human form.

The Romans took Greek architecture and improved it using concrete to fashion semicircular 'Roman arches' that were used to support bridges, villas and coliseums. They also advanced technology to solve complicated engineering problems. During their reign, many of the structures we now consider quintessentially Roman – like aqueducts, bathhouses and domes – became more widespread and sophisticated. The remarkable unreinforced dome in Rome's Pantheon remains the largest of its type, nearly 2000 years after it was built.

The Building of Byzantium

While most of Europe entered a 'dark age' after the fall of the Romans, prospects in the go-it-alone 'eastern empire' couldn't have been brighter. Building on the classical designs of their Roman forefathers, the Byzantines of Constantinople experienced an unprecedented construction boom, spearheaded by an architectural style dominated by domes, octagonal towers and attractive exterior brickwork. Unlike later European churches that were built in the shape of a Latin cross, Byzantine churches were based on a symmetrical Greek cross floor-plan, making them squarer and stouter in appearance.

Byzantium's greatest legacy, both architecturally and spiritually, is the Aya Sofya in İstanbul. Built around 537 as a Christian church, the Sofya became a mosque after the Ottoman takeover in 1453, and in 1935 was converted into a museum. It remains one of the finest European-style buildings ever constructed.

Romanesque & Gothic

After the fall of the Roman Empire, European architecture went through a period of fragmentation, lacking any continent-wide 'glue' to hold it together. Instead, specific regions began to nurture their own individual styles in isolation. Islamic geometry held sway in Spain, while Byzantine classicism dominated the East. It wasn't until the emergence of Romanesque that Europe regained some architectural commonality. Romanesque first appeared in Italy and France in the 10th century. Its subsequent spread across the continent made it the first truly pan-European architectural style since the sack of Rome. Not surprisingly, ancient Rome was an overriding influence for Romanesque builders. Not only did they revive Roman building techniques lost during the Dark Ages, they also revisited Roman style icons like the simple but sturdy semicircular arch.

While Romanesque varied from country to country and evolved gradually over the two centuries it was in vogue (c 1000–1200), there are certain binding threads that make a classic Romanesque building easy to identify. Sturdiness and scale were all-important, as was pared-back decoration. More than anything, Romanesque architecture was built to last. Classic examples include Pisa's cathedral as well as its spectacular 'Leaning Tower'.

In literature, the term Gothic alludes to horror. In architecture, its translation is a little less frightening. This grandiose, elegant, yet wonderfully flamboyant building style originated in France in the late 12th century and gave rise to many of Europe's most spectacular cathedrals. Tell-tale characteristics include the use of pointed arches, ribbed vaulting, great showpiece windows and flying buttresses.

For the full-blown Italian Gothic style, check out the cathedrals in Florence and Venice.

Torre Pendente (Leaning Tower; p182), Pisa

Renaissance & Baroque

The Renaissance led to a huge range of architectural experiments. Pioneering Italian architects such as Brunelleschi, Michelangelo and Palladio shifted the emphasis away from Gothic austerity towards a more human approach. They combined elements of classical architecture with new building materials, and specially commissioned sculptures and decorative artworks. Florence and Venice are particularly rich in Renaissance buildings, but the movement's influence can be felt right across Mediterranean Europe.

Architectural showiness reached its zenith during the baroque period, when architects pulled out all the stops to show off the wealth and prestige of their clients. The baroque movement originated in Italy in the late 17th century before spreading to France, Eastern Europe and Spain (where it adopted a more florid tone known as Churrigueresque). Most graphically displayed in churches and palaces, it was closely associated with the Counter-Reformation, the era in which the Catholic Church began pushing back against a rising tide of Protestantism. Baroque buildings were all about creating drama, and architects often employed swathes of craftsmen and used the most expensive materials available to create the desired effect.

Art Nouveau & Contemporary Innovation

Nineteenth-century architects began to move away from the showiness of the baroque period in favour of new materials such as brick, iron and glass. This was the great age of urban planning, when the chaotic streets and squalid slums of many of Europe's cities were swept away in favour of grand squares and ruler-straight boulevards.

Continent-wide, the gracefully curvaceous style of art nouveau became popular, drawing inspiration from the 19th-century British Arts and Crafts Movement and the Gothic-loving pre-Raphaelite painters, who dismissed the standardisation of classicism in favour of more naturalistic medieval forms. Art nouveau took different names in different countries but reached its apogee in Spain where it was known as *modernisme*. Inspired by a handful of talented Catalan architects led by Antoni Gaudí, Spanish *modernisme* was whimsical, highly decorative and closely associated with nature. In Barcelona, *modernisme* peaked in the first decade of the 20th century with structures such as Gaudí's peerless (and still unfinished) Sagrada Família.

In contrast to the whimsy of the modernistas, functional architecture came to dominate much of mid-20th-century architecture, especially in the rush to reconstruct Europe's shattered cities in the wake of two world wars. Somewhat thankfully, the 'concrete box' style of architecture has largely fallen out of fashion over recent decades, and now the unifying theme appears to be that anything goes. Europeans may have something of a love-hate relationship with modern architecture, but the best buildings eventually find their place, with architects (and their famous 'starchitect' siblings) expanding the built spaces and stretching the imaginations of the general public.

Grilled squid, Croatia

Food & Drink

The Mediterranean diet is listed as an 'Intangible Cultural Heritage' by Unesco, and the region is united by its passion for eating and drinking with gusto. Indeed, eating out is a way of life on the Med, and with everything from Michelin-starred restaurants, beachside tavernas, designer bistros, hipster cafes and sophisticated bars, there's no shortage of choices.

Croatia & Montenegro

The food along the coast of Croatia and Montenegro is typically Mediterranean, using a lot of olive oil, garlic, flat-leaf parsley, bay leaves and all manner of seafood.

Favourites in the region include baked whole fish, fried *lignje* (squid, the crispy tentacles coated in garlic and olive oil, or sometimes stuffed with cheese and prosciutto) and *hobotnica* (octopus, either carpaccio, in a salad or cooked under a *peka*). Other popular Dalmatian dishes include *brodet* (a slightly spicy seafood stew served with polenta), *pašticada* (beef stewed in wine, prunes and spices and served with gnocchi) and Montenegrin *riblja čorba* (a hearty, flavoursome fish soup).

Chocolates at Gay-Odin (p251), Naples

★ **Top Spots for Sweet Treats**

Pasticceria Dal Mas (p325), Venice

Pierre Geronimi (p147), Monaco

Gay-Odin (p251), Naples

Bougatsa Iordanis (p403), Hania

Karaköy Güllüoğlu (p498), İstanbul

France & Monaco

Cuisine in the sun-baked south of France, including in the independent city-state of Monaco, is laden with tomatoes, melons, cherries, peaches, olives and Mediterranean fish. Bouillabaisse, Marseille's mighty meal of fish stew, is the south's most famous contribution to French cuisine. The chowder must contain at least three kinds of fresh saltwater fish, cooked in a broth containing onions, tomatoes, saffron and various herbs, and eaten as a main course with toasted bread and *rouille* (a spicy red mayonnaise of olive oil, garlic and chilli peppers).

Before your meal, indulge in a glass of pastis, an aniseed-flavoured, 45%-alcohol apéritif that was invented in Marseille by industrialist Paul Ricard in 1932. Amber-coloured in the bottle, it turns milky white when mixed with water. Or, as an essential lunch companion, try a chilled glass of Provence's irresistibly pink, AOC Côtes de Provence rosé wine.

Greece

The essence of traditional Greek cuisine lies in seasonal homegrown produce. Lemon juice, garlic, pungent Greek oregano and extra virgin olive oil are the quintessential flavours, along with tomato, parsley, dill, cinnamon and cloves.

For a quick bite, mezedhes are small dishes, perfect for sharing. Classics include tzatziki (yoghurt, cucumber and garlic), *melidzanosalata* (aubergine), *taramasalata* (fish roe), fava (split-pea puree with lemon juice) and *saganaki* (fried cheese). Also watch for *keftedhes* (meatballs), *loukaniko* (pork sausage), grilled *gavros* (white anchovies) and dolmadhes (rice wrapped in marinated vine leaves).

For a hearty lunch look out for *mayirefta* – homestyle, one-pot, baked or casserole dishes – or stop for a souvlaki – arguably the national dish – which comes in many forms, from cubes of grilled meat on a skewer to pitta-wrapped snacks with pork or chicken *gyros* done kebab-style on a rotisserie.

Italy

Italian cuisine is dominated by the twin staples of pizza and pasta, which have been eaten in Italy since Roman times. Italian pasta comes in numerous shapes and is made with durum flour, which gives it a distinctive *al dente* bite. Italian pizza comes in two varieties: the Roman pizza with a thin crispy base, and the Neapolitan pizza, which has a higher, doughier base. Flavours are generally kept simple – the best pizza restaurants often serve only a couple of toppings, such as *margherita* (tomato and mozzarella) and *marinara* (tomato, garlic and oregano).

In Italy, *caffè latte* and cappuccino are considered morning drinks, with espresso and macchiato the preferred post-lunch options. More importantly, coffee with dessert is fine, but ordering one with your main meal is considered a travesty.

Malta

Unsurprisingly in these Mediterranean islands, fresh seafood is a staple. The most favoured of fishes is the *lampuka* (dolphin fish), and *torta tal-lampuki* (also known as *lampuki* pie) is the classic dish. It's typically baked with tomatoes, onions, black olives, spinach, sultanas and walnuts – although there are lots of variations.

Malta's national gap-filler is the *pastizzi*, a small parcel of flaky pastry, Arabic in origin, which is filled with either ricotta cheese and parsley or mushy peas and onions. A couple of *pastizzi* make for a tasty and substantial breakfast or afternoon filler. They're available in most bars or from *pastizzerijas* (hole-in-the-wall takeaway *pastizzi* shops – follow your nose).

Vegetarians & Vegans

Vegetarians will have a tough time in many areas of Mediterranean Europe – eating meat is still the norm, and fish is often seen as a vegetarian option. However, you'll usually find something meat-free on most menus, though don't expect much choice. Vegans will have an even tougher time – cheese, cream and milk are integral ingredients of most cuisines.

Vegetable-based *antipasti* (starters), tapas, meze, pastas, side dishes and salads are good options for a meat-free meal. Shopping for yourself in markets is an ideal way of trying local flavours.

Spain

For Spaniards, eating is one of life's more pleasurable obsessions, with Spain's cuisine making extensive use of herbs, tomatoes, onions, garlic and lashings of olive oil. The nation's signature dish is *paella,* consisting of rice and chicken, meat or seafood, simmered with saffron in a large pan.

Spain also prides itself on its ham and spicy sausages (including *chorizo, lomo* and *salchichón*). These are often used in making the bite-size Spanish dishes known as tapas. One of the world's most enjoyable ways to eat, tapas are as much a way of life as they are Spain's most accessible culinary superstars. In many bars in Barcelona and elsewhere, tapas varieties are simply lined up along the bar and you either take a small plate and help yourself or point to the morsel you want. If you do this, it's customary to keep track of what you eat (by holding on to the toothpicks, for example) and then tell the bar staff how many you've had when it's time to pay.

Turkey

İstanbul is the national capital in all but name and Turks relocate here from every corner of the country, meaning that regional cuisines are well represented. The only dishes that can be said to be unique to the city are those served at Ottoman restaurants, where the rich concoctions enjoyed by the sultans and their courtiers are recreated.

Mezes made with seafood, freshly picked vegetables, wild herbs and locally produced olive oil are the backbone of Turkish coastal cuisine, providing a delicious inducement for visitors. Fish dominates menus on the coast and *balık ekmek* – grilled fish fillets stuffed into bread with salad and a squeeze of lemon – is a speciality sold at stands next to ferry docks around the country.

Manarola train station, Cinque Terre (p164)

Survival Guide

Directory A–Z

Accessible Travel

With the notable exception of Croatia, which has improved wheelchair access due to the large number of wounded war veterans,

Climate

Barcelona

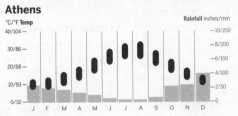

Athens

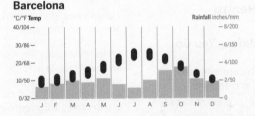

Rome

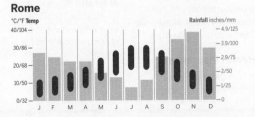

Mediterranean Europe is a tricky destination for people with mobility issues. Steep cobbled streets, ancient lifts and anarchic traffic all make life difficult for people with mobility issues. Public transport is often woefully ill-equipped, and tourist sites rarely cater well to those with disabilities.

For more information, download Lonely Planet's free *Accessible Travel* guide from http://lptravel.to/AccessibleTravel. Other useful resources include:
Mobility International USA (www.miusa.org) Publishes guides and advises travellers with disabilities on mobility issues.

Society for Accessible Travel & Hospitality (SATH; www.sath.org) Has loads of useful information, including a need-to-know section and travel tips.

Global Access (www.globalaccessnews.com) A worldwide network for wheelchair users with a monthly e-zine and tonnes of reader-generated articles.

Customs Regulations

The EU has a two-tier customs system: one for goods bought duty-free to import to or export from the EU, and one for goods bought in another EU country where taxes and duties have already been paid.

○ When entering or leaving the EU, you are allowed to carry duty-free 200 cigarettes, 50 cigars or 250g of tobacco; 2L of still wine plus 1L of spirits over 22% alcohol or another 4L of wine (sparkling or otherwise); for other goods (eg coffee, perfume, electronics) up to €430 (air/sea entry) or €300 (land entry).

○ When travelling from one EU country to another, the duty-paid limits are 800 cigarettes, 200 cigars, 1kg of tobacco, 10L of spirits, 20L of fortified wine, 90L of wine (of which not more than 60L is sparkling) and 110L of beer.

○ Non-EU countries often have different regulations and many countries forbid the export of antiquities and cultural treasures.

Electricity

Mediterranean Europe generally runs on 220V, 50Hz AC, but there are exceptions; some old buildings in Italy and Spain have 125V (or even 110V in Spain). The continent is moving towards a 230V standard.

Most countries in Mediterranean Europe use the 'europlug' (two round pins).

Embassies & Consulates

Nations such as Australia, Canada, New Zealand, the UK and the US have embassies and consulates across the region in capitals and major cities. To locate them, consult the following websites:

Australia www.dfat.gov.au
Canada www.international.gc.ca
New Zealand www.mfat.govt.nz
UK www.fco.gov.uk
US www.travel.state.gov

Etiquette

Bargaining Not common in much of Europe, but known in and around the Mediterranean. In Turkey it's virtually a way of life.

Dining Europeans take their time over dining (especially in the Mediterranean), enjoying food, family, talk and wine. Fast food, though present, is less popular.

Dress Dress modestly when visiting churches or other religious buildings. Europeans are more inclined to dress up than North Americans, be it for a business meeting or a night out at the theatre.

Tipping Less prevalent in Europe than other parts of the world. No need to leave lavish tips in restaurants or to tip the bus driver.

Greetings Vary greatly from country to country, though, in general, greetings are fairly formal and bound by long-standing etiquette.

Health

Before You Go

Recommended Vaccinations

No jabs are necessary for Europe. However, the World Health Organization (WHO) recommends that all travellers be covered for diphtheria, tetanus, measles, mumps, rubella and polio, regardless of their destination. Since most vaccines don't produce immunity until at least two weeks after they're given, visit a physician at least six weeks before departure.

Health Insurance

It is unwise to travel anywhere in the world without travel insurance. A good policy should include comprehensive health insurance, including medical care and emergency evacuation.

If you're an EU citizen, the free EHIC (European Health Insurance Card) covers you for most medical care in the EU member states, including maternity care and care for chronic illnesses such as diabetes (though not for emergency repatriation). However, you will normally have to pay for medicine bought from pharmacies, even if prescribed, and perhaps for some tests and procedures. The EHIC does not cover private medical consultations and treatment out of your home country; this includes nearly all dentists, and some of the better clinics and surgeries.

Non-EU citizens should find out if there is a reciprocal arrangement for free medical care between their country and the EU country they are visiting.

Useful Websites

The **World Health Organization** (WHO; www. who.int/ith/en) publishes the annually revised, free online book *International Travel and Health*. **MD Travel Health** (www.mdtravel health.com) provides up-to-date travel-health recommendations for every country.

In Mediterranean Europe

Good health care is readily available throughout the region.

• For minor illnesses pharmacists can give valuable advice and sell over-the-counter medication. They can also advise when more specialised help is required and point you in the right direction.

• The standard of dental care is usually good; however, it is sensible to have a dental check-up before a long trip.

Insurance

It's foolhardy to travel without insurance that covers theft, loss and medical problems. Check that your policy includes emergency medical evacuation costs, and any activities deemed risky by insurers, such as scuba diving or other adventure sports.

Worldwide travel insurance is available online at www.lonelyplanet.com/travel-insurance. You can buy, extend and claim online anytime – even if you're already on the road.

Internet Access

Wi-fi is generally easily found across the region. Check the Fast Facts box in each destination chapter for tips on finding free wi-fi.

Legal Matters

Driving Drink-driving laws apply and road checks are common in some areas. When driving, make sure you have the correct documents at hand.

Drugs Drugs are widespread. Legislation and local attitudes vary, but if you're caught with a small quantity of cannabis you might get away with a warning and/or a fine. Possession of hard drugs or quantities of cannabis deemed 'dealable' could lead to imprisonment. Note that prescription drugs that are legal in your home country might not be legal abroad – check before travelling.

Proof of Identity You are required by law to prove your identity if asked by police, so always carry your passport, or ID card if you're an EU citizen.

Theft If you have something stolen and you want to claim it on insurance, you must make a statement to the police, as insurance companies won't pay up without official proof of a crime.

LGBT+ Travellers

Discretion is the key. Although homosexuality is acknowledged and, in large part, tacitly accepted in Mediterranean Europe (with antidiscrimination legislation in place everywhere except Turkey), attitudes remain conservative and overt displays of affection could elicit hostility, especially outside of main cities.

Maps

• Tourist offices are a good source of free, basic maps.

• Good maps are easy to find in bookshops throughout the region.

Money

France, Greece, Italy, Montenegro and Spain use the euro. Croatia uses the kuna (KN) and Turkey the Turkish lira (₺).

There are seven euro notes (€5, €10, €20, €50, €100, €200 and €500) and eight euro coins (€1 and €2, then 1, 2, 5, 10, 20 and 50 cents); one euro is equivalent to 100 cents.

Tap Water

Tap water is safe to drink in most of the countries listed in this book, although in Turkey it's best to stick to bottled or purified water.

Don't drink water from rivers or lakes, as it may contain bacteria or viruses that can cause diarrhoea or vomiting.

Practicalities

Smoking Smoking bans exist in all of the countries listed in this book. The exact rules vary from place to place, so always check before lighting up.

Weights & Measures The metric system is in use throughout Mediterranean Europe.

While travelling in the region, the best way to carry your money is to bring an ATM card, credit card and cash. Internet-banking accounts are useful for tracking your spending – if you don't have one, set one up before you leave home.

ATMs & Credit Cards

ATMs are widely available in the region and easy to use (many have instructions in English). It's always prudent, though, to have a backup option in case something goes wrong with your card or you can't find a working ATM.

Much of Mediterranean Europe now uses a chip-and-pin system for added security. You will have problems if you don't have a four-digit PIN number and might have difficulties if your card doesn't have a metallic chip. Check with your bank.

Credit cards are widely accepted in most countries, but don't rely on them in small restaurants or shops. As a general rule, Visa and MasterCard are more widely accepted in the region than American Express and Diners Club.

American Travellers

US-issued 'smart' credit/debit cards with embedded chips (a technology pioneered in France in the 1980s) and PINs work virtually everywhere in France, including autoroute toll plazas, but cards with a chip but no PIN may occasionally leave you unable to pay. If your credit card is of the old type, ie with a magnetic strip but no chip, ask your issuer to send you a new, chip-equipped card – they're usually happy to oblige as the new technology is much more secure.

Tipping

There are no hard-and-fast rules about tipping.

● Many restaurants add service charges, making a tip discretionary. In such cases, it's common practice, and often expected of visitors, to round bills up. If the service was particularly good and you want to leave a tip, 5% to 10% is fine.

● At bars or cafes it's not necessary but you might leave your change or a few small coins.

● In some places, such as Croatia, tour guides expect to be tipped.

Opening Hours

Although there are no hard and fast rules respected by all countries (or even by all the businesses in any one country), most Mediterranean nations share some habits.

Note that opening hours sometimes change between summer and winter. In general, summer hours are longer with later closing times. In coastal areas, many seasonal businesses (hotels, souvenir shops, bars etc) close over winter, generally from November to March.

Banks Generally open early and either close for the day at around 1.30pm or reopen for a brief two-hour window in the early afternoon, say from 2.30pm to 4.30pm.

Museums Many are closed on Mondays.

Offices Usually operate from Monday to Friday and possibly Saturday morning. Sunday opening is not unheard of, but it's not widespread.

Shops It's common, especially outside the main cities, for small shops to close for a long lunch. Typically a shop might open from 8am or 9am until 1.30pm, and then from about 4pm to 8pm. Larger department stores tend to stay open all day.

Post

● From major European centres, airmail typically

takes about five days to reach North America and a week to Australasian destinations.

● Postage costs vary from country to country, as does post-office efficiency.

● Courier services such as DHL (www.dhl.com) are best for essential deliveries.

Public Holidays

● Most holidays in the southern European countries are based on the Christian calendar.

● In Turkey, the month-long holiday of Ramazan (Ramadan) is celebrated. Its exact timing depends on lunar events.

● August is the peak holiday period for Mediterranean dwellers.

● The major school holidays run from July to September, and many businesses simply shut up shop for much of August. Schools also pause for breaks over Easter and Christmas.

Safe Travel

Travelling in Mediterranean Europe is generally very safe. That said, petty crime is widespread in the region, so watch out for bag snatchers, pickpockets and scam artists. As always, common sense and a little

healthy scepticism are the best defence.

Emergency Numbers

The EU-wide general emergency number is 112. This can be dialled, toll-free, for emergencies in Croatia, France, Greece, Italy (for the *carabinieri* who can forward you to the other emergency services), Montenegro, Spain and Turkey (for ambulances only).

Taxes & Refunds

When non-EU residents spend more than a certain amount (around €75, but amounts vary from country to country), they can usually reclaim any sales tax when leaving the country.

Making a tax-back claim is straightforward. First, make sure the shop offers duty-free sales (often a sign will be displayed reading 'Tax-Free Shopping'). When making your purchase, ask the shop attendant for a tax-refund voucher, filled in with the correct amount and the date. This can be stamped at ferry ports and mailed back for a refund.

Telephone

Mobile Phones

If your mobile phone is European, it's often perfectly

feasible to use it on roaming throughout the Continent.

If you're coming from outside Europe, it's usually worth buying a prepaid local SIM in one European country; you'll need to have your handset unlocked by your home provider to do this. Even if you're not staying there long, calls across Europe will be cheaper if they're not routed via your home country and the prepaid card will enable you to keep a limit on your spending. In several countries you need your passport to buy a SIM card.

Europe uses the GSM 900 network, which also covers Australia and New Zealand, but is not compatible with the North American GSM 1900 or the totally different system in Japan and South Korea. If you have a GSM phone, check with your service provider about using it in Europe. You'll need international roaming, but this is usually free to enable.

Online Messages & Calls

Even if your phone is locked, apps such as 'whatsapp' allow you to send free text messages internationally wherever you have wi-fi access, while Skype enables you to make free international calls whenever you're online.

Pay Phones & Phonecards

You can call abroad from almost any phone box in Mediterranean Europe. Public telephones accepting phonecards (available from post offices, telephone centres, news stands or retail outlets) are virtually the norm now; coin-operated phones are rare, if not impossible, to find.

Without a phonecard, you can ring from a telephone booth inside a post office or telephone centre and settle your bill at the counter. Reverse-charge (collect) calls are often possible. From many countries the Country Direct system lets you phone home by billing the long-distance carrier you use at home. These numbers can often be dialled from public phones without even inserting a phonecard.

Time

Most Mediterranean Europe countries are on Central European Time (GMT/UTC plus one hour) except for Greece and Turkey, which are on Eastern European Time (GMT/UTC plus two hours).

In most European countries, clocks are put forward one hour for daylight-saving time on the last Sunday in March and turned back again on the last Sunday in October. Thus, during daylight-saving time, Central European Time is GMT/UTC plus two hours and Eastern European Time is GMT/UTC plus three hours.

Toilets

o Public toilets are pretty thin on the ground in much of the region. The best advice if you're caught short is to nip into a train station, fast-food outlet, bar or cafe and use their facilities.

o A small fee (typically €0.20 to €1) is often charged in public toilets, so try to keep some small change handy.

o Most toilets in the region are of the sit-down Western variety, but don't be surprised to find the occasional squat toilet. And don't ever assume that public toilets will have paper – they almost certainly won't.

Tourist Information

o Tourist information is widely available throughout the region. Most towns, big or small, have a tourist office of some description, which at the very least will be able to provide a rudimentary map and tourist brochures.

o Tourist-office staff will often speak some English in the main centres, but don't bank on it away from the tourist hotspots.

Visas

Citizens of Australia, New Zealand, Canada, the UK and the US do not need a visa to enter most Mediterranean Europe countries and stay for up to three months (90 days).

Nationals of countries including Australia, Austria, Belgium, Canada, India, Ireland, Mexico, the Netherlands, Norway, Portugal, Spain, Taiwan, the UK and USA need a visa for Turkey, which should be purchased online at www.evisa.gov.tr before travelling.

Visa requirements change, and you should always check with the embassy of your destination country or a reputable travel agent before travelling.

Women Travellers

It's sad to report, but machismo is alive and well in Mediterranean Europe, a region in which gender roles are still largely based on age-old social norms. But even if attitudes are not always very enlightened, a deep sense of hospitality runs through many Mediterranean societies, and travellers (of both sexes) are usually welcomed with warmth and genuine kindness. That said, women travellers continue to face more challenging situations than men do, most often in the form of unwanted harassment. Other things to bear in mind:

● Staring is much more overt in Mediterranean countries than in the more reticent northern parts of Europe, and although it is almost always harmless, it can become annoying.

● If you find yourself being pestered by local men and ignoring them isn't working, tell them you're waiting for your husband (marriage is highly respected in the area) and walk away. If they continue, call the police.

● Gropers, particularly on crowded public transport, can also be a problem. If you do feel someone start to touch you inappropriately, make a fuss – molesters are no more accepted in Mediterranean Europe than they are anywhere else.

Transport

Getting Around

Bicycle

Although cycling is a popular sport in France, Spain and Italy, as a means of everyday transport it is not common in Mediterranean Europe. Outside certain areas there are few dedicated cycle lanes, and drivers tend to regard cyclists as an oddity. Poor road conditions, particularly in the Eastern European countries, and mountainous terrain provide further obstacles.

Bike hire is available throughout the region, though – tourist offices can usually direct you to rental outlets. Ensure your rental includes a good lock and make sure you use it when you leave your bike unattended.

Car & Motorcycle

Travelling around the region by car or motorbike gives you increased flexibility and allows you to venture off the beaten path. On the downside you'll often have to deal with congestion, urban one-way systems, traffic-free zones and nonexistent city parking.

Mediterranean Europe is well suited to motorcycle touring, as it has an active motorcycling scene and plenty of panoramic roads.

Driving Licence

● An EU driving licence is valid for driving throughout Europe.

● If you've got a licence issued by a non-EU country, you'll need an International Driving Permit (IDP).

● When driving in Europe, always carry your home licence with the IDP, as the IDP is not valid on its own.

Fuel

● Fuel prices vary from country to country, but are almost always more expensive than in the US or Australia.

● Fuel is sold by the litre (one US gallon is 3.8L). It comes as either unleaded petrol or diesel. Diesel is cheaper than unleaded petrol.

Insurance

● To drive in Mediterranean Europe you'll need third-party (liability) insurance.

● In Turkey you'll also need an International Insurance Certificate, commonly called a Green Card. This is a certificate attesting that your insurance policy meets the minimum legal requirements of the country you're visiting. When you get this, check with your insurance company that it covers all the countries you intend to visit, and if you're driving in Turkey, make sure that it covers the European and Asian parts of the country.

Rental

Car-hire agencies are widespread across the region. The major international chains have offices throughout the Med, and there are any number of local firms. Note that very few cars in Mediterranean Europe have automatic transmission. To hire one, order it in advance and expect to pay more.

Motorcycle and moped hire is common in Italy,

Spain, Greece and the south of France.

Road Rules

The AA and RAC can supply members with country-by-country information on road rules and conditions.

Some universal rules and considerations:

o Drive on the right.

o In European cars the steering wheel is on the left.

o Some countries require you to have your headlights on even when driving during the day.

o Unless otherwise indicated, always give way to cars entering a junction from the left.

o Speed limits vary from country to country. You may be surprised at the apparent disregard for speed limits (and traffic regulations in general) in some places, but as a visitor it's always best to be cautious.

o Random police checks are common in some countries and many driving infringements are subject to on-the-spot fines. If you receive a fine, always ask for a receipt.

o Drink-driving laws are strict, with the blood-alcohol concentration (BAC) limit generally between 0.05% and 0.08%.

o It's obligatory to wear a helmet on motorcycles, scooters and mopeds everywhere in Mediterranean Europe. It's also recommended

that motorcyclists use their headlights during the day.

Local Transport

Most European towns and cities have excellent local-transport systems, often encompassing trams as well as buses and metro/subway/underground-rail networks. Many areas of interest in European cities can also be easily traversed by foot or bicycle. In Greece and Italy, travellers sometimes rent mopeds and motorcycles for scooting around a city or island.

In many places you have to buy your ticket before you get on the bus/boat/train and then validate it once on board (if the driver hasn't already checked it). It's often tempting not to do this – many locals don't appear to – but if you're caught with an unvalidated ticket you risk a fine.

Boat

In some parts of the region, jumping on a ferry is as common as taking a bus. In Venice, *vaporetti* (small passenger ferries) ply the city's canals, ferrying tourists and locals alike. In İstanbul, ferries are the cheapest way of getting around the city.

Bus

Buses are generally best for short hops, such as getting around cities and reaching remote villages, and they are often the only option in mountainous regions.

Reservations are rarely necessary. On many city

buses you usually buy your ticket in advance from a kiosk or machine and validate it on entering the bus.

Metro

A number of the region's major cities have metro systems, including Athens, Barcelona, İstanbul and Rome. While it can often be quicker to travel underground, it can get unpleasantly hot and crowded, especially during summer rush hours.

Taxi

Taxis in Europe are metered and rates are usually high. There might also be supplements for things such as time of day, location of pickup and extra passengers.

Good bus, rail and underground-railway networks often render taxis unnecessary, but if you need one in a hurry, they can be found idling near train stations or outside big hotels.

Uber operates in many of Mediterranean Europe's larger cities.

Train

Trains are a popular way of getting around Mediterranean Europe and are generally pretty economical. The region's rail network is comprehensive, and trains are comfortable, frequent and generally punctual. How much you pay depends on the type of train you take (high-speed trains are more expensive), whether you travel 1st or 2nd class, and the time of year (or even the time of day).

Language

Don't let the language barrier get in the way of your travel experience. This section offers basic phrases and pronunciation guides to help you negotiate your way around Europe. Note that in our pronunciation guides, the stressed syllables in words are indicated with italics.

To enhance your trip with a phrasebook (covering all of these languages in much greater detail), visit **lonelyplanet.com**.

Croatian

Hello.	*Bok.*	bok
Goodbye.	*Zbogom.*	*zbo*·gom
Yes./No.	*Da./Ne.*	da/ne
Please.	*Molim.*	*mo*·leem
Thank you.	*Hvala.*	*hva*·la
Excuse me.	*Oprostite.*	o·*pro*·stee·te
Help!	*Upomoć!*	*oo*·po·moch

Do you speak (English)?
Govorite/Govoriš — go·vo·ree·te/*go*·vo·reesh
li (engleski)? — lee (*en*·gle·skee) (pol/inf)
I (don't) understand.
Ja (ne) razumijem. — ya (ne) ra·*zoo*·mee·yem
How much is it?
Koliko stoji? — ko·*lee*·ko *sto*·yee
I'd like..., please.
Želim..., molim. — *zhe*·leem... *mo*·leem
Where are the toilets?
Gdje se nalaze zahodi — gdye se na·la·ze za·ho·di/
toaleti? — to·a·le·ti
I'm lost.
Izgubio/Izgubila — iz·*gu*·bi·o/iz·*gu*·bi·la
sam se. (m/f) — sam se

French

Hello.	*Bonjour.*	bon·zhoor
Goodbye.	*Au revoir.*	o·rer·vwa
Yes.	*Oui.*	wee
No.	*Non.*	noh
Please.	*S'il vous plaît.*	seel voo play
Thank you.	*Merci.*	mair·see
Excuse me.	*Excusez-moi.*	ek·skew·zay·mwa
Help!	*Au secours!*	o skoor

Do you speak English?
Parlez-vous anglais? — par·lay·voo ong·glay
I don't understand.
Je ne comprends pas. — zher ner kom·pron pa
How much is this?
C'est combien? — say kom·byun
I'd like ..., please.
Je voudrais ..., — zher voo·dray ...
s'il vous plaît. — seel voo play
Where's (the toilet)?
Où sont — oo son
(les toilettes)? — (lay twa·let)
I'm lost.
Je suis perdu(e). (m/f) — zhe swee·pair·dew

Greek

Hello.
Γειά σας. — ya·sas (pol)
Γειά σου. — ya·su (inf)
Goodbye.
Αντίο. — an·*di*·o
Yes./No.
Ναι./Όχι. — ne/*o*·hi
Please.
Παρακαλώ. — pa·ra·ka·*lo*
Thank you.
Ευχαριστώ. — ef·ha·ri·*sto*
Excuse me.
Με συγχωρείτε. — me sing·kho·*ri*·te
Help!
Βοήθεια! — vo·*i*·thya

Do you speak English?
Μιλάτε αγγλικά; — mi·*la*·te an·gli·*ka*
I don't understand.
Δεν καταλαβαίνω. — dhen ka·ta·la·*ve*·no
How much is it?
Πόσο κάνει; — *po*·so *ka*·ni
I'd like..., please.
Θα ήθελα... — tha *i*·the·la...
παρακαλώ. — pa·ra·ka·*lo*

Where are the toilets?

Που είναι η τουαλέτα?   pu *i*·ne i tu·a·*le*·ta

I'm lost.

Έχω χαθεί.   e·kho kha·*thi*

Italian

Hello.	*Buongiorno.*	bwon·*jor*·no
Goodbye.	*Arrive-*	a·ree·ve·
	derci.	der·chee
Yes.	*Sì.*	see
No.	*No.*	no
Please.	*Per favore.*	per fa·*vo*·re
Thank you.	*Grazie.*	gra·tsye
Excuse me.	*Mi scusi.*	mee skoo·zee
Help!	*Aiuto!*	a·*yoo*·to

Do you speak English?

Parla inglese?   par·la een·*gle*·ze

I don't understand.

Non capisco.   non ka·*pee*·sko

How much is this?

Quanto costa?   kwan·to *ko*·sta

I'd like …, please.

Vorrei …, per favore.   vo·*ray* … per fa·*vo*·re

Where's (the toilet)?

Dove sono   *do*·ve *so*·no

(i gabinetti)?   (ee ga·bee·*ne*·ti)

I'm lost.

Mi sono perso/a. (m/f)   mee *so*·no *per*·so/a

Spanish

Hello.	*Hola.*	o·la
Goodbye.	*Adiós.*	a·*dyos*
Yes.	*Sí.*	see
No.	*No.*	no
Please.	*Por favor.*	por fa·*vor*
Thank you.	*Gracias.*	gra·thyas
Excuse me.	*Disculpe.*	dees·*kool*·pe
Help!	*¡Socorro!*	so·*ko*·ro

Do you speak English?

¿Habla inglés?   a·bla een·*gles*

I don't understand.

No entiendo.   no en·*tyen*·do

How much is this?

¿Cuánto cuesta?   kwan·to kwes·ta

I'd like …, please.

Quisiera …, por favor.   kee·*sye*·ra … por fa·*vor*

Where's (the toilet)?

¿Dónde están   don·de es·*tan*

(los servicios)?   (los ser·*vee*·thyos)

I'm lost.

Estoy perdido/a. (m/f)   es·*toy* per·*dee*·do/a

Turkish

Hello.	*Merhaba.*	mer·ha·ba
Goodbye.		
	Hoşçakal.	hosh·*cha*·kal
	(said by person leaving)	
	Güle güle.	gew·*le* gew·*le*
	(said by person staying)	
Yes.	*Evet.*	e·*vet*
No.	*Hayır.*	ha·yuhr
Please.	*Lütfen.*	lewt·fen
Thank you.		
	Teşekkür ederim.	te·shek·*kewr* e·*de*·reem
Excuse me.		
	Bakar mısınız.	ba·*kar* muh·suh·*nuhz*
Help!	*İmdat!*	eem·dat

Do you speak English?

İngilizce konuşuyor   een·gee·*leez*·je ko·noo·*shoo*·yor

musunuz?   moo·soo·*nooz*

I don't understand.

Anlamıyorum.   an·*la*·muh·yo·room

How much is it?

Ne kadar?   ne ka·*dar*

I'd like…

…istiyorum.   …ees·*tee*·yo·room

Where are the toilets?

Tuvaletler nerede?   too·va·let·*ler* ne·re·de

I'm lost.

Kayboldum.   kai·bol·*doom*.

Behind the Scenes

Acknowledgements

Cover photograph: Dubrovnik, Croatia; Blend Images/Getty Images ©

Climate map data adapted from Peel MC, Finlayson BL & McMahon TA (2007) 'Updated World Map of the Köppen-Geiger Climate Classification', Hydrology and Earth System Sciences, 11, 163344.

Illustrations p54, p140, p212, p244, p414, p444, p480, p486 by Javier Zarracina.

This Book

This 1st edition of Lonely Planet's *Cruise Ports Mediterranean Europe* guidebook was researched and written by Virginia Maxwell, Kate Armstrong, Brett Atkinson, Alexis Averbuck, James Bainbridge, Cristian Bonetto, Gregor Clark, Duncan Garwood, Paula Hardy, Anna Kaminski, Catherine Le Nevez, Hugh McNaughtan, Kate Morgan, Kevin Raub, Simon Richmond, Brendan Sainsbury, Regis St Louis, Greg Ward and Nicola Williams. This guidebook was produced by the following:

Curators William Allen, Grace Dobell, Shona Gray, Anne Mason, Jenna Myers, Rachel Rawling, Kathryn Rowan, Saralinda Turner, Anna Tyler

Destination Editors Tom Stainer, Anna Tyler, Branislava Vladisavljevic

Associate Product Director Kirsten Rawlings

Regional Senior Cartographer Anthony Phelan

Senior Product Editors Jessica Ryan, Elizabeth Jones

Book Designer Gwen Cotter

Assisting Editors Heather Champion, Victoria Harrison, Amy Lynch, Anne Mulvaney, Lauren O'Connell

Cover Researcher Naomi Parker

Thanks to Ronan Abayawickrema, Vesna Čelebić, Esme Fox, Paul Harding, Claire Rourke, Genna Patterson, Doug Rimington

Send Us Your Feedback

We love to hear from travellers – your comments keep us on our toes and help make our books better. Our well-travelled team reads every word on what you loved or loathed about this book. Although we cannot reply individually to postal submissions, we always guarantee that your feedback goes straight to the appropriate authors, in time for the next edition. Each person who sends us information is thanked in the next edition, the most useful submissions are rewarded with a selection of digital PDF chapters.

Visit lonelyplanet.com/contact to submit your updates and suggestions or to ask for help. Our award-winning website also features inspirational travel stories, news and discussions.

Note: We may edit, reproduce and incorporate your comments in Lonely Planet products such as guidebooks, websites and digital products, so let us know if you don't want your comments reproduced or your name acknowledged. For a copy of our privacy policy visit lonelyplanet.com/privacy.

Index

A

Symbols & Map Key

Look for these symbols to quickly identify listings:

◉ Sights
✪ Activities
✪ Courses
✪ Tours
✪ Festivals & Events

✪ Eating
✪ Drinking
✪ Entertainment
✪ Shopping
ⓘ Information & Transport

Find your best experiences with these Great For... icons.

Art & Culture
History
Beaches
Local Life
Budget
Nature & Wildlife
Cafe/Coffee
Photo Op
Cycling
Scenery
Detour
Shopping
Drinking
Short Trip
Entertainment
Sport
Events
Walking
Family Travel
Winter Travel
Food & Drink

These symbols and abbreviations give vital information for each listing:

⌀ Sustainable or green recommendation

FREE No payment required

☏ Telephone number
⊙ Opening hours
P Parking
⊝ Nonsmoking
❊ Air-conditioning
@ Internet access
🛜 Wi-fi access
🏊 Swimming pool

🚌 Bus
⛴ Ferry
🚃 Tram
🚆 Train
📋 English-language menu
🥗 Vegetarian selection
👪 Family-friendly

Sights

🏖 Beach
🐦 Bird Sanctuary
☸ Buddhist
🏰 Castle/Palace
✝ Christian
☯ Confucian
🕉 Hindu
☪ Islamic
卍 Jain
✡ Jewish
❗ Monument
🏛 Museum/Gallery/ Historic Building
🏚 Ruin
⛩ Shinto
☬ Sikh
☯ Taoist
🍷 Winery/Vineyard
🐾 Zoo/Wildlife Sanctuary
◉ Other Sight

Points of Interest

🏄 Bodysurfing
⛺ Camping
☕ Cafe
🛶 Canoeing/Kayaking
● Course/Tour
🤿 Diving
🍸 Drinking & Nightlife
✖ Eating
🎭 Entertainment
♨ Sento Hot Baths/ Onsen
🛍 Shopping
⛷ Skiing
🛏 Sleeping
🤿 Snorkelling
🏄 Surfing
🏊 Swimming/Pool
🚶 Walking
🏄 Windsurfing
✪ Other Activity

Information

🏦 Bank
🏛 Embassy/Consulate
➕ Hospital/Medical
@ Internet
🚓 Police
✉ Post Office
☏ Telephone
🚻 Toilet
ⓘ Tourist Information
● Other Information

Geographic

🏖 Beach
⯈⯇ Gate
🛖 Hut/Shelter
🗼 Lighthouse
👁 Lookout
▲ Mountain/Volcano
🌴 Oasis
🌳 Park
)(Pass
🧺 Picnic Area
💧 Waterfall

Transport

✈ Airport
Ⓑ BART station
✖ Border crossing
Ⓣ Boston T station
🚌 Bus
🚡 Cable car/Funicular
🚲 Cycling
⛴ Ferry
Ⓜ Metro/MRT station
🚝 Monorail
Ⓟ Parking
⛽ Petrol station
Ⓢ Subway/S-Bahn/ Skytrain station
🚕 Taxi
🚉 Train station/Railway
🚋 Tram
Ⓤ Underground/ U-Bahn station
● Other Transport

Hugh McNaughtan

A former English lecturer, Hugh swapped grant applications for visa applications, and turned his love of travel intro a full-time thing. Having done a bit of restaurant-reviewing in his home town of Melbourne, he's now eaten his way across four continents. He's never happier than when on the road with his two daughters. Except perhaps on the cricket field ....

Kate Morgan

Having worked for Lonely Planet for over a decade now, Kate has been fortunate enough to cover plenty of ground working as a travel writer on destinations such as Shanghai, Japan, India, Russia, Zimbabwe, the Philippines and Phuket. She has done stints living in London, Paris and Osaka but these days is based in one of her favourite regions in the world – Victoria, Australia. In between travelling the world and writing about it, Kate enjoys spending time at home working as a freelance editor.

Kevin Raub

Atlanta native Kevin Raub started his career as a music journalist in New York, working for *Men's Journal* and *Rolling Stone* magazines. He ditched the rock 'n' roll lifestyle for travel writing and has written over 95 Lonely Planet guides, focused mainly on Brazil, Chile, Colombia, USA, India, the Caribbean and Portugal. Kevin also contributes to a variety of travel magazines in both the USA and UK. Along the way, the self-confessed hophead is in constant search of wildly high IBUs in local beers.

Simon Richmond

Journalist and photographer Simon has specialised as a travel writer since the early 1990s, and first worked for Lonely Planet in 1999 on their *Central Asia* guide. He's long since stopped counting the number of guidebooks he's researched and written for the company, but countries covered including Australia, China, Greece, India, Indonesia, Iran, Poland, Japan, Malaysia, Mongolia, Myanmar (Burma), Russia, Singapore, South Africa, South Korea and Turkey and the USA. For Lonely Planet's website he's penned features on topics from the world's best swimming pools to the joys of urban sketching.

Brendan Sainsbury

Born and raised in the UK, Brendan spent the holidays of his youth caravanning in the English Lake District and didn't leave Blighty until he was 19.

Making up for lost time, he's since squeezed 70 countries into a sometimes precarious existence as a writer and professional vagabond. His rocking chair memories will probably include staging a performance of 'A Comedy of Errors' at a school in war-torn Angola, running 150 miles across the Sahara Desert in the Marathon des Sables, and hitchhiking from Cape Town to Kilimanjaro with an early, dog-eared copy of Lonely Planet's *Africa on a Shoestring*. In the last 11 years, he has written over 40 books for Lonely Planet from Castro's Cuba to the canyons of Peru. When not scribbling research notes, Brendan likes partaking in ridiculous 'endurance' races, strumming old Clash songs on the guitar, and experiencing the pain and occasional pleasures of following Southampton Football Club.

Regis St Louis

Regis grew up in a small town in the American Midwest – the kind of place that fuels big dreams of travel – and he developed an early fascination with foreign dialects and world cultures. He spent his formative years learning Russian and a handful of Romance languages, which served him well on journeys across much of the globe. Regis has contributed to more than 50 Lonely Planet titles, covering destinations across six continents. His travels have taken him from the mountains of Kamchatka to remote island villages in Melanesia, and to many grand urban landscapes. When not on the road, he lives in New Orleans.

Greg Ward

Since his youthful adventures on the hippy trail to India, and while living in northern Spain, Greg has written guides to destinations all over the world. As well as covering the USA from the Southwest to Hawaii, he has ranged on recent assignments from Corsica to the Cotswolds, and Dallas to Delphi.

Nicola Williams

Border-hopping is way of life for British writer, runner, foodie, art aficionado and mum-of-three Nicola, who has lived in a French village on the southern side of Lake Geneva for more than a decade. Nicola has authored more than 50 guidebooks on *Paris*, *Provence*, *Rome*, *Tuscany*, *France*, *Italy* and *Switzerland* for Lonely Planet and covers France as a destination expert for the *Telegraph*. She also writes for lonelyplanet.com as well as the *Independent*, *Guardian*, *Lonely Planet Magazine*, *French Magazine*, *Cool Camping France* and more.

Alexis Averbuck

Alexis has travelled and lived all over the world, from Sri Lanka to Ecuador, Zanzibar and Antarctica. In recent years she's been living on the Greek island of Hydra and exploring her adopted homeland; sampling oysters in Brittany and careening through hill-top villages in Provence; and adventuring along Iceland's surreal lava fields, sparkling fjords and glacier tongues. A travel writer for over two decades, Alexis has lived in Antarctica for a year, crossed the Pacific by sailboat and written books on her journeys through Asia, Europe and the Americas.

James Bainbridge

James is a British travel writer and journalist based in Cape Town, South Africa, from where he roams the globe and contributes to publications worldwide. He has been working on Lonely Planet projects for over a decade, updating dozens of guidebooks and TV hosting everywhere from the African bush to the Great Lakes. He has authored several editions of Lonely Planet's *South Africa, Lesotho & Swaziland*, *Turkey* and *Morocco* guides, and his articles on travel, culture and investment appear in the likes of BBC Travel, the UK *Guardian* and *Independent*, Condé Nast *Traveller* and *Lonely Planet Traveller*.

Cristian Bonetto

Cristian has contributed to over 30 Lonely Planet guides to date, including *New York City*, *Italy*, *Venice & the Veneto*, *Naples & the Amalfi Coast*, *Denmark*, *Copenhagen*, *Sweden* and *Singapore*. His musings on travel, food, culture and design also appear in numerous publications around the world, including the *Telegraph* (UK) and *Corriere del Mezzogiorno* (Italy). When not on the road, you'll find the reformed playwright and TV scriptwriter slurping espresso in his beloved hometown; Melbourne.

Gregor Clark

Gregor is a US-based writer whose love of foreign languages and curiosity about what's around the next bend have taken him to dozens of countries on five continents. Chronic wanderlust has also led him to visit all 50 states and most Canadian provinces on countless road trips through his native North America. Since 2000, Gregor has regularly contributed to Lonely Planet guides, with a focus on Europe and the Americas. Titles include *Italy*, *France*, *Brazil*, *Costa Rica*, *Argentina*, *Portugal*, *Switzerland*, *Mexico*, *South America on a Shoestring*, *Montreal & Quebec City*, *France's Best Trips*, *New England's Best Trips*, cycling guides to Italy and California and coffee-table pictorials such as *Food Trails*, *The USA Book* and *The Lonely Planet Guide to the Middle of Nowhere*.

Duncan Garwood

From facing fast bowlers in Barbados to side-stepping hungry pigs in Goa, Duncan's travels have thrown up many unique experiences. These days he largely dedicates himself to the Mediterranean and Italy, his adopted homeland where he's been living since 1997. He's worked on more than 30 Lonely Planet titles, including guidebooks to Rome, Sardinia, Sicily, Spain and Portugal, and has contributed to books on food and epic drives. He's also written about Italy for newspapers, websites and magazines.

Paula Hardy

Paula Hardy is an independent travel writer and editorial consultant, whose work for Lonely Planet and other flagship publications has taken her from nomadic camps in the Danakil Depression to Seychellois beach huts and the jewel-like bar at the Gritti Palace on the Grand Canal. Over two decades, she has authored more than 30 Lonely Planet guidebooks and spent five years as Commissioning Editor of Lonely Planet's bestselling Italian list. These days you'll find her hunting down new hotels, hip bars and up-and-coming artisans primarily in Milan, Venice and Marrakech.

Anna Kaminski

Originally from the Soviet Union, Anna grew up in Cambridge, UK. She graduated from the University of Warwick with a degree in Comparative American Studies, a background in the history, culture and literature of the Americas and the Caribbean, and an enduring love of Latin America. Her restless wanderings led her to settle briefly in Oaxaca and Bangkok and her flirtation with criminal law saw her volunteering as a lawyer's assistant in the courts, ghettos and prisons of Kingston, Jamaica. She has contributed to almost 30 Lonely Planet titles. When not on the road, Anna calls London home.

Catherine Le Nevez

Catherine's wanderlust kicked in when she roadtripped across Europe from her Parisian base aged four, and she's been hitting the road at every opportunity since. She's travelled to some 60 countries to date, completing her Doctorate of Creative Arts in Writing, Masters in Professional Writing, and Postgraduate qualifications in Editing and Publishing along the way. Over the past 15 years she's written scores of Lonely Planet guides and articles covering Paris, France, Europe and far beyond. Her work has also appeared in numerous online and print publications. Topping Catherine's list of travel tips is to travel without any expectations.

Our Story

A beat-up old car, a few dollars in the pocket and a sense of adventure. In 1972 that's all Tony and Maureen Wheeler needed for the trip of a lifetime – across Europe and Asia overland to Australia. It took several months, and at the end – broke but inspired – they sat at their kitchen table writing and stapling together their first travel guide, *Across Asia on the Cheap*. Within a week they'd sold 1500 copies. Lonely Planet was born.

Today, Lonely Planet has offices in Franklin, London, Melbourne, Oakland, Dublin, Beijing and Delhi, with more than 600 staff and writers. We share Tony's belief that 'a great guidebook should do three things: inform, educate and amuse'.

Virginia Maxwell

Although based in Australia, Virginia spends at least half of her year updating Lonely Planet destination coverage across the globe. The Mediterranean is her major area of interest – she has covered Spain, Italy, Turkey, Syria, Lebanon, Israel, Egypt, Morocco and Tunisia for Lonely Planet – but she also covers Finland, Bali, Armenia, the Netherlands, the US and Australia. Follow her @maxwellvirginia on Instagram and Twitter.

Kate Armstrong

Kate Armstrong has spent much of her adult life travelling and living around the world. A full-time freelance travel journalist, she has contributed to over 50 Lonely Planet guides and trade publications, and is regularly featured in publications worldwide. She is the author of several books and children's educational titles. Over the years, Kate has worked in Mozambique, picked grapes in France and danced in a Bolivian folkloric troupe. A keen photographer, greedy gourmand and frenetic festival goer, she enjoys exploring off-the-beaten track locations, restaurants and theatres.

Brett Atkinson

Brett is based in Auckland, New Zealand, but is frequently on the road for Lonely Planet. He's a full-time travel and food writer specialising in adventure travel, unusual destinations, and surprising angles on more well known destinations. Craft beer and street food are Brett's favourite reasons to explore, and he is featured regularly on the Lonely Planet website, and in newspapers, magazines and on websites. Since becoming a Lonely Planet writer in 2005, Brett has covered areas as diverse as Vietnam, Sri Lanka, the Czech Republic, New Zealand, Morocco, California and the South Pacific.

← → **More Writers** ←

STAY IN TOUCH LONELYPLANET.COM/CONTACT

AUSTRALIA The Malt Store, Level 3, 551 Swanston St, Carlton, Victoria 3053
☎ 03 8379 8000,
fax 03 8379 8111

IRELAND Digital Depot, Roe Lane (off Thomas St), Digital Hub, Dublin 8, D08 TCV4, Ireland

USA 124 Linden Street, Oakland, CA 94607
☎ 510 250 6400,
toll free 800 275 8555,
fax 510 893 8572

UK 240 Blackfriars Road, London SE1 8NW
☎ 020 3771 5100,
fax 020 3771 5101

 twitter.com/
lonelyplanet

 facebook.com/
lonelyplanet

 instagram.com/
lonelyplanet

 youtube.com/
lonelyplanet

 lonelyplanet.com/
newsletter